Practicing E-Government: A Global Perspective

Mehdi Khosrow-Pour, D.B.A.
Information Resources Management Association, USA

IDEA GROUP PUBLISHING
Hershey • London • Melbourne • Singapore

ORGANISATION FOR ECONOMIC
CO-OPERATION AND DEVELOPMENT

Acquisitions Editor: Renée Davies
Development Editor: Kristin Roth
Senior Managing Editor: Amanda Appicello
Managing Editor: Jennifer Neidig
Copy Editor: Bernie Kieklak
Typesetter: Marko Primorac
Cover Design: Lisa Tosheff
Printed at: Integrated Book Technology

Published in the United States of America by
Idea Group Publishing (an imprint of Idea Group Inc.)
701 E. Chocolate Avenue, Suite 200
Hershey PA 17033
Tel: 717-533-8845
Fax: 717-533-8661
E-mail: cust@idea-group.com
Web site: http://www.idea-group.com

and in the United Kingdom by
Idea Group Publishing (an imprint of Idea Group Inc.)
3 Henrietta Street
Covent Garden
London WC2E 8LU
Tel: 44 20 7240 0856
Fax: 44 20 7379 3313
Web site: http://www.eurospan.co.uk

Library of Congress Cataloging-in-Publication Data

Practicing e-government : a global perspective / Mehdi Khosrow-Pour, editor.
p. cm.
Summary: "This book covers topics in e-government, discussing e-government's present shortcomings while exploring a renewed understanding of e-government's visions and responsiveness"--Provided by publisher.
Includes bibliographical references and index.
ISBN 1-59140-637-4 (h/c) -- ISBN 1-59140-638-2 (s/c) -- ISBN 1-59140-639-0 (ebook)
1. Internet in public administration 2. Internet in public administration--Case studies. 3. Political participation--Technological innovations. 4. Political participation--Technological innovations--Case studies. I. Khosrowpour, Mehdi, 1951-
JF1525.A8P72 2005
352.3'8'02854678--dc22

2004029849

British Cataloguing in Publication Data
A Cataloguing in Publication record for this book is available from the British Library.

All work contributed to this book is new, previously-unpublished material. The views expressed in this book are those of the authors. They do not necessarily reflect those of the publisher or the Organisation for Economic Co-Operation and Development (OECD) or the goernments of its member countries.

Practicing E-Government: A Global Perspective

Table of Contents

Preface

While the focus and purpose of e-government globally remains the same, the implementation and successes of digital governance vary widely from country to country. A common sentiment of the implementation of e-government was voiced by D. M. West, who stated, "In general, we find that e-government has fallen short of its potential. Governments are not making full use of available technology, and there are problems in terms of access and democratic outreach" (West, 2000).

In the previous decade, the concept of e-government was typically seen as a new process with unlimited potential in the rapidly expanding global environment. "Electronic governance involves new styles of leadership, new ways of debating and deciding policy and investment, new ways of accessing education, new ways of listening to the citizens and new ways of organizing and delivering information and services" (Ferguson, 1999). Now, just a few years later, although e-government is still concerned with these focuses, the processes are no longer new and we find ourselves in the phase of refining and redeveloping the foundation upon which e-government first appeared: to improve the efficiency and effectiveness of government.

To learn more about the true potential of e-government, a re-evaluation of the processes is necessary in order for e-government to continue to be accepted in the mainstream and be a more efficient system of government with access by all. If the models that were first introduced continue to be improved upon, e-government in our knowledge society will be an open and transparent institution that provides a maximum of services with a minimum of intrusion in the lives of the users.

Overall, while the basic goals of e-government have not shifted, the vision and responsiveness of the system have been forced to adapt globally in order to fulfill the public's need. Instead of a broad-based program to seamlessly interweave government workings with information technology, nations around the world now are struggling to implement Internet access, e-government interests and most importantly, safe and effective programs that serve society more efficiently.

In 2002, the Organisation for Economic Co-Operation and Development (OECD), based in Cedex France, hosted three international seminars on e-government. Government officials responsible for development, implementation and coordination of e-government initiatives joined others such as university educators and executives with expertise in this field in an open forum, to discuss ideas, innovations and solutions on ways to incorporate new information and communications technology into the changing government structures.

These seminars produced a wealth of information on this topic, most notably, "The e-Government Imperative" published by OECD in June 2003. However, with so many ideas and so much material available in excess of the report, OECD approached Idea Group Inc., a U.S.-based international publishing company, and through a cooperative effort the idea for this book was developed. In an effort to provide the most comprehensive and practical coverage of e-government issues, challenges and opportunities, the original expert participants of the OECD seminars on e-government were invited to contribute their latest work in this area for possible inclusion in this important book.

Practicing E-Government: A Global Perspective presents a variety of chapters covering many of the important topics in e-government, and is intended to elicit comments, raise concerns and open dialogue as we continue to implement e-government programs for mainstream society. Further, the book responds to e-government's present shortcomings, while exploring a renewed understanding of e-government's visions and responsiveness. The issues covered in this book are summarized:

In **Chapter 1**, *E-Government as Collaborative Governance: Structural, Accountability and Cultural Reform,* Barbara Ann Allen, Luc Juillet, Gilles Paquet, and Jeffrey Roy discuss the necessity for e-government to place an emphasis on collaboration as never before. This point of view of national governments and their organizational regimes creates a new focus on performance that, in turn, drives the need for collaboration internally. The authors remind readers of the need for a shift of viewpoint to focusing on performance rather than the typical focus on process. How national governments re-organize their own managerial regimes and organizational architectures for this new environment will determine the success of e-governance.

Chapter 2, *Performance Measurement and Evaluation of E-Government and E-Governance Programmes and Initiatives* by Tony Bovaird is based on the premise that e-government has the potential to be a major enabler in the adoption of good governance practices. This chapter focuses on the need for performance measurement and evaluation in e-government and e-governance, and is intended to help in the design of an evaluative framework. By exploring some key issues in performance measurement of e-government and e-governance, this chapter presents possible frameworks by which such evaluation might be undertaken and sets out some interim conclusions and recommendations.

In **Chapter 3**, *E-Government and E-Governance: Organizational Implications, Options, and Dilemmas*, Tony Bovaird suggests that e-government and e-governance initiatives can potentially have major organizational impacts through three major mechanisms: improved decision-making, more intensive and productive use of data bases, and better communications. These mechanisms impact on both the internal organisation of public agencies and their configuration of networks and partnerships. E-enablement therefore makes many existing organizational structures and processes obsolete and offers the prospect of transformation in both service delivery and public governance arrangements. While it seems likely that existing organizational configurations in the public sector will not be sustainable, the most appropriate ways forward will only be uncovered through much experimentation within e-government and e-governance programmes. In the nature of experimentation, many of these initiatives will turn out to be unproductive or cost-ineffective - but that is, perhaps, the necessary price to pay for the level of public sector transformation which now appears to be in prospect.

In **Chapter 4**, *Confidence in E-Government: The Outlook for a Legal Framework for Personal Data and Privacy,* Georges Chatillon writes that most users approach online services with an apprehension stemming from a lack of familiarity with government computer procedures and legal issues. Similarly, government officials' "objective" knowledge of the information technology mechanisms used by e-government is highly relative, as is their legal training in the realm of personal data protection. While the public does not really wish to know about the mysterious workings of government, electronic or otherwise, government employees are sometimes reluctant to change their work habits and adapt to new e-procedures when time-proven solutions can be found in the context of traditional government. Governments' hesitation to implement new legal status for the personal e-data processed by electronic public services has also had a detrimental effect on e-government.

In **Chapter 5**, *E-Government and Organizational Change,* Stuart Culbertson examines key aspects of organizational change required by governments to make their e-government strategies successful. The change imperative entails a hard look at many of the structures, processes, cultural issues and management practices prevailing within the public sector. This chapter identifies government success factors for several organizational entities involved in e-government and assesses the implications for organizational change on government structures, work practices and culture.

In **Chapter 6**, *Transformed Government: Case Studies on the Impact of E-Government in Public Administration,* Stuart Culbertson follows up his previous chapter with practical examples where he examines several promising trends and developments, lessons learned and key factors that have contributed to the success of e-government initiatives examined to date.

In **Chapter 7**, *Measuring E-Government in Italy,* by Marcella Corsi, the author describes her experience in establishing an observatory for the measurement of the impact of e-government policies on the efficiency and the effectiveness of the Italian public sector. Using a definition of "e-government" slightly different than the usual one, the chapter takes into account not only the mere providing of e-services, but also the whole impact of ICT in terms of transformation of public administrations. It is the hope of the author to develop a standard, transparent system, which, while it takes into account the overall level of e-government, the type and number of online services, and their ease of access and quality in the public sector.

In **Chapter 8**, *The E-mancipation of the Citizen and the Future of E-Government: Reflections on ICT and Citizens' Partnership*, by Valerie A.J. Frissen, the author considers the notion of the e-mancipated citizen against the background of current trends in social and political participation of citizens. The role of ICTs in shaping these new forms of civic engagement is discussed and the implications of these developments for e-government and e-governance.

In **Chapter 9**, *Measuring and Evaluating E-Government: Building Blocks and Recommendations for a Standardized Measuring Tool*, Christiaan Holland, Frank Bongers, Rens Vandeberg, Wouter Keller and Robbin te Velde describe research the authors have conducted on measuring e-government in The Netherlands. This research was commissioned by the Ministry of Economic Affairs and the Ministry of the Interior in The Netherlands. The authors developed a new concept and measuring tool for e-government and describe the methodological aspects of their approach in this chapter with the hope that they can create discussion on new ways to measure and evaluate e-government in an international perspective.

In **Chapter 10**, *Drop the 'e': Marketing E-Government to Skeptical and Web-Weary Decision-Makers*, Douglas Holmes addresses the risk of low public awareness and declining political interest as barriers to e-government, and considers ways governments can develop better marketing techniques to "sell" online services and the e-government concept to both groups. The term "marketing" is used loosely to mean both the presentation and promotion of actual online services to encourage people to use them, and the presentation and promotion of the theory and concept of e-government to ensure political understanding of its benefits to society.

In **Chapter 11**, *E-Government: Trick or Treat?*, author Alison Hopkins uses a consumer perspective to look at some of the principal challenges for governments in developing not just e-government but *responsive* e-government. While e-government is not a new concept, on the whole e-government services are passive — consumers can find information and download forms, but there is limited interactivity. The challenge is how to engage effectively and appropriately with consumers in an ongoing two-way process.

In **Chapter 12**, *Realigning Governance: From E-Government to E-Democracy*, Donald G. Lenihan acknowledges that over the last few decades, information and communications technologies (ICTs) have progressed at a remarkable pace. By the mid-1990s, the new technology had been used to engineer a major transformation of the private sector, reshaping markets and the basic building block of the modern economy: the corporation. Likewise, enthusiasts predicted that the public sector was about to go through a similar transformation. A new era in government was said to be dawning. For some, electronic- or e-government promised to transform government operations leading to major "efficiency gains" in service delivery. But e-government is proving more difficult and costly than first thought and the expected benefits have been slow to materialize. With some notable exceptions, the efficiency gains have been mixed. The boom in e-commerce was short-circuited by the dot-com bust. Is the bloom coming off the e-government rose? This chapter tries to shed more light on the pertinent issues and reflect a broader vision that e-government is about the transformation of government. A firm commitment from decision makers to think through the issues and steer the right course is critical or e-government could easily lose momentum or veer off course.

In **Chapter 13**, *Paradigm and Practice: The Innovative Organization to Deal with E-Government*, Valentina Mele presents a model that can be considered to be of the "transformist school," that emphasizes that leadership must play a key role in interpreting user needs before the implementation of new technology. She states that there are inherent risks in innovation and that only through strong management will failures be recognized early in the process and stopped before escalating the commitment to a doomed process.

In **Chapter 14**, *Skills for Electronic Service Delivery in Public Agencies*, Salvador Parrado deals with the needed skills to implement an e-government strategy. Although competencies and skills are used in the text interchangeably, competencies have a broader meaning. They are characteristics of an individual which underline performance or behavior at work. Competency is an observable, measurable pattern of skills, knowledge, abilities and behaviors. In this chapter, the emphasis is placed on ICT-related skills for top managers of public bureaucracies that deliver services electronically.

In **Chapter 15**, *Identifying Effective Funding Models for E-Government*, Franklin S. Reeder and Susan M. Pandy examine the central budgetary rules and processes and how they are being or could be adapted to finance investments in e-government. In particular, the paper looks at three countries (New Zealand, the UK and the U.S.) and examines the techniques and models that they are using to secure and manage funding for high priority e-government projects.

Chapter 16, *E-Government and Private-Public Partnerships: Relational Challenges and Strategic Directions,* by Barbara Allen, Luc Juillet, Gilles Paquet and Jeffrey Roy, acknowledges that there is now a growing recognition that e-government is less about electronic government in a purely technical sense and more about renewing public sector institutions for a new, more knowledge- and network-driven era. As governments formulate their own integrative strategies for moving online, coordination challenges both within and across governments are likely to grow — as will the potential for healthy competition. The new governance challenge of an effective and online public sector reside in defining the requisite mix of competitive and collaborative forces needed to realize the full potential of an online world — *one that is both digital and democratic.*

In **Chapter 17**, *What Skills are Needed in an E-World: E-Government Skills and Training Programs for the Public Sector,* Alexander Settles writes that the transition to e-government applications for public service delivery and management involves significant changes to the traditional systems of public management. The use of ICTs in combination with significant policy changes and systems of operation, has the potential to provide greater transparency and democracy. By reducing information transaction, storage, and dissemination costs, ICTs allow for greater access to information and records. In addition, the evolution of interactive communication technologies has opened additional channels for the public to access public sector information, comment on public decisions, and interact with their elected officials.

Chapter 18, *Citizen Participation in Public Administration: The Impact of Citizen Oriented Public Services on Government and Citizen* (Hein van Duivenboden), discusses electronic government services from the perspective of both government and citizens. The chapter focuses on the changing relationship between government and citizens by examining theory and practice of electronic public service delivery initiatives. Basic end-user skills will be needed of all public-sector agencies if governments intend to open e-government channels for a significant percent of government services. These employees will need the basic skills to use e-government effectively with project management and organizational skills becoming increasingly important. The quality and availability of appropriate educational and training opportunities for managers, staff, and, perhaps, even the public, provide a critical mass for potential change.

The collaboration of this book between so many experts from around the world bodes well for the future of e-government, as professionals collaborate and share best practices in an effort to take the basic concept of digital government and continue to enhance the frameworks that encourage innovation and adoption, moving e-government toward its goal of easy access for the masses. My hope is that this valuable collection of contributions in this vital emerging technology area will be instrumental in broadening our understanding of e-government technologies and potential.

Mehdi Khosrow-Pour, DBA
Editor

REFERENCES

Ferguson, M. (1999). *Developments in electronic governance.* The British Council. Retrieved from *www.britishcouncil.org/governance/edigest.htm*

West, D.M. (2000). *Assessing e-Government: The Internet, democracy and service delivery by state and federal governments.* Retrieved from *www.insidepolitics.org/egovtreport00.html*

Chapter I

E-Government as Collaborative Governance: Structural, Accountability and Cultural Reform

Barbara Ann Allen, University of Ottawa, Canada

Luc Juillet, University of Ottawa, Canada

Gilles Paquet, University of Ottawa, Canada

Jeffrey Roy, University of Ottawa, Canada[1]

ABSTRACT

In discussions on e-government, terms such as "seamless" and "joined-up" are often deployed in reference to restructuring the public sector for more effective performance. There is a critical link between delivering services online in a more client-centric fashion and government organization. This critical link often involves new coordinating mechanisms (i.e., new forms of governance) that are more collaborative than before — thus, e-government becomes collaborative government — and as such, many challenges present themselves. In government, however, collaborating is both complex and contentious, as much of public management has traditionally been premised on a command and control regime, where clear structures and rules dictate the behavior of public servants. The contentious nature of collaboration is also amplified by the political nature of government activity, and the difficulties in coordinating activities horizontally across traditional organizational units: there are structural, accountability and cultural dimensions of such coordination. E-government must be built on a fluid and constantly adapting of collaborative governance systems that respond to the twin challenges of external alignment and internal integration and cooperation.

INTRODUCTION

In discussions on e-government, terms such as "seamless" and "joined-up" are often deployed in reference to the organizational restructuring of the public sector apparatus for more effective forms of service delivery — including, of course, online channels.

Thus, there is a critical link between delivering services online in a more client-centric fashion and how government organizes and reorganizes itself to fulfill such a mission. This critical link often involves new coordinating mechanisms (i.e., new forms of governance) that are more collaborative than traditional public sector regimes of decision-making and accountability. As such, it is here where e-government becomes collaborative government — and as such, many challenges present themselves.

In government, collaborating is both a complex and contentious undertaking. It is complex in the sense that much of public management has traditionally been premised on a command and control regime, where clear structures and rules dictate the behavior of public servants. As such, collaboration becomes contentious, as it typically means acting in a manner that runs counter to the formal and traditionally accepted ways of operating.

The contentious nature of collaboration is also amplified by the political nature of government activity, and the difficulties in coordinating activities "horizontally" across the organizational portfolios (usually a single, flagship department or agency) of Ministers. In many Parliamentary regimes across the OECD, for instance, it is arguably the Cabinet or its equivalent that serves as the only meaningful venue for integrative and horizontal dialogues "joining up" all of government.

For this reason, the contours of e-government become fluid and potentially very broad, implying not only changes to service delivery models but also to the culture and structure of decision-making underpinning these models and adapting them to a more volatile and interdependent environment.

The collaborative challenges faced by national governments are immense. Yet, these linkages and relationships are not necessarily new. To varying degrees, national governments have been forced to respond to the actions and agendas of other governments and other sectors. So what exactly does e-government change?

E-government denotes an important shift in the nature of governance within such a framework in three important ways:

- First, technology, and online applications in particular, create new opportunities to link together organizations across this spectrum.
- Secondly, the policy challenges confronting cities, countries, and indeed the world demand a growing level of coordination across these levels and sectors.
- Thirdly, improving performance in the public sector, in this increasingly interconnected and relational world, requires an effective alignment of government's processes with those of its potential partners, clients, suppliers and other stakeholders.

As a result, e-government requires an emphasis on collaboration as never before. From the point of view of national governments and their organizational regimes, it is the third shift noted above, a new focus on performance that, in turn, drives the need for collaboration internally.

There are two reasons for such a claim. First, in order to be effective in responding to the collaborative challenges of working with organizations outside of its own boundaries, governments must be able to both demonstrate and nurture such an approach on the inside. Secondly, the shift to focusing on performance (a key focus of the government online movement) is a revolutionary shift in structure and mind set for public sector organizations typically focused on process.

In sum, e-government must be built on a fluid, constantly adapting collaborative governance systems that respond to the twin challenges of external alignment and internal integration and cooperation. While both points are essential and inter-linked, the focus of this report is on the latter challenge of how national governments re-organize their own managerial regimes and organizational architectures for this new environment.

Portals to Collaborative Governance

The portal is a now-familiar starting point on the path toward e-government, and it can also be used to demonstrate the potential benefits, as well as the barriers of seamless, joined-up, and collaborative governance systems. Providing a one-stop-shopping forum, which meets the needs of citizens, businesses and public employees, is a definitive part of all government's e-strategies. However, the creation of such a service requires collaboration across all agencies, heavy investment in back-office infrastructure, development of technologically uniform standards, security and inter-pretability, giving emergence to a seamless government. Examples of current and evolving portals include those of Canada, Singapore, Hong Kong, and France, demonstrating simple access points for government information and many services[2].

For many national governments, the notion of a portal typifies the front face of a public sector online. This face, focused on the needs of the client, need not reflect what's behind — within the inner workings of government. As such, portals can allow for integrative streams and service delivery based on life events, client grouping or any other appropriate grid for differentiation and delivery.

The benefits of such an approach are clear enough: if it works, client satisfaction improves, as does internal efficiency since this integrative channel for services has forged new organizational networks across boundaries in order to deliver. Essentially, bureaucracy is replaced by an innovative coordinating scheme that begins with online access, but is only realized through an appropriate organizational (re-)design that is likely to include an important dimension of collaboration.

The barriers, however, to realizing these benefits are numerous. There are three major sets of issues that must be considered:

- First, organizational and political structures must be transcended, and in some cases reconfigured in order to work collaboratively;
- Secondly, if political accountability continues to flow vertically to a single Minister, horizontal action may not come naturally; and
- Thirdly, new skill sets and a new working culture are required to facilitate the sharing of information and knowledge and the coordination of making decisions and delivering the outputs demanded of the client.

While these three points are often inter-related, their separation is the starting point for the organization of this chapter. We will proceed in three sections that will examine the structural dimensions of collaboration, the accountability dimensions of collaboration, and finally the cultural dimension. The interdependence of these dimensions will be revisited in the conclusion.

Structural Dimensions of Reform

Key questions:

- How are relationships between different administrative units formalized?
- Who takes responsibility for joined-up projects?
- How do such activities co-exist with more conventional activity?

In terms of structuring public sector activity, most Parliamentary regimes are based on a series of primarily functional units, reporting to a single Minister who, in turn, accounts to the public (often through a Chamber of elected representatives). This emphasis on a vertical reporting relationship means that actions of public servants within any particular unit are shaped almost exclusively by the interests and agendas of the Minister to whom the unit reports.

A critical question then becomes, how can more horizontal forms of coordination be achieved, joining up administrative units in a concerted and meaningful manner? Traditionally, central agencies (often dubbed horizontal agencies in some countries) have played a unique role here — coordinating managerial, financial and strategic directions across all line departments. The challenge with the central agency model is the typically top-down, centralized approach undertaken by these agencies, themselves operating under the authority of some of the most powerful Ministers in the Government (if not the leader of the Government).

With respect to e-government and horizontal coordination, a key driver is the necessity of delivering services online through portals designed in more integrative streams than the functional orientations of individual units. In response, there is new pressure for system-wide efforts to forge a shared or seamless infrastructure that can, in turn, offer services in new ways.

Importantly, however, this pressure for coordination, and its corresponding need for central action, can often run counter to a common trend over the past decade, namely giving more operational autonomy to specific units to focus on performance. In fact, here the term "agency" can be confusing given its multiple meanings as either a central agency (discussed above) or a newly empowered unit with additional operational freedoms to focus on performance with fewer process-based constraints on its actions.[3]

The resulting governance dilemma facing many national governments revolves around two central and conflicting decisions: how much authority should "central agencies" possess in imposing horizontal requirements on individual units; and what is the requisite amount of autonomy and flexibility required by individual units in order to enable them to innovate and adapt e-government strategies appropriate for their own particular function and mandate?

In countries such as New Zealand[4] where units begin with important operational freedoms, e-government has presented central authorities with the challenge of supporting horizontal coordination without any meaningful capacity to impose it. In such countries, central agencies have typically provided a monitoring and strategic advice role, with an important aim being to focus more on performance and outcomes than on process.

In contrast, in countries such as Canada, France, and Japan[5], where central agencies are much more active in shaping the operational structures and decisions of specific units, there is a different challenge. While the authority to impose rules and requirements is clearly in place, there is often a desire to genuinely find a more collaborative path, less imposing and more fostering and cooperative.

The Canadian example is interesting here, with both sides of this continuum present. On the one hand, the Chief Information Officer's Branch is located within the Management Board of the Government (Treasury Board — a central agency) that is highly involved in approving the process-based action of line departments. On the other hand, the national revenue collection authority is itself a flagship "agency" of the more performance-driven model (i.e., not a central agency) with important operational freedoms not enjoyed by other line departments.

The Canada Revenue Agency (CRA) is clearly a leading player in the government's efforts to move online and as a result, the nature of the relationship between both of these agencies will be an important dynamic in shaping the Canadian government's presence online. One can hypothesize here that in order to succeed, both organizations will need to ensure a more horizontal, collaborative relationship than has tended to be the case in the past.

But what exactly will the nature of this relationship be? Does each side have the incentives to work together, and what are the rewards and reporting relationships at play in order to ensure they do so? These key governance questions will only increase in importance. At present, there are clearly incentives, in the form of a shared agenda to collaborate. The portal is a starting point, as both actors have every interest in presenting the best possible face and capacity of a government online, thereby ensuring a growing client base for CRA in particular.

Yet, at the same time, in terms of results this unique agency is uniquely focused on its own performance and mission through both a Minister and a multi-stakeholder Board of Directors. Accordingly, in many areas of its operations such as human resource management, procurement, knowledge management and others, it could conceivably choose to exercise more autonomy than other governmental units. Recent developments include an expansion of online services to individuals and businesses, including real-time personalized tax account information using the highest form of encryption currently available, and an intensive consultation process with citizens and business titled "Future Directions."

This example is also unique given the separate agency status of CRA. With other departmental units, the relationship with Treasury Board may evolve in a different manner. An alternative example at the provincial level, still within Canada, is also revealing.

The Government of the Province of British Columbia, with a new mandate in 2002, found itself in an environment of very little central coordination of departmental units. Deeming this situation wasteful and inefficient, the Government introduced "Solutions BC Shared Services," an initiative from which a *de facto* central agency emerges as a key operational partner with individual units over most aspects of operational infrastructure.

E-government is an important driver here. The CIO function is housed within the Premier's Office (itself an important element in its degree of authority across government) and in targeting online service delivery, the Government has recognized the need for a more shared organizational architecture and it seems prepared to limit the organizational autonomy of individual units to achieve this end. One unique aspect of the B.C. approach is the contractual and competitive nature of the system. The central authority providing common services contracts with individual units (Ministries of the Government of British Columbia) through the mechanism of the Master Service Agreement, as opposed to simply imposing requirements.

Shared oversight mechanisms of senior managers from both line departments and the central authority monitor the decisions and working of this relationship, in essence introducing a body other than Cabinet (and importantly, a body at the non-political level) to overview this operational change and ensure horizontal coordination.[6]

These Canadian examples have one important theme in common — they both demonstrate that the move toward e-government is an accelerator for more horizontality in government, and potentially, a limiting force on the performance-driven trend of the past decade seeking to empower individual departments with more freedom to act independently and deliver services in the manner most efficient and effective for their own unique mandate.

Transcending Traditional Vertical: Horizontal Divides

E-government of the future will be one organized to respond to both the vertical and horizontal nature of public sector activity (as clearly, the functional pressures and line authority under individual Ministers will remain — even as it evolves in important ways). The following quote is indicative of the challenging impacts of IT on organizations and their shifting form:

"An implication is that corporate structures are becoming more heterogeneous at exactly the same time as power at the centre — over standards, systems and the like — is growing stronger. The company (organization) is becoming simultaneously more centralized and more diffuse and open. Internet technologies will enable the (organization) of the future to choose the appropriate structure in more flexible ways...Corporate leaders will constantly have to manage the tension between centralization and decentralization." (Cairncross, 2002, p. 174)

This latter point is as relevant to government as the private sector — if not more so. Structurally, in devoting resources and energies toward the design and construction of an architecture for e-government, central authorities, who will clearly be called upon to play an important coordination role, must carefully balance the need for commonality and the benefits of diversity from empowerment. One interesting model, introduced in the private sector is the so-called T-model of management, by which employees are essentially given two jobs to perform, one horizontal and one vertical (forming the T axis of the managerial regime):

"Because sharing (and collaborating) involves such contradictory behavior, one study advocates an approach that it calls 'T-shaped management,' practiced by a new

kind of executive who breaks out of the traditional corporate hierarchy to share knowledge freely across the organization (the horizontal part of the 'T') while remaining fiercely committed to individual business unit performance (the vertical part). No company seems to have given as much thought to T-shaped management as BP, the British energy giant. BP gives every manager of its business units two jobs. In addition to running the unit, managers devote between 15 and 20 per cent of their time to activities that share knowledge — and people — with other units." (ibid.)

There is a potential analogy to the provincial experiment in B.C., Canada where managers in line departments will be required to become cognizant and responsive to both their individual performance agendas as units and their shared relationships with the public authority contracting services on a government-wide basis.

In terms of role and relationships then, there is a need to embrace new forms of working relationships that transcend traditional approaches and functional orientations of public administration (Fountain, 2001). E-government will require "T-like" structures within which managers will navigate vertical and horizontal agendas in ways that are likely to be simultaneously both more formalized and fluid than is the case today.

Beyond structure, however, the application of resources to such models and the realization of shared results both take us into the realm of accountability.

Accountability Dimensions of Reform

Key questions:

- How are funding and responsibility provided to cross-unit teams and initiatives?
- How do accountability functions account for such models?

The new structural challenges create both pressures and opportunities for new partnerships — internally and externally. Within government, we have seen how e-government as a shared agenda must foster new horizontal opportunities by shifting away from traditional bureaucratic structures toward alternative mechanisms for both making decisions and service delivery arrangements.

Yet, there will be tensions between the vertical governance of traditional government and the horizontal governance needs of more joined-up and online models of service delivery.

Notions of accountability may be transformed. The manner by which accountability is perceived and exercised by government leaders determines the degree to which they embrace more collaborative models of governance (Paquet & Roy, 2000; Allen et al., 2001). Traditionalists invoke the underlying principle of Ministerial Accountability based on a clear and rigid view of vertical control and risk-minimization in order to serve and protect the interests of those leaders who are publicly accountable.

The rise of e-governance, with its pressures for a variety of initiatives introducing alternative models of decision-making and service-delivery, implies a sharing of accountability and, as importantly, a multiplicity of accountabilities. The need for collaboration, partnerships and joint ventures grows — both within government, as well as across governments (Kieley et al., 2002).

As governments have sought new partnerships to deliver services in alternative fashions, commentators are divided on the issue of whether accountability is at risk when external partners become involved. According to some, new governance arrangements threaten to undermine key institutions and practices of democratic accountability. This camp believes that any change to the existing system of ministerial accountability will damage the integrity of the system.

An alternative view, more focused on outcomes begins from the premise that collaborative arrangements can make government more accountable (Paquet, 1997). Proponents of collaborative arrangements insist that involving stakeholders strengthens accountability by virtue of the addition of partners. In particular, increased pressure for accountability to customers or clients is useful in making the starting point deliverables, results and performance — rather than the more traditional focus on process.

Notwithstanding legitimate concerns about new ways of doing things, it is difficult to conclude from these debates that the virtues of traditional accountability, namely their clarity and simplicity, can serve as justifications for their extension into an e-governance era. In the preceding section we have seen, for example, how new organizational forms will create problems for a strictly vertical model of accountability.

Such tensions also form the parameters around which new intra-governmental ties and actions are being forged. One of the critical governance quandaries of e-government and its reliance on more collaborative and horizontal processes is the political inertia of traditionally vertical lines of accountability.

Most governments exist in democratic contexts that seek to preserve accountability with an emphasis on process — rather than performance. Parliament oversight, independent offices, and media scrutiny are some of the major forces shaping this emphasis — as public sector managers face constant pressures of probity and transparency.

If this narrow and direct form of accountability is the only meaningful form in use, the emergence of e-government brings huge problems. Already, the integrative nature of portals and how services are delivered via them point to the need for different and multiple forms of accountability. Otherwise, how will government online (from a government-wide perspective) be gauged and measured?

Accountability based more on collaborative efforts and performance will invariably require new mechanisms for reporting outcomes that are more integrative and collective. There are a number of key challenges that present themselves:

- With a complex and inter-organizational government, it may be difficult to point out why things work and where things go wrong ex post facto.
- There is relatively little information on how to manage horizontally and managers are often required to think on their feet instead of relying on proven practices.
- Financial accountability is made harder when funding from several agencies is pulled together for a common venture.

With respect to the first point, the strength of the traditional model, in its clarity of control and process, becomes a potential weakness in collaborative action, particularly in the initiative is by and large informal. Effective or ineffective performance may be hidden in the transversal nature of the collaboration, at the expense a solid understanding of how the initiative is working.

Presently, this danger is not huge in many countries given the modest degree of experimentation with horizontal management, and in fact the risk is often greater when overcompensated for by a tremendously analytical and controlled approach that is deployed by partners seeking to enter into the collaboration only within the strictly defined limits offered by their home unit.

This dilemma underscores the second point above — namely, the novelty of working collaboratively across units. A common result is a form of inertia and resistance as partners find frustration in seeking to overcome the barriers presented by vertical silos. While a common and acceptable result is informally skirting rules to "make things happen," such an ad hoc approach may be useful in limited and relatively low risk initiatives, but it is likely to prove inadequate as the scope of the initiative grows in importance.

The third point points to resources — and the relatively limited funding sources typically deployed by governments for horizontal schemes (a trend e-government is beginning to reverse, albeit slowly and to varying degrees across countries). Typically, the budgetary process in most Parliamentary regimes features a speech of intensions and promises that are much more integrative than the subsequent funding allocations and implementation — which typically proceed along the lines of individual units. This dynamic is inherently political, as most Ministers seek additional resources for their own organizational fiefdom to accomplish tasks and objectives that will accrue visibility and credit accordingly.

Perhaps the single most critical shift required, then, in order to facilitate more horizontal action across government is to alter the system of allocating funds and, in a corresponding manner, to shift the emphasis from process to performance.

With respect to e-government, one important aspect of this shift is the political strength and position of the CIO or equivalent head of the e-government agenda. A Cabinet-level representation, coupled with an appropriate body and resource base would seem necessary to provide sufficient funding incentives for units to work together in a meaningful way.

Yet, collaborative efforts must have an underlying purpose and, to some degree, the willingness to collaborate must be present within individual units who must see the potential benefit in doing so. The resulting and offsetting need, then, is to allow units to have sufficient financial autonomy to be innovative in seeking collaborative arrangements across government when it is in their interests to do so — and to be rewarded in an appropriate fashion when benefits are realized.

This conundrum is at the heart of the accountability challenge facing governments: namely, striking a balance between centralized leadership and decentralized action, both of which must be linked and institutionalized in an effective manner. This balance must incorporate a shift away from vertical, rigid and process-based accountability toward shared accountabilities that are more performance-based.

Moreover, performance must be understood as based in part on the realization of results by individual units, reporting to the public via a Minister, and in part on the collective results of multiple units engaged in government-wide efforts to achieve specific goals. There is no getting around the fact that this latter dimension to realizing more shared forms of accountability, based on performance, requires political innovation to join up elected leaders as well as operational managers.

In other words, Ministers must also collaborate in order to share resources and respond collectively. For collaboration to be meaningful, there must be an expectation of collective reporting and an incentive/reward system to enforce such behavior.

Many governments have had limited experiences with horizontally driven programs, such as environmental issues or youth-based strategies. For the most part, such efforts have typically been weak — or when significant, firmly rooted in the political and administrative apparatus of a flagship Ministry (and Minister).

Such an approach is partly explained by the traditions of command-and-control authority in government and the zero-sum nature of politics and the spending process, and it is partly defended as a necessary element of clarity to explain who is in charge of what to external observers — and to the media, in particular.

Yet, such traditions are breaking down in the face of pressures for innovation and the growing realization that new governance systems are realized. But an order of caution is appropriate here. To return to the strategy of B.C., the province boldly states in its e-government strategy that citizens do not care how government works on the inside — it is the outcomes that matter and how they are treated on the outside.

While the intent here is unquestionably correct in emphasizing a more client-centric form of accountability, the reality is more complex – as often the public as well as other stakeholders *do care* a great deal about how government is organized (albeit usually when things go wrong).

The point is that the public burden of transparency requires that the need for something new must be both well explained and well understood — externally as well as internally. Ongoing mechanisms for consultation and communication become central to shifting the traditions of accountability and how it will be understood as new systems are introduced.

Shared accountabilities and how they should be defined, measured and imposed on government organizations will only be effective if arrived at through open and constant deliberative structures — engaging all relevant stakeholders. The complexities of a more Web-like government structure are not insurmountable in the face of media skepticism and public engagement, but they do require a foundation of collective learning in order to guide politicians and help bolster the political courage that is nonetheless required to introduce meaningful change.

Yet, at the same time, along with the structural requirements and accountability considerations comes an important human dimension — emphasizing a cultural shift in the roles of public servants and the changing nature of leadership in a more electronic, volatile and collaborative environment.

Cultural Dimensions of Reform

Key questions:

- What incentives can help to support and foster a collaborative culture?
- What are the changing skill requirements for public servants in a more collaborative environment?
- How are roles changing for senior managers and politicians?

The shift from vertical silos to new mixes of hierarchical and collaborative mechanisms is not one that lends itself to clarity. As management is an art, e-government will add layers of complexity and demand more creativity. A major cultural shift is under way in the public sector. While it precedes e-government in terms of a search for better policy-making and improved service delivery, the technological and social forces encapsulated in the e-government transformation accelerate this shift[7].

What are the implications for the public servant? It is again noteworthy, as a starting point, that the hierarchical and bureaucratic underpinnings of traditional notions of Ministerial Accountability are highly consistent with scientific and rational approaches to management emphasizing controlled specialization and hierarchy. In such approaches, workers are inputs to be carefully managed and controlled, often along narrow and specific tasks, with the predominant expectation being the ability to follow rules and adhere to authority.

Such a characterization is overly narrow in the sense that for some time middle managers and senior managers have exhibited a good deal of autonomy in exercising their functions. Too often, however, the ranks of public servants working for these individuals have been narrowly compartmentalized in functional units, acting to serve the direct interests of political Ministers.

Moreover, many senior public servants have succeeded in advancing through the system through loyalty and adherence to Ministerial commands (much like the traditional system dictates). Thus, the cultural transformation presenting itself under the realm of e-government (but not limited strictly to this driver) is one that requires simultaneous change at all levels of government.

On the front line, e-government may well cause a good deal of confusion, due to the conflict, potentially, between the rhetoric of customer service and decentralized authority to "front line managers" and the technological and centralizing pullback of coordinating service delivery online.

At the senior ranks, e-government is a novelty for most — and the generational divide is huge. Many senior public servants have spent their careers managing in an era where technology, often dubbed "informatics," meant backroom information systems and support functions unworthy of their attention and engagement. Such a view may be changing, but whether the rhetorical awareness of the importance of the Internet can translate into behavioral change is an important and decidedly open question.[8] New Zealand and Australia are both examining cultural reform as main tenants of public service reform.

Within the middle ranks of government exists the greatest potential for joined-up initiatives, horizontal management and collaborative action (Moritz & Roy, 2000). Often stymied by systemic rigidity, middle managers have grown most accustomed to circumventing such barriers and forging intra-governmental networks and strategies to realize their objectives. This characterization is admittedly truer within the confines of individual units, but it also extends to cross-jurisdictional processes (where such action may nonetheless be limited due to the confines of over-arching political structures and accountability systems).

The cultural challenge of e-government, then, begins with the unleashing of the creativity that already exists inside of government — and nurturing it accordingly (Werner, 2001). With the corresponding relational structures and accountability mechanisms in place, incentives can be offered for horizontal activity (as opposed to the present situation where such activity occurs informally, and thus secretively — without reward for success or punishment for failure).

Doing so requires a much more participative culture internally — in keeping with the rhetoric of e-government externally (i.e., a government listening and responding to clients, and partnering more creatively to do so). The Internet (and intranet) is a foundational tool that facilitates communication across government behind the scenes. The necessary next step is to make use of these channels in achieving formal shifts in organizational design based on creativity and innovation (Ostroff, 1999).

For public servants, in keeping with the rising importance of a knowledge workforce, the skill requirements are altering accordingly. Most managers now guiding the efforts toward moving their governments online are indicative of what is required — as many of these individuals have little technological training and are hardly rooted in careers of online service delivery.

Their entrepreneurial efforts to respond to the newly emerging opportunities are testament to the capacity of many public servants to adapt to change, create something new and navigate uncertainty. These navigational skills — requiring a blend of strong analytical abilities and even stronger communication and relational capacities, will be the premium of success in the public service of tomorrow.

At the highest ranks of public service, the burden of office weighs heavily on elected officials, particularly those serving in Government. The growing interest in e-government, coupled with the ongoing fiscal and competitive pressures for better performance, provides some fertile ground for nurturing innovation.

Yet, much depends on the actions and choices of political leaders[9]. Ideally, there will be recognition across most countries that the risks of inaction outweigh innovation. E-government is hardly a threat to elected officials, particularly at the national level. If anything, in a digital world the elected official's presence and role will be enhanced[10], and so will be the importance of the message from these individuals.

Elected officials are the agenda-setters and the communicators who must take responsibility for the broadest level of government performance. In doing so, however, there is plenty of scope to "let managers manage" and to benefit from the corresponding creativity that results. The new interface between elected officials and public servants will be a critical determinant in shaping the public sector's work environment, and the workforce of tomorrow.

CONCLUSIONS

In the private sector, some commentators suggest that the rise of e-commerce may one day render the modern corporation redundant as the key organizational unit of the 21st century. As transaction costs diminish and the need for innovation and heightened flexibilities rises, corporations could be replaced by more fluid systems that are more network-based, nomadic and neuronal in their functioning and adaptive capacities. *Is there an analogy for the traditional departmental unit in government?* While long-run visions are provocative by necessity, they often dramatically undervalue or simplify the transition — that may be quite long — during which historical traditions and their corresponding forms are not easily overcome. Yet, what is most important is the realization that governance is undergoing a profound shift in focus and in form — in all sectors.

Some commentators have depicted e-government's evolution as a bi-polar template divided by the traditions of the departmental model on the one hand and the attraction of a newly emerging, networked model on the other. This depiction is helpful in so far as it is not presented as a choice. In terms of the reform of public administration and democratic institutions, the classical department will likely continue to exist for some time to come.

Importantly, however, the departmental, vertically organized unit with a single Minister and a primarily functional purpose is already losing its place as the sole, or even the dominant, organizational mechanism. While such a change did not begin with the advent of e-government, online pressures for client responsiveness and organizational innovation will accelerate this trend and the need for innovative efforts at organizational design.

In the future, any meaningful realization of e-government will see the model of a single department or agency replaced by a myriad of more complex and collaborative governance mechanisms.

These pressures for collaboration will begin, in an online world, with the plurality of portals linking governments, businesses and non-profit organizations in shared channels of service delivery. These challenges will require shared processes of consultation and decision-making. In other words, the purpose of government action will increasingly be determined in a collaborative fashion (Batini et al., 2002).

Finally, in order to realize better performance, risks, rewards and reporting will require more collaborative architectures that will involve political as well as operational dimensions.

Thus, in realizing the promise of e-government, collaboration begins from the portal, and it extends to both defining a common purpose and realizing better performance outcomes, both within and across organizational units. In meeting this holistic challenge of collaborative governance, careful attention must be accorded to structural, accountability and cultural dimensions of this renewal.

REFERENCES

Allen, B., Juillet, L., Paquet, G., & Roy, J. (2001). E-government in Canada: People, partnerships and prospects. *Government Information Quarterly, 30*(1), 36-47.

Batini, C., Cappadozzi, E., Mecella, M., & Talamo, M. (2002). Cooperative architectures. In W. J. McIver & A. K. Elmagarmid (Eds.), *Advances in digital government – Technology, human factors and policy*. Boston: Kluwer Academic.

Cairncross, F. (2002). *The company of the future – How the communications revolution is changing management.* Boston: Harvard Business School.

Fountain, J.E. (2001). *Building the virtual state: Information technology and institutional change.* Washington, D.C.: Brookings Institution.

Kieley, B., Lane, G., Paquet, G., & Roy, J. (2002). E-government in Canada: Services online or public service renewal? In A. Gronlund (Ed.), *E-government design, applications and management.* Hershey, PA: Idea Group.

Moritz, R., & Roy, J. (2000, July). Federal IT workforce: Demography, community renewal, and leadership. *Canadian Government Executive, 4,* 12-15.

Ostroff, F. (1999). *The horizontal organization: What the organization of the future looks like and how it delivers value to customers.* New York: Oxford University Press.

Paquet, G. (1997). States, communities and markets: The distributed governance scenario. In T. J. Courchene (Ed.). *The nation-state in a global information era: Policy challenges the Bell Canada Papers in economics and public policy, 5* (pp. 25-46). Kingston: John Deutsch Institute for the Study of Economic Policy.

Paquet, G., & Roy, J. (2000). Information technology, public policy and Canadian governance: Partnerships and predicaments. In G.D. Garson (Ed.), *Handbook of public information systems* (pp. 53-70). New York: Marcel Dekker.

Werner, U. (2001). Collaboration in government. Organization: SAP public services. Retrieved from *http://www.netcaucus.org/books/egov2001/pdf/EGovWhi2.pdf*

ENDNOTES

1 At the time of preparation for an OECD Seminar in September 2002, the authors were Senior Research Fellows of the Centre on Governance at the University of Ottawa. The authors are grateful for the assistance of numerous colleagues at the Centre, and to Sayeh Minoosepehr in particular.

2 Portals as described in order: *www.canada.gc.ca*, *www.ecitizen.gov.sg*, *www.esd.gov.hk*, and *www.service-public.fr*

3 Examples of this latter trend include Executive Agencies in The UK, Crown Agencies in New Zealand, ore more mandate specific organizations such as Australia's Centrelink and the Canada Customs and Revenue Agency. On December 12, 2003, the Canada Customs and Revenue Agency (CCRA) became the Canada Revenue Agency (CRA). The customs program is now part of the new Canada Border Services Agency (CBSA). The majority of the recent e-government changes took place under the old name and institutional arrangement.

4 Example from New Zealand (*www.e-government.govt.nz*): The E-government Unit is part of the State Services Commission that is working with government agencies to achieve the Government's vision for e-government. The Unit leads, facilitates and coordinates e-government activities, but the actual delivery of e-government is the responsibility of all government agencies. The Minister responsible for the successful delivery of e-government is the Minister of State Services. The State Services Commissioner chairs the E-government Advisory Board. Its members assist him in guiding and overseeing the programme. The Board has four public service chief executives, a local government chief executive, and a private sector chief executive. The E-government Unit has people with technical IT, policy and strategy development, relationship management and project management. Two CIO (Chief Information Officer) networks support the managers who are accountable for the design and delivery of the technical and information management dimensions of e-government. The CIO networks (one for policy departments and one for operational departments) typically focus on the implementation of the interoperability framework, technical standards and guidelines, and leveraging of government IT infrastructure.

5 The Prime Minister's Office in Japan is the majority party regulating IT initiatives within the government. For reference, the government strategy is explained in the following document: *http://unpan1.un.org/intradoc/groups/public/documents/apcity/unpan002771.pdf*

6 Despite the competitive flavour of this approach, it is important to underscore that initially individual units will be "required" to contract with the public authority for shared services, from April 1, 2004 to March 31, 2006. Over time, it is expected that this requirement will become a strategic choice, allowing units to shop around between the public provider and other alternatives such as in-house development or working with the private sector (directions that would still require a mechanism to coordinate any such selection with government-wide strategies and infrastructure requirements).

7 In Canada, responding to the challenge as to why government must transform through new governance networks enabled by GOL, reports point out that government's relevance itself is at stake.
See "Connecting with Canadians – Pursuing Service Transformation" at *http://www.ged-gol.gc.ca/pnl-grp/reports/final/finaltb_e.asp*

8 New Zealand and Australia are both examining cultural reform as main tenants of public service reform.

9 It is noteworthy that the unit responsible for shaping cultural change in association with new forms of service delivery in the Canadian government, the "Organizational Readiness" organization, was transferred from the Treasury Board (a central agency) to a line department, Public Works and Government Services Canada (PWGSC) as of December 2003). As a result of structural change and decisions taken by the new Prime Minister, PWGSC may evolve toward a new status reflecting a quasi-central agency, with an increasingly horizontal scope for managing the government-wide service delivery agenda.

10 This characterization is made in reference to Ministers or those serving in Government. Whether members of the legislature will also enjoy enhanced influence is a separate debate — that varies considerably across countries and political regimes.

Chapter II

Performance Measurement and Evaluation of E-Government and E-Governance Programmes and Initiatives

Tony Bovaird, Bristol Business School, UK

ABSTRACT

This chapter explores the ways in which e-government and e-governance have been and can be evaluated and how performance measures can be developed in this field . It begins by examining the aims and objectives of e-government and e-governance, as highlighted by a number of different international bodies and governments of OECD member countries. The chapter then explores some key issues in the performance measurement of e-government and e-governance, and the options for performance indicators for e-government and e-governance. It goes on to consider the scope for evaluation of e-government programmes and initiatives, and possible frameworks by which such evaluation might be undertaken. Finally, it sets out some interim conclusions and recommendations for a range of different stakeholders.

INTRODUCTION

This chapter was commissioned by the Public Management Service [PUMA] of the OECD as part of its e-Government Task Force initiative. This initiative took as its starting point that e-government has the potential to be a major enabler in the adoption of good governance practices, with a major focus on the longer-term vision (2005-2010).

The topic for this chapter is the need for performance measurement and evaluation in e-government and e-governance. It is intended to help in the design of an evaluative framework which will have a number of complementary purposes:

- to clarify what works and what does not work
- to provide evidence for strategic choices and investments
- to highlight critical success factors in implementation
- to highlight possible side-effects and unintended consequences

The chapter begins by setting out its aims, purpose and the methodology which has been used. It then examines the aims and objectives of e-government and e-governance as highlighted by a number of different international bodies and governments of OECD member countries. The chapter then explores some key issues in performance measurement of e-government and e-governance, and the options for performance indicators for e-government and e-governance. It goes on to consider the scope for evaluation of e-government programmes and initiatives, and possible frameworks by which such evaluation might be undertaken. Finally, it sets out some interim conclusions and recommendations.

AIMS OF THIS CHAPTER

In line with these intentions, the aims of this chapter are:

- To develop a conceptual approach for the measurement and evaluation of e-government and e-governance, while taking account of the differing context in OECD Member Countries.
- To identify key themes and issues in e-government and e-governance and to suggest how they might be tackled.
- To analyze the issues, with a focus on identifying potential and existing solutions and approaches.
- To identify a library of potential performance indicators for e-government and e-governance, which are likely to be interesting to different key stakeholders in the public domain.
- To identify key information sources for performance information, current gaps and approaches which might rectify these gaps.
- To identify appropriate approaches for the evaluation of e-government and e-governance programmes.
- To make recommendations for priority areas in the measurement of the performance of e-government and e-governance and the evaluation of e-government and e-governance programmes.

The purpose of this chapter is to contribute to the overall debate on e-government and e-governance both within and between OECD Member Countries. The chapter has therefore been written with these multiple audiences in mind. The methodology used respects the need to incorporate the views of multiple stakeholders in the performance assessment and evaluation of e-government and e-government programmes.

Moreover, the final recommendations are broken down by stakeholder group, in order to facilitate exchange of views between stakeholders on what success looks like in this area of activity and how these programmes might be made more successful, within the perspectives of the different stakeholders involved.

METHODOLOGY

This chapter has used three different sets of source materials:

- OECD documents on e-government and e-governance and on other related programmes and projects
- Government and public sector agency Web sites on the Internet
- Academic and trade press literature (sometimes in print, otherwise on the Internet)
- Where material from these sources is used, they are cited in the text and full references are given. In most cases, these are references to Web sites.

In compiling the library of possible performance indicators for e-government and e-governance, the framework used was brought together from a number of sources, including:

- The good governance principles set out in the OECD document *Project on the Impact of E-Government.*
- The 2001 OECD publication, *Citizens as Partners; Information, Consultation and Public Participation in Policy-Making,* which discusses citizen engagement in policy making, provides a list of general principles for successful information provision, consultation and participation, and describes practices undertaken by some OECD Member Countries.
- The 2001 OECD publication, *The Hidden Threat to E-Government: Avoiding Large Government IT Failures*, which is based on country reports and experiences of participants, presented at a meeting in October 2000.
- The 2002 OECD publication, *From In-Line to On-Line,* which describes key service delivery objectives followed by most OECD Members countries.
- Reports emerging from the overall OECD E-Government project, including research papers dealing with the priority research topics of leadership, financing , relationships and skills (under "Strategic Implementation of E-Government") where there is a particular need to develop indicators.
- Office the e-Envoy (UK Cabinet Office) report on *Guidelines for Preparing 'Implementing Electronic Government' Statements*, listed in the References.

Aims and Objectives of E-Government and E-Governance

There is no single source which can be used as a definitive statement of the meaning and scope of the terms "e-government" and "e-governance," and the aims and objectives held by member governments in OECD countries in relation to e-government and e-governance.

Definition of E-Government

The OECD states that "the term *e-government* focuses on the use of new information and communication technologies (ICTs) by governments as applied to the full range of government functions. In particular, the networking potential offered by the Internet and related technologies has the potential to transform the structures and operation of government" (PUMA, 2001).

The World Bank suggests that "e-government refers to the use by government agencies of information technologies (such as Wide Area Networks, the Internet, and mobile computing) that have the ability to transform relations with citizens, businesses, and other arms of government. These technologies can serve a variety of different ends: better delivery of government services to citizens, improved interactions with business and industry, citizen empowerment through access to information, or more efficient government management. The resulting benefits can be less corruption, increased transparency, greater convenience, revenue growth, and/or cost reductions" (*www1.worldbank.org/publicsector/egov/definition.htm*).

These definitions from OECD and the World Bank have strong parallels with the definitions adopted by some individual OECD member governments. The Cabinet Office in the UK, for example, suggests that, "e-government ... focuses on better services for citizens and businesses and more effective use of the Government's information resources. Implementing it will create an environment for the transformation of government activities by the application of e-business methods throughout the public sector" (Cabinet Office, 2001).

The UK also makes it clear that telephone transactions may be included in e-government, if certain conditions are met. Specifically, it suggests that "electronic" service delivery means "delivery through internet protocols and other ICT methods and includes delivery by telephone if the transaction carried out is electronically enabled, i.e., the officer receiving the call can access electronic information and/or update records online there and then" (DTLR, 2002; text explaining BV 157).

The New Zealand government suggests that "e-government is a way for governments to use the new technologies to provide people with more convenient access to government information and services, to improve the quality of the services and to provide greater opportunities to participate in our democratic institutions and processes" (*http://www.e-government.govt.nz/evision/index.html*).

The Italian government uses the term "e-government" to refer to the use of modern ICTs in the processes of modernising the administration of the state and suggests that it comprises the following categories of activity (*www.pianoegov.it/UserFiles/367.zip*):

1. direct provision of information for improving the internal operating efficiency of administrative units;
2. activities which lead directly to the informatising of the delivery of services to citizens and companies, which often implies the integration of services provided by several administrative units; and
3. activities which lead directly to providing end users with electronic access to public services and to all relevant information about them.

Definition of E-Governance

E-governance, however, is a term which is used much less often and for which there are fewer definitions. This is rather odd, given that the topic of governance has been very topical for over a decade and many OECD governments have incorporated governance issues in their reform programmes (e.g., the "activating state" in Germany and the "modernising government" programme in the UK).

Richard Heeks proposes that the term "e-governance" should be seen to encompass all ICTs, but the key innovation is that of computer networks — from intranets to the Internet — which have created a wealth of new digital connections (Heeks, 2001, p. 2):

- Connections within government — permitting "joined-up thinking."
- Connections between government and NGOs/citizens — strengthening accountability.
- Connections between government and business/citizens — transforming service delivery.
- Connections within and between NGOs — supporting learning and concerted action.
- Connections within and between communities — building social and economic development.

As a result, Heeks suggests, the focus of e-governance shifts from just parts of e-administration, in the case of e-government, to also encompass e-citizens, e-services and e-society.

The joint UNESCO-COMNET-IT study of e-governance (UNESCO, 2002) defines governance as "the process by which society steers itself." It goes on to state that: "in this process, the interactions between the State, Private Enterprise and Civil Society are being increasingly conditioned and modified through the influence of ICTs." Examples of these shifts in dynamics are exemplified by:

- the use of the Internet by Civil Society, NGOs and professional associations to mobilize opinion and influence decision-making processes that affect them;
- the increasing electronic delivery of Government and commercial services and information;
- the electronic publication of draft legislation and statements of direction for public feedback; and
- on the infrastructure side, the increased adoption of e-enabled community centres, the liberalization of telecommunications markets and trends towards Web-enabled mobile telephony and digital television are facilitating this evolution.

Jim Melitski (*http://www.aspanet.org/solutions/egovworld.html*) describes the "e-government journey" as a continuum which begins with information provision when organizations and public agencies publish static information to the Internet, but then moves on as public organizations become more advanced and "are able to provide more dynamic, transactional services. Ultimately the continuum leads to organizational transformation, the transparency of public agencies, increased citizen participation in government, and facilitation of democratic processes." E-government is at one end of this continuum, while e-governance is at the other, but it is not easy, nor really worthwhile, to distinguish where exactly is the dividing line between these concepts.

However, in order to keep the distinction as clear as possible, in this chapter the term "e-government" is essentially restricted to the electronic enablement of services (both to the external stakeholders and to internal customers), while "e-governance" refers to non-service specific activities of government and public agencies.

Aims and Objectives at Supranational and Governmental Levels

The World Bank analyses the potential effects of e-government under the headings (*www1.worldbank.org/publicsector/egov/index.htm*):

- Better service delivery to citizens
- Improved services for business
- Transparency and anti-corruption
- Empowerment through information
- Efficient government purchasing

As can be seen, the third and fourth of these goals belong in the realm of "e-governance," as interpreted in this chapter.

The *e*Europe project has the following goals (European Commission, 2002):

"The overarching goal of eEurope *is to connect Europe as fast as possible to the Net. In order to do reach this goal, the action plan foresees initiatives in three areas:*

1. *a cheaper, faster and more secure Internet*
2. *investments in people and capabilities*
3. *encouragement of the use of the Internet."*

These goals and objectives clearly relate to the putting in place of infrastructure and the critical success factors which are likely to contribute to the eventual impact of the Internet, rather than to the final impacts and outcomes of e-government and e-governance.

At the country-level, again there is significant heterogeneity in the goals identified. The UK government in 2002 was committed to the three overarching objectives of the UK online programme (*http://www.e-envoy.gov.uk/ukonline/progress/anrep2001/01.htm*):

- to make the UK the best and safest environment in the world for e-commerce by 2002;
- to ensure that everyone who wants it has access to the Internet by 2005; and
- to make all Government services available electronically by 2005.

Again, these are instrumental objectives, cast in terms of putting in place a functional infrastructure.

The Canadian government suggests, very much in line with the definitions used in this chapter, that e-government (Government On-Line) can provide (*http://www.gol-ged.gc.ca/rpt/gol-ged-rpt02_e.asp*):

- "*Better service* — through more convenient, faster access to information and services

- *Reduced costs for individuals and businesses* — less search time, less time in filling out forms, faster decisions
- *Reduced costs for government* — reduced data entry costs, lower error rates."

The Canadian Government set the following targets for the end of 2000 (*http://www.comnet.mt/Unesco/CountryProfiles/Project/canada.htm*), again primarily in the realm of e-government, although the final target is more in line with public governance concerns:

- Up-to-date, accurate, bilingual information on key programmes and services available online.
- Commonly-used forms available to download and print.
- The ability to contact departments through the Canada Site.
- The Canada Site will continue to be revamped and organized around citizen needs and topics of interest. A technology and policy framework will be in place that protects the security and privacy of Canadians in their electronic dealings with government.

Moreover, and perhaps more surprisingly, the targets set for the next few years were also specified in terms of service-oriented following deliverables:

- "Key federal programs and services — the ones that matter most to Canadians — will be available on-line ... [including] ... secure and interactive transactions ... [and] ...electronic forms.
- Technical and content support will be provided through various help services ... [with] ... published service standards.
- An easy to use, advanced search capability will be available on the Government of Canada portal and all federal department and agency Web sites.
- One-stop access points (or portals) [will be] available through the Canada Site, with information and services organized according to types of activity, areas of interest and common citizen needs. Plans are already underway to develop portals for seniors, consumers, Aboriginals, the environment, and innovation resources for small- and medium-sized enterprises.
- Innovative partnerships. The Government On-Line initiative will place increased emphasis on on-line service delivery partnerships with provinces, territories, municipalities, businesses, volunteer organizations and international partners."

While essentially remaining e-government-oriented, the fourth of these points makes it clear that Canada will develop its e-services with a strong stakeholder-orientation, something which is missing from most other government strategies.

In Germany, the *Bundesamt für Sicherheit in der Informationstechnik* (BSI) states that "Electronic government refers to the use of the Internet and other electronic media to engage citizens and enterprises in the activities of government, and to enhance collaborative working within public administration" (BSI, 2002). It continues, "The core goal of e-government is establishment of a 'digital administration', which offers online access to information, communications, services and participation opportunities — in so far as they are possible and legally available — in a way which is tailored to the needs of citizens and business, i.e., the requirements of the administration's customers" (BSI, 2002). Clearly, the final sections of these goals begin to stray into e-governance territory.

As highlighted earlier, the New Zealand vision of e-government included the aspiration "to provide greater opportunities to participate in our democratic institutions and processes," which is essentially an e-governance task. The New Zealand government is committed to the mission that by 2004 the Internet will be the dominant means of enabling ready access to government information, services and processes (*http://www.e-government.govt.nz/programme/dec01-exec/exec-dec01.pdf*). It suggests that the benefits of e-government will include (*http://www.e-government.govt.nz/evision/index.html*):

- It will be easier for people to have their say in government.
- People will get better services from government organizations (and governments will have lower costs).
- People will receive more integrated services because different government organizations will be able to communicate more effectively with each other.
- People will be better informed because they can get up-to-date and comprehensive information about government laws, regulations, policies and services.

However, going beyond a pure services-oriented approach, the NZ government suggests that, "The e-government vision supports two important goals. They are:

- *Restoring trust in government and providing strong social services.* The e-government vision will play an important role in achieving this goal. It will:
  - increase collaboration between government organizations;
  - strengthen the relationship between people and the state through greater opportunities for participation; and
  - provide the state sector with an opportunity to improve the effectiveness and efficiency of their services to the public while, at the same time, reducing the cost of delivery."

Those three factors, it suggests, will help restore trust in government and provide strong social services:

- *"Helping grow an inclusive, innovative economy for the benefit of all.* The e-government vision is all about inclusion — the ability of all people to take part in our economy."

How will New Zealanders know that e-government in 2004 is delivering the right results for them? The Government has identified three broad characteristics (*http://www.e-government.govt.nz/programme/dec01-main/chapter4.html*) that mark out successful e-government:

- *Convenience and satisfaction*: *Services provided anytime, anyhow, anywhere.* People will have a choice of channels to government information and services that are convenient, easy to use and deliver what is wanted.

- *Integration and efficiency: Services that are integrated, customer-centric and efficient.* Information and services will be integrated, packaged and presented to minimize cost for people, businesses and departments.
- *Participation: Participation in government.* People will be better informed and better able to participate by having easier access to government information and processes.

Finally, we incorporate into later sections of this chapter two of the potential benefits of e-government and e-governance which are often mentioned by practitioners, although they do not feature very widely either on government Web sites or in the academic literature:

- increasing the transparency of public processes (e.g., by allowing citizen access to information on the stage reached in documentation processing or decision-taking); and
- highlighting the incidences (or possible incidences) of fraud or corruption (within the ethics infrastructure).

Aims of Other Stakeholders

So far, this chapter has focused on the aims and goals for e-government and e-governance which have been highlighted by governments. Yet it is clear that other stakeholders may have other priorities. At the very least we would expect some differentiation in the goals and the priorities expressed by other stakeholders such as:

- Parliaments
- NGOs
- civil society associations
- local authorities

The analysis which is to be found in government and public sector documents about e-government and e-governance tend to talk mainly about stakeholder requirements in very general terms — they refer to the "public" or to "people." For example, in the German context, the BSI (2002) suggests that "customers of the administration" expect online offers which allow them to use public services quickly and in an uncomplicated way, to pursue appropriate processes simply and to understand the bases of decisions which have been made — i.e., they expect service and transparency.

Consequently, governments have not been stakeholder-specific in their declared aims and priorities in e-government and e-governance. Indeed, they have often not even distinguished between citizens and business, and there have been very few attempts to target programmes at civil society through the non-profit sector. The role of the media has also been understated and probably underestimated.

One partial exception to this tendency has been the World Bank, which makes an analogy to e-commerce, where the distinction is often made between improvements which allow businesses to transact with each other more efficiently (B2B) and those which bring customers closer to businesses (B2C). Thus, the World Bank suggests (*www1.worldbank.org/publicsector/egov/definition.htm*) that e-government aims to make the interaction between government and citizens (G2C), government and business enterprises (G2B), and inter-agency relationships (G2G) more friendly, convenient, transparent, and inexpensive. However, once again there is little attempt to differentiate between the goals and the requirements of these different stakeholders.

Constructing Stakeholder-Specific Hierarchies of Objectives for E-Government and E-Governance

One of the areas of public administration which has typically been rather weak is the construction of organisational objectives, which have often been bland, imprecise, ambiguous, complex and inter-acting, unmeasurable and non-prioritised.

This is certainly the case in relation to the opportunities offered by the digital revolution. Few of the documents on e-government and e-governance which have been published by member governments to date have provided clarity on objectives and the priorities between them. Moreover, as argued in the previous section, governments have not been stakeholder specific in their declared aims and priorities in e-government and e-governance, often assuming that all stakeholders will perceive and prioritize the same benefits (and disbenefits).

The basic idea of "management by objectives" (MBO), as proposed by Drucker, was extended by Ansoff (1969) to propose that the top-level objectives in an organisation could be cascaded down through the layers of the organisation. In this approach, the objectives at the top of the hierarchy of objectives indicate the impacts which the organisation wishes to have on users and other stakeholders, including society as a whole. The achievement of these "impact" objectives should be linked clearly to the achievement of the next level of objectives, ("service-level" objectives) which are instrumental and essentially show the organisational outputs which are necessary if the "impact" objectives are to be achieved. Finally, the lowest level objectives ("logistical" objectives) should be pictured, the achievement of which will enable the service level objectives to be achieved.

The greatest innovation of the hierarchy of objectives was not that it allowed the interactions between objectives to be modelled clearly, or that it highlighted clearly the potential conflicts between some objectives, or that it encouraged performance measurement at all levels of the hierarchy of objectives (and showed how measuring performance at the lowest level of objectives might act as a proxy for measuring performance at the highest level, if this was problematic). Rather it was that it presented the map of interrelated objectives as a framework of hypotheses about "cause-and-effect" chains in the organisation (Bovaird, 2001). Since these hypotheses could be contested (and often were in practice), this approach stimulated managers and professionals to find logical arguments and evidence for their view of how the hierarchy of objectives held together. Essentially, this approach encouraged and embodied an "evidence-based-management" approach, a long time before that became fashionable.

Furthermore, by presenting a model of the hypothesised links between aspirations, the hierarchy of objectives allows stakeholders to contest the views of "reality" held by other stakeholders. The logic of the hierarchy of objectives is that each stakeholder group should construct and fight for its own vision of the appropriate corporate aspirations. Furthermore, it should attempt to gain acceptance for the ways in which the organisation might hope to realise these aspirations, i.e., the rest of the cause-and-effect chain which it hypothesises for the organisation.

This results in a set of "hierarchies of objectives" within any organisation, rather than just one. This appears much messier than the elegant simplicity of Ansoff's original idea, never mind the simple lists envisaged by Drucker.

What is the relationship between these stakeholders' hierarchies of objectives? There are three major ways in which they may be expected to differ:

- differences in values held by stakeholders may lead to different objectives being accepted as aspirations — this is especially likely to mean that stakeholder groups may place different objectives at or near the top of their hierarchies of objectives;
- differences in values or in interests may lead stakeholder groups to put different priorities on top objectives and the pathways which lead down from them; and
- differences in experience or in logical reasoning may lead stakeholders to different models of the cause-and-effect chains linking different subobjectives in the hierarchy of objectives.

This means that a multiple stakeholder approach does not simply mean the overlay of different stakeholder maps, each containing a sub-set of the overall hierarchy of objectives. In practice, stakeholder maps may differ in the objectives they contain and the logical cause-and-effect chains which are modelled within them.

Moreover, there are an infinity of maps which might be drawn by any one stakeholder to analyse different problems or different issues — a stakeholder may wish to examine the objective map for one its functions rather than for one of its products or one of its clients — and each map would present the opportunity to envisage a different formulation of what the organisation is trying to achieve.

This leads us to the conclusion that the search for "organisational objectives" has been fool's gold twice over:

- the organisation does not have objectives, only its stakeholders have objectives — so that any attempt to state "organisational objectives" is at base an attempt to impose the objectives believed by the dominant stakeholder group or coalition to be the most advantageous public expression of its own interests; and
- each stakeholder group or coalition is likely to need a different map of its objectives, depending on the problem to be solved or the issue to be addressed.

With this insight, we can then see each stakeholder's set of objectives as a set of windows into its "underlying world" of objectives. In order to illustrate this, we will use a simple hierarchy of objectives relating to one aspect of e-governance — the concern of citizens about the security of Internet transactions.

In Figure 1, we see in the background window (A) a set of objectives for reassuring the public about the level of Internet security. It contains objectives to deter fraud (partially through prevention measures, partly through detection, and partly through "high visibility policing." It also contains a different "pathway" of objectives, focusing around informing the public about the actual, as opposed to the feared, level of Internet fraud. The overall set of objectives set out in window A might, for example, be held by a government agency trying to model decide the best policies by which the public might be reassured to have greater confidence in Internet security. One set of this "window" has been highlighted in a separate window (B) — this set of objectives relates only to sub-objectives, which attempt to inform the public about how over-inflated is the common view about risks attached to Internet transactions. This narrower "window" of sub-objectives might be held by public agency which is trying to convince its users to make their payments over the Internet rather than at cashier's offices (e.g., the tax collection service).

Of course, other stakeholders will have different sets of objectives. In Figure 1, a new set of objectives has been highlighted in "window" C, relating to a different stakeholder. This might, for example, be the set of objectives held by the legal services department in the public agency, which employs an Internet monitoring agency to police internet transactions in order to detect attempted frauds. In this example, detection is the key objective which the legal services department believes should be pursued in order to reassure the public about Internet security. This stakeholder group does not see "high visibility policing of all Internet transactions" as a high level sub-objective in its own right, but only as a means of detecting fraudulent activity. Clearly, there is a dispute here about the empirical relationships which exist in the specific environment in which the map is created. And this argument really matters — the two versions of this map, at the heart of the dispute between the stakeholders involved, lead to very different strategies for reassuring the public. A "high visibility policing" policy which is given sufficient resources to actually detect significant levels of fraud is likely to require very large resourcing, whereas a "high visibility policing" policy which is essentially meant to scare off potential fraudsters might be undertaken quite cheaply. Until these arguments can be resolved, major resource wastage is likely to occur.

Clearly this example has been made simple for illustrative purposes. However, we suggest it is sufficiently realistic to demonstrate the point that it would be unwise to take at face value any set of "organisational objectives" which purport to represent all stakeholders and to aid decision making in all contexts.

KEY ISSUES IN PERFORMANCE MEASUREMENT AND EVALUATION OF E-GOVERNMENT AND E-GOVERNANCE

In this section, we outline a number of key issues which need to be tackled in developing appropriate frameworks for measurement and evaluation of e-government and e-governance:

- What criteria can governments develop to assess trade-offs in policy making, for example between efficiency and improved participation and accountability?
- How can the benefits to recipients of services, such as portals, be quantified?
- How to measure quality of services, or consultative processes, and their enhancement using e-government?
- Can progress in e-government be assessed? What are the key indicators? Can we use these indicators at both micro and macro levels?
- How can the whole of governmental e-strategies be evaluated?

Figure 1. Objective maps from three stakeholders

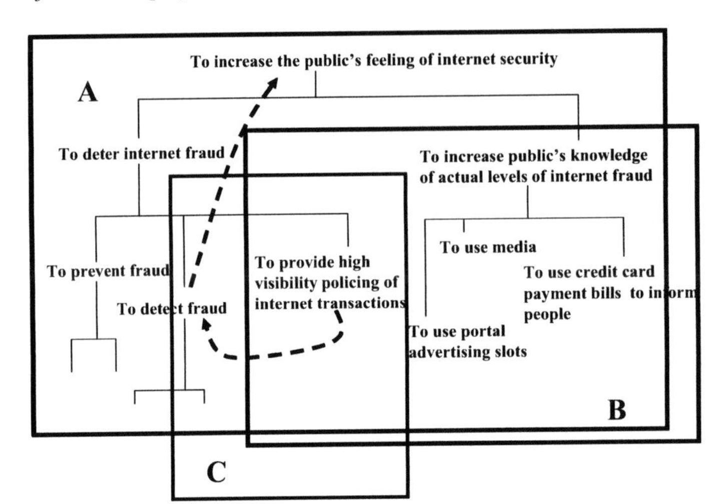

What Criteria Can Governments Develop to Assess Trade-Offs in E-Government and E-Governance?

Clearly, there are a number of difficult choices facing governments in deciding their priorities in e-government and e-governance. For example, increased efficiency might be gained if more communications could be made available only through telephone and Internet connections. However, this could disadvantage those people without telephone or Internet access. Again, e-governance mechanisms such as e-referenda could improve the interactive participation of citizens and other stakeholders in government decision-making — but it could also slow down decision-making processes and could give rise to unrepresentative pressures being placed on governments and parliaments if security systems are not sufficiently watertight to eliminate bogus or multiple voting.

In order to deal with this potential problem, governments will need to consider ways of setting priorities between the goals of e-government and e-governance. However, this will be problematic, both because the explicit setting of priorities is always difficult in a political setting and also because the goals of e-government and e-governance are so closely inter-related.

To make these trade-offs systematically will therefore require that the full portfolio of effects of e-government and e-governance programmes are be borne in mind in the decision-making process. It will be dangerous to focus on only a limited number of goals or targets at any one time, as the knock-on effects of some achievements will be so significant.

It would also be valuable if more detailed modelling were done into the cause-and-effect chains linking high level aims to low level sub-objectives in both e-government and e-governance. The absence of an agreed framework for considering these cause-and-effect chains — and for carrying out rigorous tests into their credibility — magnifies the risk involved in having to make a choice between different "pathways" in the hierarchy of objectives.

How Can the Benefits to Particular Recipients of Intermediate Technical Services be Quantified?

Many of the key steps in e-government and e-governance are intermediate outputs (for example, reducing fraud by enabling system-wide checks of behavior by welfare claimants, or increasing public confidence in financial transactions on the Internet by establishing secure systems for electronic signatures). It is often in the nature of such intermediate outputs that they are not well known to nor understood by those people who benefit from them — indeed, many of the services which produce these intermediate outputs may not even be noticed by many users.

In such cases, there are a limited number of ways in which these "intermediate outputs" can be evaluated:

a. they can be evaluated by professional peer groups who are aware of their purpose — an independent qualitative judgement process;
b. they can be evaluated through benchmarking of their characteristics by professional peer groups — an independent objective judgement process;
c. they can be evaluated on the basis of the overall impacts of the package of outputs of which they form a part, without seeking to separate out the contribution of individual components of the package — a "joint products" evaluation, based on outcome measures; and
d. they can be evaluated by testing against a "theory of change" which sets out the ways in which they are hypothesised to work, so that each link in the chain of argument can be tested.

None of these approaches is entirely convincing by itself and none will be entirely easy to undertake. In some cases, even the simplest of these approaches can be costly and can take time. Consequently, where it is important to undertake evaluations which separate out the contributions of "intermediate outputs" from "final outputs," several of these approaches may need to be combined and the evaluation may take a considerable period of time to come up with significant results.

How to Measure the Quality of Services, or the Quality of Consultative Processes, and Their Enhancement Using E-Government?

Since one of the major drivers behind e-government is improvement to the quality of services, it would clearly be advantageous to be able to measure the extent to which e-government has increased the quality of public services provided by organizations in the public sector and other providers to which services have been outsourced.

However, there is a significant gap in quality management systems in the public sector in most OECD member countries. While quality assurance systems have become very common, and they have helped to stop the occurrence of sudden "glitches" in quality levels, the measurement of actual quality levels is much less advanced. Most performance measurement systems still focus primarily on inputs and outputs (and, to a lesser degree, outcomes) which can easily be quantified, and most of these measures throw little light on the quality of services.

Although this is being partly addressed by some initiatives, such as the "results" sections of the EFQM Excellence Model, and the customer satisfaction surveys which have been built into the performance management framework for local government in the UK, these approaches are still relatively young and untried. Consequently, the determination of the success of e-government in improving the quality of public services will face major measurement challenges.

In order to take this challenge further, it is necessary for an organisation or a stakeholder to decide on the definition of quality which is going to be used. As shown in Figure 2, there are interesting and potentially valuable methods of measuring quality, whatever the definition chosen. However, without taking this first (and admittedly difficult) step of defining the concept of quality, it is unlikely that any clarity will be achieved in assessing its level and its direction of change.

Can Progress in E-Government and E-Governance be Assessed? What are the Key Indicators? Can We Use These Indicators at Both Micro and Macro Levels?

The assessment of progress in e-government and e-governance requires some measures of performance which can command credibility in the eyes of the major stakeholders who need to know whether the programmes are working.

This has been put forcibly by Di Maio: "While e-government has sparked countless best-practice exchange and comparison initiatives, which are useful in accelerating efforts in regions that are lagging behind, they risk missing the real point. Initiatives must be based on quantifying value and cost for constituents, as well as governments, and address service-delivery targets alongside the other aspects of e-government transformation. Progress must be measured against national needs, not on the basis of what other countries think and do" (Gartner, 2001, *www.Gartner.com*).

Figure 2. Measuring "quality"

Definition of "quality"	Potential measurement method
"Conformance to specification" (engineering and "contract culture" approaches	1. Level of defects ("failure rate"). 2. Full conformance to all provisions of specification or not ("yes-no" certification)
"Fitness for purpose" (systems analysis approach)	1. Scoring against each "purpose" or "objective" 2. Aggregate score against weighted set of "purposes" or "objectives"
"Meeting customer expectations" (consumer psychology approach)	1. Checking against checklist of all stakeholder expectations 2. Weighted score against all stakeholder expectations
"Producing passionate emotional involvement in the stakeholder" (social psychology approach)	1. Questionnaire to stakeholders to see if they identify with the service 2. Exploration with stakeholder to see if they would be willing to contribute (time, money, reputation) to the service, as evidence of their emotional involvement

Clearly, this assessment process will more powerful and more convincing if there is some link between the measures used to assess the success of the overall programmes and the measures used to assess the success of individual initiatives within the programme. In fact, there are two competing tendencies here:

- It is easier to measure the intermediate outputs of relatively small initiatives, since they are easier to aggregate than the large range of intermediate outputs which emerge from a national programme of e-government or e-governance.
- However, if we want to measure outcomes, then it is usually easier to do this at programme level, because at the level of projects or individual initiatives, it is very difficult to separate out the effect of individual projects on outcomes which have been brought about by a package of projects and initiatives.

Consequently, when we see to measure the success of e-government and e-governance programmes, it is likely to be valuable to pursue both the measurement of intermediate outputs and of outcomes, and to consider the relationship between them.

How Can the Whole of Governmental E-Strategies be Evaluated?

Following on from the previous issue, there is a need to evaluate not only the outcomes of e-strategies at governmental level, but also whether the strategies chosen have been well calculated to achieve their goals. This is because it is not simply important to know the end or "summative" results of a strategy. It is usually essential to know if the strategy could have been made more successful by changes which might have been brought about by the policymakers and managers concerned, so that "formative" conclusions can be reached which can allow policy learning to take place.

This requires a "theory of change," which explains in a logical and systematic way the cause-and-effect chain by means of which the initiatives within the e-programme have brought about the outcomes desired by the government.

Such a "theory of change" needs a clear statement of the elements of the "rational decision-making model" — the problems which were addressed, the objectives formulated in relation to that problem area, the options generated, the evaluation criteria used, the process of selecting an option, the implementation process used for the chosen strategy, and the monitoring and review processes which are used to check if the chosen strategy is working.

Once such a "theory of change" has been elaborated, all its elements can be tested against the evidence, including its assumptions, its problem specification, the objectives which it proposes for the programme, the alternative solutions which it generates, the evaluation criteria and the implementation and monitoring regimes. Without such a theory of change, it is very difficult to undertake a practical evaluation over any period of time, because of the likelihood that so much will change during the period of the evaluation. The "theory of change" model allows the evaluator to gauge whether the government policymakers were able to respond to these changing external factors in ways which allowed them to achieve the key results in which they were interested.

Of course, in practice governments often do not have clearly mapped out strategies — rather, they "muddle through." Even where strategies exist, they often are not prioritised and they do not have a project plan. In these circumstances, the "theory of action" may have to be hypothesised by the evaluator, who may then have to seek to validate it by checking out with a range of stakeholders as to whether it accords with their sense as to what was the original "theory of change." The greatest problem with this approach is that each stakeholder may have its own "theory of change" and may not care greatly for — or even notice — the theories of change held by other stakeholders, so that this approach to retrospective validation of the "theory of change" may not work well.

Consequently, the more shadowy is the e-government or e-governance strategy, and the more frequently it has been changed over time, the more difficult it is to evaluate whether "the strategy" worked in practice. What is then more interesting is whether the changes in the strategy were well made, given the signals from the environment — both from the external customers and from the internal stakeholders. This moves the focus away from the outcomes of a long-term strategy (which may not exist or may be very difficult to discern) towards the intermediate outputs of a set of changing short-term strategies (which are readily discernible but may hide the underlying strategy — if there was one).

PERFORMANCE INDICATORS FOR E-GOVERNMENT AND E-GOVERNANCE

Principles in Designing and Choosing PIs

The key principles in designing PIs are:

- Each PI should be relevant to at least one of the objectives of the programme or initiative.
- It should be clear whether a change in a PI indicates that the objective(s) is being achieved to a greater or lesser degree than before.
- The score on the PI should be, at least partly, subject to influence, if not full control by the politicians or managers concerned.
- The score on the PI should not easily be subject to manipulation.
- Scores should be normalized.

The key principles in choosing PIs to fit into an assessment system are:

- A portfolio of PIs should be chosen which cover all the main dimensions which we wish to evaluate, including .
    - level of activity (outputs),
    - volume of use,
    - social or other groups to which users belong (targeting),
    - quality of experience offered to users, and
    - unit cost.
- Only those PIs should be chosen which vary significantly throughout the population to be studied, so that the PI allows us to distinguish between different strategies.

Potential Uses of Performance Indicators

Performance indicators can have a number of uses within performance management systems:

- appraising potential projects, programmes or policies in advance;
- monitoring progress against predefined targets;
- increasing the transparency of public processes (e.g., by allowing citizen access to information on the stage reached in documentation processing or decision-taking);
- highlighting the incidences (or possible incidences) of fraud or corruption (within the ethics infrastructure);
- benchmarking progress against other agencies, other programmes (or even other countries);
- assessing quality against predefined standards (often in mid-project or mid-term review, since quality PIs are not easy to collect on an ongoing basis);
- measuring benefits and costs as part of an overall assessment of individual initiatives or projects (usually in mid-project and at the end of an initiative or project, since overall benefits and costs are often expensive to measure and to collate); and
- assessing overall cost-effectiveness of e-government and e-governance programmes and policies (again typically at mid-term or end of such programmes or at the stage of a major policy review).

It can be seen that these uses of PIs correspond essentially to the "appraisal, monitoring and ex-post review" stages of evaluative activity.

Scope of PIs Required

The PIs to be formulated need to cover the full range of issues in assessing e-government and e-governance. This means that they need to be able to cover at least the following dimensions:

- effects of e-government on responsiveness of governments and other key stake-holders to the needs of their users, covering such effects as:
    - more user-oriented service planning,
    - more user-oriented service delivery, and
    - more user-oriented service complaints mechanisms.
- effects of e-governance on responsiveness of governments and other key stake-holders to the needs of their citizens, covering such effects as:
    - more citizen-oriented policy-making processes and
    - more citizen-oriented processes of accountability.
- impacts on public administration made possible by e-government, which will cover inter-organisational issues such as:
    - policy cohesion across the whole of the public sector and public services (i.e., achievement of "joined-up policy-making") and

  - synergy between programmes across the whole of the public sector and public services (i.e., achievement of "joined-up service delivery").
- effects of e-government of critical success factors in service delivery (OECD draft report *From in-line to online: delivering better services*), including:
  - leadership;
  - strategy building;
  - responsiveness to stakeholders;
  - skills;
  - budget;
  - integration;
  - ICT management;
  - partnership working; and
  - change management and innovation.

Key Areas for PIs in Relation to a Range of Stakeholders

Clearly, the PIs developed should cover all the key aims and objectives specified in the previous section. As these key aims and objectives are stakeholder-specific, it will usually be important that the PIs should also reflect stakeholder interests and that PI reporting systems allow main stakeholders to see clearly how performance is being achieved in e-government and e-governance, from their perspectives. Each PI which is used should therefore be in the interests of at least one stakeholder — and often it is clear that PIs will be interesting to many stakeholders.

Under *e-government*, the areas of activity in which PIs are typically suggested are:

- General impacts on the public
  - public access achieved
  - digital divide and public access
  - public usage achieved
  - digital divide and public usage
  - developing access channels
- Impacts on corporate management system
  - corporate strategy
  - corporate leadership
  - corporate culture change
  - corporate procurement of e-government infrastructure
- Impacts on corporate communication developing joined-up communications with legislatures, other public bodies and PSOs
  - customer relations management
  - developing front-office integration
  - developing back office integration (partnership management, supply chain management, knowledge management, e-learning)

- Impacts on service planning and service commissioning
- Impacts on service delivery
    - meeting service needs of customers
    - enhancement of service quality
    - time and cost implications

Under *e-governance*, the areas of activity in which PIs are typically suggested are:

- General
    - usage achieved
    - digital divide in usage by different social groups
- Management of interface with external stakeholders
    - interactions with the public sector enabled by electronic means
    - transparency of public decision-making processes
    - ethical conduct in Internet interactions
    - establishing citizen confidence in the security of the Internet
- Developing networks with external stakeholders

Potential for Turning PIs in Some Areas into Standards

When PIs are particularly important, it may be desirable to turn them into standards, against which performance can be benchmarked. Such standards may be used as major targets in national programmes. Indeed, target values for some of these PIs are available from specific countries, e.g., the targets for the availability of e-enabled services in the UK.

However, not all PIs are suitable for standard-setting. In particular, if a PI can be easily manipulated by managerial action — e.g., through changing the dates or times at which the PI is measured, or by altering the population for which it is measured — then it is unlikely to be appropriate as the basis for a standard.

Some Silver Rules of Performance Management

While there are no "golden laws" of performance management which apply in all circumstances, there are some "silver rules" which appear to have quite widespread validity.

- *Be clear about purposes* — these may include imposing control, giving strategic direction, giving hands-off empowerment, and encouraging learning about "what works." The control purpose is likely to raise the hackles of staff and, if it is the only purpose, it is likely to be significantly undermined by the "perverse control syndrome" (Bovaird, 2004).
- *Relate PIs to objectives*, unless the objectives are poorly defined — e.g., if the objectives are vague, ambiguous, complex and interacting, partially hidden or unstated, unmeasurable or unrealistic.
- *Set targets* (i.e., target values within specified time periods) for each of the PIs in order to indicate the short and medium term pathways towards objectives — but don't allow targets to overwhelm objectives — the targets are inevitably short-termist, myopic and narrow compared to the objectives, which in the end are much more important.

- *Set balanced portfolios of PIs* — this will often involve separate PIs for economy, efficiency, effectiveness, outcomes, equity and quality.
- *Self-assessment is normally preferable to external independent assessment* because it is more knowledgeable, cheaper and involves those who will be key to implementation of lessons learned — but it requires rigorous and credible audit, in order to stop staff "putting a gloss" on their self-reported results and to ensure that alternative viewpoints are surfaced.
- *Agree on the performance management system, don't impose it*, because imposed systems will be easy to undermine by disaffected and uncommitted staff — unless it proves too difficult to agree a system, in which case an imposed system may kick-start dialogue and debate. (However, assume any imposed system which has not become agreed-to after two years has already been undermined and that its data are too contaminated to be useful, in which case the whole exercise has been damaging and counterproductive.)
- *Set priorities* for each service and assess the performance of the priorities first — you are unlikely to have the time to undertake a comprehensive assessment of all aspects of what you do. Similarly, decide what aspects of the performance management system are priorities, in terms of their likely pay-off relative to their likely costs, and implement these parts of the performance management system first.
- *Make comparisons over time and between departments/agencies* — while it is true that all comparisons are at least partly misleading, it is also the case that we only learn through making comparisons, however imperfect they may be.
- *Organise for performance management* — it will not happen automatically and performance management systems will not be taken seriously unless senior managers show that they find them interesting and use them in decision-making.
- In spite of the complications introduced by all the above "silver rules," *the overall system of performance management must remain "short, sharp, snappy,"* because otherwise it will be too cumbersome to be memorable, and unmemorable systems do not affect everyday decision-making, and are thus relatively ineffective.

EVALUATION OF E-GOVERNMENT PROGRAMMES AND INITIATIVES

Role of Evaluations

It is important to be clear why evaluations are being carried out, as the purpose will help to decide the design of the evaluation — and will also condition the response to it.

The purposes of evaluation may include:

- political and managerial accountability of organisations, partnerships and networks, through producing information on how successful (or unsuccessful) their efforts have been;

- policy learning in policy networks, through producing information on which aspects of policy have been most successful;
- supporting leadership through informing strategic direction and allowing this strategic direction to be justified to all those stakeholders who may have reasons for resisting it; and
- activation of stakeholders, through alerting them to areas in which they are less successful in receiving the benefits of projects (or areas in which they are especially likely to be bearing the costs).

As in the case of performance management in the previous section, if the first of these purposes — accountability — is interpreted as meaning that there is a hunt for a scapegoat, who will be blamed for lack of success, then the whole evaluation effort may well be undermined by the behavior of staff, who will ensure that the data provided to the evaluation obscure much of what really went on. Only if at least some of the other purposes are widely believed to be important is there a real hope that the former purpose can also be achieved.

Finally, a reflection on how such roles may be relatively short-term: Whinston et al. (2001, p. 3) suggest that, "the Internet is increasingly becoming part of the basic business model for many companies, laying the groundwork for even more impressive growth during more favorable economic conditions. The Internet is rapidly becoming a part of the traditional economy — like telephones, elevators and personal computers over the years — leading to the day when there will be no separate measure of the internet economy." The same logic may well mean that, before very long, the Internet is so much part of the woodwork in the public sector and in public services that it will no longer merit separate consideration as a key driver of change and improvement.

Key Electronic Service Delivery Issues Which Need to be Covered by Evaluation Frameworks

In the evaluation of the e-government programme, the following service delivery issues are likely to be central aspects which will need to be evaluated:

- improving access
- reducing administrative burdens
- reducing costs to administration
- providing integrated services
- improving quality of services
- tailoring services to customer needs
- incorporating citizen feedback
- ensuring privacy and security
- providing strategic direction
- ensuring oversight and control
- adapting to changes

The latter three issues may well be the most difficult, as they are areas in which it is especially problematic to devise PIs.

Key E-Governance Issues Which Need to be Covered by Evaluation Frameworks

- Need for multi-stakeholder analysis
- Transparency of decision-making
- Accountability of stakeholders to other (multiple) stakeholders
- Engagement of all stakeholders in planning, decision-making and evaluation
- Activation of all stakeholders, including those difficult-to-reach or difficult-to-reach or difficult-to-move
- Access to information within clearly agreed privacy constraints
- Joined-up working in partnerships
- Holistic perspectives on quality of life of stakeholders
- Ethical behavior and integrity
- Flexibility and adaptability of organisations, institutions and mechanisms
- Coherence of programmes
- Legitimacy of institutions

Once again, it is the latter three issues which may well be the most difficult to evaluate, as they are areas in which it is especially problematic to devise PIs.

Evaluation Methodologies

There are a number of evaluation models that are, or could be, used to measure e-government and e-governance implementation and impact.

First, there are *models for evaluating the aggregate of programme outcomes*, which typically fall into four categories:

a. *goals achievement matrix*, where there is an attempt to score the initiatives and strategies against a weighted set of goals;
b. *balanced scorecard approaches*, where there is an attempt to score the initiatives against four or five sets of performance indicators, which may or may not be linked to goals and where weighting may or may not apply
c. *cost-benefit models*, where there is an attempt to quantify most of the benefits and most of the costs in money terms;
d. *cost-effectiveness models*, where there is an attempt to assess which strategy, out of a set of strategies with approximately equal cost, is likely to score best against a weighted set of goals, *or* which strategy, out of a set of strategies judged to have approximately equal effectiveness, is likely to be least cost.

In recent years, there has been less enthusiasm for evaluation methodologies which imply aggregating across categories (such as cost-benefit analysis), on the grounds that this is an area where the decisions should primarily be political, not technical, in character.

Secondly, there are models for *measuring the individual outcomes* within each generic type of outcome which occurs in a programme. These typically fall into four categories:

a. changes in the *satisfaction levels* of users or other relevant stakeholders — these are quantifiable, subjective data;

b. changes in the *levels of certain states* (e.g., employment status, health status, educational qualifications, etc.) characteristic of users or other relevant stakeholders — these are quantifiable, objective data;
c. changes in the *attributes or features* (e.g., married or unmarried, holder or non-holder of driving license, with or without hospital appointment for condition reported to local doctor) of users or other relevant stakeholders — these are non-quantifiable, objective data;
d. changes in the *attitudes or mental conditions* (e.g., happy or sad, optimistic or pessimistic, envious or content) of users or other relevant stakeholders — these are non-quantifiable, subjective data.

Thirdly, there are methods for assessing whether the changes observed in the evaluation process are likely to have been associated with the programme being evaluated:
a. randomised trial with double-blind experimental and control groups;
b. randomised trial with single-blind experimental and control groups;
c. randomised trial with fully aware experimental and control groups;
d. area-based trials, where all residents in a particular area are in the same group, whether experimental or control;
e. before-and-after trials, with control groups;
f. before-and-after trials without control groups.

Generally, the strength of conclusions which can be drawn from an evaluation decreases as we move from a. to e. in the above list (although area-based trials can have both some special advantages and some special disadvantages in specific cases which mean that they move a little up or down this "ranking").

Using Evaluation Results

Evaluations are not of any value unless their results become used. The history of evaluations in both public sector and in the private sector shows that a high proportion of evaluations do not have a significant effect in the organisations which they were designed to help. The recent evaluation of the implementation of e-government at local level in the UK (CURDS, 2003) has concluded, along these lines, that "The disappointing take-up and use of many e-government services to date has begun to focus attention on how e-government enabled services can be *promoted and marketed* and a sense of ownership developed within local communities."

In order to make it more likely that the performance management and evaluation approaches outlined in this chapter will be put to some use, it is important that they are operated jointly by the stakeholders who will be responsible for learning the lessons which they throw up, and for implementing the consequent changes.

This means that stakeholder-based evaluation is much more likely to be successful than evaluation done to stakeholders. Of course, this brings with it some attendant dangers, particularly of lack of independence and imaginative innovation. Consequently, stakeholder-based evaluation must include such a range of stakeholders that the final evaluation is likely to have a rounded perspective and a creative search for alternative ways forward.

CONCLUSIONS

- Performance indicators for e-government and e-governance need to relate closely to a longer term strategic vision and strategic direction for government and for public service organisations. They should clearly tie in closely with a hierarchy of objectives, which sets out the aspirational agenda, rather than being stand-alone.
- Organisations do not have objectives — it is stakeholders who have objectives. It is important that the differences between stakeholder perspectives and priorities are understood when setting direction and monitoring performance of e-government and e-governance programmes.
- Performance indicators must cover a range of different objectives, including level of access (particularly across social groups), level of usage, effects on public service quality and cost, effects on organisational excellence, effects on network and partnership working and effects on key governance issues, such as stakeholder consultation and participation, transparency of decision-making, and standards of ethical conduct.
- It is possible to devise a large library of PIs which might be useful to particular stakeholders for specific purposes at a given time. However, in practice, it is unwise to try to collect and to use too many PIs at once.
- Evaluation methods can make use of essentially the same library of PIs as performance management approaches.
- Whichever evaluation methods are used, close involvement of stakeholders is essential if the results are to have any chance of influencing future behavior.
- The most popular forms of evaluation in recent years have not attempted to aggregate benefits across categories — this has been seen as an area for primarily political decision-making. This is likely to remain true in e-government and e-governance.

RECOMMENDATIONS

In this section, we make some brief recommendations for priority areas in the measurement of the performance of e-government and e-governance and the evaluation of e-government and e-governance programmes. They are broken down by major stakeholder:

For OECD

- The library of PIs suggested in this chapter should be extended and refined in consultation with stakeholders in OECD Member Countries and a range of demonstration projects should be undertaken to test the comparative success of e-government and e-governance in a sample of Member Countries which currently are taking a leading position in this field.

For governments of OECD Member Countries

- A wider range of performance measures should be used to test the success of current e-government and e-governance programmes.

- Given the cost of these programmes, and the risks which they entail to both governments and to the public, the most ambitious e-government and e-governance programmes in each country should be evaluated as a matter of urgency, using and refining clusters of the PIs in the library of PIs recommended in this chapter, so that the results can be widely disseminated.

For local government

- Given the costs and risks associated with these programmes, it is important that a range of varied and imaginative e-government and e-governance programmes be supported in each Member Country, with a careful evaluation programme, using and developing the library of PIs outlined in this chapter.

For NGOs and civil associations

- Given the potential but also the risk which e-government and e-governance programmes pose, particularly to disadvantaged and vulnerable groups, it is of paramount importance that these programmes should be designed imaginatively, to incorporate a wide degree of diversity, and should be evaluated thoroughly and quickly. Both the design and evaluation of these programmes should be a multi-stakeholder responsibility, and NGOs and civil society associations should play a major role in these processes — if necessary, raising their own resources to ensure that this evaluation is done in a way which is appropriate to reflect the interests of their members

For ICT suppliers

- Evaluation of "what works and what does not" is going to be a key theme of the digital revolution. Electronic service delivery and e-governance are intrinsically well-placed to record information on the characteristics of users. However, current systems are still not well-designed to expedite performance management and evaluation — this is an area which is likely to give suppliers a competitive advantage in the future.
- It will important to design future systems with the needs of multiple stakeholders in mind, and not just the stakeholder who is putting the most money up front. This also means the need to build in stakeholder based performance measures and evaluation criteria when the systems are being designed.

For other businesses

- Government to Business (G2B) service delivery and governance issues will grow in importance as governments catch up with the pace of change which has characterised e-commerce. It will be important for business to understand government requirements, so that the design of new digital-based information systems can reflect these likely future needs. Further, it will be valuable for business if it is made clear to government how the new e-government and e-governance systems can be designed in ways which reduce the burden of administrative costs which is entailed by public regulation. This is most likely to be effective if undertaken in collaboration with other business partners and, in some cases, with organisations in the third sector.

REFERENCES

Bovaird, T. (2001). Strategic objective maps as "windows" into worlds of cause-and-effect. Paper presented at *Reframing Organisational Performance, EAISM Conference*, Brussels, October.

Bovaird, T. (2004). Public sector performance measurement. In K. Kempf-Leonard (Ed.), *Encyclopaedia of social measurement*. San Diego, CA: Elsevier Science.

BSI. (2002). *Chefsache E-Government: Leitfaden für Behördenleiter*. E-Government Handbuch. Bonn: Bundesamt für Sicherheit in der Informationstechnik. Retrieved from *www.e-government-handbuch.de*

Cabinet Office. (2001). *E-government: A strategic framework for public services in the Information Age*. London: Cabinet Office. Retrieved from *http://www.e-envoy.gov.uk/ukonline/progress/estrategy/summary.htm*

CURDS. (2003). *Implementing electronic local government. Final Report of the Process Evaluation of the Implementation of Electronic Local Government in England.* London, Office of the Deputy Prime Minister.

CyberAtlas. (2001). E-government may not mean efficiency. Retrieved from *http://cyberatlas.internet.com/markets/professional/article/0,,5971_929471,00.html*

DTLR. (2001). *e-Government: Delivering local government online – Guidelines for preparing 'implementing electronic government' statements*. London: Department of Transport, Local Government and the Regions. Retrieved from *http://www.detr.gov.uk*

DTLR. (2002). Best value performance indicators 2002/2003. London: Stationery Office. Retrieved from *http://www.local-regions.dtlr.gov.uk/bestvalue/indicators/pi2002-03/06.htm*

European Commission. (2002). *e-Europe 2002: e-Europe Benchmarking Report*. Brussels: European Commission.

Heeks, R. (2001). *Understanding e-Governance for Development*. i-Government Working Paper Series, Working Paper No. 11. Manchester: Institute for Development Policy and Management, University of Manchester. Retrieved from *http://idpm.man.ac.uk/idpm/igov11.htm*

OECD. (2001). *Understanding the digital divide*. Paris: OECD.

OECD. (2001). *Project on the impact of e-government*. PUMA(2001)10 REV 2. Paris: OECD.

OECD. (2001). *Citizens as partners: Information, consultation and public participation in policy-making*. Paris: OECD.

OECD. (2001). *The hidden threat to e-government: Avoiding large government IT failures*. Paris: OECD.

OECD. (2001). *From in-line to on-line*. Paris: OECD.

PUMA. (2001). *E-Government: Analysis framework and methodology*. PUMA2001/16/ANN/Rev1. Paris: OECD.

UNESCO. (2002). Joint Unesco and Comnet-It Study of e-governance: Development of country profiles. Retrieved from *www.comnet.mt/Unesco/CountryProfiles/Project/joint_unesco_and_comnet.htm*

Whinston et al. (2001). Measuring the Internet economy. Cisco Systems and University of Texas. Retrieved from *http://www.internetindicators.com/jan_2001.pdf*

Chapter III

E-Government and E-Governance: Organizational Implications, Options, and Dilemmas

Tony Bovaird, Bristol University, UK

ABSTRACT

This chapter suggests that e-government and e-governance initiatives can potentially have major organizational impacts through three mechanisms: improved decision-making, more intensive and productive use of databases, and better communications. These mechanisms impact on both the internal organization of public agencies and their configuration of networks and partnerships. E-enablement therefore makes obsolete many existing organizational structures and processes and offers the prospect of transformation in both service delivery and public governance arrangements. However, the organizational changes which can be effected through the e-revolution are only just beginning to become evident. While it seems likely that existing organizational configurations in the public sector will not be sustainable, the most appropriate ways forward will only be uncovered through much experimentation within e-government and e-governance programmes. In the nature of experimentation, many of these initiatives will turn out to be unproductive or cost-ineffective, but that is perhaps the necessary price to pay for the level of public sector transformation which now appears to be in prospect.

E-GOVERNMENT AND E-GOVERNANCE: TRANSFORMATION OR DISPLACEMENT ACTIVITY?

INTRODUCTION

This chapter examines a paradox: in a period when politicians, senior public officials and management consultants appear to be competing in exaggeration about the rate of change which they will soon effect, the claims made on behalf of e-government and e-governance have been particularly grandiose. At the same time, governments such as the Blair administration in the UK continue to declare themselves dissatisfied with the rates of change actually achieved in recent times. Yet the Internet and Web-enabled operations have already been around for nearly ten years. Could it be that e-government and e-governance are not actually delivering on their promises?

This chapter sets out to examine the extent to which e-government and e-governance has already impacted upon organizational structures and processes in the public sector, to explore the potential for further change in the next few years and to examine the extent to which the promise has so far been unfulfilled. Its focus is largely, but not exclusively, on local government, with particular reference to the UK.

The aims of this chapter are:

- To identify what kind of organizational change is being proposed in the public sector.
- To develop a conceptual framework for understanding how e-government and e-governance are impacting on organizational structures and processes in the public sector.
- To identify new organizational structures and processes which are emerging to make use of the potential of e-enabled processes.

In this chapter, the following shorthand will be used for convenience:

- *e-government* will be used to denote electronic enablement of all the services provided or commissioned by the public sector.
- *e-governance* will be used to denote electronic enablement of all the other activities of government (e.g., management of democratic activity, ensuring fairness and transparency of decision-making in public bodies, etc.).

While this is a little crude, it effectively allows us to distinguish two very different ends towards which the e-revolution has been directed — the "services improvement" agenda and the "relationships improvement" agenda.

The Need for Organizational Change in Response to E-Government and E-Governance

The need for organizational change in the public sector is not widely questioned. The main arguments tend to divide along two dimensions — firstly, whether the pace of change needs to involve "step change" or, less ambitiously, "continuous improvement" and, secondly, whether the direction of change needs to be towards the "New Public Management" (NPM) set of reforms or the more recent "public governance" set of reforms.

The drivers of this push for organizational change are many and only some of them can be listed here. Adherents of the NPM school of thought tend to include:

- Belief in the supremacy of market-based procurement approaches to traditional in-house provision (a belief which may be evidence-based or purely ideological).
- Belief in "business methods" for organizing services, which normally centres around redesign of accountability mechanisms and incentive systems (both often centered in "performance management" systems).
- Desire to redesign ("re-engineer") organizational processes around the needs of service users and other stakeholders ("customers"), often through approaches such as customer relationship management (CRM).
- Concern with the inefficiencies produced by "political interference" in "managerial" decisions.
- Belief that professional groups and staff unions have dominated the processes of service planning and delivery to achieve their own ends, rather than for the good of their clients or for the public interest.

Proponents of the "public governance" school of thought tend to include:

- Concern that public services are not designed for citizens whose holistic needs must be met, but rather for users who should accept managerial/professional views of how their narrow service needs can be met cost-effectively.
- New engagement levels on behalf of stakeholders, particularly those organized on single issue lines (such as environment, transport, health care, etc.).
- Pressures toward increased transparency and freedom of information, particularly from the media and well-organized interest groups.
- Changes to authority relationships (e.g., between professionals and service users, or between service professionals and senior managers) as decisions, and the criteria on which they are based, are subject more fully to the public gaze.
- Concern that many decades of "targeting" of public expenditure have not appeared to have brought significant gains in the "equalities" and "diversity" agendas — there is still an "access divide" in the provision of services and the attainment of highly qualified employment in most public sectors around the world.

There is indeed a small set of critics, such as du Gay (2000) — and, to a lesser extent, Pierre and Peters (2004) — who suggest that the need for change is overstated and that the suggested reform programs are potentially dangerous, but their influence is minimal at the moment. Their arguments are largely based on a concern that the traditional checks and balances which allow officials in the public sector to maintain an independent position, without accepting the political line of the ruling party, are often undermined by the NPM reform program. They therefore lay great stress on the importance of "public governance" principles and show a willingness to prefer the benefits brought by these principles as a trade-off for the potential gains (e.g., in economy, efficiency and effectiveness) of NPM-type reforms. In this sense, they can be viewed a sub-group of the "public governance" reform movement, but with prescriptions which are rather different from the norm in that movement, in that they hark back to traditional forms of bureaucracy — the "old public administration" — rather than to new organizational forms.

However, we should also be aware that some of the emphasis in the last two decades on the need for organizational change may come from rather less "rational" sources. It may have sprung, to a significant extent, from political impatience with the pace of current reforms, combined with a reluctance to increase public expenditure. In these circumstances, politicians — and their closest advisers — find it relatively easy to blame the embarrassing service problems which face them on "mismanagement" or "old-fashioned and out-moded organizations."

This brings us directly to the question: how fast should be the pace of change? Those who believe that there is the potential for radical redesign in public services and other public sector activities naturally suggest major rethinking — e-enable the right processes, not the existing processes. If this tendency were dominant, there would likely be significant convergence in the organizational structures and processes of public agencies and public services, at least if there were wide agreement on what constitutes "best-in-class" in a particular service or activity.

However, such agreement is not the norm. The range of Best Value reviews which have recently been conducted in UK local government have thrown up a number of areas where current organizational structures and processes are clearly not justifiable or sustainable, but they have not pointed clearly to one single way forward for the future (Bovaird & Halachmi, 2001). It is also far from clear that public agencies have the capacity for specifying and implementing radically new ICT systems even if they agreed on what was needed. Major failures continue to be common in this area.

Pressures for ICT-Driven Organizational Change

The new generation of ICT-driven reforms has interacted with a number of other important movements which have implications for organizational arrangements in the public sector. Here we consider explicitly customer relationship management (CRM), the move to holistic needs assessment, changing public expectations with respect to service quality and new methods of staff working.

The growth of CRM: in the last 10 years, there has been a major growth in the theory and practice of "customer relationship marketing" (Stone & Foss, 2201; Stone et al., 2002), influenced by the work on relationship marketing by Christopher et al. (1991). The principal tenet of CRM is that marketing will be more successful (for both sides) if it is based on successful management of the mutual relationship between the organization and the customer. This has led to much more investigation into what relationship customers actually want with service organizations (which, in some cases such as the prison service, may be none at all) and how this relationship can be developed and used to mutual advantage in a range of ways, going well beyond the initial issue which brought the organization and the customer together. Behind all CRM is a desire to build up and to use a much more detailed knowledge base in relation to the clients' needs, wants and likely reactions to services offered.

Move to holistic needs assessment: there has been increasing impatience, particularly on the part of NGOs which lobby on behalf of disadvantaged groups, with the traditional needs assessment procedures in the public sector. They point out that clients do not particularly want "a better service" or even "a better set of services." These are rather the concerns of service-fixated professionals. Clients actually want a better quality of life, which takes into account their holistic needs (Perri et al., 2002). When clients are seen as whole persons, information which was collected for different purposes (tax, social security, population registration, etc.) is combined and integrated (Bekkers & Zouridis, 1999) and they can be offered a wider menu of services, from a wider group of providers. Clearly the integration of databases and decision making systems is essential for this to happen.

Changing public expectations with respect to service quality: partly because of changes in family life and working patterns, the public now expects public services (and indeed private services) to be available more easily and more often than previously. This may not necessarily mean "round the clock" availability but it does mean longer opening than the "normal" working day. Moreover, the public is now typically better educated and more knowledgeable about services than was the case when the welfare state was initiated and much more ready to ask questions and to be sceptical of unconvincing answers. (The level of customer knowledge is itself now often enhanced by their use of the Internet.) Consequently, staff now need to have access to wider knowledge bases (either through access to relevant colleagues or through professional databases, many of them on the intranet or Internet). It is now much less common for a member of staff to be able to act as a lone professional — the "barefoot doctor in the bush" — and much more common for professionals to demand high quality back-up in the performance of their tasks.

New methods of staff working: there are other ways, too, in which staff working is changing. Many staff now explicitly do not want (and may not accept) "normal working hours" based at an office desk some distance from their homes. They may insist upon part-time working, flexible hours, working periods dovetailed in with school terms, home working, and so on. These possibilities are all enhanced by ICT but have up to now been seen as relatively marginal in most parts of the public sector, other than in some areas of education and social care. These demands for new working patterns also affect back offices, but usually not to the same degree, given that back office working hours can usually be more flexible - at least when not based on "online" or "on-call" operations, as discussed later.

ICT Drivers for Changes to Organizational Structures, Processes and Behaviors in Public Services

What is the wellspring of the optimism about the potential of ICT? How is it that ICT innovations are able to impact upon organizational structures processes and behaviors? Although ICT may appear to be simply a resource like many others, it has two key functions in organizations. It acts as the channel for knowledge flows and, simultaneously, it has become one of the main archives for stocks of knowledge. In a knowledge-based society and economy, ICT acts therefore both as the main engine for organizational growth, through the generation of "new" knowledge, and the "iron cage" of organizational stability, based on the use of and reproduction of "old" knowledge.

There are three separate but inter-related mechanisms by means of which ICT can support — and perhaps even trigger — change in an organization:

- *improved use of databases* in the organization — here, the stocks of knowledge in the organization, at least in so far as they are embedded in the organization's databases, are more accessible and can be cross-referenced more easily. It is expected that this should help both in improving the decisions which get made and in implementing decisions more consistently;
- *better communications* in an organization — partly through the use of the organization's databases, but also because it opens up much faster, more personalized communications channels to individuals and to groups (through e-mail, interactive Web sites, etc.);
- *improved decision-making* in an organization — here, information flows are made faster, more reliable and more relevant than they were before, so that individual decisions are likely to be improved and the communications between decision makers are improved, so that decisions are more coordinated.

We can see how widespread is the effect of these mechanisms from Figure 1, which presents a model developed by the Department for Transport, Local Government and the Regions (DTLR) to illustrate the basic elements of e-government. Improved database management is a key aspect of improved transactions and successful e-business systems. Better communications are required if there are to be improved transactions and successful e-enabled business systems — the search for better communications is behind the development of e-enabled access channels. Better decision making is intended to be an outcome of e-enabled business systems. Clearly, all three of these fundamental change mechanisms require enabling technologies. Finally, none of these changes will actually make a difference in the absence of organizational leadership and capacity, which will ensure that e-government is driven by priority public needs rather than simply technocratic imperatives.

Of course, there can also be a downside to some of these changes. For example, in relation to the communications advantages of ICT, a recent report on the implementation of e-government in UK local government (CURDS, 2003) notes that "... more negatively, a number of managers talked about the 'rising tide of e-mail' and the increasing expectation of both citizens and colleagues for instant responses, leading to increased workplace stress."

New Organizational Configurations in Public Services

The drivers for change discussed in the previous section are often more potential rather than real. However, they have already had substantial impacts in the public sector in many parts of the world. In this section we explore some of the organizational responses which have been emerging. None of these can be said as yet to be "tried and tested," in the sense of having been rigorously evaluated, but some patterns are already discernible.

Some New Configurations of Front Offices

In the light of the pressures and the opportunities opened up by ICT, there have been changes to the generic configurations of front offices which are to be found in public organizations. We consider here six such configurations:

Figure 1. UK central and local government joint e-organization model

In the UK, joint work by central and local government recently produced a model of the e-organization by means of which local government (and other local organizations) can build and implement their e-strategies. In this model, the e-organization is made up of five elements:

- *Transactions* – from the citizen's perspective, service outcomes are experienced through their day-to-day transactions with councils and other local service providers. It is possible to analyze how a given priority service might be realized through a variety of generic e-enabled transactions (such as providing benefits and grants).
- *Access Channels* – these transactions might be conducted through a variety of e-enabled access channels (such as Digital TV or One-Stop Shops).
- *Enabling Technologies* – the channels can be supported by a range of enabling technologies which facilitate effective, integrated information management (such as Customer Relationship Management and Geographic Information Systems).
- *E-enabled Business Systems* – service delivery can be underpinned by a suite of core, e-enabled business systems (such as intranets, financials and e-procurement).
- *Organizational Leadership and Capacity* – successful delivery depends on organizational leadership and capacity (including the capacity to lead and manage change and to re-engineer major business processes).

Source: DTLR (2002, p. 22)

Front Office A: The Inquiry Point — where the front office simply takes inquiries and passes them on the back office. This can be done face-to-face with customers (e.g., at reception desks in public buildings), by telephone (e.g., receptionists for public offices or a call centre), by e-mail (e.g., to *info@public.org*, perhaps available on the organization's Web site). This is a very cheap solution but it is slow and the least responsive to the customer's needs. It was a very common model in public services up to the 1970s and still persists in some places.

Front Office B: The Advice Point — where the front office not only takes inquiries, but can give advice and even solve some problems (sometimes through trained receptionists, sometimes by allowing receptionists to have quick access to advisers in the back office, sometimes by putting customers in direct contact with back office staff so that their inquiries can be dealt with immediately). This approach is responsive to the needs of those customers with relatively easy inquiries and easy-to-solve problems, but it requires significant training for receptionists and also that a high proportion of back office staff become good at dealing with customers. It is typically expensive and can be very frustrating for those customers who don't get immediate help, for receptionists who have to find back office staff willing to help, and for back office staff who find that their "batch processing" work is often interrupted and who often have to stand in for missing colleagues, giving advice to customers on issues or cases with which they are not very familiar. This was the most common model in many public services from the 1970s onwards and it still persists in many places.

Front Office C: The One-Start Shop – where the front office takes inquiries not just for one service but for all the organization's services. This is equivalent to a joined-up version of the Inquiry Point. One example is the Web site *www.consumer.org* in the USA, which is a "one-stop link" to a broad range of federal information available online. It is designed so that the consumer can locate information by category, such as Food, Health, Product Safety, Your Money and Transportation. Such "one-start shops" are a convenient marketing device which makes it easy for the organization to inform all its customers of how they can get in touch. It is cheap — potentially even cheaper than a series of separate Inquiry Points, but it needs better trained and more widely informed staff.

Front Office D: The One-Stop Shop — where the front office gives advice and solves problems not only in relation to one service but in relation to all services which the organization offers. This is equivalent to a joined-up version of the Advice Point. It is a very convenient and responsive facility for most customers. (Typically, more than 90% of all inquiries and requests can be dealt with satisfactorily in one contact.) It has the advantage that it can therefore deal with cross-cutting issues and problems which involve many different parts of the organization. However, it does require very well trained staff, with the right to demand instant co-operation from staff in many different parts of the organization. If it is based on premises in main shopping centres, then it can be expensive to provide and in rural areas it is difficult to provide coverage for the whole population. If it is based on a call-centre, then it can be difficult to find staff who are both knowledgeable about a wide range of services and also good at keeping customers waiting patiently for their inquiries to bear fruit — although this may be easier where video links are installed, as has recently been done by the East Riding of Yorkshire in England (DTLR, 2001). If it is based on a multi-service Web site, then it can be difficult to make a site easy to navigate.

Front Office E: The Customer Account Manager — where each customer is given one named personal contact, through whom all future inquiries and requests are to be made. This has the advantage for both the customer and the organization of providing continuity and therefore organizational memory. It also makes the experience of contacting the organization much pleasanter for the customer, which, of course, may increase the level of contacts made — and this may not necessarily been seen as a good thing by staff in the organization. It means that the members of staff involved need to become much more powerful than in a typical front office position — and will probably have corresponding status (and therefore they may also have higher pay). It is an expensive option — basically a more staff intensive version of the One-Stop Shop. It is one of the options most frequently recommended in the Business Process Re-engineering literature (Hammer & Champy, 1993; Halachmi & Bovaird, 1998).

Front Office F: The Customer Representative — where the organization appoints a specific person to act on behalf of each client in all his/her dealings with the organization. (In the US, this is often known as the "advocate" model). The Customer Representative may be a member of staff of the organization, as in the case of a probation officer, or may be an outsider paid by the organization, as in the case of a "guardian *ad litem*" appointed by British courts to represent children in Social Services residential homes. This is a version of the Customer Account Manager where the member of staff has switched loyalties to some extent, from being largely the representative of the organization to being at least partly the champion of the customer. It is expensive in terms of the effort involved but these costs may be reduced if the representative works in a voluntary organization or as a private individual.

Changes to Back Offices in Public Services

Back offices have also been changing in public services as they have incorporated new ICT-based approaches. We can distinguish four different generic configurations of back offices:

Back Office A: The Batch Processor — all tasks are done in logical batches, when it suits the back office staff. This approach is high on efficiency but can be slow to deal with urgent work.

Back Office B: The On-Call Processor — all urgent tasks are done in real time when asked for, by staff who take a personal responsibility for the job being done and maintain personal contact with the "customer" for the job (who is likely to be one of the front office staff), while all other tasks are done in batches. This approach is high on speed and responsiveness but may require rather more staff and therefore higher unit costs than the Batch Processor approach.

Back Office C: The On-Line Processor — this model is similar to Back Office B, but with no personal contact between the front and back office staff — the urgent tasks are done in the back office anonymously and contact is essentially through e-mail. This approach is less staff-time intensive than the On-Call Processor model and therefore cheaper, but may not allow such a high quality handling of transactions.

Back Office D: The Automated Processor — this approach entails the automatic processing of most inquiries from the front office. Here, the back office acts as a designer of software systems for automating support services, and as a last resort provider of those services which cannot be automated or where the automated service breaks down. For this approach to work, front office staff must become skilled in the use of the software. This approach is likely to be cheaper in the long-term if a significant proportion of back office work can be routinized, standardized and encoded in software systems. However, it has high set up costs and requires more specialist skills in the back office (to enable back office services to be properly automated) and in the front office (to access and use the automated services appropriately). This may mean that it is vulnerable to skill shortages, especially if public organizations are reluctant to pay market rates for staff with such skills.

Clearly, most back offices have elements of each of these "ideal types." For example, most back offices have systems whereby low priority work is passed on to some staff who process it when time permits, sometimes sending batches of work off to outside firms to deal with, if a backlog is building up. Again, most back offices allow personal intervention by staff to ensure that some jobs "jump the queue" when they are considered an urgent priority. Finally, most back offices have some automated procedures, even if it is only the keeping of staff appointment diaries on the intranet or the ordering of publications on the Internet.

Configurations for Linking Front and Back Offices within an Organization

A number of strands of modern management thinking have stressed the importance of integration in business improvement — for example, the work on synergy (Campbell & Sommers Luchs, 1992) and on horizontal strategies (Porter, 1985).

There are essentially four levels of integration which can occur in the chain between service users and service deliverers — integration of users, of front offices with each other, of back offices with each other, and of front offices to back offices.

Integration of users: typically, this is undertaken by an intermediary who "represents" the customers and intercedes on their behalf with the public organization. This role is stronger the greater the number of customers whose needs are integrated in this way, since then the customer representative can speak with experience and authority about what customers want (and need) in general, which is helpful in putting demands for non-standard services into an appropriate context. This role is often undertaken by non-profit or community organizations, although some local authorities in the UK have paid voluntary organizations to undertake this acitivity on behalf of their service users, particularly for those social services aimed at people with learning difficulties or behavior problems. This is partly because these clients tend to find it particularly hard to represent their own interests when dealing with public services but also because these intermediaries are seen to have a higher degree of independence than would "customer account managers" or "customer representatives" from within the local authority.

Front Office Integration: this integration of the customer contact points is the typical "one-start shop" or "one-stop shop," in which the organization presents a single face to the customer (which typically appears to the customer as a single contact point). This can be done in a variety of different ways — through a call centre with a well-promoted telephone number, through a Web site, through a "shop" or office in the High Street, or some similar arrangement. In some cases, these initiatives can integrate contact points across other organizations in the same area (e.g., local authority, health agency and social housing organizations). This is fundamentally a communications issue. The key impacts of ICT in making these links are likely to be:

- Allowing front-office staff immediate access to past records in relation to the client.
- Allowing front-office staff to input new information about the client in real time, including all details of each new interaction as it occurs.
- Allowing front-office staff to access key expertise in the organization in real-time when it is not embedded in the electronic knowledge bases (through telephones discussion, text-messaging, Web- or telephone-based video connections, etc.) in order to solve client problems on the spot.

Back Office Integration: here, the different suppliers of back-office services are integrated with each other to provide a "joined-up" service offer to the front line staff. There was a concerted move to back office integration in UK local government in the 1990s, particularly in relation to ICT services, often associated with a move to outsourcing to a single "facilities manager."

Front Office - Back Office Integration: here, the back office service suppliers are integrated with the staff in the customer contact points to provide a "vertically joined up supply chain," which should have advantages of speed, consistency and quality control. One example of this is provided by Three Rivers District Council in England, which aimed to provide 100% electronic service delivery by December 2003 (two years earlier than the target set by the UK government) through the Web-enablement of all its services and through integrating its Web site with its corporate Customer Relationship Management System and all of its back-office systems, using industry standard software and widely used back-office systems (DTLR, 2001).

Changes in Inter-Organizational Relations and "Horizontally Joined-Up" Working

The above analysis has been couched essentially in terms of internal relationships between front and back offices in the same organization. However, very much the same framework can be applied to groups of organizations working together. Here, we need to look at how the front and back offices of a public organization work with (or against) front and back offices in other public organizations, non-governmental organizations (NGOs), voluntary sector organizations, or private sector firms. A public organization may see some of these other organizations as "partners" in the sense that they have formal alliances with them. Others may be seen as "stakeholders" in that they have reasonably durable inter-relationships with them, which means that it is worth investing some time and other resources in making the inter-relationships work more effectively. But some may simply be seen as the other party in "spot" transactions which do not merit any interest in each others' work beyond that single transaction.

Again, we can see that integration across several organizations can occur at different levels:

- Integration of service users, where intermediaries may represent users who get services from many different providers.
- Integration of front offices (e.g., several organizations sharing customer contact points, such as "one-stop shops" or highly inter-linked Web sites).
- Integration of back offices (e.g., several organizations sharing customer databases, engaging in consortium procurement from shared supplier, etc.).
- Integration of front and back offices (e.g., the UK system of local organizations establishing an all-purpose, quasi-autonomous service unit for dealing with all the needs of drugs offenders or the Finnish system, where mobile phones can be used to make payments of taxes and public sector charges from the private sector banking system) (Accenture, 2002).

Clearly these integrations are likely to be more difficult and may be less sustainable than when the integrations simply have to be achieved within the one organization. The problems of engineering these linkages become even more fraught when they involve the integration of front and back offices across different levels of government. Here, the problems are not simply about data security and data protection. A key barrier to these integration processes has traditionally been professional autonomy, but it is possible that this is now becoming at least partially eroded in the post-modern public sector organization (Bogason, 2000). There is clearly also a set of issues about agencies being reluctant to work with each other because it potentially reduces their autonomy and their power, both *vis-à-vis* individual clients (since clients can play off one agency against another to achieve more favorable decisions in respect of their own case) and *vis-à-vis* other agencies which are involved in helping the same clients to achieve a better quality of life. Games playing, in order to create or maintain "competitive advantage" in comparison to other public agencies, is common in these circumstances. While ICT can certainly help to increase the potential gains from "joining up" agencies, it can also provide fertile ground for claims of "non-compatability" of systems which, with a minimum degree of ingenuity, can be protracted indefinitely to block potential improvements.

The Role of ICT in Achieving Organizational Integration

This chapter has suggested that the three main mechanisms by which ICT can affect organizational behavior are through its ability to allow better use of databases, its ability to support better communications and its ability to support improved decision-making. We now look at how these interlinked mechanisms can impact on the integration opportunities identified so far in this section.

Table 1 sets out some ways in which ICT can be used to encourage and support functional integration within public organizations.

While containing only an illustrative selection of the ways in which ICT might support these integrations, it demonstrates the wide range of possibilities.

Table 2, similarly, demonstrates the role of ICT in supporting integration across agencies, again looking at the four different types of integration. The main differences are that in Table 2 there are extra opportunities for ensuring that public organizations take better advantage of the networks which exist in policy making, service planning, service delivery and public issue monitoring.

Table 1. ICT-based functional integration in a single public organization

	Areas of ICT impact on the organization		
Type of integration	**Decision-making**	**Database management**	**Communications**
User integration	Co-planning of services by user groups and interest groups	User monitoring of the use of personal data	Keeping networks of users of all agency services in touch with each other
Front office integration	Co-planning of new integrated service offers by different departments of the agency	Access to updated and consistent user information across all services in the agency	Providing joined-up communications to users to inform them of all services available
Back office integration	Transparent trails of all decisions made, with reasons	Updating and consistency-checking of all support service information across all support services in the agency	Transparent trails of progress of individual cases/requests/inquiries being processed in the organization
Front-back office integration	Preparation of integrated service work programs (e.g., care plans) for users	Updating and consistency-checking of all user information across all services in the agency	Ensuring that all communications to users meet "customer-first" criteria

The potential applications of ICT-driven integration which are outlined in Tables 1 and 2 have clearly only been partially realized to date. While it is natural that "silo-based" management should seek to pursue "silo-based" ICT solutions, it is also likely that most of these major opportunities will eventually be explored more fully in at least some sites. When that happens, and if it is successful, it is likely to make "silo-based management" more difficult to defend.

Implications for Governments and Public Sector Organizations

In this section, we explore a number of the implications which arise from the ICT-driven organizational responses which have been considered in earlier sections.

Separation of Service Commissioning, Purchasing and Provision

The separation of service commissioning, purchasing and provision, which was a key plank in the NPM of the 1980s, needs to be revisited. The e-revolution has already dramatically affected the cost-benefit calculations in relation to these different roles, but the final results are not yet clear. A recent example is provided in Potsdam-Mittelmark in Germany, where services that were previously the exclusive responsibility of the county are now mutually provided by the county and the municipalities, with some co-production of services (Schuppan, 2005). In the UK, the services which are most likely to be reallocated between tiers of government are the collection of tax revenues and the payment of benefits, both of which appear to exhibit significant economies of scale, and

Table 2. Use of ICT to support functional integration across public organizations

	Areas of ICT impact across organizations		
Type of integration	**Decision-making**	**Database management**	**Communications**
User integration	Co-planning of services by user groups and interest groups across all service providers	User monitoring of the use of personal data in all multi-agency units and partnerships	Keeping networks of users in touch with each other across all service providers
Front office integration	Co-planning of new integrated service offers across all service providers	Access to updated and consistent user information across all service providers	Providing joined-up communications to client groups to inform them of all services available from all providers of services to that client group
Back office integration	Transparent trails of all decisions made, with reasons, across all service providers and partnerships	Updating and consistency-checking of all support service information across all support services	Transparent trails of progress of individual cases/requests/inquiries, across all service providers and partnerships
Front-back office integration	Preparation of integrated service work programmes (e.g., care plans) for users across all service providers	Updating and consistency-checking of all user information across all service providers	Ensuring that all communications to users meet standard "customer-first" criteria, agreed by all agencies

therefore are likely to become provided by larger organizations. At the other end of the spectrum, there are strong community pressures for some services to be commissioned at neighborhood level – particularly leisure and environmental services — and this is now more possible because ICT allows easier communications between the commissioners (e.g., neighborhood groups), providers (e.g., large public agencies or private firms) and purchasers of the services who provide the funding (e.g., district or county governments).

An implication of these trends might therefore be that small-sized local authorities, so often thought to be uneconomic in these times of multi-national companies and large "efficient" municipal local authorities, may no longer need to be merged to achieve economies of scale. Rather, small local authorities may be able to articulate more effectively the needs and priorities of people in their local communities and to mobilize local resources, while simultaneously e-procurement in partnerships or consortia might allow them to enjoy least-cost provision by large regional or local service delivery organizations, which may come from the private, public or voluntary sectors. If these trends continue, it seems likely that the current allocation of functions between central, regional, local and neighborhood levels of government could be radically transformed.

Changing Roles of Public Sector and Civil Society

In the new era of public governance reforms, we are already seeing major changes in the relationships between public bodies and the other organizations in civil society which have interests in, and responsibilities for, the planning and delivery of public services. The growing understanding of the potential role of civil society, and the growing understanding of the limitations of purely public sector organizations, mean that a redrawing of the boundaries between the sectors is necessary. Added to this is the role of the private sector in providing the ICT platforms which will drive many of these changes.

This has led to a renewed interest in the use of technology to enhance the service experience of users. For example, "smart house" experiments are being conducted in many parts of Europe, in which houses are being built to incorporate a large range of features which make living easy and comfortable for people with disabilities. These are often run by non-profit organizations, using funding from the public sector.

It has also led to an understanding in the public sector that it must cut back on some activities if it is to be able to offer high quality provision in the core services which it provides. The concomitant of this is that the public sector has a duty to map, and where possible, to supplement the capacity of civil society, so that it can have a sustainable exit strategy where it intends to hand over responsibility for certain activities to organizations in civil society. These organizations, in turn, have to be able to account both to their members and to their funders for the use of their funds, the effectiveness of their decision making and the efficiency of their administration. The old picture of non-profits being run by one or two "do-gooders" in a village has been supplanted by the image of a slick marketing operation which uses its databases to run cost-effective fundraising campaigns and to coordinate volunteer efforts, employing its communications media (such as newsletters and Web sites) to keep its core members committed to the cause and using Web and e-mail links to a host of kindred organizations to inform its decisions on new ways forward.

Virtual Organizations and Reorganizations

The potential of the new ICT developments means that the redrawing of the organizational landscape will often be possible with minimum fuss and disruption. Indeed, it may largely be virtual, in that existing organizations need not disappear in the new order — only the balance of power (and of resources) between them may alter. As Michael Porter (2001) has suggested, in the e-revolution, it is now much more difficult for organizations to sustain operational advantages than previously — and therefore it is much more important that they achieve strategic positioning in the roles they choose to play. If they can achieve this, their organizational form may have much less significance than it did in the past.

Indeed, it is worth considering whether public sector organizations in the future will be so distinct — and so stable — as they were in the past. Not only has the "public-service" culture usually been seen as being very distinct from that in other sectors, but organizational cultures have usually been seen to differ significantly from agency to agency. However, structures in central and local government now appear to be becoming more fluid — take, for example, the way in which in recent years in the UK the Department of the Environment became the Department of Environment, Transport and the Regions, then the Department of Transport, Local Government and the Regions and was then split into three separate departments. In each case, within days the new department had a new logo and a new Web site. Of course, the activities in each successive organizational structure were largely unchanged, as were the staff. However, ICT made it easy to promulgate quickly the new "branding," mission and priorities of each new incarnation of these activities, both to the public and to staff. Meanwhile the interconnectivity of sub-units in these departments was unchanged because it now tends to be based more on ICT links and less on co-location.

Inter-Governmental Relationships

Inter-governmental relationships may also have to be seen in a new light, since e-government and e-governance now give to central government the possibility, so long denied, of having a direct interface with the general public, at both national and local levels. Consequently, it may be necessary for local government to think very hard about what is specifically local (and local-value-added) about its contribution to local governance. For example, central government in the UK has for some time been promulgating arrangements which would give it a direct relationship with a significant group of flagship hospitals ("foundation hospitals") and schools, taking them away from the local governance networks in which they were previously embedded.

Inter-governmental relations may become very much less important in the future (even, in the extreme, obsolete), as citizens come to insist that all their dealings with the public sector are undertaken through a single portal. This raises the prospect of a citizenry which is very sophisticated in its knowledge of what services it requires, and why, and very knowledgeable about what can be provided (and why not). In these circumstances, the public sector might have no choice but to accept "unitary" provision of services in the public sector — at least as far as service users are concerned. Meanwhile, the actual provision of these services may well be managed by a network of organizations, only some of which would ever be visible to service users. This would, however, raise serious questions of accountability, since it would be difficult for the public to hold organizations to account which they did not even realize were running the services.

Tackling the Digital Divide

These organizational responses have already demonstrated the major potential of ICT to bring about change in public sector. However, can we be sure that it is change for the better? One issue in particular has concerned many practitioners and researchers particularly — the issue of the digital divide, whereby traditionally disadvantaged groups may be further disadvantaged because they will have lower access to or make less use of e-enabled services and public activities.

Moreover, the digital divide comes with a severe cost penalty. Up to now, the introduction of new access channels has created substantial costs for public organizations and public services, with very few cost savings. This is largely because it has rarely been possible to close existing channels, in case vulnerable groups are made worse off. Of course, users of the new channels have often experienced significant benefits. However, public sector decision-making normally gives at least as much weight to cost savings as to increased quality of service. Consequently, the impact of e-government to date has been seen as problematic.

In the UK, the focus of e-government has been firmly on service delivery. However, in many other countries, and lately even in the UK as well, issues of e-governance are coming to the fore, including e-voting and referenda, e-consultation and methods of mobilizing community action on public issues, where again the digital divide threatens to disenfranchise groups which do not make use of the Web (see, for example, de Montfort University, 2002).

Research shows that the digital divide remains large in the UK (MORI, 2001) but is changing in its incidence, with very different patterns of Internet usage emerging by gender (Bimber, 2000; Jackson et al., 2001) and with problems of access rather than ownership becoming key for the "second user generation" (Attewell, 2001). However, little is known as yet about which groups are now accessing and achieving better outcomes in specific public services through the Web, which groups are not, and the drivers behind these patterns (Dunleavy & Margetts, 2002).

Tackling the digital divide has been made more complex by the emergence of different forms of strategic partnerships in electronic service delivery. These have largely been driven by the need for major investment funds, which have therefore required large-scale private-sector participation. This has typically resulted in fragmented responses to difficult public policy issues such as the digital divide.

Furthermore, the situation and behavior of the disadvantaged groups concerned are typically not well mapped nor understood in the public service organizations upon which they are usually dependent (Norris, 2001; Dunleavy & Margetts, 2002). This is because their needs are dealt with by a fragmented set of uncoordinated agencies, none of which takes a holistic view of the needs of each service user. Consequently, existing data in the public sector are usually very partial and provide little evidence on the overall problems facing members of disadvantaged groups.

If the digital divide is not to undermine the social gains which e-enablement may bring to both service delivery and to public governance processes, then it seems clear that it will have to be tackled more directly than has so far been the case in most countries, and certainly in the UK. This will entail a concerted effort to find ways in which to migrate disadvantaged groups from existing access channels to new, e-enabled channels — and to do this early in the change process, not as an afterthought. The challenge posed by this is clear but has perhaps been overstated — after all, 20 years of social policy research has emphasized that the existing access channels have systematically discriminated against or provided only limited preference to disadvantaged service users (Le Grand, 1983; Bramley et al., 1998). It therefore seems rather defeatist to suddenly defend these traditional channels as an essential bastion of an "equalities" strategy for public services. However, it will be hard to convince the groups concerned that such a migration to new channels will be in their interest. As Bellamy (2003) suggests, services for older and poorer people – such as Social Security claims, advice services or the NHS helpline, *NHS Direct* – will probably continue to be offered from call centres or face-to-face in offices, as well as on the Internet. However, this should probably be seen less as a victory on behalf of the disadvantaged and more as an indicator of the continued growth of the digital divide, and therefore of the failure to implement a successful equalities policy.

CONCLUSIONS

This chapter has argued that e-government and e-governance initiatives can potentially have major organizational impacts through three major mechanisms:

- improved decision-making;
- more intensive and productive use of databases; and
- better communications.

These mechanisms are likely to exert strong impacts on the internal organization of public agencies, requiring a rethinking of front and back office set-ups and their inter-relationships. They are also likely to affect the overall configuration of public agencies in networks and partnerships. E-enablement therefore makes obsolete many existing organizational structures and processes. While this is likely to have short-term disruptive — and expensive — effects, in the long term it offers the prospect of transformation in both service delivery and public governance arrangements.

However, the organizational changes which can be effected through the e-revolution are only just beginning to become evident. This chapter has highlighted the many different templates of configurations which are currently being adopted for front-offices, back-offices and front-to-back-office integration. All of these templates are relatively new and most remain unproven in their effects. It is still not clear which of these organizational templates will become most common, or in which circumstances they will turn out to be most appropriate. Evidence from the Best Value initiative in the UK suggest that many existing organizational configurations in the public sector will not be sustainable, either on grounds of service quality and value for money or on grounds of good governance. However, it appears unlikely that "one best way" will emerge — the most appropriate ways forward will only be uncovered through much experimentation within e-government and e-governance programmes. In the nature of experimentation, many of these initiatives will turn out to be unproductive or cost-ineffective — but that is perhaps the necessary price to pay for the level of public sector transformation which now appears to be in prospect.

ACKNOWLEDGMENTS

This chapter partly originates from a paper which was commissioned by the Public Management Service of the OECD in 2002 as part of its e-Government Task Force initiative. Some other elements of the paper arose from work commissioned in 2002 by the Office of the E-Envoy. An earlier version appeared in *Public Policy and Administration* (2003), 18(2), 37-56, and has been reproduced with permission of the editor.

REFERENCES

Accenture. (2002). *e-Government leadership – Realizing the vision.* Retrieved from *www.accenture.com/xdoc/en/newsroom/epresskit/egov/realizing_vision.pdf*

Attewell, P. (2001). The first and second digital divides. *Sociology of Education, 74*, 252-259.

Audit Commission. (2002). *Councils and e-government research so far.* London.

Bekkers, V. J. J. M., & Zouridis, S. (1999). Electronic service delivery in public administration: Some trends and issues. *International Review of Administrative Sciences, 65*, 183-195.

Bellamy, C. (2003). E-government: managing ICTs in public sector organisations. In T. Bovaird & E. Loeffler (Eds.), *Public management and governance.* London: Routledge.

Bimber, B. (2000). Measuring the gender gap on the Internet. *Social Science Quarterly, 81*(3), 868-876.

Bogason, P. (2000). *Public policy and local governance: Institutions in postmodern society.* Cheltenham: Edward Elgar.

Bovaird, T., & Halachmi, A. (1997). Process reengineering in the public sector: Learning some private sector lessons. *Technovation, 17*(5), 227-235.

Bovaird, T., & Halachmi, A. (2001). Learning from international approaches to best value. *Policy and Politics, 29*(4), 451-463.

Bramley, G., Lancaster, S., Lomax, D., McIntosh, S., & Russell, J. (1998). *Where does public spending go? Pilot study to analyse the flows of public expenditure into local areas.* London: DETR.

Campbell, A., & Luchs, K.S. (1992). *Strategic synergy.* Oxford: Butterworth Heinemann.

Christopher, M., Payne, A., & Ballantyne, D. (1991). *Relationship marketing: Bringing quality, customer service and marketing together.* Oxford: Butterworth Heinemann.

CURDS. (2003). *Implementing electronic local government: Final report of the process evaluation of the implementation of electronic local government in England.* London: Office of the Deputy Prime Minister.

De Montfort University. (2002). *The implementation of electronic voting in the UK.* London: Local Government Association.

DTLR. (2001). *Modern councils, modern services, access for all.* London: DTLR.

DTLR. (2002). *e-gov@local.* Joint Report with Local Government Association, UK-Online and Local Government Online. London: DTLR.

Dunleavy, P., & Margetts, H. (2002). *Government on the Web II.* London: National Audit Office.

du Gay, P. (2000). *In praise of bureaucracy.* Walton Hall: Open University.

Hammer, M., & Champy, J. (1993). *Re-engineering the corporation: A manifesto for business revolution.* New York: Harper Business.

Jackson, L., Ervin, K., Gardner, P., & Schmitt, N. (2001). Gender and the internet: women communicating and men searching. *Sex Roles*, *44*(5/6), 363-379.

Le Grand, J. (1983). *The strategy of equality: Redistribution and the social services.* London: Allen and Unwin.

MORI. (2001). *e-Government research review.* London: MORI for Audit Commission.

Norris, P. (2001). *Digital divide: Civic engagement, information poverty and the Internet worldwide.* Cambridge: Cambridge University.

Perri, Leat, D., Seltzer, K., & Stoker, G. (2002). *Towards holistic governance: The new reform agenda.* Houndmills, UK: Palgrave.

Peters, B.G., & Pierre, J. (2004). Multi-level governance: A Faustian bargain? In I. Bache & M. Flinders (Eds.), *Multi-level governance* (pp. 75-89). Oxford: Oxford University.

Porter, M. (1985). *Competitive advantage: Creating and sustaining superior performance.* New York: Free Press.

Porter, M. (2001). Strategy and the Internet. *Harvard Business Review,* March.

OECD. (2001). *From in-line to on-line: Delivering better services.* Paris: OECD.

Roy, J., & Wilson, C. (2002). *Making sense of smart communities.* Ottawa: Center on Governance.

Schuppan, T. (2005). Integrated local government – Steps toward IT-based service delivery in rural one-stop-offices. In T. Bovaird, E. Loeffler & S. Parrado Diez (Eds.), *Multilevel governance: Decentralising power in Europe.* Cheltenham: Edward Elgar.

Stone, M., & Foss, M. (2001). *Successful customer relationship marketing.* London: Kogan Page.

Stone, M., Machtynger, L., & Woodcock, N. (2002). *Customer relationship marketing* (2nd edition). London: Kogan Page.

Williams, J. (2001). On-line communities: The rise and rise of the internet. *Sociology Review, 10*(4), 23-24.

Chapter IV

Confidence in E-Government: The Outlook for a Legal Framework for Personal Data and Privacy

Georges Chatillon, University of Paris, France

ABSTRACT

Since the 1990s, governments have been exploring, and in many cases implementing, e-government in an effort to expand their budgeted services and efficiency. However, the desire to address these needs has often been offset with a basic lack of experience in the field of e-government, forcing governments to act relatively slowly and cautiously to migrate some of the services traditionally offered by paper-based government to e-government. In this new phase of government creation, new rules are being applied, major investments are being made, and the government agencies involved are reorganizing — not without difficulty. This chapter examines the cases of France, Belgium, Canada, the United States and Ireland and how each of these countries is extremely attentive to an important aspect of the successful acceptance of e-government — the protection of personal data — through new regulations, policies and creative, legal innovations.

INTRODUCTION

The practical need for e-government has been emerging slowly but surely since the 1990s in response to certain needs that have been expressed emphatically by users of government services (to save time and money, to get more for their taxes in the form of truly integrated government services, to do business with the government whenever they choose, to obtain information or advice, and conduct simulations). These needs, which are already long-standing, could not be met fully by "p-government" (paper-based government) and have shifted to e-government with hopes renewed by the promises of computerization and the Internet. Wishing to fulfill these needs but lacking experience in the field of e-government, governments are acting relatively slowly and cautiously to migrate some of the services traditionally offered by p-government to e-government, and to renew the content of those services. After making certain administrative forms available online, governments are instituting integrated services provided via "one-stop shops" and comprising customer request processing methods based on front-office and back-office government technology. To this end, new rules are being applied, major investments are being made, and the government agencies involved are re-organizing — not without difficulty.

In recent years, countless experiments have been attempted, successfully, by governments, despite hasty planning for lack of time and experience. Along the way, citizens have become increasingly aware of the new problems posed by e-government, using the experience acquired — sometimes the hard way — with e-businesses' online sales of products and services, and transposing it. E-customers have learned to be wary of certain e-business practices: unfair use of their personal data, and problems involving proof, merchant identity and online contracts. Many Internet users have become mistrustful of online commercial services and are projecting their fears onto e-government.

Legal solutions for the protection of personal data and privacy must be found in order to bolster citizens' faith in e-government. Regulations must take both the public's needs and those of government agencies into consideration. The rules should be different for e-services and p-services.

The cases of France, Belgium, Canada, the United States and Ireland will be examined. Each of these countries is extremely attentive to the protection of personal data. The regulatory provisions already instituted or being developed offer citizens the legal means for protecting their data, and they propose solutions that are relatively different, depending on four factors: the respective roles attributed to the State and to citizens; the prevalence of electronic commerce; the political determination to deliver public services electronically; and the type of law in force — civil law, common law, or both, as in Canada.

France and Ireland are both unitary States, whereas Belgium, Canada and the United States of America have federal structures. But the legal systems are different: France and Belgium are governed by civil law, which gives pre-eminence to the legislature; Ireland and the United States of America are governed by common law, which gives the courts the leading role; and Canada is governed by civil law and common law alike.

In each of these countries, however, and more generally across all of the OECD area, legislation to protect personal data and privacy is new and recent. Everywhere, there is a need for legal innovations. Clearly then, the central lawmaking body is the source of such protective regulations, backed up everywhere by data protection commissioners, invested with substantial power — even in France, where Act 30 January 2002 strengthens the prerogatives of the *Commission Nationale Informatique et Libertés* (CNIL), albeit without giving the Commission a major role.

Concerns for protecting personal data go hand in hand with the political determination to reform public services and develop the role of e-government and e-governance of the State (Belgium, Canada, Ireland). In the United States, there is a manifest will to develop online public services, but the status of personal data gives (perhaps) too much weight to citizens' powers of decision-making and the right to challenge decisions, as well as to businesses' promises of self-regulation. In France, the protection of personal data is relatively strong, but central government reform is taking longer than expected, and the powers devolved to territorial governments are slight. The situations thus vary widely from one country to another. It is likely that by 2005, and in any event during the period 2005-2010, most of the barriers to establishing e-government services will have vanished, or will have been transformed, and that, in practice, protective solutions will have been found — unless the current obstacles keep "e-gov" from developing.

In Canada, the Personal Information Protection and Electronic Documents Act, which received royal assent on April 13, 2000,[1] seeks to "support and promote electronic commerce by protecting personal information that is collected, used or disclosed in certain circumstances, by providing for the use of electronic means to communicate or record information or transactions and by amending the Canada Evidence Act, the Statutory Instruments Act and the Statute Revision Act." Federal institutions are subject to another law — the "Privacy Act".

In Ireland, the Electronic Commerce Act 2000 (of 10 July 2000) seeks to provide a "friendly environment" for business and a framework for the delivery of electronic government services. The Data Protection Bill 2002 has just amended the Data Protection Act 1988, adding new rules to those of 2001. The law entered into force on 1 April 2002, giving new rights to citizens and specific responsibilities to businesses.

In Belgium, since 1992 a law has protected individuals regarding the use of their personal data. Under the law, which imposes a transparency requirement, people must be alerted when information about them is being processed. The party involved must identify itself and explain why the data is being processed. The law also sets rules for the use of personal data, stipulating what may and what must be done with the data collected. In addition, it extends new rights to persons who are in registers or databases, as well as the right to access the information recorded to rectify or challenge the information, etc.

This Act of 8 December 1992 (published in the *Moniteur Belge* of 18 March 1993) was extensively amended by the Act of 11 December 1998 (*Moniteur Belge* of 3 February 1999) in order to implement the European Directive of 1995. Lastly, a royal decree of 13 February 2001 enacted the Act of 8 December 1992 on the protection of privacy (as amended by the Act of 11 December 1998 transposing the Directive).

Belgium is currently reviewing the scope of application of all laws applicable to e-government, but no definitive solutions have yet been worked out.

In the United States, the two main laws protecting privacy are the Privacy Act of 1974 and the Freedom of Information Act of 1996.[2] They apply to agencies of the federal government. At first glance, the two laws would appear diametrically opposed: the aim of the Privacy Act is to preserve the confidentiality of personal data recorded by government services, and the Freedom of Information Act is routinely used to force government to open up its files. The two laws are an attempt to achieve a balance between the public's right to know what government is doing and citizens' rights to preserve their privacy. The Freedom of Information Act (FOIA) was enacted by Congress in 1966 and amended in 1974. It is based on the principle expounded by Madison and Hamilton that transparency of government actions helps citizens to make the enlightened choices essential to democracy. The FOIA gives each citizen access to the records created by federal government agencies. In the United States of America, Congress and the President consider that e-government is the way of the future. The 1996 Information Technology Management Reform Act (ITMRA, Clinger-Cohen legislation[3]), Government Paperwork Elimination Act (GPEA, 44 USC 3504[4]) and Electronic Signatures in Global and National Commerce Act[5] (digital signatures legislation) have been adopted to overcome institutional obstacles to electronic transactions. In December 1999, the President signed a memo requesting federal agencies to post their forms on the Internet by January 2001, and all services by 2003. Congress recently wanted to institute a federal Chief Information Officer within the Office of Management and Budget in order to bolster the management and promotion of e-government services and arrange for a wide spectrum of Web-based procedures in order to encourage citizens to access government services and information.[6]

In France, the Information Society bill of 14 June 2001[7] transposed the European Directive of 8 June 2000 on electronic commerce. Its primary objective is to foster confidence in electronic trading and to help make Internet use more democratic. On 30 January 2002, the National Assembly enacted a privacy bill to protect individuals with regard to the processing of personal data,[8] amending Act No. 78-17 of 6 January 1978 on computerization, filing systems and freedoms, and transposing European Directive 95/46/EC of 24 October 1995 on the protection of individuals with regard to the processing of personal data and on the free movement of such data. France was one of the last European Union countries to transpose the Directive. While the law makes no provision that departs significantly from EU rules, there is still no bill specific to e-government and protection of personal data and privacy for users of government services.

It would appear that the protection of personal data and privacy is an issue viewed in a favorable light — at least in most of the OECD Member countries, which are under pressure to act quickly, compelled to conduct an active search for the best legal solutions. Nevertheless, the special nature of the personal data processed by government services still raises a number of questions: How can government structures be re-organized so as to generate "horizontal" treatment of work and case files that would ensure efficiency and real protection for data? Must the legal regime applicable to the personal data processed by government be aligned with that of the data processed by private businesses? How can the public and government officials be informed of their rights and obligations in the realm of data protection? How can the public be guaranteed that the rules of protection are being enforced? How can damage be corrected without interrupting data processing? Should the public play a role in the management of their personal data, and if so, how? What strategy should be adopted to enact the necessary regulations?

While the overall context is favorable to the application of legal solutions, the obstacles should not be underestimated.

Most users approach online services with an apprehension stemming from a lack of familiarity with government computer procedures and legal issues. (It would be useful to assess the semantic and legal gaps between the language used online and the "real" interpretation of that language by the public.) Similarly, government officials' "objective" knowledge of the information technology mechanisms used by e-government is highly relative, as is their legal training in the realm of personal data protection.

The public does not really wish to know about the mysterious workings of government, electronic or otherwise. At the same time, government employees are sometimes reluctant to change their working habits and adapt to new e-procedures.

Governments hesitate to propose new legal status for the personal e-data processed by electronic public services when time-proven solutions can be found in the context of traditional government.

ISSUES INVOLVED

The protection of personal data and privacy is one of the major problems that need to be solved if the goals, methods and means of e-government are to be accepted by citizens, the public and government officials. The computerization of society in general, as well as businesses and government has indeed opened the door to uses of personal data that citizens fear: constitution of filing systems, leaks, profiling, historical records, exchange and cross-checking of data between government institutions, and commercial exploitation of private data by business enterprises, etc. The public fears — perhaps with good reason — that the government or private entities will identify them, recognize them, and take decisions on the basis of this information. They fear being "over-identified" and helpless in the face of powerful and as yet insufficiently transparent public (and private) forces. It is therefore important to lessen these fears, dissipate them and, in fact, to replace them by confidence. Protection of personal data and privacy is crucial to the success of e-government. Whatever is needed must be done so that citizens feel at home in e-government. They must be able to consult and utilize government sites with complete confidence and, in any event, have no fear as to how their personal information is going to be used. One of the main goals of e-government is to conduct business remotely, but in many cases the relevant files are split up between a number of agencies belonging to different government departments. To meet this objective, remote services must search for personal information and data and match them up. It is therefore necessary to devise legal systems that would allow such operations and keep them strictly within limits so that citizens have complete faith in how the data processed is going to be used *and* benefit from the exceptional advantages of computer technology: rapidity, very great reliability, memory, instantaneous transmission and automatic storage and archiving.

It is essential to ensure that rules and means are as far possible consistent with one another in order to prevent dysfunctions from occurring.

As governments fashion legislation suitable for protecting data, it would be both timely and useful to resolve a number of relevant issues, such as the nature and extent of property rights over personal data; how data may or must be used; and the rights of governments and businesses over citizens' data.

Definitions of Personal Data Overlap from One Country to Another

From a legal standpoint, the definitions supplied by the Canadian legislation are the most specific and "concrete." The Canadian "catalogue" seems most likely to boost the confidence of the public because the items are concrete and readily comprehensible. This type of legislation could constitute a model, which would be repudiated straightaway by a number of legal cultures, such as that of France, which has grown accustomed to setting forth conceptual generalities rather than enumerating specific instances, leaving responsibility for details of implementation to the courts.

In order to bolster the confidence of e-government stakeholders, two goals need to be pursued:

- Regulation of how government can use personal data and private information on citizens: What data should be protected? What aspects of privacy? For what purposes? For what uses? What levels of protection? How to protect? Using what criteria?
- Striking a balance between the public's rights over the data processed by e-government services and the powers of government agencies. What are the respective rights of the public and of government? How can these be enforced? With what means of verification? What are the consequences?

Value criteria for personal data and levels of legal protection of privacy. The "value" of personal data is not the same in all cultures, and present-day legal systems offer highly diverse levels of protection. In some countries, the regulatory focus is on strengthening the protection of personal data in connection with contractual relationships between consumers and businesses (France, United States of America). In others, the primary concern is to strengthen the protection of personal data in connection with contractual relationships between the public and government (Ireland). Lastly, in other countries the aim is to strengthen protection irrespective of the other party involved (Belgium, Canada). Consumer-user-citizens use their own data in the social domain. The data they use in their dealings with government services and businesses are practically the same. While these data ought to be protected, protective regulations need not make distinctions that in some regards are too clear-cut between government services and private services. Clearly, the power of the State seems more compelling than that of private enterprises. But the threat that banks, insurance companies and supermarkets might try to match their customers' personal data is no less disturbing for individuals than the prospects of such matching by medical, education or tax authorities.

Breaches of privacy and improper, unlawful use of personal data are infringements of individual property, as are pirating and unlawful selling of data. Personal property, initially hereditary, made up of personal and private data, must be afforded protection under the law, and consideration must be given to the applicable legal regime. Personal data are not objective things, but subjective, individual and personal signs, symbols or representations characteristic of an individual. It is therefore important to define the principle of full freedom to use personal data and data representative of each person's privacy. The value to be protected is indeed one of personal property. The subjective, individual and personal signs, symbols or representations characteristic of an individual do not have the same property value, or the same use, in the marketplace as they do in the public domain of government that links the authorities and the public. As a result, levels of protection can be differentiated and adjusted. The property value of personal data can be determined by law, with the level of protection adjusted accordingly.

WHAT DOES "CONFIDENCE" MEAN?

In an e-government context, the public's confidence in these new procedures is based on four dimensions/conditions:

- Legal guarantees of a level of protection determined by law in the light of acceptable purposes and predetermined processing methods.
- Operational guarantees of processing that is predictable in terms of outcome and time required.
- A set of manual or automatic systems to control remote procedures and remote services, combined with performance guarantees.

Effective Application of a Set of Principles Regulating E-Government

The causes impeding greater confidence in e-government (France – Belgium – USA – Canada – United Kingdom – Switzerland):

- Lack of doctrine to guide the formulation of regulations;
- No comprehensive plan to protect personal data;
- Divergent interests between the main political, administrative and industrial stakeholders in cryptography and electronic signatures and the manufacturers of mainstream software;
- No far-reaching agreement on commercial and/or government use of personal data and the protection thereof; and
- No comprehensive and clear, constitutional or legal doctrine on the protection, security and safety of personal or government data.

The mechanisms impeding greater confidence in e-government (France – Belgium – USA – Canada – United Kingdom – Switzerland):

- The issue of national ID numbers;
- The vertical organization of government;
- Obstacles to cross-agency interface between public services;
- Competition between public services and private ones;
- Judicial excess or lack of protection for data;
- The as-yet ill-defined legal role of electronic signatures;
- Mechanisms to regulate and control encryption;
- The opaqueness of government processing;
- The lack of transparency in the government routing of case files and requests; and
- Government habits in respect of personal data.

The responses of these countries are based essentially on policies of administrative simplification; reforms of request and case file processing circuits; data protection legislation; legislation on encryption and electronic signatures; initial legal reflections on public and private government data; scattered regulations and experimentation.

Comparisons Between the Five Countries as Regards to the State of Advancement of Privacy Legislation and the Protection of the Public's Personal Data

In 2001, the United States of America adopted four laws[9] in the realm of personal data protection to begin to control certain excesses or abuses. Clearly it is extremely difficult for businesses to moderate their commercial zeal in a cultural and legal environment that puts a premium on contractual autonomy. In the European Union countries, legal systems are also based on the principle of contractual autonomy — a legal principle invented by Roman law — which affords individuals the power to enter into contracts, in the face of the State's sovereign power to impose the order of the law. The national legislation of European countries accepts the "weaknesses" of individuals and takes them into account. Consumers enjoy protection under the law, to an extent that varies from one country to another. The role of the State is to protect, and individuals are not left at the mercy of their own devices.

These considerations are important to understanding how the regulation of personal information and privacy protection has evolved. In the United States, it is necessary to strike a fairer balance between the power of large corporations and that of the public and small and medium-sized enterprises. In Europe, a better balance is needed between the power of the State, public services and the public. U.S. businesses and European States must bring their regulations in line with the major principles of personal data protection.

The laws of the countries studied try to harmonize the personal data protection rules governing relations between the general public and their suppliers of goods and services, whether they be the State, public services or businesses. But some countries, like Canada and France, make a clear distinction between rules applicable to the State and those applicable to businesses.

Others, like Ireland and Belgium, have made their laws more similar. Lastly, the United States of America is pausing to study the issue.

On the whole, it is too soon to obtain ready-made answers. In the United States, it will be necessary to wait until 2003 to revise existing legislation and propose any extensions. In Canada, it is from 1 January 2004 that all Canadians will be titled to protection of their personal information by either federal law or by provincial legislation closely approximating the federal law. In Ireland, protective legislation has been in force since April 2002, and in Belgium since 1 September 2002. In France, a few more months will be needed to know whether the new parliament will ratify or amend the legislation in force on 30 January 2002.

There remains just over a year — perhaps a year and a half — to fine-tune the principles, to bring them forward and review certain aspects of national legislation and, above all, to work towards harmonization. More than ever, the dialogue is one between America and Europe.

It would be advisable to study the legal status of the following:

- remote administrative files (administrative data + data specific to users);
- data that can and should be protected (administrative data + data specific to users);
- rules governing the use of security measures, when this is strictly necessary and legal;
- monitoring carried out by users and government departments;
- guarantees regarding the ease of filing complaints and of receiving rapid compensation; and
- rules for data storage and archiving.

ON THE BASIS OF VARIOUS LEGAL SYSTEMS AND EXISTING PRACTICES, WHAT KIND OF LEGAL FRAMEWORK WOULD GIVE CITIZENS CONFIDENCE IN LEGAL PROTECTION OF PERSONAL DATA AND PRIVACY IN E-GOVERNMENT?

In recent years, governments have steadily been implementing various aspects of e-government, such as portals, public sites and remote procedures and services, for various purposes, using different methods and in varying stages of completion. The opening of e-government sites has made possible e-mail exchanges between government agencies and Internet users, consultations with the public and surveys on the quality of services and user satisfaction. At the same time, governments and international organisations have sought to make the Internet more secure and to protect personal data, and the steps taken have given rise to a highly controversial debate on the aims and limitations of data protection.

Nevertheless, on the whole, the issues relating to e-government have not been the subject of major national debates organized jointly by governments and parliaments. Admittedly, some consultations have been held, reports have been drafted and made public, debates have ensued and laws have been passed, but the construction of e-government has predominantly been driven by the executive. Despite pressure from Internet users' associations, political parties and trade unions have only become involved belatedly. In the legal framework of traditional p-government, users had become accustomed to entrusting personal data concerning them to the State, generally without worrying about the issue of protection.

Copyright collection agencies sought and obtained protection for data on the Internet, as the Web is not secure and data can be pirated. It was then realized that this problem also concerned the data of e-government users, since the proprietary systems of government departments are not necessarily secure, and the Web is not secure. Governments rightly considered that data protection was a public mission, but they did not try to rush the process, for various reasons: government departments were not ready; identification, authentication and protection tools were not coordinated; and the back-office had not yet been organized.

Nevertheless, personal data concerning physical and legal persons are the raw materials of e-government. Computer programs must contain and apply legal instructions that govern the processing of applications and files. It is therefore necessary to make a detailed examination of the applicable law and seek to establish a legal framework that will encompass the full range of operations that data undergo.

The objectives of a legal framework for personal data and privacy protection.

To guarantee systematically the rights of users, citizens and government. The rights of citizens, users and government regarding personal data and the aspects of the private lives of individuals that these data reveal must be systematically examined so that their processing will be fully governed by the law. The current trend towards piecemeal legislation is not the best solution for data that are subject to a wide range of processing operations by various bodies and are circulated widely.

To ensure the implementation of effective good practices that do not pose legal problems. The aim is to ensure that users have confidence in e-government procedures. Both users and government officials should be able to avoid becoming entangled in complex procedures and rules. Problems must be addressed on the basis of established rules and simple solutions. The problems are similar in most countries. A small number of common basic rules should guide lawmakers and lead to simple solutions. The main obstacle remains the diversity of legal and administrative cultures and of institutional systems, such as federalism in some countries and a renewed trend towards centralization in others. No State can, on principle, be oblivious of what is going on in other countries and build an isolated legal system. The very nature of the Internet makes this impossible.

To foresee changing needs and legal solutions. The aim is to ensure that the basic legal principles remain flexible so that they can be adapted to new techniques and services that e-government may make available to users. This is the most difficult aspect.

WHAT ARE KEY PRINCIPLES THAT MUST BE RESPECTED TO PROTECT PERSONAL DATA AND PRIVACY?

The recent laws on personal data protection lay down a number of principles. The Canadian Personal Information Protection and Electronic Documents Act (2000) lays down ten principles contained in the Code:

1. *Accountability:* an organization is responsible for personal information under its control and shall designate an individual or individuals who are accountable for the organization's compliance with the following principles.
2. *Identifying purposes:* the purposes for which personal information is collected shall be identified by the organization at or before the time the information is collected.
3. *Consent:* the knowledge and consent of the individual are required for the collection, use, or disclosure of personal information, except where inappropriate.
4. *Limiting collection:* the collection of personal information shall be limited to that which is necessary for the purposes identified by the organization. Information shall be collected by fair and lawful means.

5. *Limiting use, disclosure, and retention:* personal information shall not be used or disclosed for purposes other than those for which it was collected, except with the consent of the individual or as required by law. Personal information shall be retained only as long as necessary for the fulfillment of those purposes.
6. *Accuracy:* personal information shall be as accurate, complete, and up-to-date as is necessary for the purposes for which it is to be used.
7. *Safeguards:* personal information shall be protected by security safeguards appropriate to the sensitivity of the information.
8. *Openness:* an organization shall make readily available to individuals specific information about its policies and practices relating to the management of personal information.
9. *Individual access:* upon request, an individual shall be informed of the existence, use, and disclosure of his or her personal information and shall be given access to that information. An individual shall be able to challenge the accuracy and completeness of the information and have it amended as appropriate.
10. *Challenging compliance:* an individual shall be able to address a challenge concerning compliance with the above principles to the designated individual or individuals accountable for the organization's compliance.

General principles for building confidence in e-government. The first set of principles is focused upon the personal data of users and government accountability in this regard.

Five General Legal Principles Governing the Use of Personal Data in E-Government

The principle of the unique, universal and long-lasting nature of personal data. In making personal data and their protection the focus of concern, it should firstly be borne in mind that users' personal data change little over time. Consequently, the raw material of e-government is relatively stable. There is no reason for public services to require users to provide these data over and over again throughout their adult life, i.e., over an average period of 60 years. Valid information provided by users is often stable and unchanging, and they should only have to provide it anew if it is inaccurate, false or outdated. There is general agreement on this point, and it should be possible to lay down a basic principle of e-government in this regard.

The principle of all individuals' full freedom regarding the use of personal and private data concerning them. In society, there are many situations in which people are required to divulge personal data. Users possess a right regarding the use of their personal data that is comparable to the full freedom that they enjoy in their private life. Consequently, legislation restricting the use of personal data must follow a principle of limiting such measures to what is strictly necessary to enable the State to exercise its basic rights. Otherwise, the special situations in which users come into contact with the administrative authorities would be considered as being abnormally different from ordinary situations. The issue of data ownership, and thus the possibilities governing their use must be clarified and harmonized. This is a step that is clearly necessary in France, since the law governing personal data is contradictory because of a number of divergent rules and court decisions. The same is true in Belgium. The legislation in North America and Ireland is relatively permissive.

The principle of the appropriate level of protection of personal data. All personal or private data must benefit from a level of protection sufficient to ensure confidentiality. The different kinds of personal data used, which may be of a personal, family, social, economic, administrative, political or even philosophical or religious nature, do not all have the same value. The law governing these data must take these differences in value into account. Some of the existing legislation protecting personal data does take this factor into account and ensures that there is a significant difference in the legal treatment of different kinds of data. This is the case for data considered to be sensitive in French, Belgian, Canadian, Irish and U.S. law. Certain types of data may not be released either free of charge or in return for payment. Other kinds of data may be commercialized. Specific types of law (civil, public, commercial, tax and intellectual property law, etc.) recognize these different types of ownership of personal data. The level of protection provided for these various categories of personal data should be appropriate to the legal goal being sought. North American legislation and legal thinking are sensitive to this reality. On the whole, governments are aware of this problem, but it remains to be seen which strategies governments will adopt to ensure the security of the data entrusted to them from a practical standpoint.

The principle of confidentiality. It is necessary to consolidate the scattered and sometimes outdated legislative provisions governing confidentiality in e-government (duty of discretion, professional secrecy, rules of ethical conduct) in new legislation that is adapted to the problems raised by e-government and to the recent European directives on electronic commerce, electronic signatures, data protection and copyright in the information society, so that government employees will be aware of their responsibilities and users will know their legal guarantees. U.S. legislation is exemplary in this regard. Other countries should soon follow suit. This is the case in France, where the relevant legislation is being consolidated, and in Belgium, where a general reform of public services is under way. In this regard, the relatively rapid digitalization of public data and plans in the field of storage and archiving should make it easier for employees working in e-government as well as users to "collect" useful data.

The principle of accountability. Accountability is unquestionably one of the rules that can strengthen the confidence that both users and government employees have in e-government. In p-government, it is not feasible for users to come into offices at any time to check the status of their files. The same is true of commercial sales of products and services. The digitalization of data and the use of the Internet are changing the nature of this issue. It is now not only possible, but also desirable and prudent for users to take responsibility for verifying the accuracy of the information concerning them, whether they have provided it on a compulsory or contractual basis. In some cases, they might be required to verify certain kinds of data (such as the main administrative information regarding their civil status).

The Harmonization of Rules Specific to E-Government Regarding Personal Data

The principle of the harmonization of rules specific to e-government. The differences in legal systems should not prevent countries from implementing certain common basic principles. It would be legally cost effective to conduct audits of national legal systems in order to show the legal obstacles that impede the harmonization of the principles for the construction of e-government, and, in particular, the harmonization of specific rules governing the relationship between personal data and the organization of administrative structures. Thus far, it does not seem that major organisations, such as the European Union, have carried out such studies.

The principle of the legalization and/or contractualization of administrative processing. It should only be possible to process personal and private data if this processing is specifically allowed by law or is covered by a contract between a government agency and users or their legal representatives. Application of this principle would make it possible to harmonize national legislative systems and to prevent the various government departments from creating new processing operations on the basis of their administrative needs alone, without taking into account their impact on users. Administrative processing must be structured and organized as clearly as possible if users are to have confidence in the efficiency and credibility of e-government. This aspect is regulated in various ways by government, but is not presented clearly in government information as a basic aspect of e-government, and is therefore not clearly understood by citizens. However, this issue is not simply a matter of the internal organization of government departments, since users are the main parties concerned. Admittedly, legislation is beginning to provide greater protection of personal data and the members of data protection boards are doing remarkable work. Nevertheless, it would be preferable for all processing operations to be covered by specific legislation. In this regard, the provisions of the recent French law of 30 January 2002 are not totally satisfactory.

The rules of good conduct for government agencies. Beyond the legislation governing the processing of personal data, government agencies must also comply with rules of good conduct:

- Publication of the rules governing the processing of data.
- Compliance with rules of transparency.
- Rules enabling users to monitor the status of their applications and files.
- Rules for government monitoring of the status of applications and files.

Four Principles Governing the Use of Personal Data in E-Services

The principle of the interoperability of existing practices. The practices of the various e-governments must include rules for interfacing that make it possible to take into account the different practices of government agencies and other countries, such as processing governed by legislation, processing governed by contract, processing that combines both elements (governed partly by legal and partly by contractual provisions), processing having a European label and processing by non-European countries. Most governments have developed protocols for interoperability between the computer systems of government agencies. This is a difficult, costly and sensitive task that must be focused on the rules governing the interoperability of the digital data containing the personal e-data of users.

The principle of the interconnection of government agencies. In making remote procedures and services available to users, it is necessary to guarantee that the administrative services that process applications and files are interconnected in such a way that electronic documents can circulate between offices (and, in fact, between computers) without having to remove these documents from the circuit in order to process them. This task, like that of the interoperability of computer systems, is a key to the success of e-government. It would be best to announce plans for progressive implementation in the main remote services. Governments are finding it difficult to do so, other than outlining very general plans in this regard.

The principle of simplicity. E-government departments are seeking to implement the simplest and least costly procedures, rules and techniques in the light of the available technology and the need to ensure an adequate level of security. Simplicity is equally important to users. It is not only ensures transparency for users, who would not understand highly complex internal administrative procedures for processing applications and files, but also transparency between departments. This is because of the recognized and accepted procedures used and the perfect interoperability and interconnection of departments, not only from the standpoint of data processing systems but also of decision-making processes.

The principle of the provision of the right information at the right time and place. The databases of government agencies must be updated in light of the issues raised by e-government, so that documents useful to e-government can progressively be made available both to government employees and users.

Four Principles that Mainly Concern Users in the Legal Framework of E-Government:

The principle of permanent access by users to their files.

- All users with a recognized identifier must have free access to files concerning them, without the government being able to deny them such access.
- Government departments must digitize their files so that they will be accessible at all times to the users personally concerned by these files.

The rights of access and rectification contained in the various legislative provisions studied are organized very differently. In the U.S., users may consult and make copies of their files, but they must first file an application that must be reviewed and approved by the competent authorities. The same is true in France, Belgium, Canada and Ireland. This is not conducive to users' confidence in e-government. Citizens would find it difficult to understand why they are free to consult their contractual data directly in the databases of commercial firms (under the E-Commerce Directive and countries' transposing legislation) but not able to do so in government databases containing personal data. What has been required of private e-businesses should be required of government e-services.

The principle of the free disposition of personal data by users.

The "win-win" principle of effectiveness: government must organize its services so that they meet users' needs regarding user-friendliness, rapidity and access and so that applications and files can be processed effectively.

The principle that personal data may only be processed for the benefit of users: Personal data may only be processed if it is of concrete benefit to the person concerned by the data and if the purposes of the administrative processing have been authorized and can be monitored. This principle has been enacted in the legislation studied.

Rules of good conduct for users. Users must not abuse their right of access and rectification. They must behave honestly and inform the government whenever there is a change in their personal data that will affect the processing of their files. The U.S. legislation addresses this issue, but the legislation of the other countries studied seems not yet to have done so.

The principle of mediation. To accept mediation by an independent legal expert who represents neither users nor government and is paid for out of public funds.

CREATING A LEGAL FRAMEWORK FOR PERSONAL DATA PROTECTION THAT ALLOWS E-GOVERNMENT TO FUNCTION EFFECTIVELY AND BE USED BY CITIZENS

Governments have hardly begun to address the issue of a general legal framework for personal data protection. As we saw earlier, governments had to respond to the most immediate issues raised by the development of the Internet. It is obvious that it will not suffice merely to lay down data protection rules for e-government to work effectively. It is necessary to seek out the legal obstacles that prevent e-government from functioning as effectively as possible. For example, a satisfactory practical solution has yet to be found to the key issue of online evidence or the issues of the time limits and quality of administrative electronic data processing. The issues that must be solved are interrelated, and all pertain to the central issue of the protection and use of personal data.

To create a legal framework that would give users confidence in e-government, it is necessary to address the legal obstacles preventively, to initiate policies to promote domestic and international debate, to implement timetables of legal and administrative measures and to address in depth the issue of the relationship between p-government and e-government. There are many differences between p-services and e-services and it would be useless to conceal, ignore or try to minimize them. P-services will continue to suit the needs of many users, although they may use e-government for some operations. It is better to describe these differences and keep what is best in p-government. In any event, the many faces of government will be far more diversified in the 2005-2010 period. If governments continue to transform government so that it is geared as closely as possible to users' needs, they will have to develop new responses to new situations.

Lastly, e-government services are not well defined in relation to users' needs while e-commerce services are trying to establish themselves amidst the setbacks and hopes of the Internet economy.

- What are the legal obstacles to the development of e-government?
- What must be done to create a legal framework that would give citizens' confidence in the personal data and privacy protection provided by e-government?

- What are the differences between e-services (e-government) and p-services (paper-based government)?
- How do citizens' needs in e-commerce and e-government differ?

The legal obstacles to the development of e-government in relation to personal data protection

The first obstacle is, as it were, an intrinsic one, since governments do not have a comprehensive legal framework designed especially for e-government. Nor is there a comprehensive legal framework for the development of e-government. France has begun to address the concerns of users of government services through the Act on the Rights of Citizens in their Relations with Government (the so-called "DCRA Act").[10]

There is no comprehensive legal framework for e-government. There is no legislation in the following fields:

- on the rights of citizens in their dealings with e-government;
- on the organization and functioning of e-government:
- within each ministry and with decentralized agencies;
- between ministries and decentralized agencies; and
- on the use of personal data and certain aspects of privacy in e-government.

What are the most appropriate protection policies? Five sorts of protection can be useful for building confidence in e-government from the beginning until the end of the administrative operations during which personal data are being processed:

- *Legal protection:* rights
- *Physical protection:* levels of security adapted to levels of legal protection
- *Para-legal and legal protection:* mediation mechanisms and streamlined legal procedures (rapid, simple and at the lowest possible cost)
- *Moral protection:* user assistance
- *Financial protection:* guarantees of full and rapid compensation

How can a legal framework be created that would build citizens' confidence in the personal data and privacy protection provided by e-government?

Given the need to protect personal data and simplify procedures for users inasmuch as possible, the legal framework of e-government must be organized and clarified.

Today, most online administrative operations, remote procedures and services are operations carried out by a single ministry. They are bilateral in nature (between government agencies and users), but are carried out via a direct link between the government agency and the user. These are two-way "monofunctional" operations from the viewpoint of both actors (the user and the government agency). For users, there are many administrative electronic lines that link them to the government services that they need. However, many everyday operations require the services of more than one ministry. This is the issue that e-government must settle. What methods must be developed in this regard? What systems must be implemented? These are ultimately policy issues and a legal framework must be devised to address them.

The brief description that follows is aimed at presenting a systematic approach to the main steps that must be taken and the legal issues that must be addressed in order to establish the legal framework of e-government:

- The classification of administrative procedures depending on whether they mono- or multifunctional and the need for legal security (*law governing electronic administrative procedures*) and a study of current methods of data classification (*law governing classification*);
- The classification of administrative files implemented by e-government: the legal basis of the concept of "remote administrative file," "electronic administrative file" and typology of the different kinds of files by major category — law governing files;
- Classification of file and data matching systems currently used by government — law governing file matching;
- A study on the traditional and new legal status of personal data held by the public — law governing personal "public-private" data;
- Classification of personal data depending on how they are;
- Typology of data use by category of "remote administrative files";
- A study of the means of authentication currently practiced by government — law governing authentication;
- Electronic authentication — law governing electronic authentication;
- Data storage — law governing storage; and
- Archiving of electronic data — law governing archiving.

Simple, practical solutions must be found that meet the quality criteria for e-government processing (the study of this issue is in a very advanced stage). E-government users must be given broad access; the accountability of government employees and users must be ensured; limits must be set that are subject to severe penalties if exceeded.

Law Governing Access and Modification

Under the principle of free access to personal data by persons whose identity has been authenticated (right of access), users have the right to have data changed (by the government and verified by the user) and to have material errors corrected. This principle is universally recommended. However, the practical conditions for exercising this right have not been established everywhere. This step is essential to the success of e-government, for it will enable users to see in practice for themselves one of the basic differences with p-government.

Law Governing Encryption and Passwords: File Protection

Certain predefined data may be encrypted, but to process the most sensitive operations (such as changing electronic identity cards), it is sufficient to use double passwords (like the two keys required to open a bank safety deposit box, one of which is kept by the user and the other by the bank). With regard to encryption and passwords (as for electronic signatures), the rule must be to implement the simplest possible system compatible with security. Nevertheless, some elements of remote administrative files must be concealed and placed automatically in an electronic "safe." In some cases, such as calls for tender, entire remote administrative files may protected in an electronic safe.

Transparency

Administrative procedures must be published (what is being done, who is doing it and how), as must the source codes that drive computer programs. Computer specialists in the user community must be able to substantiate the legality, fairness and accuracy of the computer programs available. Government must not be able to use proprietary software without it being possible to examine source codes, since some software may have "back doors" that can be entered without detection. Sites should also list the names of e-government staff together with their work address and telephone number and a digital photo of them.

Administrative Service Contracts

Users and government departments may sign contracts on the processing of files. This is a legitimate right since users own the data concerning them (see discussion above). It is recommended to use a standard contract procedure, although this does not allow users to ask e-government to tailor services to their needs. However, agencies can offer a list of a wide range of possible services.

Law Governing Digital Administrative Files

Law on digital administrative files is being implemented to cover a number of issues: files of correspondence exchanged; computer tracking of the status of files being processed (Where is my file? When will it be processed and by whom?) Law on storage and archiving is also being developed: Who stores files? When and how? Who archives files? When and how?

Law Governing Cookies

The use of administrative cookies is regulated. U.S. government departments currently seem to be more concerned about users' freedom than is the case on certain French sites, for example, which constantly deliver cookies, sometimes on every page. At times users must click the cookie refusal statement many times before the program accepts it and gives Internet users access to the page that they wish to consult. Users are unfamiliar with cookies. The continuing use of cookies on some government sites can give the impression that the administration wants to infiltrate into users' computers, which is unfortunate.

Cross-Agency Administrative Practices

Governments have let monofunctional administrative files develop (one agency ↔ user), which are used in remote procedures or services by individual agencies, without developing concurrently the multifunctional cross-agency communication necessary for the remote processing of files (many agencies ↔ user).

What are the differences between e-services (e-government) and p-services (p-government)?

The climate of relative confidence that reigns between users and p-government staff is due to habits of behavior of both groups and the relative flexibility of the administrative rules for processing requests and files. The sudden emergence of the Internet, the unpreparedness of both government agencies and the public and uncertainty and delay regarding legislation have highlighted the dangers of using Internet and the need to protect and secure systems and ensure that relations between government and users can be carried out safely.

E-government services transform the nature of the relationship between users and government, for government agencies will now be able to assist and advise the public and anticipate its expectations and needs and meet them more effectively. E-government services can meet the demand for high-quality services and regulation, efficiency and accountability, for it can monitor its performance continuously. The online availability of forms and remote procedures and services has already led to administrative streamlining and stimulated the demand for quality through comparison and emulation.

At present, the services delivered by e-government and p-government are used by different publics with different needs. Studies must be undertaken to assess the exact needs of the different users for e-government. Computer systems and e-services make it possible to provide users with personalized services and responses. This is one of the main differences between the practices of p-government and the future practices of e-government. Firms in the private sector are devoting a great deal of time and money to marketing so that they can meet their customers' needs. Government agencies need to do the same. This necessary policy will mean that new legal rules will have to be established.

Regarding personal data protection, p-government only has problems when personal data that should have remained confidential are disclosed or published. The monitoring of protection is *ex post*, after an incident has arisen. In e-services, there is *ex ante* monitoring aimed at preventing any incidents from occurring. This being the case, monitoring must be exhaustive and it is essential to have clear and specific rules.

WHAT ARE DIFFERENCES BETWEEN USERS' NEEDS IN E-COMMERCE AND E-GOVERNMENT?

The services provided via e-commerce and e-government are not different by nature. However, a distinction must be made between two sorts of procedures carried out via e-government, namely those responding to legal obligations imposed on individuals in the framework of public administrative monopolies (such as issuing identity papers, driving licences, etc.) and those carried out in response to requests made by individuals (such as applications for building permits). Users' needs are greatest regarding the first category of procedures (over which government agencies have a legal monopoly), which must comply exactly with legally prescribed quality criteria. For the second category, it would be useful to review the procedures and rules so that this type of e-government services would not be considered as being identical to those in the first category.

HOW EFFECTIVELY CAN GOVERNMENTS MAKE AVAILABLE ONLINE SERVICES?

This is not a legal, but a policy issue. This said, governments are now benefiting from the strong growth of new technologies and the Internet. There is a genuine, growing expectation that e-government can make a real contribution in terms of user-friendliness, security, data protection, efficiency and the rapidity of remote procedures. In the mind of the public, these expectations are linked to ideas of technical progress, government reform, participation and co-management of public affairs, all of which are ultimately legitimate expressions of each individual's personal interests and needs.

However, there are two major obstacles, i.e., the mistrust and even rejection of the computerised procedures implemented by the State, and the resistance of some government employees, polarized by their trade unions. On the other hand, the Canadian, Irish, Italian and U.S. governments have shown that it is possible to dialogue effectively with the representatives of public employees.

There remains the issue of confidence. Personal data protection is the key to success, together with effective participation of users in the work concerning their files. These two issues must be interlinked. If governments allow users to participate, the issue of confidence can be solved. This does not mean merely consulting users, but making them co-participants.

Personal data protection, confidence and user participation — these objectives will require government to engage in legislative planning and develop new concepts and practices. However, there is a danger that e-government will be perceived as government in a computerised box. The more remote procedures and services develop, the more important it will become to encourage public participation so that users can regularly meet with government officials and not lose sight of the fact that government is made up of real people working in real offices.

ENDNOTES

1 *http://www.parl.gc.ca/36/2/parlbus/chambus/house/bills/government/C-6/C-6_4/C-6_cover-E.html*

2 1996 FOIA Update, Fall 1996. The Freedom of Information Act 5 U.S.C. § 552, as amended by Public Law No.104-231, 110 Stat. 3048. Ref.: *http://www.usdoj.gov/oip/foia_updates/Vol_XVII_4/page2.htm*

3 *http://irm.cit.nih.gov/itmra/itmra96.html*

4 *http://www.uwi.com/practices/GPEA.pdf*

5 *http://www.house.gov/rules/s761cr_h3.pdf*

6 In the Senate of the United States—107th Cong., 2d Sess. S. 803 - 2001.

7 2001 14-6, National Assembly, *Projet de loi n° 3143 sur la société de l'information et exposé des motifs*, document released 18 June 2001, see: *http://www.assemblee-nationale.fr/projets/pl3143.asp*

8 *http://www.assemblee-nat.fr/ta/ta0780.asp*

9 The Confidential Information Protection Act of 12 June 2001 aims to protect the confidentiality of information obtained from the public in order to compile statistics; the Privacy Act of 14 June 2001 requires the consent of an individual prior to

the sale and marketing of such individual's personally identifiable information; the Consumer Internet Privacy Enhancement Act of 20 January 2001 restricts the collection of "personally identifiable information online" from Web site users; the Consumer Online Privacy and Disclosure Act of 31 January 2001 regulates the privacy of personal information collected from and about individuals on the Internet.

10 Loi no 2000-321 du 12 avril 2000 relative aux droits des citoyens dans leurs relations avec les administrations (1) NOR : FPPX9800029L J.O. Numéro 88 du 13 avril 2000 page 5646 .

Chapter V

E-Government and Organizational Change

Stuart Culbertson, TkMC, Canada

ABSTRACT

At varying paces, governments are aggressively pursuing e-government strategies with the expressed objective of capturing the efficiency that ICTs can provide. However, more often than not these strategies are being implemented within the existing organizational structures and practices of governments, which can, by their nature, thwart rather than advance the objectives. This chapter examines some key aspects of organizational change required by governments to make their e-government strategies successful. The change imperative entails a hard look at many of the structures, processes, cultural issues and management practices prevailing within the public sector. This chapter identifies government success factors for several organizational entities involved in e-government and assesses the implications for organizational change on government structures, work practices and culture.

Why is Organizational Change Necessary for Successful E-Government?

ICTs, by their nature, can advance reforms in the ways that governments conduct their business and relate to their citizens and clients through e-government applications. In this capacity, ICTs can serve as very useful tools for governments wishing to reform and modernize public administrations. At the same time, reforms in public administration are required to lay the administrative, policy and regulatory foundations in place to make e-government possible. Both forces working together can play a powerful role in changing the administration of government services and operations while simultaneously advancing economic development and the e-capabilities of citizenry in the information age.

This chapter summarizes some of the principal benefits that governments should expect to achieve in the implementation of ICTs in their operations. The structure and culture of government administrations pose challenging barriers, which must be overcome in order to achieve the successful implementation of e-government across the enterprise. The most prominent systemic barriers relate to the opposing forces of the "horizontal" and "borderless" orientation of ICTs within "vertical, silo-based" structures of government.

What Does the Process of Organizational Change Entail?

Successful e-government entails overcoming these barriers through changes in the organization and practices of governments. This chapter examines changes that are required in government to support the successful implementation of ICTs and e-government strategies, including:

- The alignment of e-government to public administration reform initiatives. The chances of transforming government to drive the e-government agenda are enhanced where e-government is envisaged as part of a broader, comprehensive public administration reform initiative.
- The position and power of Cabinet-level responsibilities and organizations. The more highly situated the "e-Minister" the better. However, it is vitally important that the e-Minister is seen as owning the e-government strategy along with owning, or at least able to heavily influence, the policy and funding tools to make it happen;
- The role of senior management interdepartmental coordinating organizations.
- The role of chief information officer or an equivalent position. These positions should be less "cheerleader" and more "commander" in the e-government campaign.
- The organization of the external relationship with citizens, clients and supplier/ partners in e-government — including focus groups and citizen/client feedback.

What are the Implications for Organizational Change on Government Structures and Public Administration?

Drawing from the analysis of organizational success factors and barriers to change, this chapter examines the implications for governments in addressing some of the changes in organization, administrative practice and business culture involved in effective e-government. Several of these implications are examined, including:

- Adapting to the horizontal orientation of ICTs. Fundamental to the redesign of government organization is the ability to construct, coordinate and deliver e-government across the silos of government and to ensure that the budget, management and regulatory processes of government are aligned to support, rather than thwart, this orientation.

- Impacts on organizational hierarchy and responsibility. The ability of ICTs to assist in aggregating and rapidly transmitting information throughout an organization runs counter to the conventional "chain-of-command" model that prevails within public administrations in processing their business.
- Encouraging risk and reward in government. ICTs are relatively immature technologies, which often involve innovation and risk-taking in their implementation. Public servants operate under a bright spotlight of public accountability in a business culture that rewards neither risk nor cooperation. Breaking this barrier is a tough challenge for governments.
- Meeting the expectations of 24/7 government. Citizens and clients approach e-government with high expectations of rapid action. If, however, governments feel that ICT investments will permit a reduction in their staff resources without organizational and business practice change, they may find themselves incapable of keeping up with the increased demand thereby unleashed. The ability to meet both objectives is best served when governments are able to achieve greater maturity in their electronic service offerings through electronic services featuring end-to-end transactional and citizen/client self-service capabilities. While this is being done, governments should consider how to best migrate citizens and clients to the electronic service delivery channel — through policy measures and marketing strategies.
- Human resources practices. The war for recruitment and retention of the skills necessary to drive e-government challenges often-inflexible public sector hiring practices. The move towards e-government also requires attention to training within the public sector, not only for ICT professionals but, more broadly, in order to address the concerns of those public servants who may fear technology.
- Transparency and accountability. The capabilities of ICTs to enhance access to information and accountability, as well as to jeopardize personal privacy, represent the twin horns of a dilemma facing governments embarked on e-government initiatives. Balancing the information access and privacy protection priorities requires careful attention to corporate information management strategies. The information management issue has organizational implications for governments, because such strategies must, by definition, be corporate in nature. The citizen/client is not likely to easily accept situations where different agencies of government apply different standards for privacy protection and information access.

Will governments be able to overcome the systemic, administrative obstacles to change in order to enable ICTs to play a full role in transforming governments?

The changes required for effective implementation of e-government pose challenging implications for the operating culture of public administrations. However, some factors are more important than others and merit priority consideration. These include:

- The positioning of e-government strategies, official responsibilities and authorities within government. E-government champions, both at the political and senior bureaucratic level, should be highly situated within government and clearly seen as owning the e-government strategy and owning, or at least able to heavily influence, the funding and policy tools required to make the strategy work.

Stronger inter-agency cooperation is essential to making e-government work effectively across the enterprise of government. It is likely that this cooperation will have to be forced or funded rather than facilitated into action.

- The implications of 24/7 government on the structures and practices of government must be addressed. This can be aided by increasing the number of electronic services with end-to-end transactional and citizen/client self-service capabilities.
- Recognizing the impact that e-government has on the operating cultures of government organizations. ICTs, with their orientation to data-sharing and borderless flows of information, challenge the traditional "chain-of-command" structures of government. At the same time, the immaturity of the technologies and the need to incent co-operation among agencies may require a higher acceptance of risk and reward than has normally prevailed in risk-averse public administrations. Finally, a comprehensive staff training plan will be required to address the concerns of many officials who see ICTs as a harbinger of job loss or as a complex area that they are embarrassed not to understand.
- Balancing the public priorities for increased access to information and stronger privacy protection requires careful attention to the development of corporate information management strategies that build trust among citizens and clients.

INTRODUCTION

"If we could create a public service from scratch, operationalizing the innovations in technology and management, what would it look like?"[1]

In contrast with some of the organizational transformations that have occurred in many private-sector organizations over the past decade, governments have rarely been in a position to truly ask this question and implement its answers. Even when governments change through electoral processes, they seldom are presented a "green field" opportunity on which to build new organizational structures and practices. Indeed, it seems only a matter of time before the same old conventional structures of organization re-emerge through the dust of change to frame the new government's approach to business. While governments change, they rarely transform.

The public sector is the largest consumer of information and communications technologies (ICTs) in the world, and governments, at varying paces, are aggressively pursuing e-government strategies with the expressed objective of capturing the efficiency and connectivity gains that ICTs can provide. However, more often than not these strategies, as elegant as they may appear on paper, are being implemented within the existing organizational structures and practices of governments, which can, by their nature, thwart rather than advance the objectives.

The attempt to force fit e-government into existing structures and processes may produce a new-looking electronic face to the client but will not assist governments in taking advantage of the larger transformational powers of ICTs within their organizations. Examining similar approaches in the private sector, Harvard University change management expert Rosabeth Moss Kanter characterizes such an approach as "putting lipstick on a bulldog" — noting that "a company is not transformed simply because it creates a Web site; that might be only a cosmetic change. Success requires a more complete makeover, namely re-thinking the model of how [to use ICTs] to organize the work of the whole organization."[2]

Not all governments are necessarily structured in the same way or even share the same level of commitment to transforming their relationships with their citizens and clients. Nevertheless, several common threads are emerging in the experience of e-government around the world, and they allow an examination of the important challenges and successes associated with e-government implementation. Similarly, much can be learned from the way that ICTs have transformed the operations and structures of private enterprises that have had, arguably, a stronger imperative to change driven by competitive market forces. The author also draws from his professional experience in this area while serving as Chief Information Officer for the government of British Columbia, Canada (1998-2001).

This chapter examines key aspects of organizational change required by governments to maximize the benefits of their large investments in ICTs and, in turn, make their e-government strategies successful. The change imperative entails a hard look at many of the structures, processes, cultural issues and management practices prevailing within the public sector. In this chapter, e-government success factors are identified for several organizational entities involved in e-government. The chapter then assesses the implications for organizational change on government structures and work practices associated with e-government implementation.

FRAMEWORK FOR ANALYSIS OF ORGANIZATIONAL CHANGE

The relationship between the power of ICTs to change government organizations and the reforms within public administration required to exploit the greatest benefits from the adoption of ICTs is a symbiotic one. In her study of the impact of ICT-driven organizational change on private sector firms, Marian Murphy describes this relationship as follows:

"There is a mutually beneficial relationship between organizational change in firms and ICT investments. Information technology is key to facilitating new organizational approaches, from lean production to teamwork to customer relations. On the other hand, organizational change is usually needed to realize the full benefits of information and communications technology. Complex technology requires flexible work organization and, at the same time, it increases the capacity to adopt a flexible work organization."[3]

ICTs can advance reforms in the ways that governments conduct their business and relate to their citizens and clients through e-government applications ("the push"). In this capacity, ICTs can serve as very useful tools for governments wishing to reform and modernize public administrations. At the same time, reforms in public administration are required to lay the administrative, policy and regulatory foundations in place to make e-government possible ("the pull"). The impact of both working together can play a powerful role in changing the administration of government services and operations while also advancing economic development and the e-capabilities of citizenry in the information age.

The Push: The Transformational Potential of ICTs

ICTs intrinsically operate on the horizontal plane, spanning via networks and Web-based architecture throughout an organization and challenging organizational silos in the interest of sharing information, data, business processes and systems. Drawing from the experiences of private-sector organizations, the promise of e-government holds significant prospects for the reform of public administration and the relationships of governments with their citizens and clients.

To summarize, these benefits include:

- Advanced networking power enabling the integration of information and data and a sharing of business processes and systems among governmental organizations — eliminating redundancies and saving resources;
- Ability to re-invent organizations based on a primary focus of seamless service to the citizen — not dictated or prescribed by the organizational boundaries of the agencies responsible for these services;
- More accessible and up-to-date services. The ability to provide and update information instantaneously without having to incur publishing
- and distribution costs, and the ability to serve citizens and clients at their convenience on a "24/7" basis;
- Potential for simplified business processes and citizen/client self-
- service in e-government applications — reducing costs and increasing efficiency of both the government and the client;
- Quicker response time. The ability to connect instantly with a broad range of clients and solicit their input/feedback on proposed changes;
- Ability to adapt and scale market-available ICT solutions for basic business processes — meaning that government could save time and resources in trying to build their own unique solutions;
- Opportunity to advance several key good governance goals, including enhanced accountability and openness, citizen/client participation and focus and effectiveness and responsiveness.

The Pull: Overcoming Barriers to Change

While the benefits outlined above may be appreciable in principle, governments have tended to lag behind the private sector in their ability to implement ICTs to transform their operations in practice. Indeed, it is not as if reforming government organization and implementing ICTs are two ships passing in the night. Rather, it is more an example of the proverbial irresistible force meeting the immovable object.

As governments attempt to pull the benefits of ICTs into their organizations, the effective implementation of e-government across the enterprise of government faces several prominent structural and cultural barriers. Prominent among these barriers are:

- The silo-based vertical structure of government confounds the horizontal interdepartmental work necessary to make ICTs function effectively across the enterprise. Budget, legal and policy authorities and processes are lined up with the silos, supporting turf-protection and offering little incentive for cooperation.
- Lack of budget commitment to make the change to effective e-government — lack of funding to support ICT acquisition and implementation or cross-enterprise projects and collaboration.
- Lack of training resources to help employees make the transition to transformed e-government.
- Fear of ICTs on the front lines and middle management of government — the experience of ICT implementation in the private sector suggests job loss as technology replaces front-line labor and disintermediates middle management.
- Suspicion of ICTs among many technologically illiterate senior managers.
- As operators in the largely monopolistic environment of government, these managers are not as compelled by the same "competitive advantage" sales pitch used by ICT suppliers selling to the private sector. Concerns about project failures and cost overruns leave a sense that the cost savings (if any) associated with e-government will not justify the increasing complexity brought into conventional government operations by e-government.
- The risk-averse nature of governments. While the rewards for successful innovation are meagre, the consequences of project failure under the spotlight of public accountability are grave.
- Fear that governments will not be able to cope with the increased demand and expectations for quick response from citizens and clients that ICTs engender. This is especially so if it is felt that e-government strategies are motivated by the desire to reduce labor costs.
- Who is asking for this anyway? Citizens and clients do not rank the transformation of government or e-government high on their list of priorities for action by their governments. Not all citizens and clients of government will be able to or will want to be able to deal with government electronically (the "digital divide").
- Some governments or staff may not want to encourage a closer relationship with citizens and clients or greater accountability. These governments may be happy enough limiting their e-government programs to the electronic delivery of services to citizens and clients without exploring how ICTs could be used to enhance citizen/client participation in the processes of government.

Successful e-government can only be achieved when barriers such as these can be overcome with systemic changes in the organization and practices of governments.

FACILITATING ADOPTION OF ICTs IN ORGANIZATION OF GOVERNMENTS: WHY IS ORGANIZATIONAL CHANGE NECESSARY FOR SUCCESSFUL E-GOVERNMENT?

In its 2002 survey of e-government leadership, Accenture noted that the governments it surveyed were beginning to show early signs of recognition that "e-government is not just about technology, but about harnessing technology as just one of the tools available to transform the way governments operate. Governments are learning that transformation comes not from moving services online, but from redesigning the organization and processes."[4]

Intriguing models of organizational change are now emerging as governments attempt to find the best structural ways of facilitating the adoption of ICTs and capturing their benefits. Fundamental to the re-design of government organization is the ability to construct, coordinate and deliver e-government across the silos of government and to ensure that the budget, management and regulatory processes of government are aligned to support rather than thwart this orientation.

An examination of the issues and experiences in organizational change allows the formulation of a critical list of the ideal and minimum requisite conditions that should be achieved in order for e-government to function effectively across the enterprise of government. We may consider these to be the primary e-government success factors.

Our discussion examines some of these success factors throughout various senior layers of e-government responsibility and organization within government. In a sense, these success factors might serve as objectives for organizational change and provide a guide for discussion on the types of changes in existing organizational structures that could or should be made to best advance e-government.

Changes in the Organization of Political Leadership in Government

The importance of political leadership and championship of e-government at the most senior levels of government has been the subject of much discussion. Given the immense cross-enterprise work that must be done to achieve "buy-in" for e-government, sustained senior-level sponsorship is, perhaps, the most important determinant of success for e-government.

But how is this leadership/championship to be organized in government? And where it is organized, is it empowered to go far enough and high enough in government to compel the changes required?

Alignment of E-Government to Public Administration Reform Initiatives

How is e-government envisaged in the fundamental strategy and organization of government? Is e-government seen as a fundamental tool and component of a larger public sector transformation initiative? Or is it seen as a solo effort focussed entirely on improving service to and the participation of citizens and clients in the work of government? The answer to these questions will very much determine the prospects of success of a transformational e-government initiative.

E-government initiatives will be the most effective and the impact of ICTs most powerful when e-government is clearly defined as part of a broader public sector reform initiative. In this context, e-government is most likely to receive the political attention required to justify the sometimes-dramatic organizational changes needed. Experience suggests that if e-government is not linked to a larger public-sector reform initiative, it will not carry sufficient weight among government's priorities to justify the fundamental changes necessary in the organization. As such, it also risks being relegated to a more limited, albeit useful, role of improving electronic service delivery.

Examples of e-government initiatives that have been strategically aligned with larger public sector reform processes include:

- *France.* The "electronic administration" positions information technology at the centre of state reform. The French program displays strong linkages between e-government and the reform in structures of government involved in the French Program for the Information Society.[5]
- *USA.* E-government is integral to the President's Five-Part Management Agenda for making government more focused on the citizen. [6]
- *UK.* The "Modernizing Government" plan for the renewal and reform of government embeds several key e-government components in its "information age government" approach (i.e., electronic service delivery targets; cross-government coordination mechanisms established).[7]

Strong E-Government Cabinet-Level Responsibilities and Organizations

The organization of the e-government champion is an important aspect of any successful e-government strategy. Many government leaders are keen supporters and advocates of e-government — and the support of the leader cannot be discounted. However, leaders also have to run the whole of government and cannot be expected to dedicate the time and attention required to make e-government effective. As a result, while championship may reside in the leader, the responsibility for e-government is normally delegated to a Minister, either as an exclusive responsibility or as an important priority among other responsibilities. From an organizational perspective, success factors indicate that the Minister responsible for e-government should be:

- Highly situated within government with e-government as an exclusive or priority task in the portfolio;
- The recognized "owner" of a clearly articulated strategy and enabled with the means to implement the strategy across government;
- Able to provide sustained leadership for the longer term — necessary to actually oversee the implementation of a longer-term action plan;
- In control of, or at least capable of influencing, the budgetary, legal, policy and administrative tools required to get the job done;

- Able to commit government to work in partnership with other levels of government within the jurisdiction — in service of the "single" taxpayer in a system of multiple levels of government (federal government/state/provincial/territorial/municipal).

Examples include:

- *UK*. Secretary of State for Trade and Industry is the "e-Minister" with overall responsibility for the government's e-agenda. She champions the e-agenda at Cabinet level, provides the Prime Minister with monthly progress reports, and takes overall responsibility for the government's e-strategy;
- *Canada*. The Treasury Board Minister holds ministerial responsibility for e-government. As this Minister heads a central agency with a mandate to approve and control government expenditures, there is a strong "control-and-influence" connection between e-government and the government's budgetary authorities;
- *Washington State, USA*. Since 1997, Washington State's digital government responsibilities have been led by the Department of Information Services (DIS), a Cabinet-level agency whose Director reports to the Governor. DIS's mandate is singularly focused on building digital government by providing leadership, policy and service choices for the use of information technology within state and local governments.

Changes in the Management Organization and Practices of Government

Senior Management Interdepartmental Coordinating Organizations

Inter-departmental task forces and committees are an emerging, common feature of e-government management structures within governments. These committees are normally focused on the administrative aspects of e-government: what needs to be done or changed in the organization and the processes of government to support the political direction on e-government. As such, these groups can only function effectively if they can act corporately and enable processes that will assist in deconstructing silos.

Key success factors in such organizations include:

- A clear cross-government mandate and reporting accountability to a Cabinet minister or Cabinet committee responsible for e-government.
- The seniority of the members in the committee and their ability to commit their organizations to action in cross-government projects for the common good of the strategy. Ideally, members would be drawn from the Deputy Minister or equivalent level — representing a group that has a mandate to think corporately as the administrative "board of directors" of government.
- Clear alignment — through membership and Cabinet reporting structure — with the central management agencies of government with cross-government responsibilities for budget and the machinery of government.
- A mandate to examine and make decisions and/or recommendations to the Cabinet on cross-government e-government initiatives and issues.

- Authority over budget resources to enable e-government, either with budget allocations to spend or as the primary vehicle to recommend expenditures to government's budget authorities.

Examples include:

- *UK.* Each department has identified a senior (Board level) official to act as an "e-champion." Representatives of devolved administrations and local government have also nominated e-champions;[8]
- *USA.* E-government Task Force — scrutinizes all federal IT investments to ensure that they maximize inter-operability and minimize redundancy; prioritizes all agency e-government and makes recommendations to the Cabinet on the top projects worthy of receiving funding. The Task Force was also instrumental in proposing the creation of an e-government fund specifically targeted at supporting inter-agency projects in a silo-based budget environment where appropriations are made on an agency-by-agency basis.[9]

CIO: Cheerleader, Collaborator, Controller or Commander

In its 2002 survey of e-government, Accenture discusses "the rise of the Chief Information Officer (CIO)" with cross-government authority as evidence that e-government is moving to the core of government's agenda.[10] The CIO (or equivalent) function plays a pivotal role in the corporate accountability and authority for e-government.

Several jurisdictions are moving to a CIO model, investing that office with a range of responsibilities along a continuum, which can be characterized as from "cheerleader" to "commander." As with the political leaders, a CIO who is merely a cheerleader for e-government will have a much harder time being effective than one who is a commander of e-government vested with the requisite authorities and tools to do the job.

In the middle range of the continuum are CIOs serving as "collaborators," with a mandate to facilitate cooperation among agencies to work together on specific e-government projects without specific authorities or tools to incent cooperation.

Further along the continuum, some CIOs are serving in roles that could be characterized as "controllers." They are not vested with the actual tools to do the job but are strategically positioned at vital control points in the process of e-government project approval and ICT acquisition — i.e., having to review and sign off funding requests for ICT systems and services to ensure compliance with corporate standards or to ensure that redundancy is minimized.

At the far end of the continuum sits the CIO as "commander," treating his/her role as analogous to a commander in a military campaign with key responsibilities over the budgetary, policy and procedural resources required to advance the charge.[11]

It should also be noted that, in several instances, private sector stakeholders have called on governments to establish CIO positions, largely in an effort to ensure that governments clearly place responsibility for their e-government initiatives in one office and give it some momentum.[12] A review of positions along the continuum suggests that the following minimum success factors supporting effective CIO-type organizations include having:

- A position in a senior central agency of government with an enterprise-wide view of government operations or budget — i.e., a Treasury Board or Management Board;
- Recognized authority and competencies over key governance and cross-government building blocks of e-government, including:
  - The bureaucratic "owner" of the e-government implementation plan;
  - ICT standard-setting authority;
- Responsibility for, or at a minimum, influence over key administrative guidelines and policy and legislative building blocks which support e-government, including:
  - Information management;
  - Privacy protection;
  - Security, including authentication, digital certificates, ICT systems defence;
  - Enabling legislation — i.e., electronic signatures; and
  - ICT human resource hiring practices;
- A significant role in the approval process for expenditures and financial management control of ICT throughout government — i.e., sign-off on line agency ICT budget plans and requests;
- Responsibility for a distinct budget allocation that can provide incentives to collaborate among agencies;
- Authority to aggregate ICT demand across the enterprise to ensure compliance with standards while optimizing the economies of scale in government's ICTs purchases;
- Authority to mandate the use of enterprise-wide ICT infrastructure systems and, where appropriate, force collaboration among agencies in shared business applications. The CIO does not necessarily have to operate government's shared IT infrastructure but certainly requires a strong enough governance authority to compel its usage by all. The CIO should also be in a position to review ICT application development in the silos of government in order to identify redundancies, ensure inter-operability and engineer collaboration — i.e., pulling several departments together to build a common licensing or permitting "engine" for use in issuing permits to businesses and clients;
- Recognition as an important contributor to but not necessarily the owner of transformation of government;
- Ability to forge a connection between the management of e-government and the government's economic development objectives. In this context, the CIO can be positioned to serve some of government's broader socio-economic agenda — i.e., development of e-commerce, development of local technology industries, addressing the digital divide.

Examples of offices and functions of interest include:

- *UK.* Office of the e-envoy has responsibilities across the whole e-agenda, notably e-commerce and e-government. The e-envoy resides within the Cabinet Office and reports directly to the Prime Minister, "working alongside" the e-Minister with a strong cross-agency mandate;[13]

- *US.* Director of Information Technology and e-Government resides in a central agency (Office of Management and Budget) and, among other central responsibilities, signs off privacy impact assessments for all new information-gathering processes;[14]
- *Washington State, USA.* Director, Department of Information Systems (DIS). The DIS "Digital Applications Academy" encourages agencies to work together in the construction of common business applications than can be shared once constructed.

Portal Management

Many governments are launching "single-window" service portals as a centerpiece in their e-government strategies. A variety of models exist around the world, and the best examples are very citizen-centric, focusing on citizen/client needs and services rather than the organizational structures of government responsible for delivering these outputs.

While appearing seamless from the outside-in, portals require new structural and management approaches to ensure sufficient coordination behind the scenes.

Key success factors with respect to the organization of this work include:

- Establishment of a single body who owns the portal and has responsibility for its operation and setting standards for presentation of material — i.e., ensuring compliance with common look-and-feel presentation standards (graphic design, format, navigational capabilities, content and content management);
- Establishment of a cross-government editorial board structure charged with ensuring that departmental content and presentation is consistent with portal standards set by the "owner" and that the information is current.

Changing the Organization of the External Relationship with Citizens, Clients and Suppliers/Partners in E-Government

Governments are progressively thinking about re-organizing their face to the citizen through citizen/client-centric portals emphasizing service rather than structure of government. However, only a few are contemplating the organizational aspects of bringing citizens and clients in on the planning and future direction of e-government.

Establishing a new organizational relationship between governments and their citizens and clients is an important dimension of any successful e-government program. The benefits associated with such an approach include:

- Ability to client-test approaches on issues such as privacy and authentication which could allow for useful feedback on directions under consideration in government;
- Provision of a focus group to examine client perspectives and satisfaction with government online initiatives, products, services and channels of delivery;

- Building a constructive, working relationship with clients that could result in these members, if effectively organized and mobilized, becoming more vocal, external advocates for e-government. Such a call to action coming from government's clients is likely to attract the attention of political leaders and senior public servants more than similar pleas coming from the bureaucracy;
- Building a capacity for citizens and clients to provide online feedback to governments on e-government initiatives and reports.

Success factors in structuring such a mechanism encompass:

- Ability to bring together a representative cross-section of government online *users* (i.e., small business, the legal profession, consumers, tax accountants, the not-for-profit sector) rather than government online *suppliers* (i.e., IT vendors and e-commerce companies) who may use the vehicle as a means to promote their business interests with governments;
- Instilling a sense in the bureaucracy that dealing with this group is important if for no other reason than to validate ideas under consideration. Accordingly, managers must ensure that issues identified by focus groups or citizens and clients in online feedback mechanisms will be responded to;
- Governments recognizing the groups as being legitimate representatives of citizen/ client issues and not an internally fabricated lobby group to advance e-government staff causes.

Examples include:

- *Canada.* A government online advisory panel reporting to the Minister responsible for e-government (President of the Treasury Board) has been established as a broad-based "sounding board" comprised of representatives of the public, the business community, the high-technology sector, the academic and education sector and the voluntary sector. The panel provides advice and recommendations on a wide range of e-government topics, including:
  - The scope and reach of government online;
  - The priorities and timetable for electronic delivery of government services;
  - Minimum standards for government electronic delivery of services;
  - How best to foster innovation, service improvement and increased access through information technologies and electronic service delivery;
  - Partnership opportunities and strategies for joint delivery of services with other levels of government and the private and non-profit sectors;
  - Mechanisms for assessing the government's progress in meeting its targets;
  - Strategies to promote increased awareness and use of the Internet by the public and business communities (including strategies to help address the digital divide in Canada).[15]

IMPLICATIONS FOR ORGANIZATIONAL CHANGE ON GOVERNMENT STRUCTURES AND PUBLIC ADMINISTRATION

The issues and success factors highlighted above underline several reasons why the organization of governments must change if they are to reap the full advantage of ICTs across the enterprise. In this section, we focus on some of the implications for e-government organizational change on government structures and practices. It is clear that e-government is changing the way business of government is delivered. However, what is less evident is how capable and adaptable are current administrative structures and cultures in responding to e-government.

In examining these issues, we return to the assumption that unless e-government initiatives are tightly integrated with broader public service transformation initiatives, governments are more likely to choose to adapt current structures and work practices to the new demands of e-government than to embark on a fundamental transformation of their organization to advance e-government. If some of the barriers to e-government and organizational issues discussed above are to be addressed, they will have significant implications on several areas of government work and practice and will challenge conventional practices.

Several implications are prominent and, for discussion, can be characterized around two key questions.

1. What are the Implications of Adapting to the Horizontal Orientation of ICTs?
2. How will governments achieve the cross-agency cooperation necessary for the full benefits of ICTs across the enterprise to be realized?

ICTs appear to provide function most effectively in organizations where they are allowed to integrate information and systems along the horizontal plane, capturing data from silos, aggregating information and reducing redundant systems and applications. This would appear to be the case in the private sector where the evidence suggests that ICTs have enabled several key benefits, including:

- A closer interaction among internal functions (i.e., production, marketing, finance and strategic decision-making);
- Higher levels of vertical integration and product diversification;
- More decentralization and team-working;
- Closer interaction with customers and providers of intermediate goods and services.

Citing a 1996 study on ICT investment and organizational change conducted by the Danish Ministry of Business and Industry, firms that combined organizational changes with ICT investment evidenced far higher rates of innovation: 77% of firms reported new and improved products following ICT investments accompanied by changes to management structures and work organization. ICT investments and accompanying organizational change were also credited by respondents as enabling firms to produce with greater flexibility and shortened product cycles and to satisfy changing customer tastes and requirements.[16]

However, governments generally operate on the vertical plane, structured along a series of departmental hierarchies with little incentive to engage in cross-silo cooperation. Not only are officials rewarded by keeping the best interests of their organizations foremost in their minds, the accountability structures of government reinforce the silo approach as budgets are allocated by department and ministers are made accountable by department for legislation, funding and program activity.

Given the vertical orientation of governments, cooperation and collaboration on the horizontal plane will often need to be commanded or compelled. While it is fashionable to assume that a designated e-government leader should be able to facilitate partnerships among agencies, it is more likely that these partnerships will ultimately have to be forced or funded to be effective.

Given the expenses associated with ICT projects, funding mechanisms are the most powerful instruments to incent cooperation needed. Ideally, government could provide new funding to support priority cross-government projects. However, if this option is not available, a government may choose to signal the seriousness of its intent to drive inter-agency cooperation by clawing back a portion of all departmental ICT expenditures and re-investing the proceeds into a cross-government e-government fund.

From a citizen-centric perspective, the attraction of "single-window" access to government services that e-government promises, puts significant pressure on agencies to cooperate in the back office of government so that the appearance of seamless government, unqualified by organization, can be achieved. Agencies are being asked to put the profile and interests of their organization aside in favor of presenting a service-oriented, common look and feel face to citizens and clients. This certainly has implications in the way vertically oriented agencies conventionally operate and will require new management structures and approaches to ensure that the desired end results are achieved.

As citizens access services through integrated electronic service delivery portals, they are essentially circumventing existing organizational structures through technologically enabled integrated service delivery. This, logically, challenges governments to take the next organizational step and establish an integrated service delivery agency as has been done in Australia (the Centrelink agency)[17] and the province of New Brunswick, Canada (Service New Brunswick agency).[18]

Implications on Organizational Hierarchy and Responsibility

Is Government Prepared to Adapt to E-Government's Borderless Approach to Information Flows Throughout the Organizational Hierarchies of Government?

ICTs have had the effect of "flattening" organizational structures in the private sector. ICTs enable information to be shared widely and flow faster throughout an organization, often wiping out processes and layers of middle management on the way. However, the same ability to aggregate information and rapidly transmit it throughout an organization runs against the conventional chain-of-command structures of government hierarchies. When a junior clerk can send e-mail directly to a Minister or Deputy

Minister, what are the implications of ICTs on the way agencies are managed and information flow is controlled?

The same questions arise from an outside-in perspective where citizens and clients wish to use ICTs to break down the barriers of communicating with government. In 2000, organized environmental activists in the province of British Columbia, Canada, seeking comprehensive access to government staff in certain departments, began to pressure the government to publish all e-mail addresses of government officials in the public directory. When certain departments initially refused, the groups made a successful application to the province's Freedom of Information Commissioner, who ordered the departments in question to release all e-mail addresses. This occasioned a strong reaction within the government and necessitated the development of a policy that allowed certain staff e-mail addresses to be withheld for specific reasons – including the personal safety of employees (i.e., to prevent individual harassment) and the operational need to funnel public requests in the order received through an already established response centre (i.e., for processing government medical insurance claims).

The debate held at the senior levels of the administration demonstrated how e-government challenged the culture of the organization. Some Deputy Ministers expressed concerns about their own ability to respond to an expected flood of e-mails within the immediacy time frame characterized by e-mail. Others worried about the obligations and liabilities placed on government if e-mails that alerted government to potential developments were not acted upon in time. Yet others expressed fears that e-mail access fundamentally challenged the command-and-control method of responding to public requests through the normal channels and did not want to publish e-mail addresses to further aggravate this situation. (Interestingly, in this respect, it was found that the majority of Deputy Ministers had already "published" their e-mail addresses on their business cards.)

Ultimately, the spectre of full publication of e-mail addresses through the access-to-information channels resulted in the development and approval of a new policy requiring all e-mail addresses to be published except for those exempted for tightly defined purposes of personal safety and organizational efficiency.[19]

Implications on Risk and Reward in Government

Will Government be Able to Tolerate Risk, Encourage Innovation and Distribute Rewards Involved in E-Government Projects?

Cross-government ICT projects also challenge the accountability and reward processes of government. If projects fail, are all participant agencies to share the blame equally? If they succeed, can partner agencies divide the gains? These questions confound silo-based organizations and are more likely to discourage cooperation in perceived risky ICT ventures than to encourage it.

In the private sector, rewards for innovation and tolerance of failure have often characterized successes in the implementation of ICT systems. Where risk-taking and failure may be perceived as a legitimate learning tool in technology company cultures, it is an alien concept in the public sector. Working under the bright spotlight of public accountability, the prevailing culture in government is risk-averse, with little tolerance for failure and little reward for innovation.

As noted in the OECD, PUMA Policy Brief, *The Hidden Threat of e-Government:* "Special standards of accountability and transparency apply to the public sector. This means that failure (of ICT projects) is often widely publicized and that top-level civil servants and politicians are held accountable for very technical projects over which they may have little influence."[20] This was nowhere more evident than in the Y2K experience, where often technologically illiterate ministers and senior officials were confronted with very technical questions from the public and legislators around the status of Y2K compliance in major ICT systems in government.

Again, funding can play a key role in this equation. To incent the development of innovative ICT applications, governments could introduce project funding policies that reward risk-taking. For example, an agency investing in an ICT solution that saves costs to government in the long run might be able to capture some or all of these savings for re-investment in other agency priorities. The State of Arizona, USA legislated e-government funding rules that allow agencies to recapture a large share of the savings generated by electronic service delivery projects against a commitment to re-invest part of these savings into strengthening the agency's electronic services systems and portfolio (Bill 1131 – Innovation Fund).[21] This approach represents a notable departure from the conventional model, where central treasuries generally see savings achieved in departments as a corporate windfall, while cost overruns and failures are the responsibility of the agency.

In other cases, governments have created new funding mechanisms that specifically target inter-agency projects that might be seen as too risky under conventional rules. Such is the case with the UK Invest to Save Budget (ISB) program, which provides funds to encourage two or more public bodies to jointly reconfigure elements of their work or to initiate new processes to provide innovative, or streamlined, or simply better modes of service. The program acknowledges that its role is to support projects that are sometimes deemed "too risky, or considered too marginal, to attract mainstream funding from an agency." To date, the program has invested £358m in over a few hundred partnership projects across both central government and the wider public sector — several of which have been funded under ISB's "exploiting new technologies" envelope.[22]

ICTs are relatively new technologies and, as such, often involve innovative implementation and risk-taking in this stage of the maturity cycle. Building a culture that embraces innovation and tolerates risk in the highly charged atmosphere of public accountability is a tough issue with several implications for government practice.

One example is the evaluation of business cases for ICT investment. In the private sector, the perceived competitive advantage of early ICT adoption encourages risk-takers to be more inclined to take a leap of faith on the business case for ICT investment — especially if it is known that its competitors have already made the move. However, in the high-accountability, monopoly environment of the public sector, complex ICT projects proposals are put through the conventionally conservative government methodology for evaluating business cases. This experience can be enough to thwart these projects at the outset.

Several governments have recognized this challenge and have developed templates and guidelines for ICT business case development that will assist in budget processes:

- The government of New Zealand has developed risk-based funding rules for complex ICT projects. Using quantitative risk analysis, each risk identified in the project is assessed along with its impact and probability. Thus, the fiscal impact of a project's risk can be made explicit to decision-makers.[23]
- Project and Investment Justification templates — State of Arizona, USA. This document provides the state agencies with a standardized method to report new or enhanced IT projects and investments. It is structured to report meaningful business and technical requirements, value to the public, costs, scope, risks and information on the agency's management and technical skills.[24]

However, the logical next step — and transformational move — would be to revise the business case process specifically for ICT investments to allow for more risk-taking in the evaluation of business cases.

Implications of 24/7 Government

Can Government Realistically Meet the Expectations Raised by "Anywhere, Anytime" Electronic Access to Government?

The attraction of citizens and clients to e-government is, in large part, driven by their experiences with electronic service delivery in the private sector. Through client self-service applications, private sector firms have demonstrated their capability to provide easy access to information and very rapid responses to clients while reducing labor costs in alternate service delivery channels — i.e., e-banking and the reduction of bank teller counter staff. However, for any government thinking it may be able to save labor costs by implementing ICT solutions, the expectation of rapid response certainly has implications on a department's ability to accommodate requests.

In a survey of 9,000 Canadian citizens on public service delivery expectations, respondents were asked what they considered to be acceptable reply times for a routine request to government by letter or by e-mail. While 83% of respondents found a two-week reply to a letter acceptable, 66% expected a response to an e-mail within three business days.[25] Can downsized, resource-strapped governments meet this level of expectation held by their citizen/clients?

As in the private sector, the emergence of 24/7 electronic service delivery also challenges traditional channels of service delivery within government. In actively encouraging the migration of clients to the electronic channel, many companies have captured the benefits of shifting to electronic service delivery by downsizing or closing other channels of service delivery to the client. However, given the different nature of its relationship with its clients, an attempt to migrate citizens and clients to the electronic service delivery channel would have significant implications on governments.

Citizens, as taxpayers, expect their governments to offer a range of modes of access to services. Business clients, who also pay taxes and often have no option but to deal with governments as a condition of business, expect the same. Those citizens and clients on the have-not side of the digital divide will want to ensure that governments maintain service through non-electronic channels. Hence, the pressure to keep other channels of delivery fully staffed and open diminishes the cost-saving potential of the electronic channel in the overall service delivery envelope. Despite increasing household Internet and PC penetration rates in OECD countries, it is expected that this situation will continue to confront governments for many years to come.

Nevertheless, if governments want to be more aggressive in capturing the benefits of e-government vis-à-vis their citizens and clients, there are some approaches that can be taken to encourage a shift to electronic service delivery channels. Examples include:

- Acting aggressively with business suppliers to government. Given the different nature of the business relationship between government and private-sector suppliers (as opposed to tax-paying citizens and clients), governments can more easily force a shift in service delivery channels in areas such as procurement. The UK government, in launching its online procurement service in September 2001, declared that by 2005 the online channel would be the exclusive channel available to access government tenders.[26] Alternatively, governments could choose to price e-services to the private sector at a cheaper rate than through other channels — — inducing a migration.
- Introducing more citizen self-service applications along the electronic service maturity curve. More electronic service applications that allow citizens to interact with government information systems in end-to-end transactions can help manage the pressures associated with 24/7 government. Government's relationships with its citizens and clients can be characterized along a service maturity continuum – from "passive/passive" (i.e., government publishes information and the citizen/client downloads it) to "active/active," where the citizen/client can access and complete an end-to-end transaction with government.
- As governments move along this continuum, the payoff in costs savings and increased capacity to deal with citizen/client demands will grow. As noted in Accenture's 2002 survey of e-government leadership: "Publishing services online (passive/passive) has little impact on cost — in most cases this is just a duplicate channel. Real cost savings are only realized when there is a true integration between the Web front-end and the back office systems. Achieving this end-to-end integration requires changes to administrative structures, development of new skills and re-design of processes."[27]

Marketing online services to encourage migration to electronic service delivery channels. Despite increasing the breadth and depth of the services available online, governments have done little to market the online channel to citizens and clients. In this context, marketing strategies targeting specific user groups whom government wishes to prioritize for migration to the electronic service channel will become increasingly important — as they have in the private sector. Such an approach involves both market research and communications. For example, the redesign of Canada's primary Web site involved more than 50 focus groups of citizens and clients in Canada and abroad. When then Prime Minister Chretien launched the new Canada site in January 2001, the launch was accompanied by extensive media advertising. An online citizens panel, as well as a citizen/client government online advisory group chaired by the Minister responsible for e-government, are assisting the further refinement and development of the site and Canada's e-government offerings. This approach provides Canada with a rich flow of user input into the government online strategy and an extensive outreach to citizens and clients to promote increased usage of electronic service delivery channels.[28]

Implications on Human Resources

Is government prepared to break the mould of human resource recruitment and compensation practices in order to get the necessary in-house skills to manage e-government?

The effective implementation of e-government depends on skilled professionals with certain types of skill sets being more in demand than others. The required skill sets are not confined to ICT technical skills but extend to other areas that will be required to make e-government function. For example, as governments enter new relationships with the private sector in outsourcing or supplying ICT systems, individuals skilled in contract management will be increasingly required.

Unfortunately for governments, these skill sets are precisely the same ones that are in high demand outside of government in private-sector organizations implementing e-commerce applications. These organizations often come to the market with reward and compensation packages that outpace those offered by governments.

The effective recruitment and retention of the needed skills within government implies an ability to break the mould of public sector hiring practices and innovate with competitive packages that will put government in an advantageous position for these skills. Governments that have embarked on this course have already experienced the need to challenge their conventional internal systems relating to public sector compensation and work practices.

The introduction of new technologies into government also implies a strong need to focus attention on training requirements across government. Not only is training required to help staff manage and implement new technologies, it is also an important component of the buy-in to e-government among staff who feel that their concerns and fears about technology need to be recognized and addressed. This may imply a much broader training plan for e-government than some governments are inclined to support. Nevertheless, the consequences of not proceeding with such a plan risk leaving a large part of the public sector workforce behind and, worse, dragging on e-government implementation.

Implications on Transparency and Accountability

Is Government Prepared for the Openness and Accountability Engendered by ICTs

The capabilities of ICTs to enhance access to information and public fears about the ability of ICTs to jeopardize personal privacy, represent the twin horns of a dilemma facing governments embarked on e-government initiatives.

With respect to privacy protection, the bar of public expectations is raised higher for governments than for the private sector. A citizen/client of government often has no choice but to deal with government, given its monopoly role. Accordingly, a citizen/client therefore has a higher need to trust government's information management practices than, perhaps, he/she does with respect to the private sector, where there is normally an option to switch to another competing firm if this trust cannot be established.

Citizen/client concerns over privacy protection still rank at the top of their issues list associated with e-government. Addressing this concern has significant implications for government organizations, especially if the aggregation of information held about citizens and clients in common data banks represent a large part of government's expected efficiency gains from ICTs. At what point do the privacy concerns of the citizens and clients whose information is at issue outweigh the efficiency gains on access to and management of information?

This issue came to the fore in Canada in May 2001, when the country's Privacy Commissioner revealed that one of the government's largest departments (Human Resource Development Canada (HRDC)) had developed a longitudinal file data bank that aggregated personal information about citizens from several government data banks. While citizens had provided information to individual departments relating to matters such as health, income, and employment status, the aggregation of information from these files for purposes beyond which the information was collected created a significant public outcry. This resulted in the Minister publicly announcing that she was dismantling the data bank. All the perfectly good arguments about efficiency gains and the research value of longitudinal data files could not withstand the media-fed frenzy that the government had created an intrusive "Big Brother" machine with an extensive file on every Canadian.

Yet in other areas, the linking of data across departmental silos has been publicly supported. On approval of the citizen, the Canadian government can update voter registries from information submitted in income tax files. Other jurisdictions are linking data to support other social program goals, for example, the denial of driver's license renewals to individuals not meeting child support payments (Government of Alberta, Canada).

On the other side of the coin, citizens and clients expect ICTs to produce, improve and extend access to the information holdings of government. Similarly, the provision of information through e-government represents one of the clearest areas of cost-savings that a government can expect to derive from e-government — i.e., cost savings associated with avoiding new publishing and print costs every time information needs to be updated and cost avoidance by passing the distribution and printing costs to the citizen/client as they download and print information they seek.

Many also see ICTs as a new vehicle to improve the accountability of government to those it serves. There seems to be a stronger expectation that government should report publicly and regularly on progress in e-government than in other areas of government's business. Many governments are rising to this challenge — and are going beyond simple reporting of progress by program area with the publication of related e-government information and extensive online surveys and feedback vehicles that encourage citizens and clients to identify areas where electronic service provision can be improved (i.e., the "60 second" survey on the government of Australia's home page).[29]

Balancing the information access and privacy protection priorities that citizens and clients assign to e-government requires careful attention to corporate information management strategies. Such strategies, when effective, can serve to increase trust among citizens if they feel that the personal information they have entrusted to governments is protected and that government will use e-government to expand information access not contract it. The information management issue has organizational implications for governments. Such strategies must, by definition, be corporate in nature as the citizen/client is not likely to easily accept situations where different agencies of government apply different standards for privacy protection and information access.

In order to meet high standards of public trust and to ensure compliance across the enterprise of government, many governments have chosen to go beyond simply improving policy measures and administrative practices and have legislated in this area. Meeting the tests and standards set out in privacy protection and information access legislation has certainly had organizational implications within governments. Several governments have chosen to create independent officers who report directly to legislatures rather than government executives, in order to better meet public expectations. Canada has two such independent officers or commissioners — one for information access and one for privacy protection.

Corporate information management plans also demand a high level of central coordination across agencies as well as attention to new issues brought on by e-government, such as electronic records management and data sharing. While these issues are not unique to e-government, they are closely associated with e-government in the public mind given concerns over Internet security and data aggregation.

CONCLUSIONS

In the final analysis, the key changes required for effective implementation of e-government are more closely associated with the culture and administrative practices of government than with its structure. The horizontal orientation and speed of ICTs confound many aspects of conventionally-vertical and process-bound government organizations. The fear of innovation and aversion to risk-taking in the public sector, the challenges of orienting government to a "citizen-first" rather than an "agency-first" perspective and the implications of managing enhanced citizen/client expectations in e-government pose challenging implications for the operating culture of public administrations.

There are several key factors about e-government that compel a change in structures and practices of governments in order to maximize the benefits of ICT implementation. Several of these issues have been reviewed in this chapter and yield the following conclusions for consideration:

- The positioning of e-government strategies and responsibilities within government will have a significant bearing on the likelihood that the organizational transformation required to optimize ICT investment will be achieved. Organizational change stands a greater chance of success if the e-government initiative is harnessed to a larger, public-sector reform initiative.
- The strength of the mandate, reporting relationship and authority matrix of the e-government champion, both at the political level and senior bureaucratic level, will be a crucial asset in ensuring that the e-government strategy is translated from elegant words to hard action on the ground. These offices should be highly situated within government and clearly seen as owning the e-government strategy and owning, or at least able to heavily influence, the funding and policy tools required to make the strategy work.
- Stronger inter-agency cooperation is essential to making e-government work effectively across the enterprise of government. Given that government structures and accountabilities do not generally encourage or reward cross-agency collaboration, it is likely that this cooperation will have to be forced or funded rather than facilitated into action.

- The implications of 24/7 government on the structures and practices of government must be addressed. E-government applications raise expectations among citizens and clients of rapid response and action. If, however, governments feel that ICT investments will permit a reduction in their staff resources without organizational and business practice change, they may find themselves incapable of keeping up with the increased demand unleashed.
- The ability to meet both objectives is best served when governments are able to achieve greater maturity in their electronic service offerings with more and more of their electronic services featuring end-to-end transactional and citizen/client self-service capabilities. While this is being done, governments should also pay attention to how they intend to migrate citizens and clients to the electronic service delivery channel — through policy measures and marketing strategies.
- Governments need to continue to recognize the impact that e-government has on the operating cultures of government organizations. ICTs, with their orientation to data sharing and borderless flows of information, challenge the traditional "chain of command" structures of government. At the same time, the immaturity of the technologies and the need to incent co-operation among agencies may require a higher acceptance of risk and reward than has normally prevailed in risk-averse public administrations.
- Many individuals engaged across government remain fearful of technology, either as a harbinger of job loss or as a complex area that they are embarrassed not to understand. While implementing e-government strategies, governments must pay attention to the training needs of all staff affected in order to secure the greatest internal buy-in for e-government.
- The capabilities of ICTs to both enhance access to information and accountability as well as raise public fears about the protection of personal privacy represent the twin horns of a dilemma facing e-government initiatives. Balancing the information access and privacy protection priorities requires careful attention to corporate information management strategies. The information management issue has organizational implications for governments given that such strategies must, by definition, be corporate in nature — as the citizen/client is not likely to easily accept situations where different agencies of government apply different standards for privacy protection and information access.

REFERENCES

Accenture Consulting. (2002). *eGovernment leadership – Realizing the vision.*

Bertelsmann Foundation. (2002). *E-government: Connecting efficient administration and responsive democracy*. Gütersloh, Germany.

Borins, S. & Wolf, D. (2000, May). Realizing the potentialof public sector information technology: An organisational challenge. In *Change,governance and public management: Alternate service delivery and information technology*. KPMG Centre for Governance Foundation and Public Policy Forum. Ottawa, Canada.

Chidurala, K. & Pathak, S. (2001, May). *E-government best practices: An implementa tion manual.* University of Maryland, College Park, Robert H. Smith School of

Business. Retrieved August 12, 2002 from *www.egov.gov/doc/egov_implementation_manual.pdf*

Erin Research, (2003). *Citizens First3.* Toronto: Institute for Public Administration of Canada.

France, Office of the Prime Minister, Program for the Information Society. *Preparing France's entry into the information society.* Retrieved June 23, 2004, from *http://www.archives.premier-ministre.gouv.fr/jospin_version2/GB/INFO/DPRESANG.HTM*

Global Business Dialogue on E-commerce. (2001, September). *E-government: Recommendations.* Retrieved June 22, 2004 from *http://www.gbde.org/egovernment/egovernment.pdf*

Intergovernmental Technology Leadership Consortium. *E-government: The Next American Revolution.* Retrieved June 23, 2004 from *http://www.excelgov.org/displayContent.asp?NewsItemID=3980&Keyword= ppStudies*

International Council for Information Technology in GovernmentAdministration. (2001, January). *Information and Communications Technologies (ICTs) and the Structures of ICA Member National Governments.* Retrieved June 22, 2004, from *http://www.ica-it.org/*

Kanter, R. M. (2001). *Evolve! Succeeding in the digital culture of tomorrow.* Boston: Harvard Business School.

Lenihan, D. (2002). *Realigning governance: From e-Government to e-Democracy.* Ottawa: Centre for Collaborative Government.

National Academy of Public Administration. (2001, August). *Thetransforming power of information technology: Making the federal government an employer of choice for IT employees.* Retrieved August 10, 2002, from *http://www.encmarketing.com/clients/napa/01 the_report/downloads/napa_it.pdf*

Organization for Economic Cooperation and Development. (2001). *The hidden threat of e-government* (PUMA Policy Brief No. 8). Paris.

Organization for Economic Cooperation and Development Directorate onScience, Technology and Industry. (2002). *Industry issues: Organisational change and firm performance.* (STI Working Paper 2002/14.) Paris.

Pacific Council on International Policy. (2002, April). *Roadmap for e-government in the developing world.* Working group on e-government in the developing world. Los Angeles.

United Kingdom Cabinet Office. (1999, March). *Modernising government.* Retrieved June 23, 2004 from *http://www.archive.official-documents.co.uk/document/cm43/4310/4310.htm*

United Kingdom Parliamentary Office of Science and Technology. (1998, February). *Electronic government: Information technologies and the citizen.* Retrieved June 22, 2004, from *http://www.parliament.uk/post/9802.htm*

United States Office of Management and Budget. (February 2002). E-government strategy: Implementing the president's agenda for e-government. Retrieved June 22, 2004, from *http://www.whitehouse.gov/omb/inforeg/egovstrategy.pdf*

Zussman, D. (2002, February 25). *Governance in the public service: How is technology changing the rules?* Keynote Address (Commonwealth Centre for Electronic Governance) at the Integrating Government with New Technologies Conference.

Retrieved 22 June 2004 from *http://www.rileyis.com/seminars/feb2002/ZussmanspeechFeb02.doc*

ENDNOTES

1 Borins, S. & Wolf, D. (2000, May). *Realizing the Potential of Public Sector Information Technology: An Organisational Challenge.* KPMG Centre for Governance Foundation and Public Policy Forum, *Change, Governance and Public Management: Alternate Service Delivery and Information Technology,* p. 207.

2 Kanter, R. M. (2001). *Evolve! Succeeding in the Digital Culture of Tomorrow.* Boston: Harvard Business School, p. 72.

3 Murphy, M. (2002). *Industry Issues: Organisational Change and Firm Performance.* OECD Directorate on Science, Technology and Industry – STI. (Working Paper 2002/14).

4 Accenture. *eGovernment Leadership - Realising the Vision,* p. 2.

5 Office of the Prime Minister. (2000). *Preparing France's entry into the information society – Program for the Information Society.*

6 U.S. Office of Management and Budget. *E-government Strategy: Implementing the President's Agenda for E-government,* p.6.

7 U.K. Cabinet Office. *Modernising Government.* Retrieved from *http://www.archive.official-documents.co.uk/document/cm43/4310/4310.htm*

8 U.K. E-envoy Office. Retrieved from the World Wide Web at: *http://www.e-envoy.gov.uk/ukonline/champions/e-champions_menu.htm*

9 U.S. Office Of Management And Budget. (2002, February). E-government Strategy: Implementing the President's Agenda for E-government. Retrieved from *http://www.whitehouse.gov/omb/inforeg/egovstrategy.pdf*

10 Accenture. *E-government Leadership: Realizing the Vision,* p. 16.

11 A useful survey of 11 CIO-style organisations and mandates at the national level can be found in the International Council for Information Technology in Government Administration (ICA) paper *ICT and the Structures of ICA Member National Governments.* (2001, January).

12 An example here, successfully executed, was the U.S.-based Intergovernmental Technology Leadership Consortium's call for the establishment of a central ICT "czar" in the U.S. administration. See the Consortium's *E-GOVERNMENT; The Next American Revolution.*

13 U.K. Cabinet Office, Office of the e-Envoy. Retrieved from *http://www.e-envoy.gov.uk/aboutus.htm.*

14 Accenture. (2002). *eGovernment Leadership - Realizing the Vision.*

15 Government of Canada, Treasury Board Secretariat, Government on-line Advisory Panel: Mandate. Retrieved from *http://www.gol-ged.gc.ca/pnl-grp/mandate/mandate-mandat_e.asp.*

16 Murphy, M. (2002). *Industry Issues: Organisational Change and Firm Performance.* OECD Directorate on Science, Technology and Industry – STI. (Working Paper 2002/14), p. 29.

17 Retrieved from *http://www.centrelink.gov.au/internet/internet.nsf/home/index.htm*

18 Retrieved from *http://www.snb.ca/e/4000/4002e.htm*

19 Personal experience of the author as CIO, government of British Columbia (1998-2001).

20 OECD. (2001). *The Hidden Threat of e-government.* PUMA Policy Brief No. 8. Paris: OECD.

21 Author's interview with Arizona CIO John Kelly. (July 2000).

22 U.K. Cabinet Office, HM Treasury. Retrieved from *http://www.isb.gov.uk/HMT.ISB.APPLICATION.2/about_isb/about_isb_intro.as*

23 OECD. (2001). *The Hidden Threat of E-government.* PUMA Policy Brief No. 8. Paris: OECD.

24 State of Arizona, Government Information Technology Agency. Retrieved from *http://www.gita.state.az.us/project_investment_justification*

25 Public Sector Service Delivery Council of Canada. (2003). *Citizens First 3.* Institute for Public Administration of Canada, 74-75.

26 U.K. Prime Minister Tony Blair. (2001, September) *U.K. Online Launch.*

27 Accenture. (2002). *eGovernment Leadership - Realizing the Vision*, p. 12. Accenture's "service maturity" framework measures both maturity breadth (number of services) and maturity depth (placement along the electronic service delivery continuum). In applying this framework, the report cites national examples of e-government applications in action along the service maturity continuum.

28 Accenture. (2002). *eGovernment Leadership - Realizing the Vision*, p. 44. Information on the Canadian government's government online advisory panel can be found at:http://www.gol-ged.gc.ca/pnl-grp/index_e.asp. Information on the citizen on-line panel can be found at: *http://www.gol-ged.gc.ca/rpt/gol-ged-rptpr_e.asp.* (under "responsive government").

29 Retrieved from *http://www.gov.au*

Chapter VI

Transformed Government: Case Studies on the Impact of E-Government in Public Administration

Stuart Culbertson, TkMC, Canada

ABSTRACT

E-government is, in many respects, a campaign to transform governments. For both officials inside government and the citizens and clients that these governments serve, it is vital that governments achieve "early wins" in the e-government campaign in order to lay the foundation for bolder changes that may be required to advance to the next steps. While no government has achieved full transformation, several examples have emerged that demonstrate the transformative power of e-government on the business and structures of public administrations.

WHAT DOES "TRANSFORMING GOVERNMENT" MEAN?

For the purposes of this paper, "transforming government" applies to how the application of ICT has fundamentally changed the way government operates both internally and/or externally with respect to its citizens and clients. Implicit in the notion of transformation is that an e-government application enables public administrations and the citizens and clients they serve to do things that cannot be effectively or conveniently done through more conventional channels of service delivery or approaches to internal organizations and practices.

While many governments have engaged in transformational projects, none can be said to have fully transformed their operations through e-government. As a result, at this stage in the development of e-government, it is considered more useful to examine transformation in discrete segments of e-government activity, services or operations rather than looking at a whole of government approach. The case studies examined in this chapter have been selected as exemplifying transformation in the three key aspects of e-government:

- Externally focused transformation: how e-government is being used to transform the government's relationship with the citizen/client, both from the perspective of citizen participation in the processes of government and the ability of citizens and clients to fully transact their business with government.
- Internally focused transformation: how government structures and practices are being transformed to optimize the advantage of e-government — i.e., reorganizing how common ICT infrastructure is managed and how governance structures function, advancing inter-agency cooperation and collaboration in developing "back office" and shared business applications.
- Cross-boundary transformation: how ICTs are enabling governments to work together across jurisdictional boundaries and work in partnership with the non-governmental and private sectors to better serve the comprehensive needs of their common clients.

The case studies are presented in a common format, which endeavors to:

- Paint a picture of the situation "before" transformation: what was the problem that government was trying to solve or the opportunity it was striving to advance?
- Describe the project chosen to transform the "before" picture and discuss relevant implementation issues and challenges (the Transformational Project).
- Sketch the situation "after" implementation, highlighting results achieved that signify successful transformation.
- Where appropriate, summarize key factors of success and lessons learned in the transformation project.

The case studies examined are:

Engaging the Citizen in a "New" Government: The Scottish Parliament

The establishment of the Scottish Parliament has provided a rare opportunity for a modern legislature to build a "government from scratch" — not bound by many of the existing bureaucratic structures and processes that might normally confront a new government assuming power within an established electoral process. Since 2000, the Parliament has committed to using ICTs to advance its principles of openness, accountability and citizen engagement in the Parliamentary process. In approaching this project, the Scottish Parliament has implemented an innovative e-government strategy to engage the citizen and assist the operations of the new Parliament and the government administration.

Changing the Delivery Model for ICT Infrastructure: Shared ICT Infrastructure Services in the Province of British Columbia, Canada

Governments are deploying various models for the corporate management and delivery of common ICT infrastructure across the enterprise of government. The province of British Columbia (Canada) is changing the management structure for the internal operational and transactional functions of government, including responsibility for ICT infrastructure. ICT infrastructure components have been identified and assets, resources and staff are being transferred from line ministries to the Ministry of Management Services for delivery as a "shared service" to the rest of government. This will allow all ICT infrastructures to be managed centrally on behalf of clients, allowing line ministries to focus on business applications that can plug into the shared infrastructure. An inter-agency client board has been formed to ensure that the transition to shared services meets the internal client needs.

Changing the Governance and Management Model for ICTS: Corporate and "Cluster" Chief Information Officer Functions in the Government of Ontario, Canada

The province of Ontario (Canada) has reorganized its responsibilities for ICT management. Ontario assigns cross-government accountability for ICT governance and infrastructure to a Corporate CIO in the Management Board Secretariat. It groups ministries together into "clusters" focusing on business applications. These departmental clusters report jointly to the Corporate CIO and to the Deputy Ministers of the ministries within the cluster.

Encouraging Cooperation in Cross-Government Business Application Development: Digital Government Applications Academy, State of Washington, USA

E-government initiatives around the world are changing the internal cultures of governments with innovative approaches to building cooperation among separate agencies. The State of Washington has developed a unique in-house Digital Government Applications Academy (DGAA). Departments interested in developing new business applications are brought together to build business applications for use across departments in a "build-it-once, share-it-often" approach.

Transforming the Relationship With Business Suppliers to Government: E-Procurement Reform, Ministero dell'Economia e delle Finanze, Government of Italy

Many governments in OECD member countries are adopting e-procurement applications to reduce costs, streamline management and re-engineer the business processes of dealing with suppliers. The Ministero dell'Economia e delle Finanze, government of Italy, adopted an e-procurement system in 2000 and is beginning to reap benefits inside and outside of the government.

Transforming the Business Relationship With the Citizen/Client Through End-to-End Transactional Services: Motor Vehicle Licensing Services, State Of Arizona, USA

The ability for a citizen/client to fully complete a transaction with government through an electronic service application represents a high level of electronic service maturity depth in e-government. The government of Arizona was an early e-government adopter and has transformed its motor vehicle licensing business through an innovative electronic service delivery application. The successful offering of full transactional capabilities to the citizen/client has been enabled by several significant structural and business practice transformations behind the scenes within the government.

Bundling Public and Private Electronic Services to Better Serve the Common Citizen/Client: Business Entry Point Portal, Government of Australia

As governments extend a broader range of electronic services to their citizens and clients, some governments have enhanced the convenience of electronic service delivery by integrating government service offerings from a broad cross-section of governments with related private sector services to provide a comprehensive suite of services to the citizen/client. This approach has been piloted in Australia with the "Business Entry Point" business services site.

Transactional E-Government Crossing Jurisdictional Boundaries: One-Stop Business Registration, Canada

Responsibilities for registering a business in Canada reside with both the federal and provincial/territorial levels of government. Municipal and regional governments can also have licensing responsibilities in this area. Several governments in Canada have collaborated to create a common electronic service delivery application to allow their common client to simultaneously complete most business registration and filing requirements with the appropriate levels of government. In some cases, these projects are linked into business tax payment and business change of address applications. This case study focuses on the development and implementation of one such program in the province of British Columbia — the *OneStop* business registration service.

The case studies examined highlight several promising trends and developments that exemplify the transformational capacity of ICTs in e-government applications. The lessons learned, outlined at the conclusion of these studies, summarize some of the key factors that have contributed to the success of the initiatives examined to date. While it is difficult to generalize conclusions over the diverse range of these case studies, several common points emerge as being effective contributors to capturing the transformational benefits of e-government initiatives. Governments must:

- Be prepared to support risk and innovation in a normally risk-averse public sector environment;
- Facilitate change through collaboration among peers and clients;
- Take the opportunity to re-engineer business processes while developing new e-government applications;
- Attend to the pace of transformation and build momentum from success;
- Communicate change — internally and externally. It is a key factor in successful transformational initiatives;
- Recruit and incorporate citizen/client feedback fully and quickly; and
- Increase transparency and accountability by measuring and reporting progress.

INTRODUCTION

Much has been written about the potential of Information and Communications Technologies (ICTs) to fundamentally transform the operation of business in both the public and private sector. In the relatively short history of e-government, it is clear that some areas of government program activity and organization have demonstrated a greater capacity at an earlier stage to be transformed in order to capture these benefits. In other areas, progress has been much slower, with the simple automation of paper-based processes being considered a sufficient e-government accomplishment.

E-government is, in many respects, a campaign to transform governments. For both officials inside government and the citizens and clients these governments serve, it is vital that governments achieve "early wins" in the e-government campaign in order to lay the foundation for bolder changes that may be required to advance to the next steps. While no government has achieved full transformation, several examples have emerged that demonstrate the transformative power of e-government on the businesses and structures of public administrations.

FRAMEWORK FOR ANALYSIS OF ORGANIZATIONAL CHANGE

What Does "Transforming Government" Mean?

For the purposes of this chapter, "transforming government" applies to how the application of ICTs has fundamentally changed the way that government operates internally and/or externally with respect to its citizens and clients. Implicit in the notion of transformation is that an e-government application enables public administrations and the citizens and clients they serve to do things that cannot be effectively or conveniently done through more conventional channels of service delivery or approaches to internal organizations and practices.

While many governments have engaged in transformational projects, none can be said to have fully transformed their operations through e-government. As a result, at this stage in the development of e-government it is considered more useful to examine transformation in discrete segments of e-government activity, services or operations rather than to look at a whole of government approach. The case studies examined in this chapter were selected because they exemplify transformation in the three key aspects of e-government, namely:

- Externally focused transformation — How e-government is being used to transform the government's relationship with the citizen/client, both from the perspective of citizen participation in the processes of government and the ability of citizens and clients to fully transact their business with government.
- Internally focused transformation — How government structures and practices are being transformed to optimize the advantage of e-government — i.e., re-organizing how common ICT infrastructure is managed and governance structures function, as well as advancing inter-agency cooperation and collaboration in developing "back office" and shared business applications.
- Cross-boundary transformation — How ICTs are enabling governments to work together across jurisdictional boundaries and work in partnership with non-governmental and private sectors to better serve the comprehensive needs of their common clients.

Several of the case studies examined have been profiled as emerging best practices in the e-government area and, in some cases, have received awards in national or regional competitions. The analysis of these case studies draws, in part, from two published analytical frameworks to help evaluate and assess the transformational progress of governments in their e-government initiatives.

In its review of e-government leadership across 23 countries, Accenture has developed an externally focused transformation service maturity framework for analysis. The framework measures both the breadth of service (numbers of services online) and the depth of services (in terms of the maturity of the services to move from passive to active interaction with the citizen/client). The measure of service maturity depth is indicative of the degree of transformation across a maturity continuum ranging from:

- *Publish (passive/passive relationship).* The citizen/client does not communicate electronically with the government agency and, beyond publishing information on its Web site, the government does not communicate electronically with the citizen/client. Here information is made available online in a static form and the citizen/client accesses information as desired;
- *Interact (active/passive relationship).* The citizen/client is able to communicate electronically with the government agency, but the agency does not necessarily communicate with the user. An example here would be an application which allows citizen/client to print a government form from a Web site, complete it by hand and mail or fax it back to the government;
- *Transact (active/active interaction).* The citizen/client is able to communicate electronically with a government agency, and the agency is able to respond electronically to the user. An example here would be the ability to complete a financial transaction online, such as a tax payment or a recreational campground reservation.[1]

The Bertelsmann Foundation has established a balanced e-government scorecard, which examines transformational activity with respect to:

- Benefit to citizen/client: quantity and quality of electronic services offered;
- Improvements in efficiency inside government;
- Promoting participation: how e-government more effectively engages the citizen in a closer relationship with their elected government;
- Improvements in the transparency of governments; and
- Change management: the extent to which the government takes a meaningful planned approach to the development of e-government strategies and in addressing the internal impacts and challenges of implementation.

The Bertelsmann study applies this framework to several case studies.[2]

The case studies in this chapter are presented in a common format, which endeavors to:

- *Paint a picture of the situation "before" transformation:* What was the problem that government was trying to solve or the opportunity it was striving to advance?
- *Identify the Transformation Project:* Describes the project chosen to transform the "before" picture and discusses relevant implementation issues and challenges.

- *Sketch the situation "after" implementation:* Highlighting results achieved that signify successful transformation.
- Summarize key factors of success and lessons learned in the transformational project.

The author chose the case studies. In several instances, interviews were conducted in person, by telephone or e-mail with senior officials responsible for the case study profiled.

CASE STUDIES

Engaging the Citizen in a "New" Government: Scottish Parliament

The establishment of the Scottish Parliament has provided a rare opportunity for a modern legislature to build a "government from scratch" — one that is not bound by many of the existing bureaucratic structures and processes that might normally confront a new government assuming power within an established electoral process. Since 2000, the Parliament has committed to using ICTs to advance its principles of openness, accountability and citizen engagement in the Parliamentary process. In approaching this project, the Scottish Parliament has implemented an innovative e-government strategy to engage the citizen and assist the operations of the new Parliament and the government administration. Meanwhile, the Scottish Executive, the administrative arm of the government, is advancing its e-government agenda in line with the UK online and the Modernising Government initiative, with commitments to increased electronic service delivery and improved inter-operability of systems.

Before

The process for devolution of powers to a new Scottish Parliament was formally launched with a White Paper by the UK government in July 1997 ("Scotland's Parliament").[3] Among the many issues discussed in this paper and the ensuing public debate was the need to modernize government and increase citizen engagement and participation. Consultations on this paper and other events leading up to the referendum on devolution in Scotland in September 1997 also profiled the potential of innovative use of ICTs in conducting the business of the new Parliament.

Following the affirmative referendum vote in September 1997, the Scottish Office appointed a consultative steering group to solicit views on the operational and working methods that should guide the Parliament in the exercise of its powers and mandate. The December 1998 report of the consultative steering group committee (*Shaping Scotland's Parliament)* spent considerable time focusing on how ICTs could best be deployed to meet the objectives of modernising government and increasing public participation in the democratic process. The Committee summarized its recommendations as aiming to:

"... provide an open, accessible and, above all, participative Parliament, which will take a proactive approach to engaging with the Scottish people — in particular those groups traditionally excluded from the democratic process. To achieve this the Scottish Parliament must avoid adopting procedures that are obscure or archaic. It should adopt procedures and practices that people will understand, that will engage their interest, and that will encourage them to obtain information and exchange views."[4]

The group appointed an expert panel on ICTs (with a sub-group on Democratic participation), which strongly promoted the use of ICTs in the new Parliament committee based on the principles that ICTs in the Parliament should:

- Be innovative;
- Allow the Parliament to develop its use of ICTs in a planned and coherent way;
- Seize the opportunities offered by modern, well-designed information systems for improving openness, accessibility and responsiveness to the people of Scotland;
- Aspire to be an example of best practice in Parliamentary information systems, both in terms of external communications and internal efficiency; and
- Lay the basis for delivering the business of the Parliament efficiently and effectively.[5]

The Transformation Project

The preparatory work for the Scottish Parliament clearly set the expectation that the Parliament would aspire to become a leading practice in the use of ICTs to deliver its mandate. The challenges of explaining the new roles and responsibilities of the Scottish Parliament and of engaging the citizen in new ways were significant, especially in the context of worldwide citizen cynicism in the political process as evidenced by declining voter turnout in most OECD countries. While still early days, the Parliament has lived up to this challenge with several innovative applications that can be found on its Web site. Highlights include:

- *Public education.* Explaining the functions, mandate and the authorities of a new order of government in Scotland is an important component of this initiative. The strategy to increase citizen involvement in the Parliamentary and decision-making processes could solidify support for the new governmental arrangement and instill trust and engagement of the citizens in the new system. The Scottish Parliament's Web site also targets the youth audience with special educational pages to support teaching and learning about the Parliament;
- *Web-casting Parliament and its committees.* The Parliament makes extensive use of Web-casting to broadcast meetings of the full Parliament and its committees, through its Scottish Parliament LIVE network. It also maintains a comprehensive archive of video clips of recent sessions. As well, the Web site provides an extensive itinerary of coming events on the Parliamentary calendar, listing those committee meetings and hearings scheduled for Web-cast. Where these committee hearings are inviting public input, the appropriate e-mail links are incorporated into the calendar page so that citizens can provide comments directly to the committee on issues of interest;
- *Petitions.* The petitioning of Parliament by citizens or groups of citizens is an important gateway for enhanced citizen engagement in parliamentary processes.

Since June 1999, over 550 petitions have been received by the Parliament. Its Web site contains extensive material and resources on petitioning, including:

- How to petition, including guidance and procedures for the submission of petitions and an online facility to submit petitions directly to the Parliament or one of its committees.[6] There is also a link to the International Democracy Centre, where petitioners can access the centre's e-petitioner system and resources.[7]
- Registry of petitions: the Web site posts all submissions received, either by direct transfer of online petitions or through PDF files of written petitions.
- Actions taken: Parliament or one of its committees reviews all petitions, and appropriate actions are taken. These actions taken on petitions, as recorded in Parliament or Committee minutes, are listed on the site linked to the appropriate committee minutes, so that petitioners or other interested parties can easily access information on how the petition has been dealt with and what further action, if any, the Parliament has committed to undertake.

- *Discussion groups.* Encouraging direct participation by citizens in the discussion of issues is a key principle behind the Parliament. The Parliament uses its Web site to advance this objective by sponsoring interactive "discussion boards" on a wide set of issues it is dealing with, ranging from the future of Europe to the treatment of chronic back pain in the health service. Citizens can formally register to participate in a discussion group or simply access the site to view comments. The discussion group pages also provide links to relevant committee discussions, official reports and other resources that might be of interest to citizens;
- *Contacting Members of Parliament.* There are extensive Web-based resources to enable citizens to find and contact their Members of Scottish Parliament (MSP). Citizens can search a map of Scotland or insert a postal code in order to link to the appropriate MSP. The listing of MSPs also includes the various committees or portfolios served by the MSP and links to these committees.

After

The use of the Web by the new Scottish Parliament is an innovative and evolving model of how ICTs can be used to inform and engage citizens in the democratic process. Interestingly enough, the Web site focuses entirely on engagement with the Scottish Parliament rather than the administrative structure and service delivered by the Scottish Executive. (Indeed, there is not an easily accessible link between the Parliament and the Executive on the Parliament's Web site.)

Citizen uptake in terms of e-petitions and involvement in discussion groups shows the promising potential of the use of ICTs to better engage citizens directly in the democratic process in the new Parliament. The open approach to information and reporting on Parliamentary processes and the disposition of business (i.e., how petitions have been addressed) helps to strengthen the transparency and accountability of the Parliament to its citizens. As such, the use of ICTs by the Scottish Parliament serves as a model for other jurisdictions wishing to advance similar objectives.

Changing the Delivery Model for ICT Infrastructure: Shared ICT Infrastructure Services in the Province of British Columbia, Canada

Governments are deploying various models for the corporate management and delivery of common ICT infrastructure across the enterprise of government. The province of British Columbia (Canada) is changing the management structure for the internal operational and transactional functions of government, including responsibility for ICT infrastructure. ICT infrastructure components have been identified, and assets, resources and staff are being transferred from line ministries to the Ministry of Management Services for delivery as a "shared service" to the rest of government. This will allow all ICT infrastructures to be managed centrally, allowing line ministries to focus on business applications that can plug into the shared infrastructure. An inter-agency client board has been formed to ensure that the transition to shared services meets the internal client needs.

Before

The British Columbia government has been on a decade-long journey regarding the management of common ICT infrastructure. In the early 1980s, the government assigned all responsibility for ICT to a Crown Corporation — the British Columbia Systems Corporation (BCSC) — which delivered both infrastructure and business applications to ministries. In the mid-1990s, the corporation was dissolved and responsibilities for common ICT infrastructure were transferred to a new organization within a central agency ministry — the Information, Science and Technology Agency (ISTA).

ISTA had responsibilities for ICT governance and standards (the government's CIO led the organization) and the delivery of most key components of the government's common ICT infrastructure. While ISTA delivered most common ICT services (i.e., networks, data processing mainframes, etc.), there were still elements of what could be defined as common ICT infrastructure managed separately within line ministries (i.e., workstations, help desks, file and print servers). These ministry clients were billed for services on a cost-recovery basis based on their respective shares of common ICT usage. Clients, facing budget pressures, felt that ICT service costs from the central agency were too high, compared to private sector rates. Others felt they did not have an effective role in deciding on appropriate and affordable common ICT systems and standards. Rather, they were being directed to use ICT services mandated by the central agency.

The Transformation Project

In 2001, a new government was elected to office with a commitment to make more effective use of ICTs in an expanded e-government strategy. The new government had also studied the growing phenomenon of "shared services" in the private sector, where corporations were consolidating all back-office functions placing them in a corporate body with an enterprise-wide mandate.

When the new government took office, it established a Ministry of Management Services (MMS) with a mandate to consolidate all of the key back office functions of government and develop a shared service delivery system in the areas of common ICT infrastructure, finance, administration and procurement. MMS was not only mandated to continue to provide quality support services in these areas, but also to streamline overall management and delivery of service and eliminate duplication. Ministry-based ICT functions were to be focused on business applications and strategic information management planning — plugging into the "electricity" of the common infrastructure.

Implementation Factors

The new model — the third different model in less than a decade — was greeted with some scepticism within the government. Some of the problems associated with the previous models, such as pricing and mandating technologies, had not been clearly addressed with the introduction of the new organization. At the same time, MMS needed to complete its portfolio of shared ICT services by arranging the transfer of assets and responsibilities for common ICT services that remained housed in line ministries. It was clear that a new approach needed to be taken to successfully launch the new model and that changes would need to be made in the management model and relationship with line agency clients in order to successfully launch the shared-services approach. Accordingly, MMS introduced the following features to secure client support:

- *Benchmarking internal prices against the market.* A first step was to neutralize the cost-effectiveness debate engaged by line agencies. In an effort to do this, the MMS retained an independent IT consultant (Gartner Group) to benchmark the operational costs of all common ICT functions against best practices in a representative peer group, which contained both public- and private-sector agencies. This benchmarking exercise showed that costs associated with government's current portfolio of common ICT were within 1% of the peer group. It also revealed that costs were generally higher than the peer group for those common ICT functions stranded in ministries (i.e., servers, desk top and help desk services). MMS proposed to consolidate all common ICT functions into a new shared-services entity ("Solutions BC") and committed to achieve continuous improvements in costs and quality of services. MMS committed to reducing costs over three years and to ensuring that it was well within the first quartile of peer groups in future benchmarks. The external benchmarking would be continued on an annual basis to track progress. This was seen to be a more open process than had been previously in place to test prices against best practices and secure a more open accounting of pricing.
- *Establishing new governance relationships with clients.* The Solutions BC shared-service model necessitated the invention of a new approach with respect to client agencies. The Ministry adopted a client-led transformation model and set up client advisory committees at senior and operational levels to steer the initiative. At the ICT operational level, client ministries were asked to design the best shared-service delivery model to meet their business needs within the defined budget constraints. MMS staff served as "brokers" or "agents" charged with developing and delivering the service from the client-led design exercise. This approach was designed to counter the mandated technology notion of earlier models. MMS negotiates service level agreements with all clients within the bounds of the plan and established budgets. As MMS assumes responsibility for all common ICT functions from ministries, ministries transfer assets, staff and contracts but retain operational funding in order to purchase services from MMS on a cost-recovery basis. The new model assigns clients responsibility over the whole rather than just

for their particular parts of infrastructure services. When MMS faces budget pressure, the client advisory committees are charged with the responsibility of developing new ICT service level expectations to meet the revised budget target. If a client wants to change a service or technology outside of that agreed to by the whole, it has to plead its case to its peers on the advisory group rather than to the service deliverer.

- *Mandating usage for three years.* MMS secured Cabinet approval in early 2002 for a new ICT organization within solutions BC — the Common Information Technology Services (CITS) Division — with a mandate to consolidate the complete common ICT infrastructure across government. MMS also secured a commitment from government that all agencies were required to use the new shared-services structure for a period of three years in order to give CITS enough time to prove its case. The "stick" of mandated usage of the shared-service infrastructure services accompanied the "carrot" of benchmarking and stronger client advisory structures. After three years, agencies unhappy with pricing or service will be free to leave the shared-service relationship. However, given the corporate responsibilities assigned to new client advisory groups, the departing agency will be required to first seek the approval of all fellow clients of the shared service who presumably would be concerned that their per unit costs would increase if partners leave the system.

After

The shared-service model has transformed the approach taken to delivering common ICT infrastructure in the government of British Columbia. The ICT shared-service organization, CITS, is concentrating on delivering cost-effective, quality infrastructure services while ministries concentrate their efforts on ministry-specific business applications. MMS is progressively more responsive to clients as client advisory groups made up of the "parts" of government are mandated to effectively steer and take some ownership over the "whole" of the approach.

Traditional issues about overcharging for ICT infrastructure services are now subject to a process of annual measurement against external benchmarks. The MMS has also committed to cost reductions over three years as consolidation delivers expected savings by eliminating duplication and improving the purchasing power inherent in whole-of-government economies of scale. While the shared-services model is in its implementation period, it operates under the security of a Cabinet-level commitment to the model and a restriction on ministries' ability to depart from the model for three years.

Lessons Learned and Key Success Factors

- *Significant transformational changes require time.* Implementation will best be advanced when it is done under the security of a government-imposed mandate that prevents clients from attempting to leave the transformation project mid-stream over concerns justified solely on their unique perspectives;
- *External benchmarking increases transparency and accountability to the customer.* The price charged backed to ministries by the shared-service agency is a point of contention in the relationship. An agreed-to process to benchmark the

shared-service delivery for ICTs against a peer group of best practices focuses the debate on facts rather than assumptions.

- *Transformation requires new client engagement processes.* The move from a "central agency" mandating price and technology to "shared service" reflects a fundamental change in approach. Strategies based on "client-led" transformation should be backed up with appropriate governance structures, which confer responsibilities on the clients for the "whole" of ICT service delivery rather than their particular "parts."

Changing the Governance and Management Model for ICTs: Corporate and "Cluster" Chief Information Officer Functions in the Government of Ontario, Canada

The province of Ontario (Canada) has reorganized its responsibilities for ICT management. Ontario assigns cross-government accountability for ICT governance and infrastructure to a corporate CIO in the Management Board Secretariat and groups ministries together into "clusters" focusing on business applications. These ICT clusters report jointly to the corporate CIO and to the Deputy Ministers of the ministries within the cluster.

Before

Prior to 1995, the responsibilities for ICT infrastructure and applications were distributed among ministries with limited corporate-wide responsibilities in infrastructure and governance. Corporate authority was exercised more as a coordinating function based on select ICT standards and platforms. ICT was not seen as an investment in change — one that could reduce costs and enable cross-agency business functions.

In 1995, a new government came to power with a commitment to transforming the relationship between the government and the citizen/client. It also embarked on a significant downsizing of government and challenged its ministries to work together across agency boundaries to reduce duplication and redundancy of processes and systems. The government also made a commitment to e-government not only to improve service delivery in a downsizing environment but, as a catalyst in its economic development priorities, to support the development of a high-tech "digital economy."

The Transformation Project

In March 1998, the Ontario government released a new information and information technology strategy, which defined the shape of Ontario's e-government strategy and how the government intended to organize itself to deliver.[8] Among the key objectives of the strategy was a commitment to treat ICT resources as "corporate assets to best support government priorities and directions." The ICT strategy advanced to a broad government objective to forge cross-agency cooperation in order to reduce duplication and redundancy and establish the Ontario government as an integrated organization.[9]

In this respect, the ICT initiative represented one track of inter-agency integration, along with the establishment of policy clusters and shared services in audit, financial and human resource services. The new organizational model for ICT in the Ontario government features:

- The creation of a corporate CIO function with defined responsibilities for strategy, policy, controllership, architecture, common ICT infrastructure, standards and security as well as the human resource and procurement functions relating to ICTs. The corporate CIO was designated the "owner" of the government's ICT strategy — a key enabler to driving transformation in the Ontario government;
- The "clustering" of ICT needs and services of all of Ontario's ministries into seven groups, each of which is headed by a cluster CIO.[10] The cluster CIOs have been assigned two distinct roles and responsibilities:
  - Corporately, the cluster CIOs have responsibilities for ensuring that ministries within the cluster comply with corporate ICT direction and standards, including input to and use of the common ICT infrastructure. In this capacity, they report directly to the Corporate CIO and have an enterprise-wide role in defining and advancing the government's information and information technology strategy.
  - With respect to the ministries within the cluster, the CIOs provide all business-specific ICT services and are authorized to explore collaborative business applications within the cluster. In this capacity, the CIO reports directly to each Deputy Minister within their cluster and serves on each cluster ministry executive committee. Collectively, the cluster ministries and the CIO establish a memorandum of understanding on how the cluster will operate — a mechanism which allows sufficient flexibility to form the cluster objectives and operations to meet the needs of the client ministries while conforming with corporate directions.

The Ontario government also recognized some of the pressures facing the recruitment and retention of ICT professionals in the government. However, consistent with its downsizing agenda, the government effectively challenged the bureaucracy to reduce the number of ICT managerial positions while maintaining the overall salary envelope for distribution over fewer positions — thus allowing for an augmentation of salaries. In addition, Cabinet allocated $110 million CAD over four years to develop the common infrastructure in support of the e-government directions. The funding was to be released based on a Cabinet review of whether e-government strategies, key goals and targets were being met. Some of this funding was allocated to augmenting ICT staff salaries beyond the existing envelope.[11]

Implementation Factors

- *Defining the clusters.* The composition of the clusters represented a significant challenge in a silo-based organization, accountability framework and culture of the Ontario public service. Some ministries argued for their own clusters. Smaller agencies questioned whether their service needs and priorities would be addressed in the shadow of larger ministries within the cluster. This was addressed by:
  - Establishing core criteria which envisaged that no department would be broken up;

- Establishing criteria for definition of the cluster on business lines — i.e., size and function of the agency, "affinity" of business, commonality of clients and stakeholders, office and service distribution throughout the Province;
- Bringing in an independent third party to apply the criteria and recommend the cluster composition;
- Having Deputy Ministers participating in clusters agree to the cluster composition and operational mode (via a memorandum of understanding);
- Having the cluster model approved by Cabinet.

While some compromises had to be made to address business or cultural needs (or indeed, the force of argument of some agencies), the cluster model has been in place since mid-1999.

- *Breaking the mould on recruitment and retention.* Officials faced the daunting challenge of how to improve the attractiveness of the government in the war for talent ICT skills while meeting the government's broader objectives for a leaner government. This challenge was addressed by:
    - Reducing the number of senior ICT managerial positions in the public service by almost 20% — arguing that the cluster model would capture efficiencies and reduce duplication that prevailed in the silo-based model. As noted above, the re-distribution of the salary envelope over a reduced number of positions plus the modest augmentation to salary funds contributed to a significant salary increase for ICT professionals.
    - Creating career paths and training packages for ICT staff in the new structure. This marked the first time the Ontario government had taken a comprehensive approach to the longer-term training needs of its staff in this area. Other ICT-focused recruitment and retention tools were also introduced, including a youth intern program.
- *Illustrating transformation through the hiring process.* The government was committed to challenging the status quo in its ICT organization and underlined that it was serious about transforming the way the government utilized ICT to support its business directions. Accordingly, it took a number of controversial steps in establishing the new model through its staffing practices, including:
    - Signalling the leadership role of the ICT senior managerial positions by creating a new ITX job classification level within the public service with a higher salary range. This commitment was exemplified by the decision to provide the corporate CIO position with a salary package that, in fact, exceeded the salary being offered to the chief official in the Ontario public service;
    - Emphasizing the changed organization, responsibilities and new expectations for ICT managers by declaring all management positions in the new organization as new positions and requiring all existing ICT managers to compete for all jobs in the reduced managerial compliment. This presented a particular challenge given that the same managers who often felt they were being asked to "apply for their own jobs" were also being asked to rally staff behind the new directions and strategies.

- *Challenging and changing authority within the bureaucracy.* As the clusters were being formed, management responsibilities for ICT were being transferred out of assistant deputy minister-level chief administrative officer positions throughout the government — thereby weakening the power bases of these positions at a time of considerable change within the public service. At the same time, however, the cluster CIO was designated as a member on each of the executive teams of the ministries within his/her cluster. This had the effect of elevating the importance of ICT within ministries. In addition, the success of their cluster became a part of each deputy minister's performance plan, against which he/she was measured annually and allocated salary bonuses on meeting performance targets. This helped to underscore the inter-departmental ownership of the cluster model at the highest levels within the organization;
- *Budget authorities.* While ministries agreed to participate in the cluster model, silo-based budget accountabilities made them reluctant to cede actual control of relevant budget resources to the cluster CIO. The authorizing of cluster CIO "sign off" on all ICT expenditures within cluster ministries helped empower the cluster CIO to achieve his/her objectives while keeping budget and management authorities in tact within ministries. Since the establishment of the model, at least one cluster has allocated full budget control over its constituent department ICT budgets to the cluster CIO.

After

By the summer of 2000, the transformed model for information and information technology management in the Ontario government was up and running. The challenging cultural issues raised by this transformation required much communication, patience and superior leadership skills to navigate through the various issues raised. The operations of the clusters are beginning to produce the desired efficiency gains and synergies of cross-agency cooperation. The Ontario public service has passed through the "Why cluster?" and the "Why this cluster?" phases to now exploring what more could be done within the clusters (i.e., promoting cross-ministry e-government solutions, promoting enhanced citizen engagement). A second generation of clusters is now in place through some adjustments to the initial model. The government has been satisfied enough that targets are being met to release annual additional funds for e-government based on reports to Cabinet.

Lessons Learned and Key Success Factors

- *Communicate transformation and move quickly.* The transformed management model represented a significant departure from the status quo. Organizational and administrative changes were considered necessary to fully deliver on the new e-government strategy that the Ontario government had launched. A significant communication effort on the nature and needs of transformation was mounted inside government. However, the success of this campaign was impaired by a relatively long implementation period (March 1998 – Summer 2000), which was characterized by job uncertainty and changing authority bases among the managers given the responsibility for explaining and implementing change;

- Strong corporate leadership and coordination. The roles and responsibilities assigned to Deputy Ministers to make the clusters work effectively and to own the results elevated the importance of ICTs to high levels within the government. The often time-consuming twin reporting relationship of the cluster CIO's — to the corporate CIO and their respective cluster Deputy Ministers — ensured that the strategy was implemented in a coordinated manner. Other mechanisms, such as common reporting frameworks and metrics, helped emphasize the corporate complexion of the project;
- Elevating the importance of ICTs at the executive table. The reporting relationships and assignment of responsibilities elevated the role of ICTs in ministries as the cluster CIO was assigned to the executive teams of each of their cluster ministries. This assisted in strengthening ICT alignment to program priorities within and across the ministries. In addition, the corporate CIO is a member of the Deputy Ministers Council, which consists of all Deputy Ministers from across the government;
- Alignment of ICT transformation with a strategy for broader transformation within the public service. The ICT management and governance model was one of the flagship transformational initiatives aimed at changing the way the public service worked in a downsizing environment. While the ICT model moved more aggressively than some of the other initiatives, its alignment to a broader strategy has provided significant corporate reinforcement to the changes that are being made.

Encouraging Cooperation in Cross-Government Business Application Development: Digital Government Applications Academy, State of Washington, USA

E-government initiatives around the world are changing the internal cultures of governments with innovative approaches to building cooperation among separate agencies. The State of Washington, USA has developed the unique in-house Digital Government Applications Academy (DGAA), where departments interested in developing new business applications are brought together to build business applications for use across departments in a "build-it-once, share-it-often" approach.

Before

Like many jurisdictions, the government of the State of Washington is largely composed of separate agencies operating with their own independent authority, legislative mandate and voted budget appropriations. The Department of Information Services, whose director is a Cabinet-level appointee of the Governor, leads the State's e-government initiative.

When Washington launched its e-government initiative several years ago, the then DIS Director Steve Kolodney realized that a new breed of bureaucrat would be required to develop the silo-busting cooperation needed to advance the e-government campaign. DIS took the challenge of how to allow the State to emerge as a single enterprise in a government structure composed of separate agencies, budgets and legislative authorities. To achieve this goal, Kolodney argued, "You need a way to train people to be revolutionaries in organizations" in order to make collaboration and online service delivery part of the "core competence" of all-state agencies.[12] To do this, Kolodney had the vision to create a neutral place in government where innovative staff could leave their "you-can't-do-it-that-way" agency environment and invent collaborative solutions to common electronic service delivery problems.

In December 1999, DIS began to design this neutral place in the form of the Digital Government Applications Academy (DGAA). DIS drafted an Applications Academy Charter. It elaborated on Washington State Governor Locke's commitment to digital government as a "transformational opportunity to set a course for the State that citizens really want." The charter also noted that "the success of digital government will be realized through collaboration among government entities, industry experts and customers to accelerate learning and share best practices for developing Internet business solutions."[13]

The Transformation Project

Based on this direction, DIS established an academy model focusing on inter-agency collaboration in the development of shared business applications (Decide, Build, Publish and Replicate). The initial project list included broad areas such as e-forms and lines of government service such as e-permits and e-licensing. The approach represented a significant departure from the status quo where separate agencies of the State government tended to be focused on the independent creation of the same product under their silo-based authorities. If left to exercise this authority in their own way, agencies would likely continue to duplicate effort and, more significantly, project to the citizen/client several different ways of doing the same government function, confusing citizens and clients with different requirements, formats and "looks and feels" in commonly processed forms.

In February 2000, DIS opened the doors of the academy and convened the first joint application development project on e-permits. The start-up for the academy was financed from existing DIS funds. However, in order to secure buy-in from agencies, DIS made an important decision to charge agencies to participate in academy "courses" — the facilitated workshops in which the joint application was to be developed.[14] The DIS also chose to run the academy on a voluntary basis with agencies choosing whether to participate or not. By the same token, the final product, while emerging as a *de facto* government standard, would not be made compulsory across the government. Hence, the model was focused on engaging agencies based on their interests rather than compelling participation and use of the products developed.

The process of an academy seminar is quite innovative. The objective of each seminar is to design and build a common template for the application under consideration. With business transformation in mind, agencies dissect all of the business requirements (as opposed to the technical processing requirements) involved in the application under development (i.e., authentication, payment modalities, common look and feel, legislative requirements, etc.). They agree to develop an application template that would address all of the facets required. A particular application from one of the agencies participating is chosen to be the academy class project.

As participants work on this real-life project, hidden issues and requirements that do not come up in a more conventional training course rise to the surface. These issues are resolved through collaboration among agency business and technical leaders, industry experts and customers. The collaborative decisions and approaches are built into a template. Once concluded, the sponsoring agency builds the application that was the class project using the template. Soon afterwards, other participating agencies follow suit and launch their own related applications. Participating agencies agree to at least replicate the basic patterns and guidelines in the template as they build their applications.

Another unique aspect of the academy relates to the involvement of the private sector in the seminar projects. DIS invites a business customer of the type of application under development to provide real-time input and commentary on how the application could best be developed to meet their needs. For example, in the e-licensing seminar (June – October 2001), government participants were joined by an electrical contractor who needs a contractor's license for his/her work. DIS also invites an IT applications development company to participate on a pro-bono basis in the seminar. The IT company helps direct the debate over application development, bringing in illustrations of related work that it has been involved in to assist in the shaping of the template. As the seminar aims to build a template rather than the actual final application, the IT company's involvement in the academy course strengthens its profile as a possible partner for the actual building of the application when agencies procure for a final product.

Implementation Factors

- *Facilitate rather than force collaboration.* Importantly, the project did not entail any changes in management authority or budget. Agencies are essentially free to come and go as they please with no central direction to participate in the seminars or adopt the final product as a state-wide standard. Instead, momentum driven by seminar results has encouraged a culture of collaboration in the development of shared business applications. DIS demands commitment, energy and a "leave-your-silo-at-the-door" approach from the seminar participants. In return, the academy provides a laboratory where officials can risk and innovate within a public sector environment that is not always supportive of such approaches. The tuition fee assessed for agency participation, while covering some of the costs of the academy and the seminar, more importantly signals a commitment on the part of the participating agencies to the process. The DIS reinforces the benefits of the academy corporately with proof of savings in time, money and increases in productivity associated with developing and replicating templates among participating agencies.
- *Peer engagement/peer pressure.* The academy functions as a "peer group," with each participating agency feeling that it owns the process and outcomes. The academy's graduates are among the most powerful champions for inter-agency collaboration. Agency participants have shown themselves to be both willing and able to apply peer pressure to another agency that might be considering a solo rather than collaborative approach. This dynamic supports two key outcomes of the academy, according to academy manager Dave Kirk: it develops a core competency in government to deliver service online and it changes the culture of government (with respect to cross-agency collaboration) "one person at a time".[15]
- *Engage the private sector.* The involvement of the application customer is vital to the success of the projects under development. Valuable feedback and buy-in

are achieved from the prospective user of the application, which builds a momentum for adoption once the applications are rolled out. The development of generic applications on a common "look-and-feel" basis makes it easier for clients to navigate applications if they have to use more than one. This assists in meeting the DIS challenge to make a diverse enterprise such as the State government appear as a uniform entity in the eyes of the citizen/client. The involvement of IT companies in the template development process brings in valuable applications building expertise to the project for no charge — the return for the IT company being in building its profile in front of prospective agency customers who will need assistance in actually building the application.

- *Build from success to success.* The academy model is essentially fueled by the success of previous projects. The learning-by-doing approach and the success of the pilot e-permit seminar in early 2000 sparked momentum for two further seminars based on e-forms and e-licensing. In addition, the DIS has developed a generic tool to assist in the development of digital applications. The Application Template and Outfitting Model (ATOM) helps sequence the planning steps needed for any applications development. It also provides links to relevant governance, policy, administrative authorities and technology infrastructure within the government (i.e., payment provisions linked to the State Treasury guidelines).

After

The Digital Government Applications Academy has successfully produced three common business applications (e-permits, e-forms and e-licenses). However, more importantly, it has helped establish a culture of cross-agency collaboration, which has assisted a diverse government administration to "emerge" online as a single enterprise in the face of the citizen/client — a key objective of Washington's e-government strategy.

Having completed three successful application development seminars, DIS is now extending beyond the immediate scope of the State government to engage in a project among state and local government agencies involved in business licensing. This project will transform the way collaboration is done between two levels of government and create a cross-jurisdictional template for one-step business registration. Several other State jurisdictions are examining the Washington State model for the possible establishment of equivalent academies in their jurisdictions.

Lessons Learned and Key Success Factors

- *Executive sponsorship is critical.* Governor Locke is committed to improving government services, and part of his plan is to move many of those services online. His commitment creates a major impetus for agencies to work together and avoid re-inventing the wheel;
- *Facilitating cooperation works.* The academy is not the product of a state directive mandating the common development and use of business applications. Rather, participation is engaged on the basis of agency-interest and the possibility of creating a better product for less time, money and effort. The process produces a common "look-and-feel" template that makes it easier for the State to meet citizen/client expectations for a standard interface with the State government;

- *Build from success*. The momentum behind the academy has been sparked by the success of the application templates developed and, more importantly, by the clear illustration that collaboration works. This is helping transform the culture of the silo-based government administration.
- *Encourage risk and innovation*. The academy provides a neutral place in which innovators in government can try out new ideas and take risk in developing applications. In this context, it provides a safe place to innovate in the generally risk-averse culture prevailing in governments. The "learning-by-doing" approach also enriches the employees learning experience, which assists in retention. Academy graduates are becoming active missionaries for the concept of collaboration.
- *Build customer input straight into the process*. A customer's presence in the room during the application development process provides powerful, real-time input and feedback into the development of the applications from the perspective of the future user.

TRANSFORMING THE RELATIONSHIP WITH BUSINESS SUPPLIERS TO GOVERNMENT: E-PROCUREMENT REFORM, MINISTERO DELL'ECONOMIA E DELLE FINANZE, GOVERNMENT OF ITALY

Many governments in OECD member countries are adopting e-procurement solutions to reduce costs and streamline the management of relationships with business suppliers. The Ministero dell'Economia e delle Finanze, government of Italy, adopted an e-procurement system in 2000 and is beginning to reap benefits inside and outside of the government.

Before

In 1999, the Ministero dell'Economia e delle Finanze undertook a study on expenditure processes in the procurement of goods and services for the government of Italy and its agencies. The study identified several areas in which procurement processes could be optimized to streamline costs, achieve economies of scale and stimulate the uptake of e-commerce within the business sector. The conventional practice of identifying business requirements, calling for tenders and managing complex administrative and contractual processes was replicated time after time in silo-based agencies. The procurement system did not differentiate between complex service contracts and fixed-cost "commodity-type" goods acquisitions. The approval processes for goods and services acquisition were hierarchical. Despite having sufficient spending authority to purchase supplies/services, managers were often unable to approve contracts.

At the same time, the government was interested in using its purchasing power to stimulate the adoption of e-commerce in the private sector. By being a model user of ICTs and augmenting e-government interactions with the private sector in its purchasing capacity, the Italian government saw the adoption of an e-procurement systems as a way of increasing the cost efficiency and effectiveness of its procurement systems while stimulating e-commerce in Italy.

The Transformation Project

In 1997, the Ministero dell'Economia e delle Finanze established an arms-length agency, the Public Information Services Agency (CONSIP), to provide the government with consultancy assistance and IT solutions aimed at innovation in public administration. Within the framework of the strategic policies identified by the Ministry, CONSIP was mandated to rationalize the procedures and organization of the ICT function and, in so doing, promote change and modernization in government and the development of the Information Society in Italy. The connection to economic development objectives reflected a key goal of the Italian government's e-government action plan – namely the "promotion and development of e-commerce for goods and services provisioning in the Public Administration (e-procurement)."[16]

Based on the Ministry's study, CONSIP developed a transformational approach to procurement, which both introduced ICT applications and re-engineered business processes. CONSIP examined all purchase requirements according to two main criteria: the frequency of purchase and the volatility of price and technology. With the objective of making purchases as effective and efficient as possible, CONSIP essentially separated high-volume, low-complexity purchases from those that require more traditional purchasing processes either because of price volatility or technological complexity (see Table 1). CONSIP then introduced three procurement channels or "platforms":

- *Online product catalogues.* Through a traditional tender, vendors apply to be qualified as suppliers for defined goods and services. Government customers (with appropriate spending authority) purchase products and services required directly from an online catalogue posted by a successfully qualified vendor. Product/service characteristics for this segment include high-volume, lower-price/volatility goods (i.e., office supplies).
- *E-auctions.* The end-user defines its product needs and specifications and posts the request online through a time-limited "reverse auction." The winning bidder is the one that meets the product specifications requested with the lowest priced good by the declared close of auction. Product/service characteristics for this segment include high-value, high-volatility goods with lower frequency of purchases (i.e., personal computers).
- *E-marketplace.* For high-frequency purchases with higher price volatility, the e-marketplace platform allows for a more continuous evolution in the prices and products offered by the supplier with a shorter lead time than the auction channel.

All platforms were enabled with end-to-end transactional capacity that allowed all bids and eventual purchases to be transacted online.

Implementation Factors

- *Establish a legislative framework.* To introduce the new procedures for procurement and simplify internal procedures, the Ministero dell'Economia e delle Finanze had to introduce new legislation in 2000 to provide a legal basis for the e-procurement project. Based on this legislation, CONSIP introduced a new organizational model for procurement management and a new online Web site. This allowed CONSIP to reform and centralize the purchasing process and assume a role of providing expertise for government customers and suppliers as to which platform would be most appropriate for purchases.

- *Respect agency autonomy.* While reforming and centralizing procurement policies and procedures, the Ministero dell'Economia e delle Finanze was careful to respect the budget autonomy of agencies in both the national and local governments. Thus, the authority to decide when and what quantities to purchase remains with the respective agency. The e-procurement system simply enabled a more convenient and effective process for this authority to be exercised.
- *Full transactional and e-enabled capacity.* In July 2000, CONSIP introduced a new online procurement Web site based on the platform model above.[17] The site consists of a series of electronic shops with supplier's offerings segmented by market type (i.e., office supplies, services, etc.). Users are required to register through a single sign-on mechanism, which authenticates and verifies agency and spending authority. Upon registration, users are provided a password that allows entry into the electronic shop of interest. The site informs users about the operating methods and guidelines and provides access to all documents necessary to conclude a purchase, as well as an online help function to assist the user through the transaction. This has the added benefit of ensuring compliance with procurement laws and regulations while streamlining and expediting the procurement process.

After

The e-procurement project allows the government of Italy to achieve a 30% reduction in the total cost of goods and service procured. In addition, the end-to-end transactional capacity available through the e-procurement system assists suppliers in adopting e-commerce business practices motivated by their interest in securing government business. As the government's e-procurement marketplace develops users and increases in sophistication, it is laying the foundation for future business opportunities, including collaborating with suppliers on inventory requirements and new applications to automate purchasing.

Lessons Learned and Key Success Factors

- *Respect agency authorities.* The Italian e-procurement process respects agencies' authority to purchase goods and services that fit their business needs.

  It also enables agencies to streamline approval processes based on verification that the user has the required spending authority to make purchasing decisions within the system;
- *Re-engineer business processes while introducing new online applications.* The CONSIP model provides a good example of the benefits of re-engineering business processes within government to reap the best advantage from new ICT applications. In this case, changes in legislation were required to pave the way for the new

Table 1. Segmenting procurement by platform[18]

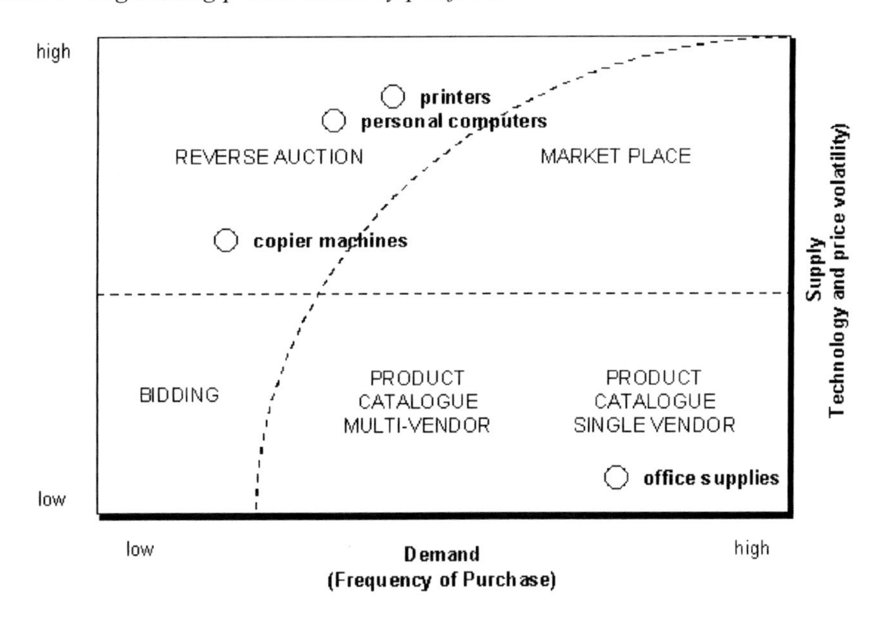

Source: Arthur Andersen, Booz Allen & Hamilton, CONSIP

business practices. As well, internal business practices were changed to segment goods and services purchases in a way that reserved the traditional process for the most complex acquisitions and provided easier access to supply for less complex and less frequent purchase. It also empowered officials, already holding required spending authority, to directly access the "shopping mall" for goods and services rather than submit to an often-tedious approval process within their agency;

- *Customer satisfaction and value is maximized when full end-to-end transactional capacity is enabled.* The Italian e-procurement example underlines the benefits of advancing electronic service delivery initiatives to the "transactional" level of the electronic service maturity curve. By being able to fully transact procurement business online, the model strips cumbersome processes from the system (as is perhaps best demonstrated in the e-auction facility). At the same time, it enables a better management of supply and demonstrates strong potential for future, closer interaction between suppliers and customers in the procurement marketplace.

Transforming Business Relationship with the Citizen/ Client through End-to End Transactional Services: Motor Vehicle Licensing Services, State of Arizona, USA

The ability for a citizen/client to fully complete a transaction with government through an electronic service application represents a high level of electronic service maturity depth in e-government. The government of Arizona, USA was an early e-government adopter and has transformed its motor vehicle licensing business through an innovative electronic service delivery application. The successful offering of full transactional capabilities to the citizen/client has been enabled by several significant structural and business practice transformations behind the scenes within the government.

Before

In the mid-1990s, the Governor of Arizona surveyed citizens for the least satisfactory Arizona state services from the customer perspective. The annual renewal of motor vehicle registration topped the list. Citizens were normally confronted with four-to-five-hour waits at Arizona Motor Vehicle Division (MVD) offices to renew vehicle registration. If information given at the counter was incorrect or incomplete, the citizen had to return later with the required updates. With the State's population growing rapidly (12% per annum), pressure on the system was getting worse. While the Governor was committed to improving service delivery, she was, at the same time, implementing a tax cutting and downsizing government agenda, which diminished the State's capacity to resource an expansion and improvement of existing services. She was also promoting expanded electronic service delivery, not only to improve service delivery but also to support an economic development platform that profiled digital government as a key instrument in developing a digital economy in Arizona and attracting high-technology investment.

The Transformation Project

In 1996, managers at the MVD decided to create a new Internet-based channel for service delivery to reduce the per-unit cost of motor vehicle transactions and take pressure off the front-line delivery offices. These were early days for Internet applications in government, and MVD managers were prepared to take risks and innovate with very little track record in electronic service delivery.

In an effort to address the backlog and service problems at MVD offices, the State made changes in the delivery model by allowing the private sector operators to open registration agency outlets and charge a "convenience fee" for their services over and above the State registration fee. In 1998, legislation was introduced that allowed private sector operators to replace the convenience fee add-on to the motor vehicle registration fee with a claim based on a share of the State fee. This change in the business model opened the door to transaction-based contract relationships with the private sector and set the stage for MVD to enter into discussions with IBM about a new model for electronic service delivery.

The Web-based motor vehicle registry project was constructed on the basis of an IBM commitment to finance the building and maintain and host the Web service, in return for a 2% per transaction return (equalling about $4.00 per transaction at the time). The citizen saw an effective reduction of the time taken to complete a registration renewal at the MVD offices (during eight-to-five MVD office hours) to mere minutes over the Web, at their convenience. Given the cost to the State of processing registrations online, which cost roughly $3.83 per transaction as compared with $10.72 for over the counter, the State saved money at both ends. It avoided the IT construction costs and achieved higher returns per transaction even after the IBM transaction fee had been netted out.[19] The

Web-based service was introduced in 1997 as the first item on a transactional portal – Service Arizona — on which further transaction-based motor vehicle products could be hosted. The State solicited ideas for new projects through a customer feedback survey conducted at the end of the transaction.

Implementation Factors

- *Overcoming internal resistance.* Web-based applications for government services were a relatively new and untried concept in 1996. MVD managers were challenged on several fronts by State financial and legal agencies with concerns relating to network security (i.e., online customers hacking into the State's network), credit card on the Web payment services and the legal aspects of a transactions-based contract with IBM. More importantly, the MVD counter staff felt threatened by the introduction of the new Internet-based channel (and an Interactive Voice Response (IVR) system that was introduced at the same). MVD managers diligently addressed the challenges — choosing to take risks on the new system. With respect to staff, MVD communicated that it did not intend to shut down or diminish the in-person counter channel, but, rather, argued that the Web-based and IVR applications would take pressure off the already stretched resources in the offices. While committing to keep all channels open, MVD embarked on a public advertising campaign to tell citizens about the Service Arizona Internet channel and encourage its use.
- *Engaging in business process re-engineering as further applications go online.* At the outset of the Service Arizona project, the MVD took an important decision to try to re-engineer business processes as they were introducing new online services. This allowed for a complete examination of the rationale behind permitting periods and processes. For example, the MVD issues restricted-use, three-day permits that allow a person to operate an unregistered vehicle from the present location of the vehicle to a specified destination (i.e., the transfer of a vehicle from one location to another for emissions testing, vehicle inspection or sales transfer). Prior to offering the permit on the Web, MVD did not track the permits once they were issued. Along with developing the Web application, MVD created an integrated database to track the permits, including those issued in field offices. The database records who purchased the permits, and when and where they were purchased, to ensure that individuals do not exceed the legal limit (three successive permits). Law enforcement agencies may, by law, access the database information to determine whether a permit is valid.
- *Strong customer focus, feedback and metrics.* The MVD chose to keep control over the "script" on the online application to ensure clear and simple directions for the user, unencumbered by technical jargon about the Web-based service. Each transaction ends with a customer satisfaction and comments survey, which provides MVD with strong public endorsement of the electronic service delivery track as well as some new ideas about additional projects to pursue online. In addition, the MVD consistently tracks motor vehicle registries over all channels, enabling MVD to measure the quick adoption of the Web-based channel once introduced.

After

From an early 2% uptake on introduction, Web-based motor vehicle registrations now account for over 20% of registrations in Arizona. The success of the online service in relieving pressure on the system has contributed, in part, to a reduction of customer waiting time at MVD offices from four to five hours to roughly 15 minutes.[20] Service Arizona has emerged as a platform for several motor vehicle transactions (replacement of lost driver's licenses, personalized plates, etc.). It has also recently ventured beyond the motor vehicle arena by mounting the U.S.'s first Web-based voter registration service.

Two of the new services merit examination, given their transformational nature:

- *Personalized/specialty license plates.* Previously, Arizona citizens wishing to obtain personalized/specialty license plates were required to submit three choices for information to be presented on the license plate as well as their choice of available license plate template. The requests were processed manually to determine whether the "information to be presented" was eligible (not already taken) and acceptable (under public appropriateness tests). If the three choices were disqualified on the above basis, the citizen had to start the request from scratch. The Web-based service allows the submission of multiple "information-to-be-presented" requests with the service replying electronically once the first such request is deemed eligible and acceptable. The citizen then can perform an on-screen projection of the "information to be presented" against several available license plate templates before confirming the order.
- *Restricted-use, three-day permits.* Rather than having to go to an MVD office to secure a temporary document for this purpose, Service Arizona allowed the citizen to not only apply for a temporary permit over the Web but to print a valid permit out from his/her personal computer printer.

Lessons Learned and Key Success Factors

- *Listen to the customer, and keep communications simple.* MVD has continually improved its Web-based service by drawing from real-time customer feedback via surveys at the end of transactions. (There is a 40% response rate to these surveys.) MVD has also recruited and acted on ideas for new e-service offerings through this feedback (i.e., the personalized plate application process.) MVD's commitment to control the script and keep the direct interface with the customer as simple as possible has helped the user-friendliness of the system and avoided needless technical jargon that is evident on some Web-based e-government applications.
- *Measure and report.* MVD rigorously tracks comparative use both of its service channels (Web, counter, phone, mail) and customer satisfaction. This information feeds directly into the Governor's overall commitment to improve customer satisfaction and increase electronic service delivery.
- *Engage in business process re-engineering while introducing new electronic services.* Arizona has specifically challenged business processes in its electronic service delivery offerings, choosing to improve business aspects of its services rather than simply automate existing processes.

- *Take risk.* MVD managers, working with a relatively new technology, clearly took risks in mounting the Service Arizona platform in the face of internal resistance and concern. The ability to demonstrate quick up-take of the service by citizens without the realization of security concerns, helped managers get over internal resistance and deliver a valuable service.

Bundling Public and Private Electronic Services to Better Serve the Citizen/Client: Business Entry Point Portal, Government of Australia

As governments extend a broader range of electronic services to their citizens and clients, some have enhanced the convenience of electronic service delivery. They've done so by integrating government service offerings from a broad cross-section of governments with related private sector services to provide a comprehensive suite of services to the citizen/client. This approach has been piloted in Australia with the Business Entry Point business services site.[21]

Before

The Business Entry Point Web site was established by the federal government in 1998 to provide a "one-stop shop" for Australian small businesses to discover information about government compliance issues. The need for such a service was recognized in a 1996 report by the Small Business Deregulation Task Force. It found that businesses were struggling to find information about, and comply with, regulation administered across three levels of government.

Integral to the Australian government online strategy is the objective of removing the need for the client to understand the structure of the Commonwealth, State and local governments in order to access the service required. The Business Entry Point (BEP) established agreements with federal and state agencies to aggregate business-related information from other Web sites and make it discoverable through a central, federally managed Web site.[22]

The Transformation Project

Working from the inter-jurisdictional agreements above, the BEP provides a fully integrated gateway to the business services provided by all agencies of the Commonwealth, State and territorial governments. The BEP also features several innovative applications, including:

- *The transaction manager.* This enables clients to discover, manage and complete online transactions with relevant Commonwealth, State and local government agencies for business licenses and permits, including:
    - Registration for payroll tax;
    - Local rates payments;
    - Business name renewals;
    - Grants and assistance applications;
    - Company registration, returns and change of details; and
    - Building and development applications.

- *Client-specific profiles.* Using Customer Relationship Management (CRM) applications offered through the BEP, clients can:
  - Store their multiple personal and business details in profiles to auto matically pre-fill and complete online transaction forms as they become available;
  - Search for transactions that have been registered with the system;
  - Group and execute a series of transactions; and
  - Maintain records of completed, incomplete and visited transactions.
- *Capability to extend beyond governments.* The BEP also recognized that the portal approach was not necessarily the most efficient way of providing access to government information. Rather, it realized that injecting the information into the business process when and where it was most needed was a more appropriate and effective approach. For example, government information about starting a business (registration, tax compliance, licences, etc.) was syndicated on the Web sites of banking institutions so it would be accessible when the business approached the bank for start-up finance. The bank is able to offer a value-added service, and the business customer has all the relevant information — both government and non-government — in one place. Thus, in addition to offering seamless service across jurisdictional boundaries, the BEP has entered into partnerships with a number of non-government and government agencies, resulting in valuable, aggregated government content published on a range of other sites. While the BEP is an intergovernmental initiative, the Commonwealth of Australia has solely absorbed the costs associated with it.
- *User-friendly content themes.* In addition to recognizing the need to make information more accessible to businesses, the BEP realized it needed to change its approach to classifying this information. Essentially, the information needed to be logically categorized into specific business-related activities. These activities — or "themes" — now form the basis of content found on the BEP site itself as well as the content that is syndicated to other organizations. Content themes include information about specific government compliance obligations and other information associated with specific business activities. For example, the exporting theme includes information from federal and State government agencies on grants and other assistance schemes that are available for exporters, as well as customs requirements.

Implementation Factors

- *Marketing to the client through multiple channels: syndication.* Over the years the BEP Web site has rated highly in both government and business assistance Web rankings. However, market research undertaken in the first years of operation consistently demonstrated a lack of awareness about the site. This can be attributed to a number of factors, not the least of which are the resource and logistical implications of marketing a service like the BEP to a target audience as diverse as new and existing small businesses. Recognizing the continuing need to make government information more accessible, the BEP decided to use XML standards to take its content to the sites that businesses do know about and visit regularly. These include sites that already provide a range of information and services for small businesses, such as financial institutions, industry associations and local government agencies.

By syndicating content in this way, the BEP is moving away from the portal philosophy and creating multiple access points for the same information. The BEP has entered into partnerships with a number of non-government and government agencies, resulting in valuable, aggregated government content published on a range of other sites. The syndicated content is structured in a way that is relevant to business. It includes information on starting and registering a business, paying tax, getting licences and permits and finding out how to obtain government funding and a range of other topics. High-level descriptions and a direct link to the relevant government resource are syndicated to the partnering organization's Web site using technology that ensures that the content takes on the "look and feel" of the partner's site. Ultimately the decision to syndicate content to a private sector organization remains within the BEP, which evaluates potential partners on the basis of the value brought in, making BEP content available to partner clients. BEP's only firm criterion is that its content must not be sold.

- *Feedback from clients and partners.* The BEP coordinates two groups to address the needs of clients and stakeholders: the BEP Consultative Forum and the BEP Advisory Committee. Both are part of the BEP's governance structure as endorsed by Federal Cabinet in 1998. The BEP Consultative Forum provides an opportunity to discuss and resolve issues impacting partner and user participation in elements of the BEP program. It also keeps stakeholders up to date with developments and enables the exchange of information among members. Members are drawn from federal and State government agencies, industry, business and professional associations and local government. The purpose of the BEP Advisory Committee is to influence the direction of the BEP and provide guidance to the BEP's decision-making process. Members represent government agencies, business and industry associations. Three to four meetings are held each year.

Decisions about relevant business themes have been made following market research among businesses and intermediaries (accountants, advisers, etc.), as well as feedback received directly from businesses through the BEP's "e-mail a business question" facility. The BEP also offers a useful "jargon buster" on its home page, which provides definitions of government, business and computing terms that clients may come across when dealing with government over the Internet.

Qualitative research has been undertaken among business clients to assess the value of the syndication content. Feedback on this has been very positive. Businesses see considerable value in providing information grouped under headings that relate to specific business activities.

- *Managing partnerships.* During the early conceptual stages, a small number of government agencies raised some minor concerns. These were based on the assumption that in syndicating aggregated information, the BEP might be either directing traffic away from other sites or breaching the copyright of material owned by other government agencies. In reality, the syndication project drives considerably more traffic to other government sites simply because information about

> those sites is now available through many more access points. In addition, the syndicated content consists of a general description of a government service or resource and a link leading directly to that resource. Such content does not lead back to the BEP but directly to other government agencies. Through consultation and regular briefing with Commonwealth and State agencies, concerns about the project have been alleviated.

When the BEP was established in 1998, it forged relationships with government in each state and territory. These relationships continue. An advisory committee comprised of representatives from each state and territory government, as well as other federal government stakeholders, oversees the BEP initiative as a whole.

After

The syndication project has received full commitment and support from Ministers and senior management. Arrangements with partnering organizations are managed through a memorandum of understanding that sets out responsibilities so that the content is always available, maintained and current. Partners maintain responsibility for ensuring the content integrity (i.e., not changed in any way when published on partner sites), currency and appropriate branding. The MOUs also include a mutual disclaimer of liability, and BEP insists that partners provide links to its disclaimer, privacy and copyright statements.

The syndication process has been running since July 2002, although not all partners have been publishing content since that time. At this point, no evaluation has taken place among business users. However, feedback from syndication partners is very positive. Over the next six to eight months, BEP plans to undertake more market research in conjunction with syndication partners. It also intends to develop an interactive CD-ROM that will enable potential partners to better understand the benefits of the project without the need for initial face-to-face communication.

From the client's perspective, the BEP effectively makes redundant the challenge of understanding which level of government offers which service in Australia. The service is not only more convenient to the client but dramatically reduces the time normally taken to fill in government forms, as the "Transaction Manager" enables clients to store relevant details in a client profile that can pre-fill and complete online forms as they become available.

This provides a useful information management service for the client whose records of inquiries, completed transactions and associated receipt numbers are managed in one Web page through the online history tool. Also, the non-governmental partnerships that BEP has struck allow the client to easily access related business services in the private sector and thus enrich the value of the electronic service offering.

Lessons Learned and Key Success Factors

- *Build strong partnerships*. Strong partnerships are integral to the success of the BEP and the syndication initiative. While these partnerships are governed, to a certain extent, by formal agreements, the strong sense of mutual benefit among partners is a key factor of success in the program. If governments are perceived as trying to bypass or take over services traditionally offered by other organizations, they will diminish the support they need to make collaborative systems like the BEP work.

- *Innovate and commit to continuous improvement.* While the BEP consistently achieves good results in overall business and government Web rankings, management and staff are continuously looking at innovative ways to improve processes and to offer businesses new opportunities to make effective use of online technologies. Other government ministries and stakeholders have been kept informed of progress throughout the project and consulted regularly.
- *Get feedback from clients and give it to partners.* The BEP is developing a strong process of recruiting and circulating relevant information that will assist in improving client satisfaction and solidifying partner commitment. As more reporting tools are brought on-stream (i.e., the recently introduced URL "bounce" system), partners will receive real-time feedback on client use of their online services. BEP's advisory structures bring together the owners and users of business information provided through the BEP syndicated network.

Transactional E-Government Crossing Jurisdictional Boundaries: One-Stop Business Registration, Canada

Responsibilities for registering a business in Canada reside with both the federal and provincial/territorial levels of government. However, municipal and regional governments can also have licensing responsibilities in this area. Several governments in Canada have collaborated to create a common electronic service delivery application to allow their common clients to simultaneously complete most registration and filing requirements with the appropriate levels of government.

The federal government is collaborating with several provinces in developing and delivering cross-jurisdictional business registration services. In some cases, these projects are linked to business tax payment and business change of address applications. This case study focuses on the development and implementation of one such program in the province of British Columbia: the *OneStop* Business Registration service.[23]

Before

The *OneStop* program originated following discussions held by British Columbia's former Ministry of Small Business, Tourism and Culture (MSBTC) with small businesses in the province regarding red-tape reduction. In discussions with the Minister in 1994, the small business sector complained about the complex process to register a small business in Canada, which, in British Columbia, involved several different agencies at three different levels of government (federal, provincial and municipal). Establishing a business tax account (federal and provincial), registering with the Workers' Compensation Board, registering a new business (provincial) and securing operating licenses (municipal) were cited as key examples where information had to be filed separately. The business sector called for collaboration and an integrated solution that would effectively harmonize the information needs of business registration programs within the levels of government and reduce the complexity of the process.

The Minister agreed to champion a solution focused on allowing businesses to simultaneously register for required licenses and accounts at different levels of government. Given the Ministry's concurrent interests in augmenting its electronic service offerings to businesses, it was agreed that an ICT solution would be sought at the outset to solve the problem.

The Transformation Project

The Ministry established a vision for the project and objectives that sought to reduce red tape, paper burden and administrative costs for business clients and the government. The fundamental vision of the program was to design and deliver a process that would allow a new business to enter business application information once into an integrated system. It also aimed to have that information accepted by the federal, provincial and municipal government agencies that shared authority over various business registration filing requirements and associated permits. The program initially started as an integrated extranet system within government offices, requiring registrants to physically come to a government office to make the application on government computer terminals. Then, in May 2002, the program was introduced through in an online application channel accessible from home or office Internet connections.

Implementation Factors

- *Developing the process for collaboration.* The commitment to approach the project on the basis of intergovernmental cooperation was significant given that there was no coordinated intergovernmental forum or liaison on these issues. Nor was there any push by Ministers to cooperate in this area. Similarly, inside the provincial government no formal process existed to encourage inter-ministry cooperation. This was significant because the sponsoring ministry, MSBTC, did not actually own the key business registration programs. These resided in the federal Canada Customs and Revenue Agency (CCRA), provincial Ministry of Finance and Corporate Relations, Ministry of Provincial Revenue, British Columbia Workers' Compensation Board and various municipal governments.

MSBTC chose to approach the key federal department in this area — CCRA — to see how the provincial government's business registration process could be aligned with the CCRA's business tax requirements. The CCRA was also interested in collaborating with provincial/territorial governments on tax policy and tax compliance issues. Securing the support of a key "anchor tenant" for a collaboration process assisted in bringing other ministries on board at all levels of government. Similarly, MSBTC chose to partner with the 12 municipalities constituting the Greater Victoria region (the provincial capital) and five other municipalities as pilot projects to integrate the service.

- *Building the partnership: Start small and build momentum.* Having secured commitments to collaborate from a major partner, MSBTC strategically paced the project roll-out, keeping the number of partner agencies at a manageable level to ensure that pilot projects could be delivered successfully and create momentum for additional partner subscriptions. In the initial phases, the partnership was quite informal, with officials securing required commitments from their ministries. Operating within existing budgets and management authorities allowed agencies to come to the table without fear that their budgets could be negatively affected or accountabilities changed. However, as momentum was established, the need to formalize the arrangement became pressing.

As the number of government partners increased, *OneStop* extended its reach to include private sector agencies such as Chambers of Commerce and domain name registries to provide a more extensive list of partners and services to new businesses.

- *Moving along the e-service maturity curve.* While MSBTC had committed to develop a Web-enabled product offering full transactional capabilities, other partners were satisfied, at least initially, with publishing their forms online for clients to print, fill out and return by fax or mail. This presented a service delivery challenge, as some partners would be offering services at the transactional end of the continuum while others remained at the more elementary print-and-fill end. To encourage migration to the *OneStop* channel, the partners committed to delivering faster approvals and responses for applications delivered through the OneStop channel than the phone and counter channels.
- *Business culture issues: "We're not going to change our form?"* The project involved harmonizing the client information data requirements on a variety of business registration forms. In some instances, partners argued that their agencies had unique requirements, sometimes enshrined in legislation that prevented them from changing their particular forms to conform to a common standard. Others demanded an ink signature on the business application. MSBTC respectfully challenged these positions from its position as a neutral sponsor, given that it did not own any particular application where it could be perceived to be forcing others to align to its systems. It also allowed the Ministry to serve as a broker for solutions – for example, convening a joint application development process with six municipal governments that resulted in the adoption of a common business license application process that required no ink signature. This solution has now been spread to 65 local government partners, as signature requirements have now been removed from all partner application forms.
- *Legislation.* The move to electronic signatures and Internet-based payment on business applications required a change in several pieces of provincial legislation relating to e-signatures and payment procedures. These legislative barriers had to be identified early to ensure that they could be made in time so as to not hold up implementation. (In fact, implementation of the Internet-based service was delayed for a few weeks until the provincial legislature could pass the required legislation.)

After

The *OneStop* Business Registration Project has transformed the process of starting up a business in British Columbia. With integrated, Web-enabled access to the application requirements and business assistance services of more than 200 public and private sector agencies, it is hard to imagine how such a service could be offered in a non-e-government environment. There has been a rapid uptake of *OneStop*'s Internet-based service since it was introduced in May 2002, and over 40% of new business applications are now done over the Internet from home or office locations. Moreover, 30% of these applicants have used the system after conventional government office hours, allowing the partners to get a good measure of 24/7 demand for government services.

OneStop surveys its clients with online questionnaires at the end of each application. It is important to solicit quick feedback, because most applicants use the service only once, given that business registration is not a repeated function. More than 75% of users of the program have responded to these questionnaires with 96% rating the service as either good or excellent. The feedback section of the survey also allows business applicants that have just been through the process to provide ideas for further improvement.

OneStop's success has allowed the partnership to evolve into new ventures that would not have been imaginable before this project. For example, the three levels of government have now developed a common business number for business clients. In May 2004, the common business identifier, across all levels of government and partners, along with an enhanced *OneStop* Business Address Change service was implemented at a new Web site: *www.bcbucinessregistry.ca.*

Lessons Learned and Key Success Factors

- *If you don't have a process, invent one.* The *OneStop* project would not have succeeded unless operational-level partnerships were established with key players. If the project champions had to "wait" for their political or senior-official masters to design a collaboration process, they would probably still be waiting.
- *Neutrality of the champion/sponsor.* There is merit in having a neutral champion or sponsor of the program. MSBTC's interests here were in streamlining applications processes for its clients. However, the Ministry did not own any of the application processes in question. Hence, it was in a position to challenge the orthodoxy of forms and related issues from a position of no vested interest and could not be accused of trying to convert other partners to their way of doing things.
- *Start small and build the momentum.* The success of the program was greatly advanced by an early decision to actually limit the number of partners and services in the start-up phase to ensure sufficient project management focus on the pilot projects. The resultant pilots' success fueled momentum for the program, allowing the management team to scale up the program with the addition of new partners at a realistic pace.
- *Recruit external validation and feedback immediately after the client has completed the transaction.* In this case, it is vital to capture the client after the *OneStop* experience, as business registration, by its nature, is usually a one-time event. The feedback mechanism provides real-time customer satisfaction data and valuable feedback for process improvement.

CONCLUSIONS

These case studies highlight several promising trends that exemplify the transformational capacity of ICTs in e-government applications. The lessons learned, outlined at the conclusion of these studies, summarize some of the key contributors to the success of the initiatives examined to date.

While difficult to generalize conclusions over the diverse range of case studies examined, several common points emerge as being effective contributors to capturing the transformational benefits of e-government initiatives. Many of these factors deal with changes in the culture and business practices of governments rather than the structure of administrations.

- *Be prepared to support risk and innovation.* Transformational projects, by definition, seek to fundamentally change the status quo. In some electronic service delivery applications, these types of projects offer the citizen/client a value-added service or mode of access to such a service that could not be easily replicated in a non-electronic form. Such projects break new ground and require risk and innovation. However, the intense spotlight of public accountability prevailing over public administrations is more likely to breed a culture of risk-aversion rather than risk-taking. Some government leaders clearly have been prepared to take risk over internal resistance. Others have created special environments or collaborative structures that offer a safe place to innovate.
- *Facilitate change through collaboration among peers and clients.* Transformational projects in the back-office or infrastructure layers of government may be driven by broad government objectives. However, a thoughtful process of facilitating and encouraging change utilizing peer engagement rather than central agency command enhances their ultimate success. Such an approach ensures that issues are addressed in a collaborative environment and that ownership of the ultimate project or process is broadly shared. While centrally mandated ICT standards and processes are important in driving e-government, the development of these products and activities can be done collaboratively among peers to ensure broader buy-in. Respecting agency autonomy and authority over budgets and business programs sends a strong signal that e-government is intended to enable agencies to do their jobs better rather than command them to do their jobs electronically.
- *Take the opportunity to re-engineer business processes while developing new e-government applications.* Transformative e-government is not about automating existing business processes. It is about using ICTs to fundamentally change the way business is conducted and service is delivered. Several of the case studies examined have conducted a simultaneous business process re-engineering exercise while developing new e-government applications. This process has, in some cases, required changes to administrative business practices. Others have committed to continuous improvement objectives that extend throughout the implementation process.
- *Attend to the pace of transformation and build momentum from success.* Project managers have often realized that transformational service platforms could be jeopardized if forced to carry too much weight in early days. An approach that focuses on a limited number of key pilot projects and ensures that sufficient

management attention is paid to their development is more likely to succeed. With each successful project, the foundations of the e-government platform are strengthened, enabling additional partners' projects to be adopted. This can be characterized as a "start-small, succeed-and-then-scale-up" approach. Similarly, fundamental changes in the internal structures and processes of government should be announced and implemented quickly, but given the benefit of a reasonable length of time to work before any future revisions are considered;

- *Communicating change is a key factor in successful change.* Internal to government, transformational e-government initiatives, by definition, change the status quo. Change can be threatening to officials in other service delivery channels if they fear that the introduction or augmentation of an electronic service delivery channels jeopardizes their jobs and programs. Similarly, if e-government initiatives are launched in the context of an overall downsizing environment or a public service reform initiative, these concerns could manifest themselves more broadly through the organization. Communications in support of change must address such concerns, especially since in some cases, those responsible for explaining directions may feel threatened themselves.

External to government, attention should be given to marketing new e-government applications to citizen/clients to encourage their adoption and use. Applications that provide full end-to-end transactional capacity and that allow citizens and clients to do things they could not feasibly do with government through more conventional service channels merit special profile. These are the transformational drivers of e-government. Attention should be paid to the actual wording and communications of directions to the citizen/client in new electronic service-delivery applications, so that the scripts are kept as simple and technically jargon-free as possible.

- *Recruit and incorporate citizen/client feedback fully and quickly.* Several of the case studies examined paid great attention to recruiting the feedback of citizen/client users and incorporating these ideas into re-engineered business processes. In transactional applications, efforts have been made to capture the customers at the conclusion of a transaction to provide real-time reports of customer satisfaction. Other initiatives have directly involved prospective application customers in the actual design and development of new electronic service offerings. In any event, quick and thorough recruitment of customer feedback serves several purposes in improving services, engaging the customer's interest in accessing future e-government applications and validating e-government initiatives from the perspective of the customer;
- *Increase transparency and accountability by measuring and reporting progress.* A commitment to measuring progress, benchmarking against external indicators and reporting to government leaders and the public makes transformational projects more transparent and accountable. Public reporting also serves as a marketing tool to encourage broader utilization of e-government applications. Benchmarking against peer group standards can assist in supporting internally focused transformation where a new e-government initiative is challenging or changing existing authority structures, roles and responsibilities.

REFERENCES

Publications

Accenture Consulting. (2002). *e-Government Leadership – Realizing the Vision.*

Bertelsmann Foundation. (2002). *E-government: Connecting Efficient.* Administration and Responsive Democracy. Gütersloh, Germany.

Caldow, J. (2001). *Seven e-government leadership milestones.* IBM Institute for E-government. Washington, DC. Retrieved October 5, 2002, from *http://houns54.clearlake.ibm.com/solutions/government/govpub.nsf/Files/egov_milestones/$File/egov_milestones.pdf*

Commonwealth Centre for Electronic Governance, Commonwealth Secretariat, London. (2002). *E-government 2002: Part II Applications of e-government in five countries and a review of electronic democracy.* Retrieved June 30, 2004, from *http://www.electronicgov.net/pubs/research_papers/index.shtml*

Case Study References and Resources

In many cases, information for the case studies was gathered through personal interviews with officials involved. These interviews are noted, where appropriate, in footnotes in the respective case studies. Published and Web-based material used as resources for the studies were as follows.

Engaging the Citizen in a "New" Government: The Scottish Parliament

Scottish Office. (1998). Shaping Scotland's Parliament: Report of the Consultative Steering Committee on the Scottish Parliament. Retrieved June 30, 2004, from *http://www.scotland.gov.uk/library/documents-w5/rcsg-00.htm*

Government of Scotland. Scottish Parliament Website. Retrieved June 30, 2004, from *http://www.scottish.Parliament.uk/index.html*

United Kingdom Parliament, Parliamentary Office of Science and Technology. (1998). *Electronic Government: Information Technologies and the Citizen.* Retrieved October 2, 2002, from *http://www.Parliament.uk/post/9802.htm*

Changing the Delivery Model for ICT Infrastructure: Shared ICT Infrastructure Services in the Province of British Columbia, Canada.

Government of British Columbia, Ministry of Management Services, Common IT Services Division. Retrieved from *https/cits.gov.bc.ca/*

Government of British Columbia, Ministry of Management Services, Shared Services Initiative and discussion paper. Retrieved October 1, 2002, from *http://www.mser.gov.bc.ca/bcss/*

Changing the Governance and Management Model for ICTs: Corporate and "Cluster" CIO Functions in the Province of Ontario, Canada.

Government of Ontario, Management Board Secretariat. (1998). *Using information technology to transform government for the 21st century.* Toronto, Ontario.

Government of Ontario, Cabinet Office, Restructuring Secretariat. (2000). *Working together – An integrated organisation.* Toronto, Ontario.

Government of Ontario, Management Board Secretariat, Office of the Corporate Chief Information Officer. (2002, August). *Leading the way – Transforming the information and information technology organisation of the Ontario Public Service (Draft Paper).* Toronto, Ontario.

Encouraging Cooperation in Cross-government Business Application Development: Digital Government Applications Academy, State of Washington, USA.

State of Washington, USA, Department of Information Services. Digital Government Applications Academy. Retrieved June 30, 2004, from *http://www.wa.gov/dis/academy/*

Douglas, M. (2001, April). E-government 101. *Government Technology Magazine.*

Transforming the Relationship With Business Suppliers to government: E-procurement Reform, Ministero dell'Economia e delle Finanze, Government of Italy.

Ministero dell'Economia e delle Finanze Website. Retrieved June 30, 2004, from *http://www.acquistinretepa.it/servlet/page?_pageid=57&_dad=portal30&_schema=PORTAL30&macrosection= off&p_subid=7244&p_sub_siteid=74&menu=7244*

Microsoft Corporation, Case Study. Retrieved June 30, 2004, from *www.microsoft.com/resources/casestudies/CaseStudy.asp?CaseStudyID=13031*

Transforming the Business Relationship With the Citizen/Client Through End-to-End Transactional Services: Motor Vehicle Licensing Services, State of Arizona, USA.

State of Arizona, USA, Motor Vehicle Department, Service Arizona Website. Retrieved June 30, 2004, from *http://www. servicearizona.com/*

Symonds, M. (2000, June 22). Government and the Internet: The Next Revolution. *The Economist.*

Bundling Public and Private Electronic Services to Better Serve the Citizen/Client: Business Entry Point, Government of Australia

Government of Australia, Department of Industry, Tourism and Resources, Business Entry Point Home page. Retrieved June 30, 2004, from *http://www.business.gov.au/BEP2002/Home/*

Transactional E-government Crossing Jurisdictional Boundaries: One-Stop Business Registration, Canada

Government of British Columbia, Ministry of Finance Website. Retrieved June 30, 2004 from the World Wide Web at: *http://www.onestopbc.ca/.*

ENDNOTES

1 BERTELSMANN FOUNDATION, *E-government: Connecting Efficient Administration and Responsive Democracy,* Bertelsmann Foundation (2002).

2 *http://www.scotland.gov.uk/government/devolution/scpa-00.asp.*

3 Scottish Office, *Shaping Scotland's Parliament: Report of the Consultative Steering Committee on the Scottish Parliament,* December 1998 – Section 2.4.

4 Shaping Scotland's Parliament – Annex J.

5 *http://www.scottish.Parliament.uk/official_report/cttee/petit99-00/petitfrm.html*

6 *http://www.e-petitioner.org.uk/*

7 The link to the operations and services of government as provided by the Scottish Executive is: *http://www.scotland.gov.uk/pages/default.aspx*

8 Government of Ontario, *Using Information Technology to Transform Government for the 21st Century,* Management Board Secretariat (March 1998).

9 This strategy was eventually published in 2000: *Working Together – An Integrated Organisation.*

10 Clusters formed were: Community Services (including Education); Economics/ Business (including Labour and Economic Development); Central Agencies (including Finance and Management Board); Human Services (including Health and Family Services); Justice (including Attorney General and Public Safety); Land/ Resources (including Agriculture, Environment, Energy and natural Resources) and Transportation (including Highways).

11 Based on an estimated $ 750 million CAD ICT budget, this represented a less than 5% increase. However, given the significant budget cuts being delivered overt that period, an increase in budget was rare. What was key here was that officials were successful in securing a net new funding for e-government vs. the contention that e-government would reap immediate savings that could be drawn from to invest in further activities.

12 Merrill Douglas, E-government 101, *Government Technology* Magazine (April, 2001).

13 State of Washington, Department of Information Services. *The Applications Academy Charter*, at: *www.wa.government/dis/academy/charter/htm.* (As retrieved 29 December 2004 from the World Wide Web.).

14 Seminars generally take place one day per week over 12 weeks.

15 Interview with Dave Kirk, Manager, Digital Government Applications Academy (September, 2002).

16 Italian e-government action plan as quoted in "*Financial aspects of e-government implementation in Italy*" OECD E-government Project Short Paper (June 2002 seminar), OECD PUMA E-government project Website at: *http://Webdomino1.oecd.org/comnet/pum/egovtf.nsf/Documents/[022]%20June%20Seminar%20-%20Summaries/$File/June%20Seminar%20-%20Financing%20Summary.pdf*

17 Ministero dell'Economia e delle Finanze Website at: *http://www.acquistinretepa.it/servlet/page?_pageid=57&_dad=portal30&_schema=PORTAL30&macrosection=off&p_subid=7244&p_sub_siteid=74&menu=7244*

18 Ministero dell'Economia e delle Finanze at: *www.acquistinretepa.it*

19 The Economist, *Government and the Internet: The Next Revolution,* June 22, 2000.

20 Data provided in an interview with Penny Martucci, Arizona Department of Transportation, Motor Vehicle Division (September, 2002).

21 Much of the background for this case study was drawn from e-mail correspondence with Barbara Grundy, Manager, BEP Syndication, Web and Marketing, e-Business Division, Department of Industry, Tourism & Resources (September, 2002).

22 *www.business.gov.au*

23 Much of the background for this case study was drawn from interviews in September 2002 with Mike Cowley, then-Director, OneStop Business Registry Project, Government of British Columbia.

Chapter VII

Measuring E-Government in Italy

Marcella Corsi, LUISS G. Carli, Italy

ABSTRACT

This chapter describes our experience in establishing an Observatory for the measurement of the impact of e-government policies onto the efficiency and the effectiveness of the Italian public sector. Such an Observatory is based on evaluation procedures different from those used in other measurement exercises, such as e-*Europe or those belonging to the Big Five consultant groups. Moreover, the adopted definition of "e-government" is slightly different than the usual one, as it takes into account not only the mere providing of e-services, but also the whole impact of ICT in terms of transformation of Public Administration — both at a "front-" and at a "back-office" level. What has made us think about a new evaluation method is the desire for a standard, transparent (i.e., one that everyone understands) system, which, while it takes into account the overall level of e-government, the type and number of online services, and their ease of access and quality, also considers policy actions which flavor the spread of electronic government applications, both inside and outside the public sector.*

INTRODUCTION

ICT is opening new and interesting scenarios in terms of the relationship between citizens, businesses, and Public Administrations (PA). These agents now have to interact more than ever among them, using the advanced systems which technological progress has put at their disposal, with an undeniable increase in efficiency and effectiveness.

E-government is making giant strides in all the most advanced corners of the globe, laying down the first technological substrate for the Digital Society to be able to come about. As far as Italy is concerned, this process is to be seen in the many innovations from 1997 onwards which have characterised changes in the PA, whether in its internal and external dealings, or — more precisely — with a view to bringing them into line with Italy's decentralization and development requirements. These two trends when taken together (local government computerization and restructuring) are the most powerful motor for change in the public sector.

The models currently being used to evaluate the impact of these two drivers of change, however, do not seem wholly adequate, and they can be broken down into two groups: (a) those which measure the state of advancement of online services, as is the case with *e*-Europe benchmarking, and (b) those which tend to make more "qualitative" judgements, although still only in online services, and their completeness and sophistication, as is the case with the methods developed by the Big Five consultant groups. In both cases, something is missing from these approaches. The first type of measurement risks tying the judgement of transaction-type evolution in innovation strategies to the provision of a series of public services, but completely leaving out, for example, any measurement of how widespread the service is, how it is carried out, or how closely it measures up to what the constituency actually need. The second type of method is a little more "obscure," given that it measures parameters which private companies do not fully publicize. The danger here is that judgements about the "overall maturity" of online public services often mean the questionable reduction of some countries to second-class status.

What has made us think about a new evaluation method then is the desire for a standard, transparent (*i.e.,* one that everyone understands) system, which, while it takes into account the overall level of e-government, the type and number of online services, and their ease of access and quality, also considers policy actions which flavor the spread of electronic government applications, both inside and outside the public sector.

In an area which is undergoing such rapid evolution, laying the foundations for measuring what the impact of new technology on the PA is (and especially what it will be), it is vital that the future policy direction of central and local government be measured. With such a long-term view, then, an Observatory has been established within the Italian Office for the Innovation of the Public Administration (UIPA) in order to examine the impact of ICT on the PA, taking into account all impulse, control, and updating policies for the paths the Italian PA will have to undertake to improve its internal and external efficiency.

The guiding objective in the early stages of the project is to work with a restricted number of central and local PAs in order to see how well the model could work, so that the civil servants involved could evaluate performance improvements brought about by the introduction of new technology. Any improvements would be both in the provision of a public service (mainly to citizens and business, but also to other branches of local and central government), and in increased efficiency within the PAs themselves. In the long term, when the model has proven to be effectively able to show the main reasons for change brought about by the introduction of ICT in the PA, the Observatory could help policy makers in the decision-making process, as the real effect of efficiency policies could be shown to each and every branch of local and central government.

STRUCTURE OF THE CHAPTER

When considering the impact of ICT on the PA, both at a "front-" and at a "back-office" level, we specifically decided to try to find the cause and effect of improvements in effectiveness.

In this direction, we came across three different kinds of assessment to be made:

- Service level to constituents (e.g., Is the service what they need? Are they using it? Does it provide greater value at the lower cost than off-line service?)
- Operational efficiency (e.g., Are online transactions reducing government costs?)
- Macroeconomic return (e.g., Is e-government increasing consensus? Are there any positive effects on the economy and the society at large?)

Based on the experience we have gained up to now, this chapter is divided into three main sections.

The first section looks at the effectiveness of the single service. We do not refer just to online services, but namely to every public service provided through seven main channels (desk, telephone/fax/call center, mobile or wireless systems, Web, ATM, Digital TV and, finally, through an intermediary). The model we describe tries to recognize the way in which the introduction of e-government policies can improve the performance of every one of these channels. This choice has been made also to consider the desiderata of every part of the constituency (citizens, enterprises and PAs), which seem to expect a wide range of supplying ways. Moreover, we try to stress the importance of the introduction of some welfare consideration, based upon a segmentation within the constituency, and the confrontation of the "social cost" users bear to obtain a service and its "value" (as users attribute to it).

The second section focuses on the operational efficiency of the public sector. After having considered every single service, the outcome of the evaluation should be taken into account as a whole, referred to any single administration, in order to evaluate the average internal efficiency of the PA, and the structural transformation induced by the introduction of the ICT (personnel reduction and/or mobility, cost savings, technological investments, reductions of "delivery" time and so on). In order to measure this second kind of parameters, we try to establish a "self-assessment tool" for every administration, in order to take into account PAs' "actual experience," *that is,* the feedback they receive from the intended categories of users.

The third section deals with the estimation of the macroeconomic return of e-government. Even if at a very early stage, the Observatory tries to evaluate the socio-economic impact that a more efficient public sector may have, especially at a local level. First of all, this chapter looks at the improvement in terms of "technological cohesion" among different members of the constituency (citizens, enterprises, government), which could be caused by the spreading of e-government. Afterwards, an attempt is made to emphasize what kind of parameters should be considered in the future to build up a consistent dataset for regressions.

ASSESSING CONSTITUENT SERVICE LEVELS

In our analysis, we try to classify services according to three characteristics: *depth, maturity and efficiency*. The "depth" of a service mainly refers to the number of channels used for providing it and the kind of constituency that it is targeted for. "Maturity" looks at how advanced services are in terms of level of interaction. "Efficiency" implies some welfare considerations based upon the confrontation of the "social cost" users bear to obtain a service and its "value" (as users attribute to it), as well as more "traditional" measures of service availability and dynamicity.

Depth of a Service

How the Service is Provided

By contrast with *e*-Europe, the definition of e-government used in our model does not merely look at the provision of online services. Instead, we consider the application of advanced technology both at a "front-" and at a "back-office" level. At the base of this approach, then, is the idea that new technology can improve efficiency within the PA and bring services closer to the public, not just by increasing the number of online services provided, but also by improving the efficiency of operations carried out via other channels.

Every service is therefore classified according to whether they are present in one of the following channels: desk, telephone or facsimile, mobile phone or *wireless* system, ATM, Internet, digital TV, or another intermediary. The availability of the service through several channels is added to by indications of the effective use that is made of the channels, based on the number of transactions carried out.[1] Particular attention is given to the comparison between online and other types of channels. Indeed, it will become possible to measure how much a completely online channel brings about a reduction in other channels, and to see exactly which ones.

These are important considerations, for at least two reasons. Firstly, although online channels may well be the objective in innovation policy objectives, in the medium term it might actually be better to keep many channels open to narrow the digital divide, which is seen in certain sectors of society. In this sense, the bringing in of new technology alongside more traditional channels would guarantee both efficiency improvements and a better range of services for the widest possible range of users. Secondly, the movement of users between channels, and in particular the use of online services, is on the one hand a direct indicator of the quality of electronically provided services (and thus of e-government policies). On the other hand, it is an indirect indicator of the ability of other policies (concerning education, infrastructures, or consciousness-raising) to drag people towards a more mature use of new technology.

The Kind of Constituency the Service is Intended For

Our model looks closely at the division into types of constituency, although at the moment this is done indirectly. This aspect is particularly important when considering certain welfare problems.

Generally speaking, a service can be offered to citizens (C), businesses (B), or government departments (G). Furthermore, when considering special services used by departmental operators (*e.g.*, viewing a database at the Land Registry), there are also services for staff (E).

Alongside this widely used classification, we would like to adopt one of our own, which looks more closely at the kind of dealings which occur among the different users involved. In this sense, (C) may broadly define the expected constituency, whether citizens, business, or other PAs, when dealings with the provider are of the "consumer" type (e.g., a person or firm who applies for a licence, or a Local Authority that wants a health certificate from a Health Service Trust). (B) and (G) identify dealings concerning the "productive" activity of the PA, such as a company which supplies a particular PA department or, in an "integrated" service, two PAs which exchange information via the Internet.

Maturity of Services

The level of effectiveness induced by the use in the PA of new technology is often directly proportional to the level of maturity of the services on offer. To explain this observation, we must shed some light on what we mean by "maturity" and explain why it may be spoken of only in certain cases and only for certain channels.

With particular reference to online services, we have classified these according to their state of advancement, a subdivision similar to that carried out under *e*-Europe and the one adopted by OECD. In general, a service provided without a desk channel can be catalogued according to the following categories.

Information-type state (1st): only information about access to the service is provided (the opening hours of a local government office, for example). No form of interaction is possible.

One-way interaction state (2nd): the user may download a form, but this must be filled in and sent back at a later stage (such as, for example, a form used to inform the Local Authority of an official change of address).

Two-way interaction state (3rd): the user may open an electronic form, fill it in, and send it back electronically (as is currently happening with personal details via the Web).

Transaction-type state (4th): unlike the simpler two-way interaction, this state guarantees not only the uploading of data, but also their real-time processing. A particularly good example is to be seen with online economic transactions, such as the payment of taxes and local rates.[2]

Integrated-type state (5th): this category is even more complicated, based as it is on the open exchange of information between various government branches. Here, information networks of the various PA departments work together to provide a neutral service for the user, thus "taking an enormous weight off the shoulders" of those administrations who currently provide the service. It can involve either two-way or transactional traffic.

It can therefore be seen how measurement of the various "service states" looks primarily at online services, and their interactive abilities, and — where this has been adequately implemented — how safe the servers are for users to send sensitive information across. It must be said, though, that other channels (mobile/wireless more and more, but also digital television and the telephone) can provide services which are not merely giving out information. Measuring this element for any channel (except the desk) will let us monitor how things will evolve over time independently on the channel used today.

Efficiency of Services

Welfare Considerations

Two special indicators allow us to make mention of the *welfare* impact of e-government, which undoubtedly comes to the fore in technology policies in the PA.[3] For each service, an *average social cost* and an *average service value* (for the constituency) must be defined.

The *average social cost* of a service measures how much its provision "costs" the end-user. To obtain this value, an approximation is made by multiplying the average waiting time per channel, "weighted" by the percentage every channel is used, by the average opportunity cost per user. The formula is as follows:

$$ASC = \Sigma(\text{average waiting time per channel} * \%\ \text{use of channel}) * \Sigma(\text{average hourly remuneration per user category} * \%\ \text{user category})$$

Briefly, a weighted average is calculated for each service. This is obtained by working with the relative PA department to find out what average waiting times are per channel,[4] how much each channel is used, and then calculating the cost in money terms, by using an opportunity cost. This is connected, on the one hand, to an objective element (average hourly remuneration per user category taken from nation-wide statistics), and on the other hand to an analysis of the percentages of user categories using the service (this information must be provided by the PA departments involved). Once a series of money values have been obtained, they are "standardized," *i.e.*, converted to an absolute scale of values. In this way they can be compared with the *average service value* per user, which *per se* is only indicative of the quality of a service.

The *average service value* is a service measurement for those who use a particular service. In discussions to date, this indicator has been one of the biggest problems encountered within the Observatory. At a first glance, we thought to calculate an "objective" (money) value by looking at services provided by intermediaries, almost as the sum paid to a middleman represented an "opportunity cost" for the end user, and could be associated with the value he/she gave the service provided (usually to speed things up). We did not think this solution was very good, first of all because not all services can be obtained via a middleman and, secondly, because the cost of a middleman can change according to outside influences (such as inflation, the elasticity of demand for a service, *etc.*), and thus limits the objectivity of the indicator obtained in this way.

We feel the best solution currently available would be to involve PA departments to define a table of "perceived values" for each service they provide, according to the kind of constituency. Although it is very subjective, this method appears to be the only way to take into account PAs' "actual experience," i.e., the feedback they receive from the intended categories of users. As well as this, our option seems to be much more economic than a poll obtained by "sampling" the users themselves. The *average service value* should therefore be an indicator provided by PAs' self-assessment, according to a scale of values which can be compared with the cost of the service (which is "standardized" on purpose).

The final result should be the finding, for every service examined, of a ratio between average service value and its social cost, which we have called the *value/cost ratio*, which may be considered a measure of "external efficiency" for the PA. Over time, in fact, it should be checked, at least for the most important services for the constituency, whether any innovation brought about by technological and administrative changes would modify the ratio related to their provision.

However, no simple interpretation can ever be possible here. Indeed, *if the value/cost ratio increases*, any changes over time will only be important as far as the perceived *value* remains constant (or better increases), and the *cost* decreases. Where the ratio increases due to an *increased value*, with *cost* remaining the same, the situation would be rather negative, given that the PA would appear unable to improve its procedures in order to provide greater access to a service whose value is increasing. *If the value/cost ratio decreases*, the policy implications of a negative situation where *value* remains constant (or worse decreases) and *costs* increase are quite straightforward. The problem arises with constant *cost* and decreasing *value*: the reduction of cost could be meaningless, since the value of the service is on a downward trend.

As well as similar dilemmas, we could add other difficulties by types of constituency. For example, by distinguishing between entrepreneurs and housewives, even more complicated results could be obtained for the "value" and "cost" of a service. By choosing an "average" value (for the moment at least), we have tried to avoid these complications.

Leaving aside for the moment the great amount of attention this indicator might receive, we must also mention the importance of intuition that it requires, i.e., when allocating resources for new technology, the PAs cannot ignore the impact this will have on users. Unlike what has usually been done up to now, a self-assessment tool such as the one we are describing here could give useful information on how to invest in ICT, especially when considering who the various services are intended for. This will mainly benefit efficiency improvements for services where efficiency is important, and this makes a lot of sense where the PA's budget must be considered. Furthermore, such an indicator should take into consideration how the constituency will use them. For example, a department must evaluate whether or not to invest in new technology which will reduce waiting times via a traditional channel rather than promoting policies which shift the demand for services onto faster channels, such as the Internet.

ASSESSING PA OPERATIONAL EFFICIENCY

Moving away from *e*-Europe type of measurement, our Observatory tries to measure the impact of new technology, not simply on services provided (and therefore from a "front-office" point of view), but rather on the consequences of the application of ICT at the "back-office" level, *i.e.*, within the PA itself, which is considered as the "apparatus" which must react in different ways with the type of constituency for whom the various services have been set up.

In the previous section, we have dealt with "external efficiency" induced by new technology, and we now move on to talk about methods for measuring how innovations bring about "internal" or "operational efficiency." When moving on to look at this aspect, we shall no longer consider the services taken individually, but rather the local or central government department which provides them. To do this, we shall bear in mind certain things, including: internal efficiency (in terms of costs), induced restructuring, and the integration level between the various type of constituency.

Internal Efficiency

Just as one of the main aspects of external efficiency was *welfare*, when speaking of internal efficiency induced by new technology the effects on transactions are a crucial point. As well as this, the trade off between this type of operational efficiency and welfare effects may create the greatest amount of policy questions.

Internal efficiency can be measured by three parameters: the *cost per completed transaction*, the *number of transactions per employee* (civil servant), and the *average transaction time* (i.e., the time required to carry out a transaction, on average).

Before moving on to a more detailed description of these indicators, we must mention some of the obvious difficulties with measuring them. As it is currently set up, our model puts the measuring of transactions at the centre of the whole system, where "transaction" is to be understood as the *sum of operations, whether inside or outside a department, necessary to provide a service*. One cannot fail to note the amount of "abstraction" necessary for identifying the path followed in providing each service. The idea is to find for each service, which has previously been measured in terms of "external" efficiency, a model which permits us to reconstruct specific internal routes, taking into account average costs, the number of employees involved and the processing times.

To collect these data, we must involve PA departments in a very active way, since they are the only agents able to reconstruct, for a given subset of services, the operations usually required.

Cost per transaction is the first parameter we shall examine, and it estimates overall costs (and not merely ICT costs) borne in carrying out a single transaction. Here we must stress two points: the first is practical and concerns the difficulty in making measurements. Indeed, this parameter can be measured from two points of view, as an index of the economic efficiency of a single service provided by a PA department, or an index of the average economic efficiency of all services provided by that department. In particular, this latter usage of the term gives a result which can be obtained carrying out an analysis on average values. The second concerns the way one looks at the cost per transaction. There are two possible effects: on one side, it is a real "cost," for services carried out by a department where there is always a certain amount of inefficiency (such as, for example, an increase in costs which is not bound up with increased productivity). Then, on the other side, rather than costs, one may talk of "investments" (although this is a difficult distinction to make within a PA), that are public expenditures aiming to increase the productivity of a certain process (such as that concerning the use of new technology).

Here, too, then, policy decisions which are linked to an indicator such as *cost per transaction* must not be taken out of context. They must rather be the aim of overall evaluations which take other elements into account. Generally speaking, we might state that a *reduction* in *costs per transaction* may represent an index of internal efficiency within a department. However, especially in the short run, there may be a trade-off between external and internal efficiency. This is the case, for example, with a service which is characterised by an increasing value/cost ratio (external efficiency), in the presence of increasing *service value* and still relatively high *social costs*. Here, a reduction of social costs, suitable for a further increase of external efficiency, might be obtained by the use of new technology and might indeed turn out to be — in the short run — a *greater cost* for the department involved (e.g., in terms of investments). But in the long run it may provide for increased internal efficiency and greater satisfaction for the users. A self-evaluation tool, such as the one under examination here, should force PAs to take on policies which balance, in the medium- to long-term, the objective of internal efficiency, and the satisfaction — in as brisk a time as possible — of users' requirements.

The *number of transactions per employee* is another indicator of operational efficiency, and roughly it aims at measuring labour productivity in a department. Here, too, what we said above holds true again, i.e., about making a first "averages" measurement (total number of transactions divided by number of employees), rather than measuring each service individually. As far as interpretation of the index is concerned, it is quite straightforward. There is a range of suitable values, leaving aside extremes,[5] where an *increase* in ratio can be seen only as a positive element for productivity.

Average transaction time is a more accurate way of measuring *delivery time*, in other words the time the department involved takes to provide a service, from when the application has been received. Here again, the difficulty lies in providing as good a measurement as possible of the time needed to deal with a procedure, and here, too, the involvement of the PA departments will have to be deep. The parameter is important and completely objective when measuring the impact of ICT on the PA. The introduction of new technology ought to reduce execution times for a transaction via any channel. It also indirectly shows the effects of computerization at the back-office level. Completely interactive PA departments should see human interventions in the various processes decrease, and the speed of transactions should thus increase. This could clearly be tied up to an increase in costs (i.e., in investments) per transaction.

Induced Restructuring

The impact new technology has on internal processes is measured in our model by two indirect indicators, which will require further specification. The first refers to the *number of organisational units*, and should consider — in the light of the problems we have already mentioned — how ICT impacts on internal processes via the reduction or restructuring of organisational units. The second indicator is *staff mobility*, defined as the number of people who, in a year, leave an office (either to retire, to change occupation, or because of a dismissal) or who start work there (new staff, transfers, etc.). We know from previous parameters what route a transaction must follow, and since we know what technological innovations have been made to bring this about, we can use *mobility* figures to infer what impact it has had on reduction in staff numbers or in their transfer. It is easy to understand that this factor must be cautiously examined, because it might be due to other extraneous influences such as mobbing or early pension schemes. However, the long term trend might show a systematic link (substitution or compensation) between PA computerization and staff changes.

Degree of Integration

A particularly important element in defining e-government strategies is the calculation of how little they represent simple re-styling operations for public services, and rather of how much they are a flywheel for redefining relations with different types of constituency, i.e., citizens, business, and the PA itself.

Actually, the idea of integrating services is quite far from being openly accepted in government plans. However, in our model, we have tried to consider it by inserting an *integration index*, which we feel should show not only how integrated various government departments are in terms of electronic data-sharing, but also how much the introduction of new technology is to be seen in the integration of the PA with the world around it. This can surely be seen as an index of growing PA efficiency, given that both internal and external efficiency means to be able to guarantee a better level of services (especially more user-based), and faster procedures to provide them, especially via the Web.

Making this index — the details of which have yet to be defined — takes several aspects into consideration. On the one hand, there is a whole series of context indicators, bound up with the in-house use of e-mails, and Internet and intranet Webs by the public. On the other hand, there is also another series of measures bound up with the number of electronic dealings between different government departments (G2G), or within a department for internal needs, between the department and its business suppliers (G2B) or its own employees (G2E). A G2G/(G2B+G2E) ratio might be useful in showing the number of induced electronic dealings in PA departments, i.e., in what direction a department is going in order to bring about an electronic "environment."

There are, of course, some details to consider. At first it must be stressed that "dealings" are measured by approximation looking at the number of e-mails sent and received, and the number of "hits" on the department's Intranet or Extranet. Secondly, we must remember that the total amount of dealings with the constituency, G2C, can actually be measured by the number of dealings carried out via the electronic channel obtained by aggregating those provided to different kinds of constituencies. According to this point of view, therefore, a comparison between G2C and the G2G/(G2B+G2E) ratio could be interesting as a measure of the dynamic nature of a department when activating the all-pervasive strategy of e-government.

ASSESSING MACROECONOMIC RETURN

To analyse the macroeconomic return of e-government means to look at both socio-economic factors and information and communication technology factors. The major goal of the Observatory is to improve understanding of these interactive socio-technical processes and effects and their implications for citizenship, and to produce recommendations for maximizing opportunities and minimizing risks associated with the use of ICTs within the PA.

In pursuit of this goal, the project is designed to achieve the following specific objectives:

- To provide an improved understanding of the interactive processes and effects between the key social and economic factors relating to e-government and the technical factors associated with ICT use, and to identify the implications of these socio-technical processes and effects for citizenship.

- To provide sets of predictions and observed outcomes of the social and economic effects of ICT use for modernising public administration, and to establish their implications for the relations between citizens, institutions and organisations.
- To recommend measures to improve access, usability and socio-economic outcomes of ICT and the relationships between citizens and institutions, at the local and national levels.

To deal with these issues implies taking into consideration the availability of know-how, the eligibility to services, the role of regulatory and financial systems, the consequences on social behaviors and on organisational structures. These processes impact on the national citizenship by creating a common information background and by facilitating information and knowledge sharing and by expanding the field of competition at the local and national level.

At a very first step of the analysis we can imagine that macroeconomic return could be assessed against three groups of parameters.

Public relations. The Observatory aims specifically to investigate how the Internet affects public relationships, by examining not only its impact upon work, but also how the Internet may benefit or undermine social and family relations. Modern society is confronted with an evolutionary change resulting from globalization and the challenges of ICT's diffusion. This change requires a deeper understanding of the new ways of interacting and grouping that are emerging in people's every-day life and the consequences that these new models of communication and interaction produce on our social model and structure. One dominant concern about ICTs is that features of the technology, such as physical isolation and the impersonal aspect of the medium, will lead to a weakening of social ties. Time spent communicating on the Web may mean less time spent communicating with family and friends in the local environment. According to this view, the broader use of the Internet tends to result in less social engagement and poorer psychological well-being. Despite these negative accounts, the ICTs also provide a means by which to reach others with shared interests and from similar categories. Through the Internet and intranets, individuals and organisations increasingly participate in new forms of social networks which can lead to the emergence of "virtual communities" that are only accessible via computer. In these cases, the Web provides more than simply a means of communication, it fosters a network of social support for those in similar positions, and with similar problems, providing a means to raise consciousness, organize politically and promote collective actions. These mixed observations call for deeper investigations on the social implication of ICTs with respect to public relationships and social structure.

Closing the digital divide. ICTs provide a basis for a greater connection and cohesion as well as reflecting isolation and fragmentation. While new technologies are an opportunity for integrating marginalized people, the access to ICTs seems to privilege only the skilled and richer classes. The project aims to highlight policies and measures to enhance the social cohesion by avoiding new forms of social isolation and inequality. In this context, one of the research goals of the Observatory is to explore which groups in society are included and which are excluded, not only by access to the ICTs, but also to the opportunities that flow from their use. Ethnic minorities, the poor and uneducated may not have access to the Internet and/or they may lack the necessary skills for its use.

Citizenship. By focusing on the ICT's impact on citizenship, the Observatory aims to evaluate the role of new technology in fostering and reinforcing political and social integration and to provide suggestions and indications on the possibilities to support this process by means of specific policies. This issue is considered in relation to a number of domains such as participation in the democratic process, as well as participation in social and community life. ICTs provide a means of increasing participation, for polling, online referenda, as well as perhaps even more direct participation in decision-making. Moreover, they provide a means for a more direct contact and offer the opportunity to promptly and efficiently access information on a broad range of initiatives promoted at national and local level. ICTs transcend regional boundaries and provide people the means to get in contact with others with shared interests and agendas and to promote group process and identification among citizens in the virtual environment.

As it is easy to see, our assessment relates to the *e*-Europe objective regarding access to the Internet, the equipping of citizens with required skills to live and work in the digital society, and stimulation of use of the Internet. However, an important feature of our project is that it both relates to and goes beyond the objectives of *e*-Europe. The project anticipates future issues in the development of *e*-Europe by investigating the social factors affecting Internet adoption and use by citizens, as well as the social impacts of Internet use upon citizens. Thus, the research goes beyond numerical indicators of availability (of a cheaper, faster Internet, or the number of public services online, etc.) identified for *e*-Europe. The project considers what are the social factors affecting take-up of the facilities and services that are made available, and how take-up of the Internet and its services affects the social and work lives of citizens who do adopt, and those who are excluded from online information and communication.

Indeed, some of these data, such as that associated with closing the digital divide or with citizenship, may be difficult to relate to e-government action. However, quoting Aristotle, we believe that only "what is difficult to obtain is highly valued."

ENDNOTES

1 "Transaction" is used here to mean, simply, the application for and provision of services, for example obtaining a certificate, if the service provides for this, or a piece of information, with a news service. Naturally enough, this measurement can more easily be made when electronic channels are involved. Otherwise, the PA involved will have to make the measurement more carefully.

2 Care must be taken with the terminology used, given that it may confuse. Here we use the term "transaction" in the economic sense, i.e., as a monetary operation. When talking about state 4 in general, however, we must understand "transaction" as the modification of documentary PA databases. This is different again from two other meanings used in the rest of the text, given that it indicates: (a) the set of operations (i.e., the various "internal" stages from receiving an application to the elaboration and supply) necessary to obtain a product linked to a specific service, or, more simply, (b) the number of operations carried out by users at the department concerned for a single service. Within the text, we shall explain which meaning we are using every time we quote the term. In the future, we shall also try to provide terminology which may better dissipate these ambiguities.

3 No less important are other indicators used in measuring the efficiency of such services. We shall mention them only briefly: they examine the *availability* of the service per channel; *ease of access* of the same, especially for disables; how *dynamic* it is in terms both of *transactions directly provided by the department* and of *connectivity between pre-prepared forms per service/total forms per service.*

4 By "*average waiting time per channel*" is meant *queuing time*, or how long it takes to obtain a procedure which provides a service. In other words, it is the average time a user must spend when making an application. It can be very different from the *delivery time*, i.e., the time it takes the department from receiving the application to providing the service applied for. Here, since we are dealing with opportunity costs, we have decided to make a distinction between these two time factors. Whereas *delivery time* has no particular interest for the end-user, since he/she can spend this time in other revenue-generating activities (a crucial aspect, given that the social cost is calculated in money terms), *queuing time* implies the direct and continuous presence of an end-user, i.e., his/her "distraction" from other activities. Naturally enough, there are special cases, such as the entrepreneur who suffers a "loss of earnings" due to the time spent in obtaining a certificate from a PA department. In such cases, *queuing time* is a lot less important than *delivery time*, and should be swapped for it.

5 If we take the lower limit for granted, the trend towards an "infinite" number of transactions per employee indicate reduced efficiency within a department and proof of a lack of personnel. The effects on work productivity can only be negative.

* I am grateful to Elio Gullo and Andrea Gumina for their help in drafting this chapter. Usual disclaimer applies.

Chapter VIII

The E-mancipation of the Citizen and the Future of E-Government: Reflections on ICT and Citizens' Partnership

Valerie A.J. Frissen, Erasmus University Rotterdam, The Netherlands

ABSTRACT

In this chapter, the author considers the notion of the e-mancipated citizen against the background of current trends in social and political participation of citizens. The role of ICTs in shaping these new forms of civic engagement is discussed and the implications of these developments for e-government and e-governance. This chapter argues that in exploring this new frontier, e-government risks seem to take the wrong direction. Up to now, government largely seems to ignore actual developments in citizens' participation that are taking place both in the off-line and online worlds. In this chapter these trends were brought together under the headings of sub-politics and life-politics and their political character was described mainly in terms of the "empowerment" of citizens.

INTRODUCTION

In the current discussions on e-government we can observe a growing awareness of the need to develop a more citizen-oriented perspective towards policy making. The e-government discourse assumes that modern citizens are well-informed, educated and thus rational, self-assertive individuals. They are quite capable of framing and expressing their needs and goals and they are more and more inclined to critically assess government policies and to be actively involved in the process of policy making. Moreover, modern citizens now use information and communication technologies (ICTs) to inform and organize themselves, to scrutinise government actions, and to bring specific issues to the attention of policy makers. In this view the modern citizen is therefore truly "e-mancipated." An example of this discourse can be found in the OECD-publication entitled, "Citizens as partners":

"Citizens are increasingly demanding greater transparency and accountability from their governments and want greater public participation in policies that affect their lives. Educated, well-informed citizens expect their governments to take their views and knowledge into account when making decisions on their behalf. Engaging citizens in policy-making allows governments to respond to these expectations and, at the same time, design better policies and improve their implementation" (OECD, 2001:9).

The last sentence illustrates how much a citizen-oriented perspective has become the cornerstone of a debate on "good governance." However, looking a bit more closely at this debate, it becomes clear that not only the happy occasion of the rise of the e-mancipated citizen has stimulated governments to rethink their principles of good governance. The renewed interest in the citizen results also from market mechanisms in the public sector, which has pushed governments and public organisations to shift from a bureaucratic and supply-oriented perspective to a more dynamic and flexible demand perspective, involving notions such as customer friendliness, flexibility, efficiency and effectiveness of service delivery. From this perspective, the e-mancipated citizen is conceived of primarily as a critical customer who wants to be served well. Moreover, the focus on citizens in the current government discourse can be explained by serious worries about an ever declining voter turnout at elections, falling membership of political parties and a loss of confidence in public institutions that is increasingly shown by citizens. This problem is commonly referred to as the "crisis in democracy" or the "democratic deficit." This crisis tends to endanger the legitimate position of governments in representative democracies and therefore has forced governments to think of ways to strengthen their weakened relations with citizens. In the e-government debate there is a slightly desperate tendency to look towards ICTs as the "killer app" for restoring the more or less troubled relationship between citizens and government and to cope with an apparent loss of legitimacy. The e-government and e-governance rhetorics hammer on the unequalled potential of ICTs to improve transparency, accountability, responsiveness, efficient and customer friendly service delivery and the active involvement of citizens in the decision-making process.

While the notion of the e-mancipated citizen is quite central in this discourse, it is more complex as it may look at first sight. Especially when focussing on "active participation" — as we will do in this paper — the e-mancipation of citizens is rather problematic. Although there is an undeniable tendency towards self-realization and freedom of individual choice among citizens, it is much less evident that this has also increased their willingness to actively participate in decision-making processes. The assumption that modern citizens expect governments to take their views into account and want to be included in policy-making processes is largely contradicted by the striking lack of interest in government policies and politics that citizens have shown over the last decades. Moreover, in spite of the ever increasing access of citizens to ICTs, there is virtually no sign that ICTs have led to any serious improvement of the engagement of citizens in political processes.

How can we understand this paradox of the e-mancipated citizen who is not the least bit interested in actively participating in policy- and decision-making processes? To answer this question, in this chapter the notion of the e-mancipated citizen is considered against the background of current trends in social and political participation of citizens. Furthermore, the role of ICTs in shaping these new forms of civic engagement is discussed, as well as the implications of these developments for e-government and e-governance.[1]

OUTLINE

In the next section current developments in citizens' participation are described and analyzed. This analysis shows that we are not so much witnessing the premature death of civic engagement, but a fundamental change in the *nature* of the engagement of citizens, which involves new channels, new platforms and new modes of operation. Secondly, the role of ICTs — and particularly the Internet — in these developments is discussed. It is argued that the Internet increasingly functions as the backbone for these new and diverse forms of civic engagement. Following this, we take a closer look at the use of ICTs for *political* participation. Three types of ICT-mediated political engagement of citizens are distinguished here and discussed in terms of their implications for e-government and e-governance.

REINVENTION OF CITIZENS' ENGAGEMENT

Over the last decades a common assumption in debates about citizens' engagement has been that participation of citizens is generally declining. This assumption has inspired gloomy formulations such as "the crisis in democracy" or the "balkanization" of the public interest (Putnam, 2000). Conservative politicians and authors often relate these processes to a decline in shared values and a loss of *Gemeinschaft*. These developments are assumed to be enhanced by some of the characteristics of post-modern society, such as fragmentation and individualization.

However, these assumptions need to be reconsidered. If we look for instance at socio-cultural developments in The Netherlands, as monitored by the Dutch Social and Cultural Planning Agency (SCP) for government purposes, we must conclude that the level of participation of the Dutch has never been as high as in the last decades (SCP, 1998). According to the SCP, the only decrease in citizens' participation that can be observed, is a decrease in what we may label *formal* political participation (voter turnout, membership of political parties, taking part in policy and decision-making processes, etc). When civic engagement is defined in a broader sense, as the SCP does, participation includes the involvement of citizens in different types of civil society organisations, including political ones. From this angle, there is a strong tendency towards "active citizenship," claims the SCP, which is expressed in all kinds of new social movements, single-issue and single-event types of involvement of citizens, "bank-account" activism (charity) and a wealth of local, small-scale citizen initiatives. Moreover, what has fundamentally changed over time is the *nature* of involvement of citizens with these kinds of issues and organisations. Citizens' participation is more than before based on changing individual preferences and is thus more temporary and volatile. Furthermore, participation is less rooted in face-to face-interactions between citizens and less based on formalized and institutionalized membership. What we see here is a paradoxical combination of a tendency towards individualizations on the one hand and the blooming of new kinds of citizens' associations on the other hand. This is what we have called the "paradox of individual commitment" (Frissen & Van Bockxmeer, 2001).

These conclusions are supported by other studies, such as the large scale, longitudinal research on the social consequences of Internet use reported by Katz and Rice (2002) in the USA. These authors conclude that Internet use tends to increase civic engagement, community involvement and online political involvement, while off-line political involvement is not affected significantly by Internet use.

On a more global level, according to Norris (2002), civic participation is not declining either, but is searching for new channels and modes of operation[2]:

"Indicators point even more strongly towards the evolution, transformation and reinvention of civic engagement rather than its premature death. Multiple newer channels of civic engagement, mobilization and expression are rapidly emerging in post-industrial societies to supplement traditional modes." (Norris, 2002)

Or, as Anheier et al. have put it:

"What we can observe in the 1990s is the emergence of a supranational sphere of social and political participation in which citizens groups, social movements, and individuals engage in dialogue, debate, confrontation, and negotiation with each other and with various governmental actors — international, national and local — as well as the business world." (2001, p. 4)

What is new about this phenomenon seems to be its more diverse and fragmented character on the one hand and its unprecedented scale and scope on the other hand. According to Anheier et al., the number and reach of international and supranational NGOs has grown substantially over the past decade. Furthermore, the number of organisations and individuals who are part of the global civil society — mainly measured through membership of international NGOs such as Greenpeace or Amnesty International — has never been bigger. And finally, the network linking the organisations to each other is becoming denser as well (Anheier et al., 2001:4). Colas differentiates between on the one hand more "traditional" social movements, politically embedded and directed at *grand* political projects and the reshaping of the system and, on the other hand, international NGOs, whose action is directed at realizing a specific goal and for whom the political component is much less important (Colas, 1997, p. 277). Particularly the new social movements and international NGOs tend to concentrate on single and easily marketable issues.

How can we explain these shifts in civic engagement? Giddens distinguishes between three major sets of developments which are crucial for understanding this kind of social changes in what he calls "late modernity." These three developments — in which the media and ICTs play a crucial role - are: globalization, the detraditionalization of social organizations and what Giddens calls "social reflexivity" (Giddens, 1991; Beck, Giddens & Lasch, 1994). The implication of globalization in this context is that the boundaries of time and space have become less determining for social participation and for building new forms of social association. The media and ICTs enable individuals and organizations to participate in global, or at least distant social associations and networks. This leads to new relationships and interaction patterns, and thus, according to Giddens, to new forms of uncertainty for citizens. Related to this is that the natural logic of traditions, and the forms of authority which were rooted in these traditions, are more and more questioned. In an open, cosmopolitan and global society, people are confronted with a vast amount of information and thus a multiplicity of sources to answer their questions and to give meaning to their place in the world. The result of this is that uncertainty has entered every aspect of the everyday life of individuals and that these individuals are thus forced to continuously make choices, to sort out their priorities and to redefine their opinions and values. This is what Giddens refers to as "social reflexivity": "...individuals are forced to negotiate lifestyle choices among a diversity of options" (Giddens, 1991). In this light, increased possibilities of self-realization and individual choice are the inevitable parameters of the late modern *condition humaine.*

This brings us to the question what it is that connects people in these times of uncertainty and reflexivity. What is the late-modern basis for "collectivity"? We can understand this in terms of what we have described elsewhere as a shift from traditional *communities of birth*, based upon a shared history, territory and cultural heritage, towards more loosely organized and fragmented *communities of interest* (Frissen & Van Bockxmeer, 2001; Van Bockxmeer et al., 2001). Communities of interest are a typical phenomenon of late-modernity, as described by Giddens. These interest- and issue-based associations also imply that the identity of an individual person is less confined to one, single community but more to a set of loosely organized communities. In late modernity, you can be part of the Muslim community, a citizen of Amsterdam, a fan of techno-house music, a supporter of Greenpeace and a member of a women's network of ICT-professionals, all at the same time. With all these identities you can participate in different communities, and ICT is one of the means for doing so. An interesting feature of current forms of social association is that the management of these multiple identities seems to be quite unproblematic for modern citizens: diversity of interests and identities is a defining characteristic of the way the way these citizens engage in associations with others.

ICT AS ENABLING TECHNOLOGY

In this context, ICTs and particularly the Internet play an interesting role. The characteristics of the Internet more or less reflect the socio-cultural changes I have described in section 2. The Internet thus may function as the "*backbone*" for new and diverse forms of connecting with others on the basis of shared interests or shared identities, connections which are not dependent anymore on real-life, face to-face interactions, and are much less restricted by the boundaries of time and space. Thus the Internet is developing as one of the major platforms where new civic engagement is taking place. The internet enables the fast and efficient mobilization of fragmented individuals around single issues and events.[3] The structure of the Internet corresponds with these loosely organized and decentralized forms of commitment and participation. The Internet is informal, low key, it is easy accessible and it creates less obligations than in the real world. The following characteristics of the Internet are fundamental here in our view.

First, the *network character* of the Internet makes it is very easy to get in touch with people with a similar interest. The network potential of the Internet is particularly strong because of its independence of time and space. For the formation of networks and new forms of participation, this characteristic is fundamental. Communities can be built and can grow without physical contact or time constraints of participants. "Meeting people" is defined fundamentally different. The network-potential of the Internet may empirically be understood in terms of *interactivity between people* (possibilities for interaction, such as discussion forums, chats, guest books, e-voting, emailing, etc.) and *interactivity between texts* (hypertext links to other, related places on the Web). Both features support the building of new networks both in terms of social relations and in terms of a hypertext. A second relevant feature of the Internet is its potential towards *horizontalisation.* The Internet can be used to transform the traditional chain of supply and reception of information. Users have more choices and are able to offer and distribute information themselves. In terms of citizens' participation, this enlarges the possibilities for bottom-up initiatives and for active participation of "members." Thirdly, the *virtual character* of the Internet offers possibilities to be anonymous or to play with one's identity. This increases the possibility of participating in groups which in real life would possibly be more closed. Another aspect of this virtuality is that it is much easier to connect with others without the social obligations and rules of real life. And finally, the *multimedia character* of the Internet increases the possibilities of cultural representation. On the Internet it is quite easy to construct "images of oneself," by using a vast array of textual and audio-visual symbols. Together, these characteristics of the Internet make it a strong, enabling technology for the formation and functioning of new forms of social association.

According to Van Audenhove (2001) many authors writing on the *global* civil society also emphasize the importance of the Internet. As Norris puts it:

"Digital technologies may serve to strengthen the institutions of civic society, widening the opportunities for information, communication, and participation in the electronic public sphere, allowing well-organized and nimble David's to run circles around lumbering corporations and international bodies. The characteristics of the Internet to shrink costs, maximize speed, broaden reach and eradicate distance provides transnational advocacy networks with an effective tool for mobilization, organization and expression that can potentially maximize their leverage in the global arena." (2001)

This possibly over-optimistic view of the Internet as an instrument for global civic empowerment brings us to the question what ICTs imply for the *political* participation of citizens. In the next section this will be discussed in greater detail.

ICTS AND POLITICAL PARTICIPATION

Political participation here refers to the more or less organized actions and associations of citizens in the policy- and decision-making arena, actions that are oriented towards influencing the policy- and decision-making process. The analysis of trends in citizens' participation in the former sections has already made clear that some fundamental changes have taken place in the way modern citizens shape their engagement and seek to meet their objectives, and that ICTs play a remarkable role here. First, we have described a shift towards "communities of interest," loosely organized and more temporary associations based on shared values and interests, a shift which in political terms has resulted in the blossoming of a large array of single-issue and single event-like associations. ICTs fit in with and support these developments and furthermore provide the possibility of virtualization. Through the use of the Internet, loose and fragmented associations of individuals and groups — organized around quite diverse types of issues - can become a powerful network organisation in the (global) civil society. A striking example here is of course the anti-globalization movement, which mobilizes quite diverse associations of people to come into action when a specific event occurs (such as an economic or political summit). Second, existing associations can extend their working geographically through ICTs, to organize on a larger scale, to build (global) coalitions with like-minded organisations, to mobilize beyond its own constituencies and to spread information on a larger scale, thus creating and/or supporting larger public spheres (Norris, 2001; Warkentin, 2001; Warkentin & Mingst, 2000; Calabrese, 1999; Anheier et al., 2001: 6).

ICTs offer citizens not only the means to organize themselves, but also to produce cultural codes to represent themselves. *Identity politics* has become an important feature of these new forms of citizens' engagement. Another characteristic is that they have a networking, decentered form of organisation and intervention, which makes it hard to identify their *collective* ambitions or goals. The formulation of goals is more decentralized and fragmented. The shared identity is the only thing that binds participants together and not necessarily shared views on specific issues or topics. They do not necessarily use the traditional channels of political representation and decision making to reach their goals and are more issue- and event-oriented. Manuel Castells has observed that these forms of non-partisan politics seem to win increasing legitimacy, thus redefining what citizens perceive as politics. He uses the phrase "informational democracy" here, pointing to the centrality of the media and ICT in these new forms of citizens' participation (Castells, 1996, 1997).

At first sight these new types of social association appear to be non-political in the classical sense. They do not fit into the formalised framing of political issues that is characteristic for representative democracy. We may, however, understand these shifts better as a "reinvention of politics." Beck observes a "non-institutional renaissance of the political" in all kinds of citizen initiatives and possibilities to voice particular issues. These initiatives no longer define politics in terms of formal political and corporatist interests, institutions and practices. According to Beck, both agents outside the formal political system and individuals increasingly become crucial actors in the political arena. Beck refers to this political undercurrent as "sub-politics."

"Sub-politics means shaping society from below. Viewed from above this results in the loss of implementation power, the shrinkage and minimization of politics. In the wake of sub-politicization, there are growing opportunities to have a voice and a share in the arrangement of society for groups hitherto uninvolved in the substantive technification and industrialization process." (Beck, 1994, p. 23)

Moreover, in our research on ICT and citizens' participation we have observed another shift: citizens' engagement has moved from a focus on "liberation" of domination and equality of chances, which was more typical for the social emancipation movements of the 20th century, towards a focus on diversity and freedom of choices in the new social movements. Giddens (1991) refers to this as a shift from "*emancipatory politics*" towards "*life politics*." Life politics to a certain extent presumes an emancipation from the fixities of tradition and from conditions of hierarchical domination. Emancipation thus has created the condition for *a politics of choice*, which is essentially what life politics is about. While emancipatory politics is focusing on equal chances, life politics is focusing on the diversity and freedom of choices in lifestyles. [4] The concept of life politics also implies that people tend to formulate political goals more in terms of the "project of their life" in terms of self-realization (shared with others) and in terms of identity politics. This explains the more issue-oriented approach and the interest in human interest issues, considered relevant in everyday life in many current forms of citizens' engagement.

Although they do not fit into the traditional framing and addressing of political issues, characteristic for representative democracy, sub-politics and life politics are not un-political. What they particularly do is contribute to the *empowerment* of citizens. Sub-politics and life politics have substantially increased citizens' possibilities to voice issues and interests, to associate with others who share this interest and to find alternative modes of expression and representation. Furthermore, the issues that are binding these associations together are not abstract, but rooted in everyday life experiences (for instance at the local level), which seems to increase the willingness of citizens to participate. Sharing individual experiences with others can make the political element in personal experiences explicit, visible and easier to address. In this sense the effectiveness of these types of engagements can be experienced by citizens as quite high, without any contact with the formal political, decision-making arena. On the other hand, platforms which at first seem to have a primary "identity politics" objective can suddenly become highly issue- or event-oriented and can be used for mobilizing people to come into action, for instance to get an issue on the formal political agenda or to make formal politics or governments responsible or accountable for certain policy decisions or actions. This implies that new forms of political representation are presenting themselves here, which can largely ignore the classical procedures of representative democracy and look for direct, concrete and short-line interactions with actors in the decision-making arena.

E-GOVERNMENT AND E-MANCIPATED CITIZEN: A NEW DIGITAL DIVIDE?

The types of engagement described in the former section particularly seem to contribute to the empowerment of citizens — and as ICT can be seen as an important enabler of this empowerment — we can indeed speak of an *e-mancipation* of citizens. However, the question to be addressed in this chapter is whether this is the same kind of e-mancipated citizen that the e-government discourse is referring to and whether e-government policy does take these new forms of citizens' engagement (effectively) into account.

To understand the way ICTs can be used for political participation of citizens, we have made a distinction here between three types of political engagement of citizens [5]:

- *Government politics:* refers to the active participation of citizens in processes of policy- and decision-making, initiated by government. ICT is used here to modernize and "revive" the classical political participation of citizens (voting, opinion polling, the involvement of citizens and their interest- and lobby groups in policy-making, co-production, deliberation, etc.). The initiative for citizens' engagement in this case lies with government, in contrast to the other two forms of engagement, where the citizens themselves are the initiators of political action;
- *Sub-politics*: refers to what Beck has called the "non-institutional renaissance of the political." ICTs create new opportunities for citizens to voice certain issues and put them on the political agenda, through what Castells has called "informational democracy." This implies that new and less clearly defined political actors with new unconventional political methods and tools can enter the political arena and to a certain extent redefine this political arena (e.g., the anti-globalization movement);
- *Life politics*: refers to the framing of political issues by citizens in terms of the "project of their life," which makes these issues highly relevant to them and substantially increases the potential of mobilizing them for particular actions. This

Table 1. Typology of political engagement of citizens

TYPE OF POLITICAL ENGAGEMENT OF CITIZENS	ORIGIN IN OFF-LINE WORLD	ORIGIN IN ONLINE WORLD
Government politics	*Web sites informing citizens about consultation processes, asking feedback, etc.*	*E-voting/referenda, Digital discussion platforms* *"Communities of practice" ("virtual policy communities")*
Sub-politics	*NGO's using ICT to consult citizens or to organise debates between citizens and policy makers*	e.g., Independent Media Centres of the anti-globalisation movement
Life- and identity-politics	Existing communities using ICTs to enhance their activities and objectives	Virtual communities based on shared identities, issues, interests or "self-help"

> implies also that "the irrational, the emotional and the trivial" dimensions of everyday life become more fundamental drivers of political processes. The "grand ideologies" that have inspired traditional representative democracy are increasingly irrelevant for citizens. Life politics thus may bring about fundamental changes in the way citizens want to be represented. Furthermore, from a life politics perspective citizens are acting more than before as a watchdog of governments when it comes to issues that directly touch their everyday life. Traditional politics is experienced as too abstract and distant. This implies that concrete results and, related to that, accountability of governments' actions to solve these everyday life problems become more important.

The following matrix shows a typology of the "new" forms of citizens engagement described in this chapter, in which ICTs play a crucial role. We have made a distinction here between, on the one hand, the types of political engagement as described above and, on the other hand, the role ICTs play in these types of engagement. We distinguish here between the origin of a citizens' association in the off-line world (existing organisations that have now started to use the Internet to reach their goals) and an origin in the online world (organisations that started to exist because of the platform and network-possibilities of the Internet).

This typology is useful to categorize the ways ICTs can be used for different types of political participation and engagement of citizens. When applied to e-government, we may conclude that most initiatives in the e-government field are only taking place in the first layer of this typology (government politics) and maybe a little in the second layer, as far as governments use NGOs as an organizer or mediator of debates or other interactions between governments and citizens on policy issues. In the typology, italics are used to mark these activities. Until now, e-government has not paid much serious attention to the other forms of civic engagement that — at least in the eyes of e-mancipated citizens — have become highly relevant over the last decade. Moreover, the OECD states that in the e-government thinking and actions until now in most countries the mere notion of "active participation" and the principle of partnership between governments, citizens and civil society organisations is still rare and thus represents a "new frontier" for e-government (OECD, 2001, p. 5).

Furthermore, if we take a closer look at what is the actual effect of the e-government actions undertaken to increase the active involvement of citizens, the results are usually quite disappointing. Research on, for instance, digital discussion platforms (Brants, 2001; Bekkers, 2001) has shown that both in terms of participation and in terms of the actual influence of citizens on the policy- and decision-making process, the expectations have been proven to be much too high. First, the number of participants in these discussions is usually quite low. Second, the profile of the participants is often rather elitist and has raised the question whether these forms of civic engagement do possibly only increase the participation of those who are already highly interested in politics. Third, looking at the possibilities these platforms offer for actual influence, the conclusion is that there is often no clear connection of citizens' contributions with or embedding in the actual policy process. Fourth, politicians and policy makers are underrepresented in these discussions and there is often no real debate but only a consultation of opinions. And finally, the quality of the discussions and deliberations is often not very high (Bekkers, 2001, p. 253).

On the other hand, if we look at citizens' engagement in the sub-political and life-political field, another picture emerges. The number of citizens participating in these platforms is often high, the profile is much less elitist and the platforms are experienced as highly relevant for citizens' empowerment, although this empowerment is not defined in terms of actual influence on the formal political decision making arena. The quality of debates in these new forums, however, is often not very good either. From the perspective of e-government, theoretically the domains of sub-politics and life-politics offer politicians and policymakers a new and rich source of deliberation, public debates, problem definitions and directions for potential solutions. Besides, they constitute a public to address when certain issues need to be actively communicated and when governments want to account for certain actions they have undertaken. Looking at the potential these associations of citizens have for a government which is increasingly focusing on the redefinition of good governance, it is surprising that there is so little attention in e-government actions for these new types of civic engagement.

This section is concluded with two examples of citizens' associations focusing on life-politics to illustrate the potential of these new forms of civic engagement. In the concluding remarks of this chapter, I shall get back to these examples.

Case 1

The URL *www.nieuw-volendam.nl* is a discussion site of a local newspaper in a small (27.000 inhabitants) fishing village just north of Amsterdam. New Year's Eve 2000, this closely knit community was struck by a fire in a local pub, filled with young celebrating locals. Twenty people died and many more had severe burns; disfigured youngsters are now a common sight in a village very popular with tourists. With many inhabitants someway interrelated, everyone knows at least one of the victims. The Web site of the local newspaper had already existed for some time, but quickly became a site of mourning for both locals, ex-pats and all those who sympathized and wanted to share their condolences; the latter mostly turned to a separate virtual register of condolences. The discussion site probably reflects the reality of everyday life discussions: the participants switch their topic constantly, from whether or not to hold the annual fun fair to the question of who is responsible for preventive policies of fire control, and in between local, non-disaster related issues are discussed. But at the same time, the site of mourning can, from one 'minute' to the next become a site of anger and blaming. After a few weeks of extending and exchanging sorrow and coping with public mourning, the discussion widened from the disaster and the personal tragedy to include the municipality, political parties, civil servants, organisations and individual villagers who become part of a process of shaming and blaming, and of exonerating and defending. The personal (sharing, victim information, help), the social (organisations, religion, education, the village) and the political (municipality, political parties, politicians) are difficult to separate, implode as well as explode. If one can speak of an aim of the site, which it officially not has, it would be the function of an 'exhaust pipe' for feelings of sadness, anger, impotence and indignation. Over a period of four months since the disaster, there have been 1,500 postings; on average 12 a day in a community of around 25.000 people (NB: with a relatively small number of participants contributing a large amount of the postings). There is a wide variety of discussion themes — in total 125 different topical discussion lines were traced over the four-month period - debated by around 98 out of the 340 registered participants. Surprisingly, the more political the topic the longer the discussion line: the discussion about the responsibility and accountability of a local political party in the fire, drew 220 postings. These postings were usually very negative *vis-a-vis* political authorities and generally showed a high level of political cynicism. (This case is based on a study done by Brants, 2002.)

Case 2

Since the 1960s, a substantial number of people have immigrated to the Netherlands from Morocco. For several reasons (low education, unemployment, criminality, traditional values) the image of the Moroccan community in the Netherlands is not very positive. In the Spring of 2000 two young Moroccan businessmen started a very popular "life-style magazine" on the Internet called *Maghreb.nl*. They aim to bridge the gap between the Dutch and Moroccan community. The purpose of the Web site is to show the community in a positive way, to be open to other cultures and to let them know what the Moroccan culture and religion is about, and also simply to earn money. They especially aim at young people and at the issues they consider important in their everyday life. The Web site has several multimedia options and many possibilities for relatively un-moderated communication between participants. There is news and information, entertainment (games, Miss Moroccan contest, music) and even a Cyber-Imam. The site is an example of how the Internet can be used by migrant groups who are trying to integrate two different worlds and at the same time want to express their own cultural identity. The virtual character of the community enables young people to ask questions which are more or less taboo in the real-life communities they are living in, communities that are experiencing a confusing mix of Moroccan, Islamic and western elements. Questions about religion and, for instance, sexuality can be raised and answered here anonymously by the "Cyber-Imam" or by peers, and without the social pressure of the real-life community. These characteristics, enabled by the Internet, have made this Web site extremely popular. A striking feature of *Maghreb.nl* is its hybrid character. There seems to be no distinction between expert-knowledge and knowledge based on personal experiences. Serious and light subjects are discussed and there are remarkable combinations of intimacy and public debate. The boundaries between emotions and rationality, between individual and common interests, between information and communication and between commercial and public messages are blurring visibly. Topics addressed range from the weather in Casablanca to the place of girls and women in Islamic culture and, recently, the aftermath of the 11 September attacks for the position of Arabic people in the Netherlands (this case is based on our own research, Van Bockxmeer et al., 2000).

NEW FRONTIER: IMPLICATIONS FOR E-GOVERNMENT

Governments in all OECD countries are currently under pressure to rethink the relationships between governments and citizens. An important element in this new vision is the strengthening of citizens' active input and participation in policy- and decision-making processes. ICT is assumed to be an important instrument here. The OECD considers active participation of citizens as a relationship based on partnership with government: "an equal standing for citizens in setting the agenda, proposing policy options and shaping the policy dialogue." It also concludes that only a few countries have actually begun to explore these possibilities and that experiences to date are limited to a few pilot cases (OECD, 2001, p. 12). Engaging citizens in policy deliberation and active participation requires specific tools to facilitate learning, debate and the drafting of concrete proposals (e.g., forums, consensus conferences, citizens' juries, etc., integrated with ICT-instruments such as online discussions, interactive games) (OECD, 2001, p. 13). This chapter argues that in exploring this new frontier, e-government risks seem to take the wrong direction. Up to now it largely seems to ignore actual developments in citizens' participation that are taking place both in the off-line and online worlds. In this chapter these trends were brought together under the headings of sub-politics and life-politics and their political character was described mainly in terms of the "empowerment" of citizens.

The e-government discourse and actions until now mostly seem to focus on a perspective in which governments set the policy agenda and consequently try to organize civic consultation or engagement around these issues. However, research has shown that the level of citizens' interest in these initiatives is not very high. This has led to disappointed reactions concerning the expected democratic potential of the Internet. There are until very few examples of an actual *co-production of policy,* which is based on an "equal standing" of government and citizens (and which uses the existing patterns of engagement of citizens in a constructive way). A possible direction for this may be the so-called "virtual-policy communities" as described by Bekkers (2001): *communities of practice* which organize themselves around a specific and usually "fuzzy" or "wicked" policy issues. This community is a network of involved actors, using ICTs for communication, social learning, knowledge sharing and the co-production of policy. The purpose is to look at an issue from different perspectives and use the manifest and latent knowledge and experience of the different actors involved in the network. All actors need to have access to the same data (not only the politicians and public servants). There also needs to be an openness to competing ideas and competing solutions. Participation in these communities, according to Bekkers, can be guaranteed by connecting with existing networks. The foregoing sections have stressed that — enabled through ICTs — there is now a sheer unlimited amount of networks in society in which citizen engagement is taking place, focusing on virtually any relevant policy issue that we may think of. Connecting with existing networks therefore cannot be the problem.

If we take the Volendam case as an example: in the aftermath of the pub fire, many failures to prevent this disaster on the part of the local government were revealed. The citizens' Web site, which originally functioned as a platform for the sharing of grief and sympathy, evolved into a platform for voicing public criticism and demanding accountability. The high level of involvement of the local citizens with this issue and the organisation and voicing of this engagement through ICTs could have been used more effectively. The Internet may have been a useful instrument to develop new policies to prevent future disasters and to develop instruments for accountability of both *public actors* (e.g., by publishing government permits for pubs on the Web) and *private actors* (e.g., by publishing the fire measures that pubs have taken on the Web). Citizens might add to this by using the Web site to qualify pubs in terms of safety measures, etc. This co-production of a "risk policy" would involve a certain shift in the government-citizen relations. Government in this case would account for its policy not through the classical political process (accounting for its actions to the local council) but directly to citizens. Citizens would then take over some of the classical inspection and surveillance roles of the government.

Unfortunately, more often these forms of civic engagement and their potential for the co-production of policy are not so much experienced as a challenge, but more as a threat to government. This is not surprising as they may have some radical effects for future governance. To name some of them:

- Citizens (or representatives of citizens) are more directly involved in the policy process and could possibly even take over specific government functions (such as surveillance), which implies a loss of control by governments and politicians.
- Citizens' networks tend to have a quite fluid and dynamic character, which evokes uncertainties concerning the basis for and sustainability of policy decisions.
- The democratic character of citizen networks (and of other actors participating in "policy communities") is not guaranteed in the same way as it is in representative democracies and thus new guarantees are needed.
- A focus on co-production of policy and possibly "virtual-policy communities" implies the displacement of politics to networks outside the classical political system, which leads to a marginalization of the elected political representatives.
- This displacement may also involve a stronger role of government officials, who are more directly addressed by citizens as they are "closer to the fire" and they have to operationalize political issues in concrete actions and measures and are therefore potentially more interested in cooperation with citizens. Moreover, these officials tend to operate more autonomously in these networks, which has an effect on the principle of "ministerial accountability." It is impossible to function in a virtual-policy community without an enlarged mandate and an increased autonomy, as these networks are dynamic and constantly changing. The whole process of policy making within these networks would be obstructed by the slow and bureaucratic procedures of the classical governmental hierarchy.

These issues inevitably address the key characteristics of our democratic system, and the risks and challenges resulting from the new forms of civic engagement described in this chapter. Therefore, future e-government strategies inevitably have to take into account e-democracy and e-governance issues as well. Even more substantially, these strategies have to include debates about the basics of our democratic system. Often the representative democracy model is taken for granted in the debate on e-government and there are indeed very good reasons to do so, as this system has proven to be very strong. Nevertheless, the developments in civic engagement as described in this chapter have produced some serious challenges to this model. We cannot afford to avoid these challenges, as the current activities in the field of e-government have not brought any solution for the democratic deficit yet.

REFERENCES

Anheier, H., Glasius, M., & Kaldor, M. (Eds.). (2001). *Global civil society 2001.* Oxford: Oxford University.

Audenhove, L. van, Cammaerts, B., Frissen, V., Engels, L., & Ponsioen, A. (2002). *Transnational civil society in the networked society.* Study in the framework of Terra 2000 (EU Project under IST 2000).

Bardoel, J., & Frissen, V. (1999, Second Quarter). Policing participation: New forms of participation and citizenship and their implications for a social communication policy. *Communications & Strategies, 24,* 203-227.

Beck, U. (1994). The reinvention of politics: Towards a theory of reflexive modernization. In U. Beck, A. Giddens, & S. Lasch (Eds), *Reflexive modernization. Politics, tradition and aesthetics in the modern social order,* (pp. 1-55). Cambridge: Polity.

Beck, U., Giddens, A., & Lasch, S. (1994). *Reflexive modernization. Politics, tradition and aesthetics in the modern social order.* Cambridge: Polity.

Bekkers, V. (2001). Virtuele beleidsgemeenschappen. Over responsieve democratie en digitale participatie. *Bestuurskunde, 10*(6), 252-260.

Bockxmeer, H. van, Frissen, V., & Staden, M. van. (2001). *Nieuwe media en gemeenschappen.* Delft, TNO Strategie, Technologie en Beleid.

Brants, K. (2002). Politics is E-verywhere. *The European Journal of Communication Research, 27*(2), 171-188.

Brants, K., & Frissen, V. (2002). *From e-politics tot un-politics?* Paper presented to a meeting of the European Science Foundation Network on Changing Media, Changing Europe, Amsterdam, February.

Calabrese, A. (1999). Communication and the end of sovereignty. *Info, 1*(4), 313-326.

Castells, M. (1996). *The rise of the network society. The information age: Economy, society and culture* (Volume I). MA: Blackwell.

Castells, M. (1997). *The Power of identity: The information age: Economy, society and culture* (Volume II). MA: Blackwell.

Colas, A. (1997). The promises of international civil society. *Global Society, 11*(3), 261-277.

Frissen, V., & Bockxmeer, H. van. (2001, Second Quarter). The paradox of individual cCommitment. The implications of the Internet for social participation. *Communications & Strategies, 42,* 225-258.

Frissen, V., Van Lieshout, M., Staden, M. van., & Ponsioen, A. (2001). De Schaduwdemocratie. ICT en Maatschappelijke Participatie. In S. Zouridis, P. Frissen, N. Kroon, J. de Mul, & J. van Wamelen (Red.), *Internet en Openbaar Bestuur: een Vervolg.* Den Haag (8 delen).

Frissen, V., & Ponsioen, A. (2003). *Schuivende Panelen: Maatschappelijke Organisaties in de Digitale Wereld: Uitdagingen Voor Politiek en Bestuur.* Den Haag: Ministerie van BZK.

Giddens, A. (1991). *Modernity and self-identity. Self and society in the late modern age.* Cambridge: Polity.

Katz, J., & Rice, R. (2002). *Social consequences of Internet use, access, involvement and interaction.* Cambridge, MA: MIT.

Norris, P. (2001a). *Digital divide? Civic engagement, information poverty and the Internet in democratic societies.* Cambridge: Cambridge University.Available at *http://www.pippanorris.com/*

Norris, P. (2001b). *Giving voice to the voiceless. Good governance, human development and mass communictions.* Pippa Norris. Retrieved from *www.pippanorris.com.*

Norris, P. (2002). *Democratic Phoenix: Political activism worldwide.* Cambridge: Cambridge University. Available at *http://www.pippanorris.com/*

OECD. (2001). *Citizens as partners. Information, consultation and public participation in policy-making.* Paris: OECD.

Putnam, R. (2000). *Bowling alone. The collapse and revival of American community.* New York: Simon & Schuster.

Sociaal Cultureel Planbureau. (1998). *Sociaal en Cultureel Rapport 1998. 25 jaar sociale verandering.* Rijswijk: SCP.

Warkentin, C. (2001). *Reshaping World Politics: NGOs, the Internet, and global civil society.* Lanham: Rowman & Littlefield.

Warkentin, C., & Mingst, K. (2000). International institutions, the state, and global civil society in the age of the World Wide Web. *Global Governance*, (6), 237-257.

ENDNOTES

1 The chapter is based upon empirical research carried out at TNO Strategy, Technology and Policy, in cooperation with others. One project (*The Shadow Democracy),* focuses on the consequences of ICT for new forms of citizenship and social participation in the Netherlands and the implications this may have for democracy (Frissen et al., 2002). This project is part of a wider research programme called "Internet and Governance" which is a joined progamme of Dutch universities, research organisations and several Ministeries. The second project, (*New Media, New Communities)*, focuses on the implications of ICTs for the formation and functioning of (new) communities (Van Bockxmeer et al., 2001). This study was commissioned by the Dutch public broadcasting organisation KRO. Furthermore, this paper draws on joined research with the University of Amsterdam for the European Media Technology and Everyday Life Network (EMTEL) on *ICT and Citizens' Participation* and on research for the EC-funded research project TERRA, in cooperation with Infonomics and SMIT, on *ICT and the Global Civil Society (*Audenhove et al., 2002).

2 Arguments on the "global civil society" in this chapter are primarily based on Audenhove et al. (2003).

3 Based on a study for the Dutch Ministry of the Interior among Dutch NGOs, which was a combination of a large-scale survey among NGOs and several in-depth case studies (Frissen & Ponsioen, 2003).

4 The definition of life politics as given by Giddens is: "life politics concerns political issues which flow from processes of self-actualisation in post-traditional contexts, where globalising influences intrude deeply into the reflexive project of the self, and conversely where processes of self-realisation influence global strategies" (Giddens, 1991, p. 214).

5 Brants & Frissen (2002).

Chapter IX

Measuring and Evaluating E-Government: Building Blocks and Recommendations for a Standardized Measuring Tool

Christiaan Holland, Dialogic Innovation and Interaction, The Netherlands

Frank Bongers, Dialogic Innovation and Interaction, The Netherlands

Rens Vandeberg, Dialogic Innovation and Interaction, The Netherlands

Wouter Keller, Argitek, VU Amsterdam, The Netherlands

Robbin te Velde, Perquirimus Ltd., The Netherlands

ABSTRACT

In this chapter we describe research we have conducted on measuring e-government in the Netherlands. This research was commissioned by the Ministry of Economic Affairs and the Ministry of the Interior in the Netherlands. There are many aspects and benefits of e-government which are missing in existing measuring tools and concepts. Existing benchmark studies lack a theoretical basis and merely look at the supply side of electronic government: the availability of electronic services. Actual use or the impact of electronic public services is not captured. We therefore have developed a new concept and measuring tool for e-government. This tool is being used in a benchmarking study, the results of which will be published by the end of this year. For this reason we* *have only described the methodological aspects of our approach here. We believe our experience in this research project and this measuring tool can contribute to the discussion on new ways to measure and evaluate e-government from an international perspective.*

INTRODUCTION

If you can't measure it, you can't manage it. *Peter Drucker*

The hype about e-business may have died down (and even given way to negative hype), but the high expectations concerning e-government have certainly not diminished. Electronic government is a subject that is high on the political and administrative agenda in various countries. Expectations are high regarding the presumed effects or promises it has to offer. The quality of service provision is improving, transparent government is emerging, less business has to be conducted over the counter and the relationship between the public authorities and the citizen can be improved. Out of this transformation, it is claimed, a completely different type of government is reckoned to be finally appearing, one that is better able to perform public tasks to the satisfaction of all relevant target groups. Customer satisfaction for citizens, reduced administrative loads for businesses and efficiency gains and reduced costs for government should be some of the resultant benefits — to name only the measurable ones. However, the road to this ideal situation is strewn with obstacles (though fortunately with opportunities, too). The crucial point is that it must be possible to ascertain whether promises are really being turned into reality, and what further effects are still emerging. In short, there is a need for measurements to be performed.

Measuring tools offer an important gauge for gaining an understanding of the state of affairs and undertaking policy actions ("what gets measured, gets done"). Little by little, measurements of electronic government are beginning to take shape in various countries. These measurements sometimes consist of evaluations of programs or individual national studies, in which a country surveys its progress in the area of electronic government. One particular feature of these studies is that they are usually repeated over time. Then there are the international benchmark studies, often conducted by big consultancy firms, in which the current state of play with respect to electronic government is compared in different countries. Strikingly, these benchmarks often lack the necessary depth, have scarcely any theoretical foundation, and often confine themselves to the supply side of electronic government. Frankly speaking, most of these studies are no more than a tally of government Web sites and the content and services that the government has chosen to display "in the shop window." It is like trying to ascertain the success or added value of a company by simply looking at the breadth of its product range.

At the international level, therefore, there is a growing need to improve on the current measuring tools and then, obviously, to make regular use of them. For policymakers, this would have two significant advantages. Firstly, regular measurements can reveal the progress of electronic government in a country. Using this information (measurement is knowledge), policymakers can determine the areas in which an additional effort is required. Secondly, these measurements can be used to reveal the differences between countries, enabling countries to learn from one another. The administrative culture, the approach to governance and government control, the presence of basic records as a basis for service provision and the legal framework are all factors of importance for the development of electronic government. It is interesting, for example, that in the United States, specific laws have been adopted that have placed the subjects of electronic government, the reduction of red tape and performance measurement higher on the agenda. Notable examples of this are the Government Performance and Results Act of 1993 and the Clinger Cohen Act, which specifically deals with the role of ICT in a variety of government programs. Furthermore, the GPEA (Government Paperwork Elimination Act) stipulates that all government services must be offered in electronic format by 2003.

At present, however, there is no coherent and soundly constructed measuring tool on which international bodies such as the OECD can agree. Attempts are being made in individual countries to record the current state of the information society, including electronic government (examples here include the framework of the British e-Envoy and publications by the Australian National Office of the Information Economy). However, the various individual research projects and benchmarks are not particularly well suited to make proper comparisons possible, since each country employs its own definitions and measuring tools, producing measurements that cannot be compared with one another. Moreover, these measurements lack any robust theoretical and operational foundation. The customary approach used in existing benchmarks is that data is gathered from secondary sources, with aspects and indicators being included which "happen" to be present in those sources. This is not very satisfactory. Sooner or later, primary research will also have to be conducted, in which international teams use identical conceptual frameworks and tools to produce truly comparable research results. These results will need to relate not just to the supply of services, or the "exterior" of electronic government, they will also need to direct the spotlight "behind the scenes" of service provision (the organization of the back-office), and on the intensity of use and effectiveness of electronic services.

We performed research in the Netherlands on behalf of the Ministry of Economic Affairs and the Ministry of the Interior and Kingdom Relations (Dialogic, ZenC & Argitek, 2002). For this benchmark, the assignment was (with the help of secondary sources supplemented with national studies) to create as accurate a picture as possible of the state of play with electronic government in the Netherlands and its position compared with other countries in the benchmark. The other countries are: Australia, Canada, Germany, Finland, France, Japan, Singapore, the United Kingdom, the United States and Sweden. Because we are not yet in a position to present the results, we confine ourselves in what now follows to discussing the approach and methodological aspects of this research. On the basis of our experiences, we offer suggestions regarding an appropriate international approach and recommendations about the measuring tool and method.

This chapter is organized as follows. In the following section, we deal with the purpose of the chapter. We focus on three questions: What do we want to measure? How will we measure? And what methods are suitable? In Section Three, we look at five existing benchmark studies and seek to compare these with one another. Because these existing studies have considerable limitations, we proceed in the ensuing sections to devise the building blocks for a more robust and standardized way of measuring. The definition and elucidation of concepts is the subject of Section Four. Section Five is devoted to a number of methodological points. Section Six focuses on our conceptual model, while Section Seven deals with devising the measuring tool in indicators. Points regarding the approach and the research methods are dealt with in Section Eight, and the final section is devoted to the issue of processing research data: from measurement to evaluation.

The Purpose of This Chapter

A sophisticated information society — and, as an element of that society, electronic government — requires a sophisticated set of research tools which will do justice to the complexity and variety of ICT in society. This chapter constitutes a first step towards the constitution of such a measuring tool for electronic government. It deals with three questions:

- What do we want to measure? (The theory: what do we mean by electronic government?)
- How do we want to measure? (The practice: how do we operationalize electronic government?)
- What methods are suitable? (The approach: primary or secondary data collection, qualitative/quantitative?)

The response to these questions should produce a framework within which electronic government can be measured and evaluated. The framework is intended to produce a survey of the state of progress with regard to the development and penetration of ICT in the public sector in a given country. It relates to the "state of the art" in the development of electronic government. An important feature is that the tool must be applicable in more than one country. It must therefore provide comparable information, regardless of the administrative culture and structure. As we develop this framework, we shall make sure that we draw attention to its advantages and disadvantages. After all, electronic government is never complete. Technologies and services are subject to continual change. A measuring tool therefore needs to be flexible, and to grow together with its subject.

Electronic government can be measured in two ways: absolutely and relatively. Absolute measurement primarily means hard figures that contain clear information, such as the time of a stage-winner in the Tour de France. Often, though, it is also interesting and instructive to see how others have scored in the same section, such as the second- and third-placed cyclists and the pack. One can then see how much of a gap the stage-winner has put between himself and the competition. At the same time, the competition can see how well the winner has done and, if they look a little further, why. This process of comparing measurements and drawing lessons from them is called benchmarking.

Existing Benchmark Studies Compared with One Another

In measuring the phenomenon of electronic government, we do not, of course, have to start from scratch. International organizations such as the European Union and the

United Nations (and, shortly, the OECD) are seeking to establish the progress their member states have made in developing electronic government. Market research and consultancy firms (such as Gartner and Accenture) present fairly regular rankings of countries in this area.

For this chapter, we have looked at a number of benchmark studies which are often cited in international contexts. These studies contain elements which may be of value for our measuring tool. They are the following comparative studies[1]:

- Accenture (2002), eGovernment Leadership — Realizing the Vision;
- CID/Harvard University (2001), The Networked Readiness Index;
- Cap Gemini/Ernst & Young (2002, April), Web-Based Survey on Electronic Public Services, results of the second measurement;
- Gartner/IMD (2001), E-Government in the EU: An Unlikely Gold Rush; and
- UN/DPEPA (2001), Benchmarking E-Government: A Global Perspective.

These five different studies measure countries' *overall* performance in the area of e-government. Countries are ranked on the basis of indices constituted from various individual indicators. A different set of indicators is used in each study, and the scoring method, weightings and so on also differ from study to study. If the studies are aggregated to produce an overall score, this provides an indication of external validity. If completely different types of measurement produce comparable results, the (presumed) reliability of the aggregated overall score is greater. Equally, substantial differences between the individual final scores would point to a less reliable outcome.

As part of our work to determine the Netherlands' position with regard to ICT in the public sector, we performed an aggregation of this kind. Figure 1 provides an overview

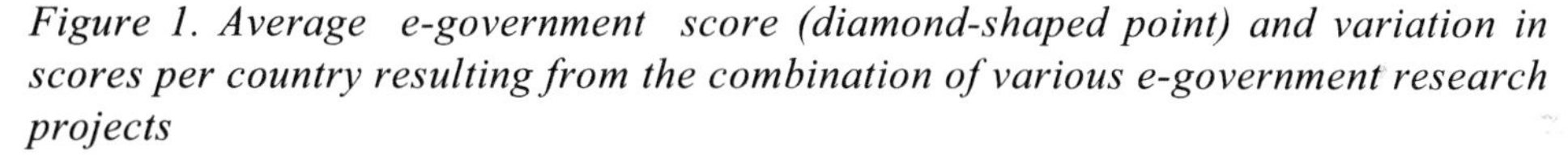

Figure 1. Average e-government score (diamond-shaped point) and variation in scores per country resulting from the combination of various e-government research projects

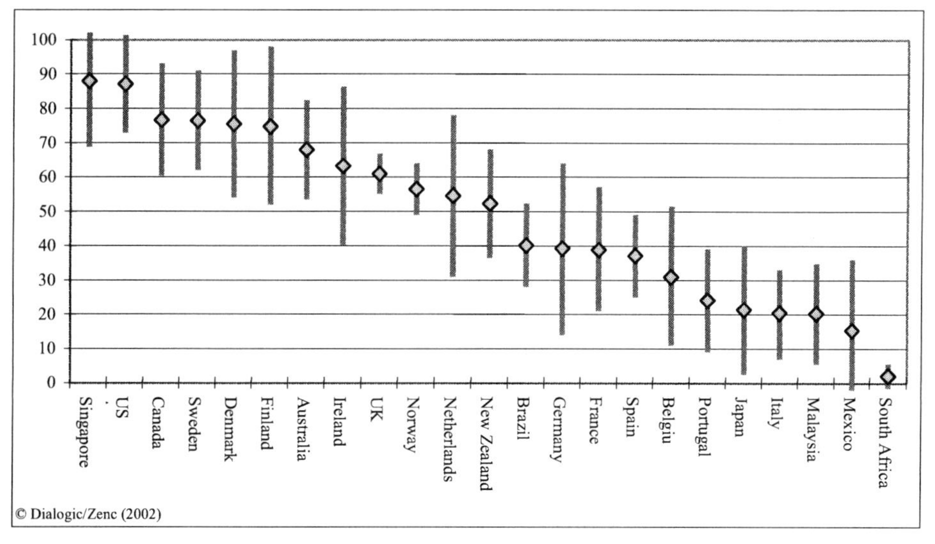

Table 1. Scenario: Average scores

	score	range
1 Singapore	88	(1-2)
2 USA	87	(1-2)
3 Canada	77	(3-5)
4 Sweden	76	(3-6)
5 Finland	75	(3-6)
6 Denmark	75	(4-8)
7 Australia	68	(7-8)
8 Ireland	63	(7-10)
9 UK	61	(5-11)
10 Norway	56	(9-12)
11 Netherlands	55	(9-12)
12 New Zealand	52	(10-12)
13 Brazil	40	(13-15)
14 Germany	39	(13-15)
15 France	39	(14-16)
16 Spain	37	(14-17)
17 Belgium	31	(16-17)
18 Portugal	24	(18-19)
19 Japan	21	(18-21)
20 Malaysia	20	(20-21)
21 Italy	20	(19-22)
22 Mexico	15	(20-23)
23 South Africa	2	(22-23)

© Dialogic/Zenc (2002)

of 23 countries, ranked on the basis of their aggregated overall scores — shown as diamond-shaped points in the middle of the vertical bars. The length of these bars shows the standard deviation between the individual final scores, providing an additional gauge of the reliability of this specific measurement value.

In general, the extent of divergence between the studies is considerable — the United Kingdom and Norway are the only countries with a robust overall score. The final scores and ranking shown in Table 1 should thus be treated with due caution. The differences are largely attributable to the substantial differences between the indicators on which the indices are based.

If ranking were arranged on the basis of maximum and minimum scores (the top and bottom of the vertical bars), this might produce different orderings. The variable "range" shows what positioning the most positive and negative scenarios produce.

However, we found that most of the existing benchmarks are fairly *partial* and superficial. Their superficiality derives from the fact that only a small number of specific elements are taken into consideration, and that those elements are external (i.e., they do not involve looking *behind* the Web site). There is a tendency to use traditional datasets (mainlines, Web hosts, etc.) because these are easily available. However, as an indicator they have little or nothing to do with e-government. This way of proceeding is all the more dangerous given that most of the studies pass over the specific qualitative differences between countries. Their partiality resides in the fact that the figures only relate to the Internet, and that counting focuses on the supply of services. Moreover, no distinction is made on the basis of the relative importance of the services in question. It makes sense to draw an analytical distinction between high-frequency interactions between government and citizens (or businesses) which are relevant to a broad target group (usually referred to in Anglo-Saxon countries as "high impact" services) and more or less "exotic" (sporadically occurring) services. To put it another way, an address change should be regarded and counted differently from a sex change. To give a concrete example, in one study (Accenture, 2002), the possibility of electronic interaction with the national ombudsman (a facility that probably involves no more than a few dozen e-mails per year) is given an equal weighting in the overall score for the Netherlands as, for instance, the electronic submission of income tax declarations — a service with 3.7 million users. A theoretical weakness of all the studies is that, in order to assess the degree of advancement of e-government (i.e., of government Web sites), they unquestioningly assume the validity of the familiar cumulative scale which runs from "flat" information via interaction and transaction through to "integration." However, it is highly questionable whether the final step (integration) automatically follows on from "transaction." It may be that the developmental phases in e-government simply cannot be recorded on a unidimensional scale of this kind. Rather, one tends to find a divergence, in which the final two phases are more or less mutually exclusive.

Defining and Clarifying Concepts

A more thorough approach to research into the development of electronic government in different countries starts with a clear definition of the research field. In the course of our search, we encountered a great many different definitions of e-government. They vary from the very broad ("making life better for citizens") to the very narrow ("the offering of public services via the Internet"). A neat definition is provided by the Flemish government: "E-government is best defined as the redesigning of the public sector's internal and external relations, based on network processes via information and communication technology, with the aim of ensuring better government and optimal service provision, and increasing citizens' involvement" (Flemish Government, 2000).

Atlin (2000) has made a comparison between the approaches to and definitions of electronic government in a number of Anglo-Saxon countries.

US: Creating an Electronic Government: Government will be transformed by electronic means for doing business and provide the public with better access to the government, similar to how "amazon.com" transformed bookselling.

UK: E-government "focuses on better services for citizens and businesses and more effective use of the Government's information resources … the transformation of government activities by the application of e-business methods throughout the public sector."

New Zealand: "E-government is a way for governments to use the new technologies to provide people with more convenient access to government information and services, to improve the quality of the services and to provide greater opportunities to participate in our democratic institutions and processes."

Canada: "E–Government

- begins with digitizing information
- leads to delivering services – but certainly doesn't end here
- interactive tool for engaging citizens in the development of policies, programs and services
- leading, ultimately, to E-democracy
- as well as promotion of e-everything, and
- effect on economy and society."

source: Atlin (2000).

Our definition is as follows. We speak of electronic government when a government organization, for the conduct of its public tasks — and, beyond them, its operational processes, services and interaction with citizens and businesses — makes use of ICT, combining the new media with the old media.[2] It thus relates to internal operational processes, external service provision and the supply of information by government institutions via open and/or closed electronic networks.

The interest in e-government is of course primarily attributable to the possibilities and the rapid rise of the Internet. The government is able to use Internet technology in support of various processes, involving various different relations between the various players. However, we must widen our scope to include more than just the Internet.

Definition: The Technique of Electronic Government

ICT is a wide-ranging concept. Central to it is the computer. Infrastructures and network services connect computers with one another. In addition, all kinds of information and communication services, some of them featuring audio and video technology, also fall within the scope of ICT. In this analysis, the term ICT is used in the broad sense, to mean all technologies with which information — data, text, images and sound — can be stored, processed and (re)presented, and all technologies used for communication. ICT is more than just the Internet. Within the field of electronic government, interesting developments can also be identified in closed networks (e.g., EDI for the tax and customs authorities) and non-Internet related services and platforms (mobile communication, smartcards, etc.).

Definition: Players and Relations

Electronic government can also be described and categorized with reference to the various *players* involved in it. These are G (*government*), E (*employee*), B (*business*) and C (*citizen* or *customer*).

- G-C and G-B relate primarily to the service counter or performance function of government with respect to the target groups of citizens and businesses. (In addition, C-G should be kept distinct so that a positioning can be attributed to e-democracy.);
- B-G relates primarily to purchasing (e-procurement), in which the government in fact operates as a market player;
- G-E relates to applications for government employees (found on intranets, etc.);
- G-G relates primarily to the exchange of information between governments and public organizations and to the streamlining of processes.

It is striking that this categorization into players and their relations is becoming an increasingly prominent feature of e-government policy in different countries. In Singapore and the USA, for example, activities in e-government policy are clustered on the basis of these interaction models.

Definition: Goals, Areas (Public Functions) and Phases of Development

One relevant aspect of the definition and delimitation of terms is the question of what goals are set. These goals may be very broad and far-reaching, or highly restricted and narrowly defined. Within these definitions, we discovered considerable differences in countries' level of ambition. Measuring tools must obviously reflect the underlying objectives of e-government. These may be as follows:

- Improved quality of service provision by government organizations, because they are set up to respond to citizens' concerns (a demand-driven user perspective).
- Enabling services to be integrated, streamlined and individualized (e.g., location-based services).
- Reducing costs of service provision (e.g., by improving the effectiveness and efficiency of government organizations), resulting in a lower price for the user (e.g., reduction of transaction costs).
- Lowering the threshold of access to services and current information by ensuring that these are provided in a way that is independent of time and place.

Table 2. Goals and progress of e-government policy

	Objective (national, unless otherwise specified)	*Status*[1]	*Measurement*
Netherlands	1. 25% electronic service provision at central and decentralised level by end of 2002 2. 75% electronic service provision at central and decentralised level by end of 2006 3. 15% interactive policy in policy-making bodies by 2002 and 100% by 2006 4. all municipalities online by 2002 5. 25% lighter administrative burden by 2006[2] 6. 10% productivity increase in executive services 7. 5 million e-ID cards by 2006	Partially reformulated	1. Attained 4. 85%
Germany	By 2005, all administrative transactions that are suited to ESD are online	New	-
Finland	A significant proportion of all forms and applications should be processed electronically by 2001	Unchanged	-
France	All government bodies accessible for services and documents by 2000	Unchanged	Attained via Service-Public portal
Japan	The most advanced e-government in fiscal year 2005	New	
UK	100% electronic service provision by 2005	Unchanged	42% in 2000 73% expected in 2002[3]
USA	Public access to government services and documents by 2003. Possibility of submitting forms electronically	Unchanged	
Sweden	No specific objective for e-government. Modernisation of the government regarded as an objective, however.	Unchanged	
Australia	By 2001 all services that are suited to ESD are online	Unchanged	Attained
Canada	1. All significant government services completely online by 2004 2. 10% more customer satisfaction by 2005	Unchanged	2. biennial measurement of customer satisfaction
Singapore	1. To transform Singapore into an advanced information society 2. 100% electronic service provision in fiscal year 2002	Partially reformulated	2. 85% in fiscal year 2001

- Improving policy- and decision-making processes.
- The horizontal and vertical integration of government institutions. Horizontal integration relates to multiple policy areas or public tasks, while vertical integration involves the combination of (services provided by) multiple layers of government.
- Improving relations between citizens and the government, and revitalizing democratic processes and institutions.

What immediately strikes one's notice is that most of the goals are formulated in terms of means. The overwhelming majority of targets are formulated with respect to the supply of services and information — and hence with respect to readiness indicators, rather than to use (intensity) or the effects of use (impact). In practice, the use of technology (the electronic channel) is elevated into a strategy in its own right. A second striking point is that, although all kinds of ambitions are formulated, there is usually no associated measurement of progress.

A subsequent aspect of definition (in addition to goals) concerns the fields in which the government is involved. Which public tasks should be taken into account in the analysis? In the Netherlands, we tend to distinguish e-government from areas such as e-learning and e-health. In other countries, it is different. In the USA, for example, the tendency is to take all public tasks into account, and to include all fields of application, including e-health, e-learning, "e-military" and even "e-court" under the heading of e-government.

Finally, there is the question of maintaining a dynamic perspective. E-government is never complete. It is an ongoing innovation that needs to be fed by learning processes. The following steps or phases in this process are often distinguished:[6]

- Information provision (the government is the transmitter)
- Interaction (the recipient starts to communicate back)
- Transaction (interaction involving a financial element; more complex)
- Integration (cooperation between government institutions)
- Transformation (the government decides on new forms of organization)

These elements should also appear in the measuring tool. The approach to measurement must have a certain degree of "in-built" sensitivity to the developmental stages at which the activities and players concerned are located. We shall return to this point in Section 6. First, though, we wish to set out a number of methodological points about the pros and cons of measuring activities undertaken to date.

METHODOLOGICAL POINTS CONCERNING E-GOVERNMENT BENCHMARKS

"Benchmarking is systematic research into the performance and underlying processes and methods of one or more leading reference organizations in a certain field, and the comparison of one's own performance and operating methods with these 'best practices', with the goal of locating and improving one's own performance." (Camp, 1989)

These elements of benchmarking stand out all the more clearly when measurements are repeated periodically, revealing the subject's relative progress compared with others and compared with previous periods. A country may have made progress in absolute terms, but may at the same time have been overtaken by other countries on both sides. The longitudinal perspective is thus of importance. A single measurement is simply a snapshot, and does not provide much information. However, a few points need to be made regarding the measuring of electronic government in an international perspective.

Firstly, a remark is called for on the unit of analysis - the individual country. It might be more logical to compare regions or metropolitan areas. There is something odd about comparing the Netherlands with countries the size of Canada, the USA and Australia. In terms of relative scale, it would be more obvious to compare the former with an individual state or province in one of the latter countries. Singapore has more in common with a large city or a small region than with a nation state. And there are enormous differences between regions in big countries. The USA and Australia have both highly advanced and very backward areas with respect to the development of electronic government. How much sense does it therefore make to refer to the USA or Australia as individual countries? From the methodological viewpoint, this problem is insoluble, given the availability of sources. When interpreting the results, then, allowance will have to be made for this variation.

The second point concerns the incorrect identification of the term electronic government with the Internet. This is found in numerous sources, and frequently leads to considerable errors of measurement. Closed networks (EDI) and stand-alone applications can also be important. Furthermore, it is important to look "behind the Web site" at how service provision actually works. How valuable is the possibility of obtaining a copy of a birth certificate via the Internet, if a two-month waiting period and a trip to an office is then needed in order to collect it? Finally, there is the question of the *efficiency and intelligence of the whole service-production system,* and not just the presence or attractiveness of the Internet as a layer of presentation.

This brings us to a further point. Truly intelligent solutions are not very visible, and that makes them difficult to measure. Technology plays less of a leading role here. It is more a question of organizational and process-related adjustments. An example here is child allowance, which was originally dealt with by a separate organization in the Netherlands, and was then provided via a tie-in with the GBA (Municipal Basic Registration) as a proactive service (there is no need to apply for it - you receive it if you are entitled to it). A few more examples (and nuances): more intelligent than an electronic form is a direct link between files, as is aimed for in the Netherlands by the Elektronische Heerendiensten Project for the electronic delivery of mandatory information by SMEs. Fewer services (or integrated service provision) might well be better and more efficient for the target groups than an enormous range of (partly overlapping) electronic services. A total solution is preferable to any number of partial solutions. Smarter than the one-office principle is the no-office concept, in which the customer's knowledge (data in a record) is directly (without interaction) converted into a value-added service. "Intelligent" records, which ensure that large quantities of data no longer need to be called up separately, or make the reuse of data (single delivery) possible, are of course superior in terms of efficiency and the reduction of administrative tasks, but are also less visible and are hard to measure. In our own research, we have sought to make this visible by also analyzing concrete services.

A fourth comment relates to the fact that multiple parties have an impact on progress in the field of electronic government. This applies both to the infrastructure of electronic government (ISPs and broadband providers, for example), but also to service providers in areas such as payment traffic (banks), safety and so on. It is also possible for market players to be brought in to perform all or part of public tasks — an example here is *certification authorities*. If this is done successfully, should it count as (electronic) government or not? For the target group — whether they are citizens, business leaders, or the employees of other government bodies - the identity of the service provider makes no difference: all they judge is the result. In this research (in the national studies) we have investigated whether use is made of PPP arrangements. Where public activities are carried out by private organizations in the form of a PPP, we have regarded this as a part of e-government.

Our next point concerns the making of pronouncements about the results or performance of electronic government. In our research, we have identified impact indicators which should tell us something about matters such as efficiency gains and the reduction of administrative tasks. The difficulty here is that we lack proper zero measurements and, above all, a "calibrated" tool that is sensitive to differences in the starting position of countries in the benchmark. If a highly efficient service provision process already exists in Country A, the added value of efforts in the area of electronic government will be relatively limited. By contrast, if Country B has highly inefficient operating processes, it will be easy to make a considerable leap forwards by providing services electronically. To put it another way, a 50% efficiency gain in Country B need not be better than a 10% gain in Country A — it depends on the starting point. There is no adequate solution to this problem. Measuring makes more sense the more often it is repeated over time. It is not just the relative positions that are of interest, but also the shift in relative positions over time.

Finally, obvious errors of measurement may also be committed if insufficient consideration is taken of factors such as administrative structure (e.g., the degree of centralization), culture (e.g., the general confidence of citizens in the government) and extent of government (such as the number of governmental tasks and available means for performing them) in a country. In particular, differences in the extent of the public sector in the different countries can lead to distortion.

TOWARD A CONCEPTUAL MODEL

What, ideally, would you wish to measure when considering progress in the policy area of electronic government? As a researcher, you would like to be able to pronounce on the effects of policy drives and new developments. If so, however, you have to conduct research into what the target groups of electronic government (citizens, businesses and people within the government, itself) *experience* in terms of gains and increased convenience (as always, we leave pleasure out of the picture). What gains of time and efficiency are realized? What cost savings result? To what extent can citizens be seen to be more involved in decision-making? What is the quality of the services that - preferably, of course, in integrated form - are provided? In short, what added value is created? Note well that, for these target groups, it is irrelevant whether the added value is generated via electronic means or not. They want their problem to be solved, and are mainly interested in an intelligent (proactive, thoughtful, integrated, etc.) government (and not directly in electronic government as such). These pronouncements concerning effects are called impact indicators. Unfortunately, these effects or impact indicators are almost never researched systematically. In this area, new primary research is therefore required.

Slightly less ambitiously, we seek measurement data that will tell us something about the use (or rather, intensity of use) of services and processes that are offered electronically. This involves research topics such as the use that citizens and businesses make of specific electronic services, the extent to which the government uses ICT in connection with interactive policy development, and so on. We call these indicators intensity indicators. Unfortunately, the source material that is available on these points is highly sporadic in nature. Thus, it is only very rarely that we encounter figures for the number of visitors to government Web sites. This is another area in which new primary research is needed.

What certainly is possible at this current stage in the development of electronic government is research into the prerequisites for electronic government. These criteria can be divided up into aspects that have a direct influence on the policy area of electronic government and those that have more to do with the information society in general. Examples of these include Internet penetration, public attitude, citizens' ICT skills, privacy and safety laws and available electronic infrastructure. We call these prerequisites readiness indicators. We shall regularly refer to this distinction in types of measurement.

Coherence Between Indicators: Conceptual Model

In the introduction, we claimed that there is no robust and well-defined measuring tool available. What we do find in various places are lists of indicators which — taken

Figure 2. Electronic government flywheel

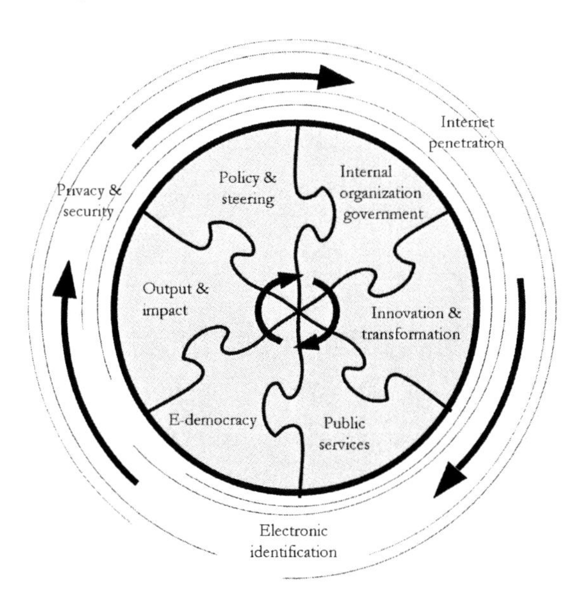

together — represent the beginnings of a measuring tool. However, we have not yet arrived at any proper understanding of how these indicators relate to one another. To take a step in this direction, we have devised a "complete overview" of topics, indicators and explanatory variables, represented in the form of a flywheel. This flywheel indicates what needs sorting out in order to achieve further progress in the area of electronic government.

As prerequisites for electronic government in the outermost ring in Figure 2, we have identified a number of factors that are of importance for the development of electronic government. These are factors over which the government is able — to a greater or lesser extent — to exert influence in its policy on electronic government. Before service provision is possible by electronic means, there must be sufficient connectivity (Internet penetration in households and businesses); for transactions, an electronic identity (electronic signature) is required; for citizens, it is vital that privacy can be guaranteed; and there must of course be a certain critical mass of available services.

Within the flywheel, various themes are identified which *taken together* provide a picture of the development (or level of sophistication) of electronic government. These themes should be regarded as "pieces in the puzzle," and are thus closely interconnected. As our starting-point, we have chosen policy and the method of control. Policy partly affects the prerequisites, but also leads to new applications within the government — which in turn create the conditions for external service provision. Within government, not only does new technology need to be introduced and information provision and exchange optimized, but operational processes and organizational structures also need to be changed. We call this (business process) reengineering the "innovation and transformation" of government. For example, it may relate to cooperation between government institutions in order to arrive at integrated service provision. This organizational change is scarcely visible — let alone measurable — but nonetheless is ultimately of central importance within the conceptual model and hence the measuring tool. Once the citizen has experienced new forms of service provision, and is familiar with new interactive possibilities, the demand for involvement in policy- and decision-making (e-democracy) will also increase. Within the subject area of e-democracy, the openness of government information is also of relevance, together with other factors which contribute to the transparency of government machinery. This side of electronic government is regarded of great importance by citizens in particular. If all these links in the flywheel do their work properly, this will lead to the effects (customer satisfaction, increased efficiency, a reduction in administrative tasks, etc.) which we earlier identified as impact indicators, and these will in turn set off a new round of policy and governance measures.

TRANSFORMATION INTO A MEASURING TOOL

We have, where possible, translated the subject areas from the conceptual model in Section 6 into "'underlying" indicators. The list of indicators (i.e., our measuring tool) looks as on the next page.

Subject 1. Policy and control
- policy objectives and progress
- budget
- government control and organisational coherence
- relevant legislation and regulations
- policy on public-private partnership

Subject 2. Prerequisites
- Internet penetration in households
- Internet penetration in businesses
- electronic signature (citizens and businesses)
- privacy
- percentage of Web sites for government institutions

Subject 3. Provision of services to citizens
- penetration of electronic service provision
- level of sophistication of service provision
- use of electronic service provision (concentrating on four[1] specific services)
- (examples of) integrated service provision

Subject 4. Provision of services to businesses
- penetration of electronic service provision
- level of sophistication of service provision
- use of electronic service provision (concentrating on four[2] specific services)
- (examples of) integrated service provision

Subject 5. Internal government functioning
- quality of services offered; presence of government portal, product catalogue, electronic forms
- chosen solutions for identification/authentication (government-side PKI)
- streamlining of basic data
- intranet among government institutions
- policy on standardisation

Subject 6. E-democracy
- policy on openness
- percentage of members of parliament with their own Web site
- policy on ICT in policy development
- availability of legislation and regulations on the Internet
- availability of policy information on the Internet

Subject 7. Output/impact
- effects of provision of electronic services to citizens (customer satisfaction)
- effects of provision of electronic services to businesses (reduction of administrative load)
- gains in efficiency and productivity increase within government

Each of these indicators obviously requires further elaboration. Agreement on the details is required between those countries that wish to be monitored and compared internationally. The following considerations should be made for each indicator:

- the definition to which the object relates;
- how we want to measure the object (method);
- the unit in which the measurement is expressed, or the measure which indicates what we want to know about the object;
- where applicable, the standard which defines the performance which is acceptable or which is being aimed at.

In this area, therefore, a common system of concepts needs to be developed, as was previously done, for example, in connection with the measurement of R&D (the Frascati manual).

The major drawback of having an enormous series of measuring tools and summaries of indicators, is that you are no longer able to see the forest for the trees. The major advantage is that you end up with a nice checklist of all the factors which are involved in the measurement of e-Government, and that you gain a picture of the requirements that you need to set for the measuring tool and the method. This is the subject of the following section.

RECOMMENDATIONS ON THE PROPER APPROACH

Each of the various indicators from the previous section requires its own approach. In any case, the research will have to use a combination of quantitative and qualitative methods. There are numerous methods with which it is possible to measure and compare the state of play with regard to electronic government at the international level. In the foregoing, we have already discussed one frequently used method: that of a benchmark on the basis of secondary analysis. This means using desk research (Internet and literature research) to collect and analyze as many sources and publications as possible about electronic government. This analysis should be conducted on the basis of the aspects and indicators we have included in our measuring tool. As far as possible, the secondary source material must meet the following requirements:

- The reliability and validity of the measuring tool and measurement results. The measuring tool that is used measures what it is supposed to measure, and the results are generally applicable. Ideally, the publication gives an insight into the research method that has been used (e.g., the extent of sampling);
- Repeatability. As we want to have regular (e.g., biennial) updates of a benchmark, preference is given to research which is likely to be repeated in the same manner every few years;
- Topicality. We should collect research that is as up-to-date as possible. In any case, it should not predate the previous benchmark. The shelf-life of many ICT figures, such as Internet penetration, is particularly short;
- Completeness. As far as possible, the research that is collected should cover countries included in the benchmark. The advantage of this is that the same measuring tools are often used in different countries.

Experience teaches that working with secondary sources does not suffice to provide the detailed input for our measuring tool. There is scarcely any quantitative material available, at either the international or national level. The few internationally comparable publications about electronic government that exist scarcely, if at all, meet the criteria, as they often cover only a very limited proportion of the requirements (at best a few readiness indicators). One consequence of this is that we are compelled to fall back on qualitative individual national studies. These national studies are highly valuable in themselves, but the results are hard to compare with those from other national studies. Moreover, the international sources are not based on our tool (and often not on any e-government measuring tool). This sometimes calls for a lot of juggling with the data, which undermines the reliability and validity of a benchmark.

Fortunately, there are sufficient alternative ways of gaining insight into the development of electronic government in an international context and, above all, of drawing comparisons. They call for intensive international harmonization and research coordination, for instance, within the setting of the OECD. In order to measure electronic government, the OECD countries need to arrive at an agreement about a measuring tool in which all relevant aspects and indicators of electronic government are described in context with one another and operationalized. To this end, we have described an example of a common reference framework. Each country would then be responsible for measuring and analyzing the national situation with regard to electronic government. The same set of research tools would be used in each country, preferably during the same time period. If necessary, the measuring tool could be adapted to the national context. For example, large countries could use a larger sample than smaller countries. The results would then be collected and compiled at the international — i.e., OECD — level. In their report to the OECD, countries would be able to contextualize the results in the light of specific national characteristics, such as the structure and extent of the government.

An important consequence of this approach is that the benchmark for electronic government would be based on *primary data collection* in the individual countries, whose results would be comparable with those of other countries. Obviously, some thought would be required concerning the methods for primary data collection. One possibility would be *panel research* among different electronic government target groups (citizens, businesses, government employees). They could be given the opportunity to respond to written, telephone or Web surveys about electronic government. Another method would be the collection of *Web statistics* about electronic government. Other possibilities include the straightforward counting of purchased electronic services and transactions. In terms of impact, a survey could be conducted of the gain in efficiency (time and money) resulting from use of the electronic channel as compared with other, traditional channels with respect to a selection of services.

It must be borne in mind that the measurements should have a *longitudinal character*. Serial measurements alone are capable of providing insight into (shifts in) the absolute and relative position of the benchmark countries in comparison with one another. Furthermore, the measuring tool must be flexible enough to take account of new developments in electronic government in subsequent measurements. In this way, the emphasis can shift from readiness indicators via intensity indicators to impact indicators.

- Gathering together the building blocks from the previous sections and combining them with our recommendations, the measuring tool must take the following considerations into account:
- The supply and demand sides of e-government: in other words, not just the supply of services, but also the need for them, the use that is made of them and the relevant characteristics of the target group;
- The development perspective: readiness, intensity and impact. In other words, the various phases in which e-government activities may be situated;

- As regards readiness indicators: the identification of prerequisites for the development of e-government and the contextualization of goals and means. The key causal relations (goals and means, inputs and outputs) must be expressed here;
- As regards impact indicators: the identification of different types of effect or effectiveness for different target groups;
- The multiple roles of government (service provision, e-democracy) and interaction patterns with different players (citizens, businesses and other governments) should be distinguishable;
- Ultimately, measurement must take place at the right aggregation level: measurement makes most sense at the level of specific services;
- Policy relevance: the sum of indicators must provide the government organization in question with relevant information;
- Relevant structural characteristics and environmental variables which may explain differences between countries or regions should be taken into account in qualitative descriptions.

CONCLUSIONS

The results provided by the measuring tool need to be analyzed and interpreted. Only then will it become clear what a country's position is in the international context. This process of judgement is hence a form of evaluation. The simplest evaluation is to compile a country ranking for each aspect and/or indicator. For each indicator, an average score is calculated. Countries can see whether they are higher or lower than this score. These rankings are aggregated to a single level, as was the case in Figure 1 for example. Although this appears to be the most objective measure, it does have a number of drawbacks. We have referred in the foregoing to the different weightings that can be assigned to indicators. The scores cannot simply be added up, without any weighting. However, a complicating factor is that the assigning of weighting may differ from country to country. Some countries may attach more value to a particular indicator than others (an example here is the diminished importance attached to the protection of privacy in the USA in connection with the War on Terror).

There are still further ways of arriving at a final judgement. If required, these may be used in combination with one another. However, these are somewhat more laborious. Firstly, a selection of e-government goals can be made. The scores of countries are then compared with this standard. The e-government goals would be determined within the OECD. They would be based on what is technically and organizationally feasible with regard to electronic government and what is realistic at the time of measurement. The measuring tool would focus on these goals. An important advantage of this is that with each measurement, the goals and the measuring tool would "automatically" evolve together with the current possibilities in the area of electronic government.

Another form of evaluation is possible by relating the measurement results to national objectives as set by the governments themselves with regard to electronic government. However, this is a less objective measure. As we have seen, national objectives differ in terms of both content and ambitiousness. Countries with less ambitious objectives will score better than ambitious countries. Moreover, objectives may be adapted between measurements.

In any case, it is important to take the specific context into account in the final evaluation of a country with regard to electronic government. An evaluation is not just based on a list of tables. A benchmark offers space for supplementary information. In the Dutch benchmark, this supplementary information is found in a qualitative description of the situation with regard to ICT and the government in each country. This makes it possible to provide nuances and supplementary considerations, so that the position of each country is described as comprehensively as possible.

REFERENCES

Accenture. (2002, April). *E-government leadership: Realising the vision.*

Advies Overheid.nl. (2001). *De Overheid op Internet. Kwaliteitsmonitor Overheidswebsites en Juryrapport Webwijzer Aard 2001*, The Hague.

Atlin, D. (2000). *Governance in the digital economy.* Digital Foresight (presentation).

Camp, R. C. (1989). *Benchmarking: The search for industry best practices that lead to superior performance.* Milwaukee, WI: Impressum.

Cap, Gemini, Ernst & Young. (2002). *Web-base survey on electronic public services: Results on the second measurement.* Brussels: Europese Commissie.

Central IT Unit. (2000). *International benchmarking report.* Cabinet Office, London.

Dialogic. (2001). *E-government: de Vraagkant aan Bod. Een Inventarisatie van de Wensen en Verwachtingen van Burgers Over de Elektronische Overheid [about: A citizen consultation on e-government].* Utrecht: Dialogic in opdracht van het ministerie van Binnenlandse Zaken en Koninkrijksrelaties.

Dialogic. (2001). *What gets measured, gets done: Quick Scan Meetinstrumenten Elektronische Overheid.* Utrecht: Dialogic in opdracht van het Ministerie van Binnenlandse Zaken en Koninkrijksrelaties.

Dialogic. (2002). *Burgers aan Het woord: Oordelen en Klachten Over de Elektronische Overheid [about: An inventory of citizen's judgements and complains about the electronic government].* Utrecht: Dialogic in opdracht van het Programmabureau burger@overheid.

Dialogic. (2002). *Surfers in de Delta. Benchmark toegang en Vaardigheden ten Behoeve van ICT Toets 2002 [about: An ICT access and skills benchmark in 10 OECD countries].* Utrecht: Dialogic in opdracht van de ministeries van Economische Zaken en Onderwijs, Cultuur & Wetenschappen.

Dialogic, ZenC & Argitek. (2002a). *Pijler E: Rapportage ICT-toets Pijler E: Stand van Zaken Elektronische Overheid [about: An Egovernment benchmark in 10 OECD countries].* Utrecht: Dialogic in opdracht van de ministeries van Economische Zaken en Binnenlandse Zaken en Koninkrijksrelaties.

Dialogic, ZenC & Argitek. (2002b). *Bijlage I Pijler E: Rapportage ICT-toets Pijler E: Stand van Zaken Elektronische Overheid - Landenstudies.* Utrecht: Dialogic in opdracht van de ministeries van Economische Zaken en Binnenlandse Zaken en Koninkrijksrelaties.

Di Maio, A. (2001). *E-government in the EU: An unlikely goldrush.* (Paper voor het Gartner Symposion ITXPO 2001). Stanford: Gartner9.

Kirkman, G.S.,Osorio, C.A., & Sachs, J.D. (2002). Harvard report Chapter 2. The networked readiness index: Measuring the preparedness of nations for the networked world. In *The global information technology report 2001-2002: Readiness for the networked world*. Oxford: Oxford University Press[10].

UN/DPEPA. (2001). *Benchmarking e-government: A global perspective*. Washington DC: UN.

ENDNOTES

* The report on which this chapter is based was published in 2002.

1 Accenture (April 2002); Kirkman G.S., C.A. Osorio & J.D. Sachs (2002) (aka: CID/Harvard University (2001)); Cap, Gemini, Ernst & Young (2002); Di Maio, A. (2001) (aka: Gartner/IMD (2001)); UN/DPEPA (2001).

2 Roughly speaking, anything to do with the Internet may be regarded as new media. The old media represent the traditional automation techniques as used by government since the late-50s.

3 Compared with previous benchmark in 2000.

4 This objective is not exclusively bound up with the use of ICT, but can also be achieved, for example, by simplifying regulations.

5 Office of the e-Envoy (July, 2002).

6 As we mentioned in Section 3, this need not necessarily be a unidimensional development process.

7 Income tax, vehicle registration, changes of address and extracts from the Register of Births.

8 VAT, customs, registering (starting) a business, electronic procurement.

9 A.K.A.: Gartner/IMD (2001). *E-government in the EU: An unlikely goldrush.*

10 A.K.A.: CID/Harvard University (2001). *The networked readiness index: Measuring the preparedness of nations for the networked world.*

Chapter X

Drop the "e": Marketing E-Government to a Skeptical Public and Web-Weary Decision Makers

Douglas Holmes, www.dougholmes.com, France

ABSTRACT

This chapter was prepared originally for the 2002 Task Force of the OECD Project on the Impact of E-Government and was updated in 2004 for inclusion in the book, Practicing E-Government: A Global Perspective. The chapter addresses the risk of low public awareness and declining political interest as barriers to e-government, and considers ways governments can develop better marketing techniques to "sell" online services and the e-government concept to both groups. The term "marketing" is used loosely to mean both the presentation and promotion of actual online services to encourage people to use them, and the presentation and promotion of the theory and concept of e-government to ensure political understanding of its benefits to society. The chapter has two parts plus an initial Executive Summary that summarizes the points raised in both sections. Part A discusses demand-side issues: the lack of awareness and confusion among users and potential users of electronic services and how these issues can be addressed with various marketing techniques. While the greatest factor contributing to low take-up of electronic services continues to be poor Internet access and a lack of computer skills, the purpose of this report is not to address social exclusion issues. It is recognized that the digital divide is gradually being bridged and therefore the chapter primarily considers the person who has access to a computer but, for a variety of reasons, does not use it to access government services. Part B looks at the supply side and ways to market the concept of e-government to decision-makers — politicians and senior level bureaucrats — who are responsible for supporting and funding the development of online services and for removing remaining regulatory and legal barriers. The chapter does not address culture change within the public sector and the need to shift the mindset of government employees from traditional department-centric thinking into more customer-centric and user-friendly approaches. Overcoming employee resistance to new working methods requires more management skills than marketing skills. But marketing techniques can be used to address the risk of a backlash against e-government as declining political interest in the Internet generally and in e-government specifically coincides with the need to develop more complex and expensive electronic services and information systems. *The author would like to thank Stefan Czerniawski, David Hickman, Chris Roberts, and Rod Quiney for their contributions.*

EXECUTIVE SUMMARY

Part A. Demand Side: Marketing E-Government Externally to the Public

Most people who access government Web sites do so primarily for information purposes or, at most, to download a scanned form. Few are prepared to take the next step to conduct electronic two-way transactions that may require a payment or submission of personal data. For such interactions, most people still opt to wait in line at a government office and complete paper forms by hand.

Uncertainty of the take-up of electronic services makes it difficult to measure the benefits of e-government. There is a risk of overstating efficiency gains as a result of overestimating take-up, especially where existing delivery channels have to be retained. If take-up is lower and slower than expected, the benefits from investments in new technology will take longer to be fully realized.

Low take-up can be attributed to a number of factors, including people not having access to a computer or the skills to use one. But even the most experienced Web user may not trust security on the Internet, or they may not trust government with their electronic data. The desired services might not be available, service offerings may be of poor quality or a Web site may be too difficult to use. Quite often people are simply not aware that an electronic service exists or they don't see the advantage of using it.

The vast majority of visitors to government Web sites are first-time users, and they are not entirely sure what to expect. But few e-government strategies include a marketing component and, when applying for project funding, rarely is an agency asked to say how it intends to promote a service it intends to move online. Government tends to "inform" the public of changes to a process rather than "sell" a new service.

To encourage take-up, governments need to view their electronic services in much the same way that a private company would launch a new offering or product line: with much promotion and publicity. While still largely unsure how to go about it, some governments are at least starting to recognize they need some kind of a marketing strategy for e-government. Such a strategy should include:

1. *Traditional marketing practice*. Online services can be promoted through existing correspondence with citizens such as renewal notices, as well as advertising campaigns and through government's own touch points and front office staff. Governments can also do more target-marketing by adopting more sophisticated segmentation of different groups within society.
2. *Incentives*. Financial rewards can be given to citizens for using electronic services and non-financial incentives could include guarantees for faster and more reliable service. There is a need to guard against disparities that might negate the benefits of e-government and result in a disincentive to use electronic services.
3. *Personalized service and added value*. A number of intentions-based portals allow citizens to customize online services to their particular needs and tastes. CRM is still largely untested by government, but it can enhance intentions-based portals and enable segmentation beyond the established G2C, G2B and G2C categories. An emerging school of thought says government departments are not structured to operate outside their silos and it might be better to leave them as "wholesalers" of public services while creating a separate government "retailer" to package and deliver offerings from across the public sector based around life events, user intentions, segmentations, etc.
4. *Multiple delivery channels*. E-government should create new means of access and support traditional means of accessing public services. Through the use of such segmentation, governments can determine the most appropriate deliver channel(s) for a particular user group, e.g., wireless technologies to reach students. Few governments have developed an explicit channel strategy. Ultimately it will be necessary to integrate the different channels to provide citizen choice. Governments can also leverage their efforts to close the digital divide to encourage take-up of electronic public services.
5. *Use of intermediaries*. The mixed economy and network of third-party intermediaries that have developed to reach a critical mass of citizens in the physical world will ultimately be the best way to reach a critical mass in the virtual world. A commercial Web site can reach as many citizens in one day as a government Web site can in one month or a year, and a private company can provide added value to government services by packaging them with its own products and services, making them more market-focused and attractive to individual consumers. Ultimately public, private and voluntary sectors will be judged on the same standards by citizens/consumers/clients who don't care who's providing a service so long as it's good. An effort should therefore be made to bridge the gap between e-government and e-commerce, through the greater use of government content syndication and intermediaries to deliver public services.

Part B. Supply Side: Marketing E-Government Internally to Decision-Makers

E-government emerged as part of the late-90s Internet boom, which also coincided with a political priority to improve the quality of public services. Soon, e-government became the most prominent and radical IT initiative ever undertaken by the public sector, and it has helped to drive change and carry forward the reinventing government agenda.

If the success of e-government is to continue, it requires sustained political backing and executive sponsorship. Many practitioners believe it is not realistic to expect a consistent level of leadership over the long term. Anecdotal evidence suggests political interest is already on the wane. The reasons for declining enthusiasm in e-government can be attributed to a lack of understanding of the benefits, and the fact that many of the anticipated benefits — especially cost savings — have not so far materialized. The burst of dot-com bubble has had a spill-over effect: the Web is no longer a novelty.

Finally, there are changing political priorities. The events of September 11, 2001 propelled security concerns to the top of the political priority list, and it still takes precedence, at least in the US. In Europe, illegal immigration and race relations have become more important topics, and the economy and related issues are of greater concern everywhere. All of these have served to relegate the improvement of public services — and by extension, e-government, to the back-burner.

Just as proponents of e-governments need a marketing strategy to address the demand side of e-government and ensure take-up of online services, they also have to consider how they will address the supply side of e-government and ensure ongoing support from those who fund the development of online services. Even if it is not characterized as "marketing" in the traditional sense, more strategic and systematic approaches are needed to maintain high-level interest in e-government so that it keeps its place on the political agenda.

Internal marketing efforts should cover a range of activities and include the need to:

1. *Speak the "customer's" language.* Proponents of e-government need to view political leaders and senior-level managers more like customers and sell them on the concept of e-government. For the sales pitch, they need to tone down their technical jargon and speak a language that decision-makers understand. The way in which an e-government strategy is be communicated internally should be detailed within the strategy document itself. In many countries, this often entails keynote addresses, executive breakfast seminars, etc.
2. *Make friends, isolate enemies.* E-Government needs allies so that enthusiasm for it becomes infectious. Senior director-level champions need to be identified for every government department, and MBA's rather than engineers should be appointed as departmental IT heads — or, preferably, someone with knowledge in both areas. The more e-ministers the better, ideally one for each department, and backbench parliamentarians and opposition members who carry weight should be targeted. Antagonists can be neutralized by exercising diplomacy and working around them.
3. *Develop projects to improve decision-makers' own work.* Politicians and senior managers have to be educated and shown how the Internet can improve their work, including by automating decision-making processes such as the circulation of parliamentary papers and cabinet documents. Rather than lug kilograms of papers to every cabinet meeting, ministers should bring just their laptops or use touch screen terminals installed in the meeting room to call up documents, access minutes from past sessions, consult articles of laws, and communicate with officials. They can even participate in cabinet meetings from remote locations using videoconferencing. Such scenarios are already a reality in some of the emerging democracies such as Estonia and Croatia where they are not burdened with either decades-old technology infrastructures or centuries-old parliamentary traditions

and protocols. Technology can then be rolled into the country's parliament, perhaps using tablet PCs due to a lack of space for terminals on the members' benches. Once computers make it into the legislative chamber, securing political backing for e-government initiatives should come faster and easier.

4. *Better analysis of costs and benefits.* Because the required level of investment in e-government is increasing at a time when budget surpluses are diminishing, executive sponsorship of e-government initiatives will increasingly demand more formal cost benefit analysis, with business cases required to measure return on investment (ROI) and cost recovery. Political and senior management backing will also require better assessments of non-tangibles such as user satisfaction, take-up rates, improvements in speed and accuracy, alignment with the agency's mission and strategies, and opportunities for sharing applications across agencies.
5. *De-emphasize the link with public services.* The main factor motivating e-government has been to improve public services, which are now being supplanted at the top of the list of political priorities by more immediate concerns — the economy, security and the fight against terrorism, illegal immigration, etc. Because e-government is associated almost exclusively with service delivery, it has suddenly found itself out of fashion and on the wrong side of today's major issues. Champions and proponents of e-government must follow the new funding trails and re-position e-government to focus on those areas that now matter politically.
6. *Drop the "e" and re-brand e-government.* E-government has a fixation on technology. Initiatives such as integrated service delivery, CRM, process re-engineering and even public procurement are approached as technical challenges rather than organizational, cultural and political issues. By stressing the electronic, change agents create the risk that decision-makers will look at technology as an end in itself rather than an enabler. The "e" in e-government becomes more of a liability than an asset as it puts e-government on par with e-commerce or, at best, e-business. While e-government still has legs in countries which are at an early stage in the process, many decision-makers from developed countries are starting to experience "e-gov fatigue." Everything in politics has a shelf-life, and e-government is approaching its expiry date. Now might be a good time to drop the "e." To safeguard executive leadership and maintain the momentum for change, a new brand image for public sector reform should be sought to succeed e-government.

PART A: DEMAND SIDE: MARKETING E-GOVERNMENT EXTERNALLY TO THE PUBLIC

Introduction

Many governments today have a defined vision of e-government and have established a lead agency to drive the vision forward. Many also have departmental champions and targets to improve service and efficiency. Governments at all levels are deploying portals to provide a single point of entry, with new online service offerings added regularly. Increasingly, citizens and businesses can go onto a government Web site to register vehicles, renew drivers' licenses and passports, apply for planning permissions, file tax returns, and so on. The focus for many agencies is now shifting from getting services online to addressing the more specific needs of the users of public services.

Yet most people use government Web sites only for obtaining information or, at most, to download scanned forms. For research purposes, government Web sites are extremely popular. When the British Public Record Office put the 1901 census for England and Wales online on January 2, 2002 (census material is only released after 100 years), the site crashed on its first day under the weight of 30 million hits from people searching for details about their lives of their ancestors. If nothing else, the agency learned that it is difficult to predict the demand for online services and when peak levels of demand will occur.

Relatively fewer citizens are prepared to move beyond the "pdf-stage" and take the next step to conduct electronic two-way transactions, which may require a payment or submission of personal data. Surveys suggest people are interested in the idea of doing business with government electronically. A KPMG-MORI poll split the British population nearly evenly into three groups: 35% enthusiasts (those who were prepared to use six or more electronic government services annually); 29% pragmatists (prepared to use between one and five electronic government services); and 31% e-reluctants (not prepared to use any electronic government services). The remaining 5% didn't know (KPMG Consulting, 2002).

But people saying they're interested in doing something is not the same as actually doing it, and for two-way interactions with government, the majority of people by far still choose to wait in queues at a government office and complete paper forms by hand than do everything over the Web. The Pew Internet & American Life Project in 2002 indicated that only 16% of people in the United States who regularly access government Web sites have filed their taxes electronically and only 12% have renewed their automobile registration online (Larsen & Rainie, 2002). The KPMG-MORI poll found that only 7% of people who use the Internet regularly had renewed their TV licence electronically, a year after it was possible to do so. Almost everywhere, the number of citizens and businesses accessing public services over the Internet has been lower than expected.

Uncertainty of take-up makes it difficult to measure the benefits of e-government. There is a risk of overstating efficiency gains expected from e-government projects as a result of overestimating expected take-up, especially where existing service delivery channels have to be retained. If take-up is lower and slower than expected (or higher and faster, if it causes the system to crash!), the benefits from investments in new technology will take longer to be fully realized.

Governments are starting to recognize the problem. The National Audit Office (NAO) in the UK has called on the British government to establish take-up targets for electronic services to complement targets already in place for making services available online. The National Office for the Information Economy (NOIE) in Australia is undertaking a study into the take-up of electronic services in order to obtain a better understanding of how demand levels have impacted and will continue to impact e-government, particularly on a whole-of-government basis. The methodology and results of the study will be used by the Australian government as part of an ongoing process to determine future demand and to assist service delivery agencies to tailor their services to the specific needs of their clients.

Reasons for Low Take-Up

Low take-up of electronic public services can be attributed to a number of factors. Broadly speaking, people do not conduct business with government online because:

1. The digital divide — they do not have access or do not have the skills to access the Internet
2. They do not trust security on the Web
3. They do not trust the government
4. The electronic services they want are not available, or they do not know what they want
5. Service offerings are poor quality or the Web site is too difficult to use
6. They are not that aware an electronic service exists, or not aware of the advantages of using it

Digital Divide

In most countries, the digital divide remains the primary barrier to the take-up of electronic government services and attempts to increase take-up are often lumped in as one of the (many) justifications for launching larger initiatives to spread computer use throughout society — establishing public access points, IT skills training programs, putting computers in classrooms, etc. Yet, as Internet penetration rates increase, the issue of take-up becomes less of a social exclusion and education issue. There are plenty of well-connected, computer-literate citizens who won't go anywhere near a government Web site. There are other factors at work; factors that call for more specific responses.

Web Security

Many citizens are reluctant to conduct online transactions with government because they are not yet comfortable with the idea of sending confidential information such as income and Social Security data over the Internet. The ability to provide effective electronic services often runs in conflict with the need to ensure security, forcing organizations into a Catch-22 situation: take-up is affected if security controls make a service too difficult to use, but it is also affected if security is perceived as being inadequate.

Some pragmatism is required on government's part. Not all transactions require the same level of security and the level of security must be appropriate to the service concerned. People should not have to provide the same level of authentication to buy a fishing licence online as they do to apply for a passport.

Authentication becomes less of an issue as e-commerce moves more into the mainstream of the economy and the private sector comes up with solutions for greater online security. Government has the opportunity to follow in the slipstream of commercial successes in getting people's comfort level up. For example, it is easier to convince somebody who does their banking over the Internet to conduct financial transactions with government, such as filing income taxes over the Internet as well.

It should also be recognized that security breaches can and do occur and organizations should have a response ready for when and if it happens to them. A failure in a key online service is probably the worst thing that can happen to the reputation of e-government. It can destroy years of trust-building efforts in a swoop. Any interaction with an electronic government service is a major predictor of trust, and hence of continued use. The Inland Revenue is one of the UK's pioneers in providing transactional electronic services and its online tax return service is seen as a flagship project. But the department now faces a much more difficult task to encourage take-up after the service was suspended for several weeks in June 2002 when it was discovered that some users logging on to update their records had been presented with other taxpayers' details. While the problem affected only about a dozen of the 70,000 taxpayers who use the service, the publicity surrounding the breach forced a number of tax advisers to warn taxpayers to treat the service with suspicion. Ernst & Young cited a lack of security as one reason why it would not use the system.

Data Protection and Privacy

In July 2002, the Japanese government launched "Juki Net" to allow any ministry, agency or municipality in the country to access the same citizen data (name, sex, address, date of birth, etc.) in order to provide seamless services. The network attracted controversy because a privacy bill was not enacted prior to the system going live and, in protest, six municipalities refused to implement a government directive to link their systems with the national network. Citizen groups expressed concern that, without proper safeguards, agencies could use Juki Net to create alternate databases, perhaps matching them against other existing records. Juki Net carried echoes from two years earlier in Canada, where it was revealed that a now-disbanded database called the Longitudinal Labour Force Files contained information on citizens derived from different departments and different levels of government but held centrally by the federal Department of Human Resources. The data (which included people's ethnicity, movements in and out of the country or between Canadian provinces, and health and tax data) was used for policy research purposes and the government gave assurances that the files were secure. But newspapers reported that police and the security service had access to database and dutifully labelled it the "Big Brother files." The Quebec provincial government demanded that files on its residents be destroyed, and thousands of people from across the country jammed government phone lines trying to find out what information was being held on them. Bowing to public pressure, the government dismantled the database and the pieces of information were sent back to the agencies and provincial governments from where they had originally come. The government's information-sharing arrangement between agencies was put under review and the Department of Human Resources' own policy analysis and research data was henceforth kept as "separate, secure and unlinked files."

While one of the guiding principles for e-government is to take a whole government approach and incorporate services from all areas of the public sector, it must be recognized that in many countries people are uneasy about the idea of a single super-database and how information they provide electronically could be used. Governments have always tracked citizens from cradle to grave, and there is much public misunderstanding about the purpose of correlating database information, but it's a reality that many people trust government with their personal data even less than they trust private-sector companies. This has become apparent to some governments that have introduced a change-of-address service for all of government only to discover that nobody used it because when people move home, they often only want to inform selected agencies, when and where they see a clear benefit.

Government inefficiency — issuing different identity numbers for different purposes, for example — has traditionally served to protect people's privacy by ensuring data isn't used for purposes unrelated to the reason it was obtained. Even countries where citizens have a national identification number, such as France, different codes are used for tax, health care, and social benefits. Governments legitimately want to make their services more efficient by, for example, limiting the number of times a citizen has to give out the same information to different departments. But if government is now all of a sudden going to conduct business efficiently, it needs to tell people how it will go about ensuring their personal security. The loss of privacy is a tangible, so without guarantees that it will be protected, government risks provoking a boycott — whether organized or spontaneous — of its online services. There is a need for greater openness and clarity about how far government and society is willing to go to share the data across different agencies. In order to gauge what is an acceptable balance between people's right to privacy and the need to provide citizen-centric services, governments might need to initiate some kind of a national debate on the issue. This shouldn't be difficult as it could be an extension of deliberations started in the wake of the events of September 11, 2001, in respect to the balance between privacy and the need for government to enhance its ability to protect citizens through better co-ordination of data.

Availability of Services

That some public-sector Web sites receive so many hits while others get so few suggests that governments still have difficulty knowing which online services will be popular and which ones won't. A focus group in Fairfax County, Virginia, found that residents primarily wanted the ability to go online to sign up for a tee-time at the public golf course. In most of America, access to Social Security accounts is the most frequently cited service that people would like. (The Social Security Administration allows citizens to request statements via the Internet, but the information is then sent only through the post, due to concerns about the confidentiality of the data.) In the UK, the KPMG-MORI poll found that 37% of those surveyed would like to go online to book an appointment with their doctor while 21% said they'd file their income tax return over the Web. Similarly, research in May 2001 by Gartner Dataquest found that citizens of the UK, Germany, France, Italy and the Netherlands would rather make a health care appointment online than complete their tax returns electronically (National Audit Office, 2002). Yet most government priorities are the exact opposite — they have enabled the e-filing of taxes while e-healthcare remains a long-term vision.

People have the right to change their minds and what they wanted to access electronically last year is different from what they want this year, which is different again from what they will want next year. Many citizens simply do not know what services they want from e-government. Many do not even know the possibilities.

In the private sector, successful companies constantly assess customers' tastes and preferences before putting their merchandise into the market, and they continue to monitor them until it is time to discontinue the product line. In the public sector, catering to the personal preferences is only one of several, often competing, considerations when determining what services to put online.

Before moving up the ladder to tackle complex and expensive e-government projects, organizations prudently try to abide by the principle of starting with "low-hanging fruit." So the most frequently used services (e.g., medical appointments) and those with high-volume transactions (e.g., vehicle registrations) are put online first in order to ensure some quick wins that will encourage further public use of online services and maintain senior-level support of e-government. If government is viewed as an institution that takes money in with one hand (tax, licence fees, fines, etc.) and pays money out with the other (social benefits, pensions, farm aid, etc.), then it is usually technically simpler to Web-enable the money-in systems rather than the money-out systems. So the people get online vehicle registration whether they want it or not.

The concern about whether citizens are getting the electronic services they want diminishes as more and more services go online and governments get closer to meeting their targets of having 100% electronic service provision. Ultimately e-government caters equally to the person who once a year files a tax return, to the person who once a month books a family doctor's appointment, and to the person who once a week tees off at the public golf course.

Quality and Presentation of Services

Low take-up raises questions about the quality and usability of online public services. While many government Web sites are as well-designed and as easy to navigate as the best e-commerce sites, many more are huge immovable beasts that force users into multiple mouse-clicks through pages of extraneous information. It is often difficult for people to find what they are looking for on a government Web site, and frequently they do not know what they are looking for but can't find where to look for help or advice. It is not unusual for people to log off a government Web site frustrated and empty-handed.

Many government Web sites need to be sophisticated to deal with complicated transactions (tax returns, for example), although it is too often assumed that users have a high degree of computer confidence coupled with a proficiency in government jargon: individuals and small businesses are often not sophisticated in their dealings with either government or the Web.

It's often said that government Web sites simply are not "fun." In fact, "Belief in seriousness — rather than fun — runs straight through virtually all UK government organizations' approach to the Web. Government sites are conservatively designed, use bureaucratic language and contain no incentives other than strict functionality for users to explore the site" (Margetts & Dunleavy, 2002).

Many Internet users log off government Web sites frustrated without completing a transaction, either because they did not know how to navigate through the pages or the sites lacked the content they required. That veteran Internet users are no more successful than rookie surfers suggests more of a lack of useful content (Larsen & Rainie, 2002).

Often, a Web site designed by a regional office provides more information and better service delivery than an agency's headquarters site. The Web site of the Gulf Coast regional office of the US Minerals Management Service, for example, offers forms for bids on oil leases in the Gulf of Mexico — something which no other Minerals Management Service site provides. The regional office initiated the service on its own because it couldn't get buy-in from management to put it on the agency Web site. Some claim this demonstrates why centralized rules on government Web site designs should not be imposed, while others say it's a good reason why they should.

Sometimes people's expectations about what can be delivered electronically is unrealistically high in terms of both what is cost effective and what is allowed by legislation on privacy and data protection. For example, almost all governments have attempted to organize services and information around the needs and expectations of citizens, which requires incorporating services from different agencies, grouping them as life events, and making them accessible through a single portal. Usually different departments and perhaps regional and local governments have a link off the portal to their own site, but users must still enter their information more than once. While governments are increasingly deploying portals that ask for "tombstone" information which can be distributed through a gateway, this is a costly development and it raises privacy concerns as mentioned above.

Not Aware of Online Services and their Advantages

In most countries today, government is the single largest provider of electronic services. But it does not have the largest share of the Internet market. For numbers of both visitors and transactions, government Web sites trail far behind those for banking, travel and tourism, sporting and other events, books and music, computers, news and information, and so on. Call them uninitiated or uninterested, but most of us in society are more interested in logging onto commercial Web sites than looking to see what the government has on offer. Low demand for an electronic public service should not be confused with low demand for the service itself. Generally speaking, government services — electronic or otherwise — have a low profile because people use them so infrequently. A Web site that's going to be accessed only once a year isn't going to be saved on the "Favorites" list of too many people's Web browsers, regardless of whether it's public or private.

It is probably the barrier that receives the least attention even though (or perhaps, because) it is the least controversial, but the biggest reason why people do not access online government services is that they simply do not know a service exists. Or they have forgotten it exists. Or they know it exists but can't find the URL. Even though almost every local government in the US is now online, only a half of Internet users are able to say whether their municipality has a Web site at all (Larsen & Rainie, 2002). In the UK, only one-third of Internet users know about the existence of the British central government portal (KPMG, 2001).

There is also the person who knows about an electronic service but doesn't think it's worth his or her bother to learn to use it. Human behavior studies show that people are often reluctant to make the initial personal investment required to learn a new technology or change their way of doing things, even when they know they will benefit in the long run. In the United States, 70% of those who filed their taxes electronically in 2001 said they saved time, including about half who said they saved more than an hour. Yet despite this clear timesaving benefit, only 16% of Internet users file their taxes electronically (Larsen & Rainie, 2002). The best way to persuade the remaining 84% is to market the service to them.

Creating an External Marketing Strategy

Whether it entails standing in long queues or completing multiple paper forms, citizens and business feel comfortable with their established, if inconvenient ways of dealing with government. Even though society has changed, and there are public demands for higher quality government programs to respond to societal changes, it is difficult to ask people to change their habits and interact in an entirely different way to which they are accustomed. It should be remembered that the vast majority of visitors to government Web sites are first-time users, and they are not entirely sure what to expect. Government organizations need to view their electronic services much like a new product line. In the private sector, when a company is ready to release a new service or product, the first thing it does is market the thing. Then it markets it some more. And it keeps right on marketing it, long after it has reached a critical mass of consumers and has achieved high brand awareness.

The most popular education Web site in UK isn't run by the government. It's a commercial portal called Schoolsnet.com that provides interactive lessons, project ideas, study tips on how to study, even school sports reports. It competes with, and is arguably no better or worse than, the government's National Grid for Learning site, but Schoolsnet has more users because it markets itself better. To raise awareness of the site and its services, Schoolsnet launched itself by sending out 30,000 coffee mugs, 55,000 posters and 600,000 branded exercise books directly to 5,000 secondary schools. Governments do these sorts of things on occasion — usually to promote something new, big and important such as the launch of the euro currency. News flash: taken as a whole, e-government is new, big and important.

Very few organizations' e-government strategies include a marketing component and, when applying for project funding, rarely is an agency asked to say how it intends to promote a service it plans to move online. Even when a communication strategy is required, it is often the first thing to be cut or scaled back when budgets get tight. (In the private sector, when business is slow, the marketing budget is the first thing to be ramped up.)

Marketing isn't really a public sector strength. Organizations tend to "inform" the public of changes to a process (often simply by issuing a press release without any follow-up) rather than "sell" them the benefits of trying out a new service. While still often unsure how best to encourage take-up, some government are starting to recognize that they need some kind of a marketing strategy for e-government, which takes into account:

1. Traditional marketing practice
2. Incentives
3. Personalized service and added value
4. Multiple delivery channels
5. Use of third parties and intermediaries

Traditional Marketing Practices

The most common way to market a new online service is through existing correspondence. This includes the obvious, such as changing the agency letterhead to include an e-mail contact and Web site URL. Some organizations will also promote the departmental Web site on the envelope or outside packaging a tax return, for example.

The process of mailing millions of pieces of paper to individual citizens to tell them about an electronic service is a complicated and expensive endeavour so rather than do an extra mailing, most organizations will add a flyer or re-print an existing renewal notice with an extra line to say "see our Web site." There are good ways and bad ways of doing this, and the provincial government of New Brunswick, Canada, has had experience of both. In 1994, the government pioneered a system that let moose hunters apply for an annual hunting license electronically using an interactive voice response (IVR) telephone system or, later, over the Internet. The ability to apply in person remained in place, but take-up of the electronic service was 86% in the first year and 98% by the second year. Around the same time, the government introduced an electronic system for the registration of motor vehicles. The technology was almost identical to that used for the hunting licence application, and the system was just as convenient to use. Yet, in its first year, only 10 % of New Brunswick motorists chose to register their cars over the phone — the rest stood in line in a government office as they had always done.

Why the difference? Why did the citizens of the same jurisdiction — often the very same people — choose to embrace a new, simpler way of doing business with government for one service yet refuse it for another service? After analyzing the methods used to deploy both systems, officials concluded that it all came down to basic marketing. With the launch of the hunting licence system, all the old paper cards and information sheets were discarded and replaced with a new form telling people that they could now apply over the phone. A line of small print at the bottom of the page informed people they could still apply in person at a government office if they so wished. For the motor vehicle registration, the government did not re-design the renewal notice that it mailed out to motorists. Instead, it announced the new delivery channel on a separate piece of paper and slipped it into the envelope with the renewal form — much like when a person receives their credit card statement and there’s a wad of promotional literature offering all sorts of goods and services (financial services, water treatment, air conditioning, leather wallets, etc.). Swamped by superfluity, people tend to extract the bill from the envelope and automatically toss the rest into the bin without looking any of it. And that’s basically what New Brunswickers were doing when they received their motor vehicle registration notices. So people didn’t know about the electronic service, until the following year when the government printed a new notice form, on a different kind of paper, with the new, electronic way to register highlighted in a prominent place on the page.

Besides traditional mailings, some government are running print and broadcast advertising campaigns to promote their portals or specific services such as e-filing. Results have been mixed. In France, the number of visits to the French government portal more than doubled from 400,000 to 1 million hits per month after a TV advertising campaign. On the other hand, the Canada Customs and Revenue Agency reported no significant increase in the electronic filing of income tax after it ran TV ads. (Any comparison could suggest that encouraging people to visit a Web site is one thing, getting them to conduct a complicated transaction is quite another.) Most mass media campaigns to promote online services have been small and modest. Many agencies are constrained by the fear that blitz advertising will result in public complaints that taxpayer’s money was being wasted. (Tax agencies are especially sensitive to this charge.) We are not selling soap, they say, and we can’t afford the sort of advertising campaign that soap companies conduct.

Governments, however, do have many highly visible and unique platforms, that are available to them exclusively for communication purposes, even if they are not traditionally thought of as a medium for marketing purposes. For example, few Pennsylvania residents go a day without seeing the URL for their government’s portal: it’s stamped on all state vehicle license plates.

Beyond changing written words on papers (and licence plates), organizations can revise their spoken scripts to promote an online service while answering a public query over the phone or in person. All that's need is a simple mention that the service the person is looking is now available online. And while an airline customer who is put on hold listens to an automated voice saying their ticket can be purchased online, citizens phoning into a government office are put on hold and get dead air or, if they're lucky, Vivaldi's *Four Seasons*.

The private sector is driving take-up of online transactions in the broad public market, and government should be able to leverage some of the commercial marketing efforts. It will be easier, for example, to sell the benefits of filing income tax online to someone who banks over the Internet than to someone who still hands a deposit slip over to a bank teller. There might also be opportunities for joint public-private marketing initiatives, to promote Web security, for example, in order to help get people's comfort level up to start using the Web for a wide variety of financial transactions.

It is always easier and cheaper to market to targeted audience with common interests than it is to a general public of diverse and changing tastes. Advertising in the mass media isn't necessary for most G2B (government-to-business) services because the lead agency can work through chambers of commerce, trade bodies and professional associations to target-market to specific groups. In Italy, for example, some 130,000 authorized intermediaries (accountants, professional tax preparers, trade associations, tax assistance centres, etc.) sit between the tax collector and the taxpayer. When the Finance Ministry introduced an electronic tax filing service, it launched a publicity campaign with 85,000 mailings, 9,000 posters, 3,000 brochures, 5,000 leaflets, 2,000 CD ROMs, trade press advertisements, booths at exhibitions and trade fairs, and information-based seminars – all aimed at the intermediaries. The tax administration Web site became an information hub with additional services made available for tax professionals and, at its peak, a toll-free telephone assistance service dealt with 28,000 enquiries per week. It was a massive marketing effort, but not nearly so much as it would have been trying to promote the service to the country's 38 million taxpayers (36.6 million individuals and 1.5 million companies).

Governments could do more target-marketing, even in the G2C (government-to-citizen) area, by adopting more sophisticated segmentation of different groups within society, such as students or the elderly, and promoting electronic services that are directly relevant to their lives. Governments are often reluctant to do almost any kind of target-marketing because of the perceived need to communicate with all citizens in the same manner. But failing to market electronic services sufficiently to key groups of citizens results in the paradox that those services are not fully used by any citizen.

The message is, of course, as important as how it is to be delivered. Any information campaign must not only make the target audience aware of a service, but it must also convince people of the benefits of using the service. The value proposition for going online must come through loud and clear, perhaps by prominently highlighting the top three or four benefits — easier, faster, cheaper, 24/7, or whatever. The use of language is important and there is always room for an eye-catching slogan like: "No More Waiting" or "Always Open." The Netherlands tax authority should probably win a prize for the best catchphrase for promoting an electronic public service: "We can't make it fun but we can make it easy."

Incentives

If they can't make them either fun or easy, organizations can always *pay* people to use their services. Financial incentives have long been a common private sector practice, from grocery store coupons to utilities offering a reduced tariff for those who pay by direct debit. In New Brunswick, the government there charged moose hunters a $6 fee to apply for a hunting licence electronically compared to $10 if applied in person — a 40% discount. The British government introduced a rebate to shift people away from paper tax returns — £50 to companies that file VAT returns electronically and another £50 for submitting employer's tax. Individual taxpayers received £10 off for e-filing self-assessment income tax. The chance to win a lot of money attracts attention: the Inland Revenue Authority of Singapore enters every e-filer in a cash draw where S$235,000 in cash prizes are given away, with a top prize of $20,000. Those who file early get additional chances in the draw, and a taxpayer is given yet another chance to win if he or she participates in the "Help-A-Friend-To-E-File" Scheme and gets someone else to file electronically. It's not surprising that one in two taxpayers in Singapore submits their returns electronically.

The argument for providing financial incentives is that an organization should pass on to citizens as much as possible any cost savings realized by delivering services electronically, which in turn will increase take-up and further reduce the cost of delivering the service. But the cost savings to be derived from e-government are difficult to estimate and agencies tend to view them more as a long-term benefit since online services usually require a high initial outlay in technology, help-desk staff, marketing campaigns, etc. Many fee-collecting agencies are also now wrestling with the question of who will pay the service charges levied by banks for credit card transactions — something they often never had to worry about when services were provided over the counter or through the post and people paid their fees by cheque, money order or cash.

Public sector organizations need to be realistic. Financial rewards probably will not work if the money received is offset by other expenses such as credit card fees or the need to buy additional software or a digital certificate. If this is the case, then organizations should be honest with their customers and promote the rebate as assistance to help them with their transition costs.

Non-financial incentives can also be effective at encouraging citizens to access services electronically. Again, the principle is often that government ought to share the benefits of going digital with its customers. If e-government speeds up processing times, organizations should be able to guarantee a shorter waiting time for the issuing of a driving licence, passport, business licence, etc. Singapore allows taxpayers an extra three days to get in their tax returns in if they're submitted electronically rather than by paper. Other governments, including The Netherlands, Australia, Canada and USA, promise that anyone due a tax refund will receive it by a certain date if they file electronically.

The Canada Customs and Revenue Agency advertises that it will issue a tax refund within five to 10 days of receiving an electronically-filed return, compared to the performance standard of six weeks for paper return. However everyone knows that, with recent efficiency gains, the agency can now turn even around a paper return around in 10 to 15 days. The agency has, in a sense, become too efficient for its own good as the shorter waiting time for an electronic return has been all but cancelled out. While it would likely seem politically unacceptable to intentionally slow down the processing of paper returns, it might not be such a bad idea. Prof. Margetts and Prof. Dunleavy say: "Once electronic services are underway, agencies need to look out for possible disparities developing between electronic and non-electronic transactions... which can work against incentives. Again, explicit recognition of disparities and even the introduction of matching negative incentives into paper-based transactions may be required."

At the very least, governments must guard against disparities — real or perceived — which serve not only to negate the benefits of e-government but also result in a disincentive to use an electronic service. In the US, there was a perception that tax returns filed electronically were being scrutinised more closely than paper returns, which likely contributed to a 3% decline in electronic tax filing during 2000-01. And rather than give money away, some agencies are charging a "convenience fee" for accessing services over the Web. For example, to pay for digitized mapping program, a lands department might charge people to view topographic maps online. This will only encourage people to come into the office to look at the old paper maps for free.

Personalized Service and Added Value

The sheer size and complexity of government has long been a barrier for many people trying to access public-sector information and services. Most central governments have about 70 or 80 different departments or agencies, each of which nowadays has its own Web site with an URL that's impossible to guess or remember. There can be just as many additional organizations at state, regional and local levels and different agencies may be involved in providing a service, each requiring the completion of different forms. They all expect people to communicate with them in turn rather than take the initiative to deal with each other. Thus, one of the most compelling incentives for conducting business with the government over the Internet is the opportunity to receive more personalized and "added value" services.

Most governments now have an established Web portal or single entry point, built originally to enable people to find the needles in the public-sector haystack. Many remain information portals rather than delivery channels providing services that cut across the boundaries of different organizations. There have been some efforts to present services according to what is important to the citizen rather than from a bureaucratic viewpoint, with transactions arranged by subject or life event. Singapore's eCitizen Centre portal grew gradually until it encompassed 49 life events, including giving birth, attending school, registering for national service, looking for a job, pursuing a "first class" career, going overseas, employing people, and retiring from the workforce. When logging on, the site automatically detects the user's connection speed (high or low bandwidth) and adjusts its graphics accordingly. The US state of Virginia pioneered the concept of a personalized, or intentions-based government portal with its My Virginia Homepage, which lets citizens tailor online government services to their particular needs and tastes. Launched in July 2000, it allows users to add, update or remove links as the see fit. People can request to have reminders to renew permits sent to them electronically and there is an automated legislative tracking service linked to the Virginia general assembly with e-mail notification of government-related announcements. Pennsylvania followed suit in October 2000 with the launch of a new portal called PAPowerPort which includes a facility like Virginia's to let users customize the site as well as value-added services so people can check the news, weather and stock market quotes, and open e-mail accounts, participate in chat rooms, view Web-casts, design their own Web pages and even manage their finances online. The governments of Singapore, Hong Kong, France, and The Netherlands each now have portals with intentions-based designs. The Dutch portal allows citizens to customize the site by zip code to display relevant local and regional information.

Yet, the drive for further personalization and added value seems to have slowed down, if not come to standstill. This is attributed primarily to the greater focus now being placed on cost savings and cost recovery in light of the volatile economy and new post-September 11 realities. The portals are there and governments can't very well switch them off, but rather than continuing to add new "whiz-bang" functionality, governments are now taking stock and trying to figure out how they can add and remove content and run their portal as efficiently and cost-effectively as possible.

While attracting interest as a potential tool to integrate and reorganize services around citizen needs, Customer Relationship Management (CRM) is still largely unexplored and untested by government. CRM can enhance intentions-based portal designs and enable segmentation, an increasingly common practice in the private sector to allow companies to skim the cream of their customer base and seek out the "high-value" ones. While seemingly at odds with the public sector imperative to serve all citizens equally, segmentation (or "mass customization") allows government to deliver tailored services based on the requirements of individual citizen groups, such as students, single parents, farmers, SMEs, war veterans, etc. Segmentation already exists on many government portals, albeit on a rudimentary basis, catering to citizens (G2C), businesses (G2B), and often civil servants (G2E). Canada, Singapore and the state of Florida each include an extra gateway for non-residents (tourists, immigrants, investors, etc.).

Government still has a long way to go to match many of customer service innovations being embraced by the private sector. For example, eBay, the online auction site changes the look of its homepage as market opportunities arise — nearly everyday in some cases. The Web merchant opened a new storefront devoted to Michael Jordan memorabilia the very morning after the basketball star announced his retirement from the Chicago Bulls. This "eBay effect" (Sawhney, 2001) has been replicated by other companies (not only e-commerce sites) and it would an effective tool for government, especially when the need arises to get information, services and emergency assistance out quickly in times of crisis or natural disaster.

One emerging school of thought is that government departments and agencies are simply not structured to think and operate outside their silos in a way needed to provide joined-up, personalized public services. Attempts to blur organizational boundaries, the thinking goes, is destructive and lowers the performance of individual departments because each has its own culture, skill sets, business processes, strategies, and politics. Given that a joined-up service is only as efficient as the most inefficient agency, a small number of governments are starting to believe that it might be better not to disturb the silo structure and instead think of departments as "wholesalers" or "manufacturers" of public services while a government "retailer" is created to sit above the overall government structure. The retailer would have a free hand to arrange and manage all service delivery and package offerings from across the public sector based around life events, user intentions, segmentations, eBay effects, or whatever. It would act as the government's customer relationship manager, marketing personalized services, measuring service quality, and providing the administration with a more complete view of citizens and businesses.

The Canadian province of New Brunswick was perhaps the first to tread down this path when it created Service New Brunswick (SNB) in 1998 out of the former New Brunswick Geographic Information Corporation (NBGIC). The mandate of the new government-owned corporation was extended from managing property registries to become the government's front-office provider of basic services to citizens and businesses. Today, it is market-driven organization providing 120 public services on a semi-commercial basis through a network of 36 service centres (one-stop shops), a call centre and Web portal. Similar public service structures have since been, or are being, developed in other jurisdictions, usually by smaller or regional governments. In the autonomous regional authority of Catalonia in Spain, a government-owned company called .Cat is setting up a similar central customer service structure. In Ireland, a new agency called Reach has the mandate to develop a "Public Services Broker" to deal with different departments on behalf of citizens and agencies. A number of multinational corporations with highly decentralized management and diverse product lines (e.g., 3M) are also trying to make their companies more responsive by managing information so that customers see a united front, but without breaking down the walls between units. Could large national governments be next?

Multiple Delivery Channels

Electronic public services are designed primarily for accessing through the Internet from a personal computer, but the need to cater simultaneously to those with and those without a computer remains a key challenge for government. Technology can and should be used both to create new means of access and to support traditional means of access. Web-enabled call centres and one-stop shops are important aspects of any e-government strategy, and front-office staff need to have access the same resources as what's available through a government Web site, to ensure a standard approach to dealing with enquiries, whether online, over the phone or face-to-face. Yet few governments have developed an explicit strategy to ensure coherence in the delivery of public services through multiple channels.

Multiple delivery channels can broaden the scope of e-government. The emergence of mobile technology, for example, creates an opportunity for government to provide real-time information and services relevant to peoples' daily lives, such as traffic updates, tourist information, energy alerts, lottery results, etc. In many countries, university campuses are becoming a key testing ground for wireless technologies, due to the mobility of students, faculty and researchers. Students, for example, can remain in range of a wireless network as they move from dorm to lecture to pub. Through the use of segmentation, governments can determine the most appropriate deliver channel(s) for a particular user group. In other circumstances, interactive voice response (IVR) telephone systems might be more suitable channels. Television will remain the medium of choice for a majority of people for some time to come, so governments and broadcasters need to coordinate the delivery of electronic public services through digital TV. Ultimately it will be necessary to integrate the different channels to provide citizen choice and to ensure no limitation is put on how online information and services are accessed. Thus it is important that the implementation of one delivery channel is leveraged to develop the next, with a single Web-based underlying technology supporting the various channels.

Governments can also look to leverage the effort and money they spend on closing the digital divide to encourage take-up of electronic public services. This could be done in much the same way that easyJet, the discount airline, launched a chain of cybercafés to give people without Internet access the opportunity to buy plane tickets online. Customers would pay a nominal rate for using the Web but could visit the easyJet site for free. (The company was selling two-thirds of its airline seats online within two years of launching its first transactional site.) Today, governments buy and install PCs in libraries, post offices, schools, telecottages, and other public spaces to help push Web access out to the community, but there is no encouragement for users of these public Internet access points to use them for public services. At the very least, their home pages could be set to the government portal.

In Singapore, the government makes its online tax filing system available to citizens through computer rooms located at polytechnics, community clubs, shopping malls, and a community service program (Student Volunteer E-Filing Service) provides free assistance to taxpayers who may need help to submit their returns electronically. There is also an "E-Filing coach," a bus equipped with 10 Web-connected PCs and Inland Revenue Authority staff to help people submit their taxes electronically. The bus is parked in office parking lots during working hours, including at Changi International Airport to serve the 2,000 airport staff and other taxpayers who work or pass through the vicinity.

Governments could also work with private cybercafés to encourage citizens to use these facilities to access government Web sites free of charge. A government could purchase time and space on their computers in the same way that schools buy slots at private leisure centres and swimming pools. Citizens could be issued vouchers that they could use to access government sites from the cybercafé, telecottage or one-stop shop of their choice. Move over school-voucher programs!

Use of Third Parties and Intermediaries

If e-government is about allowing citizens to interact with government in the way they want, what about those people who would rather not interact with government at all (or as little as possible)? In the off-line world, it has long been standard practice to grant concessions to retailers, banks and even gas stations to provide all sorts of public services. People may pay their bills and parking fines through their bank, they get their vehicle safety inspection certificate from a mechanic, or they buy their fishing license from a tackle shop. The mixed economy and network of third-party intermediaries that have developed to reach a critical mass of citizens in the physical world is also be the best way to reach a critical mass in the virtual world. Many people already have experience of transacting with banks and retail outlets on a day-to-day basis and a commercial Web site can reach as many citizens in one day as a government Web site can in one month or even one year. A private company can provide added value to government services by packaging them with its own products and services, making them more market-focused and attractive to individual consumers.

According to the NAO: "Government organizations have to think creatively about increasing their "nodality," the extent to which they are at the centre of social and informational networks. This may actually require a substantive change to thinking about Web development — rather than focussing on their own Web site, organizations might have to think in a "de-centered way" about the extent to which their services are offered on the sites of other organizations. So an environmental agency that gives advice on sustainable products might need to liaise with a variety of retailers to ensure that their information is presented.

The Federal Election Commission (FEC) in the US was one of the first public bodies to use Internet intermediaries, or "private doorways," by allowing third-party entities to incorporate the voter registration application (National Mail Voter Registration Form) and a voter registration information service on their home page. Rock the Vote, an organization founded by the recording industry to mobilize young people to respond to political issues and encourage them to exercise their right to vote, provided the first online voter registration service in 1996 (even before the FEC itself had one). It re-launched the site for the 2000 presidential election, through which 164,000 new voters were registered. Another 20,000 young people also used the site to apply for absentee ballots. The Rock the Vote site interfaces with the technology services company election.com, which in turn links to the FEC. The voting public does not see or deal with these behind-the-scenes organizations. They simply go online as they would in the course of leading their regular lives, and they are able to conduct a government transaction that is relevant to the particular activity of the Web site they are visiting.

In South Africa, taxpayers who wish to submit their tax returns via the Internet register with one of five companies appointed by the South African Revenue Service (SARS) to provide e-filing services. By opting to appoint a number of private service providers, the government sought to cater to its Web-enabled citizens and businesses while avoiding the high costs of developing and managing (and marketing) the service itself. The service providers — consortia of different accountancy and technology firms — charge a fee for the service and each is responsible for marketing its own offerings: some only target the business community, for example, while one does not offer its service directly but through third (fourth?) parties such as accountants. The ability to link into to a government tax agency appeals to the financial sector as it is increasingly looks for ways to provide added value services to customers. Rather than just sell a cheque and savings account, today's financial services companies tend to provide banking, insurance, financial planning, tax preparation, etc., all under one roof. The e-filing of a customer's taxes is one more service offering to add to the portfolio. The Canadian government does not allow the filing of taxes directly through banks — people must still use the government Web site for that — but it does allow the payment of *taxes electronically* through a financial institution's telephone or Internet banking service. Different banks have different service offerings based on what they think is useful to their customers, but all are listed with links on the Customs and Revenue Agency's Web site. This allows people to easily compare the services of the different banks, and the competition has had an effect in that each bank now has a large number of online tax offerings available.

Just as a government transport agency would not give a certain chain of service stations the sole right to issue car safety certificates, the various public and private players within an online government service network shouldn't strike agreements with each other on an exclusive basis. There should be terms and conditions guaranteeing service quality standards, such as to ensure the service is up and running 24/7 or to comply with privacy and data protection regulations. (The South African Revenue Service requires e-filing service providers give each customer an electronic signature and run a 24-hour help desk to answer any Web-related queries, while questions specific to a return or payment remain limited to government working hours.) But the principle is that, in order to reach out to the maximum number of citizens, any capable service provider or commercial Web site ought to be allowed to provide a franchised service.

The voluntary sector can be used in the same way to provide essential public services, particularly health and social services. For example, the UK government is financially supporting the National Council for Voluntary Organizations (NCVO) to launch a Web site that provides online services delivered by public and voluntary sector partnerships.

Ultimately public, private and voluntary sectors will be judged on the same standards by citizens/consumers/clients who don't care who's providing a service so long as it's good. To ensure people consistently receive the better quality and more dependable services that they demand, the sectors need each other. A greater effort should therefore be made to bridge the gap between e-government and e-commerce, through the greater use of government content syndication and intermediaries to deliver public services, and government-led initiatives that deliver a mixed e-economy.

Conclusion

This chapter is a call for e-government practitioners to sharpen their external marketing skills. Low take-up is becoming a political concern, especially as Internet penetration rates continue to climb but use of electronic public services stay static. Business cases underpinning investment in e-government projects will increasingly require a marketing component.

Most visitors to government Web sites are first-time users, and they don't know what to expect. As such, organizations need to view their electronic services in much the same way as a private sector launches a new service or product line: with great fanfare and much promotion.

Matters to consider whilst devising an external e-government marketing strategy include:

- Online services can be promoted cost-effectively with existing correspondence such as licence renewal notices, and through government touch points like front office staff. It's also worth looking at opportunities for joint public-private marketing initiatives, e.g., to promote Web security.
- It's easier and cheaper to market to a targeted audience with common interests than it is to a general public of diverse and changing tastes. Consider adopting more sophisticated segmentation of different groups within society, and promote electronic services that are directly relevant to their lives.
- Promote the benefits of using a service loudly and clearly with eye-catching slogans, e.g., "Don't stand in-line, go online." Guarantee the benefits, e.g., through performance standards for processing times. Where necessary, *pay* people to use an electronic service, either through reduced fees or a straight cash-back offer.
- Guard against disparities that negate the benefits of e-government and serve as a disincentive to use electronic services, and introduce matching negative incentives into paper-based transactions if necessary.
- Let citizens tailor online services to their needs and tastes by deploying an intentions-based portal. Use CRM to enhance an intentions-based portal and enable greater segmentation (or "mass customization") to deliver tailored services based on the requirements of individual citizen groups.

- Departments are not structured to operate outside their silos and it may be worth leaving them be as "wholesalers" of services while a separate government "retailer" delivers and packages offerings based around life events, user intentions, segmentations, etc. The retailer would act as the government's customer relationship manager; marketing personalized services, measuring service quality, and providing the administration with a more complete view of citizens and businesses.
- Governments should develop a multiple-channel strategy to ensure technology is used to support new and traditional means of accessing public services. The channel strategy should take into account different citizen groups, e.g., mobile technology can be exploited to provide services to students. Governments and broadcasters need to work together to co-ordinate electronic service delivery through digital TV. Ultimately it will be necessary to integrate channels, thus it is important that one channel is leveraged to develop the next, with a single Web-based underlying technology.
- Money and effort spent on closing the digital divide should be leveraged to encourage take-up of electronic public services. Governments could buy time and space from cybercafés and issue vouchers so citizens could access government Web sites free of charge.
- Rather than focus on their own Web sites, governments should establish a network of third-party intermediaries to reach a critical mass of citizens, and let these "private doorways" add value to government services by packaging them with their own products and services.

Reflecting on the "Field of Dreams"

The film, "Field of Dreams," starring Kevin Costner uses baseball as a metaphor to tell us something about who we are and what we need — about the "dreams" that elude us. In the film, the Iowa farmer played by Costner hears supernatural voices telling him that if he builds a baseball diamond in his cornfield then the legendary Shoeless Joe Jackson, one of the greatest players of all time, will appear. "If you build it, he will come," the farmer is told. Many commentators today speak about the film to illustrate how not to do e-government. They claim that e-government is not a field of dreams and that people will not come to use online services just because they have access to them.

The pundits are wrong — they need to watch the film again, to the end. After building the baseball diamond, Shoeless Joe in fact did not come. The voices in Costner's head continued, urging him to "go the distance" and attract people to his cornfield to see Shoeless Joe and his teammates play. In particular, the Costner character was to seek out a reclusive writer (J.D. Salinger, in the novel). He travels to the east coast to find the writer, explain to him his unlikely dream, and bring him — kidnap him, really — back to Iowa. So the message is that it's okay for governments to have fields of dreams: visions for efficient, seamless, citizen-centric, electronic services. But to turn the e-government dream into reality, governments need seek out the reluctant public and entice them to interact with them electronically. If you build it, they will come — so long as you do some clever marketing.

PART B: SUPPLY SIDE: MARKETING E-GOVERNMENT INTERNALLY TO DECISION-MAKERS

Introduction

In the late-90s, people were told that the Internet would change everything. In many ways it did. It enabled new ways to communicate, work, shop, learn and play. It completely changed the way companies did business. It all happened with breathtaking speed. Government felt it could not be left behind. It had to jump in with both feet and radically change the way it did business too. Senior government officials incorporated the Internet into their vocabulary, presidents did Web-casts, prime ministers participated in online chats, and e-government visions were launched.

The emergence of the Internet and e-government happened to coincide with a timely political priority in many countries to improve the quality of public services. Many governments' performance — and chances for re-election — were being measured by their ability to improve long-neglected public health care, education, public transport, crime prevention, etc. As a result, e-government, with its focus on improving service delivery, has become the most prominent and radical IT initiative ever undertaken by the public sector. It has helped drive change and carry the reinventing government agenda forward.

Committed political backing and executive sponsorship needs to be sustained if e-government is to enjoy continued success. Support at the highest level is required to approve financial resources, guide change management, ensure adequate staff training, and remove the final regulatory and legal barriers to e-government. Yet many e-government practitioners and implementation teams believe it is not realistic to expect a consistent level of executive leadership over the long term.

Reasons for Declining Executive Support

No hard data or surveys are currently available that measures the attitudes towards e-government of political leaders or senior-level bureaucrats. However, anecdotal evidence suggests that high-level support, while initially dependable and solid, is starting to wane.

The underlining reasons for a decline (or risk of a decline) in political and management enthusiasm for e-government can be attributed to:

1. A lack of understanding of the benefits
2. The anticipated benefits — especially cost savings — have not materialized
3. Burst of dot-com bubble; the Web is no longer a novelty
4. Changing political priorities and "events, dear boy"

Lack of Understanding of the Benefits

Many politicians and top bureaucrats have come to recognize the importance of e-government to drive reform. Yet many more still don't understand its aim, or they thought they understood it but are now starting to question its value.

It is often difficult for politicians and senior managers to see what business problems and political issues e-government can solve, and many of the solutions being developed seem rather trivial. While paying lip service to the importance of the Internet and the new economy, too many senior-level government people see cyberspace as simply new space to work in the same old way. They have not taken the initiative to understand the way e-business and e-government work to adjust their public duties accordingly. When the decision-makers and the IT experts get together, they often fall into a tense "Venus and Mars" type of relationship. Ministers and managers still delegate their word-processing and get their secretaries to print out their e-mail for them to read while the techies obliviously talk right past them with opaque talk of PKI and XML.

Anticipated Benefits have not Materialized

While the external pressure to deliver e-government has been to meet citizens' demands for improved service delivery, internal expectations have hung primarily on the promise of e-government to achieve cost savings. The IT industry promised cost reductions, often based on the experience of e-business. In the private sector, e-business led to savings for many companies because it allowed them to make do with far fewer staff and to target their most profitable customers and reject the unprofitable ones, including the socially excluded and those who lacked Internet access. Neither of these are options for government, and making transactions available online doesn't remove the need to provide them off-line.

Seen as an additional activity, e-government costs at least as much money as it saves. There's an initial investment in technology, restructuring costs, staff training costs, not to mention the cost of marketing new services to the public. There is now a general acceptance that no cost savings will be realized in the short term, and long-term savings resulting from greater efficiently and automation are difficult to predict. With the economy now in decline and many governments facing budget shortfalls, some decision-makers are adopting draconian measures to balance budgets — with e-government initiatives among those receiving the chop.

Burst of Dot-Com Bubble, Web No Longer a Novelty

Just as the e-commerce hype created a crisis mentality in the private sector, there was a feeling about the Internet among politicians and senior bureaucrats that they "had to be there." Since the burst of the dot-com bubble, the inclination has been more towards "anywhere but there." The high-tech bust has rippled through different industries (software, hardware, telecoms, energy trading, etc.) and it is now starting to rub off on government. Rather than press on regardless with e-government and risk being caught out like a Silicon Valley start-up with dubious business plan, many government leaders are now stressing their public duty to consult, to protect, to cut taxes.

It may seem paradoxical, but the greatest political interest in e-government today is probably in countries where Internet penetration rates are the lowest. In countries playing "catch-up," it is more important for political leaders to appear technologically progressive. In the more connected societies, the novelty of the World Wide Web has worn off and has become mainstream, and has thus lost its political lustre.

In July 2000, Robert L. Mallett, then Deputy Secretary of Commerce, speaking at conference on e-government in Washington DC, said: "We are encouraging them (government employees) to think out of the box. We're saying forget about boundaries and bureaucracies, stop thinking about serving your own departments. Think big picture.

Identify your customers, figure out what government-wide services they use, and use the new smart technologies to serve these customers quicker, cheaper, and faster."

It is difficult to imagine any senior federal government official in the United States uttering such words today.

This new emphasis of caution is a source of irritation for many e-government practitioners whose projects were driven through faster than otherwise might have been advisable due to political imperatives. Some services, such as electronic tax filing and online vehicle registration, were often viewed as a measure of success of e-government as a whole. A widely praised online vehicle registration system in Arizona prompted California's governor to order his state's motor vehicle department to establish one. And the British parliament's Public Accounts Committee criticized the Inland Revenue's electronic self-assessment service for being introduced too quickly to meet a government promise that the service would be available by April 2000, which contributed to a series of technical glitches that affected public confidence. The committee called for future systems to be more rigorously tested, including consultation with users, to reduce the risk of a repeat of implementation problems.

It might not be fair, but a few e-government failures (due either to political pressure resulting in haphazard implementation or simply because trailblazers sometimes step on landmines) creates the risk of a change of political heart and reluctance to implement further, more complex online transactional services.

Changing Priorities and "Events, Dear Boy"

The new economy and e-government emerged at a time of unprecedented prosperity and relative peace and stability in the world. Most governments were not preoccupied with any particular economic problems or foreign relations crisis. Public finances were in order and issues such as tax cuts and the environment were not prominent in the public mind. Save the occasional food-related health scare and predictable sex, lies or corruption scandal, the key issue keeping decision-makers awake at night was the quality of public services. Better services, with the added bonus of appearing modern, became the political motivation for e-government.

Service quality, particularly in the areas of education and health, is always a public concern but it often pushed off the political agenda when a government is confronted with an unforeseen predicament. The government's fate is often then determined by its handling of the new issue. As the British Prime Minister Harold Macmillan once famously put it: it's "events, dear boy, events," and the events of September 11 propelled terrorism and homeland and global security as top issues, relegating public service quality — and by extension, e-government, to the back-burner. While security concerns are still of primary concern in the US, further "events" have occurred in Europe which have put illegal immigration, race relations, and the rise of the far right onto the political agenda. Meanwhile, economic problems (and related issues such the burst of the dot-com bubble, stock market volatility, abuses of corporate governance) and natural disasters (floods in Europe, wildfires in America, typhoons in East Asia) have made it very difficult to drum up political interest in e-government.

And in politics, there are elections. Ballots have been cast in most jurisdictions since the first e-government action plans were introduced, often resulting in a change of government. While e-government is non-partisan and does not (or should not) favor one political party over another, inevitably e-government strategies become associated with the governing party that initiated them. The political need for the in-coming people to distant themselves from the out-going people has contributed to, at best, a slow down in implementation of e-government and, at worse, a complete set-back if the strategy was too closely associated with the defeated administration or a previous minister. Italy is not alone, but it is typical in that the change of government there in May 2001 effectively delayed the implementation of e-government for nine months as a new Department of Innovation and Technologies was set up to take over primary responsibility from the Department of Public Administration. The previous e-government strategy was amended to put greater stress on the need to identify and measure results and benefits, and compare them to costs. But the most marked change was a shift in emphasis from "build" to "integrate," with a reduction in the original e-government plan's budget of 690m euros to 413m euros (drawn from the auction of 3G mobile licenses). More than half (258m euros) was allocated to local and regional government projects, with a first call for proposals (covering just 120m euros) finally made in February 2002.

Creating an Internal Marketing Strategy

Just as proponents of e-governments need a marketing strategy to address the demand side of e-government and ensure public take-up of online services, they also have to consider how to address the supply side of e-government to ensure ongoing support for those who will fund the development of online services. Rarely are any formal or systematic tactics taken to keep e-government on the political agenda and attempts to shore up top-level interest are not generally brought together under a "marketing" label. But it may be worthwhile to start thinking in marketing terms to promote e-government to this all-important, elite target group in order to maintain the momentum for change and ward off a looming political backlash against e-government.

Internal marketing efforts should cover a range of activities and include the need to:

1. Speak the "customer's" language
2. Make friends, isolate enemies
3. Develop projects to improve decision-makers' own work
4. Better analyze costs and benefits
5. De-emphasize the link with public services
6. Drop the "e" and re-brand "e-government"

Speak the "Customer's" Language

It's a marketing adage to "speak the customer's language," and government decision-makers need to be seen much like a customer for internal marketing purposes. While political leaders and senior-level bureaucrats would almost certainly benefit from learning some basic facts of IT life, they cannot be forced. In reality, it may take a generation or more before all politicians are computer literate. Therefore the onus falls on the practitioner to convey a better understanding of e-government to the decision-maker. It is extremely difficult for the uninitiated and non-technical person to get his or her head around even the most basic explanations of concepts such as PKI and XML. Proponents of e-government need to tone down the jargon and focus much more on the business and political benefits.

A good way of making e-government more visible to senior officials and ministers is to require departments and agencies to develop an e-business strategy (which is also important in its own right). In some countries, including the UK, the departmental strategy document itself is expected to include how the strategy will be communicated internally. Approaches often include organizing or encouraging others to organize events such as conferences, keynote addresses, and executive breakfast seminars that impart the benefits of e-government to both parliamentarians and senior decision-makers as well as to those directly involved in service and program delivery.

Make Friends, Isolate Enemies

As with any large-scale public works project, IT implementations can be intensely political. Their success depends on having allies in the field — ministers, parliamentarians, senior managers, public-sector union leaders and influential employees who can generate further support. Some of the people whom need to be on side are obvious: an online tax filing system requires the support of the minister of finance or revenue. People respect their peers, so a political lightweight cannot be sent in to win the support of a political heavyweight. Unfortunately ministerial responsibility for e-government is often piled on top of other duties and given to a junior minister sitting at the far end of the Cabinet table.

The UK takes a rather more pervasive approach with at least 22 central government ministers having some kind of responsibility for e-government. The Secretary of State for Trade and Industry, one of the most senior cabinet portfolios, is the "e-minister" who has overall responsibility for the government's e-strategy and who provides monthly progress reports to the prime minister. There is also a junior minister responsible for e-government located within the Cabinet Office. Both sit on a formal cabinet committee on electronic service delivery, chaired by the chief secretary of the Treasury, and which includes membership of five other junior ministers or parliamentary under-secretaries from different departments. Furthermore, each government department has nominated a junior e-minister to provide political leadership within their departments. They have day-to-day responsibility within their department for the e-agenda and support the overall e-minister in delivering and developing policy and work with colleague departmental e-ministers to facilitate joined-up approaches. In the ranks of senior management, each UK government department identifies a director or director-general to act as an "e-champion" for their department, to encourage both opinion leadership and specific delivery. Representatives of the devolved administrations (Scotland, Wales, Northern Ireland) and local government have also nominated e-champions. The group is chaired by the Cabinet Office's e-envoy and they too support the e-minister in driving forward the UK online strategy. This all-encompassing high-level representation of politicians and bureaucrats serves as an important vehicle for communicating internal marketing messages and for rounding up support across government.

Of course, even with an army of champions, e-government will have its antagonists — individuals and groups who, for whatever reason, prefer the status quo and who have some authority or influence to obstruct change. Implementation teams should expect resistance among upper management, where some executives may view information sharing and integrated service delivery as a threat to their fiefdoms. Such opposition is best neutralized by exercising diplomacy — let them critique the project and vent their concerns, and then proceed to isolate them and work around them!

Too often parliament is seen as an enemy of e-government, or at least a necessary evil for resource allocation. Backbench and opposition members of parliament may not have an official role within government but they often carry moral authority and credibility with their colleagues. Little effort is made to court them to share in the mission to achieve e-government, and to participate as speakers at executive breakfast meetings.

The system of representative democracy in most developed countries requires parliamentarians to represent many stakeholders with often competing interests and this makes it difficult to find any politician prepared to go the distance to constantly champion e-government. Hong Kong enjoys the advantage of having a legislative council in which half of its 60 councillors are elected through regular ridings based on geographic boundaries and the other half through "functional" constituencies of various interest groups in society (health, education, organized labour, business sectors, etc.). Sin Chung-kai has been the legislative councillor representing the IT community since 1998 and he previously represented a geographic constituency. He is also a central committee member of the Democratic Party and its spokesman for economic and financial affairs, and information technology. As a result, one of Hong Kong's longest-serving politicians and best known advocates for democracy is also one of its loudest cheerleaders for e-government.

While they may not able to do much about their parliamentary systems, organizations in other countries can stop treating IT as a support function and departmental IT heads as support officers. Some agencies are starting to appoint business managers as their IT head or CIO, rather than an engineer who may not be able to think strategically and politically. Ideally, an IT head should be both — someone with an engineering knowledge who understands what's possible from a technical standpoint combined with an MBA who can maintain an open relationship with their director-general or minister to provide strategic advice on a daily basis and distinguish achievable goals from industry hype. Very few public-sector CIOs have this level of authority, nor can they be considered equivalent to their boardroom counterparts in the private sector.

Develop Projects to Improve Decision-Makers' Own Work

It has been recognized that e-government requires a fundamental change in government employees' work and training programs have been devised to help them adapt and develop computing skills. The reduction of routine tasks, more enriching jobs, financial incentives and rewards for innovation are all helping to convince civil servants of the benefits of e-government. Yet that level of effort has not been made to persuade the decision-makers. Many politicians and senior level bureaucrats remain suspicious of e-government because they don't use computers themselves and they don't understand how e-business works. Many view new technology as all gadgets and an annoyance that they wish would simply go away. The nay-sayers who fear change have to be educated and shown how the Internet can improve their own work. This requires wiring their stuffy old buildings and automating their stuffy old procedures.

The processing and circulation of parliamentary papers and Cabinet (executive sessions) documents are among the oldest processes in public administration, and in most countries they continue to be carried out with the same inherently inefficient paper-based protocols as ever. Seeing ministers lug four kilograms of papers to each cabinet meeting prompted the Irish Department of the Taoiseach (prime minister) to launch an e-cabinet initiative in which memoranda and processes such as briefing, agenda and decisions are circulated to ministers electronically. In cabinet meetings, ministers will soon call up documents using silent touch screen terminals. The e-cabinet is already a well-established scenario in some of the emerging democracies of central and eastern Europe where they are unburdened by decades-old technology infrastructures and centuries-old parliamentary traditions and protocols. Estonia had virtually no modern technology when it regained its independence in 1991. Government offices were sparsely equipped and there were just two mobile phones in the entire Ministry of Foreign Affairs. Today Estonia is one of the most wired nations in the world with an ambitious e-government plan. Rather than having a token e-minister, it said to have an entire e-cabinet. Since August 2000, all ministers have packed only their laptops to cabinet meetings, where they electronically check agendas and cabinet documents and log onto the Internet to communicate with and consult their officials. They can also participate in cabinet meetings from remote locations using videoconferencing. A similar situation has existed in Croatia since the end of 2001, except ministers access documents using a touch-screen interface on terminals installed in the cabinet meeting room. After the third or fourth session, ministers were asking for more functionality, in particular the ability to access minutes from past sessions and to consult articles of laws and the Constitution. Building on the momentum, the technology is being extended to Croatia's parliament, perhaps using tablet PCs due to a lack of space for terminals on the members' benches. Once computers have made it into a country's legislative chamber, securing political backing for e-government initiatives should come faster and easier.

Better Analysis of Costs and Benefits

Because the required level of investment in e-government is increasing at a time when budget surpluses are diminishing, executive sponsorship of e-government initiatives will increasingly demand greater returns on investment (ROI) and cost recovery. Some legislatures are even starting to deal with IT funding proposals on a case-by-case basis.

More formal cost benefit analysis will become the norm for e-government projects, with business cases required to measure the development, implementation and maintenance costs of providing an electronic service as well as compensating costs for transferring transactions to the Web. If implementation of an electronic transaction is sold on its potential to save money on data-entry staff, the decision-maker will want to know how much of the saving will be off-set by the need for additional help-line staff to answer citizens' queries about how to use the new online service. Assessing this requires more reliable information than what is currently available on the costs of delivering existing services, together with a considered opinion on how e-government will affect those existing costs. Proponents of e-government projects will have to be careful not to overstate efficiency gains, and they will have to admit that sometimes ROI may take years to be realized.

Support for e-government will also require a harder sell of the non-tangibles: user satisfaction, expected take-up rates, improvements in the speed and accuracy of the service, alignment with the agency's mission and strategies, and opportunities for sharing applications across agencies. Business cases will also have to assess the ability of an online service to simplify or reduce existing functions rather than complicate them.

Until recently, some political leaders and senior management were convinced that too much planning led to too little progress, and organizations were encouraged to work on "Internet time" to develop online services. Now the prevailing view is that a lack of planning leads to an uneven development of e-government. It's hoped that more discriminating scrutiny will benefit e-government in the long-run by contributing to project stability. Evaluating initiatives on specific criteria prior to approval should especially help reduce the risk of project derailment for non-technological reasons.

De-Emphasize Link with Public Services

The main factor motivating e-government efforts has been to improve public services. While public services are always important, they have been supplanted (for now) at the top of the political priority list by more immediate concerns — the economy, security, etc. Because e-government is almost always associated with service delivery, it is now suddenly out of fashion and on the wrong side of today's most pressing issues. Champions and proponents of e-government must follow the new funding trails and re-position their focus on areas where it now matters.

E-government has become a component of almost every government IT project, with core pieces involving the development of online applications and Web infrastructures to support a mission. It can therefore be anticipated that IT initiatives will increasingly not be called "e-gov" projects at all. Rather they will be called "homeland security" projects or "economic development" projects or "immigration control" projects or whatever kind of project that addresses the political priority of the moment.

In the United States, of course, tax dollars are being spent hand over fist to shore up homeland security and guard against potential threats such as bio-terrorism. Homeland security relies heavily on data sharing among different agencies to combat terrorist threats, which by extension creates an unprecedented opportunity to integrate data, establish a culture of cross-agency cooperation, and address business process re-engineering issues across government. Similarly, biometric technology has gained much attention since September 11, which could be leveraged to serve e-government through the technology's ability to identify and authorize.

The billions of dollars being spent each summer to put out wildfires, coupled with the ensuing damage to property and environment, is an emerging issue in the American West, where it is already more important than the quality of public services. The issue prompted the National Wildfire Coordination Group to implement a Web-based application called the Resource Ordering and Status System (ROSS), which integrates data across agencies to allow federal, state and local firefighters to quickly locate and deploy people and equipment to fight wildfires. The system fits the definition of e-government, but nobody has ever called ROSS an e-government application. The $4.7 million to design and develop the system plus an annual $2.2 million for deployment and maintenance did not come from some small pot of money reserved for e-government projects — it came from a large tub earmarked for the wildfire crisis. If the project was sold internally as an e-government initiative, it probably would not have received executive support or financing.

De-Emphasize Link with IT: Drop the "e" and Re-Brand E-Government

It is often said that technology is only an enabler and the real focus for e-government is to establish good structures, processes and people who can apply the technology. But in reality, e-government is totally fixated on technology. Far more attention is paid to network speed or software implementation, for example, than to consulting users about system designs or giving employees customer service training. The major investments are in technology, not people. Initiatives such as integrated service delivery, customer relationship management (CRM), process re-engineering and even public procurement are approached as primarily technical challenges rather than organizational or cultural ones. The marketing muscle of the IT industry has influenced much of the public sector reform agenda, and government change agents have in many ways been willing conspirators. If the only way to drive change is to stick an "e" in front of your project, then you stick an "e" in front of your project.

For the past decade or more, reinventing government has been a broad-scale reform movement taking on many shapes and appearances — including privatization, outsourcing, decentralization, the creation of independent agencies, civil service reductions, accruals accounting, and so on. Some of these have enjoyed high level commitment, although they are rarely sustained over time. In this context, e-government has had an extremely good run. With the possible exception of privatization, no other reform tool has enjoyed such a high public or political profile. In countries where Internet penetration rates are just now starting to escalate to a critical mass, e-government presents new opportunities and political and public support remains strong. The IT industry is waking up to the fact that there are 6.2 billion people on planet and it has been focusing on less than 1 billion of them. Software and technology companies are now wooing governments in developing countries and the international market is seen as the battleground of the future, especially as the developed world becomes awash with technology.

Yet everything in politics has a shelf-life, and e-government will eventually reach its expiry date everywhere. Many decision-makers in developed countries are already experiencing "e-gov fatigue," and the "e" in e-government is become more of a liability than an asset. The emphasis on the electronic implies that technology is an end in itself rather an enabler. It conjures up negative connotations, putting e-government on par with e-commerce or, at best, e-business. Clearly, e-government is concerned with much bigger issues: economic development, social inclusion and empowerment, democracy, openness and transparency, and public trust and confidence in government. If e-government isn't about making government electronic *per se*, then why the letter "e"? Now may be a good time to drop it.

Public-sector reform may not now provide immediate political reward, but governments today have little choice but to carry out change since to avoid it would create even greater problems. However, if reform loses executive leadership because of a backlash against e-government, then it will slow to a crawl, and creeping reform can soon become no reform at all. Therefore, to maintain momentum and persevere with everything that e-government aims to achieve, it will be necessary to re-tag e-government and realign it to today's political priorities. In other words, a new "brand name" will have to be launched to replace an out-of-fashion e-government range. But re-branded as what? "Seamless," "integrated" or "joined-up" government won't capture the imagination of neither politician nor press nor public. The marketing people might be able to do something with "citizen-centric" or "customer-friendly" government. Or if the next brilliant idea fails to emerge, the promotion of a mixture of labels may be required. While e-government was a home run, public sector reform from now on may have to be won by grinding out the singles.

CONCLUSIONS

This chapter is a call for e-government practitioners to sharpen their internal marketing skills. Even if it is not characterized as "marketing" in the traditional sense, a more strategic approach is needed to maintain high-level interest in the objectives of e-government and keep them on the political agenda. A loss of executive support would adversely impact the success of e-government and could jeopardize the whole government reform movement.

Matters to consider whilst devising an internal e-government marketing strategy include:

- Think of political leaders and senior level managers as customers to whom the concept of e-government needs to be sold. Then tone down the technical jargon and speak the customer's language.
- How an e-government strategy is to be communicated internally should be included within the strategy document itself. The internal communication plan could entail keynote addresses, executive breakfast seminars, etc., for senior decision-makers.
- Identify e-champions, and an e-minister if possible, for every government department. Don't neglect parliament — many backbench and opposition members carry weight.
- Appoint business managers as the department IT head rather than an engineer (or, ideally, someone with a knowledge of both).
- Neutralize antagonists by exercising diplomacy, and then work around them.
- Educate ministers and managers by showing them how e-business can work for them, including automation of their own processes and the establishment of an "e-cabinet." Put technology into the parliamentary chambers.
- Conduct more formal cost benefit analysis of e-government projects, with business cases measuring ROI and cost recovery. Don't over-state cost savings and efficiency gains. Do stress non-tangibles: user satisfaction, take-up rates, improvements in the speed and accuracy service, alignment with the agency mission, and opportunities for sharing applications across agencies.
- Recognize that events have pushed public services down the list of political priorities so re-position e-government to follow the new funding trails and focus on areas that are now more important.
- End the fixation on technology. By stressing the "e" in e-government, the technology is seen as an end in itself rather than an enabler.
- Recognize that everything in politics has a limited shelf-life; e-government is approaching its expiry date as more and more political leaders and senior-level bureaucrats experience "e-gov fatigue." To safeguard executive leadership and maintain the momentum for change, consider dropping the "e" and crafting a new brand image for public sector reform to succeed e-government.

REFERENCES

Accenture. (2002). *eGovernment leadership – Realizing the vision.*

Atkinson, S., & Mortimore, R. (2002, July 19). What's worrying the people? *Poll Digest.* MORI, London.

Economist. (2002, August 10). There's always someone looking at you – and the people don't like it. 47-48.

Emery, G. R. (2002, July 9). E-Gov: Beneath the surface. *Washington Technology, 17*(9).

Holmes, D. (2001). *eGov: eBusiness strategies for government.* London: Nicholas Brealey.

Kelly, C. (2000). *E-government: Creating digital democracy.* META Group and Federal Sources.

KPMG Consulting. (2002). *Is Britain on course for 2005? - Third annual KPMG Consulting e-government survey.* KPMG LLP, London.

KPMG Consulting. (2001). *E-government for all – the KPMG consulting e-government survey 2001.* KPMG LLP, London.

Larsen, E., & Rainie, L. (2002). *The rise of the e-citizen - How people use government agencies' Web sites.* Washington, DC: Pew Internet & American Life Project.

Lowe, C. (Ed.). (2003). Take-up of eGovernment in Europe. *Report of the e-Forum Working Group on Take-up and Benefits.* Brussels: e-Forum Association.

Margetts, H., & Dunleavy, P. (2002). Cultural barriers to e-government. *Better Public Services through e-government.* London: The Stationery Office.

National Audit Office. (2002). *Better public services through e-government.* London: The Stationery Office.

Sawhney, M. (2001, July-August). Don't homogenize, synchronize. *Harvard Business Review,* 101-108.

WEB RESOURCES

Canada Customs and Revenue Agency: *www.ccra-adrc.gc.ca*
Inland Revenue Authority of Singapore: *www.iras.gov.sg*
Federal Election Commission: *www.fec.gov*
National Office for the Information Economy: *www.noie.gov.au*
Office of the e-Envoy: *www.e-envoy.gov.uk*
Rock the Vote: *www.rockthevote.org*
South African Revenue Service: *www.sars.gov.za*

Chapter XI

E-Government: Trick or Treat?

Alison Hopkins, National Consumer Council, UK

ABSTRACT

This chapter approaches the topic from a consumer perspective, looking at some of the principal challenges for governments in developing not just e-government, but responsive e-government.

SETTING THE CONTEXT

Consumer, in the context of this paper, is a broad term overlapping with citizen, and includes individual users or potential users of government services. Public services need to respond to the diversity of consumer demand, so it is more meaningful to think about the plurality of individuals as consumers, service users, stakeholders, and individuals concerned with the wider public interest, rather than using differentiated identities for the roles people have in their daily business (NCC, 2004).

E-government is not a new concept. In the UK for example, the government issued a consultation paper called Government.direct in 1996. E-delivery has become a key plank of government policy — for local as much as central government — and is essentially a top-down development aiming for efficiency, speed and convenience, with meeting consumer need as one goal. On the whole e-government services are passive — consumers can find information and download forms, but there is limited interactivity. E-government has the capacity to make services much more user-led, and to be much more responsive, but has a long way to go to realize its potential (OECD, 2003).

Responsive e-government is about the quality of interaction between public administrations and their clients, including how far the needs of clients can be satisfied within policy frameworks, the comprehensibility and accessibility of administration, the openness of administration to client participation in decision making, and the availability of redress. It is also about a different way of thinking and organizing services which will require an overhaul of systems and professions.

Responsive government will need to take the e-government agenda several steps further than merely providing online services. Crucially, if governments are to be responsive they will need to engage consumers or clients at each and every stage of policy development and determination. The OECD project on e-government started from the point that e-government has the potential to be a major enabler in the adoption of good governance practices, and that developing responsive administration is integral to its achievement (OECD, 2001). The challenge is how to engage effectively and appropriately with consumers in an ongoing two-way process.

KEY ISSUES FOR CONSUMERS

Generally speaking, consumers have limited interest in and experience of government services — particularly central government services. Most consumers interact with central government on an infrequent basis, and only when it is mandatory, for example to pay taxes, apply for a passport, register a birth, marriage or death, or apply for a driving licence — or for essential services such as health and social welfare. Contact with administration at a local level is much more frequent. In the UK, it is estimated that local authorities handle 80% of government-to-citizen transactions (Socitm, 2003).

Services that are delivered or experienced locally like refuse collection, street lighting and policing are much more likely to register in the mind of the public than the more remote and rarely experienced services of central government. E-government programs, therefore, will need to overcome public disinterest if they are to attract widespread support and public engagement.

Gaps in Trust and Confidence

There is broad agreement that the current lack of user trust and confidence, especially among specific sectors of the population, is a significant inhibitor to the widespread growth in use of electronic services in many OECD countries. The end of the "dot-com" boom, coupled with the high profile given to failures and security breaches, continues to exacerbate existing consumer concerns.

Many consumers will need to be persuaded of the benefits of dealing with government electronically. In part this stems from the general reluctance to venture online but governments are also going through what might be called a crisis of credibility in their relations with citizens and consumers. There are questions about governments' ability to deliver what consumers want or expect, or to be responsive to their needs. Also in many countries the experience and history of government IT projects is not a happy one with projects being well over budget or failing to deliver. In addition the steady erosion of trust and confidence in institutions — public and commercial — and low voter turnout in elections is seen as evidence of a more general apathy. This trend is widespread if uneven across OECD countries, and has been evident for decades (Putnam, 2000; Zuboff & Maxmin, 2003).

Security and Data Protection

In our research on e-commerce, conducted in 2000, the main consumer concern was the remote nature of e-transactions — with no apparent physical presence, there is no obvious way of checking the identity of whom you are dealing with, or how to sort out problems if they arise. Poor security of credit card and personal details, and the potential for fraudulent activity were also at the front of consumers' minds. Although the research was restricted to the UK, the findings are not peculiar to UK consumers (NCC, 2000).

It seems that public perceptions about e-commerce have changed little since then. Recent research indicates that consumers do care about what personal information is collected or stored, and whether it is sold on to others (RSGB, 2004; DCA, 2003; PIU, 2002).

Findings by the European Commission into the impact of the EU Data Protection Directive show that most respondents said they were aware of "invisible" data collection through the use of cookies and spy ware technologies, and a majority expressed concern that their personal data might be misused (Privacy laws, 2003). Public concern about the nature of online transactions is persistent, as people feel they have no control over what happens, or if something were to go wrong.

This should not be surprising, as we are developing ever more sophisticated ways of capturing and using personal data. Each time we respond to a marketing offer, fill in a questionnaire, use a loyalty card, or use the Internet we are laying down a rich seam of information that can be used for other purposes — for example to provide us with better services, or for unsolicited marketing purposes. Public services at local and central levels gather an enormous amount of information — from those who pay general taxation and council tax, car owners and drivers, patients and social benefit recipients. The growing use of electronic communications means information can be captured and shared more rapidly than ever. There may be benefits in terms of efficiency but the perceived loss of control in an electronic environment, and poor understanding of how online transactions are processed, or how data protection legislation applies have heightened public uncertainty about how personal information is collected and used. For example:

- 84% of the population in Britain think they have less privacy now compared with 10 years ago.
- 78% felt the had lost control over how their personal information is collected and used by organizations.
- 58% said they felt they did not really understand how their personal information is collected and used by organizations (RSGB, 2004).

There are other concerns about how an individual gains access to information about himself or herself, especially as government agencies are perceived as overly bureaucratic, reluctant to provide open access to files or to explain how decisions are made.

You would probably spend a good half hour on the phone to someone, being passed from department to department. And nobody would want to give out that information (NCC, 1999).

These perceptions present a critical challenge, especially as data sharing is intrinsic to the notion of public service reform and the e-government agenda. Government must be able to demonstrate that their services are safe and reliable to use. Concerns about privacy and security will be difficult to overcome and may remain unresolved if governments rely solely on technological solutions to reassure the public. Strong accompanying legal guarantees and authentication will need to supplement other measures. Most importantly, providers need to find ways of building confidence, and engaging users in the design and development of security systems.

Rights and Redress

A regulatory framework needs to be in place to provide reassurance that if something goes wrong, individuals have some means of finding out, of putting it right and gaining redress. Things happen quickly and invisibly in electronic communications, with no obvious audit trail. Government will need to lead by example to set standards for others to use as a benchmark for other providers.

Regulation needs to take account of the converged communications environment and work out how to support consumers in an environment where responsive online government can flourish. Consumers will need to feel their interests are effectively recognized and protected or they will be reluctant to engage. Simple, easy to use systems of redress will be reassuring as long as they are effective. Complaints handling should be an integral element of e-government strategies, building on and extending best practice while adopting flexible and responsive working methods. Frontline staff must have the power and discretion to make decisions and to guide consumers to a satisfactory resolution, without passing them round a succession of fruitless encounters.

Access

Bridging the digital divide will require time and resources. Responsive e-government will require a societal infrastructure with universal access to information and communications technologies that are convenient and easy to use, and a population with the necessary skills and confidence to take part.

Access is a multi-dimensional concept, and is fundamental to the development of e-government. It includes physical access for all to the technology as well as the knowledge and skills to use it effectively, regardless of age, wealth, experience of sensory or physical impairment, cultural diversity, education or geographical area.

Governments are concerned about how universal access can be achieved. Issues of social exclusion and the digital divide underlie e-government strategies, including how to promote the take up of digital technologies and the drive to improve relations with consumers and citizens.

The relatively low level of penetration of information and communication technologies is, to a degree, a transitional phenomenon. The divide between those who do and do not have skills and home access is likely to diminish gradually over time as digital devices become integral to our daily life at work and at home. Countries and regions with low levels of access will, at varying rates, catch up. But this development may not be either universal or inevitable. Technology is continuously developing and is introduced rapidly into the market. The poor and the less able or less well educated are always left behind. Public policy measures and investment will be required to ensure universal access goals are achieved and people or communities are not left out if e-government services are to be universally accessible.

Digital television, broadband and mobile telephony will extend access but may not provide the anticipated solution to access and interactivity. Internet access via digital TV or wireless technologies is an additional service at additional cost, and does not yet offer a viable alternative to computer-based Internet services because of the limited range of services and the relatively poor visual quality of Web content. And there are added complications such as the low security of phones, and compromised confidentiality. These factors, combined with technical limitations such as access to broadband or other high-speed connections mean that universal access at home will take some time to achieve.

There are other questions about whether consumers will want to communicate online, even if they have Internet access. Some people will not want to go online — and others may be unable to, particularly poor people, older people, and those with learning or reading difficulties. Others feel disillusioned about the Internet as their experience fails to live up to expectations, or the novelty wears off. UK research suggested that people are starting to turn away from e-mails in favor of face-to-face meetings (CA, 2001). In addition, concern about privacy and security affects online behavior. People avoid giving their personal details if they can find a way round it. In a recent survey of the general population in Britain, 62% of respondents said they either falsify personal information or refuse to answer questions (RSGB, 2004).

Regardless of how good the strategy may be, the road to responsive government is pitted with potential diversions and discontinuities as human factors come into play.

KEY CHALLENGES FOR GOVERNMENT

Governments need to find ways of addressing these consumer issues — especially the gaps in trust and confidence, in structures and systems to enable responsiveness, and in shared understanding of what responsive e-government means for administrations and for consumers. This cannot be achieved without entering a continuous process of engagement with consumers, and a radical change within government.

As many consumers are not yet interested in or convinced about the need or the advantages of going online, e-government services need to be attractive, easy to use, and useful so that people want to use them. Such services cannot be built without involving consumers at all stages of design and development. Government will need to be an exemplar in its delivery of electronic services. Their services must set and deliver the highest standards of quality in security and systems management including incident response handling and contingency planning when something goes wrong.

Apart from having to deal with current perceptions and prejudices about government in general — including its ability to deliver what consumers or users want – governments will also need to overcome negative perceptions of e-commerce. In many countries the e-economy is still in its infancy and to a certain extent consumers, business and governments are "learning as we go." Government strategies need to be sufficiently flexible to cope with a changing environment, and major concerns regarding user trust and confidence will need to be regularly reassessed and addressed as change occurs.

Trust and Confidence

Confidence won't be won unless governments get the organizational and professional culture right. The right kind of organizational changes must be implemented within government, among its institutions, staff and policies. Consumers are on one side of the equation — they need to be persuaded of the benefits of e-government and to have the right kind of access to use services — but government itself needs to be convinced too.

The stereotypical impression of government is of institutionalized bureaucracy, unwilling and unable to change — or at least to change rapidly. Its institutions and processes are rooted in traditional modes of operation. Public bodies have been slow to take up new technology or new ways of working and are associated with cultural inertia rather than innovation. This way of working has evolved partly through necessity. The public sector has to demonstrate it uses public money prudently, resulting in a tendency to wait until new techniques and technologies have been tested, to do things as cheaply as possible, and make them last as long as possible.

Parts of government still see electronic delivery as an optional extra, not a central aspect of their role. Some see it as about the channel, about technology instead of transforming the service. Changing the mentalities and habits of public servants and government agencies is a challenge across the world. Such a change entails a revolutionary turnaround, not merely adjusting staff attitudes and the mechanics of government delivery — no trivial challenge in itself.

Apart from these hurdles, the sheer number and complexity of government services presents another challenge. Government may lag behind the private sector but their task is of a different order. Central and local government provide a number of very different services to a wide range of users. For example, a typical unitary local authority in the UK has 706 functional areas, compared with 12 in a bank (PIU, 2001).

Security and Data Protection

Personal information is one of the most valuable commodities in society today. Government is a repository of sensitive and confidential information about businesses and consumers. The development of digital communications makes it increasingly possible to collect large volumes of information about individuals, their families and their use of services. Protection against unauthorized data gathering and sharing will be increasingly important, both to protect people's fundamental right to privacy and to engender trust in new technologies.

At the same time, data sharing and data transfer between public bodies and private or voluntary partners will play a key role in the government's plans for e-delivery of services. But how will data collectors and service providers convince consumers and other service users their personal details are safe? How far should public bodies be allowed to share data? What are the limits of informed consent as a model for legitimizing information use, and how will consumers be able to assess the costs, risks and benefits of all the different options and permissions that are likely to arise in different contexts? It will be crucial to have the right systems in place but governments have to find ways of taking people with them, inside and outside the administrative circles.

With the notable exception of the USA, data protection legislation is almost universal in OECD countries — though, in common with much other legislation, is little understood by most consumers. Governments can help to improve awareness and understanding by publicizing legal provisions, explaining clearly how they apply to personal data obtained through electronic interaction with government.

Clear rules will need to be developed for the public and for staff on what information is collected, who is given information, and how government and its agencies use it. Consumers will also need to know how they can access and amend their personal data.

The problem is that public service organizations vary in the importance and priority they attach to consent and transparency which means there is a risk of inconsistency and confusion about standards.

Integrated care records in the UK health system are an all too rare example of good practice. The Integrated Care Records Service is an electronic health records initiative that includes a confidentiality code issued by the NHS Information Authority. This is a consumer friendly code giving patients a right to ask that certain pieces of information should not be shared with particular agencies. Their requests can only be overridden in an emergency, and with a safeguard that the decision can be challenged and held to account.

An early UK Performance and Innovation Unit report envisaged that a similar approach would be applied consistently across government. The report suggested drawing up a Public Services Trust Charter which would promise to give consumers notice of data collection, choice about how data is used, access to their own data, and guaranteed security of data (PIU, 2001).

Unfortunately, these original plans for joined-up, holistic privacy protection to keep pace with possible incursions on privacy have been watered down into a set of protocols for particular services. This means that data sharing issues are likely to develop on a case-by-case basis, and that consumers will be deprived of a single, easy to understand point of reference on data sharing within government.

However, this kind of approach, based on some type of contract or agreement between individuals and government should engender trust — especially if consumers were actively involved in developing and designing the "contracts." There would also be a spin-off in terms of raised awareness of privacy issues and what kinds of protection exist. Consumers themselves must be properly identified to gain access to e-services but they also need to be sure they are dealing with an identifiable entity. A common standard would be a preferable way to tackle this kind of shared challenge, especially in an environment where service integration and multi-agency delivery are likely to be much more commonplace.

Few people have a comprehensive understanding of the technology, security systems and potential risks to make an accurate judgement about the risk to personal information through using electronic channels. Codes of practice and security devices must be developed with involvement of consumers so they know how to use them, and feel confident in their effectiveness. But there may need to be a trade off between demands for "perfect" security and a system that is affordable and flexible. Governments will have to invest time and resources to convince service users that systems are safe and secure — and will certainly have to demonstrate and maintain the highest possible standards. Whatever approach is used, the standards must be effectively monitored to ensure compliance. Models for effective risk handling and risk communication should support both consumers and professionals as they develop new skills and responsibilities in a more responsive environment (NCC, 2003b).

Integrating Services

Greater co-operation throughout the public sector is required for e-services to be delivered effectively and in response to need. But there are practical obstacles to fundamental change in the way governments and their departments are organized, and integration brings potential risks as well as benefits.

Government is deliberately compartmentalized, partly in the public interest to avoid inappropriate data sharing and over-centralization. So, for example, welfare records are kept separate from those of the Inland Revenue. The financial implications of integration are important too, as departmental and agency budgets are hard-won and closely defended, touching sensitive issues about the structure, independence and competencies of each department or agency.

This suggests that funding strategies, especially for technology or e-government projects, will need to change. At the moment it is often ring-fenced within each department, with only a limited amount of crosscutting responsibilities and money, reinforcing the fragmented approach to building e-services.

Governments need to avoid a harmful dislocation between consumer expectations and public policy as they develop their e-government strategies. Joined-up government will need to strike the right balance to protect individuals and to convince staff that the benefits are in their, and the public, interest. There is in-built tension to the idea of responsive government, between integrated multi-agency services requiring more data sharing and the risk to privacy and confidentiality. The strategy will need to take into account, for example, how far the public will tolerate data sharing and the only way to do this is to have an effective dialogue.

Reducing boundaries between departments may improve coherence and efficiency in service delivery but at the same time it reduces accountability for a wide range of functions with different statutory bases. It will be essential that people know precisely who is responsible for a particular service, to whom they can complain and how to gain redress when things go wrong, and that staff are trained and empowered to respond effectively. Strong leadership, enthusiasm, commitment and co-ordination at the highest levels of government will help to promote change but investment in training, implementation and delivery will be essential at all levels and across sectors including local and central government and voluntary or other agencies.

Universal Access

The delivery of e-services and responsive government will affect the whole of society, meaning it is essential to ensure that everyone can access the services they need, and engage in dialogue with responsive government agencies. This does not mean that everyone will want to engage, and certainly not on every issue, but access to the means of communication with government is an essential first step to enabling responsiveness. One way to ensure access is to promote and provide electronic access in the home and community, but alternative channels will need to be open too.

Consumers are not a homogeneous group. People have highly differentiated needs and attitudes so e-services must be sufficiently flexible to respond appropriately. The attitudes and needs of each person also vary according to the services they use and the perceived advantages of using one channel rather than another. For example renewing road tax or a vehicle licence, or contacting government departments for business needs online is more acceptable than using electronic channels for services catering for personal needs. Those claiming welfare benefits express greater concern and unwillingness to interact electronically or to provide personal information online, especially if they feel confidentiality is compromised, at a public access point for example (PIU, 2001; DCA, 2003).

Design issues and ease of use will be prominent in e-government strategies, particularly as the changing age profile of many countries means that a greater proportion of citizens will have some direct experience of disability. Disabled or older people may be less likely to have home access to ICTs because of additional equipment costs. Local and central government will need to develop initiatives to address their specific needs, and work with major IT suppliers to design new systems and devices to meet the needs of disabled people, rather than re-engineer them at some cost at a later date. This applies as much to the design of smart card systems as to public access kiosks and digital navigation and input devices. The increased capacity for consumers, and particularly for disabled people, to become actively engaged should make "design for access" a norm rather than an exception or add-on (Demos, 1999; ITC, 2002).

Access means more than having equipment. Education and training opportunities need to be readily available to all sections of society and governments will need to be flexible and creative in their strategies. Governments and consumers will need to be pragmatic. Access will revolve around a combination of channels and devices which people will use at different times for different purposes, depending on need.

In addition, there will always be a proportion of the population without access to electronic means of communication, or who choose not to use them. But government services are so important that it is unjust and undemocratic to provide only one channel of access. No pressure should be put on people to conform and use electronic channels, for example, through introducing additional charges for an alternative service, or a reduced quality in services delivered by other channels.

Access to interactive communications technologies will provide access to essential lifeline services for consumers to function effectively and participate in society. Connectivity services are run by private-sector companies which need to be regulated in a way that improves access for consumers, ensuring they provide a range of initiatives that benefit disadvantaged consumers. Governments will need to develop strategies to ensure these services are, and remain, accessible and affordable to all consumers, instead of relying on ad-hoc and ineffective measures, as described in the National Consumer Council's agenda for inclusive access (NCC, 2003).

GETTING THE INFRASTRUCTURE RIGHT

Building trust and confidence in government and e-services will be a gradual process. Government will need to implement specific measures, such as ensuring the legislative and institutional frameworks are appropriate to the protection of consumer and citizen rights in the "information age." But the way in which change is communicated and the degree of government responsiveness will influence how that process of building confidence develops. Governments will need to actively promote responsive e-services to the public and to public sector staff, and to achieve the organizational and cultural changes required to make e-government happen. Most importantly, trust will depend on governments' ability to deliver. Public education programs must be supplemented by education and training for staff so they, too, feel confident in using and delivering new services.

Governments need to develop effective ways of communicating with their consumers. Many people are confused or ill-educated about government and what it provides, or about the differences and relationships between central and local government. The capacity of new technologies to capture and process data also raises questions about the motive for introducing e-government. There are real public concerns about the potential threat to civil liberty and personal privacy implied by e-government and multi-agency delivery. Is it primarily about serving consumers better, or is it more connected with surveillance and security measures, policing and immigration control? These questions have become much starker in the debates on international and national security measures being developed since September 2001.

Quality Standards

Trust and confidence derive, in part, from the quality, reliability and track record of service providers. Governments have some catching up to do in this respect. E-government should be about improving the quality and not just quantity or speed of services. Quality standards, developed in conjunction with consumers and staff, must be incorporated into the planning, implementation and delivery of e-services, followed by effective monitoring for compliance.

Governments have already set up online service quality initiatives. For example INFOCID in Portugal has standards for speed and quality of responses and Switzerland has standards for the quality of information. Standards need to be developed across the board – from appearance and ease of use to transactions and security. The Netherlands and Australia, among others, have developed standard components for their online services that can be reused by different agencies in different services. These include usability standards, navigation routes and aids, and online transactions (OECD 2002). In the UK the Central IT Unit (CITU), now part of the e-government office's responsibility, develops cross-departmental standards for national government and the Central and Local Information Age Partnership (CLIP) aims to ensure that online standards are suitable for both central and local government (PIU, 2001).

Adequate systems and resources such as in-house capacity for information management will also be essential to maintain quality standards. In the end it is the quality of user experience that matters, from ease of navigation and the usability of the technology to the responsiveness of systems and support staff. Services need to match consumer expectations and meet their needs — particularly in privacy, security, and accountability.

Clear and well-publicized rules on liability, complaint handling, dispute resolution, and redress for damage or injury are essential for promoting openness and trust. Overall public reporting will be another important contributor to public confidence. At the same time, service quality must be maintained.

Evaluation and Oversight

Audit and evaluation are important for government accountability, and provide the most effective way of finding out what works. A thorough evaluation process assesses the relative incidence of success and failure and helps to identify any unexpected consequences of introducing new ways of working. The findings also form a solid basis on which to plan future projects and improvements. Scrutiny by an external body adds an element of accountability, not only reinforcing a commitment to openness and transparency, but also helping to demonstrate compliance with legislation, regulation and current best practice standards. In the UK individual government departments are regularly assessed on a number of requirements, such as their Public Service agreements, and on progress to their targets for getting services online. The Cabinet Office publishes annual reports but in addition the National Audit Office conducts, and publishes, detailed value for money studies which are independent of government (Office of the e-Envoy, 2003; NAO 2002).

Responsive government may require dedicated resources to monitor and evaluate new ways of working. Independent scrutiny adds credibility to such measures. For example, an ombudsman or commissioner to oversee e-government services, with a duty to report publicly on their findings, similar to the existing arrangements for monitoring compliance with Data Protection and Freedom of Information legislation in the UK would strengthen confidence. They could also act as a central point for dealing with complaints that cannot be resolved by internal procedures.

The final evaluation rests with service users, however, and they must be involved in assessing the performance and effectiveness of e-government. Governments could introduce a consumer impact assessment tool (in the same way that most apply regulatory impact assessments) to help them assess the impact of policy proposals and decisions on their service users. More involvement of the public should further strengthen the openness and accountability of government but most importantly will help to ensure that consumers' needs are met. But this will require effective communication channels and a greater degree of responsiveness in government, as well as a greater degree of sophistication than the ubiquitous user satisfaction survey.

ENGAGING AND COMMUNICATING

Governments are under pressure to integrate public input to the policy-making process and respond to public expectations that their views be considered. In addition, "Engaging citizens in policy making is a sound investment and a core element of good governance" (OECD, 2001a, 2002). Most governments already involve consumers, to varying degrees and with varying effect through public opinion polls and other surveys, in written consultations on specific policy issues or proposals. These are invariably initiated, controlled and defined by government, and there is little feedback on whether and how the information is used. This leaves consumers feeling as if they have wasted their time, and discourages them from getting involved again.

Modern technologies offer huge potential for greater public consultation, and for consumers to take more initiative in communicating with government. The OECD report, Citizens as Partners, lists ten principles for successful information, consultation and participation for citizens in policy making. Success depends on having clarity about the objective for involving consumers, and to build involvement into the policy making process, as described in the NCC's list of key ingredients (NCC, 2002). A framework for communication will be essential, not least to ensure the information collected from the public is used and that public expectations do not exceed their rights and obligations. Governments will continue to be responsible for ensuring the public is properly informed, with access to objective and reliable information they are able to understand and respond to. But service users and citizens will be much more meaningfully engaged in a responsive system of policy-making and delivery.

Technology provides government with a wide range of feedback mechanisms, offering greater flexibility and opportunity for the public to be involved in policy making. A mixed approach will be necessary, partly to allow consumers to choose how they want to communicate with government but also to capture a broad range of views and inputs. The various methods will need to be adaptable to different situations, local traditions and practices (OECD, 2002). New channels will complement, not replace, more established routes such as surveys, public hearings, focus groups, citizen panels and workshops that may take place online or off-line. Ways of integrating methods and of finding the balance between online and off-line opportunities for involvement will also need to be found.

Governments will need to develop realistic strategies, making consultation meaningful and relevant to consumers, learning how and when to engage with the public. The challenge is how to get people interested in policy and policy making in the first place.

Getting People to Engage

Can governments develop and maintain personalized relationships with consumers? Government may want to develop an interactive dialogue with their citizens, but the feeling may not be reciprocated, especially given the general decline in trust, respect and deference.

Responsive government will need to find ways of communicating on a consensual basis — so that interactions are of direct interest to the individual, and of some mutual benefit (DCA, 2003). Issues and opportunities need to be relevant and timely so that consumers understand what the issue is, what they have to do, and what will happen afterwards. Making it easy for people to participate is just as important — so all kinds of potential barriers need to be assessed and removed or, if that is not possible, reduced (NCC, 2002; 2004).

NCC research into consumers and involvement found that people are more inclined to become involved with local issues or those that affect them directly (NCC, 2002). It will be difficult for governments to interest people in issues at a national level and they will need to be imaginative and experimental in finding ways of motivating the public. One of the leading policy bodies in the UK has suggested it might be more appropriate to start by supporting e-experiments at neighborhood level to engage people, and to support community network content development to stimulate more civic engagement locally before trying to engage people in national issues (IPPR, 2002). Local pilot schemes have been successfully implemented but often prove unsustainable after an initial burst of enthusiasm, instead of establishing enduring interest and commitment.

Service providers will need to develop a better understanding of consumer behavior in order to engage effectively. The UK Government is beginning to show some awareness of this particular challenge and recently published a discussion paper exploring some issues in detail but much more needs to be done in this area (PIU, 2004). The effective exercise of responsiveness relies on people's ability to deploy skills, capacity and inclination — attributes that are unevenly distributed among the population. Consumer appetite for involvement varies, and not everyone has the time, commitment or confidence to take on new responsibilities. Government and providers will need to provide help and support for people, to make sure they can be responsive, to avoid a bias toward those who shout the loudest and to generate motivated consumers who feel sufficiently "e-government literate" to be able to engage to good effect. Equally, consumers need appropriate and trustworthy information and support to engage responsively and responsibly. A responsive system will require commitment from professionals to educate, inform and guide consumers too. In the end, trained advocates and intermediaries will also be needed to help individuals deal with the new environment.

The NCC recognized this skills gap some time ago and developed a generic training program aimed at consumers taking on a role representing others. The package has been used by a wide range of organizations from community bodies to formal boards and professional bodies (NCC, Stronger Voice, 2003a). It aims to develop the skills, confidence and ability to enable consumer representatives to hold the ring for stakeholders, to champion the needs of users and take on the full responsibilities required of a board member. To support consumers' needs and to help build trust in risk decision-making processes and bodies, the NCC has developed a model for risk governance, and government has recognized that the management of risk has become increasingly important to the business of government (PMSU, 2002; NCC, London, 2003b). These essential building blocks must be widely disseminated and communicated at all levels.

User involvement needs to be matched by a mature understanding of responsibility and risk sharing if individuals are to take on greater responsibility for decisions, especially where they affect others. This is partly about accepting responsibility for one's own decisions, choices and actions, and partly about the stakeholder or governance level where individuals need to balance conflicting and collective needs, and to make decisions on behalf of others.

In addition to opening up a dialogue with users and citizens, responsive government will need to include representative organizations and individuals in their plans for greater participation. Civil society organizations (CSOs) make an important contribution to policy discussions. Their particular interests, skills and experience will need to be weighed against those of individual citizens, but they also play a role in encouraging informed participation in debates. CSOs are well positioned to contribute to the design of e-services and consultative mechanisms, to help with disseminating information, offering alternative policy options and evaluating public policy. They often act as watchdogs and independent monitors of government activity and have multiple roles to play in helping to develop responsive services and educate responsible consumers.

Managing Impacts

Responsive working methods, processes and procedures will transform government organizations. Frontline staff will need to be empowered to make accountable decisions or judgements — accountable because responsiveness implies there should be clarity and transparency about decisions and their consequences. In addition, feedback from frontline staff is valuable information about service delivery and should be integrated into the consultation and evaluation processes. Organizational structures will need to adapt, adopting flatter hierarchies, wider structures, and more team working, although effective management and leadership will continue to be essential.

Feedback and engagement must be managed effectively. It requires trained staff with the capacity for making prompt and competent replies or interventions, and a change in culture for public bodies unaccustomed to openness and transparency. Communication has to be a genuine two-way process for consumers to put trust in e-services and become engaged in policy-making. Equally, consumers will need to have a clear understanding of the process and level at which policy decisions are made (OECD, 2002).

Public bodies will need to find new ways of developing policy proposals, building in sufficient time to digest, evaluate and take into account responses from a wide and disparate public. Time and resources will also need to be devoted to working out how to integrate responses into policy making and accountability processes. Guidelines, rules and standards for information provision, feedback and consultation need to be built in. For example, the UK government, in collaboration with consumer organizations and others, has developed a code of conduct for engagement in written consultations, but its use is optional rather than a requirement for good practice.

Professionals must be technically competent, but this by itself is no longer enough. Responsive government needs professionals who are responsive to the needs of consumers as individuals, who can develop relationships built on respect rather than control, and who can work in partnership with consumers. These interpersonal skills must be embedded in competencies through education, training, and continuous professional development, and reflected in the practice of professional bodies (NCC, 2004).

Managing New Service Models

The implementation of e-government provides new opportunities to put service users at the centre of service design and delivery. There will be opportunities to systematically create and develop new services, for example to match consumers with services and with other people who share a particular interest or who live in a particular area. Personalized or customized services could be developed, pulled together either by the service provider or by the individual consumer. There is also much greater potential for allowing people to express their views and influence future service development.

New service models will be essential to support responsive government, something more radical and imaginative than public access points and public-private partnerships. Public bodies will be much better equipped to work in partnership with consumers and providers to develop responsive services. Local networks could be developed with differing levels of "hands-on" engagement by service users, whereby communities or individuals take much more control of their own services. This could range from users collectively delivering services themselves, effectively working on behalf of service provider organizations, producing the services themselves, or buying in expertise as and when required. In such circumstances government could be providing a support role for new modes of enterprise.

Not all public services will be provided electronically, either because it is not cost-effective or the service relies on human interaction. But ICTs can help to improve even these services. For example outreach service providers and those who deliver personal social care could take Internet-enabled lap top computers on their home visits to access information and input client records. Trained and trusted mediators working locally can provide face-to-face support and reassurance for those least likely to possess digital technology or the skills to use it — who tend to be those who use government services most.

There are many tensions implicit in potential new models of delivery and governments must monitor their performance and standards as well as how the public responds. Solutions will vary between States and services, and the OECD has started to bring together comparative information on what works, developing international benchmarks and guidelines (OECD, 2004). Agreements and contracts may need to be made on a case-by-case basis and should involve effective consultation with users and potential users of each service. Income and cost recovery should not be allowed to compromise the probity and impartiality of public service delivery. Governments will need to convince consumers that e-government is about better services, not about saving money or allowing private profit to influence service delivery. It will also be crucial to guard against a two-tier service, where unprofitable services and sectors of the population could be excluded from access to, or receive lower quality, public services.

The long-term effects could exacerbate the existing breach in relations with government. The public may feel even more distant from their governments, partly because they will be dealing directly with the service provider but particularly if e-services are badly designed or poorly executed by third parties, or if consumers have to pay for added value services. Effective and holistic engagement strategies will play an important role in helping to mitigate negative or unintended impacts.

Managing Expectations

Governments will need to effectively manage the expectations of their partners and of the public in respect of e-services. The potential for users to influence delivery is considerable but there is a limit to the capacity of governments and service providers to adapt. Disillusioned consumers may disengage if they do not understand how the process works. Developing new e-services throws up a range of searching questions about government relations with their consumers and citizens. For example:

- It will be possible to take a "bottom up" instead of "top down" approach, putting more control, participation or initiative in the hands of the user. But are governments and other public bodies ready to cede control or delegate decision-making, and where will they have to draw the line? How will the role of the professional evolve?
- Governments' willingness and ability to invest the necessary resources to continually adapt online services to the needs of consumers will be limited; responsive services will be resource intensive. What are the limits of customization? How can responsiveness be balanced with the drive to deliver services more efficiently and cost-effectively?
- And how far can the State go in delegating responsibility for service delivery or policy development onto the citizen or consumer? Are consumers ready and able to handle their new role? What about vulnerable people, some of whom may not have the skill or aptitude or will to engage? Will they be even more excluded than they are now? Will the information society exacerbate the democratic deficit in societies?

Responsive government does not remove the potential for inequality or unfairness but if these are to be managed, consumers will need to play their part, and once again, open and transparent communication is the key. The range of potential need and desire outstrips what services can deliver, so criteria to support decision making must be developed. For example, individual needs will need to be balanced against aggregate needs and professionals will need clear guidance in applying their professional judgement, possibly supported by a set of shared values and approaches to collective priority setting, such as those suggested in the Policy Commission report to NCC (NCC, 2004).

A VIRTUOUS CIRCLE

If implemented effectively responsive government could set in motion a virtuous circle of improvement. Opening up communication with government and its decision-making processes will make a significant contribution to greater openness within administrations. In turn decision making will be made more open to scrutiny by individuals, directly or indirectly via the media and any bodies with oversight. A greater degree of consumer involvement could lend credibility to the process of government decision making, depending on how it is handled. In theory, the quality of decisions should also improve as consumer participation in turn brings a wider range of information, perspectives, priorities and solutions to bear on policy. More information, consultation and participation in policy making can ensure better implementation and compliance because more people are aware of the policy and will demand to know what is happening (OECD, 2001, 2002). Most importantly, service quality should improve, delivering better services overall, services that are more appropriately designed to meet consumers' needs, and that are better understood and supported by the general public.

However, none of this is inevitable. It will require determination, resources and imagination to make public bodies capable of active participation with consumers. There is a risk that a policy of engagement and interaction with the public could have unintended consequences unless it is not only well designed and carried out but done so with genuine commitment (NCC, 2002).

CONCLUSIONS

Achieving responsive e-government is not an inevitable consequence of introducing e-services. The social and cultural environment will need to be receptive to the idea, service users and citizens must be motivated to become involved, and those who provide services — from the highest levels of responsibility to the frontline staff — must be fully committed to participating and responding. Systems need to be in place but human factors cannot be underestimated.

Responsive e-government is not just about delivery channels, automating existing systems and processes, doing the same things cheaper, faster and more conveniently. The primary objective is to meet the needs of consumers. In doing so governments will need a better insight into consumer needs, learning to engage and communicate effectively with their public. More responsive services should make a real and tangible improvement to the way ordinary people live their life. Working with greater openness and transparency may result in improved relations between consumers and government, but these favorable outcomes are not inevitable. Governments will have to invest time, resources and imagination to developing responsive services.

Designing and implementing responsive e-government presents huge challenges for public policy. There is no single solution, and responsive government cannot be achieved overnight. It will take time to evolve and adapt as internal processes and methods of working are transformed. In the process a number of core challenges, both anticipated and unanticipated, will arise. If the challenges can be met, the potential benefits for consumers and for providers are substantial. If not, the gap between the public and public policy could become unbridgeable. Government must now show courage, leadership, honesty and innovation in taking consumers into genuine partnership.

REFERENCES

Consumers Association. (2001). Online survey.

Demos. (1999). An inclusive future? Disability, social change and opportunities for greater inclusion by 2010.

Department for Constitutional Affairs. (2003). Privacy and data sharing – survey of public awareness and perceptions.

Independent Television Commission. (2002). Easy TV research report, Consumers Association and ITC.

Institute for Public Policy Research. (2002). Code Red.

National Audit Office. (2002). Better public services through e-government.

National Consumer Council. (1999). Privacy in the information age.

National Consumer Council. (2000). E-commerce and consumer protection.

National Consumer Council. (2002). Involving users – everyone benefits.

National Consumer Council. (2003). Life Lines, an agenda for affordable energy, water and telecommunications services.

National Consumer Council. (2003a). Stronger Voice - training for consumer representatives.

National Consumer Council. (2003b). Winning the risk game.

National Consumer Council. (2004). Making public services personal - Report of independent policy commission to NCC.

OECD. (1998). Impact of the emerging information society on the policy development process and democratic society. PUMA, (98), 15.

OECD. (2001). E-government: aAnalysis framework and methodology.

OECD. (2001a). Citizens as partners; information, consultation and public participation in policy making.

OECD. (2002). Citizens as partners: Engaging citizens in policy making.

OECD. (2003). The e-government imperative.

OECD. (2004). Managing conflicts of interest in the public service.

Office of the e-Envoy. (2003). UK Online annual report, Cabinet Office.

Performance and Innovation Unit. (2001). E.gov, electronic government services for the 21st century. Cabinet Office.

Performance and Innovation Unit. (2002). Strategies for reassurance: Public concerns about privacy and data sharing in government. Cabinet Office.

Performance and Innovation Unit. (2004). Personal responsibility and changing behaviour: The state of knowledge and its implications for public policy. Cabinet Office.

Prime Minister's Strategy Unit. (2002). Risk: Improving government's capability to handle risk and uncertainty. Cabinet Office.

Privacy laws and Business. (2003, May/June).

Putnam, R. (2000). *Bowling Alone, the collapse and revival of American community.* New York: Simon and Schuster.

RSGB. (2004). *Personal information omnibus survey for NCC.* (Unpublished).

Society of information technology managers. (2003). Better Connected: Advice to citizens.

Zuboff, S., & Maxmin, J. (2004). *The support economy.* London: Penguin.

Chapter XII

Realigning Governance: From E-Government to E-Democracy

Donald G. Lenihan, Centre for Collaborative Government, Canada

ABSTRACT

In this chapter, the author acknowledges that over the last few decades, information and communications technologies (ICTs) have progressed at a remarkable pace. By the mid-1990s, the new technology had been used to engineer a major transformation of the private sector, reshaping markets and the basic building block of the modern economy: the corporation. Likewise, enthusiasts predicted that the public sector was about to go through a similar transformation. A new era in government was said to be dawning. For some, electronic- or e-government promised to transform government operations leading to major "efficiency gains" in service delivery. But e-government is proving more difficult and costly than first thought and the expected benefits have been slow to materialize. With some notable exceptions, the efficiency gains have been mixed. The boom in e-commerce was short-circuited by the dot-com bust. Is the bloom coming off the e-government rose? This chapter tries to shed more light on the pertinent issues and reflect a broader vision that e-government is about the transformation of government. A firm commitment from decision makers to think through the issues and steer the right course is critical or e-government could easily lose momentum or veer off course.

SETTING THE STAGE

Toward a Broader Vision of E-Government

Over the last few decades, information and communications technologies (ICTs) have progressed at a remarkable pace. A quarter of a century ago, huge expensive systems that filled several floors of an office building were needed to perform tasks that can now be done by a handheld calculator. The growth in raw computing power has been awesome and it continues to increase exponentially.

By the mid-1990s, the new technology had been used to engineer a major transformation of the private sector, reshaping markets and the basic building block of the modern economy: the corporation. In 20 years, we have gone from centralized multinationals with regionally defined markets, to "borderless" corporations organized around "just-in-time" production in a global economy.

Only a few years ago, enthusiasts predicted that the public sector was about to go through a similar transformation. A new era in government was said to be dawning. For some, electronic- or e-government promised to transform government operations leading to major "efficiency gains" in service delivery. Others prophesied of a coming boom in e-commerce that would revolutionize how business was transacted and make information services the basis of the new economy. Government, they said, had a major role to play in creating the infrastructure. As a result, governments in OECD countries have been revving up for e-government. Many have committed themselves to major ICT programs, especially in service delivery.

In 20 years, we have gone from centralized multinationals with regionally defined markets, to "borderless" corporations organized around "just-in-time" production in a global economy. Before we pass judgement on e-government, we need greater clarity on what it is and where it may lead.

But e-government is proving more difficult and costly than first thought and the expected benefits have been slow to materialize. With some notable exceptions, the efficiency gains have been mixed. The boom in e-commerce was short-circuited by the dot-com bust. Is the bloom coming off the e-government rose?

That conclusion would be hasty. Indeed, the policy community is not well-equipped to hold an informed debate on the question. The prevailing vision of e-government has been influenced too much by early successes in online service delivery and misleading analogies with the private sector. It fails to do justice to the scope of the transformation implied by e-government or the opportunities and challenges it poses. Before we pass judgement on e-government, we need greater clarity on what it is and where it may lead. This chapter tries to shed more light on the issues. It sets out a storyline that helps us arrive at a richer, more complete account of e-government — a broader vision of the terrain.

Before we pass judgement on e-government, we need greater clarity on what it is and where it may lead.

In that vision, e-government is about the transformation of government. Indeed, it may well be the biggest transformation since the democratic revolutions of the late 18th century. But as with all revolutions, many outcomes are possible. We can be more confident of some than others. For example, ICTs are very likely to lead to more efficient service delivery. It is not at all clear that they will lead to a form of government that is more open, transparent, accountable or democratic than conventional government.

Addressing such issues poses many challenges. To meet them we must have leadership that is committed, informed and engaged, especially at the political level. Providing such leadership may be the single biggest challenge on the horizon. A firm commitment from decision makers to think through the issues and steer the right course is critical. E-government could easily lose momentum or veer off course.

So the argument in these pages is that, in one form or another, e-government will come. But that form is undecided. Some options are better, some worse. A serious effort to describe e-government as a whole cannot ignore this reality. As a result, the chapter is a sometimes uneasy mix of analysis and advocacy, though there is an effort to keep the two separate. If, on one hand, it provides a descriptive account of the state of the art, on the other hand, it is also peppered with prescriptive arguments and comments regarding the kind of government we want for the future. As such, it is at once a piece of public administration and a call to arms — an attempt to think rigorously and clearly about an extremely challenging task and a challenge to rise to the task. Nevertheless, it is hoped that the descriptive part is anchored well enough in fact and analysis to make the framework that emerges from it a useful and solid one, even if there are doubts about the value of the more prescriptive parts.

Getting the Whole Picture

What is e-government? A few years ago, the word was largely unknown. Now it is part of the working vocabulary of public policy. Nevertheless, its meaning is neither simple nor obvious. Depending on whom you ask, the answer can range from "putting services online" to "renewing democracy." No one has seen it; hence no one is in a position to declare just what it looks like.

Someone once said that where you stand depends upon where you sit. The point is worth recalling as our experience with e-government progresses and our views on it evolve. Not surprisingly, people with different interests have very different views on how information and communications technologies (ICTs) should be used to improve or change what governments do: the business community wants better services, journalists want more access to information, policy developers want more information on societal trends, "e-democrats" want more online consultations and voting.

The story of the blind men and the elephant comes to mind, a story in which each of several blind men had his hands on a different part of an elephant — ears, tail, trunk, leg, etc. Since none of them could see the whole beast, they began to argue over what it looked like. A passerby explained that, although none was wrong, each man was describing only a part of the beast.

The story has a least two important lessons for e-government. First, to get a clear picture of a new or unfamiliar thing, we often need to combine the experiences and perspectives of a variety of people who are in contact with it. Such is the case with e-government. If we rely too much on the viewpoint of one or two players in the field, we will miss the bigger picture. A satisfactory effort to describe the e-government beast will take into account as many of its parts as are known, connecting them together where possible.

To get a clear picture of a new or unfamiliar thing, we often need to combine the experiences and perspectives of a variety of people who are in contact with it.

Second, the whole is greater than the sum of its parts. Although it is useful — even necessary — to analyze the various parts, that process alone is not enough. The more we know about how the parts combine and interact with one another, the better we will be at designing, constructing and managing the entire beast.

Although it may be too early to construct a complete or clear picture of the e-government elephant, enough is known about its various parts and how they combine to explore them in some detail and to provide an outline of the beast; at least that is the assumption and goal of this paper.

Three Aspects of E-Government

We can begin by identifying three aspects of e-government under which our discussion will be organized:

1. *Improving service delivery:* building the new public infrastructure
2. *Information:* a new public resource
3. *E-democracy:* extending public space

These aspects are treated as themes that have emerged from discussions with many individuals who are working on or thinking about how ICTs can improve what governments do. They identify how people with different interests in government approach the topic of e-government. We can call such people "e-government stakeholders."

E-government stakeholders have a professional interest in how ICTs are being used to transform government. They include public servants, politicians, journalists, the business community, academics, voluntary organizations and the international environmental movement. There is a growing awareness among them that the new ICT networks and databases are creating a new public "infrastructure," which is the basis of e-government. They want to be sure that, as the infrastructure develops, their interest will be taken into account.

There is a growing awareness among them that the new ICT networks and databases are creating a new public "infrastructure," which is the basis of e-government. They want to be sure that, as the infrastructure develops, their interest will be taken into account.

There is no perfect way to summarize the interests of all these stakeholders, but the three aspects are a useful start. They help us see how the different communities are actively shaping the e-government discussion and how they imagine the future. This, in turn, helps us assess how the technology is being put to work to achieve different public policy goals, and it shows us some of the issues and challenges being raised.

Idea of the Storyline

Some of the biggest challenges of e-government arise from the way that various aspects interact and how they affect one another. How we design our service delivery systems, for example, may limit the options, say, for electronic voting. So as we think about how to design one part of e-government — such as the new service delivery channel — it is important that we think about the impact it might have on other parts. In short, we need to think about e-government *holistically*, as an integrated and evolving organism. This is not an easy task.

As we think about how to design one part of e-government — such as the new service delivery channel — it is important that we think about the impact it might have on other parts. In short, we need to think about e-government holistically, as an integrated and evolving organism. This is not an easy task.

The three aspects provide a helpful starting point. Although they are interconnected and interdependent in all kinds of ways, they can be usefully separated and considered one at a time. We can tell a kind of logical story about how one leads to the other that connects them into a series of steps. It is not without fuzziness and sometimes the sequences may seem a bit contrived, but a single storyline appears to be emerging.

The storyline begins with a view of e-government that focuses on simple tasks like paying a parking ticket online. It then moves through the three aspects of e-government in steps, ending with a discussion of e-government as a tool for democratic consultation and engagement. If there is a main conclusion on the descriptive side, it is that ICTs seem to be moving industrialized countries toward a transformation of modern government. In western democracies, this goes well beyond simply reengineering or reinventing government. It pushes citizens and governments toward a realignment of some fundamental aspects of representative democracy.

At the same time, concerns about the impact of ICTs on key democratic values such as openness, inclusiveness, accountability, transparency, personal privacy and voice draw the evolving storyline in and out of a more prescriptive engagement of the issues, options and challenges along the way. Hopefully, the tension between descriptive and prescriptive passages is a creative one and the difference between them is relatively clear.

IMPROVING SERVICE DELIVERY: BUILDING NEW PUBLIC INFRASTRUCTURE

The Origins of E-Government

There is no authoritative or single place to begin telling the story of e-government. This version begins about a decade and a half ago, when a government reform movement was sweeping through OECD countries. The UK, Australia and New Zealand were among its most enthusiastic champions. Having turned to the private sector for ideas on how to improve government, the reformers distilled what they had heard about service improvement into a few basic principles that have had an enormous impact on governments of both the left and right. Our "potted history" of this period is as follows.

Policy is supposed to be about what government does. Service delivery is about who does it and how it is done.

First of all, a clear distinction was drawn between two basic tasks of government: policy and service delivery. Policy is supposed to be about what government does. Service delivery is about who does it and how it is done. The distinction is not a new one. Indeed, it has a long and somewhat controversial history in public administration. The reformers found it convincing, revived it, and made it a basis for much of their thinking.

They took the view that liberal democracies should care less about the who and how of government than the what. For example, if streets need repairing, citizens do not care much about who repairs them (i.e., a public- or a private-sector firm). Nor are they greatly concerned about which tools or business strategies are used to complete the job, as long as it is done effectively and efficiently and in a manner that is consistent with the liberal-democratic commitment to government that is transparent, open, accountable and respectful of personal privacy.

By contrast, deciding what government should do — policy-making — is what the reformers sometimes called a "core function" of government. It is not enough that policy-making be carried out in ways that are transparent, open, accountable and respectful of personal privacy. Deciding what government should do also requires a *democratic mandate* and is the prerogative of elected officials. Unlike service delivery, policy-making cannot be handed off, say, to private sector firms just because they can do it more effectively or efficiently. That would be an affront to democracy. First and foremost, democracy is about exercising public authority in a way that reflects the will of the people. This means that only those who have been given such a mandate have the legitimacy to make such decisions. The most that others should be allowed to provide is advice on which decisions will lead to which consequences.

It is not enough that policy-making be carried out in ways that are transparent, open, accountable and respectful of personal privacy. Deciding what government should do also requires a democratic mandate and is the prerogative of elected officials.

Separating policy and operations in this way allowed reform-minded governments to experiment with new ways of delivering services, including privatization, contracting out and public-private partnerships, while maintaining that the core function of government (i.e., policy-making) remained solidly in government hands. David Osborne and Ted Gaebler, two leading thinkers in the movement, famously summed up the approach this way: Government should do more steering and less rowing.[1]

A second cornerstone of the movement — a principle also borrowed from the private sector — was the idea of client-centered service. Because governments enjoyed monopolies in many areas, the reformers maintained that they lacked adequate incentives to provide high quality services to citizens or to deliver them efficiently. In this view, governments had gotten into the rut of ignoring their "clients" and instead had become too focused on their own priorities. The client-centered approach was supposed to reverse this trend by declaring that governments exist to serve citizens, not the reverse.

A key goal of client-centered service was to make government user-friendly by reorganizing it around citizens. According to the reformers, government had been allowed to organize around its own priorities and interests long enough, ranging from administrative convenience to jurisdictional disputes. As a result, citizens had come to regard government as an impenetrable maze of departments and offices. In a famous Canadian case, one person had to visit over half a dozen government offices involving three levels of government to get a business license! Reformers argued that government, rather than citizens, should be responsible for the "integration." It should be done behind the scenes so that, from the client's perspective, the operation is seamless: a single transaction, provided at a single point of access.

A key goal of client-centered service was to make government user-friendly by reorganizing it around citizens.

This movement has heavily influenced the dominant vision of e-government in countries such as Canada. The close relationship between the service-reform movement and e-government appears to have been forged during early experiments that used Web sites and kiosks to improve service delivery by making it more client-centered and more efficient. In Canada, for example, Human Resources Development Canada placed some kiosks in malls across the country in the early 1990s and used them to make available information on employment insurance and job postings.

Kiosks and Web sites represented an innovative way to deliver services, a method that caught on quickly. The new approach was called ESD — electronic service delivery. Those who started it thought it was quite consistent with the principles and outlook of the reform movement. First, the new mechanisms for delivery — kiosks and Web sites — were regarded as separate from the policy behind the service and they provided a faster and cheaper way of delivering it. Second, ESD made services much more accessible and so it was certainly more client-centered than conventional service delivery. Finally, it had some remarkable successes in reorganizing government around citizens. Several services could be made available at a single Web site or kiosk. Because of this, ESD quickly earned a reputation as a new and promising way to promote seamless government.

By the mid-1990s the separation of policy and service delivery and the commitment to client-centered service had fused with ESD to create a vision of citizen-centered, seamless government. In this view, although government services are scattered over many departments and multiple jurisdictions, real people do not engage the world this way. For them, it is a seamless whole. If governments used the new technology to reorganize services to fit the citizen's viewpoint, rather than their own, government services would also appear as a single, consistent and well-organized set of options, managed and delivered from one source. This vision has inspired public servants around the world to reorganize, redesign and reinvent government. We now call this the e-government movement.

If governments used the new technology to reorganize services to fit the citizen's viewpoint, rather than their own, government services would also appear as a single, consistent and well-organized set of options, managed and delivered from one source.

Seamless Government: The Eldorado of the Reform Movement?

It is noteworthy that the services most frequently put online through ESD involve a simple transaction (e.g., renewing a driver's license or passport), acquiring information (e.g., a weather report or business digest), posting information (e.g., income tax returns), or securing forms and documents. If the thing to be exchanged in the transaction can be reduced to a bundle of information, the technology is well-suited to improving the service. The tasks involved can be defined clearly and separated easily. For example, a client enters a request for a document, government receives and processes the request, transfers the document back to the client, and the service is delivered. Such services are often referred to as the "low-hanging fruit" of e-government because they are "easily reached" by officials looking for some "quick wins" on service improvement.

As the low-hanging fruit gets picked, governments have begun to pursue what looks like the next step in the evolution of ESD: not only should different services be available at the same Web site or kiosk, but they should be integrated or clustered to make government more seamless.

For example, if a spouse passes away, the surviving partner will be required to complete several tasks, such as registering the death, notifying a number of government departments, requesting a transference of assets, perhaps considering a name or address change, etc. Would it not be more client-centered to have government(s) cooperate to integrate these tasks in the backroom? Ideally, the client would go online, complete a single form and submit it. Government(s) could ensure that the form requested all the information needed to complete the various tasks. The different levels of government could then share the information among themselves and their departments as required.

A logical extension of this idea is to create a single "portal" or "secure government channel" on which all or most services can be made accessible. Rather than sending citizens to a variety of kiosks or Web sites, they would be able to access government services through a single point. Within that portal, services would be integrated or clustered to make them as seamless as possible.

A logical extension of this idea is to create a single "portal" or "secure government channel" on which all or most services can be made accessible.

Over the last five years some governments have made big commitments in this direction. In Canada, for example, the federal government intends to have all services linked so that they are available through a single point of access by the year 2005. The "no-wrong-window" idea thus imagines government as an integrated series of electronic portals through which all or most services would be accessible. A number of other OECD countries have made similar commitments, including the United States, Great Britain and Australia.

In this network of portals, related services ideally would be "clustered" so that citizens would not have to complete a series of separate transactions to receive what, from their viewpoint, appears to be a single service. Thus one would not have to go to 10 different government departments, involving three levels of government, to get a single business license. Citizens would experience government as a seamless whole.

However, the task of integrating services is turning out to be far more complex than imagined. With a few notable exceptions,[2] in Canada, at least, most federal departments have some distance to go to make serious progress on integration. Most are scrambling just to meet the more modest goal of getting basic services online by 2005. The more governments experiment with integration, the more obstacles arise. To some, the quest after seamless government is beginning to look like the search for Eldorado, the fabled City of Gold, which, it seemed, existed only in the imagination of those who sought it.

To some, the quest toward seamless government is beginning to look like the search for Eldorado, the fabled City of Gold, which, it seemed, existed only in the imagination of those who sought it.

Moreover, the tendency to talk as though all services could be provided online is misleading. Renewal of a driver's license can be fully digitalized. Other services however, such as medical services, cannot. Surgery, for example, requires face-to-face contact. Talk of putting all services online thus really refers to the extent that information related to them can or should be online. One could, for example, register for surgery online. As we will see in the section "Information: a new public resource?", a richer vision of e-government requires a more searching debate over how ICTs should be used to support such services. For example, should there be a national system that contains the health records of all patients? If so, who should have access to it?

In conclusion, achieving *single-window access* to government services will not coincide with the launch of a new era of *seamless government.* It will be more like a comprehensive directory of government services, a single entry point into government. But what happens then? Is that the final result of 15 years of work on reforming service delivery? Is integration an unrealistic goal? What makes it so hard? What can be done about it? Is the revolution over?

The remainder of Section 2 of this chapter explores some of the obstacles standing in the way of seamless government. For convenience, we categorize them under three basic headings:

1. Change management
2. Concerns over the governance system
3. The lack of clear and committed leadership

Change Management

Legacy Systems

The most easily understood problem for integration is interoperability; that is, technical differences that prevent separate systems from communicating. Departments or governments cannot share information or integrate services if their systems are not compatible. In fact, many are not. Many programs still rely on systems that were designed for intradepartmental use only. When they were built, little attention was paid to ensuring compatibility with systems in other departments or governments. As a result, information transfer and sharing is often difficult, if not impossible.

The most easily understood problem for integration is interoperability; that is, technical differences that prevent separate systems from communicating.

At one level, the interoperability problem is a technical one. It is about the vintage of equipment, the design standards, computing languages, etc. But ensuring interoperability also has political and managerial aspects.

First, to permanently resolve the issue, universal standards must be adopted for a wide variety of purposes, ranging from how information is tagged and stored to the kind of software systems that should be used to manage data. Achieving this kind of coordination across a government — let alone, across different governments — is a major political and managerial challenge. For one thing, all vendors have a major interest in promoting the standards used by their products and in discouraging the use of their competitors' products. Vendors are among the most active and aggressive defenders of the status quo precisely because they compete with one another for market share. But winning market share is based upon emphasizing the differences between products, not their sameness.

Second, replacing outdated "legacy" systems is usually very costly and time-consuming.

Neither of these issues has a simple solution. They require ongoing attention and engaged leadership at the senior management and political levels. An effective strategy is needed to ensure that universal standards are set, and that procurement policy promotes the development of a single, universally compatible system.

From Seamless Services to Seamless Government

The lack of universal standards and the problems around legacy systems are significant and costly to fix; however they are, in principle at least, resolvable. The issue of program coordination presents a far bigger obstacle on the path to seamless government. What is it and why does it matter?

Let us return to the case of registering a death. Beyond interoperability, information sharing of this sort does not present insurmountable technical problems. Departments could be linked by a single information system with a mechanism for sending incoming information to the right points in the system. That raises concerns around privacy — which are noted below — but let us suppose that they can be answered. If so, how easy would integration be?

The lack of universal standards and the problems around legacy systems are significant and costly to fix; however they are, in principle at least, resolvable.

In the case of registering a death, integration may be quite achievable. It involves a cluster of services that can be linked through a single transaction (i.e., the exchange of a bundle of information) because they share the same simple goal of registering a single event. However, there are many services that, at first glance, look like good candidates for integration, which turn out to be quite challenging instead.

Consider services for disabled persons. Hundreds of such programs exist in Canada. Yet many disabled persons are unaware of more than a handful of them. They do not know which ones they are eligible to access, where they can find out about the services, from whom the services are available or what purposes they serve. As a result, disability programs lie scattered across Canadian federal, provincial, territorial and municipal governments like seeds in a field.

Presumably, integrated service delivery should help disabled people cope with such problems. It seeks to bring relevant services together — to cluster them — around key needs so that citizens encounter government as a single, integrated whole, rather than as a maze of programs and departments through which they must find their way. As a first step, all of these programs should be available through a single point of access: an electronic portal or window.

It seeks to bring relevant services together — to "cluster" them — around key needs so that citizens encounter government as a single, integrated whole, rather than as a maze of programs and departments through which they must find their way.

But if integrated service aspires to be more than just a large directory — a telephone book — of government services, it should make access to and delivery of the range of options as seamless as possible. As we have seen, from the client's point of view, a cluster of services would appear as a single, consistent and well-organized set of options, managed and delivered from one source. This certainly would be an improvement over the status quo. But what would it involve?

Suppose a disabled person wanted to apply for two separately organized government programs. Suppose that person also needed to use special government transportation services sponsored by one department to report to a new job-training program for persons with disabilities, sponsored by another department. What burden does integration place on the two departments to ensure that the services are streamlined and coordinated?

Should the disabled person be able to fill out only one application form for the two services? If letters of support or recommendation are required for both, should he or she need to provide two sets of them? If the person plans to use the services together as part of what appears to him or her as different aspects of a single task (i.e., an effort to become more employable) should that person expect the government to make them mesh? For example, suppose that the transportation service is only available after 9:00 a.m., but that the training course begins at 8:00 a.m. As a client of both departments, should the disabled person expect the services to be coordinated so that he or she can use the van to get to the course? How far are such programs supposed to be complementary? Should integration commit governments to aligning or harmonizing program objectives?

What about duplication and overlap? How far should it be minimized or eliminated? Does it make sense for two departments to use public money to offer a client what is effectively the same service? When a client of a program finds that they do, should that person reasonably expect them to eliminate one? How would that be decided?

Or suppose that it is the municipal government who sponsors the special transportation services that the disabled person needs, but the provincial government who sponsors the job-training program. As a citizen and taxpayer of both governments, how far should that person reasonably expect the two of them to work together to coordinate such programs for his or her benefit?

As these examples suggest, providing clients or citizens with what *they* regard as seamless service would require much higher levels of coordination and cooperation between departments, governments and other service providers in the private and voluntary sectors than now exist.

Furthermore, as the examples also make clear, the pursuit of seamless service quickly pushes us beyond service delivery and into the realm of policy. In this context, the client-centered services principle, stating that policy and service delivery can be separated, is more than a little misleading. As the examples show, any serious effort to integrate services beyond a very basic level will involve policy choices as well.

The pursuit of seamless service quickly pushes us beyond service delivery and into the realm of policy.

Consider the transportation example. Whether the van is allowed to pick the disabled person up at his or her home before 8:00 a.m. is not just a question about how the service will be delivered. It raises questions about why the service exists, what it is supposed to achieve and who has access to it. Providing answers to such questions will launch us into a discussion of the *policy goals* behind the program. Moreover, suppose that, in the interests of efficient and effective service, delivery has been passed to another department, level of government or private or third sector partner. Should they be permitted or expected to make such decisions? Would this amount to an unacceptable transfer of the core business of government to someone else — someone without a public mandate to make decisions about what government does?

Such considerations suggest that to treat integration as merely the next step in the evolution of ESD is misleading. It makes it sound like the issues around integration are practical ones about how to provide services more efficiently and effectively. Where services can be integrated through information sharing, such as registering a death, this may be the case. But for a great many services, it will require policy coordination. Thus, if governments really want to take the citizens' point of view, they must recognize that seamless government is about more than efficient or accessible service delivery. It also implies coordination at the policy level and, as such, is as much a policy vision as a service-delivery vision.

So unless the concept of seamless government is to be confined to services that can be reduced to simple exchanges of bundles of information, efforts to create it through e-government lead us beyond a discussion of the impact of ICTs on one part of government — its operations — and toward a discussion of *e-government as a different kind of government*. They invite us to begin considering what such a government might look like. What kind of organizational features and infrastructure would it have? What kind of capacity must be added to the machinery that now exists in order to coordinate and integrate across departmental, intergovernmental and even private and third sector boundaries?

Early experiences suggest that such a system would include a wide range of new mechanisms, such as joint committees, information sharing networks and integrated delivery systems. In the old world of telephone calls, photocopies, fax machines, filing cabinets and bricks and mortar, seamless government was not a realistic option. However, early experience with ESD suggests that ICTs can be used to provide critical new infrastructure that could make such a system possible. Taking this idea seriously moves us beyond a discussion of experimenting with ESD to one that focuses on e-government *as a robust new public infrastructure of ICT networks and databases.*

So unless the concept of seamless government is to be confined to services that can be reduced to simple exchanges of bundles of information, efforts to create it through e-government lead us beyond a discussion of the impact of ICTs on one part of government — its operations — and toward a discussion of e-government as a different kind of government.

The (Internal) Governance System

As we have seen, when governments began using ESD, they regarded ICTs as a tool to improve client services and the efficiency of government operations. This was consistent with their view that policy is separate from service delivery, and that e-government is about better services. However, if governments are serious about integration, the boundary between service delivery and policy must be crossed. In fact, integration raises questions about a number of boundaries that are basic to conventional government. An equally important case involves those boundaries that underpin personal privacy and public accountability.

Conventional government is organized into parts, which are based on functions or roles. For example, the Department of Health is a separate entity that exists to cure disease and promote well-being. The department is divided into smaller parts or sectors, which are then divided into smaller subsections and so on. This separation of parts goes all the way down to individual jobs, each of which has a special role to play in the system. Together, the parts make up a single system. If the parts have been designed well and all of the workers do their jobs properly, government should perform like a well-oiled machine.

This metaphor that government is like a big machine has had enormous influence on its evolution and design. Indeed, in most governments there is a high-level policy shop–(often called "Machinery of Government") whose job it is to examine, adjust and refine the parts to ensure that they mesh.

The systems that ensure respect for personal privacy and public accountability are linked to the machine model and intertwined with it. Consider the system for protecting personal privacy. It is based on the idea that each official has a separate function or job. He or she is allowed to collect only as much personal information about a client as is needed to do that job. Officials cannot collect additional information on clients nor are they allowed to share the information that they have with other officials. Keeping their functions separate, thus, is essential to keeping information private.

The same system is essential to preserving public accountability. In the machine model, the various parts of government are organized hierarchically so that each person reports up the ladder to the next one, who is responsible for the actions of the first, and so on, all the way up to the Deputy Minister and ultimately the Minister. If the reporting relationships get blurred, for instance, because roles or functions have become unclear, the lines of accountability also become blurred.

Seamless government cuts across the boundaries that separate different jobs or functions in the conventional machine model. ICT-based systems are able to support seamless government precisely because they can be used to organize people, jobs and information flows into *networks*, which are less respectful of legislative or administrative boundaries and less hierarchical. But this blurring of roles and functions, and sharing of information and tasks, undermines the conventional methods of protecting privacy and ensuring accountability. As a result, what appears as a gain in client-centered service as a result of seamless government or integration may be offset by a loss in, perhaps, privacy or accountability.

ICT-based systems are able to support seamless government precisely because they can be used to organize people, jobs and information flows into networks, which are less respectful of legislative or administrative boundaries and less hierarchical.

The emerging conclusion is that integration is laying the infrastructure for a different kind of organizational model, one whose organizational structure more closely resembles that of a network than a machine. If so, this raises fundamental questions about the future: Does the "new system" threaten the integrity of the existing one? More specifically, does it threaten government's commitment to respect personal privacy or public accountability? Are there alternative ways of meeting these commitments? If so, what are they and how do they work? Can the old and new systems be integrated? Do we need a balance between the two? If so, how would that be achieved?

Much of the debate over e-government today revolves around such questions. Collectively, there is a sense among officials that the move toward seamless government is necessary — probably even inevitable — but that building the infrastructure is going to be a very challenging job because, as we have seen, it is not just a matter of reengineering service delivery.

The privacy and accountability issues have been barriers. Although some progress is being made, much discussion, reflection and research is still needed. For one thing, it is not clear how much of the information that governments would need to share to integrate services is of a personal nature. Information that is of a general nature compromises no one. Where information is of a personal nature, there is still much disagreement over how difficult it is to keep it secure in a more integrated system. In some cases, information that has been kept separate for privacy reasons is now shared because citizens have given their consent in order to receive better service. In Canada, a question has been placed on federal income tax forms requesting that some personal information be integrated, with positive results. Perhaps citizens are less concerned about personal privacy in some cases than has been suggested.

It is not clear how much of the information that governments would need to share to integrate services is of a personal nature.

Nevertheless, it is clear that the privacy issue is a barrier. There are real concerns over the erosion of personal privacy. At the same time, privacy can and sometimes is used as an excuse to not provide or share information. A broader more open discussion of the issues is needed. It should be led by politicians, who are well-positioned to consider the issue, rather than by public servants who do not have this authority.

The accountability issue is another one that has given many thoughtful people pause, when considering the goals of e-government. There seems little doubt that the networking model of government that it implies stands in tension with the hierarchical, chain-of-command kind of accountability that liberal-democratic governments have relied on for the last two centuries. But, as we will see below, e-government may give rise to an alternative form of accountability. The Office of the Auditor General of Canada has referred to it as "public accountability."[3] It may be that public accountability is a satisfactory way of offsetting — even improving upon — the loss to chain-of-command accountability that e-government implies.

Leadership: From the Public Service to the Political

We have seen that key obstacles standing in the way of progress toward e-government include the inoperability problem, the need for new mechanisms and processes of policy coordination, and new approaches to privacy and accountability. It should be clear by now that e-government is about much more than plumbing. On the contrary, it seems to imply a transformation of government, as we know it. Indeed, many senior people working on the file now speculate that the redesigning and reorganization of the whole system may be required, ranging from new plumbing to new horizontal governance systems. This exercise will require everything from a new approach to procurement to a major rethinking of the principles and values underlying key pieces of privacy legislation. Such a transformation cannot be accomplished by the public service alone. It requires strong, committed and informed leadership at the political level.

It should be clear by now that e-government is about much more than plumbing. On the contrary, it seems to imply a transformation of government, as we know it.

As the research for this chapter was underway, we heard repeatedly that the e-government file needs engaged political leadership. We heard that, without it, there is a risk that the project will lose momentum and bog down. Yet it is not always clear why this leadership is needed or what role it should play. Why do we need more engaged political leadership on the e-government file?

In general terms, political leadership is required because it can perform tasks that the public service cannot. For example, politicians can:

1. Make horizontal decisions more easily;
2. Publicly debate and champion various policy options; and
3. Make policy decisions.

Some of the key challenges now facing e-government — such as policy integration — require action that cuts across organizational boundaries. Public servants are too constrained to achieve this alone. They lack the authority to make decisions that reach beyond departmental boundaries and mandates. Negotiating interdepartmental or inter-governmental changes to set common standards, align policies or integrate programs is therefore a long, slow process for them.

E-government needs some significant and visible successes that demonstrate its value to the broader policy community and the public at large. One approach would be to identify a few key areas where progress is possible on achieving seamless service across jurisdictions, such as, perhaps, disability. If a non-partisan group of elected officials could be formed to champion integration in such an area, progress might be more rapid. This, in turn, would provide a public demonstration of the benefits that can flow from e-government, and would help governments arrive at a better understanding of the challenges and opportunities involved.

Awareness of the broader issues and opportunities among politicians is very limited. By-and-large, they tend to regard e-government as "a plumbing issue," albeit a large and costly one.

Getting to seamless government will require strong political leadership at the senior level to drive the process. At present, however, awareness of the broader issues and opportunities among politicians is very limited. By-and-large, they tend to regard e-government as "a plumbing issue," albeit a large and costly one. They are, of course, in favor of better services, but beyond that, e-government is barely on their radar screens. As one politician remarked: "When my constituents come to see me, it is not to ask about e-government." As a public issue, e-government has a very low profile.

The discussion in this section helps us see why e-government has such a low priority. Over the last decade, advocates from the public service and the private sector have made the case for expanding the use of ICTs largely in terms of their ability to improve government operations and service delivery. Not surprisingly, that is the level on which political leaders have taken notice and responded. It is now clear, however, that e-government is multifaceted. The new infrastructure is a foundation on which whole new levels of government activity are being built. Indeed, it is now common for those working in the field to regard the discussion as one over *how to imagine, envision and build a new kind of government*. Such a debate — and such a project — requires clear and committed political leadership.

INFORMATION: A NEW PUBLIC RESOURCE?

Refocusing the Discussion on Information

We have been telling a story about the growth of e-government, with service delivery as the point of departure. It led us to explore some tensions between the vertical organization of conventional governments and the new horizontal or networked one of e-government. This is a valid, useful and important way to approach e-government. But it is not the only way. The new infrastructure creates far more than new plumbing; it also creates a dynamic and powerful new capacity to collect, create, integrate, share and store data and information, which we will call the new information capacity.

The new infrastructure creates far more than new plumbing; it also creates a dynamic and powerful new capacity to collect, create, integrate, share and store data and information, which we will call "the new information capacity."

This capacity promises to change what governments know about themselves and, indeed, the world. Using the new information capacity rather than service delivery as the point of departure for discussion sheds a new light on e-government, leading us to look at the role and value of information as a new public resource.

Our comments are divided into four sections, each of which considers a particular challenge that the new information capacity poses for government. The four challenges are:

1. To make government a pre-eminent source of quality public information;
2. To make government "smarter";
3. To make government more transparent and accountable; and
4. To make government information a *public* resource.

The first challenge proposes that the new information capacity could lead to a new, or at least much expanded, service to citizens. The second considers how it can lead to government that makes more informed decisions and learns from experience. The third focuses on how the new capacity could make government more accountable, transparent, open and fair. The fourth asks what it means for governments to take seriously the idea that government information should be regarded as a public resource.

E-Government as a New Information Provider

Governments Should Liberate Their Information Holdings

Some say that information is to the knowledge-based economy what oil was to the industrial-based one. If so, the capacity to provide high-quality information for a wide range of purposes is destined to make information services of all sorts an increasingly important part of what governments do.

Modern governments contain huge amounts of data and information. They are currently stored in a host of separate systems, many of which are the equivalent of nooks and crannies in the vast edifice of government. The more integrated government becomes, the more accessible these nooks and crannies will become. Increasingly, e-government will penetrate them, liberating much of the information from isolation and obscurity.

Indeed, it is not science fiction to imagine government eventually operating as a single system, in which vast amounts of information and knowledge that were scarcely imaginable only a decade ago have become available to governments.

Furthermore, the capacity to integrate data from various streams will grow at an exponential rate, as will the ability to collect and add new streams. Indeed, it is not science fiction to imagine government eventually operating as a single system, in which vast amounts of information and knowledge that were scarcely imaginable only a decade ago have become available to governments. An obvious and immediate task for them is to begin to collect, integrate and organize the information that now lies scattered across departments and investigate the best ways to make it available to citizens — and, indeed, many departments and governments are doing just that.

In OECD countries, the mounting wave of new information will have a major impact on all policy fields and sectors of society, including health, education, community services, transportation, agriculture, research and development, historical analysis, economic and business trends. The more the new capacity comes into focus, the more questions it raises:

1. How will data be collected, integrated and combined?
2. What things will citizens and governments learn that they did not know before?

3. Who will decide what counts as authoritative information on a given topic and what does not?
4. Who will have access to the new information and knowledge?
5. Who will own or control it?
6. What will it be used for?
7. Who will decide how questions such as these are to be answered?

An example might help clarify the role of government as a provider of public information.

CanadaPlace: A New Information Service for Citizens

CanadaPlace is an Internet portal where Canadians and others can learn about Canada by accessing authoritative information on a wide range of topics and themes relevant to its past, present and future. As such, CanadaPlace is an electronic version of a traditional public archive (i.e., a digital archive) that is intended to provide an important public service.

As such, CanadaPlace is an electronic version of a traditional public archive (i.e., a digital archive) that is intended to provide an important public service.

As a public archive, it is quickly becoming a rich source of digitalized information about Canada, beginning with key reference sources such as the *Canadian Encyclopaedia and the Historical Atlas of Canada.* At its launch, CanadaPlace will also include information from the National Archives, the National Library, the Canadian Broadcasting Corporation and other members of the federal Department of Canadian Heritage portfolio. All material will be indexed to facilitate easy access to the most relevant information on cultural or social topics. CanadaPlace will also be linked to a wide range of other sites to provide users with easy access to additional information and sources.

Reliable, authoritative information is a critical resource in the Information Age. Taken together, the Department of Canadian Heritage and its 16 portfolio agencies constitute a vast storehouse of information about Canada. Much of this information is of authoritative or reference quality. Putting the storehouse of material from the Heritage portfolio online through CanadaPlace will liberate it.

The material will be integrated, aggregated and assembled, using a set of indexing standards aimed at retrieving the most relevant material. A national advisory board will oversee the process. In addition, Canadian Heritage is funding a variety of organizations, including members of the portfolio, to ensure that the process of digitization conforms to indexing standards.

Canadians (and others around the world), ranging from genealogists and historians to journalists and school children, will be able to access documents, film clips, tapes and other archival material, using their home computers. This kind of access could hardly be imagined a decade ago. It sets a new standard for user-friendly access to authoritative information on themes, issues, events, places and persons with a particular relevance to Canada.

It sets a new standard for user-friendly access to authoritative information on themes, issues, events, places and persons with a particular relevance to Canada.

The quality and volume of information that will become available through CanadaPlace can be expected to have a major impact on Canadian businesses and activities, ranging from entertainment to education. For example, it will add value to a wide range of products for the knowledge-based economy and provide a key learning resource to help Canadians (and others) understand our history, laws, institutions, culture and practices. It will also support informed public debate on key public policy issues.

A central goal of the mission of CanadaPlace is to become the pre-eminent source of authoritative information on Canada, and especially on Canadian cultural content. In this regard, the digital archive may prove to be a peerless service provider. It may also serve as a model for other departments, who seek to provide a similar service in a variety of other areas.

Government as a Manager and Guarantor of Information

The example shifts attention away from issues about service delivery and the installation of new "pipes" and on to questions about the content that will flow through them and its impact on Canadian society. Will e-government result in massive new levels or sources of content? Where will it come from? What will it look like? How different will it be? What impact might it have on the way governments view, discuss or understand issues?

As we move into the Information Age, a key role that citizens may expect governments to play is that of a manager and guarantor of quality information. The prospect of being overwhelmed by so much information — much of it contradictory — that it is impossible to make informed decisions or feel a part of discussions and debates is very real. Moreover, in a world where advocacy and private interest will drive the collection and dissemination of much information, citizens may find themselves turning to governments for help in the expectation that they will act as reliable and trusted authorities on the management and quality control of information of all kinds. They want someone to provide reliable guidance on what information is authoritative and relevant in a variety of contexts. This may be one of the most important public services governments will perform in coming years.

As we move into the Information Age, a key role that citizens may expect governments to play is that of a manager and guarantor of quality information.

More immediately, a key challenge that the new information capacity poses for governments is to begin treating their information holdings, and their information capacity, as a major public resource that should be put to use supporting citizens, businesses and other organizations. This will require that the range and nature of various kinds of information that governments can and should collect be further explored and defined and that policies be developed to guide the development of this new — or changing — government role.

For example, information that is collected from Statistics Canada is different from internal administrative data on various government programs. Personal information about Canadians that can be collected and matched through various government departments is another kind of information, and Memoranda to Cabinet and records of Cabinet discussions are yet another. Decisions must be made, for example, as to what kinds of information can or should be considered a public resource or whether the public should be charged for it.

Government as Smarter Government

Good Policy-Making

A second place that the new capacity should be put to immediate use is in promoting *smarter government.* What is involved?

Seamless service is an effort to organize service delivery around the needs of citizens. It begins with single-window access and then progresses to services that can be reduced to transactions involving information. However, we saw that programs such as those to help the disabled pose a problem. Integrating programs leads beyond service delivery to the harmonization of policy goals. From the client or citizen's perspective, such coordination would certainly improve government services and is thus a desirable goal. But realizing it required us to broaden the vision of seamless government to include more than service delivery. We concluded that it must also be seen as a policy vision.

Integrating programs leads beyond service delivery to the harmonization of policy goals.

There is therefore a difference between the value added by coordinating or integrating services and the value added by good policy-making. *Smart government is about good policy-making.* It is about the policy vision behind seamless government. What is it and how can e-government help us promote it?

Good policy-making involves choosing the options that will do the best job of achieving the goals and priorities that a government has set for itself. Such goals and priorities might include, for example, a stronger economy, a healthier or more educated population, a more innovative business community or a deeper respect for democratic equality among citizens.

Good policy-making involves choosing the options that will do the best job of achieving the goals and priorities that a government has set for itself.

Suppose that a government declares that promoting a healthier population is a priority. To do this, it wants to strengthen its health care system. This is currently the case in Canada. Promises have been made to take steps to make the health care system more efficient and more effective so that rising costs can be contained. How should the government decide what to do?

A variety of policy options are being debated to improve health care in Canada. One is to introduce user fees, which advocates say will discourage patients from overusing the system. Another suggestion would allow private clinics to compete with public ones (supposedly the competition would result in more effective administration by the public sector). A third proposal is to create centralized electronic patient records, which would give doctors a much clearer picture of a patient's past care and present needs, thus improving diagnosis and treatment.[4]

All three options are at least superficially plausible. How then should a government decide which one or combination is the right one? Determining which policies are most likely to get the right result involves assessing options on at least two levels:

1. Choosing the most effective option; and
2. Ensuring that the option fits or meshes with existing policies.

Good policy-making requires the right combination and balancing of these two imperatives. We will consider them one at a time, beginning with the first. It is useful here to start with a summary of past experience.

The Evolving Role of Information in Policy Debate

A century ago, public debate and decision-making in countries such as Canada relied mainly on two kinds of evidence: anecdotal and ideological.[5] The first proceeds from a few examples based on anecdotal reports to a broad generalization. Suppose that a government program is launched to help farmers in financial trouble. Farmers Jones and Wilson, who are in financial trouble, fail to meet the criteria of the program and so are forced into bankruptcy. They report this to their MP, who then raises the issue in Parliament. On the basis of this evidence, he argues that the program is a failure. His assessment thus moves from a couple of cases to a generalization about the whole program. As a basis for public debate, this is better than nothing but a long way from reliable.

At the other end of the spectrum lie ideological arguments. They start with broad generalizations about history, economics, social life or human nature and use them to draw conclusions about specific initiatives. For example, someone might argue that, because humans are basically self-interested creatures, smaller government and more reliance on market forces is the best way to create wealth. In this view, humans are motivated by personal gain. If smaller government creates more opportunities for them to profit by performing a service, it will also make them more industrious, innovative and efficient. This, in turn, will create more wealth for the society as a whole.

Whether such a conclusion is true or false will depend upon the truth of the supporting claim that human beings do in fact act mainly out of self-interest. But that claim is simply too broad to be known to be either true or false. It remains controversial. The usefulness of ideological generalizations such as this is therefore limited. They can help to clarify beliefs and values that may have a legitimate role in public debate, but as statements of fact, they are unreliable.

For the first two hundred years of modern government, public debate had little to rely on beyond anecdotal and ideological evidence. Then, during the 20th century, governments began collecting and compiling information on a wide range of economic and social trends, ranging from employment and inflation levels to birth rates and levels of education. These new pools of information have become a critical resource that helps guide public debate and decision-making.

These new pools of information have become a critical resource that helps guide public debate and decision-making.

Yet as we enter the 21st century, information is still too often incomplete, unreliable or altogether nonexistent. To return to the example of the three options for improving the

Canadian health care system, at present there is at best partial evidence to support the claims that advocates make on their behalf. In fact, we really do not know how well any of them will perform. As a result, governments could easily spend tens of millions of dollars experimenting with one or another, only to find that it fails to deliver on the promises. The history of modern government overflows with such examples. More information is needed before a final judgement could be made.

The new information capacity could help us overcome this barrier. It promises to increase vastly the quantity and quality of information that is available on the performance of policies. As a result, many information gaps could be filled, giving decision makers a more complete picture of the issues, risks and opportunities that they need to consider. As we have already seen, governments could use the technology to liberate data and information from myriad sources within themselves and across society, and integrate it into new forms of knowledge. In addition, they could collect vast amounts of new information previously unavailable.

Toward a More Holistic Approach to Policy

If the new information that is generated is to lead to good policy-making, much work needs to be done on identifying the kinds of systems and databases that will be needed. In particular, governments need to gather more complete and reliable information on what we can call "societal outcomes" and the trends that produce them. Societal outcomes are the result of many factors, including actions by various governments, the private and voluntary sectors and individual decisions. Examples include safer communities, a healthier or more educated population, and a cleaner environment.

If the new information that is generated is to lead to good policy-making, much work needs to be done on identifying the kinds of systems and databases that will be needed.

Reliable information on such outcomes and the trends that produce them is sketchy at best. Filling this gap would provide a much richer context in which to evaluate how policies and programs interact with one another, and to achieve a higher level of coordination between them. Once again, health care provides a convenient example.

The conventional approach to health policy is reactive and focused on curing illness. That is changing. Most governments now aim at promoting wellness or well-being as a societal outcome. As an outcome or goal at which policy should aim, well-being is much richer than curing illness. It includes a proactive approach to being and remaining healthy. Policy analysts who take this approach seek to identify "health determinants" or the conditions that affect good health. These can include poverty, environmental factors, sports and recreation opportunities, diet, stress levels and education.

As is evident, this goes well beyond the traditional responsibilities of departments of health. It requires an interdepartmental and, indeed, multi-sectoral approach, in which officials from the various departments, governments and sectors work together to assess the impact of their activities on one another, by assessing their impact on common goals or societal outcomes.

For example, the objective of a community day-care program for single mothers may be to give them an opportunity to seek employment, and thereby help them raise themselves out of a poverty-level existence. At the same time, a community education program to help single mothers understand the nutritional needs of their children may aim at reducing child illness. Uniting both programs under the common goal of promoting well-being or a healthier population sets them in a larger, shared context that allows the sponsoring governments or departments to focus on how their respective programs might be better coordinated to produce the overarching goal, say, by sharpening or adjusting particular policy goals.

As this example clearly demonstrates, we have now returned to the point where we broke off our discussion of service delivery: policy coordination. But there is a difference. This time we have arrived through a discussion of policy-making rather than service delivery. As a result, the task of integrating policy objectives no longer seems like an uninvited guest at the dinner table. On the contrary, integrated policy is at the heart of the holistic approach we are considering. As such, it is the natural soul mate of seamless service; it is the other half of the seamless government vision, which, as we have seen, requires integration at both the service delivery and policy levels.

The task of integrating policy objectives no longer seems like an uninvited guest at the dinner table. On the contrary, integrated policy is at the heart of the holistic approach we are considering.

The new information capacity is a critical resource for achieving that vision. It allows us to collect quality information on the broad outcomes that specific policies and programs are supposed to support. That information is what allows policy-makers to become more effective at identifying where they could strengthen, adjust or coordinate their efforts to get a better result.

In conclusion, the new information capacity created by ICTs can be expected to generate a second, much larger wave of new public information as we move into the 21st century. Preparing for it may be among the biggest and most pressing challenges that e-government poses. *A unique opportunity exists to engineer a quantum leap in the quality and quantity of information that is available to support public debate and decision-making. This should translate into a quantum leap in our capacity to produce good policy.*

E-Government as Transparent and Accountable Government

We have been discussing ways that the new information capacity could be used to strengthen public debate and policy-making. It may seem like a small step from this optimistic talk about major increases in the accuracy, scope, quantity and availability of information about government performance, to the claim that ICTs should make government more transparent and accountable. And there is no shortage of people who have made such a claim. But the gap is bigger than may first appear.

In conventional governments, accountability rests on what we have already called the machine model. It establishes a clear chain of command that runs from the Minister all the way down to the person who purchases the paperclips. If the chain is broken, accountability is lost. But the kind of horizontal relationships and exchanges of information that we have been discussing threaten to do just that. They cut across organizational boundaries, blurring distinctions that are essential to the chain of command. Thus, a key issue raised in our discussion of seamless service was that integration could undermine the systems that support accountability and transparency.

Thus, a key issue raised in our discussion of seamless service was that integration could undermine the systems that support accountability and transparency.

On the other hand, the discussion in this section suggests reasons to be optimistic. The emergence of the new information capacity could make it possible for the public to learn more about the performance of government policies and programs, and, indeed, about the internal operations of government, than could be contemplated a decade ago. The new information systems could give rise to a whole new system of accountability and transparency.

The question therefore arises: Is e-government likely to make government more or less accountable and transparent? Does the prospect of more information on operations and performance act as a counterbalance to concerns over a possible loss of vertical accountability?

Much, it seems, will depend on the choices that are made as the new system is built. In any event, it seems clear that the new capacity for information should be viewed as more than a tool for smart government. It is also a key tool for providing oversight. This needs further discussion and debate. In particular, defining the terms of access to government-controlled information for elected officials, stakeholders or the general public is likely to be a key issue. A much more open approach than now exists could have far-reaching consequences for government transparency and accountability.

A much more open approach than now exists could have far-reaching consequences for government transparency and accountability.

In conventional government, ministers and departmental officials decide what issues should be the subject of reports. In addition, they collect, organize and present the data and information the reports contain. As information becomes more abundant and accessible, it will be possible to allow public access to it. Indeed, it may be difficult to prevent it! This would be a big step beyond traditional reporting practices, in which governments control the information that will be made available. It would shift some control over the new resource to the public.

Governments could go even further. The technology exists to allow members of the public to begin to pose their own questions to government. It is quite possible for governments to design search engines that would help citizens seek out and integrate data to create new information that would answer the questions *they* would like to pose to government. Is this a good idea? What risks, opportunities or costs might it involve?

Making Government Information a Public Resource

If ICTs could be used to enhance greatly the transparency and accountability of government, getting there poses a major challenge. Not only will it require significant changes to longstanding government practices, but also in the culture of secrecy and control that sometimes inhabits them.

Top-down management in large bureaucracies (private or public), requires centralized control over "messaging," such as communication of the strategic plan or the various responsibilities of different parts of the organization. Too much information or the wrong kind of information circulating throughout the organization can create serious problems. Modern governments have organized around this principle for two hundred years. Knowledge is power. As a result, governments are often hierarchical, secretive and controlling about information that is regarded as sensitive. Although almost no one disagrees that some information is sensitive and should be regarded as secret, that category is often expanded far more widely than it needs to be. Moreover, the processes by which information has been used to arrive at decisions are often less than transparent.
Knowledge is power. As a result, governments are often hierarchical, secretive and controlling about information that is regarded as sensitive.

E-government requires a different kind of culture — one that is less controlling and more collaborative, less hierarchical and more horizontal, less secret and more transparent. Making e-government work will require more than a change in management practices or organizational design. It will require a major change in culture.

DEMOCRACY: EXTENDING PUBLIC SPACE

ICTs increase connectivity — across organizational boundaries and between governments and citizens. In our discussion of the first aspect, "Improving service delivery," we saw that ICTs are being used to create a new delivery channel. As a result, citizens will be able to access government services from their homes or offices (e.g., they may be able to file income tax returns online or order government documents).

Under the second aspect, "Information: a new public resource?", we explored three other ways that the new infrastructure and databases might be used to create new forms of connectivity: to provide new information services, promote smart government and enhance public accountability.

Our discussion of these aspects shows that ICTs are changing how governments work. Ideally, they will lead to government that is more client-centered, more responsive, smarter, more transparent and accountable.

There is yet a third level on which ICTs could change how governments work. They could be used *to extend public space* in ways that might promote consultation and dialogue and between citizens and their governments. Through this dialogue citizens and stakeholders might express their views, propose ideas, explore differences or participate more directly in decision-making, that is, in governance. It could contribute — perhaps very significantly — to the revitalization of democracy and to the strengthening of the legitimacy of government. Our discussion of this aspect begins with a few brief comments on democracy. [6]

Through this dialogue citizens and stakeholders might express their views, propose ideas, explore differences or participate more directly in decision-making, that is, in governance.

The Test of Democracy

In our discussion of smart government we said that it requires effective policy-making and a holistic approach. The missing ingredients here were better information, and more of it. But if that is the basis of smart government or good policy-making, it is not enough to ensure *good governance*.

Because citizens disagree about some of the key values that they think government should foster, their differences over policy options often would not be solved by more complete information or evidence. Choosing between policy options often involves a choice between competing *values*. Such judgements are controversial in the sense that there is insufficient evidence for deciding authoritatively the rightness of one value over another. Is capital punishment right or wrong? What responsibility does the state have to ensure that citizens have an equal opportunity in life, say, through state-sponsored education or employment equity? How much do considerations of equality trump those of individual liberty?

Democracy can be viewed as a way of resolving policy disputes arising from this kind of pluralism. It is a way of making decisions in the midst of uncertainty and disagreement, so that the choices:

(a) treat everyone's interests and concerns fairly; and
(b) are binding on everyone, including those who disagree with them.

Democracy proposes to achieve this goal by placing three fundamental conditions on public decision-making:

1. All voices should have a fair chance to be heard in the debate that precedes a decision;
2. Each person should have an equal part in the act of decision-making: one person, one vote; and
3. In order to participate in such a process, each individual must agree that, if the first two conditions are met, he or she will accept the outcome of the process as legitimate and binding.

Let us call these conditions the test of democracy. Passing this test is the ultimate challenge for any democracy. To the extent that democracy succeeds, legitimacy increases. To the extent that it fails, legitimacy decreases.

Of course, there are endless debates over how to ensure that the conditions are met and the test is passed. Indeed, it is the stock and trade of much political debate. For example, there are disputes over how fairness is affected by campaign financing, concentration of ownership in the media, differences in levels of education or access to elites. Moreover, there are as many different systems of democracy as there are democratic governments. Basic models include British parliamentary democracy and the American congressional system, each of which is capable of endless variations. Some theorists have even defended the view that "one-party democracies" can pass the test.

In short, there are ongoing disagreements and debates over which practices, rules, institutions and systems best realize democracy. Nor is a final resolution of these debates likely. After two or more centuries, the moral seems to be that the practice of democracy is itself given to pluralism. As a concept, it is a simple and flexible idea that is capable of many variations.

ICTs introduce a whole new dimension into the discussion. They raise new concerns and opportunities for democracy. We saw, for example, that they could massively affect the quality and quantity of information that will be available to decision-makers. Because high quality information is a critical resource for informed public debate, the control and supply of information will become an increasingly important issue in everything from election campaigns to the tabling of annual reports.

The control and supply of information will become an increasingly important issue in everything from election campaigns to the tabling of annual reports.

However, such considerations suggest that the impact of ICTs on democracy focuses on the *process of public debate* that precedes decision-making. Nothing stated so far implies that they will change the practices and procedures around the *act* of decision-making — or, in particular, the practice of voting. In fact, ICTs are likely to have a major impact on this aspect of democracy as well. Before considering this implication, we need to describe one more aspect of the longstanding debates over meeting the test of democracy: the distinction between participatory and representative democracy.

Participatory vs. Representative Democracy

In participatory democracy, citizens participate directly in decision-making, usually by voting. The act of voting is seen as distinct from the public debate that precedes it. Voting is the quintessential democratic act. It is the primary expression of our belief that citizens of a democracy are free and equal.

Supposedly, the democracies of ancient Greek city-states, such as Athens, were essentially participatory. Citizens gathered together to debate and then vote on key issues. However, with the rebirth of democracy in the 18th century, states were no longer cities, but whole countries with large and sometimes culturally diverse populations. In addition, most had developed bureaucracies, and considerable holdings and responsibilities.

Participatory democracy was not feasible in such a society. Populations were usually much larger than in the Greek city-states and citizens did not have the time, expertise or inclination to participate in every debate or vote. In addition, they lived in different cities, often separated by considerable distances, so that the process of voting would have been preventively expensive and slow if every citizen had to be present for every vote. This issue was resolved by allowing citizens to choose representatives to stand for them in government and act on their behalf.

It is worth pausing to underline that not even ancient Greek democracy was fully participatory. There is always some delegation of authority to an official who is empowered to make decisions on behalf of citizens and who, in this sense, is a representative. Given the number of decisions that must be made in any modern government, it is hard to imagine how things could be otherwise. But neither is any democracy fully representative. At the very least, citizens must participate in elections to choose their representatives. Most democracies contain a host of other participatory mechanisms, ranging from referendums to community-based partnerships.

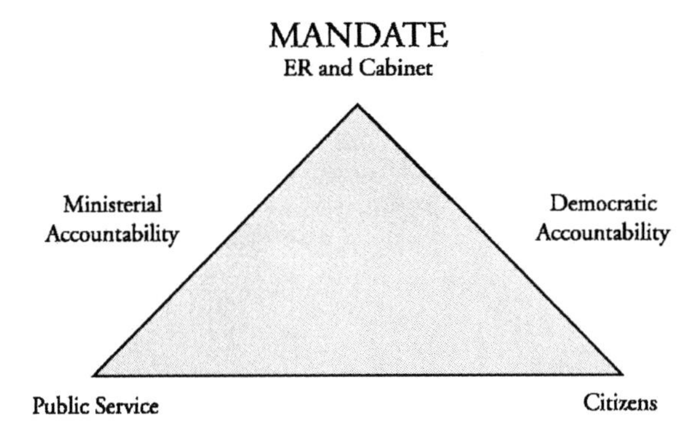

There is always some delegation of authority to an official who is empowered to make decisions on behalf of citizens and who, in this sense, is a representative.

The two models of democracy therefore are best viewed as ends of a continuum. Most modern democracies are a complex combination of the two that has evolved over the years. Thus, in Canada, there are federal, provincial and municipal legislatures with elected representatives. Even so citizens also participate in public decision-making in all kinds of ways, ranging from national referendums to the management of regional health organizations or community day-care groups. In the end, most of the really interesting debates about the future of democracy are not abstract ones over which form of democracy is better, participatory or representative, but practical ones about how, where, when and why a particular decision-making body or process should favor one approach over the other.

The Governance Triangle

The basic relationships that underlie modern representative government as it was conceived in the 18th century can be represented visually in the diagram provided.

The three points of the triangle mark the three cardinal points in the division of labour underlying representative government. The theory goes something like this:

The Governance Triangle begins with citizens, whose task (and right) it is to choose representatives who will be empowered to speak and act on their behalf. This authority is invested in representatives through the electoral process. In that process, candidates must present themselves for office, informing citizens what they stand for (usually done by presenting an electoral platform). At the end of the debate surrounding the campaign, citizens make a choice based upon their beliefs about which candidates and platforms will best represent their interests. For citizens, making this choice — casting a ballot — is the quintessential democratic act. By participating in the process in this way, they invest representatives with a *democratic mandate*, based upon the platform and debate of the campaign. This mandate provides governments with the legitimacy and the right to exercise the public authority necessary to realize the mandate. Finally, representatives remain *democratically accountable* to citizens in that the period of their mandate is limited. If they wish to remain in office, they must seek a new mandate by presenting themselves again as candidates.

The second stage of the Governance Triangle involves setting the agenda. After being elected, a new government turns its platform into a series of specific policy goals and directions. It must set priorities for action and allocate resources for that purpose (usually through a budget).

In the third stage, the project is handed off to the Public Service, which, under the direction of the appropriate elected officials, turns these instructions into programs, services, measures and (proposed) laws. Finally, these flow back to citizens, completing the triangle of governance.

Of course, this is an overly simplistic description of how any actual democracy works — particularly today. It ignores many things that can and do complicate the relationships between the three stages of the process and the principal parties involved. For example, no mention has been made of the role played by "civil society," lobby groups, political parties or the media. Nor have we mentioned the complicated relationships that exist between regular elected members of a legislature and the executive, various houses or levels of government, the political influence of the bureaucracy or the place of the courts or the constitution.

Nevertheless, there is an elemental logic in the Governance Triangle that cannot be ignored. It has underpinned the moral legitimacy and the assignment of roles and responsibilities of the cardinal players in representative democracies for two hundred years. However simplistic they may sound, these basic relationships in the Governance Triangle remain essential to how politicians, journalists, bureaucrats, policy advocates, academics and others officially explain, justify and assess their various roles and responsibilities in the process of representative government. The Governance Triangle still defines the basis of our democratic discourse, notwithstanding the fact that virtually every system of democracy has departed in various ways and degrees from it.

It has underpinned the moral legitimacy and the assignment of roles and responsibilities of the cardinal players in representative democracies for two hundred years.

So, on one hand, the Governance Triangle remains the foundation of what we can call the social contract behind representative government: citizens choose representatives at election time; elected representatives set big policy directions, define the resources available to realize them and make the laws. The public service designs and delivers the programs and services that implement these decisions.

On the other hand, the basic relationships in the Governance Triangle have been altered and obscured by two centuries of evolution in government, sometimes to the point of Byzantine complexity. As a result, the model's power to explain and justify government decisions has weakened.

For example, citizens are often skeptical of a government's appeals to a mandate to justify a decision. Campaign debates are filled with vague promises and commitments. In any event, things change too quickly for long-term plans to carry much moral authority. For their part, elected representatives often complain that they are not setting the government agenda or deciding how resources will be allocated. In particular, many feel that the bureaucracy has too much control over such decisions or that authority is too concentrated in a few individuals. Public servants complain that politicians meddle in management decisions but refuse to make the hard decisions and choices necessary to set government direction and provide leadership.

There is no need here to take sides in such debates. The point is that the vast increase in the complexity of modern governments over the last century — and, indeed, of modern societies — has made the elementary division of roles and responsibilities in the Governance Triangle unclear, confused and increasingly ineffective. The original Triangle carves out a region of public space that 200 years ago must have seemed wide open. Today, it is crowded by intricate subsystems and a complex array of players, including political parties, "civil society," media giants, lobbyists and the private sector. The elaborate numbers of participants, issues and interests in the governance process make it hard to decide exactly who is responsible for what, and hard to hold anyone accountable. Given the pace of change today and the complexity of the process and issues, the Governance Triangle seems almost quaint.

The vast increase in the complexity of modern governments over the last century — and, indeed, of modern societies — has made the elementary division of roles and responsibilities in the Governance Triangle unclear, confused and increasingly ineffective.

ICTs are not likely to improve this situation. In fact, they will likely lead to further erosion of the model. In particular, critical concepts such as "representation" and "electoral mandate" will be weakened as the relationships between the three principal players in the Triangle are eroded further. Let us briefly consider why.

IMPACT OF ICTS ON THE GOVERNANCE TRIANGLE

The Changing Nature of Political Representation

When representative government was invented, the world was a simpler place. For one thing, it was populated by more culturally and ethnically homogeneous societies. The idea that a single individual could meaningfully represent the values, interests and perspectives of a significant number of his or her co-citizens for a period of four years, on the basis of an electoral mandate, seemed plausible.

Today, societies are socially, culturally and economically more complex. An MP in the Canadian Parliament from a riding in the City of Toronto represents perhaps 120,000 people. The social, cultural and economic interests, concerns, backgrounds and values of such a community are bewilderingly complex. Furthermore, the pace of change in a city such as Toronto is so rapid that within a year of having been elected a party's platform may become obsolete or irrelevant. One need only think of how the events of September 11th in United States turned government agendas upside down.

Generally speaking, governments such as the Government of Canada must make decisions daily, as a result of rapidly changing circumstances and information. At the same time, because populations are so much more diverse, their views on issues are less stable and far less homogeneous. It is often very difficult to know how various communities will react to or view a new policy decision. The idea that a single MP can represent 120,000 people for four years under such conditions on the basis of an electoral mandate begins to stretch credulity.

The idea that a single MP can represent 120,000 people for four years under such conditions on the basis of an electoral mandate begins to stretch credulity.

Changing Nature of Consultation in Representative Government

At the same time, the new infrastructure and the information resources being created by e-government can — and almost certainly will — be used to connect citizens and governments in ways that go beyond service delivery or the use of information as a new resource. More specifically, they will be used to connect citizens and government in various forms of consultation processes.

Of course, such processes are not new. Public involvement processes have always played a role in government planning. They serve a variety of purposes, such as testing ideas or building awareness. Insofar as citizen- or client-centered government strives to be more responsive, such processes can make an important contribution to good governance. But what may begin as a practical effort to bring government in touch with citizens as quickly as possible can be regarded by citizens as an invitation or an opportunity to influence policy development. *What starts as an exercise aimed at developing more responsive programs and services becomes an exercise in governance.*

Consider the kind of process that was traditionally used by countries such as Canada to create new international trade agreements. First, it would involve teams of officials from each of the countries. Second, negotiations would be held behind closed doors, sometimes for years, until an agreement was reached. Third, the final product would be presented to the public as a *fait accompli*; perhaps at a summit, where leaders from the participating countries would endorse it.

In recent years, protesters, such as those in the anti-globalization movement, have taken aim at such processes, calling them elitist and anti-democratic. At the Quebec City Organization of American States Summit in 2001, they were particularly effective, forcing OAS countries to agree to release a draft text of a proposed new Free Trade Agreement for the region. Getting this text released was something of a coup for the protesters and it almost certainly sets a precedent so that, in future, no such text is likely to remain secret for long. Stakeholders, such as the protesters, will argue that drafts should be available on the Internet as they evolve. Such demands are likely to meet with increasing success. The Internet provides a whole new medium through which the public can circulate and discuss such a text.

Now it is a very short step from demanding that the text be made available, to demanding that it be made available *for public comment*. Indeed, it is hard to imagine that governments could consent to the former without implicitly consenting to the latter. But if stakeholders and citizens are being invited to comment, they will expect governments to take their comments seriously; that is, to listen to them, and to act on them. The Internet thus could quickly become more than a tool for disseminating documents. It could become a venue for discussion, debate and engagement — *an extension of democratic public space.*

The Internet thus could quickly become more than a tool for disseminating documents. It could become a venue for discussion, debate and engagement — an extension of democratic public space.

Such a dialogue could be very inclusive. It is possible to hold comprehensive, ongoing consultations with a wide array of citizens and/or stakeholders on policy issues on the Internet. As the possibilities become clearer, stakeholder groups will almost certainly intensify the push for governments to use the technology in this way. It will be difficult for governments to resist. To do so will appear elitist and anti-democratic. Indeed, opposition parties are already beginning to see the political point behind this. Casting ICTs as an instrument of democracy to engage stakeholders may be a powerful way to win support from activists outside government. If so, opposition parties will begin to make promises to use it for these purposes if elected. In Canada, at least one opposition party at the provincial level that is well-positioned to win the next election has made such promises.

These reflections raise serious questions over where, when, why, to what extent and for how long governments can or should resist moving in this direction. In trying to frame some of the key issues, it is useful to view the situation through the prism of the Governance Triangle. In that model, decision-making is the responsibility of elected officials, who receive their mandate from citizens in an electoral process. In the kind of consultation process we have just been sketching, citizens connect directly with government officials. As already noted, citizens or stakeholder groups who participate in such consultations are not likely to view their input as merely an opinion sample to inform governments about what the public may be thinking. The line between having a discussion and giving instructions is likely to blur very quickly and they will view themselves as giving directions — a mandate — to the government officials who have consulted them. They will expect governments to act on this mandate.

The line between having a discussion and giving instructions is likely to blur very quickly and they will view themselves as giving directions — a mandate — to the government officials who have consulted them.

They would view such a consultation as analogous to that between citizens and elected representatives at election time. In other words, stakeholders or citizens could argue that they are giving government officials a democratic mandate through the consultation process. The process thus would be treated as a form of participatory democracy.

This poses many questions. For one, such a mandate could altogether bypass elected representatives. That would not only threaten to undermine the basic governance relationships defined by the Triangle, it could also undermine the concept of a democratic mandate, on which the legitimacy of the government rests. What would happen, for example, if the instructions given to government officials conflicted with those that an Executive believed defined the mandate it received at election time? Who would have the "real" mandate?

The scenario shows that ICTs are reconfiguring the basic relationships that define the old division of labour in representative governance. As the new relationships develop, they could come into conflict with the old ones, undermining the democratic legitimacy of elected governments. What is the right response?

Toward a More Participatory form of Government?

One response is to adopt a policy of disallowing the use of ICTs for any kind of engagement processes that might have a bearing on policy development. One assumes that in countries such as Singapore or China this would be close to the government's position. At least in democratic countries, however, it is hard to see it as anything other than a "finger-in-the-dike" strategy. For one thing, we saw in our discussion of seamless government that policy and operations cannot be kept separate for long. Efforts to use the technology for operational or other non-policy purposes are likely to creep quickly into the policy domain.

Efforts to use the technology for operational or other non-policy purposes are likely to creep quickly into the policy domain.

Moreover, given the willingness of opposition parties to make hay with the issue, it is highly unlikely that the attempt to suppress the use of such processes by government fiat will be effective. A government that adopts this approach will quickly be made to appear controlling and antidemocratic. The political reality is such that, if enough people outside government want the technology to be used this way, it will — and perhaps it should — happen.

This will sound worryingly like technological determinism to some. There is a measure of determinism here. The view that history seems to be moving developed democracies toward greater connectivity runs through this chapter; as does the view that this connectivity is erasing many organizational boundaries and changing the relationship between citizens and governments. To say that history is moving in this direction, and that it is to a great extent driven by the technology, is to admit a measure of determinism — just as it is deterministic to say that the printing press or steam engine changed the course of history in earlier centuries.

The view that history seems to be moving developed democracies toward greater connectivity runs through this chapter; as does the view that this connectivity is erasing many organizational boundaries and changing the relationship between citizens and governments.

But if this way of looking at things implies that the future is in some sense "already defined" by the technology, it does not follow that it is "fully defined." It is perhaps true to say that, as a result of the Internet, options for the future have narrowed. Even so there are still many possible futures. For example, if broader public engagement in policy development is likely to occur because of the technology, it is not at all clear who will be involved in such processes, what kind of processes they will be, what sort of information will be made available to the participants or how the results will be decided. And that part of the history of 21st century democracy is far from written. There is a huge and critical need here for reflection, debate, experimentation, learning and—most of all—leadership.

Where To Go From Here?

Two Approaches to E-Democracy

In rising to this challenge, a key task will be to revisit some of the basic concepts underlying the old Governance Triangle, such as the idea of a *mandate or of political representation*. If a more direct relationship is developing between citizens or stakeholders, on one hand, and government officials, on the other, what does that mean for the role of an elected representative, and how is a government to define its mandate?

On the Canadian political scene, some views and options are taking shape around such questions. Some observers have been impressed at how the new technology can instantly register and tabulate citizens' views on key issues. Should we settle policy disputes through electronic voting, they wonder? Would this be more democratic? Is it a way of being more inclusive and less elitist? One provincial opposition party has already promised that, if elected, it will make electronic voting a key part of its agenda for change. Let us call this the "e-voting" approach. In essence, it seeks to make decision-making more democratic by using the technology to allow more people to directly participate in more decisions through mechanisms such as electronic voting.

Other interested groups, such as the anti-globalization protesters and some social policy advocates, have recognized that ICTs could link citizens and/or stakeholder groups directly into government discussions and negotiations. As a result, such groups are beginning to argue for a "virtual space" in which to allow participation in such discussions to happen more frequently, on a greater scale and in greater depth. Let us call this the "e-consultation" approach. Essentially, it seeks to strengthen democracy by enlarging the policy development process so that more people get a say in what goes into a final product, such as a trade agreement.

Essentially, it seeks to strengthen democracy by enlarging the policy development process so that more people get a say in what goes into a final product, such as a trade agreement.

Both approaches have merit and both raise questions. Broadly speaking, the former has the virtue of being more inclusive but risks taking democratic societies like Canada too far in the direction of populism. The latter has the virtue of being more deliberative but risks slipping backward into a worrying kind of elitism. We need to examine the two a little more closely.

The Risk of Populism

Contemporary Canadian populists have tended to rest their case for more inclusive decision-making on an appeal to the "common wisdom" or "common sense" of the common people, or some reasonable facsimile. They seem to hold that if politicians would only heed this wisdom, public policy would improve. Mainstream politicians do not listen, they tell us, because they are beholden to elites, including bureaucrats, special interest groups and lobbyists. Once a politician comes under the influence of such elites, he or she tends to lose touch with the common wisdom and, by implication, ceases to represent truly the people who elected him or her.

Once a politician comes under the influence of such elites, he or she tends to lose touch with the common wisdom and, by implication, ceases to represent truly the people who elected him or her.

In response, many populists seek to reconnect common wisdom and public policy by increasing citizens' direct control over or input into decision-making, using mechanisms such as parliamentary recall, constituency surveys and referendums. ICTs could facilitate the use of such tools, but there are risks.

First, the appeal to a common wisdom suggests that there is an underlying consensus on values, beliefs, perspectives, concerns and priorities. As we saw above, if such a consensus ever existed, it is in rapid retreat. A range of new forces, including globalization, changing demography and the ICT revolution, are combining to make issues and interests far more complex, nuanced and differentiated than in the past. In Canada, we have seen this in a host of debates, including constitutional reform, health care, taxes, the role of courts, abortion, language policy, aboriginal self-government, gun control, and free trade.

The populists' appeal to a common wisdom is thus something akin to myth — the idea that there exists a quiet consensus among the majority. Perhaps a greater degree of consensus did exist when countries such as Canada were culturally, socially and economically more homogeneous. In the 21st century, however, they will be far too diverse to assume such a consensus or to rely on it to produce good governance. The world is a far more complex and diverse place than it was even 30 years ago. The pace of change, tools of mass communication, mobile populations, economic diversity, varying levels of educations — these all contribute to making the idea of such an underlying consensus on more than a few basic values and practices unlikely.[7]

The populists' appeal to a common wisdom is thus something akin to myth — the idea that there exists a quiet consensus among the majority.

Allowing large numbers of people simply to express their "democratic will" on key issues through regular electronic voting is not likely to produce good governance.

Individual citizens are unlikely to become directly involved in more than a handful of such exercises.

If e-consultation processes are to enhance democracy, a way must be found to ensure that they are not simply taken over by interest groups, who may be committed and articulate, but who have no real claim to represent citizens.

To the extent that such a consensus is to be found, it is more likely to involve a common commitment to the principles and values of democracy, understood as a way of ensuring the fairness and legitimacy of decision-making in the midst of such pluralism. Although democracies tend to be in a state of ongoing discussion around the best way to meet the test of democracy, most citizens in these countries agree with the three basic principles we set out above. On the other hand, there is abundant evidence that consensus will be rare in most of the key policy areas, from education and health to regulation of the environment or levels of taxation. In short, allowing large numbers of people simply to express their "democratic will" on key issues through regular electronic voting is not likely to produce good governance. Nor is it likely to increase the legitimacy of governments. On the contrary, passing the test of democracy requires more than fair or regular opportunities to vote. It also requires that decision-making be preceded by an *open and informed debate.* That is a crucial condition of good governance in complex, diverse and changing societies like Canada.

The Risk of Elitism

The e-consultation approach raises different questions and concerns. Those who advocate it believe that giving citizens and/or stakeholders a more direct voice in the policy process would make it more democratic and thereby strengthen legitimacy.

On one hand, opening up such processes to greater public participation could be democratically liberating. On the other hand, individual citizens are unlikely to become directly involved in more than a handful of such exercises. They do not have the time, interest, expertise or inclination to pursue direct democracy beyond a few special cases. The likely participants in such an arrangement are so-called stakeholder groups.

Many such groups are formally committed to changing government policy and are already seeking a seat for their organizations at government negotiating tables. Often this is justified on the basis of claims to inclusiveness, or by virtue of a mandate to speak for some part of the population. Just as often, such claims are unsubstantiated and doubtful. Additionally, these groups are often ideologically motivated, highly partisan, exclusive and controlled by professional policy advocates. Giving them a "virtual seat" at government negotiating tables is therefore unlikely to enhance the legitimacy of such processes. Indeed, it may heighten the sense of elitism that already surrounds them.

At least two morals can be drawn from this discussion. First, if e-consultation processes are to enhance democracy, a way must be found to ensure that they are not simply taken over by interest groups, who may be committed and articulate, but who have no real claim to represent citizens. Many questions need to be answered: How much influence should they have? Which groups should be allowed to participate? What is the role of government in such discussions? What is the role of elected representatives?

Second, the diversity of interests in contemporary democratic societies such as Canada suggests that good governance often requires getting more than a simple "yes" or "no" from citizens about their views on a particular issue. Experiments with e-democracy should emphasize the importance

Finding the Middle Ground: Between Populism and Elitism

None of this discussion denies that ICTs could be a powerful tool to strengthen democracy. On the contrary, they can extend the reach of sophisticated new techniques of citizen engagement, ranging from complex opinion polling exercises, to focus groups, lengthy deliberative processes and referendums. As such, they are potentially a powerful tool for extending public space and making it more inclusive. Much work will have to be done to learn to use them effectively, but models for such processes already exist and have been used with considerable success in other forums.

ICTs can extend the reach of sophisticated new techniques of citizen engagement, ranging from complex opinion polling exercises, to focus groups, lengthy deliberative processes and referendums.

Finally, it is worth reflecting briefly on how such a process might affect the role of elected officials. In fact, it seems to suggest a new one that is less representative and more interactive. If they are to succeed, such processes will require strong leadership and skilled facilitation. First, politicians could champion such discussions, leading governments to experiment with the technology. Second, if these processes rest on the premise that good governance is the result of hard work and reasonable compromise, thoughtful and skilled facilitators will be needed to help participants work through the issues in a constructive way.

Elected representatives could play a key role here, helping citizens to understand the issues and to engage one another in ways that will develop the kind of interpersonal and fair negotiating skills that are needed to forge consensus. The ancient philosopher Socrates comes to mind here. He disliked being called a teacher and, instead, saw himself as a "midwife to ideas": someone whose job was to help his fellow citizens recognize the implications of their own beliefs. Perhaps politicians should see themselves less as policy-makers and more as policy midwives. Perhaps they need to consider how the shift from the metaphor of the machine to that of the network as a model for the organization and functioning of government changes their relationship to citizens and, indeed, the nature and practice of democracy.

CONCLUSIONS

This chapter is an effort to provide a clearer picture of e-government. It should now be evident that although e-government shares many features with conventional government, the two differ in very important respects. First, the network-like structure of e-government means that it is more horizontally organized. Although this has been presented as a challenge, it is not to be taken as a suggestion that vertical government should be exchanged for horizontal government. Rather, the challenge is to build a new horizontal dimension into existing vertical structures, without compromising key values, such as privacy, transparency and accountability.

Second, e-government involves a shift from a more closed to a more open system. Conventional government is, relatively speaking, a closed system. In it, information and decision-making are hierarchically controlled so that contact, for instance, between middle management and organizations outside the system (government) is monitored, limited and regulated to ensure that central control is not undermined. This approach is essential to the effectiveness of all command-and-control systems.

By contrast, e-government seems likely to produce a wide range of new connections that will involve government officials in relationships with organizations and individuals outside of their usual organizational boundaries. This is changing the way information enters and flows around the system of government, introducing new — and sometimes uncontrollable — influences into decision-making.[8]

Finally, by opening up the boundaries of conventional government in this way, e-government weakens its traditional command-and-control structures. E-government thus is shifting conventional government toward an organizational model that is more collaborative in style and in which decision-making could become more *distributed* — a concept that should be distinguished from *decentralization.*

E-government thus is shifting conventional government toward an organizational model that is more collaborative in style and in which decision-making could become more distributed — a concept that should be distinguished from decentralization.

Decentralization involves the transfer of authority from one command-and-control centre to another, such as from central agencies to line departments, or from federal to provincial governments. In decentralization, the transferred authority remains centralized, but is moved to a new centre (or a series of new centres). By contrast, *distributed governance* takes some of the centralized authority and spreads it around the system.

Conventional government, with its management system of paper filing systems, fax machines, top-down planning committees, hierarchical reporting relationships and departmental silos is too hierarchical to permit a significant deconcentration of authority and too slow and mechanical to ensure that, if it were attempted, it would remain responsive, transparent and accountable. As a result, conventional government could only decentralize. Not surprisingly, since the beginning of modern government, debates over government reform have usually been framed in terms of centralization vs. decentralization. *Perhaps the most exciting and far-reaching feature of e-government is the prospect of creating a communications and management infrastructure that could support a more distributed approach to governance.* Such a development could be as momentous in the history of liberal-democratic thinking as the revolutions of the late 18th century.

In conclusion, all three points raised here pose fundamental questions about the future of liberal-democratic government:

1. How far do such governments want to go in the direction of e-government?
2. How fast should they move?
3. What can they do to facilitate (or prevent) e-government?
4. What tools and options are available for managing such a change strategically (or preventing one from happening)?

The principal aim of this chapter has been to provoke a richer and more wide-ranging discussion of the issues that such questions raise.

ENDNOTES

1 *Reinventing Government: How the Entrepreneurial Spirit is Transforming Government*

2 For example, see the section on CanadaPlace.

3 For some examples of the AG's evolving thoughts on the subject of accountability, see, for example, Chapter 1 of the *Report of the Auditor General of Canada, 2002*; or Chapter 5 of the *Report of the Auditor General of Canada, 1999*. In addition, a discussion paper on the subject was produced by the AG's office in conjunction with the Federal Treasury Board Secretariat. It is entitled 'Modernizing Accountability Practices In The Public Sector' and is available at *http://www.tbs-sct.gc.ca/rma/account/OAGTBS_E.html*.

4 If this seems to be more of an administrative than a policy option, its implementation would require many policy changes, including privacy.

5 See *Measuring Quality of Life: The Use of Societal Outcomes by Parliamentarians*, by Carolyn Bennett, Donald Lenihan, John Williams and William Young; Library of Parliament and the Centre for Collaborative Government, Changing Government, Vol 3, November 2001. Also available at *www.crossingboundaries.ca*.

6 The use of ICTs to create a new cultural and political institution along these lines is explored in *Post Industrial Governance: Designing a Canadian Cultural Institution for the Global Village*, by Donald G. Lenihan, Centre for Collaborative Government, Changing Government, Vol 5, January 2002. Also available at *www.crossingboundaries.ca*.

7 of deliberation, the need to achieve compromises and to work through the issues as a group. Such processes must be designed to promote genuine discussion, learning, negotiation and compromise, while remaining open, inclusive and accountable. The changing nature of collective and individual identity and its connection to new forces such as ICTs, globalization and population mobility are discussed at length in *Leveraging Our Diversity: Canada As A Learning Society*, by Donald G. Lenihan (with Jay Kaufman), Centre for Collaborative Government, Changing Government, Vol 4, February 2002. Also available at *www.crossingboundaries.ca*.

8 These ideas are discussed in *Opening the E-Government File: Governing in the 21st Century*, by Reg Alcock and Donald G. Lenihan, Centre for Collaborative Government, Changing Government, Vol 2, February 2001. Also available at *www.crossingboundaries.ca*.

Chapter XIII

Paradigm and Practice: The Innovative Organization to Deal with E-Government

Valentina Mele, Parthenope University, Italy, and
Bocconi School of Management, Italy

ABSTRACT

The contribution starts from assessing the reciprocal influence between organizational change and the adoption of information and communication technologies (ICTs) in Public Administrations. ICTs cannot work without a proper organizational change, but at the same time, ICTs are usually one of the main drivers of such change in public administrations, as they provide the political momentum and act as catalyzer or enabler. After reviewing the role that New Public Management experts granted to the ICT in fueling, or rather in following public sector reforms, the work identifies a possible evolution of the model from New Public Management to Innovative Public Management. This model is based on the adoption of technological and organizational innovation at three levels, namely the operational choice, the collective choice and the institutional choice levels. Thereby, the chapter presents some of the current and future impacts of ICTs on institutional configuration, on policy and decision making, and on the organizational/managerial structure. Finally, the ecosystem for an innovative public administration is re-interpreted in the light of recent ICT changes.

ICTS AND ORGANIZATIONAL CHANGE: A RECIPROCAL INFLUENCE

Papers and articles about E-government often present the leitmotif that organizational change is the *condicio sine qua non* for a successful adoption of Information and Communication Technologies (ICTs) by Public Administrations. While sharing this view, the present contribution emphasizes that it works also all the way around: ICTs can't work without a proper organizational change, but at the same time ICTs are usually one of the main drivers of such change in public organizations.

Bureaucracies all around the world wave their e-government policies, projects, *ad hoc* units and probably part of this fuzz is merely a tool for consensus building. Nonetheless ICTs are providing the political momentum and often represent the catalyzer for Public Administration change. This remark does not fall in the realm of the "chicken or the egg" questions, but rather clarifies the assumptions of this chapter, which acknowledges the reciprocal influences of PA reform processes and ICTs developments.

The starting point has been the model of Van de Donk and Snellen (Figure 1), who applied the van Parijis model of causal and functional links on ICTs in Public Administration.[1]

According to the model, ICT developments change the production functions in Public Administration since a causal relationship exists between autonomous ICT developments and their cost structure on the one hand, and the possible cost-savings on the other. At the same time a causal relationship links cost-profiles and cost savings possibilities of ICT in the cost optimum, service optimum and democratic optimum, as ICTs improve best practices in the public sector by exerting a constant attraction. In order to exploit the possibilities created by ICTs to enhance efficiency, service provision and democratic standards, Public Administrations need to undergo institutional adaptations. However the model should also be read in the opposite sense, accounting for the autonomous political, legal, economic and professional developments of public admin-

Figure 1. Model of causal and functional links applied on ICTs in public administration (Snellen & Van de Donk, 1998)

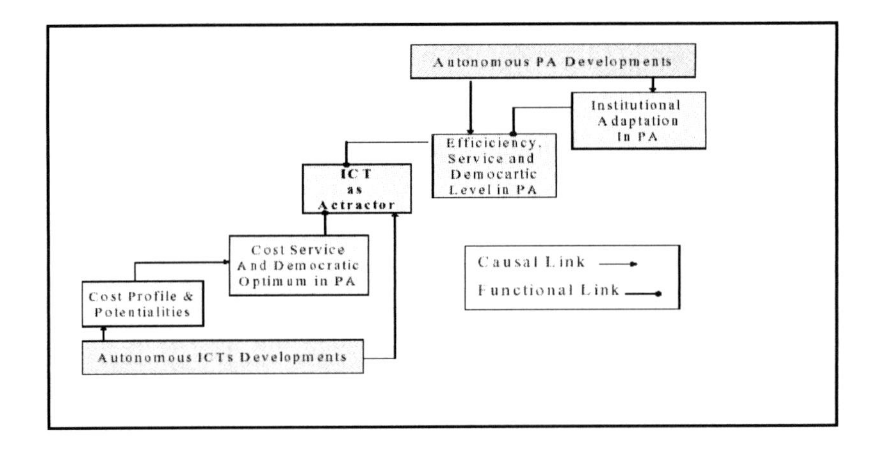

istration, which "provoke institutional adaptations and ICT applications to improve cost, service and democratic levels in public administration."

This view can be included in the "transformist school," a Solomonic approach according to which the spread of ICTs determines smooth transformations of the pre-existing socio-economical structures in a way which is not disruptive nor negligible.[2]

FROM NEW PUBLIC MANAGEMENT TO INNOVATIVE STATE MANAGEMENT

The model illustrated above also pioneered the importance of the reciprocal influence between ICTs and the autonomous transformations of Public Administration. Yet, there is an even more controversial level which concerns the public administration reform paradigms, as saying New Public Management (NPM), and the role played by new technologies. Most of the literature recognizes the role of ICTs in driving or fueling the reforms which go under the umbrella of NPM.

"Admittedly, the administration sector found itself at the center of much reform in the 1990s, though this had little to do with ICT and more to do with organizational changes in the way of New Public Management. Only recently it has been recognized that the decentralization of responsibilities, the construction of finance controlling, and many other reform measures can not being contemplated without the support of ICT" (Killian & Wind, 1996, 1998). It is also argued that the perception of technological needs and related priorities is related to the state of the art of administrative reforms so that the development of NPM is going to influence how critically ICTs are assessed, until the point where "the realization of organizational changes will bring about new investments in ICT."

Recent assessments of New Public Management (Ferlie & Fitzgerald, 2002) explicitly include ICT as one of the main drivers of NPM archetype: "...within the sphere of technology new forms of performance management have been made possible by more powerful IT and Information Systems. We see the creation of increasingly sophisticated comparative databases used for external audit, performance review and benchmarking.[3]" Here, besides the operational improvement, the potential impact of ICTs on the very NPM guiding principles does not seem fully understood.

Some, in depicting the current trends and future prospects of new public management, ignore the role played by ICTs. For example, McLaughlin, Osborne and Ferlie claim that the NPM shouldn't be limited to an approach linked to the public services' marketization, arguing that, "...NPM is fundamentally concerned with the shift from the unitary government provision and management of public services to the concepts of the plural state and the governance of public service, rather than their management."

The ICTs — missing from the previous sentence — could play an important role in such shift, by allowing decentralization in the passage from unitary to plural state, by enabling networks among public, private and non-profit sectors for the governance of public services delivery, and, even more important, for inspiring this shift which is embedded — as Castells would say— in an information economy, society and culture.

By contrast there is a vision pushed by *IT utopianists*[4] which defines NPM as a very product of the informatization process: "NPM can be interpreted as a special and prominent case of an attempt to deliver the transformational properties of informatization.

Full-blown NPM is an information-intensive reform of the structures and processes of governance, demanding new and complex horizontal and vertical flows of information in and around government organizations.[5]"

What emerges from these examples, whether the ICTs are held accountable for the development of NPM or vice versa, is that a preexisting framework of analysis is adapted to the new tools, which are mostly seen as instrumental to achieve administration goals. Dunleavy and Margetts (2000) firstly identify possible Web-enabled scenarios which acknowledge that a paradigm shift is, or at least should be, there.

Beside the choice of the ever-present "paradigm shift" label, which often corresponds to a conceptual panacea, it seems relevant to recognize that the evolution of the technologies leads to "critical features of Internet and Web impacts on public management which represent a qualitatively different kind of shock compared to previous initiatives." In *the advent of digital government: public bureaucracies and the state in the Internet age*, the authors ground their forecasts on the assessment of a relationship between NPM's impact and the development of ICTs which has not lived up to the expectations. First of all, investments and technological developments of the information systems of governments between 1980 and 2000 did not result in a proportional transformative impact in NPM countries or agencies. Second, diminishing ICT costs and the diffusion of processing power among public-sector officials through PC-based systems did not bring comparative productivity increases in the public sector organizations — nor in private ones. Also large scale computer systems inside public agencies, at least in Britain and in the U.S. Federal Government, were often working against NPM trends. A caveat against large IT projects comes also from the OECD's policy brief on *The Hidden Threat to E-Government — Avoiding Large Government Failures*, which warns Governments to avoid the "risks connected with large public IT projects...if they want to harvest the huge potential of going online."

For example in the UK large-scale computer contracts mixed with the oligopolistic feature of government computer service markets undermined the competition.[6]

After recognizing the missing synergies between New Public Management goals and new technologies development and applications, Dunleavy and Margetts forecast two possible scenarios emerging by the intersection of Web-enabled government change and extent of change (radical/transformative or slow/partial): the *Digital NPM Scenario* and the *Digital State Paradigm*.

The *Digital NPM Scenario* would take place in case the rapid development of Internet and the online versions of public services transactions were to shift the demand of current physical services into electronic substitutes, aiming at costs and public agency personnel cutbacks. Also, "the push to Web-enabled public bureaucracies would give a further strong twist to the contracting out/privatization elements of NPM" due to the Government attempts to attract private finance initiatives in order to finance equipment and capital costs for creating effective intranets, public service online versions and Web-enabled databases. One proof of the continuity of the NPM digital scenario in comparison to the previous PA reform issues is given by the principles heralded by Ostrom in the mid-70s, where, by simply adding the prefix "ICT-enabled" we can easily fill the worldwide first generation of e-government action plans:

- an entrepreneurial approach to government;
- a quality and performance-oriented approach to public management;

- an emphasis on improved public service delivery and functional responsiveness;
- an institutional separation of public demand, public provision and public service production functions;
- a linkage of demand and supply units by internal contract management, agencification or contracting-out; and
- whenever possible the retreat of government institutions in favor of commercial market enterprises and various form of social organization and self governance.[7]

Major risks related to this approach are the "public veneer" and the "McDonaldization" of public services, where the first refers to the government-branded delivery of so-called public services produced by several private suppliers, and the second effectively conjures up the government purchase of pre-defined packages of services provided by large corporations (Ritter, 1997; Dunleavy, 1994). In both cases, with respect to the effects on citizens, and more dangerous that the decrease in public service quality, seems to be the ambiguity, if not he lack of transparency, of these operations and the progressive transition toward a hollow state which grants its reassuring brand and limits its mission to determining the citizens' eligibility for service delivery and their secure identification. The resistance against the online delivery in this scenario comes from "non-connected" constituencies, such as the elderly, SMEs and all the social players that do not have access or skills to be part of the so-called information society. These authors also operate a distinction between those countries of "long-lived liberal democracy" where inclusive policies require that multi-track access is to be maintained at least in the short-run, and countries as Singapore or Hong-Kong. Such countries are less politically cautious about inequalities arising from requiring citizens to use electronic transactions, and would use centralized Web-based initiatives to push the competitiveness and to update people skills "using a public sector Web-presence overtly as the catalyst to create an e-based society" (Dunleavy & Margetts, 2000).

The Digital State Paradigm, instead, represents a Web-enabled change within government that takes the place of NPM as dominant public administration paradigm. This transformation reflects the vision that the Web development is reversing the trends of NPM, by imposing an integrated approach. Such a model of joined-up government is opposed to the fragmenting tendencies of NPM that "placed a premium on single organizations handling discrete service tasks in a financially independent way with minimal policy integration with partner agencies." The Web is a medium which would allow public personnel or agency staff to get in touch with the customers and to include their feedback in re-engineering public services. According to this model the government would use Web-based changes "to enhance citizens competencies and to radically cut policy complexity" (Dunleavy & Margetts, 2000). An example of such simplification is the possibility to notify the address changes to all the public authorities the citizens have to deal with, simply by sending one form.

Dunleavy and Margetts assert that complexity reduction would stem from the digital state paradigm, and this would be confirmed by the first examples of citizen-centered Web-portals, organized as "one-stop shops" where citizens, business and non-profits can access the available online services and information grouped around "life-events," as pioneered by the *uk-online* portal.

The main achievement of this setting is that citizens or businesses can access the services with no need to identify the involved agencies or to track the procedure steps.

Nonetheless, this complexity reduction carries the risk that users do not perceive the organization structures nor the processes underlying the one-stop shopping. Such risk seems very similar to the side effects common to policy regimes change, both in terms of citizen competence and in terms of institutional and policy complexity. Maybe this is the price to be paid in order for e-government to develop its potential: make it necessary. But, in a transition phase when the traditional PA organizational structures and, over all, sectors are still in place and are implementing e-government as their brand new project, it sounds a bit ambitious to declare that "public organizations must become their Web sites.[8]"

If the Internet is held responsible for a progressive depersonalization of human relations, we might also think about de-institutionalization as a collective loss of consciousness on public organizations, their structures and their interactions in the era of service-oriented portals.

Also, couldn't we consider it a neo-Weberian vision of bureaucratic machine which, though extraordinarily flattened, ensures a non-maneuverable, non-discretionary execution of the public mandate? Zuurmond, in his work on the passage from democracy to *infocracy,* is rather detecting a neo-Hobbesian vision, since "boundaries are disappearing and in one sense public administration has grown to one organization, like a Leviathan.[9]"

Finally, it seems that the Dunleavy Digital NPM scenario is described as ineffective and unable to keep the pace with the Internet revolution, while the Digital State model would better fit the ongoing changes. However, it may also be seen as a chronological rather than paradigmatic distinction: politicians and public managers professionally grown-up with the NPM principles are using this paradigm to deal with the Information Society innovations. But this can be considered a temporary solution until the transition to e-government has been completed. Then, new managerial tools, skills and, over all, cultures emerge constituting the dominant policy paradigm (see Figure 2), which, in turn, generates transaction and transition costs.[10]

Figure 2. Evolution of the e-government paradigm (Mele, 2002)

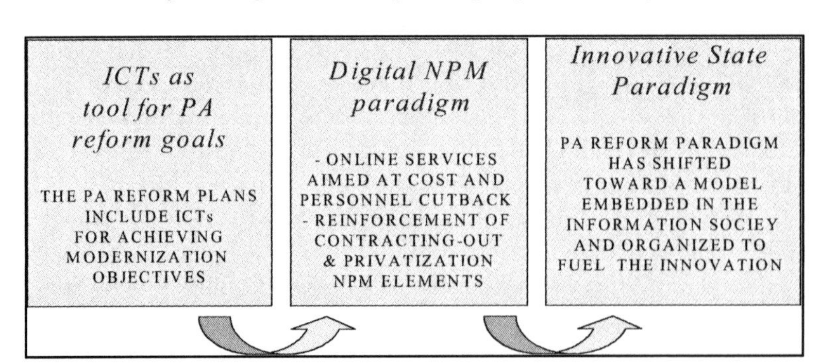

LOCUS AND FOCUS OF E-GOVERNMENT IMPACTS

In order to assess the impacts of e-government on the organizational structure of public administrations, which is the main goal of this chapter, it seems important to place these changes in the proper *locus*.[11] The distinction of Toonen (1998), who reframes the Kiser and Ostrom (1982) three worlds of action — operation choice, collective choice and constitutional choice — shall be used.

The level of operational choice is the world of daily activities and decision making with a given framework of rules and institutional setting. "...This is what we generally refer to as administrative practice where general rules, policies and programs are applied and enforced with respect to concrete objectives and issues.[12]"

The level of collective choice concerns the joint decision making on collective policies such as law, plans, regulations and rules, with direct consequences on the operational level called to enforce these decisions.

The level of constitutional choice refers to processes of joint decision making about principles and rules guiding the collective and operational choices. "The world of institutional choice is about *metadecisions*: decision on how to take collective decisions and conduct joint decision making."

However, the three world approach does not operate necessarily as a strictly integrated hierarchy with sequential order of events, and this increases the usability of the framework for the schematization of the e-government impacts on Public Administration, which indeed couldn't be forced into a hyper-sequential or highly hierarchical structure.

Figure 3. Locus and focus of e-government impacts (Mele, 2002)

Locus: / Focus:	*CONSTITUTIONS* INSTITUTIONS & ORGANIZATIONAL CONFIGURATIONS	*POLICIES* POLICY & DECISION MAKING	*MANAGEMENT* IMPLEMENTATION & OPERATION
Within Public Administration	- Creation of *ad hoc* institutions for e-government at the National and Local Level - ICT-driven changes in the organizational configuration	- Policies for increasing the internal efficiency through ICTs, policies for public officials training on e-government	- Intranets - Interorganizational co-operation - Knowledge Management
PA relations with Citizens, Business and Non Profit	- Online mechanisms for democratic participation - Changes in the check and balance system	- Policies for increasing the quality of services and promoting e-procurement	- Online service delivery - E-procurement
External to the PA	- Online communities	- Guidelines for including all the social categories in the information society, policies for the job enhancement, for updating the educational system, for the economic development and system competitiveness	- Interventions for enabling citizens and territory to participate to the information society

The table provided sums up the intersection of the *locus* of operational, collective and institutional choice with the *focus,* the digital state approach. The focus is composed of three levels, internal to the public administration, from the public administration to citizens and business and, finally, external to the public administration.

E-Government Impacts on Institutional and Organizational Configuration

The creation of *ad hoc* institutions for e-government at National and Local level represents the intersection between the e-government institutions and organizational configuration change and the level internal to the public sector. Generally, Public Administrations have appointed *ad hoc* groups and task forces to preside over these issues which, anyway, are progressively penetrating, in the form of tools or in the form of program goals, in most Ministries, Agencies and Departments. In Italy the Authority for the IT in the Public Sector, established in 1993, has been joined by the work of the Public Administration Department (First E-Government Action Plan, 2000) and, since 2001 by the Ministry for the Innovation and Technologies also in charge of e-government matters. In the UK the Central IT Unit became the E-Government Group in 1995 and joined the Office for the E-Envoy, which collaborates with the E-Minister, in the year 2000.

As for the e-government-driven changes of institutions and organizational configurations, at the level of PA relations with Citizens, Business and Non-Profits, there are online mechanisms for democratic participation.

E-democracy has become a rather popular word, and originates many controversial issues. However, most of the problems apparently related to the "e" suffix, seem to derive more from the evolution of deliberative democracy and of the informed citizenship, both well known before the advent of Internet. Today, indeed, democratic institutions are facing a choice between politically unequal but deliberative elites and politically equal but hardly deliberative masses, where the trade-off is between the quality and the equality of the deliberation.

A first approach to this problem states that the solution lies in elections and that the deliberation comes from discussions among elected officials. But since in most democratic countries elected officials often pursue their own pet interests or the interests of lobbies above those of the majority of their constituents, the equality reached through the elections turns out to be subverted. Alternatively, elected representatives follow the polls' dictates renouncing to a meaningful and rational deliberation. The problem here is not much the lack of rationality of the public decision expressed through the poll, but rather the lack of public decision expressed through the polls, which "stand in generally unknown and often quite limited relation to the views people would hold if they had the chance of learning, thinking and talking about the issues.[13]" Thereby, the decision-making stage would be a no-win, since ignoring mass-preferences vitiates equality while following them vitiates deliberation. This school of thought then proposes deliberative polling, an ancient solution based on the lot in the Athenian democracy and by random sampling in modern terms.[14] The idea of gathering citizens in small groups to discuss policy issues provides an incentive for the participants to be informed and think about the issues.

Another approach acknowledges that there has to be some distribution across people and across issues of the cognitive demands of self-government, affirming that if democracy requires "omnicompetence and omniscience from its citizens, it is a lost cause.[15]" The main argument is that we buy chicken and milk in the supermarket, trust in the metropolitan water supply, so "why, then, in public life, do we expect people to be political backpackers?" (Schudson, 1999).

One solution is represented by the concept of "monitorial citizen," who engages in environmental surveillance more than information-gathering. This kind of citizenship might be less heavy than in the era of political parties, but for sure the commitment is year-round and day-long, due to such a frequent messaging of traditional and new media.

New technologies and particularly the Internet might play a role in both approaches. The first solution, deliberative polling, can use the Internet for online forums and other forms of virtual interaction which could substitute or integrate the vis-a-vis groups.

The second solution, monitorial citizenship, can use the Internet for increasing the "monitorial capacity" of the citizens, since there is potential for a more rapid diffusion of the news and, over all, ICTs can improve information gathering and knowledge management.

The second solution, thus, is better shaped for the "digital state paradigm." Nonetheless, it presents some side-effects related to the time of the decision making, which might need a time lag in order for the issues to be understood and for a conscious opinion to be formed. There is the risk that citizens "will use the set-top boxes on their Internet televisions to engage in frequent plebiscites that will be poorly understood and easily manipulated behind the scenes.[16]" Alternatively the access for information will be plentiful and cheap, so that political participation, including voting, can be made easier. Still, there is a question of inequality and opportunity that arises, replicating online, under the name of digital divide, the problems deliberative democracy still has to solve.[17]

The question of Web-enabled political participation is also necessary to counter-balance the *infocracy* (Zuurmond, 1998). According to the Weberian model, the power of the bureaucracy served as barrier to the power of the political leader, and in its turn needed to be compensated through the exercise of the liberal liberties by the citizens, such as freedom of speech, freedom of union and assembly, freedom of press and so on. Now that the bureaucracy is evolving toward *infocracy*, also the political leader and the individual citizens should be enabled to use the ICTs to strengthen their position, thereby reshaping the original "checks and balances" system.

Yet, on the side of the debate around the individual citizen position and citizens aggregation through the Internet, a major issue is represented by online communities. Again, the online prefix is only partially accountable for the crisis that communities, either voluntary or local, are experiencing.

According to the Hirschman model of voluntary communities characterized by an exit/voice option, the current voluntary communities in industrialized countries tend to be exit-like ones, and this trend would be strengthened by Internet-based communication. Three, in fact, are the main features of a community: entrance costs, exit costs and mechanisms of internal functioning, which are generally not hierarchical and based on the mutual adjustments of participants' interest.

The online communities are often presented as low entrance and exit costs, since it is easy to become a member, participate and leave the group. Such easy exit would also affect the internal rules of the community whose members, instead of being pushed to the interests' homogenization would leave the group when the pursued interests either are realized or are dismissed by the community.

This is why online communities, initially welcomed as the alternative to contiguity-based groups, able to overcome the geographic boundaries and to create extremely variegate groups of individuals and interests, are now considered a reality where "the ready availability of exit tends to produce internally homogeneous groups that may not even talk with one another and that lack incentives to develop shared understanding across their differences.[18]" But content matters. If one decides to take part in an off-line voluntary community, the chances of quitting the group increase as the activities pursued or the mission lose their interest. Then he/she will stop going to the meeting or paying the year subscription, but does this exit ontologically differ from the online one? The charge on the exit seems to be the real point, and whether this is posed on or off-line may not be dramatically different.

So, if there are reasons why, for instance, a city council or another public organization, wants to keep an online community alive, which better way than offering value-added services, information, contact, updating to the participants? Then, the burden of quitting the group by choosing the *exit* option might seem disproportionate with respect to the costs of exerting the *voicing* option. This is why online community might be considered an oxymoron (Mele, 2002).

Certainly, a subject that decides to invest resources for the development of online communities is the local public administration, thus combining "place and cyberspace" (Galston, 2002). The reasons that might call for the public intervention go chiefly under the label of "accelerated pluralism.[19]" According to this view, the Internet, by decreasing the transaction costs, allows the democratization of group politics. But the lower costs of organizing like-minded individuals would result in a lower political coherence and stability, due to ephemeral issue-groups' high turnover: "...the power of more traditional public and voluntary sector institutions that enjoy some stability over time and work to integrate (or at least broker) diverse preferences is likely to erode.[20]" The local administrations thereby can benefit by continuous and lively online communities which represent a valuable resource for its citizens and that combine the voluntary character with the local roots.

The evolution of community networking leads to the identification of trends and possible future pathways, related to the information society in which they are embedded.[21] The characteristics of community networking, have, in fact, been partially shaped by how the information society has been driven either by business, by public bureaucracies, or by civil society. Many experts have issued a *caveat* about the dangerous overlap that can be observed in the emerging relationships between the information society, information economy and the information state.

In some development models, as in the U.S., economic goals drive ICT innovations in a way that "is useful for designing chips and companies, not information societies, and produces a digital divide" (Serra, 2000).

In other development models, and particularly in the EU welfare states, a common feature seems to be that public bureaucracies are producing a "digital and innovation lag." The "Telecities" model in Europe is, according to this analysis, better shaped to serve the Information State than the Information Society. [22]

Lastly, the "third way" of the Information Society proposes community networks that promote "leadership of new societal organizations, establishing alliances and getting funding from the corporate sector and from the state for fueling this societal change — they are organizations that will serve societal needs" (Serra, 2000).

E-Government Impacts on Policy and Decision Making

In terms of policy, the Internet and ICTs impact on the process of policy and collective decision making. This is linked to the issues we considered above, such as the changes in the political participation and the strengthening of interest-group politics. There are ICT-related impacts on policy and decision making also in terms of tools for the information gathering and storage through knowledge management and for maximizing the speed and the acknowledgment of the public service users' feedback, both enable more efficient and more respondent policy design. Finally, ICTs and the Internet are the subject of an increasing number of policies:

- policies for increasing the internal efficiency through ICTs and for public officials training on e-government;
- policies for increasing the quality of public services through ICTs and for promoting e-procurement; and
- guidelines for including all social categories in the information society or are included as instruments in the policies for job enhancement, for education system modernization and for the economic development and country competitiveness.

Certainly the flourishing of national and regional plans for e-government is evidence of a more mature approach to these issues compared to the first period of the public sector recourse to the Internet, most of the time limited to a self-celebrating Web site.

Managerial Impacts of E-Government

At the level of operational choice internal to the public administration, e-government developments have relevant impacts on the management style and tools. One example is given by the implementation of knowledge management (KM) through computer networks. What does KM mean? We refer to knowledge as the ideas or understandings that an entity possesses, which are used to take effective action, in order to achieve the entity's goals. This knowledge is specific to the entity which created it. Knowledge management, instead, is the systematic process of finding, selecting, organizing, elaborating and presenting information in a way that improves an employee's comprehension in a specific area of interest. Knowledge management helps an organization to gain insight and understanding from its own experience.[23] Specific knowledge management activities, according to this perspective, help focus the organization on acquiring, storing and utilizing knowledge for such things as problem solving, dynamic learning, strategic planning and decision making. It also protects intellectual assets from decay, adds to firm intelligence and provides increased flexibility.

Narrowing the focus on the public sector, knowledge management is a management modernization, which involves adapting classic management tools in a way that systematically promotes knowledge sharing, and which relies heavily on the use of new ICTs. But, while there is evidence that the great majority of leading private-sector firms are now actively pursuing knowledge management, many doubt that the same systematic organizational changes are taking place in the public-service institutions, as showed by the PUMA study *Knowledge Management: Learning-by-Comparing.*[24]

If this is true, governments are at risk of falling behind leading-edge companies in managing their knowledge. This could affect the competitiveness of public organizations and lead to a reduction in citizens' trust in public institutions.

Knowledge management is strictly linked to e-government.[25] As government managers are challenged with structuring information that can be shared agency-wide, they typically realize there is room and need for creating an intranet and to integrate it with an online front-office. There is also an issue related to knowledge management, which can highly benefit from the synergies with e-government: the benchmarking/benchlearning activity.[26]

Public service provision is also strongly affected by ICTs, both in production and in delivery. Speaking about two clearly separated phases in Fordist terms might be simplistic, since the Internet and the new technologies are often considered a strong accelerator of the "Toyotism" process. The immediateness of the customer/producer communication and of the producer, and of the user feedback on the product/service can lead to a cycle where the demand drives the production rather than the supply drives the consumer choices.

This is one of the ICTs' impacts which private and public sector share the most and that requires dramatic organizational changes. As for public services, there is often confusion on the impacts of new technologies. However, it would be useful to apply the traditional distinction among the core service, the ancillary service and the communication of the service, to the extent of the ICTs impacts. Considering a health care service, for example, one might include the ICTs impacts on:

- the core service through telemedicine applications;
- the ancillary service through electronic patient record or online registration and booking; and
- the service communication through patient relationship management application or health online communities.

The observations on the trends of online communities and of Internet-based, de-intermediate politics apply also to "direct medicine" (e.g., the attempt to avoid as much as possible the intervention of hospitals and off-line health care experts, versus the exchange of experiences and advice with other patients and the recourse to online expert opinions about certain health care matters).[27]

Another important clarification should be made about the Internet and ICTs' impacts on the service and on the channel. Most of the times, indeed, what is considered a new service results in being rather a traditional service delivered online. Figure 5 shows the possible intersections between traditional/innovative service with traditional/innovative channel.

Lastly, particular emphasis should be given to interventions for enabling citizens and businesses to be part of the information society, typically represented by programs for spreading Internet access and digital literacy.

Such interventions are based on the assumption that efficient online public service delivery needs a critical mass of users. Until the multi-tracking delivery is needed also for those services which do not require it and their online version is just a *plus* that on-the-pace administrations offer to the already connected citizens, e-government won't activate a virtuous circle. This is why many administrations are launching, particularly

Figure 4. Mix of channel/service technological innovation (Mele, 2001)

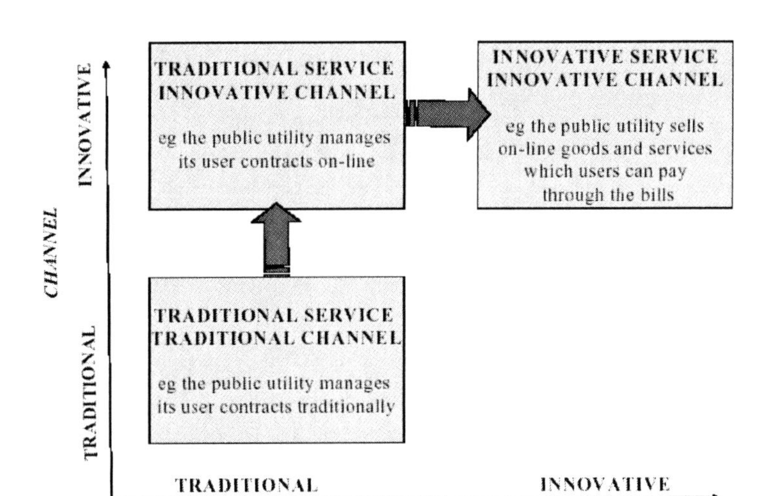

at the local level, projects for Internet access such as kiosks, public office connections, distribution of connected PCs in the schools and so on, as well as initiatives aimed at spreading digital literacy.

ORGANIZATIONAL IMPACTS OF ICTS ON PUBLIC ADMINISTRATIONS

It is possible to define two categories of ICT-related organizational changes, one concerning the organizational structure of public administrations, and one affecting the relations among different administrations.

As shown in Figure 3, the framework about locus and focus of e-government impacts included the changes of institutional and organizational configuration. A common feature of these changes is the establishment of departments or units explicitly dealing with e-government, together with the introduction in the organizational chart of new functionaries experts of ICTs.

For example, in Italy, a research on the organizational and training models for e-government at the local level has assessed the role of e-government in organizational terms, by measuring the presence of staff dedicated to the Information Systems and to the Training. According to the research findings, the administrations where these functions are carried out by *ad hoc* professionals, where these professionals are positioned in the organization chart directly below top management and where both IS and Training functions are subject to the same hierarchical level, turned out to be better equipped to deal with e-government changes.[28]

But, while new functionaries are introduced in the organizational structure, there are increasing concerns toward a general de-skilling process that can be witnessed, since the computer applications and the work-flow management tools tend to appropriate much of the knowledge that belonged to the professionals in the old work process.[29]

The second category of e-government-related organizational impacts is structured around interorganizational cooperation. Killian and Wind from the University of Kassel state that computer networks can simplify and increase the effectiveness of working practices without changing the organizational structures, by making it possible to access data beyond the organizational boundaries and to improve cooperation within the administrative system.

According to this vision, computer networks represent a unique opportunity to solve the conflict between specialization/differentiation versus integration. OECD countries, indeed, are facing the growth of increasingly complex tasks, which they tackle mainly by establishing hyper-specialized departments and units. On one hand, this organizational segmentation is needed to adequately deal with complex matters, thereby meeting the citizen expectations. On the other hand, though, it increases organizational tensions, since these tasks are highly interdependent, so that "different administrative units require the same data or rely on other departments to supply them with data.[30]" Computer networks can be considered one solution to relieve such organization tensions, by easing the access to information irrespectively of departmental boundaries.

It is also important to specify that different kinds of computer network require different levels of interorganizational coordination. For example, networks set for resource sharing or for communication improvement do not call for a high degree of cooperation, since they represent mainly supportive infrastructures. On the opposite, computer networks which support the transactions or that allow access to information irrespectively of time, space or personnel restrictions, require more efforts to gain coordination since they re-define interorganizational information flows.[31]

Introducing these computer networks and re-defining interorganizational information flows in the public administrations might have disruptive consequences. It breaks the information monopoly of street-level bureaucrats limiting their discretional power and, more in general, it weakens the power of the departments that possessed nearly exclusive access to specific data.

An example is given by the introduction, in Italy, of the Digital Unified Booking Centre for Public Healthcare Services (CUP), which is operating in several regions.[32] The Metropolitan Cup of Bologna, the first to be established, ensures a widespread access Network to health care services. The network is composed of hundreds of desks covering the Provincial area and a Telephone Call Center. With CUP, it is possible to book from these desks approximately 2,000 different types of health care services delivered by the National Health System, by some private facilities and registered private facilities, and pay the fees of booked services from the desks.

The benefits for citizens include increasing the choice on how, where and how to access the requested provision, minimizing citizens' traveling from poorly served areas and reducing queues service booking/payment. But what really makes the point is that, wherever this system has been implemented, one of the most critical aspect has been the willingness of the different departments to give up selection criteria and management of the openings for services and referrals delivery.

Traditionally, this function carries a big deal of power, since the management of waiting lists, when it does not grant patronage favors, represents a leverage within hospitals and health care structures, able to speed up or slow down activities and workflows. Concentrations of power are often hidden beneath the surface of trivial administrative functions such as these openings management, so that the resistance to digital systems are inspired more by concerns about the loss of control than by mere operational inertia.

These trends forecast an even more explosive scenario in organizational terms, as the legitimacy of the authorities and agencies whose main purpose is to coordinate other authorities or to distribute information, might be threatened by computer networks increased ability to share and exchange the information when, where, for what and by whom is needed.

But, as some experts emphasized, this is about a possible future, while we are still in a transition phase where the new institutional and organizational rules coexists with the previous ones.[33] It is likely that we will witness a dramatic improvement of the transparency degree in administrative transactions due to computer networks, but whether this will be joined by extended freedom ensured to decentralized units or by more constraints in the devolution process through Web-enabled tighter control from superior authorities, remains to be seen.

Yet, at the level of interorganizational relations, ICTs are eroding the very concept of organizational boundaries. As Scott Morton forecasted in 1991, "...boundaries of organizations are becoming more permeable; where work gets done, when and by whom is changing." Then he analyzed the impacts on the four levels of private firms' value chain:

1. Organizational boundaries *within the value chain* are blurring, and we can relate to the one-stop-shop Web sites and portals where administrations and departments are connected to deliver online public services. In addition to the space barriers, also the time barriers are changing their meaning since the present communication and transactions between government and citizens or government and business are freed from office hour constraints.
2. *End-to-end links of the value chain* between organizations are also enabled by ICTs. Public administrations, indeed, have been coping with the flood of data by shifting much of their routine data processing and business transactions to computer-based information systems. However, differences in information systems required that trading partners frequently translated from one system to another manually, greatly reducing both the speed and the reliability of information exchange. Electronic Data Interchange (EDI) grew out of a need to address this problem. EDI standards enable fast and accurate exchange of routine, relatively simple business transactions between different automated information systems. Also, the infrastructural networks are massively migrating toward multi-provider networks which enable peer-to-peer connections among the members.
3. *Value chain substitutions* via alliances or contracting-out are also facilitated by computer networks, though, as previously considered, these public/public or public/private partnerships are easier to hide under an integrated interface. Nonetheless, ICTs offer the opportunity to faster and cheaper coordination among the different levels of the value chain, as showed by the example of the Office for the Relations with the Citizens of the Italian municipality of Modena. The Municipality maintains the accountability, the planning and the implementation of the Office Information System structure, while a consortium of private firms manages

the informative service delivery and the back-office research. In this example, computer networks facilitate the value chain substitution via subcontracting to the private sector, by allowing a strict interaction between public decision makers and the private consortium employees, as well as by enabling interactions between the citizens and the consortium, in charge of the service delivery to final users. Computer networks also support value chain substitution within the public sector, by reinforcing the "transmigration effect.[34]" The phenomenon counterbalanced the downsizing efforts that many countries put in place since the early 90s. Though ICTs can not be held accountable for it, they strengthen the internal and external networking capacity of public administrations, de facto enabling the transmigration effect. In Italy, for example, the number of ministries has been reduced and the new structures, often deriving by merging functions and sectors have an organizational set-up better suited to their own mission. But it is also true that new Agencies and Authorities focusing on a vast array of sectors — such as telecommunication, public works, health care, utilities — have been established, so that the overall downsizing has not been as dramatic as firstly conceived. The same applies to local governments, since the combined effect of contracting out, contracting in for such activities as local police, information technology and support services, creation of enterprises and foundation led to the "enlarged organization" phenomenon. Thus, the Municipality becomes the strategic centre of a network of various organizations. By the way, works such as Paul Light's book on *The true size of government*, inform us that the phenomenon is not a unique Italian feature.[35] In the U.S. federal downsizing attempts, for example, the matter is about the "shadow of government," crowded by non-federal employees working under federal contracts, grants, and mandates to state and local governments.

4. *Electronic markets* are the last level of the value chain according to Scott Morton. Certainly e-procurement represents in several countries and in different sectors a first relevant example of market place, where the private supply and the public demand meet each other, typically in the virtual arena of the *vortals*. Yet, there is no electronic market for public services, mainly for the non-voluntary, non-price-identifiable, still scarce competitive character of the public service offer.[36] We can think about a near future where, at least, different public suppliers offer their services online, leaving to the user the choice to pick-up the most convenient supplier either for geographical location or for price/quality rate.

INNOVATIVE ORGANIZATION TO DEAL WITH E-GOVERNMENT

The innovative state model results in the parallel impacts on public organizations, which are hardly summed up in a single path of e-government related organizational change, since ICTs are not uniformly shaping the organizational chart nor the inter-organizational coordination.

Nonetheless, there is a common feature in worldwide e-government projects and policy: it's about innovation policy and innovation management. What is innovation, and what is innovation in the public sector, keeps puzzling field experts and schools. This research field has generally dealt with private sector innovation, but there is a growing interest in non-profit and government innovation, mainly stimulated by the Ford Foundation. Traditionally, the literature has been much concerned with the single act of innovation than with the organizational settings in which those acts take place. Another common feature is the focus on the importance of the individual actors in making innovation occur. But the stress on the potential role of the single manager in challenging the prevailing wisdom has the counter-effect of underestimating the organizational reform work.

More recently, the focus of innovation management studies has moved to the organizational components involved in the innovation process, as well as on the tools that an administration should develop in order to facilitate the internal innovation. "Sustaining innovation: Creating Nonprofit and Government Organizations that Innovate Naturally" (1998) is Paul Light's paean, encouraging a reorganization of public agencies able to capture and to stimulate the innovative momentum. The model, thereby, derives from the assumption that "the key to stimulate innovation lies in the mundane work of organizational reform" (Light, 1998; Meneguzzo, 2002), and emphasizes the need for a shift from the innovation-event to the innovation-process. This result comes from creating and embracing competition, flattening hierarchies, giving permission to make mistakes and establishing learning systems. Light's way of sustaining innovation is based on a kind of ecosystem in which organizations' innovativeness depends on four factors that ignite and sustain new ideas, namely external environment, internal structure, managerial tools and leadership. Public administrations shifting to the *innovative state model* might consider using this "conscious" vision in approaching e-government.

The *external environment* is represented by the expectations of citizens and business accustomed to communicate and transact online. There is a global economic setting which calls for a new role of government in the digital economy, as opposed to the traditional mission of governments in the bricks and mortar economy.[37] The role of public administrations, as effectively summed up by Stiglitz, changes as the economy moves toward information-based production, since "the prevalence of public-good-type and informational concerns loom larger." Public goods are characterized by zero marginal costs and non-excludability, so that information can be considered as such. The shift from an atom-based to a bit-based, knowledge-intensive economy could therefore show some inconsistencies with a laissez-faire approach: who will invest to obtain information if no returns or minimal returns are expected? This situation might lead to information imperfections. Another danger of an Adam Smith-like paradigm is represented by network externalities, arising when the value of using a specific type of products depends on how many other people are using it. Again, the markets might not be efficient and keep producing a certain technology neither because it is more accessible to the most, nor because it is better performing, but because everyone else is using it. This phenomenon, labelled as QWERTY effect, is often coupled with the *winner-take-all* or *superstar effect*, where "zero marginal costs combined with the possibility of exclusion imply that small differences in quality produce large differences in returns.[38]"

All these aspects of the information economy seem to require an active role of the government, though Stiglitz acknowledges that government failure may be even more pronounced in the context of rapidly moving information-based markets, since it needs innovation and change abilities often missing in the public sector.

In terms of *internal structure and internal management systems*, besides the considerations exposed in the previous paragraph, the tension should be kept on designing a structure, a set of management tools and of interorganizational dynamics able to shift the focus from the disruptive act of innovation to the continuing innovation.

An interesting example of this vision is the user-led model applied to public services. The model is an old acquaintance of private management theories. Von Hippel, for example, in his 1986 article on "Lead Users: A Source of Novel Product Concepts," pinpoints this category of users, whose present strong needs will become general in a marketplace months or years in the future. Since lead users are familiar with conditions which lie in the future for most others, they can serve as a need-forecasting laboratory for marketing research, as well as provide new product concepts and design data as well. Other authors developed a user-led innovation model for the public sector (Corrigan, Joice, McNulty & Rose, 1999), identifying citizen needs as the innovation drivers. "It is the responsibility of managers to help identify users' needs at the point of service delivery. This has to happen because, in our model, the political/citizenship relationship at the level of running the organization is so weak that it does not have strength to define users needs. This leaves managers having to be involved in the direct negotiation of user needs, not just directing front-line staff on what to do in order to execute the policy of politicians.[39]" Not only are new technologies and particularly the Internet extremely useful in identifying and improving the delivered service, but the very target of connected users can act as lead-users of online public service, since they have access and digital literacy, both conditions hopefully diffused in the near future.

In the model, a key role is played by our forth variable, the *leadership*. Public manager are responsible for interpreting and selecting user needs, and, even more important, in charge of transforming the single user-led innovation into an ordinary practice, by boosting the "learning organization" paradigm.

The learning organization is grounded on managing innovation-related risks and debacles, a *trait d'union* among turbulent and highly uncertain contexts. Silicon Valley managers as well as worldwide professional gamblers assume that failure is a component of innovation, which requires a great deal of discipline. Failures have to be stopped early, to avoid the risk of escalation of commitment. "Fail fast, fail cheap, move on!" also applies to the initiatives to implement innovation policy in the public sector.

ENDNOTES

1 Philippe van Parijs (1981) combines in his model causal and functional reasoning and Snellen and van de Donk, in their *Public Administration in an Information Age* (1998) use this model to show how and why the existence of a technology as a potential improvement attracts certain social and technological reactions in the form of "socio-technical realizations." The causal line connects prior situations with later consequences, while the functional line connects later states of affairs to prior situations. "In other words causal reasoning explains later occurrences by former ones while functional reasoning explains former occurrences in the light of later ones."

2 While schematizing the schools of thought about the impacts on our society of ICT, at that point still labeled "IT," Miles, Turn, Rusher and Bessant presented the *continuative*, the *revolutionary* and the *transforming* approaches, quite obviously opting for the last one.

3 Ferlie and Fitzgerald, "The sustainability of the NPM in the UK." In McLaughlin, Osborne and Ferlie *New Public Management. Current Trends and Future Prospects*. Routledge, 2002, p. 341.

4 Dunleavy and Margetts speak about IT *utopianists* that, together with practicing managers, would see informatization and NPM as "inextricably intertwined." *The Advent of Digital Government: Public Bureaucracy and the State in the Internet Age,* paper presented to the Annual Conference of the American Political Science Association. Washington, 4 September 2000.

5 Bellamy G., and Taylor J., *Governing in the Information Age*. Open University Press, Buckingam, 1998.

6 Bastow S., Dunleavy P., Margetts H., and Tinkler J. The Advent of a Digital state and Government-Business Relations, paper to the Political Studies Association Conference at LSE. London, 10-13 April 2000.

7 Ostrom V. *Intellectual Crisis in American Public Administration* (1970), In T. Toonen, *Network, Management and Institutions: Public Administration as 'Normal Science'* (1998).

8 Dunleavy and Margetts report this observation of an Australian public official about the Australian Tax Office (2000).

9 Zuurmond. A., From Bureaucracy to *Infocracy*. Are democratic institutions lagging behind? (1998) p.269.

10 See Scott, J., *Seeing Like a State* (1998), for the analysis of side implications such as transaction and transition costs generated by policy regime changes.

11 Toonen, T. In *Network, Management and Institutions: Public Administration as 'Normal Science,'* affirms that "the study of public administration may be viewed as an approach as well as subject matter, a focus as well as a locus. Government in action has been defined as the locus of the study of public administration since Woodrow Wilson in 1887" (p. 234).

12 Ibid.

13 Fishkin, J.S., and Luskin, R.C., *The Quest for Deliberative Democracy. Symposium on Deliberative Polling*, 1999 (p.4).

14 See Hansen, M.H., *The Athenian Democracy in the Age of Demosthenes* (1991).

15 See Schudson, M., *The Social Construction of the "Informed Citizen"* (1999).

16 Nye, J.S., *Information technology and Democratic Governance* (2002).

17 See Norris, P., *Digital Divide: Civic Engagement, Information Poverty and the Internet in Democratic Societies* (2001).

18 Galston, W.A., *The Impact of the Internet on Civic Life: An Early Assessment* (2002) p. 47.

19 Bimber, B., *The Internet and Political Transformation: Populism, Community and Accelerated Pluralism* (1998). In W.A. Galston, *The Impact of the Internet on Civic Life: An Early Assessment* p. 55.

20 Ibid.

21 See Mele, V., *The Modena E-Network for Strengthening Local Governance and Citizen Participation* (2002).

22 *Telecities* is a European network of cities which promotes a wider awareness of the potential of ICT to ensure that these reflect a balance between economic competitiveness and social needs - *http://www.telecities.org*.

23 A vast literature inquires about the very definition of knowledge and knowledge management. Scholars throughout the '90s have been busy in sharpening these semantic distinctions as witnessed, among the others, by Alain J. Godbout, *Information Vs. Knowledge: Small contribution to an old debate* (1996) or Robert J. McQueen, *Four Views of Knowledge and Knowledge Management* (1998).

24 *Knowledge Management: Learning-by-Comparing Experiences form Private Firms and Public Organizations* –Summary Record of the High Level Forum. Copenhagen, 8-9 February 2001." PUMA-OECD.

25 For explicit references and state-of-the-art discussion on the topic see also the contributions to the yearly workshop in "Knowledge Management in Electronic Government" at its III edition (May 2002).

26 See Meneguzzo, M., *Innovazione Managerialità e Governance* (2000).

27 Recent studies start to prove that, besides the virtual feature of the Internet, individuals recur to the Internet in order to take part to the health care choices that concern them and to obtain a more human and personalized assistance.

28 The research of Formez and Dipartimento Funzione Pubblica (June 2002) is titled: *E-Government, new organizational and training paradigms in the regions and in the local administrations.*

29 See Zuurmond, A., *From Bureaucracy to Infocracy*, 1998, p. 265.

30 Killian, W., and Wind, M., Changes in Interoganizational Coordination and Cooperation, 1998, p. 274.

31 An example of transaction support computer networks is represented by EDI-Electronic Data Interchange-systems, while an example of computer networks for the access to information is represented by MIS (Management Information Systems).

32 For the English version of the website: *http://www.cup2000.it/cup2000/cup2000(e).asp.* CUP works roughly as follows: a citizen goes to any CUP desk - manned by operators or in a pharmacy — with the CUP Card (an identification magnetic card replacing the health care book) and the request by the physician. Users not residing in the Municipality of Bologna must present the health care card, instead of the CUP Card. The CUP operators, or the pharmacist, present the user with the display of available openings in the different town facilities, so that the user can choose the most convenient options. The citizen is issued a booking receipt and the charge payment slip, if due. There are desks managed by operators, desks in the pharmacies and one telephone call centre to book from home. The town's health care facilities send CUP 2000 the openings for different services and referrals. CUP 2000 makes them available to citizens, via the desk network. Via its operational units processing data and managing resources, CUP 2000 links service demand and supply (namely the user's request and the available openings in health care facilities) by organising the access to services.

33 Killian, W., and Wind, M.

34 Mele, V. In V. Mele and M. Meneguzzo, "Designing and Implementing Innovation Policy in the Public Sector: the Italian Experience" Paper presented at the International Public Management Symposium. Edinburgh, March, 2002.

35 Paul Light, The True Size of Government. Brookings Institution, Washington D.C. (1999). In this book — the first that attempts to establish firm estimates of the shadow work force — he explores the reasons why the official size of the federal

government has remained so small while the shadow of government has grown so large. Light examines the political incentives that make the illusion of a small government so attractive, analyzes the tools used by officials to keep the official headcount small, and reveals how the appearance of smallness affects the management of government and the future of the public service. Finally, he points out ways the federal government can better manage the shadow work force it has built over the past half-century.

36 See Borgonovi, E., *Principi e sistemi aziendali per le amministrazioni pubbliche* (2000).

37 Stiglitz, J.E., Orzag P.R., and Orzag J.M., *The Role of Government in a Digital Age,* 2000, p. 39.

38 Ibid., p. 44.

39 Corrigan, P., and Joice, P., 1997

Chapter XIV

Skills for Electronic Service Delivery in Public Agencies

Salvador Parrado, Spanish Distance Learning University, Spain

ABSTRACT

The text analyses the strategy of OECD countries in order to introduce the needed skills for launching e-government services at the national level. The chapter further establishes the four sets of e-government related skills that are needed within the three relevant communities of public servants: information technology community, information management community and service community. It additionally discusses the framework to identify skill gaps through the revision of different assessment toolkits. Finally, it offers an overview of how ICT-related skills can be outsourced. This chapter draws on documents, policy papers and interviews with experts and managers of national e-government strategies from OECD countries.

INTRODUCTION

This chapter deals with the needed skills to implement an e-government strategy. It was commissioned by the Public Management Service [PUMA] of the OECD as part of its e-Government Task Force initiative. The present text, as an updated version, benefits from numerous comments and questions gathered from seminar participants and interviewees.[1] It highlights the most important strategies of OECD countries in relation to e-skills.

Although competencies and skills are used in the text interchangeably, competencies have a broader meaning. They are characteristics of an individual which underline performance or behavior at work. Competency is an observable, measurable pattern of skills, knowledge, abilities, behaviors and other characteristics that an individual needs in order to perform successfully work roles or occupational functions (Barker, 2001). According to this definition, general competencies could be oral communication, problem solving, customer service, while technical competencies are, for instance, infrastructure design, network management, and systems integration. In this chapter, the emphasis is placed on ICT- (Information and Communication Technology) related skills for top managers of public bureaucracies that deliver services electronically.

Two different dimensions have been assigned to electronic service delivery (ESD) or e-government (see Bovaird & Lenihan). One dimension refers to the electronic provision of services and the new capacity to collect, integrate and manage information for the use of the public or for tracking broad societal changes and evaluating governmental actions. Another dimension has a wider meaning. It implies the use of ICT to expand public space enabling the direct participation of stakeholders — citizens, businesses, mass media, NGOs (non-governmental organizations), and other levels of government — in government activities. For the sake of simplicity the concept of "e-government services" encompasses both dimensions in the text.

ESD needs that the right skills are in place. The search for generic skills for the Information Age Society is mostly the concern of Anglo-Saxon countries like Australia, Hong Kong, the United States, Canada and the United Kingdom. In other OECD countries, the work on skills is not emerging, or the search for the right skills is narrowed down to ICT-specific skills for the IT community. While there is recognition that government strategists and business managers are not always fully aware of the implications (software, hardware, relationships with other stakeholders and citizens) of the ICT, the content of training of these professionals lack IT-related contents. Different reasons can be offered for this. Some interviewees have underlined the strong division among IT specialists and generalists and the relatively high control of the formers not only on the technical aspects of e-government strategies but also on the non-technical dimension, i.e., on the overall service strategy. In many non Anglo Saxon countries, the launch of e-government service has been seen as an opportunity for IT specialists to control service delivery.

In order to tackle the issue on skills, four questions will be addressed in the chapter. How can different groups or communities of public servants be identified in relation to e-government services? What ICT skills are linked to different communities? Which instruments could assess the existence of e-skills in those groups or communities? How could the gap of needed skills be filled?

COMMUNITIES OF PUBLIC SERVANTS AND E-GOVERNMENT

The introduction of ICT in the public sector to achieve e-government has facilitated the further specialization of different communities of professionals and has fostered the need of increasing communication needs among communities.

The Canadian government (Treasury Board of Canada Secretariat) has identified three communities [information technology (IT) community, information management (IM) and community and service community (SC)]. Other governments, however, tend to merge the IT and the IM community and accordingly, their skills, under the same label of IT specialists. The differentiation of these two communities proves to be useful for rightly approaching the topic on e-skills.

The information technology (IT) community is relatively easy to recognize. It is basically formed by technical staff that work primarily in fields such as information technology supplies and services, telecommunications, IT consultancy, multi-media and Internet-based products and services. The limits of the information management (IM) community are more blurred. Specialists and managers responsible for the provision of information management services constitute this community. The work of IM professionals encompasses professions like librarians, archivists, and access to information and privacy specialists, communication managers and records managers among others. The members of this community hypothetically have the role of shaping the content management to be produced for different output media.

The service community (SC), formed by general managers and front line staff, provides services to citizens and other stakeholders by traditional or electronic means. The SC is made up of generalists. They develop the whole life cycle of a service. All legal, financial, managerial and other professional experts typically belong to the service community.

The first two communities share the "supply side." They have to meet the business requirements of the demand-side or "end-user" organizations, i.e., the service community.

The boundaries among communities are less clear than suggested by the definitions. For instance, an IT specialist may be appointed (or promoted) to a generalist position. In this post, he ought to master both business- and ICT-related skills. Likewise, it is, for instance, quite difficult to determine whether the design of a portal should be led by an IT specialist, an IM specialist or a generalist. While the IT specialist can claim the connection of the hardware and software to the existing hardware and software of the organization, the IM specialist may focus on the content that should be published in the different output media and the service community member may claim that the portal is another, different interface for service delivery. In many instances, the technological and the content sides of a portal are defined by an IT specialist if the organization lacks IM specialists or IT knowledgeable general managers to face the e-challenge.

These overlaps entail at least one consequence on skills. There are some skills that all three communities should share because they are pursuing the common enterprise of delivering better services through electronic means. Therefore, the more technical communities should be aware of business skills, while general managers should have acquaintance with technical skills.

CLUSTERS OF E-SKILLS

Three sets of skills relate directly to e-government: information technology (IT) skills, information management (IM) skills and information society (IS) skills. Although boundaries among IT, IM and IS skills are blurred, a common-sense distinction has been

Figure 1. Communities and skills

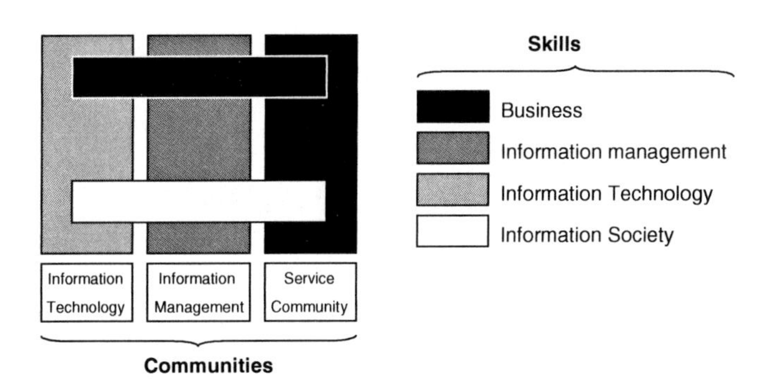

used to link IT and IM skills with "hard" (technical) skills and IS skills with the "soft" ones. IS skills refer exclusively to the ability of recognizing how to make better use of technology for information systems and service provision of the organization.

E-government service requires a combination of skills in each community (see Figure 1), and business and IS skills are cross-cutting for the three communities. The service community should at least have some IS skills, while business skills should be added to the repertoire of the IT and IM communities

The focus of the section will be on IT, IM and IS skills. The skills will be clustered around four sets: (a) strategy and planning, (b) system development, (c) system implementation and (d) service and user support. These clusters are an adaptation of materials from the British Cabinet Office and the Skills Framework for the Information Age (SFIA).

Information Technology (IT) Skills

Information Technology (IT) skills (see Box 1) must be accompanied by business skills for the success of an e-government service. IT skills cannot improve a poorly designed service, and can never replace business skills altogether. IT specialists should take into account the overall service strategy in drafting the IT system (strategy and planning), and establishing networks, databases, and acquiring appropriate software and hardware (system development). Furthermore, IT specialists have to integrate the technical infrastructure with the service requirements (system implementation) and the support of the customer organization, the end-users and the customers (citizens) in the use of ICT systems (service and user support).

IT specialists should have "hard" technical skills that help to design and implement the technical elements (hardware, communication and software) of the e-government service. Moreover, they should have "soft" skills (IS and business skills) for understanding and matching the business strategy to the new technologies.

Information Management (IM) Skills

IM skills allow the adequate deployment of knowledge resources between the different parts of the organization and between the organization and other partners,

Box 1. IT skills

a) Strategy and planning:
It implies understanding the principles of…
- … the service strategy, facilitating thus the implementation of the e-government service.
- … the organisational information system.
- … change management for helping to design the transition from traditional service delivery to e-government services.

Also…
- Designing the technological strategy of the organisation by developing the ICT architecture in terms of components, interfaces, standards, data security and payment for services.
- Auditing existing technological instruments and their adequacy to the strategy of the organisation
- Exploring the existing IT software solutions in the market, in the partners, in other stakeholders and in the public sector in order to achieve the goals of interoperability and interchangeability of data and information with other departments and organisations.

b) System development:
- Establish the communications network of data, voice, text, image and the like.
- Design the database structures and foreseeing its maintenance.
- Design or acquiring and adapting the adequate software in order to meet the service needs.
- Define the terms for the adequate acquisition of external supply of hardware, software, operational and maintenance services when applied.
- Test e-services using a variety of mechanisms like Web sites, digital TV, electronic kiosks, and digital signatures.
- Design instruments in cooperation with partners and stakeholders for integrating processes and exchanging data.
- Facilitate the communication exchange between IT managers, end-users of the service community and customers.
- Design the electronic system to redress customers.

c) System implementation:
- Install new hardware and software, changing components of hardware and software and integrate them with the existing hardware and software systems.
- Administer the network of the organisation and maintain the database structures.
- Implement the security measures of the system in terms of authorisation, provision of authentication of services, investigation of unauthorised access and the like.
- Implement the e-payment policy of the organisation.
- Help to implement or implementing the Web sites and other output media.
- The continuous evaluation of the system through selected performance indicators.

d) Service and user support:
- The maintenance of hardware and software systems.
- The reception of problems reported by the users and the provision of technical fixes.
- The training of end-users to make an appropriate use of technology and designing proper tools for continuous computer literacy policy.

stakeholders, customers and the general public. In the road from dispersed to integrated electronic services, IM skills play an extraordinary role. Leadership in IM means understanding the business-related issues associated with the management of information and ensuring that IM functions and services are positioned to address those issues, especially in an e-government context.

IM skills complement business skills. The IM community should take into account business skills to deliver e-services effectively, while the service community needs some IM skills in order to plan and implement e-services adequately.

The Canadian government has undertaken promising work on IM skills and the contribution of IM leaders to e-government. An IM Competency Working Group was set up to oversee the project on Competency Profile. As a starting point, an online repository of actual work descriptions was established. The committee is identifying common traits in the work descriptions for positions that are aligned to the needs of e-government. According to an interviewee, the work seems to show that these positions will require more specialized skills, a higher use of technology, involve advisory functions and carry a higher level of accountability (see also TSCS, 2004).

Ed Fine (2003) suggests that IM leaders should be aware of a mix of traditional and emerging roles, including responsibility for: "strategies, policies, standards, good practices; enterprise-wide, integrated information architecture; managing information

Box 2. IM skills

a) Strategy and planning: IM specialists should take into account the overall service strategy in drafting the IM system strategy by:

- Understanding the business, the processes and the overall strategy of the organisation in order to better design the information system.
- Helping to identify relevant sources of information and relevant information to the business of the organisation and to the external stakeholders, partners and citizens.
- Filtering and codifying information in line with the service strategy of the organisation.
- Designing the strategy for information management in the organisation by developing the formats for exchanging, retrieving and sharing information within the organisation and with external partners, stakeholders and customers.
- Auditing existing information management systems and their adequacy to the strategy of the organisation.
- Exploring the existing information management practices in the market, in the partners, other stakeholders, and the public sector in order to achieve the goals of interoperability and interchangeability of data and information.

b) System development:

- Designing the system of retrieving and keeping information electronically for future use.
- Helping to establish the contents to be provided for various output media and target groups.
- Designing the technical system to update and maintain information in different output media.

c) System implementation and maintenance:

- Administering and maintaining the archive system composed of traditional and electronic means.
- Administering and maintaining the knowledge content from external and internal sources of information and making sure that content is available to relevant groups.
- Implementing the content management system for various output media and target groups.

d) Service and user support: Finally, among the IM skills should be included the support of the customer organisation, the end-users and the customers (citizens) in the use of information. Thus, IT skills should imply:

- The continuous evaluation of the system through selected performance indicators.
- The maintenance and the update of the information.
- The reception of problems reported by the users.
- The design of training programmes to facilitate an appropriate use of information through the new tools by helping the service community, and eventually the citizens, in navigating and interrogating information sources, assessing and evaluating information, creating, recording and storing information, i.e., designing proper tools for continuous information literacy policy.

flows within core business processes; enabling innovation and risk management through information sharing and supporting service delivery with content rich extranets."

Corporate information flows are complex and there is an increasing need to understand and manage them. IM skills (see Box 2) are distributed among different professions, especially librarians and archivists. While librarians have focused largely on the acquisition and the distribution of external information; record managers (archivists) have developed their own particular discipline from an inner perspective in many public agencies, while in others they are involved in the design and implementation of portals. Advisory cabinets, internal advisers, consultants, strategic planners are also examples of information rich areas that often set up their own information systems away from the organizational systems. The concepts of information sharing, utilization and creation imply a level of information handling skills which has been taken for granted but not explored in depth.

Although Librarian and Information Specialists (LIS) and Record Management (RM) skills are of enormous importance in an e-service strategy, it seems that both professions have had little impact on the management of information and knowledge of public organizations. The service community seems to rely little on LIS and RM professionals, because of their perception as professions that seldom engage with "the business" (TFPL, 1999).

Information Society (IS) Skills

IS skills imply, especially for the service community, the ability of recognizing how to make better use of ICT resources in order to implement a responsive e-government strategy. IS skills complement the business skills and intersect at some points with the IT and IM skills (Figure 2).

An e-government strategy requires that the whole organization gain information and computer literacy. Four sets of IS skills are key for the service community (see Box 3):

a. Relationship management with suppliers, with end-users, with customers and with other stakeholders.

Figure 2. Skills for e-government initiatives

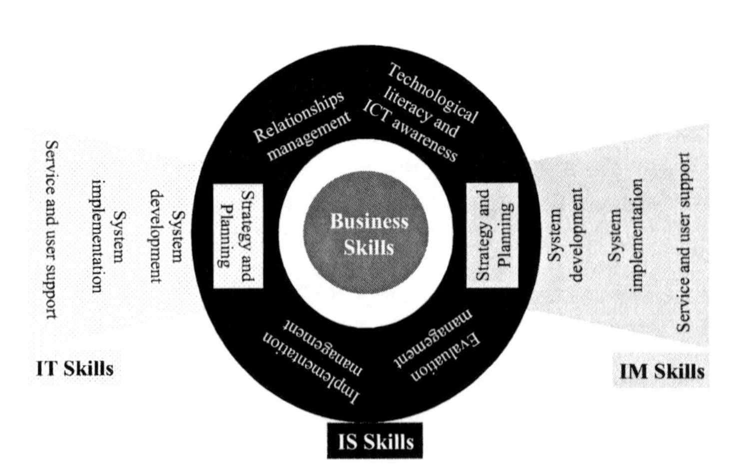

b. Technological literacy and ICT awareness to support the business strategy.
c. Implementation management.
d. Evaluation management.

These sets of IT, IM and IS skills, or similar ones, should enable the relevant managers to ensure that the information systems are beneficial to the activities of the organization, that the relevant technologies are contributing to the effective e-govern-

Box 3. IS skills

a) Relationships management: An e-government strategist should…:
(regarding citizens-customers)

- Decide the level of involvement of customers in decision-making and in consultation of e-services.
- Decide the level of responsiveness *vis à vis* customers in e-services.
- Consult citizens on how e-government services should be planned.
- Help to design the frameworks for redressing customers.

(regarding suppliers)

- Establish long-lasting relationships with ICT specialists from outside and from in-house. In case of external supply, this entails ensuring the efficient acquisition of ICT supplies and defining the basic and broad requirements of ICT-based services (based on Smart Cards, Call Centres, Cell Phones, Webs, etc.) to be delivered.
- Define the level of ICT integration with suppliers of different services (not necessarily ICT services) and other stakeholders.

(regarding end-users or in-house staff)

- Ensure that the in-house end-users of information systems have the adequate support and training.
- Involve all end-users in the use of the information system. End-users should not only be able to get information from the system but also give inputs to it.
- Consult end-users on how the e-government service should be planned.

(regarding partners)

- Identify common sources of cooperation to achieve seamless government.
- Help to establish governance principles of transparency, responsiveness, responsibility and equity among different partners.

b) Technological literacy and ICT awareness to support business strategy and management: An awareness of ICT and the acquisition of the right technological literacy implies an understanding of:

- the meaning of technology developments in terms of the information system of the organisation and also in regards to the e-government service strategy. This also includes a continuous scanning of technological tools that could support the business strategy.
- the principles underlying the ICT architecture of the organisation and the possibility of innovation and expansion.
- the broad technical aspects of ICT supply and provision in order to do an adequate monitoring of the activities of suppliers.
- the principles of an information system strategy.
- the limits of the use of information by staff, suppliers, customers, and partners.
- the standards for security, privacy and authentication work, so that these standards can be met.
- the principles of risk management that are ICT–related.

c) Implementation management: The e-government strategist should …

- Establish the relationships and responsibilities between the supply-side (technology) and the demand-side (e-services).
- Ensure that the end-users deliver e-services in an appropriate manner by meeting quality standards.
- Combine traditional channels and electronic channels of e-government service delivery.

d) Evaluation management: The e-service strategist should be able to…

- Identify and apply a library of indicators (with other stakeholders if necessary) in order to adequately evaluate the impact of a strategy of e-services.

ment service, that the information resources are managed in an effective and efficient way, that the agreements between the supply and the demand side are effectively negotiated and that the organization can successfully plan and implement an e-government service. While the three sets of skills are of great importance, it is taken for granted that IT/IM specialists are aware of the new technologies and the potential use for delivering e-services. However, top managers of the service community seem to be unaware of the potential of new technologies and the training and recruiting programs do not often include IS skills.

ASSESSMENT OF CURRENT LEVEL OF E-SKILLS

The development of an e-service strategy should entail an assessment of the current capability (skills availability) of the organization. Several national approaches assess the current level of skills: the British Cabinet Office focuses on available skills and skill gaps; the Canadian government concentrates on competencies and jobs skills profiles; and the KPMG proposal for the German BundOnline initiative analyses the readiness of an organization to deliver e-services with mention to e-skills.

The E-Business Skills Assessment Toolkit

This toolkit was developed as an instrument to help Departments identifying the skill gaps in their organization as part of developing an e-service strategy. Besides, the toolkit should deliver a cross-government view of skill-related issues and gaps to the British Cabinet Office. The toolkit provides a comprehensive checklist of all possible requirements, and it assesses separately two sets of skills: technical professional skills and business system management skills. The British Central IT Unit (CITU) of the Cabinet Office merges the IT and IM skills in the first set and the business and IS skills in the second one (Cabinet Office, 2000).

Each set of skills (technical and business) is broken down into seven clusters or areas of skills. For each cluster, a questionnaire of nine questions assesses the relevance of listed skills for the successful implementation of the organizational e-strategy, the critical skills for that success, the internal or external availability of these skills and the skill gaps among other aspects. The assessment of each question is marked in a three-point scale. Unavailability of a critical skill indicates that the organization should fill the gap as soon as possible. An aggregate result of unavailability of certain critical skills across different departments and agencies requires also further central action.

According to an interviewee from the Cabinet Office, many departments incorporated the results of their analysis using the toolkit into their early e-service strategies. This allowed them to consider skills issues as part of the risk analysis and for remedial action to be taken where necessary. Departments had to assess their skill needs in the context of whether the technological systems had been outsourced or were still provided by the in-house staff. In the event of outsourcing, some of the responsibility for identifying and addressing skill needs would rest with the provider. The current situation seems to suggest that things have moved on more generally. Besides monitoring the requirements for skills with the skills assessment toolkit, departments and central government are increasingly focusing on taking action to address a broader range of skill needs that are included in the category of business skills and information society skills. These skills include: leadership, project and program management, related commercial skills and IT literacy. In other words, the British agencies realize that more technical skills (hard skills) are important, but not enough to address an e-service strategy. The business strategy should have priority, while IT awareness is an important complement.

The toolkit provides a very useful and detailed checklist of almost every single skill that an e-government service would require. However, it is not very clear who should fill in the questionnaire, based on a self-assessment exercise. While it would make sense that the human resource unit co-ordinates the exercise, extensive consultation with specialists and business managers is required. Finally, the process of self-assessing the skill needs of the organization seem to represent a burden for some organizations, especially those that are unable or unwilling to undertake such an enterprise. Perhaps a more simplified version would help some agencies in identifying skill gaps.

The IT Job Competency Profiles

Canada's Treasury Board Secretariat (2000) explored the adoption of a community-led, competency-based approach to HR Management for the IT Community. IT Job Competency Profiles are one key element of the process. A competency-based approach has potential to allow the flexible, adaptable responses required in dynamic modern organizations. It also reflects an assumption that the knowledge and experience of individual public servants will be more critically important. Furthermore, the role of managers will increasingly involve encouraging and supporting individuals willing to take initiative to manage their own development and career progression. Competency profiles can help to identify optimal candidates in staffing processes; link development and training to sustained high performance and provide valid foundation for recruitment, selection and training (Barker, 2001).

The IT Job Competency Profiles provide a common basis for comparing requirements for similar positions within and across departments and jurisdictions. Improved awareness of the skills and competencies needed in various types of positions allows IT professionals and managers to make better informed decisions about learning and training plans to meet both individual and organizational goals. But competencies are only useful if the competency profiles are kept up-to-date, and if there is a consistent, effective and accepted way of assessing competencies of applicants for positions, and of employees for development and for effective performance management and work assignments.

Processes are being developed to assess and record individual competencies which, if successfully implemented across the community, could reduce the substantial time and other resources devoted to retesting job applicants and employees for competencies they have already proven. Moreover, Canada is implementing the first version of a Web-based self-assessment tool to allow individuals to compare their personal qualifications to the competencies required in IT positions for which they may wish to prepare themselves.

Adopting a community-wide competency taxonomy should help to reinforce the Canadian government's commitment to lifelong learning by providing an incentive to improve qualifications in anticipation of a range of career possibilities, rather than focusing on training individuals for specific positions. The organization benefits from having individuals with increased ability to perform in their current positions, and from the flexibility of being able to draw on pre-qualified individuals when positions come open. The IT Competency Profiles and the accompanying assessment tools being developed in Canada have the potential to provide the basis for an inventory of individual competencies and learning plans. Such an inventory would put both individual departments and the overall IT Community in a better position to predict skill gaps, allocate learning resources and do succession planning.

Canada's competency-based approach identifies skills for particular types of jobs, while the British Skills Assessment Toolkit is a generic tool that assesses whether the required skills exist in the organization. It does not matter whether these skills are in one particular job or not. Unlike the British toolkit, Canada's approach makes possible very detailed career and training plans customized for each individual in each hierarchical level and an overall assessment of specific capacities across the community. This richness of information entails a considerable amount of work, making it more suitable for agencies already used to the competency approach and more generic job descriptions, but probably less suited for public agencies that still use traditional job assessments.

The types of information that the competency-based approach can provide include whether a candidate for a position has the competencies and skills or has the potential to attain those competencies and skills required; the types of training and/or development an individual would need to qualify for a specific position; and whether there is a career path for the individual within the particular organization or whether they should expect to move outside that organization to achieve career goals. In contrast, the e-skills assessment toolkit has a broader focus and it provides information about whether the candidate's particular skills exist somewhere in the organization, in a team or in an individual position-holder. The Canadian approach allows not only the organizational-level HR planning possible with e-skills assessment, but also allows significant HR planning at the individual and group level in order to meet changing job requirements.

The Net-Readiness Analysis

The Net-Readiness Analysis has been devised by KPMG for the BundOnline 2005 strategy of the German Government and has been placed in the e-government manual of the German Federal Office for Information Security (*Bundesamt für Sicherheit in der Informationstechnik*). The Net-Readiness analysis is a self-assessment instrument that should help to evaluate the e-government capacity of an organization.

The analysis is undertaken through a questionnaire that could be answered either by single individuals or by teams within the organization. The analysis follows the four dimensions of a model (technology, learning skills, leadership and organization). Each part is structured around 10 questions and each one accounts for 50 points. With the overall addition of points, a Net Readiness Scorecard can be built up. For each position in the final scale, there is a label of the organization in terms of Net Readiness and a subsequent list of recommendations can follow after working out the position of the organization in this scale.

For instance, a "visionary organization" (more than 180 points) is, according to KPMG, an organization that is a pathfinder in e-government services and is very successful in its Internet activities. This organization may serve as a model for other agencies. A "savvy organization" (between 120 and 179 points) has awareness for the potential results that e-government can trigger and the organization is able to follow and understand what the competitors or similar organizations do in terms of e-government services. In this kind of organization, some resources have been allocated for e-government strategies and some processes are under study of being changed or have already been changed. The challenges would be to extend these partial initiatives to an overall picture.

This instrument offers a first approach to the e-capacity of a specific public organization. However, there are some problems linked to the ICT skills in this instrument. Firstly, skills represent a minor part of this assessment tool, and although there are recommendations to improve the skills of the organization after the exercise, this cannot be followed from the questions for each dimension. Secondly, this instrument is based on numeric overall points that give a general idea of how "agnostic" or "visionary" an organization is in terms of e-government. An overall numeric mark does not help very much in terms of searching for the specific gaps of the system. Therefore, this instrument could be used as a starting point, but—in terms of skills—more specific tools are needed.

Assessing ICT-Related Skills: Getting the Fittest Instrument for the Organization

It is difficult to establish the same and unique guidelines that could be followed by different countries. Some governments are designing central systems to identify and assess the level of ICT skills in public organizations while other governments are fully unaware of how to plan the improvement of ICT skills in public agencies. The research into OECD countries showed that most countries have not given much importance to the need of IS skills for the service community (especially for top managers). In some organizations, human resource managers are used to dealing with job profiles or with self-assessment tools, while many public agencies have never undertaken a self-assessment of any kind. In these conditions, there is not a best-for-all tool. Each organization should select and use an adequate instrument to fit the current HRM practices of the organization.

The assessment of e-skills gap for the three communities is an urgent job for many public agencies. In some cases, the specific needed skills are very obvious and any common sense self-assessment exercise can tell that without any specific methodology. In other cases, some instruments may help identify the skills gap. The British and the Canadian tools seem to be good instruments to tackle this question but at the same time they are complex (too many questions, too many sets of skills) and hard to use for inexperienced or busy managers. That was at least the reactions of managers in related ICT services in countries where self-assessments for required skills have not been implemented.

At OECD seminars, an easier-to-use tool was presented (Parrado, 2002). It can be summarized as follows. The more detailed lists of skills (from the Skills Assessment Tool, for instance) are useful for those organizations that are used to work with skills; other newcomer organizations should focus on the core skills.

Once the short list of skills has been decided upon, a decision should be made on the appropriate questions that could help identify the skills gap. The organization could use four parameters to assess the importance of particular skills for the e-strategy, the availability of these skills, the need to maintain them in-house and whether or not the organization should undertake further actions.

Further actions could be graphically represented by a traffic light system. Red meaning that urgent actions should be enacted; amber implying that further actions should be planned and/or implemented; green meaning that the organization has the proper capacity in these skills.

The self-assessment exercise should be undertaken by representatives from each community: IT, IM and SC.

The output cards should show that the different sets of skills cannot always be seen isolated, as there are strong connections among different sets of skills and different communities (see Figure 2). It is not necessary to ascertain exactly whether a skill is very important or not. Several outside observers may think differently about one particular skill, even though it is important in the perception of the leading staff of the organization (from the three communities). If a particular skill is important and not available, something must be done.

Nevertheless, in some public agencies, some questions still remain. Would the leadership be able to clearly link importance and availability of skills to their strategy? Would they be able to undertake such an exercise or would they need external help for this self-assessment? They could always seek for advice from consultancy firms from the private sector. There are other solutions from within the public sector through different means of recruiting and training (see Settles) or by means of competence centres (see next section).

OUTSOURCING E-SKILLS?

Once skills gap have been identified, can the organization fill the gap with in-house skills or does it need to buy those needed skills from an external contractor?

It was previously suggested that the skills assessment tool could contain a question on whether a specific skill (or set of skills) should be taken care of in-house or not. This requires further explanation. It is almost impossible to offer a list of those skills that should necessarily remain in-house for all kinds of organizations and services in all countries. This issue should be examined through an assessment exercise of the concerned organization.

The Finnish Ministry issued a policy decision of the Council of State on the Development of Information Management of State Administration in which concerns were developed around the idea of outsourcing information management tasks. The document explicitly mentioned that attention should be "paid to the maintenance of adequate leadership, planning, acquisition and information-security know-how in the office. In outsourcing, the risks and total costs thereof, the tasks of the office and the nature of the services subject to outsourcing as well as especially the possibilities of the office to steer and inspect the appropriate handling of the outsourced services and information security shall be taken into consideration." The Ministry of Finance announced that regulations and instructions relating to outsourcing would be issued.

According to interviewees from the Finnish Ministry of Finance in the Finnish government, the analysis of outsourcing of IT functions has been done for five agencies.

At first, the Ministry of Finance analyzed the skills these departments currently have and which ones would be required in 2006. Apparently, the differences were not daunting. Basic skills that should remain in-house were: project management, data security, IT strategy and procurement skills, although these skills may change for different agencies.

Outsourcing is then an important strategy to buy skills that cannot be found in-house but it also entails risks if the outsourced skills are core to the e-government service and the external provider fails to provide them adequately. There are then two different questions: What questions do we pose to know if specific skills could be contracted out? Once a decision has been reached to contract out, what checklist of questions could be used to do a pre-outsourcing exercise?

Regarding the first question, some dimensions could be offered. These dimensions relate to risk management issues, to the privacy, confidentiality and security of data on customers and to the relationship between the business skills and ICT-related skills under scrutiny. By checking those dimensions against the list of skills, any organization should have a fair idea of what could be outsourced or not.

Regarding the second issue, the pre-outsourcing exercise, a checklist of different items grouped in four sets could help an organization to identify how the IT services could be outsourced (see Box 4). Two basic skills are involved in the exercise: Are the skills available in the organization to do the pre-outsourcing exercise? Are the skills available to monitor the contract? (Adapted from Gramatikov, 2002.)

The first issue of Box 4 is critical. If the team considering outsourcing lacks decision capability, external aid should be sought. Ideally, the drafting team should consist of people from the different identified communities (IT, IM and the Service Community). At least one member of the team should have a legal background, while another person at least should be a financial expert. While it is assumed that the managerial, legal and financial expertise can be traditionally found in any organization, the required ICT expertise may be absent. Moreover, the outsourcing team should check if the hard skills of the clusters "Strategy and planning" and "System development" are present in the IT community of the organization so that the outsourcing exercise can be safely made.

Box 4. Check-list for outsourcing ICT related skills

Pre-outsourcing question on skills
• What is the skill level of the organisation for deciding the pre-outsourcing conditions?
IT function and the e-government service
• Is the organizational IT function clearly defined or definable? • How critical is the IT service level for the performance and the strategies of the organization? • What are the strengths and weaknesses of the internal provision of IT? • What are the middle- and long-term perspectives of the internal and external provision of IT?
Cost of e-government services and market competition
• Does the market provide for cost optimisation? • What is the total cost of operating the service? • What is the total cost of ownership of the IT assets? • What is the level of competition on the market?
Skills level to manage the contract
• What are the experience and the skill level of the organization in management of complex contractual relations?

The second issue of Box 4 refers to the present relationship of the IT function and the service. In this regard, the outsourcing team should collect performance indicators of the current IT infrastructure and question whether the current level of IT is enough for the organization and can help to satisfy the services demand. A list of indicators can be helpful in this regard (Gramatikov, 2002) (see Box 5).

This kind of information will help to compare the bids and to decide whether the market can provide the service at a sufficient quality.

Regarding the third issue of Box 4: "Cost of e-government services and market competition," the outsourcing team should be able to ascertain the total cost of ownership for hardware, software and network components of the IT and to assess the different offers from the market. A vague perception of the cost of the services is of little help when the public manager has to conduct cost-benefit analysis. Thus, price and levels of service performance are the two components of the outsourcing decision. In order to ease this task, the outsourcing team can break down the IT services to be outsourced into functions and separate from the rest those generic functions for which there are more standardized parameters and the outsourcing decisions are easier to handle. The list of Box 6 offers some suggestions (Gramatikov, 2002).

The final set of questions (Box 5) refers to whether the outsourcing team has the required skills for managing the contract. This means to:

- Draft the specifications of the IT services which will be transferred outside and determine, for instance, the Service Level Agreements that provide the regulation of responsibilities of the parties according to the demand for and supply of the service within the contract.
- Determine the incentives for excelling performance and penalties against under-performance.
- Set up and maintain an effective system for controlling the IT-provided services.
- Finish the outsourcing contract in due time (for updating the system) or in case of risk of disruption of the e-government service.

The outsourcing exercise is a complex task and some help from other public agencies is welcomed. The German government has devised Competence Centres in order to coach

Box 5. Indicators for assessing current IT infrastructure

- number of servers and desktops in use in the organization
- percentage of uptime
- request for desktop help per day
- lines of source code
- proprietary and off-the-shelf applications used in the organization
- transactions per second, hour, day or week
- mean bandwidth capacity
- mean delay time for processing, storing, publishing, printing etc. requests
- time for learning the system
- interoperability with existing internal or external systems
- level of compliance with planned IT systems
- level of standardization required for the organization IT system

Box 6. Functions of IT services

- Desktop maintenance, application development and implementation, data warehousing, transition from legacy systems to client-server environment, network access services, helpdesk services, LANs and WANs, virtual private networks, identification and authorization services, Internet and intranet,
- Applications development and maintenance, EPR systems, payroll processing, accountancy applications,
- Various data centre and databases applications, electronic fund transfers, B2Government applications, e-procurement, etc.,

and complement in-house e-skills of different agencies. These centres could also be of help in outsourcing exercises, although their primary functions are rather different.

The five competence centres designed by the German government have the following features:

1. *Processes and Organization.* The competence centre should help the agency to align the processes of the organization through analyzing the workflow and undertaking process reengineering when necessary with the designed e-government services.
2. *Job Processing and Document Management.* The competence centre should foster the cooperation between those involved in document-intensive processes in accordance with specific rules and methods. Its activities should cover those that establish the order in which individual steps of a job are to be processed and which staffing, material and organizational resources are needed for implementation.
3. *Data Security.* The competence centre on this issue will help agencies to ensure and get the citizens' trust on e-government services through the correct set up of the encryption and authentication instruments, the enhance of confidentiality by protecting data against unauthorized access, the establishment of integrity by protecting data against incorrect manipulation and the assurance of authenticity by ensuring that a message actually comes from the person or institution claiming to be the sender of the communication.

In the three previous competence centres, activities are centrally planned but locally provided. However, the next two competence centres offer basic components that are suited for central planning and central provision.

4. *Content Management System (CMS).* The CMS is to provide topical, relevant content for various output media and target groups, as well as implementing their creation, requirement for the provision and the ongoing updating of considerable information offerings of authorities on the Internet. Some public agencies may not have the CMS, therefore, a centrally provided solution might be of great help.
5. *e-Payment Platform.* The provision of a central platform for payment requires that different interfaces are integrated within the respective application.

The competence centres will be staffed with 25 to 30 experts from the German public administration and external industry experts/IT consultants. The centres will initialize, monitor and coach projects from different federal agencies. In doing so, these competence centers would be an optimal solution to help the organization in two ways: either fostering the in-house work for implementing the e-government services or assessing them in the outsourcing exercise. Thus, the skill gaps can be filled with external aid under public sector supervision.

CONCLUSIONS

This chapter has collected and analyzed leading experiences of OECD countries in identifying communities of public servants, in using instruments to assess e-skill gaps (at the individual- and agency-level) and offering some ideas about how to fill those skill gaps.

The identification of three different communities: information technology (IT), information management (IM) and service community (SC) should help to further identify their leaders, the sets of skills they need for e-service strategies, and the gaps in e-skills for individual-, organizational- and community-levels.

From the different international experiences it seems that four sets of skills are needed for e-service strategies: information technology (IT), information management (IM), information society (IS), and business skills. These sets of skills (except business skills) have been kept to the most meaningful ones and have been broken down into four clusters in this chapter. IS skills are important because they constitute the link between technology and business from the perspective of the service community. Business skills are relevant for members of the IT and IM community in order to adequately integrate the technology into the service. IT skills have been sufficiently developed in some countries while IM skills are rarely attracting the attention from governments. These skills seem to hold the key to the future of e-government services as they should be able to connect communities of public servants, stakeholders and the general public.

There are basically two approaches for identifying skill gaps. One is based upon job Competency Profiles, which is used for the individual-, the organizational- and the community-level (Canadian approach). The other approach is based upon skill needs of an entire agency (British approach). It has been suggested that both approaches are useful instruments, but they should match the current HRM practices of the organization. For agencies with less developed HRM, more easy-to-use tools are advised.

In order to fill the skill gaps, we have discussed just one option: outsourcing (while training and recruitment have been dealt with in the chapter from Settles in this book).

For the outsourcing exercise, it is recommended to build up a pre-outsourcing team with members from the three communities (IT, IM, Service community) from the organization that should go through a check-list. The team should check the dangers of outsourcing particular skills, the relationship between the IT and the service, the costs of different providers and the capabilities of the organization in order to monitor the contract. In the pre-outsourcing exercise, public competence centres, shaped after the German experience, could be of great help.

REFERENCES

Barker, S. M. (2001). Information technology competency-based job profile. Retrieved June 25, 2004, from *http://www.opm.gov/compconf/postconf01/it/sbarker.htm*

British Computer Society. (2004). Retrieved June 29, 2004, from *http://www1.bcs.org.uk*

BSI. (2002). Chefsache E-Government: Leitfaden für Behördenleiter. E-Government Handbuch. Bonn: Bundesamt für Sicherheit in der Informationstechnik. Retrieved June 26, 2004, from *www.e-government-handbuch.de*

Bundesregierung. (2001). Umsetzungsplan für die eGovernment-Initiative [Implementation plan for the "BundOnline 2005" eGovernment initiative.] Retrieved June 25, 2004. from *http://www.bmi.bund.de/downloadde/16396/Download.pdf*

Cabinet Office. (2000a). Successful IT: Modernising government in action. Retrieved June 29, 2004, from *http://www.ogc.gov.uk/index.asp?docid=2632*

Cabinet Office. (2000b). E-business skills assessment toolkit. Retrieved June 20, 2004, from *http://e-government.cabinetoffice.gov.uk/Resources/Guidelines/fs/en*

Cabinet Office. (2000c). Skills in the information age. Retrieved June 20, 2004, from *http://e-government.cabinetoffice.gov.uk/Resources/OtherPublications/fs/en*

Fine, E. (2003). The IM leadership initiative. Retrieved June 27, 2004, from *http://www.cio-dpi.gc.ca/oro-bgc/imli-ilgi/pres/initiative/page01_e.asp*

Gramatikov, M. (2002). Outsourcing of public information systems. UNPAN. Retrieved June 26, 2004, from *http://unpan1.un.org/intradoc/groups/public/documents/untc/unpan003861.pdf*

Melitski, J. (2002). The world of e-government and e-governance. Retrieved June 26, 2004, from *http://www.aspanet.org/solutions/egovworld.html*

Ministry of Defence. (2000a). Modernising defence training: Report of the dDefence training review (volume 1). Retrieved June 26, 2004, from *http://www.mod.uk/linked_files/dtr_vol1.pdf*

Ministry of Defence. (2000b). Modernising defence training: Report of the defence training review (volume 2). Retrieved June 26, 2004, from *http://www.mod.uk/linked_files/dtr_vol2.pdf*

Ministry of Defence. (2001). Armed forces e-skilling (chapter 4). Retrieved June 26, 2004, from *http://www.mod.uk/linked_files/deb2001_ch4-10.pdf*

Parrado, S. (2004). ICT related skills for e-government. Paper presented for the *OECD E-Government Project at the Seminar on Reform of Public Administrations OECD*, Paris, September 23-24.

Skills Framework for the Information Age. (2004). Retrieved June 20, 2004, from *http://www.e-skills.com/cgi-bin/wms.pl/335*

Treasury Board of Canada Secretariat. (1999). Strategic directions for information management and information technology: Enabling 21st century service to Canadians. Retrieved June 26, 2004, from *http://www.tbs-sct.gc.ca/Pubs_pol/ciopubs/TB_OIMP/sdimit_e.html*

Treasury Board of Canada Secretariat. (2000). IT job competency profiles. Retrieved June 26, 2004, from *http://www.cio-dpi.gc.ca/oro-bgc/learning/jswg-gtpc/it-comprofil-ti/it-comprofil-ti00_e.asp*

Treasury Board of Canadian Secretariat. (2004). Retrieved June 26, 2004, from *http://www.cio-dpi.gc.ca/oro-bgc/im/im_e.asp*

ENDNOTE

1 I would like to acknowledge the help from Santiago Segarra, Ernesto Abati, Luis Felipe Paradela, Tomás Muñoz, Tony Bovaird, David Hickman, Ed Fine, Helen McDonald, Sandra Bogdanovic, Ralf Kleindiek, Timo Hauschild, Olavi Köngäs, Olli-Pekka Rissanen, Masaaki Nakagawa and Brigid Feeny. I am also very thankful for the help of Elizabeth Muller from OECD. Errors of this document are entirely mine.

Chapter XV

Identifying Effective Funding Models for E-Government*

Franklin S. Reeder, The Reeder Group, Inc., USA

Susan M. Pandy, Virginia Polytechnic Institute and State University, USA

ABSTRACT

Historically, and some would argue quite properly, most major information technology investments have been considered and allocated in the context of the particular programs that those investments would support. As some OECD countries have made electronic enabling government processes (e-government) a visible priority, alternative, more horizontal, approaches to securing and managing the required investments have emerged.

INTRODUCTION

This chapter, part of an overall OECD project on the impact of e-government, examines the central budgetary rules and processes and how they are being or could be adapted to finance investments in e-government. In particular, the chapter looks at three countries (New Zealand, the United Kingdom and the United States) and examines the techniques and models that they are using to secure and manage funding for high priority e-government projects. In each country, we examined: (1) strategies and policy initiatives for e-government; (2) structures and processes for financing capital investments and, in particular, investments in information and communications technology (ICT); and (3) how those processes are being modified or adapted to address the imperatives of each government's e-government initiatives.

Beyond describing those processes, this chapter seeks to identify public management issues, including the tension between central management and control and decentralized funding. This is not a comparative analysis. These countries were chosen because they, as well as other OECD countries, have made a strong, high-level commitment to implementing e-government.

Drawing on some illustrative examples, this chapter presents a range of approaches to managing and creating incentives for e-government and identifies public management issues that arise in that process. The ultimate purpose of this chapter is to provide conceptual and definitional guidelines for complementary research which may include case studies and other types of data collection.

In the countries that we examined, we found a continuum of budgeting practices ranging from traditional vertical approaches, where financing is evaluated only in the context of a particular organization or program, to more horizontal approaches where financing is drawn for a number of agency budgets to central funding of cross-agency or government-wide initiatives. Each approach has its advocates and advantages. *Vertical* funding requires ICT investments to compete against other claims for investments within the same program (e.g., should we buy a piece of surgical equipment or a computer for a hospital) and sharpens the discussion of the business case for a proposal in terms of how it will contribute to the program or organizational objective (e.g., improving public health) but makes it difficult to finance ICT investments that benefit more than one agency or program, whether for commonly used infrastructure or even applications that might be used by multiple agencies (e.g., loan portfolio management). *Horizontal* funding addresses this deficiency in vertical funding by encouraging pooling of resources. It retains the advantage of having investments compete against other priorities within a program. We found limited use of a third option, *central funding*, where a central unit of government allocates a pool of resources to high priority or innovative e-government initiatives that are not likely to obtain initial financing using other approaches.

Among the innovative approaches to financing e-government investment that were found were the use of central innovation funds, to finance projects that were highly innovative or cross-cutting and not likely to gain funding using conventional means. The portion of ICT investment funds allocated through this mechanism is still quite small. Notwithstanding all the rhetoric that might suggest otherwise, traditional vertical funding remains the primary means of financing e-government projects. Private-sector financing remains an important source of funding but not in the way one might imagine. While there is much discussion of concepts like joint-ventures, co-branding, and gain-sharing, private financing manifests itself most importantly through leasing and other similar arrangements and in the government's growing reliance on private investment in the basic ICT infrastructure on which e-government projects increasingly rely.

WHY A CHAPTER ON FINANCING E-GOVERNMENT?

Arguably, the issues around financing investments in information and communications technologies (ICT) or e-government projects should be no different from those involved in financing any capital project. And to a significant degree, that is the case. But it is also the case that the process of obtaining financing is a critical element in whether or not a project will succeed or even get off the ground at all. As this chapter will presumably demonstrate, however, the process and politics of budgeting for ICT are materially different in a number of important respects and, therefore, are worth examining as a separate subject.

Financing ICT projects differs from other capital projects in several important respects:

(1) Existing structures and budget decision-making processes often do not readily accommodate these initiatives because the current wave ICT projects often cross traditional programmatic and organizational lines.

(2) These projects are seldom self-contained, in the sense that constructing a building or dam often is, because they usually rely on the existence of other ICT infrastructure.

(3) Risk management is inherently different in large, complex ICT projects than it is in brick and mortar projects. and

(4) Financing, or the lack thereof, is often seen as an impediment to the current wave of e-government projects.

Thus, we would argue that the issues and challenges in the budget process faced by government officials seeking to advance e-government are sufficiently different to warrant an examination of how that dynamic has played out in OECD countries.

DEFINING BASIC TERMS

For the Purposes of This Chapter

Capital and *capital budgeting.* The U.S. President's Commission on Capital Budgeting defines *capital* as follows: "Spending that yields benefits beyond the typical reporting period (such as a year) should be considered to be investment, and 'capital' refers to the assets created by this spending." Accounting standards typically take a narrower view that capital is physical and certain intangible assets. Rather than engaging in the debate as to whether or not an information system is a capital asset, we take the view that ICT systems do indeed produce benefits beyond the period in which they are financed and that budgeting for them is a capital budgeting question.

E-government "focuses on the use of new information and communications technologies (ICT) by governments as applied to the full range of government functions. In particular, the networking potential offered by the Internet and related technologies has the potential to transform the structures and operation of government" (OECD – PUMA(2001)10REV2). Some countries have identified a specific subset of their ICT projects as e-government initiatives. This chapter seeks to examine the current state of the practice for financing the totality of a government's ICT portfolio, not just those projects labeled as e-government. Thus, while the terms are not entirely synonymous, ICT and e-government are used somewhat interchangeably throughout this chapter.

Horizontal approaches *refers to efforts to finance and manage projects across organizational (ministry, department, or agency) lines.*

Vertical approaches means the traditional structures of managing projects and information within organizational boundaries, often also referred to as stovepipes.

SUMMARY OF COUNTRY FINDINGS

This section summarizes our findings in examining the e-government financing policies and practices in three countries — New Zealand, the United Kingdom and the United States. Specifically, we have attempted to learn about each government's:

1. strategies and policy initiatives for e-government — brief description of major government-wide initiatives that establish the overall e-government policy framework;
2. structures and processes for financing capital investments and, in particular, investments in information and communications technology (ICT); and
3. approach as far as how those processes are being modified or adapted to address the imperatives of each government's e-government initiatives.

New Zealand

E-Government Laws and Policies

E-government in New Zealand has its origins in work by the State Services Commission on public sector information management, conducted in conjunction with the Chief Executives' Group on Information Management & Technology (now defunct), during 1997/98. This work culminated in a briefing paper to the Minister of State Services and Minister of Information Management and Technology in December 1999, which provided the first outline of an overall e-government program for New Zealand. The briefing advocated using e-government initiatives to shift government from a "silo" model to a networked model.

New Zealand's e-government strategy was first released in April 2001 and subsequently updated in December 2001. The Strategy is built around a four-phased approach to developing e-government over the long-run. The first phase involves developing a Web presence across the public sector. Phase II involves interaction, or the capability of agency Web sites to provide online access to critical information and downloadable forms and to be able to contact the agency by e-mail. The third phase is transaction, or the capacity for entire transactions or processes to be completed online. This phase will be aided by the imminent enactment of the Electronic Transactions Bill, which will ensure that electronic and non-electronic transactions are given equal legal status where they are functionally equivalent. Phase IV is about transformation, in which government processes and service delivery are ultimately redefined.

The New Zealand Government identified three key characteristics of e-government that it hoped to achieve through the E-Government Strategy: (1) convenience and satisfaction; (2) efficiency and effectiveness; and (3) participation. The E-Government Unit (EGU) of the State Services Commission has overall responsibility for implementing the e-government strategy to achieve this vision. It has identified 16 initiatives, or "work streams," which have become part of the overall e-government program and are aimed at supporting various stages of this four-phased model. For instance, the e-procurement project is currently being developed by the EGU on behalf of all interested departments. Officials suggested that if the project "proceeds to full implementation it is likely that departments would meet costs through annual subscriptions...[t]he intention [being] that departments would achieve annual benefits that at least meet their subscription costs." Table 1 lists the 16 work streams and Table 2 illustrates where they fit in relation to the four-phased model that informs the overarching strategy.

Table 1. New Zealand E-Government Initiatives (Source: New Zealand E-Government Strategy, December 2001 Update) (Available at http://www.e-government.govt.nz/docs/e-gov-strategy-dec-01/chapter5.html#Heading288)

- Strategy and Business Planning
- Governance and Operational Arrangements
- Interoperability Framework
- Web Guidelines
- Geospatial Metadata
- Portal: NZGLS and Thesaurus; Portal: Metadata; Portal: Delivery
- E-services
- Authentication
- Change of Address
- E-billing
- Shared Policy Workspace
- Secure Electronic Environment (S.E.E.) Mail
- Secure Electronic Environment PKI (S.E.E. – Public Key Infrastructure)
- Secure Electronic Environment (S.E.E.) Directory
- Procurement
- Assessment and Monitoring

Source: E-Government Strategy (December 2001 Update and E-Government Website: http://www.e-government.govt.nz/docs/e-gov-strategy-dec-01/chapter12.html).

While Table 2 indicates target dates for completion of various initiatives in relation to the four phases, New Zealand has avoided setting arbitrary targets for agencies, as this does not fit well with its approach to public management, which requires that agencies integrate e-government into their strategic plans and implement it at a sensible pace.

Several work streams in Table 1 are currently providing support for the "interaction" phase including e-procurement, the new portal development, interoperability framework, the secure electronic environment, the NZGLS Metadata standard, and the authentication framework. The E-Government Strategy identifies the fact that several issues will need to be addressed before government can successfully embark on the "transformation" phase of e-government. These include matters of funding, governance, privacy, data quality, and enterprise architecture.

The New Zealand Government portal (New Zealand Government Online, referred to as NZGO, *www.govt.nz*) is an e-government initiative developed by a group of agencies led by the Department of Internal Affairs in 1997 to facilitate greater participation in government. The State Services Commission assumed responsibility for NZGO in 2000, and the EGU announced the development of the new Internet portal in December 2001, which was expected to be fully implemented by July 2002. In the first instance it will be used to direct information searchers to the government information and services they are seeking. The portal is notable for two things: (1) its emphasis on the importance of helping people find information and services, not the agencies that provide them; and (2) the fact that it will be built out of metadata that government agencies will create about their information and services, as per the requirements of the New Zealand Government Locator Service Metadata Standard — a relatively innovative practice at the national

Table 2. New Zealand's Four-Phased Model for E-Government (Source: New Zealand E-Government Strategy, December 2001 Update) (Available at http://www.e-government.govt.nz/docs/e-gov-strategy-dec-01/chapter5.html#Heading288)

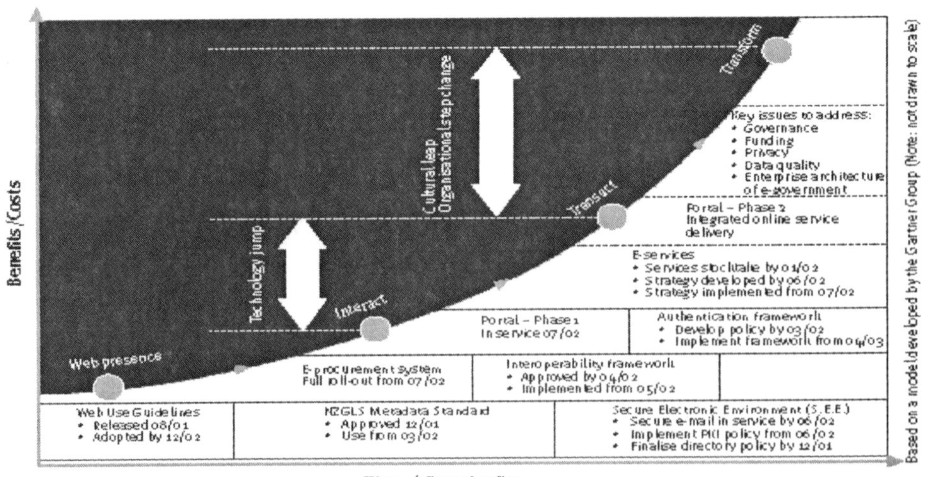

government level. (See *http://www.e-government.govt.nz/news/2001121901.asp* for more details.)

Aside from the goals of the Strategy, a key message in the New Zealand approach to e-government is the importance of effective collaboration across agencies in the use of ICT. This message was formalized in a keynote address delivered by the Minister of State Services in October 2001, "[f]or years now we have seen the debate between centralization and decentralization as the best approach to public management. A new approach suggests that neither is inherently superior, and that collaboration between agencies no matter how they are structured and governed will yield the best results. This is the philosophy behind e-government, which you are all going to have so much to do with over the next few years" (as noted in the E-Government Strategy December 2001 Update).

Furthermore, the Strategy notes that, "[t]he e-government program is about managing the process of change within the public sector, as we move towards becoming a 'knowledge society.'" To assist in managing this change, and the need for greater collaboration between agencies, the E-government Advisory Board, chaired by the State Services Commissioner, is the main governance arrangement to aid cross-agency e-government initiatives. Two networks of senior departmental staff, (the E-government Agency Leaders network and the Chief Information Officer network), were also created by the EGU to facilitate cross-agency collaboration. Furthermore, many of the projects being led by the EGU have steering committees comprised of agency chief executives. Consideration will be given to whether current public-sector governance arrangements are sufficient to encourage a networked type of organization under e-government.

While there is not yet an overall strategy and plan for leveraging IT investments across government agencies, a path to achieving a better ROI on these investments is set forth in the E-Government Interoperability Framework (e-GIF), published in February 2002. The e-GIF will develop common standards for enabling sharing of information, applications, and technology across the public sector, or standards for "interoperability," described as "[t]he ability of government organizations to share information and integration information and businesses by the use of common standards." This initiative mirrors the UK Government's development of its e-Government Interoperability Framework. The New Zealand Government has identified the adoption of common standards across the public sector as a critical factor in laying the foundation for e-government.

Overall funding of e-government initiatives is an important matter. There is a strategic focus on the question of how to fund across agencies, or take a horizontal approach to ICT investments. Active agency management of e-government projects is emphasized in order to maximize benefits across government, and agencies are responsible for identifying the fiscal and economic benefits of their e-government application portfolios over time. While the Strategy acknowledges the need for more creative approaches to funding e-government initiatives, it anticipates that e-government investments will be recovered through improved efficiency in the use of taxpayer funds and through the growth of access, thereby making savings a tangible goal.

Budgetary Processes and Practices

According to our correspondence with New Zealand officials, Vote State Services has appropriations of around $17 million (GST inclusive) over four years with $5.6 million appropriated for fiscal year 2000/01 and the remaining $11.4 million for out-years 2001/02 to 2003/04. It has been appropriated for the development, coordination and evaluation of initiatives in relation to the use of information and communication technologies in the State sector. A further commitment was made for additional funding of $25 million over fiscal years 2001/02 to 2004/05 and out-years. The E-Government Unit has primary responsibility for the delivery of this output class and works with departments to identify those e-government projects that are consistent with the Government's E-Government Strategy so that they can be advanced.

Government agencies are already funded for ICT as part of their business infrastructure through traditional budgetary baselines and appropriations. Under the current budgetary process, the Government has the capacity to plan for the period ahead and to align resource allocation with policy priorities, which then requires spending approval by Parliament. Appropriations are requested in the Estimate of Annual Appropriations presented to the House of Representatives at Budget time. Vote Ministers seek appropriations from Parliament for expenses, expenditure and liabilities, for all purposes including classes of outputs detailed in the Estimates. Appropriations are typically limited to one year, consistent with the annual Budget cycle. However, multi-year appropriations are provided for in the Public Finance Act of 1989, with a maximum term of five years.

The question of how much expenditure will actually be directly attributable to e-government in the future is currently unanswered. The State Services Commission will be getting preliminary information on this from Public Service departments later in 2002. This information will help inform development of Budget strategy for the 2003/04 fiscal year and, perhaps, beyond. It should be noted that, to date, New Zealand has not said that e-government is going to require major new investments over and above the quantum of funding (capital and operating) that already goes into ICT in government agencies.

New Zealand's approach to e-government has identified that some savings are anticipated in the shift from an individual agency, to more collaborative, networked models of government. Mechanisms to facilitate cross-agency initiatives already exist, with Ministers determining the priority of joint initiatives. Typically, an initiative is undertaken by a lead agency, which develops the initiative on behalf of all participating agencies. As part of the development of the 2002/03 Budget process, Treasury will examine whether funding processes need to be strengthened across strategic areas, Votes and agencies.

The costs associated with business process redesign, particularly as more services are delivered by multiple agencies must be outweighed by net benefits before new e-government initiatives are approved. Thus new costs would have to be weighted against gains in overall improved efficiency in government. Given that the portfolio of new e-government initiatives is due to be identified in mid-2002, these costs and savings are still to be calculated. When compared to other countries, New Zealand has stood out as the "country that has never said e-government is going to cost lots of extra money." Any new funding will primarily be spent developing the foundations of the e-government program at the central level, such as shared infrastructures, the new portal, or the interoperability framework.

This perspective reflects the top-down management of spending aggregates in New Zealand, which is largely a product of the changes in budget management that resulted from the implementation of the Public Finance Act of 1989 (PFA) and the Fiscal Responsibility Act of 1994 (FRA), according to Budget Management That Counts: Recent Approaches to Budget and Fiscal Management in New Zealand (Treasury Working Paper 01/24). This paper details the shift in financial reporting created by the Public Finance Act from an input to an output basis. In the past, departmental appropriations were based on three types of inputs (personnel, operating costs, and capital). The PFA required appropriations to be based on the nature of departmental outputs, or goods and services.

According to a 1996 Report, *Putting it Together: An Explanatory Guide to New Zealand Public Sector Financial Management System*, the PFA provides the legal framework for the financial management system and the basis for the appropriation and management of public resources. Furthermore, it prescribes the reporting requirements for the Crown, departments and Crown entities to publish and regularly update information about specific fiscal indicators and forecasts over a three-year planning period. Atkinson (1997) has succinctly summarized the Fiscal Responsibility Act (FRA) as "established principles of responsible fiscal management, and required transparent and detailed explanation by the government of the day about the reason for any departure from these principles and about how it proposes to return to them."

Putting It Together noted that at that time, department heads had been employed for up to five years based on fixed-term contracts. These contracts established the ministerial expectations for departmental performance. The budget allocation that enables the department head to finance those services is set out in the annual Estimates. Department heads are granted considerable discretion to manage this budget allocation. Departmental financial positions are reported at least annually through a balance sheet prepared according to Generally Accepted Accounting Practices (GAAP). This balance sheet reflects the assets and liabilities under the department's control, the difference representing the taxpayer's investment in the department. This level of investment is effectively approved through the appropriation system.

The chief executive of each department bears sole responsibility for their respective department's financial management and for ensuring the capacity of each department to meet future demands. Chief executives are, therefore, extended adequate authority to make decisions on the structure of the balance sheet to allow them to manage this responsibility (e.g., the management and application of the department's working capital, and the timing and manner of replacement of plant and equipment as it is consumed).

The authority held by chief executives is controlled by the allocation of resources through the budgetary process and, thus, the level of the approved investment in the department. The New Zealand financial delegation system requires, amongst other criteria, approval by the Cabinet Minister for capital investments over $7 million and approval by the Cabinet for investments over $15 million. Capital contribution through the budget process is the only option available to departments unable to finance capital expenditures from its balance sheet. In this event, the department must submit a sound business case for the expenditure for review by Treasury officers, followed by Cabinet approval.[1] This allows the Treasury to analyze and optimize the net benefits for the total set, or portfolio, of e-government initiatives. Accordingly, initiatives are ranked so that those with the highest net benefits proceed.

The 2001 *Guidelines for Managing and Monitoring Major IT Projects* emphasizes the need for departments to link their major IT projects to their business strategy as well as to broader Government strategies, which includes e-government. The guidelines stress the importance of risk management and sound project management practices, which includes centralized monitoring of major IT projects. Centralized monitoring is important to provide assurance that the ownership interests of the Government and the accountability of Chief Executives in terms of these initiatives are being met. Furthermore, these guidelines provide "lessons learned" from IT projects that are disseminated to all departments. The three central monitoring agencies are the State Services Commission, Treasury, and the Department of Prime Minister and Cabinet (DPMC). The Office of the Controller and Auditor-General also shares an interest in sharing best practices and developing reports regarding the management of public sector IT projects.

The E-government Unit of the State Services Commission plans to have identified potential e-government initiatives that may require funding in 2003/04 and fiscal out-years by mid-2002. According to our respondents, further approaches for funding e-government initiatives for the 2003/04 fiscal year may be designed by Treasury as part of the 2003/04 budget process. The State Services Commission will work with the Treasury in this regard. For those e-government initiatives occurring in the 2003/04 fiscal year and beyond, a range of budget processes and types of funding will become available to agencies. Funding will come from within baselines (existing funding), new government funding (individual or cross-agency initiatives), and partial or full non-government funding (including user pays and public/private partnerships). Given that the budget process is already designed to evolve each year to match changes in the Government's policies, few new practices are expected.

E-Government Financing Innovations

When the New Zealand Government adopted Generally Accepted Accounting Practices (GAAP) under the Financial Reporting Act in 1993, the principles of accrual accounting were incorporated into its budget process. The accrual-based budgeting system used in New Zealand has been recognized as a method to support performance-based management by more accurately reflecting total cost of inputs. In this way, appropriations can be more specifically allocated to provide for specific output levels of goods and services.

Output appropriations reflect acceptance of the full accrual cost of the specified outputs, not just the cash required for inputs, as described in the 1996 report, *Putting It Together*. In effect, accrual budgeting and output budgeting in New Zealand support a more decentralized management system, ensure accountability for results by managers, and reduce controls over inputs. FRA also mandated the adoption of Generally Accepted Accounting Practices (GAAP) used by the private sector, which required both accrual and cash accounting, separate current and capital budgets, and provision of balance-sheet information as well as income and operating expenses.

Furthermore, the accrual budgeting concept is widely considered to be a useful mechanism for examining the treatment of the term, "investment," especially when considered on equal footing to spending within budgetary structures. A budgeting expert, with whom we consulted, suggested that one could question the value of "investments" in e-government, especially as that term is used in budgetary or economic parlance.[2] Nonetheless, the basic underlying value of accrual-based budgeting is that it allows investments, however defined, to be directly compared to spending and further provides a framework and criteria for ranking investments.

Investments for complex projects are generally ranked according to risk-based funding rules, which require the use of quantitative risk analysis to assess each risk along with its impact and probability. This allows department heads to explicitly demonstrate the fiscal impact of a project's risk to decision makers (OECD PUMA Brief No. 8 March 2001). Risk analysis that generates a normal distribution of the likely outcomes is required for each major project. Appropriations are determined from the expected value of the project, with limits around the amount drawn down over time. Quantified risk analysis is preferred ahead of a contingency funds approach because allowing departments to draw from a contingency fund provides only weak incentives to control costs. Under the quantified risk analysis approach, additional costs need explicit Ministerial, Cabinet or Parliamentary approval.

Part of the mandate of the State Services Commission's E-government Unit is to integrate information and service delivery across the whole-of-government. Treasury noted that integrated e-government initiatives are financed in the same basic way as single-agency initiatives (i.e., from agencies' balance sheets or baselines, or via the Budget process). Costs are typically allocated in proportion to the net benefits that agencies expect to receive resulting from successfully implemented initiatives. Our respondents consider that "there will be few truly innovative practices that are unique to the funding of e-government initiatives" resulting from a budget process that is designed to evolve each year to match changes in the Government's priorities, new sources of funding and new practices.

Funding for e-government initiatives are more likely to be funded than other ICT projects, based on an imperative delivered by the Government that stressed ICT projects should be aligned with the E-government Strategy, which is a major priority for the Government. Accordingly, e-government initiatives that have not yet been identified do not receive special treatment and any new initiatives must include consultation with the State Services Commission's E-government Unit regarding the alignment of any proposed initiative with the E-government Strategy. Initiatives that fit within the Strategy are looked upon favorably, over those that do not satisfy the Strategy, "either because they assist agencies toward fulfilling the goals represented within the Strategy, or fulfill the strategy itself."

Further, The December 2001 *Report of the Advisory Group of the Review of Centre* provides a wider context for the E-government Strategy. This Report identified five key issues for attention for the public sector management system. These issues included: (1) the establishment of networks among related agencies for policy integration, delivery and capability-building in the State sector; (2) the reduction of structural fragmentation in the State sector by a careful process of structural consolidation, including the preparation of criteria to be agreed by Ministers; (3) the improvement of the governance of Crown entities with particular attention to improving the clarity of relationships between Ministers, departments and Crown entities; (4) the reduction of barriers to resource reallocation within budget processes; and (5) the investigation of the need for additional mechanisms to improve the quality of evaluation undertaken by State agencies, taking into consideration the newly created Social Policy Evaluation and Research Committee.

The E-government Advisory Board, chaired by the State Services Commissioner, is the main governance arrangement to aid cross-agency e-government initiatives. Two networks of senior departmental staff, (the E-government Agency Leaders network and the Chief Information Officer network), were also created by the E-government Unit to facilitate cross-agency collaboration. Furthermore, many of the projects being led by the E-government Unit have steering committees comprised of agency chief executives.

Consideration will be given to whether current public-sector governance arrangements are sufficient to encourage a networked type of organization under e-government.

Structural and legal mechanisms for "pooling of resources" do not exist under the current system and essentially, the E-government Strategy should encourage such practices. The lack of mechanisms does not preclude departments and agencies working together where there is a shared need. New Zealand has consistently said that e-government should, in general, sell itself to agencies based on its business benefits, some of which are expected to arise through more efficiency and effectiveness gains from collaboration in development and use of "back-office" resources (data and ICT), and design of multi-agency business processes for integrated service delivery. The e-procurement initiative provides an example of a system that is being developed that can be utilized by all departments.

Current budget processes and accountability arrangements may be somewhat more attuned to funding individual agencies, therefore, indicating the necessity to examine whether there is any need to strengthen funding processes across strategic areas, votes and agencies. Finally, no special mechanisms exist to encourage departments to pursue creative financing options, although the New Zealand system already encourages creative thinking about options. Departments are generally free to determine whether their information technology needs are met by in-house suppliers or contracted out.

United Kingdom

E-Government Laws and Policies

Electronic government has long been a priority of the UK government dating back at least to the creation of an e-Government group in the Central IT Unit in 1995. In 2000, that group was transferred to the Office of the e-Envoy (*www.e-envoy.gov.uk*), an arm of the Cabinet Office, charged with "leading the drive to get the UK online, to ensure that the country, its citizens and its businesses derive maximum benefit from the knowledge economy."

In a white paper on *Modernising Government* (March 1999), the government stated five commitments including an "information age government [that] will use new technology to meet the needs of citizens and business...." It articulated a vision of "organizing government activities in new, innovative and better ways and for making life easier for the public by providing public services in integrated, imaginative and more convenient forms like single gateways, the Internet and digital TV." That report set a target that "by 2008 all [government] services (with exclusions for policy or operational reasons) should be available electronically." In March of 2000, the Prime Minister announced that the deadline should be advanced to 2005.

A number of laws enacted both by the UK government and the European Commission have given further impetus to e-government initiatives:

- The Electronic Communications Act 2000, enacted in May of that year, brings legal equivalence to online and off-line ways of doing business, and encourages the establishment of a self-regulatory accreditation scheme for providers of online authentication and confidentiality services.
- The European Commission's E-Commerce Directive was adopted on 8 June 2000 and was due to be implemented in the UK by January 2002 The Directive will ensure that Information Society services benefit from the Internal Market principles of free movement of services and freedom of establishment and it will ensure that Information Society services can be provided throughout the European Union if they comply with the law in the service provider's home Member State.
- The Regulation of Investigatory Powers Act updated the law on the interception of communications to take account of technological change such as the growth of the Internet. It also puts other intrusive investigative techniques on a statutory footing for the very first time, provides new powers to help combat the threat posed by rising criminal use of strong encryption, and ensures that there is independent judicial oversight of the powers in the Act.

In December 2000 the Departments of Trade and Industry (DTI), and Culture, Media, and Sport (DCMS) jointly published the Communications White Paper. The White Paper sets out the Government's vision for developing the most dynamic and competitive communications and media market in the world, while at the same time ensuring universal access to high quality, diverse services, and ensuring that citizens and consumers are safeguarded.

The National Audit Office's report, *Better Public Services through e-Government*, published in April 2002, uses case studies of ESD approaches in private and public sector organizations as the basis for recommendations on ways forward for the e-Envoy's Office and for individual Government departments.

As part of the UK online strategy, the Government is committed to making the UK one of the world's leading knowledge economies. The approach is to provide an effective light touch regulatory regime in which those in the UK may engage in e-commerce and use the Internet safely and securely. It is deemed by the Government to be essential for growth and inward investment that the policy framework ensure consumer confidence and trust in e-commerce and use of the Internet. The UK is already updating existing legislation and regulation to facilitate electronic communication and data storage through the work of the Modernising Our Laws for the Information Age (MOLIA) Group.

To give further impetus to its e-government initiatives, the government has set up a Ministerial Committee on Electronic Government to review key projects. While it has no direct budgetary authority, that Committee meets monthly and, by virtue of having minister-level participation, elevates the level of management attention to e-government projects.

Budgetary Processes and Practices

Budgeting for government program is done on a three-year basis with Spending Reviews conducted every two years. Year three of the previous three-year cycle becomes year one in the succeeding review. "The introduction of Spending Reviews (beginning with the Comprehensive Spending Review in 1998) also led to significant changes in the framework for planning and controlling public spending. The 2000 Spending Review set new three year spending plans up to 2003-04, using 2001-02 (the last year of the plans set in the 1998 CSR) as the first year of the new plans." Spending Reviews are currently under way for the three-year budget period beginning in April of 2003. In addition to traditional, vertical department-by-department reviews, the government conducts a series of cross-cutting reviews. In 2002 they will focus on seven areas:

1. Children at Risk
2. Improving the Public Space
3. Role of the Voluntary Sector in Delivering Services
4. Public Sector Labor Market
5. Science and Research
6. Services for Small Businesses
7. Tackling the causes of Health Inequalities

Separate allocations are made for capital investments and operating costs. The total moneys available for investment are determined by the Treasury based on overall debt and cash flow considerations and the individual capital allocations for each department are made based on draft departmental investment strategies that each submits. ICT investments are considered as part of the overall capital allocation. ICT projects may also be financed using a department's operating budget or other revenues. To assure that departments are getting value for money, all projects that entail acquisition, including ICT projects, once approved, are subject to scrutiny by the Office of Government Commerce (OGC). OGC administers a five-step review called the *Gateway Process* "The process applies equally for those organizations that already have strategic partnering arrangements in place. The Gateway Process examines a project at critical stages in its lifecycle to provide assurance that it can progress successfully to the next stage. It is designed to be applied to projects that procure services, construction/property, IT-enabled business change projects and procurements utilizing framework contracts."

E-Government Financing Innovations

According to the e-Envoy's office, there is no centralized funding specifically for e-government initiatives. Consistent with the government's e-government (Electronic Service Delivery) target of making all of its services available online by 2005, we were told that "bids for the funding of projects, which are directly linked to Government targets will tend to be more successful than other ICT bids where projects may be perceived as less essential." The reviews of the Ministerial Committee on Electronic Government, described above, while not directly linked to the Spending Review process, can put subtle pressure on ministries to give priority to in their spending plans.

The various government departments bid for ICT funding in the same way as for any other planned expenditure, as part of the UK's Three-Year Spending Review process, supporting these bids with business cases. Statistics are not collected in a form to enable one to calculate the percent of Government expenditure accounted for by ICT. The publication of *Successful IT: Modernising Government in Action* (*http://www.e-envoy.gov.uk/publications/reports/itprojects/index.htm*) in 2000 set new guidelines for the management and review of ICT projects. These guidelines were included in the "dual key" procedure following the 2000 Spending Review.

According to the e-Envoy's office, in its cross-cutting review of departments' progress towards the 2005 target for putting all Government services online, the Government is: (a) targeting services that are likely to be most attractive to citizens (thereby accelerating the take-up of e-services), and (b) encouraging departments to structure their services in a more "joined-up" way that will facilitate movement across government Web sites, rather than simply being based on conventional departmental responsibilities. Financing would still be based around the 3-Year Spending Review, and departments would still bid for funding in the same way, but users would not need to know the details of organizational structure or departmental responsibilities in order to acquire information or access e-services.

Horizontal or multi-department projects are being funded by putting the resources into the budget of a single, or lead department. For example, the new *Business to Government Portal* is being funded through the budget of the Department of Trade and Industry, although it will deliver services from other departments including Inland Revenue and the Department of Employment. Staff from other departments who work on the project will be assigned to the Department of Trade and Industry. While no direct transfer of funds will occur from the other participating departments, presumably the fact that the direct demand on them for certain services will be diminished will be considered in the Spending Reviews and reflected in their spending allocations.

Other moneys for ICT investments come from bids to the Capital Modernization Fund (see *www.hm-treasury.gov.uk*) and the *Invest to Save Budget* (*www.isb.gov.uk*).

In 1998, the government set up a separate *Capital Modernisation Fund*, apart from the allocations given to individual departments, to finance innovative investments based on project proposals submitted by the departments. These funds, which were available as a result of under-spending from the conventional capital allocations, have been used extensively for ICT projects. According to the Treasury Web site, "[t]he Capital Modernisation Fund was set up in the Comprehensive Spending Review to support capital investment to improve public services. An additional £200 million was added to the Fund for 2000-01 as part of the Budget 2000 announcement to take the total size of the Fund to £2.7 billion over 1999-00 to 2001-02." The Fund is allocated on a competitive basis and on the following criteria:

- the extent the project applies genuinely innovative approaches to service delivery;
- the quality and strength of the economic appraisal of the project;
- the impact on the efficiency and effectiveness of the service;
- how far the project contributes to the department's objectives;
- how far the project is genuinely additional; and
- the robustness of arrangements for delivering, managing, accounting, monitoring and evaluating the project.

While by no means focused on e-government *per se*, successful projects using the Fund have included e-government initiatives. The first round (1999-2000), funded a number of e-government projects including: "£470 million as part of the National IT Strategy to provide 1,000 IT learning centres across the country;" "£1.1 million to pump-prime various e-commerce procurement initiatives across Government - in particular to develop a Government 'Shopping Mall' to provide electronic tendering of low-value transactions to and from Government, which could save over £10 million a year" and

"£600,000 for electronic procurement by Foreign and Commonwealth Office posts overseas." In the second round, £23.3M was allocated for Transforming the Crown Court, "a package of three enhancements designed to reduce delay in the criminal justice system by more effective management of cases through the Crown Court and improving the quality of service to court users. These are: a PC-based system for prosecution, defence, judge, jury, defendant and witnesses, allowing the electronic presentation of evidence producing significant savings in court time in complex cases; electronic transcripts of court proceedings through a digital audio recording of the official record and improved information distribution through displaying relevant information on how cases are progressing, public information kiosks and a read-only access IT source."

The *Invest to Save Budget* (ISB) stipulates a partnership approach to bids and therefore incentivizes "joined-up working."[3] The ISB is "venture capital for the public sector" run by both the Treasury and the Cabinet Office. A committee, chaired by the Treasury, assesses bids in consultation with the Cabinet Office using a pre-determined set of criteria. "Bids are invited from partnerships made up of two or more of the bodies listed below:

- central Government departments and their Agencies;
- non-departmental public bodies;
- health authorities;
- fire authorities;
- police authorities; and
- local authorities ; [and].
- voluntary sector bodies."

Over its first five years, the ISB expects to put more than £380m into innovative partnership projects.

The Performance and Improvement Unit's 2000 report *Electronic Government for the 21st Century* also recommended the creation of "an ESD incubator ... as a home for start government ESD [electronic service delivery] ventures [to] fund jointly with the private voluntary sector, prototypes ..." A unit to manage this effort has been set up, although it has not yet undertaken any ventures pending decisions on basic policies and negotiations on funding levels in the current Spending Review.

User charges will fund certain services — e.g., for passport applications/renewals, the UK Passport Office, as an executive agency, operates a net running-cost regime, requiring them to fully recover costs through passport fees. As of this writing, the UK government is developing policies for joint funding with the private sector, but private venture capital does not represent an important source of financing for e-government at this time.

United States

E-Government Laws and Policies

The United States Federal government expects to spend $49 billion on information and communications technology (ICT) in fiscal year 2002 (ending on September 30, 2002) and the President's budget proposes spending of approximately $52 billion for ICT in fiscal year 2003. Notwithstanding those substantial expenditures, the *President's Management Agenda* published in August of 2001 noted that this level of spending had "not produced measurable gains in public sector worker productivity." To address this concern, the Bush Administration announced the creation of a task force of government personnel that, among other things, was to "create easy-to-find single points of access to government services for individuals, reduce the reporting burden on businesses..., share information more quickly and conveniently between federal and state, local and tribal governments...' [and] automate internal processes to reduce costs internally..." This initiative, which came to be known as Project Quicksilver, was not the first U.S. effort to promote the use of ICT to streamline government operations and simplify interactions with non-governmental entities including the public.

The previous (Clinton) Administration had already made creating portals for access to government services a priority in the creation of *FirstGov* (*www.firstgov.gov*). Since substantially modified by the current administration, *FirstGov* used a search engine that had been developed in the private sector to create a single point of entry for anyone seeking governmental services or information. A key design criterion of *FirstGov* was that it did not require the searcher to know or understand the structure of government or government programs.

The principal statutory basis for U.S. Federal e-government initiatives can be found in the Government Paperwork Elimination Act (or GPEA), a 1998 law that broke ground on two important fronts. GPEA requires that within five years, or by October 1, 2003, (1) agencies must allow anyone submitting information to the Federal government to do so electronically "when practicable as a substitute for paper;" and (2) agencies must provide "for the use and acceptance of electric signatures, when practicable." Through a series of implementing documents issued by the Office of Management and Budget (OMB), agencies have been required to create plans and projects so that the major transaction processes in which they engage can be electronically enabled by the statutory deadline.

The Bush Administration's *Presidential Management Agenda*, issued in August of 2001 established "expanded electronic government" as one of its five government-wide initiatives and said, in part, that the "administration's goal is to champion citizen-centered electronic government that will result in major improvement in the Federal government's value to the citizen." An interagency e-government task force, established in July of 2001 (dubbed Project Quicksilver), took that mandate, reviewed e-government projects and identified 24 initiatives in four broad areas: government to citizen (G2C), government to business (G2B), government to government (G2G), and internal efficiency and effectiveness (IEE). In addition, e-authentication, as well as a cross-cutting projects on developing a Federal architecture, were identified by the Government Performance and Results Act as "initiatives that address barriers to e-government success."

While these projects, listed in the February 27, 2002 "E-Government Strategy" report, do not define the totality of the government's e-government program, the Quicksilver task force found that "...the federal government could significantly improve customer service over the next 18 to 24 months by focusing on [these] high-payoff, government wide initiatives..." Examining the underlying objectives of these initiatives and the inherent management challenges they create, particularly given their intergovernmental context, will provide deeper insight into the changing environment of IT investment and budgetary processes in the U.S.

Each e-government initiative has been assigned to a lead agency or "managing partner," and a "portfolio manager" at the Office of Management and Budget coordinates each group (i.e., G2G, G2B, G2C, and IEE). See Table 1.

The U.S. Federal government operates on a cash budget using an encumbrance (obligation) accounting system to control spending authority.[4] This system, basically unchanged since the Budget and Accounting Act of 1921, makes no special provision for capital spending.

Department and agency budgets are constructed on an organizational and program basis and undergo an elaborate review process, first by the Office of Management and Budget, which compiles the President's budget, and then by the Congress which divides the budget into 13 separate appropriations bills, which ultimately become the laws that authorize spending. Most appropriations are annual — the funds must be encumbered during the fiscal year for which they are appropriated — although a few accounts allow for multi-year or even non-expiring (no year) appropriations. A 1972 bill, the Budget Reform Act, created a process for setting overall spending limits, but actual spending authority can only be conferred through one of the 13 appropriation acts.[5]

Table 1. Organization of U.S. E-Government Initiatives

U.S. E-Government Initiatives (Managing partner in parentheses)
Government to Citizen
Recreation One-Stop (Department of the Interior)
Eligibility Assistance Online (Department of Labor)
Online Access for Loans (Department of Education)
USA Services Online (customer relations management) (General Services Administration)
EZ Tax Filing (Internal Revenue Service)
Government to Business
Online Rulemaking Management (Department of Transportation)
Expanding Electronic Tax Products for Business (Internal Revenue Service)
Federal Asset Sales (General Services Administration)
International Trade Process Streamlining (Department of Commerce)
One-Stop Business Compliance Information (Small Business Administration)
Consolidate Health Informatics (Department of Health and Human Services)
Government to Government
Geospatial Information One-Stop (Department of the Interior)
e-Grants (Department of Health and Human Services)
Disaster Assistance and Crisis Response (Federal Emergency Management Agency)
Wireless Public SAFEty Interoperable COMmunications/Project SAFECOM (Department of the Treasury)
e-Vital (Social Security Administration)
Internal Efficiency and Effectiveness
e-Training, (Office of Personnel Management)
Recruitment One-Stop (Office of Personnel Management Enterprise HR Integration) (Office of Personnel Management)
e-Payroll (Office of Personnel Management)
e-Travel (General Services Administration)
Integrated Acquisition Environment (General Services Administration)
Electronic Records Management (National Archives and Records Administration)
Initiatives That Address Barriers to E-Government Success
e-Authentication (General Services Administration)
Federal Architecture (Office of Management and Budget)
Source: *E-Government Strategy*, Office of Management and Budget, February 27, 2002

Funding capital projects has long been a controversial matter under the U.S. system. As reported by the General Accounting Office (GAO) in November 1996, agencies have been required to budget for the full cost of most capital assets before acquiring them (referred to as up-front funding), a practice that has been in place now for over 100 years under the Adequacy of Appropriations Act and Antideficiency Act.[6] Advocates of budget discipline and control argue that a project should not be begun unless all funds necessary to complete it, or some usable portion of it, have been appropriated. Since a major capital project, including a large ICT project, may require a large up-front investment, the net effect of such a discipline is to create a large one-year increase or spike in an agency's spending authority, which will result in substantial spending in future years, leaving little discretion for new spending in the budget and thereby making it difficult to finance the life of the project. Up-front funding essentially does not allow agencies or departments to recognize the benefits that may accrue over many years beyond the period in which then money is spent. Accordingly, there is a recognized need to address the problem of financing capital projects, particularly in an environment of capped resources.[7]

Recognizing the problems in the U.S. budgeting structure for capital assets, the GAO examined the potential to improve this condition and suggested that the selection and evaluation process of capital projects was in need of improvement. The GAO reported that this need was addressed by the Federal Acquisition Streamlining Act of 1994, which requires agencies "to develop cost, schedule, and performance goals for their acquisitions and requires OMB to report to Congress on the agencies' progress in meeting these goals." While acknowledging the need to provide fiscal control, the GAO determined that the end result is "budgetary costs that differ from measurement of full, annual program costs that will be needed to successfully execute the Government Performance and Results Act of 1993 (GPRA)."

Incremental funding for capital asset acquisitions, on the other hand, may allow a project to be undertaken, but, in the eyes of the budget disciplinarians, understates the future cost impacts. It is very difficult, for example, to refuse to fund future increments to complete a building or other public work if the foundation has been dug and there is a gaping hole in the ground. Thus, advocates for a capital project will often seek partial funding just to get a project started in the hope that political momentum will guarantee future funding as needed. An important advantage of incremental funding is that it builds in checkpoints at which those responsible have to make a decision as to whether or not to provide funding to proceed. Full, up-front spending authorizations, create a presumption in favor of completing a project even if it may prove to be of questionable merit.

The Office of Management and Budget (OMB) and the GAO generally take the view that capital projects should be funded up-front in their entirety and support incremental funding in only two cases: (1) if the increment buys a usable portion (e.g., one building on a multi-building campus or one fully functional segment of a multi-function information system); or (2) the project is of such high risk involving, for example, new technologies, that require further design and testing before full deployment can be authorized.

According to a February 2001 GAO report, incremental funding for high technology capital projects is justified in some cases. The report characterizes these projects as being closer in nature to research and development, rather than actual tangible assets. The logic provided in the report follows that although the costs of such projects are highly uncertain, the funds are not necessarily wasted, even if no additional funding is provided because of the gains acquired in overall knowledge.

In our interviews with the staff of the GAO, they helped us appreciate an interesting distinction between ICT and other, primarily, brick and mortar, capital projects. Advocates of physical projects, like buildings or dams, often prefer even small initial funding recognizing the political dynamic noted above. To the ICT project manager, incremental funding is often not an attractive option, preferring instead the certainty of full up-front funding. We think that this is because, unlike brick and mortar projects, a partially finished ICT project is less visible and therefore, less likely to produce the kind of pressure on the political system that a partially completed public work might.

The foregoing overview of capital budgeting provides a broad context for turning our discussion to the challenges the U.S. government faces in financing e-government initiatives The next section will explore the evolving framework of public sector finance and innovations that support the e-government strategy in the U.S., beginning with a brief overview of the statutory context from which it originated. This statutory context has stimulated the adaptation of management concepts that have been borrowed from best practices employed in the private sector. The following section discusses the move to "portfolio management" in the U.S. for modernizing its governmental operations to achieve greater cost savings in the long-term and provide more efficient electronic services to its citizens in the short term. In essence, portfolio management and enterprise architecture provide the foundation for the e-government financing innovations that are taking root in the U.S.

E-Government Financing Innovations

Concerns about ICT acquisition and capital planning gave rise, in 1996, to the enactment of the Clinger-Cohen Act (formerly known as the Information Technology Management Reform Act). The Clinger-Cohen Act required each cabinet level department and major agency to designate a "chief information officer" and repealed a previous law, which had established a highly centralized process for approving the acquisition of ICT. In effect, departments and agencies were given greater autonomy. However, funding arrangements, as described above, remained largely unchanged, although the Office of Management and Budget (OMB) was directed to develop "a process for analyzing, tracking, and evaluating of all major capital investments made by an executive [branch] agency for information system." Hence, the Clinger-Cohen Act prompted the OMB to create a database of ICT projects that it now uses in conjunction with its annual review of budget proposals.

Furthermore, the Clinger-Cohen Act, implicitly encouraged multi-agency projects by directing OMB to issue "guidance for undertaking...multi-agency and Government-wide investments in information technology..." thereby prompting the OMB to issue guidance on capital planning as part of its omnibus policy document on information resources, *Managing Information Resources* (OMB Circular No. A-130). The Act also gives OMB the authority to re-direct funds from one agency to another to finance multi-agency projects. Finally, the Clinger-Cohen Act permits joint agency funding of projects, known as "pass-the-hat" funding, a practice otherwise prohibited under most U.S. appropriations laws, which tend to require single agency funding and accountability for projects.

The authority to re-direct funds has, until recently, not been used. In May of 2002, OMB did invoke this authority in support of an e-government initiative, online rulemaking management.[8] In July of 2002 OMB announced its intent to use its Clinger-Cohen authority to support the realignment of government functions envisioned by the Administration's proposed Department of Homeland Security by limiting individual agency investments in projects that will need to be consolidated.[9]

The "pass-the-hat" authority in the Clinger Cohen Act has also played a role in financing e-government initiatives in at least two important ways. It is being used to finance the activities of the Federal CIOs Council (*www.cio.gov*), the principal coordinating body for Federal ICT activities and to fund the FirstGov initiative described above. That authority is also being used to finance some cyber-security initiatives that have government-wide utility.

Even though the e-government initiatives are listed in the President's budget for fiscal year 2003, which was submitted to the Congress in February 2002, no new funding is identified for those projects. To the extent that the projects were already part of the program of the participating departments or agencies, resources are contained in those agencies' budgets. The Budget does endorse the 24 e-government projects and funding for them was in the individual agency budget requests, although, according to OMB staff, they are not specifically enumerated because it was too late to put these numbers together. A request for a limited "Electronic Government Fund" ($45 million or less than 1/10 of one percent of the total ICT budget) is contained in the budget for fiscal year 2003, although some of those interviewed voiced skepticism as to whether even that small amount would be enacted. In the current fiscal year, $5 million was appropriated to this fund, of which $4.1 million has been allocated to five projects.[10]

In the U.S. model, e-government initiatives continue to be funded through the traditional, largely vertical funding channels. Funding across agencies or programs remains limited. (See discussion, above, of the use of the Clinger-Cohen Act authorities.) Even vertical financing faces challenges as it competes with other priorities within a department or with other agency programs. Especially if full, up-front funding is required, a new ICT project may represent a substantial portion of an organization's budget. Several techniques have been devised to deal with this inherent "spikiness" in capital spending:

- *Working Capital Funds* are authorized to sell services, usually administrative, for fees, which they can then use to cover operating costs and to amass working capital to replace systems as they become obsolete. This usually requires the appropriation of an initial infusion of operating funds.
- *Capital Acquisition Funds*, a relatively new innovation in which a group of agencies pool a portion of their annual appropriation each year and then, in turn, finance larger projects. This requires that the participants be willing to put in resources knowing that some of them will not benefit directly until some date in the future.
- *Pass-the-Hat*, a technique for financing projects where multiple organizations with separate appropriation accounts are the beneficiaries of the investment.
- *Private financing.* While we are not aware of any efforts to date to seek private capital for governmental ICT investments, in recent weeks, the administration has been seeking ways to engage the private sector and leverage private sector

investments. On April 11, 2002, OMB's associate director for information technology and e-government, Mark Forman, urged managers of e-government projects to consider contracting with Web portal companies to host government Web portals in "co-branding" arrangements. Such partnerships would presumably take advantage of the private sector investment and thus reduce the need for new capital

Given the bias that the U.S. budgeting system creates against large, long term investment, in recent years OMB has substantially changed its processes for reviewing capital spending in an effort to ensure more favorable consideration of meritorious proposals. Budget preparation guidance has, in the words of one official, been "revolutionized" to place greater emphasis on building a business case.

The latest management innovation in the U.S. falls under the rubric of "portfolio management," which some we spoke to see as the "cure-all" for making decisions about the proper levels of spending on IT services and products. Portfolio management in the U.S. has its origins in the Clinger-Cohen Act of 1996, which specifically mandated senior executive involvement in agency IT decision-making and the adoption of a capital planning and investment control process. The 2003 budget defines a capital planning and investment control process as "a collective decision making process for ensuring that IT investments integrate strategic planning, budgeting, procurement, and the management of IT in support of agency missions and business needs" (p. 393).

Portfolio management is more fully described in the February 2002 *E-Government Strategy,* and practical applications in terms of "lessons learned" are provided in the March 2002 report issued by the Federal CIO Council.[11] The Report defines IT investments as "all funds being committed to ICT programs, projects, and systems for the benefit of the Agency" and promulgates that "it is only when IT investments are managed as a portfolio can an optimal return even be approached" (p. 4). Accordingly, a portfolio will include a collection of initiatives or projects.

The March 2002 Report by the Federal CIO Council also illustrates a move towards more decentralized ICT decision making among U.S. agencies, citing the Customs Service and the Bureau of Land Management as examples. According to the CIO Council, this shift from centralized to decentralized ICT investment decision-making is made possible by the presence of an enterprise architecture, which provides a better understanding of ICT investment opportunities and impacts according to the report. Under the Clinger-Cohen Act and OMB policy, enterprise architecture is a tool that will ensure the effectiveness and modernization of agency management. The Federal CIO Council credits agencies such as the Department of Housing and Urban Development, Department of Labor, and the Department of Education, as having been successful in their capacity to create enterprise architectures that have enabled IT portfolio managers and investment decision makers to "assess opportunities *within* and *across* organization's mission areas and business lines" within a useful framework [emphasis added]. The report notes that the enterprise architecture serves other useful purposes as well, such as "to help formulate and target investments to improve data and information management and sharing, application development and deployment, and the ongoing operation and maintenance of the organization's technology infrastructure" (p. 9). The 2003 budget likens enterprise architecture to an "agency-wide roadmap or blueprint" that propels the agency toward achieving its mission and improving its core business processes and effectively using IT.

The final piece of the U.S. approach to rationalizing the ICT management and governance process, according to the 2003 budget, is performance management. The 2002 budget revealed that "less than 20% of the IT investments identified any performance goals and measures." Significant strides have been made in performance metrics according to the 2003 budget, with a large number of agencies projecting performance information in three areas: "(1) GPRA [Government Performance and Results Act] and agency performance goals; (2) contracts that are performance based with measures; and (3) IT projects goals in terms of increasing customer service, reducing process time, and reducing burden on citizen by standardizing data and reusing it to address multiple business processes" (p. 393).

The Department of Housing and Urban Development (HUD) is cited by those we spoke to as a useful example of how enterprise architecture has been adapted as part of an agency's portfolio management, as described in the March 2002 report. HUD has integrated the enterprise architecture with its capital planning process and is used to identify performance gaps, redundancies, and opportunities. Regular enterprise architecture analyses allow HUD to make decisions about proposed initiatives for improving business processes. The enterprise architecture is updated following each portfolio review reflecting the agency's current "to-be" state (p. 9).

While an enterprise architecture approach, portfolio management, and performance-based budgeting arguably offer promise for identifying opportunities to consolidate and harmonize ICT initiatives across traditional organizational and program boundaries, they do not, in and of themselves, address the challenges of financing those initiatives. Interestingly, many of the officials we interviewed stated that there is no need for additional funding for e-government initiatives, but suggested that more pooling of resources across agencies and more tracking and monitoring of project management and outcomes would be sufficient. Two important obstacles remain:

- A budget process in which capital investments are inherently at a disadvantage because, in the U.S. system, they "score" as the funds are disbursed rather than as benefits accrue.
- The difficulty in obtaining funding for initiatives that cross organizational or program boundaries and the understandable reluctance of those who ultimately control the purse strings to give up control over funds under their stewardship.

DEFINING A CONTINUUM OR TAXONOMY OF POLICY AND PRACTICE

In the countries that we examined, we found a continuum of budgeting practices ranging from traditional vertical approaches, where financing is evaluated only in the context of a particular organization or program to more horizontal approaches where financing is drawn for a number of agency budgets to central funding of cross-agency or government-wide initiatives. Each approach has its advocates and advantages:

Vertical funding requires ICT investments to compete against other claims for investments within the same program (e.g., should we buy a piece of surgical equipment or a computer for a hospital). It sharpens the discussion of the business case for a proposed investment in terms of how it will contribute to the program or organizational objective (e.g., improving public health). Vertical funding is also consonant with the core management principle of holding an organization or official accountable for achieving some organizational objective and giving that organization or official the resources to accomplish it. A major deficiency of vertical approaches is in financing ICT investments that benefit more than one agency or program, whether for commonly used infrastructure or even applications that might be used by multiple agencies (e.g., loan portfolio management). Unless the benefits overwhelmingly accrue to a single ministry or department that is willing to make the investment, the project is not likely to be funded.

Horizontal funding addresses this deficiency in vertical funding by encouraging pooling of resources. It retains the advantage of having investments compete against other priorities within a program. Opponents fear loss of control as resources are shifted to the principal financing agency. At the same time, the other contributors may have less interest in contributing their share of the resources for the investment. A proposed investment becomes "*their*" project as opposed to "*our*" project. A disadvantage of both the horizontal and vertical approaches is that high priority government-wide e-government initiatives may not always win in the competition for resources.

Central funding provides an assured source of financing for high priority and infrastructure investments. It allows a central authority to set priorities for e-government, at least to the extent of the resources allocated to the central fund. Central funds can also foster innovation as e-government project advocates seek to outdo one another in the creativity that they show. Given that the total available resources for governmental spending are limited, central funds are in effect a tax on other spending authorities. Some argue that this method of financing e-government results in technology push — developing projects that are technologically interesting — rather than meeting the real needs of the public. A variant on direct central funding are so-called *Innovation funds*. These may be used to provide seed financing for single agency or multi-agency ICT projects with the expectation that the investment will be repaid, sometimes with interest, and the fund replenished, from user fees or savings that accrue from the resultant ICT system.

Each of these models has substantial implications for the manner in which financing decisions are made. Perhaps most significant are the differences in incentive structures. Projects that require funding through the traditional organizational budget justification process must be sold in terms of their contribution to the mission and goals of the funding program or organization. In some cases, this can lead to sub-optimization.

The most significant difference among the funding models is the extent to which each reflects a different set of priorities. Notwithstanding formal rules, authorities and organizational structures, most budget experts will agree that the golden rule applies to the financing of e-government projects: "Whoever has the gold, makes the rules." A mandate to achieve some broad objective, no matter how sincerely and passionately articulated, is not likely to be achieved without adequate funding. And to the extent that such a mandate (e.g., implementing e-government) competes with other compelling public policy objectives (e.g., improving public health), in the context of individual ministry or program budgets, it is likely to lose. Where those goals are in consonance, the need for central funding becomes less compelling.

Issues and Challenges

Our analysis revealed a number of issues and challenges that face proponents of investments in e-government. Some are inherent in the financing of capital projects, whether for e-government or more traditional public works and some unique to ICT investments.

- *Capital is limited.* By definition, capital projects are multi-year in nature. This requires commitments to spend resources over a long period, sometimes well beyond the budgeting horizon. Whether a government operates on an accrual or cash basis, a commitment to a capital projects represents a commitment to expend future revenues. Governments — and businesses and individuals for that matter — are quite understandably reluctant to tie up a significant portion of future spending and thus limit their discretion to address future needs.
- *Capital spending is inherently uneven from year to year.* Over the life of a project, spending tends to be relatively low at the outset when initial planning, requirements analysis and design are the main tasks. During the development stage, when software is acquired or developed and hardware is obtained, spending tends to peak. Spending then levels off during implementation when maintenance is the major cost.
- *Capital projects entail varying degrees of risk.* In some cases, that risk is technological, where the techniques (hardware or software) are not well understood. Often, even if the technology is well-known and perceived to be low risk, the scale of the project or the nature of the change in processes being made results in substantial *organizational* risk.
- *The expected benefits from the project may be difficult to quantify.* Benefit-cost analysis and return on investment are typically readily calculable for "brick and mortar" projects like dams and roads, but less obvious for e-government initiatives where the expected benefit may be public convenience or even improved public perceptions of public services.[12]
- *Benefits often do not accrue to the organization being called up to make the investment.*

Financing strategies we learned about in our examination seek to address one or more of these challenges. The predominant method of budgeting for e-government initiatives remains *vertical funding* through traditional organizational and program budgets. This has the advantage, noted above, of competing against other program priorities so that e-government projects thus financed presumably have the support of the official who is accountable for that budget.

In the UK and New Zealand, *capital budgets* are separate from operating or running cost budgets so that the cost of a project can be amortized over the life of the investment rather than treated as a one-time expense. This tends to put expenses and investments on a more equal footing. The use of *accrual accounting,* where the expense is recognized as the resources is consumed rather than when the resource is acquired, has a similar effect. Nonetheless, the government as a whole must institute controls, usually in the form of limits on total capital spending and/or requirements for high-level approval of capital projects, lest the commitments to amortizing capital investment encumber an unacceptable portion of future spending.

We found few real examples of *horizontal spending* to finance projects that cut across organizational or program boundaries. More typically, a lead department or agency was expected to finance a project even if it served multiple organizations. This was done either by explicitly putting resources in the budget of the lead agency or, more often, by expecting the lead agency to take the resources "out of hide."

Central funds or *Innovation funds*, while widely discussed as a means of financing multi-organization projects or projects that are too risky to gain financing through traditional channels, remain an insignificant factor in financing e-government. Ultimately, given that all public budgets are constrained in the aggregate, such funds represent a tax on budgets for other segments. Absent a strong advocate, one can anticipate continuing difficulty in allocating substantial funds for investment through this channel.

A potentially important technique is *incremental funding*, where only a portion of an initiative is financed and the next portion is not made available until the previous portion is complete or nearly complete. If misused, this approach can lead to abuse by understating the real cost of a project, as when funds are sought only to construct a portion of a building, say the foundation, leaving future decision-makers little real discretion lest they suffer the embarrassment of having a partially completed structure. Used properly, such as to finance a usable portion of a new project or to fund the initial phase (e.g., proof of concept) in a highly risky project, incremental funding can make eminent sense.

- *New resources vs. re-allocation.* For the most part, the governments we examined were forced to look to re-allocation of existing resources for e-government projects rather than some entirely new sources of funding. This is a result of larger, macro-economic factors (e.g., stagnant or shrinking economic growths, reduced tax revenues), which have put most governments in the position of having to operate with level or even shrinking budgets. The result is to increase the tension claims for e-government projects and other claimants.
- *A note on private sector financing.* While we have heard much discussion about using private capital to finance investments in e-government, we found relatively few actual examples. Some innovative work, albeit on a small scale, is being undertaken under the rubric of *gain-sharing*, where an investment is expected to yield efficiencies in operation and the government agency provides in its tender, that any savings will be shared with the successful contractor. In those cases, presumably, the expected gain is reflected in the prices bid and the government's up-front investment is reduced. The U.S. has begun to talk about *co-branding*, an arrangement in which a private sector partner gains some commercial advantage from a partnership with a public agency and presumably reflects that gain in the price the government pays. Two other techniques, not always thought of as private financing, are far more widely used.
- *Leasing or renting capital assets.* This shifts the investment burden and risk to the owner of the asset. If the term of the lease is short and the amortization period for the asset is long, the government can expect to pay a substantial risk premium to protect the lessor against the contingency of owning an asset for which there is no customer. Often, the government will enter into a long-term lease, in some cases known as a *capital lease*, and even issue ownership of the asset at the end

of the lease term. Budget purists see this as a form of subterfuge to avoid reflecting on the government's accounts the true nature of the encumbrance that the government is assuming. An interesting twist on leasing can be found in the recent trend to a concept known as *seat management*, for the acquisition of network computer services including desktop software and hardware. Rather than purchasing hardware and software and hiring staff to operate a computer network, the department or agency purchases a package of services and the contractor purchases all of the capital assets, even agreeing to replace technology as it becomes obsolete.

- *Reliance on private infrastructure.* Although not typically thought of as a method of raising capital for financing e-government, by far the most important form of private financing comes from the use of privately-developed and financed infrastructure to support government ICT applications. One of the early successful applications of e-government, the U.S. electronic benefits transfer system, uses the privately developed and funded point of sales and electronic banking system.[13] Similarly, the innovative Australian electronic visa system was only possible because of the existence of automated reservation systems. Indeed, one could argue that much of what we now call e-government depends on the private sector investments in the infrastructure of the Internet. For example, we were told that: "The expansion of broadband access in the UK will be key to the use of e-services and fostering public access to online information, so that the challenge will be to facilitate the roll-out of broadband across the UK, requiring a new, flexible approach to funding which allows for quicker responses to changes in technologies and markets." Much of that funding will, per force, come from private sector investment seeking to exploit the commercial potential of broadband access.
- *Using private sector intermediaries.* We are beginning to see government agencies look to the private sector as part of their delivery systems in new and innovative ways. Finland, for example, has developed a promising project of using private sector companies as value-added information consolidators so that entities that report to various government agencies can consolidate reporting by engaging trusted third parties to produce reports in electronic form. This has two important advantages: (1) public sector investment in the information consolidation and conversion process is virtually eliminated and agencies receive information in electronic form; (2) information providers, in this case businesses, provide all of their data to a trusted third party with the assurance that only relevant portions of the data will find their way to each government agency; and (3) those business are able to benefit from the efficiencies that these intermediary organizations offer rather than having to prepare a variety of specialized reports. Similarly, in the U.S., private sector tax preparers and, in recent years software companies, have long been an important link between businesses and individuals with complex tax returns, on the one hand, and the Internal Revenue Service on the other. In recent weeks, the government announced that, rather than attempt to compete with these preparers, it would cooperate with them. [14]

Potential Future Work

An obvious limitation of this work is that it is based on the experience to date in three countries. Time and distance also limited the scope of this inquiry in other ways suggesting a number of questions that might be the subject of a broader survey of e-government financing practices in OECD countries. To name a few:

- How have innovation funds been used in other countries where they represent a more substantial portion of the ICT investment budget?
- Are there innovative examples of cost-sharing across levels of government, whether national, regional, or municipal?
- Is the notion of joint-venturing or co-branding to take advantage of the commercial potential of e-government being pursued elsewhere and, if so, to what effect?

REFERENCES

Organization for Economic Cooperation and Development (OECD). (2001, December 13). *Project on the Impact of E-Government,* PUMA 10/REV2.

OECD. (2001, March). *The hidden threat to e-government: Avoiding large government IT failures.* Public Management Policy Brief No. 8. Retrieved from *http://www.oecd.org/puma/Risk*

Harvard Policy Group on Network-Enabled Services and Government, John F. Kennedy School of Government. (2000). *Eight imperatives for leaders in a networked world: Guidelines for the 2000 election and beyond. Imperative 4: Improve budgeting and financing for promising IT initiatives.* Retrieved from *http://www.ksg.harvard.edu/stratcom/hpg/index.htm*

New Zealand

Atkinson, P. E. (1997, April/May). New Zealand's radical reforms. *OECD Observer, 205*, 43-48.

Cabinet Office Circular. (2001, April 10). Monitoring regime for major information technology (IT) projects. *CO,* (01) 4. Retrieved from *http://www.dpmc.govt.nz/cabinet/circulars/co01/4.html*

Cabinet Office Circular. (2000, Noveber 23). Guidelines for changes to baselines. *Co,* (00) 12. Retrieved from *http://www.dpmc.govt.nz/cabinet/circulars/co00/12.htm*

E-government in New Zealand Online. Retrieved from *http://www.e-government.govt.nz*

New Zealand Chief Executives' Group on Information Management and Technology. (1999, December). *Electronic government: Briefing to Minister of State Services and Minister of Information Technology.* Retrieved from *http://www.ssc.govt.nz/documents/government_information_and_technology_management.htm*

New Zealand Government Online. Retrieved from *http://www.govt.nz/*

New Zealand Office of the Controller and Auditor. (2000, April 20). *Governance and oversight of large information technology projects.* Retrieved from *http://www.oag.govt.nz*

New Zealand State Services Commission. (1999, September). *Vision statement – Electronic government in New Zealand.* Retrieved from *http://www.e-government.govt.nz/programme/vision.asp*

New Zealand State Services Commission. (2001, December). *New Zealand e-government strategy*. Retrieved from *http://www.e-government.govt.nz/docs/e-gov-strategy-dec-01/strategy-dec01.pdf*

New Zealand State Services Commission and Treasury. (2000, April). *The chief executive accountability framework and the budget process as they relate toinformation technology projects.* Retrieved from *http://www.ssc.govt.nz*

New Zealand State Services Commission and the Treasury. (2001, August). *Guidelines for managing and monitoring major IT projects.* Prepared for the State Services Commission and the Treasury by Synergy International Ltd. Retrieved from *http://www.ssc.govt.nz/documents/itguidelines/guidelines.html*

New Zealand Treasurer. (2001, December 31). *Report of the advisory group on the review of the centre.* Retrieved from *http://www.treasury.govt.nz/publicsector/reviewcentre/*

New Zealand Treasurer and Minister of Finance. (2001, December 18). *Budget Policy Statement 2002 and December economic and fiscal update 2001.* Retrieved from *http://www.treasury.govt.nz*

New Zealand Treasurer and Minister of Finance. (2001, May 24). *Budget 2001.* Retrieved from *http://www.treasury.govt.nz*

New Zealand Treasury (2001). *Budget management that counts: Recent approaches to budget and fiscal management in New Zealand.* Working Paper 01/24. NZ Treasury. Authors: Angela Barnes and Steve Leith. Retrieved from *http://www.treasury.govt.nz/workingpapers/2001/01-24.asp*

New Zealand Treasury Circular. (2002). Format of financial recommendations for cabinet and other policy papers, 4. Retrieved from *http://www.treasury.govt.nz/circulars/*

*For a general overview of the budget process, see *Putting it together: An explanatory guide to the New Zealand Public Sector Financial Management System.* 1996. Available on *http://www.treasury.govt.nz/publicsector/pit/*

*For daily news updates, see *New Zealand Information Weekly.* Available on *http://www.stuff.co.nz/inl/index/0,1008,0a10,FF.html*

United Kingdom

European Commission (2000). *The electronic commerce directive* (00/31/EC). Retrieved from *http://www.dti.gov.uk/cii/ecommerce/europeanpolicy/ecommerce_directive.shtml*

Government on the Web. Retrieved from *http://www.governmentontheweb.org/*

United Kingdom Cabinet Office. (2001). *E-Government International Benchmarking Report: Government Service Delivery for the 21st Century.* Retrieved from *http://www.cabinet-office.gov.uk/innovation/2000/delivery/intro.htm*; *http://www.e-envoy.gov.uk/publications/int_comparisons.htm*

United Kingdom Cabinet Office. (1999, March). *Modernising government.* White Paper. Retrieved from *http://www.archive.official-documents.co.uk/document/cm43/4310/4310.htm*

United Kingdom Cabinet Office. (2000, April). *e-government: A strategic framework for public services in the Information Age*. Retrieved from *http://www.e-envoy.gov.uk/ukonline/strategy.htm*

United Kingdom Departments of Trade and Industry (DTI), and Culture, Media, and Sport (DCMS). Communication White Paper. A New Future for Communications. Retrieved from *http://www.communicationswhitepaper.gov.uk/*

United Kingdom Her Majesty's Stationery Office. *Electronic Communications Act 2000*. Retrieved from *http://www.uk-legislation.hmso.gov.uk/acts/acts2000/20000007.htm*

United Kingdom Her Majesty's Treasury. *Invest to save budget*. Retrieved from *http://www.isb.gov.uk/*

United Kingdom Office of Government Commerce. *OGC Gateway Process*. Retrieved from *http://www.ogc.gov.uk/index.asp?id=377*

United Kingdom Her Majesty's Treasury. Retrieved from *http://www.hm-treasury.gov.uk/budget/bud_index.cfm*

United Kingdom National Audit Office. (2002, April). *Better public services through e-government*. Retrieved from *http://www.nao.gov.uk/whatsnew.htm*

United Kingdom Office of the e-Envoy. (2000, April). *E-government strategic framework*. Retrieved from *www.e-envoy.gov.uk/ukonlin/stragey.htm*

United Kingdom Office of the e-Envoy. (2000, May). *Recommendations of successful IT: Modernising government in action*. Retrieved from *www.e-envoy.gov.uk/publications/reports/itprojects/index.htm*

United Kingdom Office of the e-Envoy. (2000, September). *E.gov: Electronic government services for the 21st century*. Retrieved from *www.e-envoy.gov.uk/publications/reports_index.htm#2000*

United Kingdom Office of the e-Envoy Website. Retrieved from *http://www.e-envoy.gov.uk/*

United States

Clinger-Cohen Act of 1996. (1996). Information Technology Management Reform Act, Public Law 104-106, Section 5125, 110 Stat. 674.

Electronic Government Task Force. Retrieved from *http://egov.gov/task/*

Federal CIO Council. (1999, January). *ROI and the value puzzle*.

Federal CIO Council. (1999, September). *Federal Enterprise Architecture*, Version 1.1.

Federal CIO Council, Committee on Capital Planning and IT Management. (2000, October). *Smart practices in capital planning guide*. Retrieved from *http://www.cio.gov/Documents/smart%5Fpractices%5book%2Epdf*

Federal CIO Council, Council Committee on Best Practices. (2002, March). *A summary of first practices and lessons learned in information technology portfolio management*. Retrieved from *http://www.cio.gov/*

Frank, D. (2002, April 15). OMB floats e-gov 'branding' strategy. *Federal Computer Week Online*. Retrieved from *http://www.fcw.com*

Government Paperwork Elimination Act of 1999. (1998). Public Law 105-277, enacted October 21, 1998.

Information Technology Resources Board. (1999, December). *Assessing the risks of commercial off-the-shelf applications*. Retrieved from *http://www.itrb.gov/documents/cotsfinal%2Edoc*

Intergovernmental Advisory Board, Federation of Government Information Processing Councils in cooperation with the Office of Intergovernmental Solutions, Office of Governmentwide Policy, U.S. General Services Administration. (1998, January). *Innovative funding approaches for information technology initiatives: Federal, state, and local government experiences.*

McFarlan, F. W. (1981, September/October). Portfolio approach to information systems. *Harvard Business Review, 59*(5), 142-151.

McGill, R. (2001). Performance budgeting. *International Journal of Public Sector Management, 14*(5), 376-390.

Miller, J. (2002, March 18). Latest e-gov task: Finding funding. *Government Computer News Online*. Retrieved from *http://gcn.com/21_6/news/18194-1.html*

Miller, J. & Menke, S. M. (2002, March 20). E-gov projects likely to end up in a bell curve. *Government Computer News Online.* Retrieved from *http://www.gcn.com/vol1_no1/daily-updates/18221-1.html*

Porteus, L. (2002, April 2). Legislation driving Bush administration e-gov efforts. *National Technology Journal Daily.* Retrieved from *http://www.govexec.com/dailyfed/0402/040202td2.htm*

President's Management Agenda Fiscal Year 2002. (2001, August). Retrieved from *http://www.whitehouse.gov/omb/budget/index.html*

Ross, J. W. & Beath, C. M. (2002, Winter). Beyond the Business Case: New Approaches to IT Investment. *MIT Sloan Management Review*, 51-59.

U.S. GAO. (n.d.). *Information Technology Investment Management: A Framework for Assessing and Improving Process Maturity.* (Exposure Draft). Retrieved from *http://www.gao.gov/special.pubs/ai10123.pdf*

U.S. GAO. (1994). *Improving mission performance through strategic information management: Learning from leading organizations.* Retrieved from GPO Access.

U.S. GAO. (1996, November). *Budget issues: Budgeting for federal capital.* Retrieved from GPO Access. GAO/AIMD-97-5.

U.S. GAO. (1998). *Budget issues: Budgeting for capital, testimony before the President's Commission to study capital budgeting, statement of Paul L. Posner, Director, Budget Issues, Accounting and Information Management Division.* Retrieved from GPO Access. T-AIMD-98-99.

U.S. GAO. (1998). *Executive guide: Measuring performance and demonstration results of information technology investments.* Retrieved from GPO Access.

U.S. GAO. (1998, December). *Leading practices in capital decision-making.* Retrieved from GPO Access. GAO/AIMD-99-32.

U.S. GAO. (2000, February). *Accrual budgeting: Experiences of other nations and implications for the United States.* Report to the Honorable Benjamin L. Cardin, House of Representatives. Retrieved from GPO Access. AIMD-00-57.

U.S. GAO. (2001, February 26). *Budget issues: Incremental funding of capital asset acquisitions.* Retrieved from GAO-01-432R.

U.S. General Accounting Office. (2002, March 21). *Information technology: OMB leadership critical to making needed enterprise architecture and e-government progress.* Testimony of Randolph C. Hite and David L. McClure before the

Subcommittee on Technology and Procurement Policy, Committee on Government Reform, House of Representatives. Retrieved from GAO-02-389T

U. S. General Services Administration. *IT Policy On Ramp*. Retrieved from *http://www.gsa.gov/Portal/content/policies_content.jsp?contentOID=117087&contentType=1006&PMKE=1&S=1.*

U.S. Office of Management and Budget. (2000, September). *Budget of the United Statess Fiscal Year 2003*. Retrieved from *http://www.whitehouse.gov/omb/budget/fy2003/index.html*

U.S. OMB. (1997, July). *Capital programming guide*. Retrieved from *http://www.whitehouse.gov/omb/ciculars/a11/cpgtoc.html*

U.S. OMB. (2000, November 28). Circular A-130. *Management of federal information resources*. Retrieved from *http://www.whitehouse.gov/omb/circulars/a130/a130trans4.html*

U.S. OMB. (2001, July 17). Circular No. A-11, Transmittal Memorandum # 74. *Preparing and submitting budget estimates (Part 3): Planning, budgeting and acquisition of capital assets*. Retrieved from *http://www.whitehouse.gov/omb/circulars/a11/01toc.html*

U.S. OMB. (2002, February 27). *E-government strategy: Simplified delivery of services to citizens*. Retrieved from *http://www.whitehouse.gov/omb/inforeg/egovstrategy.pdf*

U.S. White House. (1999, February). *Report of the president's commission to study capital budgeting*. Retrieved from *http://clinton3.nara.gov/pcscb/report_pcscb.html*

ACRONYMS

CIO	Chief Information Officer
ICT	Information and Communications Technology
EA	Enterprise Architecture
OMB	Office of Management and Budget
GAO	General Accounting Office
GSA	General Services Administration
GPRA	Government Performance and Results Act (US)
GPEA	Government Paperwork Elimination Act (US)
I-TIPS	Information Technology Portfolio Management System
IT	Information Technology

INTERVIEWS

We would like to acknowledge and thank the following people for their contribution to the organization, through their interviews, writing, and editing of this document.

New Zealand

Vivien Wynne, Principal Advisor, Public Sector Management, The Treasury
Russell Craig, Senior Advisor, E-government Unit, State Services Commission

United Kingdom

Catrina Bowman, Policy Advisor, Office of the e-Envoy
Chris Carr, Funding Scrutiny, Office of the e-Envoy
Robert Pope, Funding Advisor, Office of the e-Envoy
Michael Thornton, H.M. Treasury

United States

Christine E. Bonham, Assistant Director, Strategic Issues, U.S. General Accounting Office
Mayi Canales, Acting Chief Information Officer, U.S. Department of Treasury
Daniel J. Chenok, Chief, Information Policy & Technology Branch, Office of Information and Regulatory Affairs, U.S. Office of Management and Budget, Executive Office of the President
Tony Frater, Government-to-Government (G2G) Portfolio Manager, Information Policy & Technology Branch, U.S. Office of Management and Budget, Executive Office of the President
Ursula S. Gillis, Program examiner, Treasury Branch, U.S. Office of Management and Budget, Executive Office of the President
Susan Irving, Federal Budget Issues Director, U.S. General Accounting Office
David L. McClure, Ph.D., Information Technology Management Issues Director, U.S. General Accounting Office
Mark J. Schwartz, Chief, Treasury Branch, U.S. Office of Management and Budget, Executive Office of the President
G. Martin Wagner, Associate Administrator, Office of Governmentwide Policy U.S. General Services Administration

ENDNOTES

* The observations and conclusions in this chapter reflect the state of the practice in the three governments examined as of 2002. There have been developments with regard to both policy and funding in each, e.g., the U.S. E-Government Act of 2002.

1 Cabinet Office Circular CO (00) 12, released in November 2000, outlines the guidelines for changes to budget baselines. According to this circular, new capital resources require a sound business case and strategic business plan to support all capital contribution requests. Requests for additional capital should only be considered as a last resort option. While capital decisions may require greater flexibility regarding the extent of resources that can be sought, the preference is that these decisions be considered in the Budget. Furthermore, projects with a major IT component are expected to follow a more rigorous approval process set out in Cabinet Office Circular CO (01) 4 and the SSC Chief Executive Circular CE

2000/10, which involves a two-stage Cabinet approval, the use of quantitative risk analysis and breaking large projects into smaller modules.

2 The *American Heritage College Dictionary* defines investment as, "Buying or sacrificing something today, with the intent of: (a) creating a stream of wealth in the future; or (b) preventing wealth destruction in the future."

3 In *Modernising Government* (March 1999) "joined-up government in action" is described as "including a clear commitment for people to be able to notify different parts of government of details such as a change of address *simply and electronically in one transaction*." For more on the ISB see *www.isb.gov.uk*.

4 This discussion applies only to the U.S. Federal government. States and localities often have very different budgeting and accounting systems.

5 Spending authority is also created in what are called "permanent appropriations" for so-called entitlement or mandatory programs, like old age and disability pensions, which are not subject to annual appropriations. These are not relevant to the discussion of financing e-government since ICT projects are funded out of the discretionary accounts.

6 The General Accounting Office is an arm of Congress and the Auditor-General for the United States.

7 According to a 2001 GAO Report (GAO-01-432R), "Capital acquisition funds can be used to help alleviate 'spiking' issues…a department level CAF would borrow from the Treasury, as provided in appropriation acts, to purchase an asset needed by a department subcomponent. The subcomponent would 'rent' the asset, paying sufficient rent so the CAF can repay loan principal and interest to Treasury. Full funding is preserved and 'spiking' at the sub-component level is eased. Discretionary caps could be adjusted to reflect a concept change for appropriating interest" (*Incremental Funding of Capital Assets*, p. 41).

8 See Office of Management and Budget Memorandum (unnumbered), "Redundant Information Systems Relating to On-Line Rulemaking Initiative," dated May 3, 2002, *http://www.whitehouse.gov/omb/pubpress/2002-27.pdf*.

9 See Office of Management and Budget Memorandum (unnumbered), "Reducing Related IT Infrastructure Related to Homeland Security," dated July 19, 2002, *http://www.whitehouse.gov/omb/pubpress/2002-46.pdf*; and Memorandum M-02-013, "Review and Consolidation of Business Management Systems for the Proposed Department of Homeland Security," dated July 30, 2002 *http://www.whitehouse.gov/omb/pubpress/2002-51.pdf*.

10 "OMB hands out e-gov funding," *Federal Computer Week,* April 19,2002. Retrieved from the World Wide Web at: *http://www.fcw.com/fcw/articles/2002/0415/web-egov-04-18-02.asp*.

11 See *http://www.cio.gov/* and select "Best Practices" to find document available in pdf format.

12 An interesting debate has raged, for example, about the economic value of "small time savings." If the public, on average, spends 30 minutes less time in line waiting for a driver's license to be issues, are those small increments truly recoverable and put to other economically productive uses? Put another way, if 100,000 individuals save 30 minutes once a year, has the economy realized the equivalent of 25 work years in savings?

[13] EBT is used to provide credits for food to eligible individuals by issue them a card that can be used in grocery stores in lieu of the paper coupons that were previously issued. Not only does this application save time and money and reduce fraud, it helps avoid stigma of using *food stamps* since, to the casual observer, their transactions are indistinguishable from credit card transactions.

[14] See *IRS e-file for Business Partners,* "The Internal Revenue Service has entered into partnership agreements with these companies to foster electronic filing." Retrieved from the World Wide Web at: *http://www.irs.gov/elec_svs/bizptnr.html.*

[15] For reasons of timing and cost, interviews outside the U.S. were conducted either by e-mail or telephone.

Chapter XVI

E-Government and Private-Public Partnerships: Relational Challenges and Strategic Directions

Barbara Allen, University of Ottawa, Canada

Luc Juillet, University of Ottawa, Canada

Gilles Paquet, University of Ottawa, Canada

Jeffrey Roy, University of Ottawa, Canada[1]

ABSTRACT

E-government creates both new pressures and new opportunities for partnering — within governments, between governments and across sectors and the citizenry. In particular, new relational mechanisms are required to shape effective ties between governments and the vendors of IT systems and solutions that are more pervasive, fluid and demanding in terms of the level of collaboration and trust required between private sector vendors and public sector clients. The complexity and sophistication of such solutions produce many strategic choices for governments about how to deploy IT and the degree to which in-house capacities should be balanced and complemented with externalized skills and solutions. Thus, partnerships are now central to public management: In a digital world, effectively dealing with more relational organizational architectures becomes the core competency of a continually renewed and enabled public service. This chapter first explores the main challenges facing governments in such an environment, followed by a sketching of the main strategic directions required to address them.

INTRODUCTION

E-government is an umbrella term for a wide range of initiatives — driven by both emerging technology and social ingenuity — that carry the potential to fundamentally alter relationships within government, between governments, and across all sectors and the broader public. In fact, there is now growing recognition that e-government is less about electronic government in a purely technical sense and more about renewing public sector institutions for a new, more knowledge and network-driven era.

As governments formulate their own integrative strategies for moving online, coordination challenges both within and across governments are likely to grow — as will the potential for healthy competition. The new challenges of an effective and online public sector reside in defining the requisite mix of competitive and collaborative forces needed to realize the full potential of an online world - *one that is both digital and democratic.*

As a starting point, *governance* may be defined as effective coordination in an environment where both knowledge and power are distributed. Every organization is built on governance, whether formal or informal, ineffective or successful. The rise of *e-governance* refers to new processes of coordination made possible or even necessary by the advent of technology — and the spreading of online activities in particular.

As a result, e-*government* in the broadest sense refers to an IT-led reconfiguration of public sector governance — and how knowledge, power and purpose are redistributed in light of new technological realities. In summarizing what has been written about the information age and/or digital world to date, our perspective is that there are three main sets of inter-related forces driving the emergence of e-governance and the search for new organizational models across all sectors:

- *Spatial:* geography and place
- *Digital:* communications and time
- *Cognitive:* knowledge and education

Globalization drives new spatial considerations that are changing our notion of place as economic and, to some degree, social and political forces for integration create new interdependencies beyond national borders. As a result, identity and community are less bound by geography, with new and far more complex networking patterns emerging.

More instantaneous communication and changing perceptions of time are related considerations — as the expression "*Internet time*" redefines many organizational activities in the private sector, and in government as well. A digital world implies instantaneous decisions and accessibility, and speed and responsiveness become the hallmarks of performance (Guillaume, 1999; Tapscott & Agnew, 1999).

Changing cognitive capacities are the third set of contextual forces driving change — as the rapid expansion of both information and education empowers populations to become less passive and better educated. Organizations struggle to define and retain the right mix of competencies in a knowledge-based workforce increasingly characterized by mobility, diversity and assertiveness (Rifkin, 2000; Rosenau, 2000).

These simultaneous forces are at the heart of the struggle to adapt to a new governance environment. *For governments, however, there are inherent contradictions in each that must be recognized.*

New notions of place mean that e-government emerges not within a traditional order of national processes, rather within a more complex picture of both globalizing and localizing pressures. E-government, at the national level, means interfacing with the new global possibilities and pressures, while empowering cities and regions with the tools to act collectively in order to prosper.

Governance in a digital world is bound to encompass a growing number of multilevel processes, heightening the need for coordination and learning across traditionally separate public sector systems (Weil & Broadbent, 1998).

New notions of time also result in contradictory pressures for government. While "Internet time" stimulates service delivery and the desire to be more customer-oriented, public interest considerations and more citizen-oriented government often heighten complexity and time requirements. Using technology to engage citizens in more deliberative forms of democracy may well require more time — and more patience.

Similarly, demographic trends signal new challenges as an emerging knowledge society takes shape. Driven by the so-called Internet generation, the citizenry is becoming less homogenous, less passive and less accepting of traditional forms of authority and representation, and more contradictory in its demands (Lenihan, 2002). Government will be challenged to not only respond, but to also redefine the social contract of the new millennium — meaning both the rights and responsibilities of a connected citizenry.

The struggle to define a vision of *e-government* reflects our search for better ways to adapt in order to meet new spatial, digital and demographic realities. As the proceeding discussion implies, e-government cannot simply be derived from the imposition of new technology on existing organizational models. As the public sector adapts itself to a new environment, it must also serve as a catalyst for guiding all stakeholders toward a common path. Therefore, e-government is intertwined with the broader governance transformations reshaping and joining our economy, our society, and our polity.

Comparative reviews undertaken by the OECD and other organizations demonstrate both the growing scope of e-government and its potential importance. As Internet usage widens, so too does the set of opportunities for delivering services in digital formats, rethinking how such services are created and packaged, and considering the need for new services and policies that may be required.

In terms of where we are at presently, there appears to be convergence on three broad points:

- First, e-government is accelerating as a key priority for governments around the world, and as a key driver for public service reform;
- Secondly, governments remain at an early stage of online evolution; and
- Thirdly, the future prospects of e-government are tied to a variety of structural and cultural factors that go well beyond getting on the Internet.

Within such parameters there is a struggle with terminology. We suggest that the term, *digital government,* reflects a *partial re-configuration* of the public sector through new information technologies. This new digital architecture is a crucial component of the e-government challenge — *but it is also incomplete.* It is crucial since the investments made into IT will lay a foundation for a less hierarchical and more flexible organization. However, it is incomplete since hardware and software alone cannot ensure better performance and ongoing learning.

The Partnership Imperative

E-governance and the resulting emergence of e-government create both new pressures and new opportunities for new partnering — within governments, between governments and across sectors and the citizenry (Allen et al., 2001). Within government, IT fosters new horizontal opportunities by shifting away from traditional bureaucratic structures toward alternative decision-making models and service delivery arrangements.

The growing possibilities for consultations with both stakeholders and the citizenry are also expanded with new technologies. Moreover, online delivery implies integrative channels within government, linking external users across sources and systems internally. These trends mean IT forces are both dispersing and centralizing – fostering a need for integrative action. Put another way, these forces create tensions between vertical accountability predominant in traditional government and the horizontal action made both feasible and essential by the advent of e-government.

The challenge is two-fold: e-government requires action and strategies at the level of individual departments and agencies, but such efforts must be orchestrated within the parameters of government-wide leadership and coordination.

Accountability is a key element of such a balance. The manner by which accountability is perceived and exercised by government leaders will determine the degree to which it embraces more collaborative models of governance. Traditionalists invoke the underlying principle of Ministerial Accountability based on a clear and rigid view of vertical control and risk-minimization in order to serve and protect the interests of the publicly accountable political leader.

The rise of e-governance, with its pressures for a variety of initiatives introducing alternative models of decision-making and service delivery, implies a sharing of accountability. The need for collaboration, partnerships and joint ventures grows within government, and often between private and public organizations (Jayes, 1998).

There are also important debates around the issue of whether accountability is at risk when external partners become involved in the governing and shared delivery of government programs and services. According to some, new governance arrangements threaten to undermine key institutions and practices of democratic accountability (Globerman & Vining, 1996).

Many in this camp believe that any change to the existing system of ministerial accountability will damage the integrity of the system. There is some question as to whether the *ad hoc* nature of the ever-increasing number of partnership arrangements between sectors challenges accountability mechanisms or can be absorbed in traditional models of decision making with adaptations to risk mitigating strategies.

An alternative view is that collaborative arrangements can make government more accountable (Armstrong, 2000). The proponents of collaborative arrangements insist that involving external stakeholders strengthens accountability to citizens by virtue of the addition of partners. In particular, private- and civic-sector partners bring additional pressure for accountability to customers or clients (Paquet & Roy, 2000).

Notwithstanding legitimate concerns about new ways of doing things, it is difficult to conclude from these debates that the virtues of traditional accountability, namely their clarity and simplicity, justify their extension to e-governance.

These tensions shape ties between governments and the vendors of IT systems and solutions. IT solutions, however, are more pervasive in demanding closer collaboration between private vendors and public-sector clients (Mornan, 1998; Jelich, Poupart & Roy, 2000). The complexity and sophistication of such solutions produce many strategic choices for governments about how to deploy IT both in and across public sector operations.

Main Challenges

A key variable in the e-government equation is how and why private-public partnerships must be envisioned and effectively managed within the realm of e-government. This section addresses this question by breaking it down into the following set of strategic sub-issues that include the:

- Philosophy behind public-sector procurement and pressures to reform and strike new capacities to partner;
- Approaches to accountability, less vertical and more horizontal, capable of balancing the constraints of contracting with the opportunities of collaboration;
- Ownership and financing implications of private–public partnerships in an increasingly online environment;
- Centrality of human capital and the altering skills requirements of public service to operate in a more partnership-intensive environment; and
- Stakeholder perspectives that shape the context of private-public partnerships, including labor organizations and non-governmental organizations.

Procurement

A key variable at the heart of the partnership challenge lies in the reality that for the most part, traditional procurement processes shape the choices that governments make — in terms of which products, services and solutions to buy, and on what basis to make this selection.

Traditionally, government procurement functions do little to distinguish between various types of goods and services — and so the manner by which pens and buildings are bought for government departments and agencies can differ little from how technology services and organizational solutions are selected.

A necessary starting point, then, is to consider the possibility that the technical and cognitive architecture underpinning the emergence of e-government represents a process of such strategic importance that it cannot be managed within traditional processes, even as many reforms are undertaken to adapt them to new realities.

Such reform may well be inadequate and counter-productive: inadequate, since the inertia of procurement cannot be easily improved at the margins; counter-productive, since this traditional approach to buying goods and services may well still be relevant for large amounts of more static inputs that governments still require to operate.

Accordingly, there is much confusion about the evolution of procurement in an online world. And this argument is in no way meant to refute the potential benefits of e-procurement. E-procurement is online and centralized — and it can be centralized for all of government, or even for many governments (as many American states are showing).

Centralization of such processes can be more efficient — discriminating across instantaneous marketplaces — electronically — to seek greater value. Yet such processes are not the same processes as those required to fundamentally redesign service delivery strategies, managerial systems, outsourcing versus insourcing strategies, and the need for constant adaptation in an increasingly dynamic environment.

This differentiation distinguishes procurement from partnering in an e-government context. An exploration of partnering begins with notions of accountability.

Accountability

Most national governments exist in democratic contexts that seek to preserve accountability with an emphasis on process — rather than performance. Parliament oversight, independent offices, and media scrutiny are some of the major forces shaping this emphasis — as public sector managers face constant pressures of probity and transparency.

This process-based accountability underpins, of course, traditional procurement architectures that focus on cost minimization, risk avoidance, and competitive maximization. In other words, governments cannot play favorites when contracting: they must be fair and open in deploying the public purse.

If this process-based accountability focuses on costs and inputs alone, the emergence of e-government brings huge problems. For each new IT initiative involving purchasing or partnering with an outside vendor, managers must provide blueprints for their precise "specifications" over time and demonstrate precisely how each phase of implementation will occur, and to what end for the organization.

A shift to partnership-based accountability implies focusing less on the inputs and controls and more on the outcomes and expectations. In many respects, results-based management, in an increasingly digital world, must begin with the procurement function.

Yet beyond this purchasing and managing continuum, there must also be political reform in order to alter the way reporting for results occur. In most OECD countries, public accountability, even when results-based, takes place in a silo-like fashion: each Minister reports to their political chambers for the inputs and outputs of their particular jurisdiction (usually underpinned by a flagship department).

Accountability based more on partnering and performance will invariably require new mechanisms for reporting outcomes that are more integrative and collective. Only when governments begin to share accountability within their political structures will they be in a position to truly share accountability with partners in industry or civil society.

The private-sector perspective must also be considered. From an otherwise excellent and forward looking discussion of what is termed as transformative outsourcing, the following definition reveals a degree of separation that will be consequential in shaping the nature of any collaboration.

For Accenture Consulting, then, outsourcing may be defined as:

Contracting with a private-sector firm to take responsibility for a function or process for which the government remains accountable.[2]

This quote and the philosophy behind it shape the second level of accountability (between partners) in important ways. The implication is a role for the private sector in contributing to public interest outcomes — without an according degree of shared responsibility for the outcomes stemming from their involvement.

Sharing accountability means moving from away from a traditional focus on contracting toward one of partnering. While there is no commonly shared or adhered-to definition of outsourcing with respect to IT and e-government, and the growing complexity of the systems being put in place, it is useful and necessary to embrace a relational philosophy that extends beyond contracting.

The following continuum is a useful comparative portrait[3]:

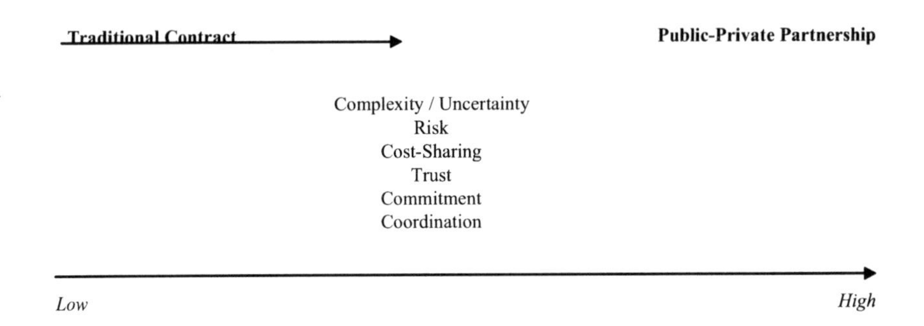

The emerging context of e-government is quite clearly a move toward a greater reliance on partnering and, as such, toward a more strategic focus on outsourcing. The term, outsourcing, is regarded as poisonous by some due to both notorious political and managerial implications of this more relational-based forms of governance. While all governments outsource, what is occurring today is an intensification of pressures to outsource larger and more strategic components of its operations.

Labelled co-sourcing or co-sharing by some IT service providers, outsourcing arrangements are much closer to the notion of private-public partnerships than traditional contracting relationships. Successful outsourcing relationships between governments and industry seem to share, at their core, the three following characteristics:

- An emphasis on outcomes and results-based compensation;
- A stipulation of minimum service requirements and long-term goals and expectations; and
- A capacity to continually deliberate and adapt as circumstances change.[4]

A useful depiction of this relational evolution is provided by Stevenson (1998) who differentiates between three scenarios or types of interactive arrangements — markets, alliances and partnerships (Figure 1).

Market-based activities certainly do not lose their place in the e-government context. This is the context of e-procurement, suitable for static, high-volume goods and services easily defined and readily attainable.

The limitations of transacting in this market manner (electronic or otherwise) explain the shift toward alliances of various sorts, including those between companies and those

Figure 1. Stevenson scenarios

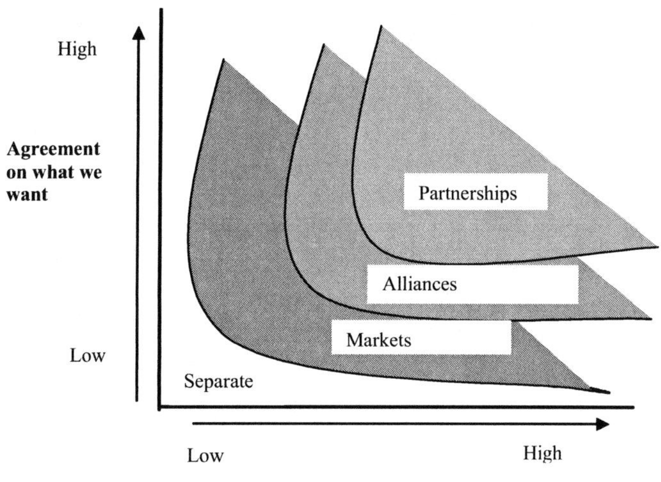

joining companies and governments. More agreement is required about both how the world works and about what the different parties want if one is to forge a relationship. Yet, the relationship is likely not long-term and it may or may not emphasize performance outcomes.

In The United Kingdom, government's usage of the private financing initiative (PFI) for traditional forms of infrastructure might fit well in the alliance category: the relatively static and clear deliverables (usually hard forms of infrastructure such as schools and roads, etc.) lend themselves to the extension of contracting to alliances of private and public resources. Others may be inclined to place PFI in the partnership zone (and the true placement probably varies from one example to the next).

The depiction above underscores that shared accountability between partners requires shared frames of reference that can only be developed through high degrees of trust. Trust, in turn, only comes about in a deliberative environment where contracting is not a measure designed to attempt to envision every conceivable outcome and risk, but rather one element of a broader arrangement designed to move parties forward in a common direction with the expectation that the relationship will evolve, and co-evolve over time.

The third and final level of accountability involves the collective responsibility that partners have to their over-arching set of stakeholders (and shareholders, surely, in the market sphere of activity).

Here a significant share of the burden shifts from government to private sector partners who must accept what are often unique realities of doing business in the public sphere:

The private sector must expect that, when it deals with the State, the disclosure requirements cannot merely be those that pertain to commercial transactions...if the accountability arrangements are the same, insufficient weight will to be given to the need for the State to be accountable to the citizen.

Those in the private sector who seek to gain commercial advantage from dealings with the government cannot to escape the level of scrutiny that prevails in the private sectors. Such scrutiny is required because of the non-commercial nature of much government activity, the non-voluntary relationship between individuals and their government and the different rule of law which applies in the public sector from the private sector.[5]

The important lesson, with respect to partnering between industry and government in an increasingly technology-driven and interdependent environment, is relational: codified agreements — contracting — are insufficient to withstand the change and uncertainty prevalent and likely to increase as e-government takes hold.

At a minimum, then, in order to effectively collaborate there is a need for a mechanism that shares accountability across all key stakeholders and links it, in part, to performance outcomes (rather than purely process-based inputs and controls).

Financing and Ownership

A major challenge in private-public partnerships centres on ownership, and the importance that governments attach to maintaining a deed on critical aspects of their national and local infrastructure. Accordingly, the UK's PFI program is rather innovative in rethinking this approach in a manner that attempts to blend public purpose and private return in new ways.

E-government is a peculiar and at times contradictory challenge. On the one hand, many governments are keenly "contracting" to build their own secure channels in order to possess the necessary infrastructure internally to go online. On the other hand, the rapid growth and expansion of Internet usage is blurring ownership lines like never before.

Although the Internet is viewed as the new and necessary public infrastructure for the 21st century, its presence and effective deployment requires a good deal of private investment and market-based activity. In a digital world, government ownership will decline in relative terms — although, the state can augment its role through other means such as regulatory powers and direct interventions when markets fall short.

Portals are a good illustration. Governments around the world are fiercely attempting to create attractive and functional entry points into their online domains. Yet, usage of these portals remains modest, and in an early stage of growth — leading some commentators to suggest that many portals now in place, or just being created, will be redundant in just a few years.

A major factor for the explanation is the growing presence of private-sector portals and Internet channels, and the possibility for partnering the necessity of public provision and the creativity of private promotion. In other words, some portions of online public services can be better managed through private-public alliances of one sort or another[6].

Even where governments choose to build their own portals, partnerships can be deployed. A major determinant is whether a government views a portal as a process or an asset: in the latter, subcontracting its design may prove sufficient. Conversely, a more integrative process between portal development and organizational redesign is the focus of a growing set of outsourcing relationships between public agencies and private specialists.

Different countries and cultures will vary in their approaches and relative balances between their private and public components of their online architectures. Whatever mix achieves the required capital investments should be pursued and the requisite recipe will, by necessity, differ across jurisdictions.

Still more contentious choices surround the ownership of intellectual capital: *namely, knowledge and people.* For instance, gaining access to highly skilled workers is used as an argument both for and against outsourcing IT-laden systems. Governments want to tap into the expertise of specialists without becoming entirely dependent on outside organizations for their capacity to operate.

Here lies the necessity of people and human resource management's central place in the e-government equation — and the willingness and capacity to partner in particular.

Human Capital

E-government's evolution is largely dependent on a nexus of technology, governance and people. Thus, human resources management must be integrated holistically with all elements of strategy to adapt the public sector for these new challenges.

As government engages in new forms of collaborative arrangements, work teams comprise sets of individuals with a variety of formal, informal and overlapping reporting relationships. Moreover, more workers contributing to government may do so from outside the traditions of a core, full-time public service.

Many studies demonstrate this rise in a partially external workforce of non-core staff. One such analysis claims that from 1997-2002, senior managers expect an increase from 10 percent to 25 percent in non-core (meaning non-traditional full-time, or external) workers.[7] This *crescendo* of the external workforce will likely accelerate with technology-induced pressures for organizational innovation and flexibility. The pressures for e-government transformations will tie organizational design issues on the one hand, beginning with the utilization of new partnerships, and human resource management reform on the other.

How decisions are made will also change due to such trends. For example, recent research on public-sector IT management demonstrates how traditional structures of vertical hierarchy are being impacted not only by horizontality within government, but also by the growing power of external consultants who serve as key intermediaries between public servants, external vendors and politicians (Jayes, 1998; OECD, 2001).

Consequently, a more complex mix of agendas and incentives will emerge that explains the growing emphasis on inter-personal skills such as negotiation, facilitation, and consultation. These skills are forming the basis of a "*new public servant*" as reported by a major study on public-sector leadership in the coming decade:

One of the most important will be teamwork. Successful partnerships will often require government workers to work in teams with outsiders or civil servants from other departments. Survey respondents also cited technology skills as being very important by 2010...For governments to manage their swelling numbers of technology alliances and outsourcing arrangements successfully, they need employees with enough technology sophistication to manage such projects. [8]

The importance of such skills will escalate in areas such as project management, network design and implementation, and database management as well as in areas that are key to bringing government online — information and data systems, privacy and security, Web-enabled application design and client training. Moreover, demographic trends facing many national governments underscore the need for more innovative efforts to find and keep skilled workers — and hiring pressures will only intensify.

What is interesting and somewhat worrisome to observe across most national governments in the OECD is the separate treatment of e-government challenges on the one hand, and human resource management on the other. The changing shape of the public-service workforce is both strategic and controversial — running counter to traditional parameters of public-sector employment in many OECD countries such as the merit principle, competitive and open hiring, and job security (at least in relative terms versus the private sector).

The link between human resources and outsourcing and partnerships is a crucial one in the transformation to e-government. It is unlikely that outsourcing the entire IT infrastructure of a government is feasible for most jurisdictions.[9] Yet, it is equally unlikely that any government can efficiently and effectively internalize its entire workforce in a network-centric world.

Stakeholder Engagement

The central place of procurement and contracts, coupled with the reality that a significant portion of the technical expertise for e-government's infrastructure resides in IT market-based specialists combine to explain the over-arching focus on business–government relationships as the focal point of private-public partnerships.

Yet, there are other stakeholders as well — whose input and role can be determinant in whether a partnership can be undertaken, and eventually succeed. First and foremost, a unique aspect of IT partnering and outsourcing in the public sector is the power and perspective of labor organizations. This aspect is characterized as unique since many outsourcing deals between private companies may take place in the absence of unions.[10]

The level of union authority within a public sector, and the ties between labor and the government in power have, to some extent, politicized the environment for partnering. The ideological term for one form of partnering — privatization — is synonymous with the right of centre governments to remove functions from the public sphere, place them into the marketplace, and thereby remove itself from any further role or responsibility (though reality is rarely so simplistic).

It is noteworthy, however, that unionization need not translate into a barrier to partnering or even to outsourcing public servants from public-sector to private-sector organizations. Yet, the challenges unique to such circumstances must be carefully accounted for. For example, prior to its significant activities in the UK, one IT multinational followed a non-union corporate policy for itself and its client selection. Today its significant public-sector presence is global, transcending partisan boundaries.

E-government and the growing presence of IT-based solutions provide at least the potential for distinguishing between politically extreme models of the past and the necessary partnerships for tomorrow. The main driver for such optimism is the blurring of private/public boundaries in cyberspace — or perhaps more accurately, the need to rethink and rebalance the private and public interests at play in a digital society.

The main requirement is dialogue and inclusion. There are enough lessons from outsourcing experiments in the United States, an environment not generally deemed as labor friendly, to underscore the reality that if a partnership is viewed as a strategy to circumvent or diminish labor's presence, the result is likely to be highly confrontational and divisive. The probability for failure thus heightens dramatically.

Aside from labor, the roles of the public and their elected representatives are also important considerations. Such is particularly relevant for those political systems with some degree of separation of powers within the Executive branch or with strong oversight mechanisms from the Legislative Branch.

The reasoning is similar to the logic of labor involvement. A deal to contract out functions or partner with a company that is undertaken in secrecy is virtually assured to attract more critical inquiry for skeptics than those that result from vigorous and open public debate.

To an increasing extent, the degrees of freedom of governments to even consider, let alone undertake, new forms of partnership arrangements will be determined, to a significant degree, by the level of public awareness and debate generated by them in a proactive manner.

Strategic Directions

The world of e-governance marks an important turning point for many governments — particularly those at the national level. After years of fiscal contraction and modest spending levels, particularly on new organizational infrastructure, the drive to modernize the state, particularly in terms of a more innovative and digital public sector, requires substantial investments of fiscal, human and cognitive resources.

The following five directions are discussed as starting points for reform in addressing the challenges outlined above and in building a framework for more effective partnering:

- Shifting beyond procurement
- Decentralizing authority
- Balancing risk & results
- Remembering people & politics
- Realigning for performance

Shifting Beyond Procurement

There is nothing inherently outdated about the procurement function in government, as public-sector agencies will continually buy a range of inputs in order to fulfil their missions. Yet, there is a growing disconnect on the one hand between traditional contracting mechanisms and controls and the need for more collaboration on the other. Recognizing the existence of this disconnect and addressing it is a precursor to effectively adapting to a world of e-governance.

A useful starting point for many governments to consider is the creation of a new organizational unit to overview partnering. It may simply not be feasible for existing procurement authorities to take on the additional and dramatically different partnering requirements of e-government (though they remain an important stakeholder in the transformation).

A cautionary point is a fear in many circles that creating such unit to devise and oversee e-government strategies means proceeding via highly centralized mechanisms (Langford & Harrison, 2001). Thus, e-government policy shops operating within existing central agencies may face particularly acute challenges in orchestrating action in a collaborative manner — as the willingness to do so may run counter to historical legacies and inertia.

Decentralizing Authority

This logic leads to the second direction — that while it may be appropriate to centralize certain forms of procurement for static inputs, effective and innovative forms of partnerships are best realized in decentralized settings — where creativity can be maximized. Decentralized can mean either within a particular government (central agencies versus departments and special agencies), or across levels of government.

The degree of flexibility with new forms of partnerships will likely fluctuate inversely to the amount of resources at stake. As such, in many governments we are seeing sub-national governments leading experimentation with innovative partnering schemes while, quite naturally, the multi-billion dollar apparatus of national governments offers more resistance and higher degrees of caution.

The research on IT project management demonstrates that while IT can be a centralizing force for many organizations, success rates (or more accurately, the least frightening failure rates) seem to take place in those jurisdictions that have either decentralized procurement/partnership choices to individual department levels (New Zealand as a case in point).

Federalist jurisdictions are compelling cases — as while many sub-national units explore partnership avenues, central governments aggressively promote e-government agendas, raising questions about the relative equilibrium between centralization and decentralization that it is likely to emerge.

At a minimum, coordinating bodies must exist not only across individual governments, but also across all levels of state activity. The governance of e-government must weigh the need for central leadership and coordination on the one hand, and the advantages of flexibility on the other, particularly in partnering, inherent in more decentralized settings.

Balancing Risk & Results

The third direction, more centered on accountability, focuses on the need for a cultural shift in the public sector to renew the balance between risk and results. Government must find ways to overcome the traditional inertia of minimizing the former. In a world of shared governance and an immense amount of private-public partnering, clear accountabilities must give way to truly shared forms of accountability.

One positive way to share accountability is to focus less on the rules of inputs and controls and more on the outcomes of a collaborative experiment. While business and government will never be unique in this regard, an enabled public sector in the digital world will be more nimble, and freer to seek new solutions for new circumstances.

Designing and constantly adapting solutions to changing circumstances requires shared decision-making processes between all agents involved in shaping them. A new compact requires expanded freedom for public servants to involve private-sector organizations in designing solutions — in exchange for some shared sense of responsibility that the private partners will not only enjoy the possibility of benefits, but also comply in sharing the costs of negative outcomes.

Critics of collaboration charge that such risks are unacceptable in many democratic regimes that seek clear accountability and openness and transparency in decision-making processes. Moreover, the media — traditional channels — present a powerful force always prepared to expose failures and to apply blame.

The response can only be that the risks of applying traditional notions of control and blame to a more dynamic and instantaneous world of governance far outweigh the risks of innovation. An informed public will be better placed to pass judgment on a creative government that fails — provided it is capable of defending actions and assessments, and provided that government consults adequately and openly prior to moving forward.

Remembering People and Politics

Building on this place for consultation, the fourth direction is the need to include and account for people and politics. Too often, such inclusion implies "communication" — informing the public and stakeholders about government needs and government choices, and by extension successes and failures.

Yet, collaboration requires more than communication — it also requires consultation in a meaningful manner. The dialogue necessary to underpin and defend innovation in the public sphere of our governance is critical — and it must extend beyond the private-public agents that are negotiating to include the public and their representatives in office.

An open dialogue prior to choosing a path can be illuminating. If politicians oppose more private-sector involvement in public pursuits, as is often the case in outsourcing initiatives, what is the alternative? Is it to spend more in internal government operations to build new capacities or is it to just not pursue new forms of technology? There is room here for legitimate democratic debate, and it's the deliberation that will create more degrees of freedom through a wider understanding of the choices and risks in play.

Presently, debates around private-public partnerships seem to fall into one of two camps: either ideologically laden extremities by those simply for or against on principle, or more specialized and technical communities of experts, as is common in the IT environment. The imperative of moving toward e-government means that such debates must become more mainstream in political dialogues — with more nuance and reflection and less immediate reaction.

As such, large-scale, private-public partnerships should include public consultation and oversight mechanisms that emphasize openness. The private sector should be accommodating here, as companies who face public inquiry in a more proactive manner will find themselves in better places to respond and contribute to the debate, as opposed to being captive to problems that emerge if and when secrecy is exposed.

Similarly, governments, by definition, must be prepared to defend the need for partnering and explain the requirements at hand, the risks at play, and the intended result. A central focus must be less on process and more on performance.

Realigning for Performance

The move toward results-based management is occurring at various speeds across the OECD government, as is the trend toward more citizen engagement in policy-making. E-government requires acceleration on both fronts.

There is a danger inherent in many jurisdictions that in the absence of bold and open discussions about the nature of the transformation ahead, an incremental approach to moving government online will take hold. As Blake Harris reminds us:

Moving industrial society government onto a digital platform would simply produce a digitized industrial government — a form of governance that would be increasingly out of step with the changing realities of citizens and businesses alike.[11]

An incremental trajectory is likely to be cautious and it is likely to both emphasize process and be shaped by tradition. Yet, to some extent, incremental thinking is appropriate, as surely e-government does not imply leaving behind all traditions of public administration. Yet, what is required is an ability to look ahead and to think about the sorts of objectives that are likely to dominate the public agenda in a digital world.

At any level — that of a single department, an inter-agency network, or a national jurisdiction as a whole, more partnerships are likely to take hold. A key success factor will be finding the resolve to think about what these partnerships are to accomplish, and then design the appropriate governance mechanisms to get there.

An equally important success factor will be devising new approaches to partnership management that properly account for shared accountabilities, uncertainty and change, and the need for constant innovation. Here, what little academic research has been done on the measurement and evaluation tools appropriate for e-government partnerships has been shown to be highly inadequate (Langford & Harrison, 2001).

A partnership must be viewed, by definition, as a learning affair. And in an increasingly digital world, much of traditional project management is about planning and evaluating actions according to highly a specified blueprint of the path ahead.

Partnership management must be about gauging progress toward agreed-to objectives while defining and redefining such objectives in a collaborative manner. Performance drives process with constraints arrived at through deliberation and adaptation.

CONCLUSIONS

What are the lessons to be drawn? First, realizing the promise of digital government is perhaps best viewed as an evolving process characterized by a difficult mix of innovation on the one hand and incrementalism on the other. As digital connectivity grows, the holistic challenge lies in organizational innovation while recognizing that redesigning governance requires buy-in and ongoing support, as much from public servants as from clients of their services and the partners with whom they are delivered.

A major difficulty for partnership results from the notorious lack of specific targets in the public sector. The uncertainty so prevalent in a digital environment also challenges relations between business and government. If the public and its political leaders possessed a clear blueprint of what it wanted to achieve, with few unknowns, then it would be relatively easy for industry to be able to promise to help reach specified targets. The absence of certainty makes collaboration a challenge.

From the perspective of industry, one of the most common frustrations with traditional procurement is the necessity of providing specific technical solutions in a highly precise fashion despite the uncertainty inherent in the environment. The shift to partnership and outsourcing provides a more relational mind set with a stronger capacity to address uncertainty in a joint fashion.

Yet, outsourcing deals are hardly absent of contracts and technical specifications. As discussed, outsourcing arrangements often attempt to balance and minimize service level guarantees with the possibility of shared rewards if they are surpassed. To some degree, such sharing can also be specified and codified in the legal underpinnings of a partnership.

The growing experiences to date, however, with IT partnerships, those most likely to underpin the emergence of e-government, suggest that if parties are relying solely on contract specification to guide their progress and gauge results, success is unlikely. The more intricate the solution and the higher degree the complexity, the greater the likelihood that legal specifications at the outset of a relationship will prove inadequate in providing a roadmap of the path ahead.

Here lies the central importance of learning and adaptive capacities in partnership-based governance models. In fact, the capacity to learn and adapt is perhaps the most important component to envision in designing an architecture for e-government based on new models of decision-making and service delivery that is based to any significant degree on outsourcing elements of support or strategic functionality.

An effective relationship requires — *commitment, trust, and flexible innovation.*

A strong commitment is itself derived from three sub-elements: clarity in purpose and objectives in partnering, courage in undertaking justified risks and innovations, and conversation to facilitate learning and adaptation over time.

The first point, clarity of objectives, speaks to the need for government leaders to ensure that partnerships are a means to other, specified political and policy outcomes (as opposed to simply being perceived as the end in itself). There is also a need for courage — as the political and media scrutiny of the public-sector environment can magnify attention devoted to errors and minimize that of successes.

Many of those governments, for example, quickest to explore outsourcing with IT specialists are those same governments often under fire in the popular press and scholarly communities.[12] Much like the risks and rewards, courage must be shared across all stakeholders.

The importance of conversation can also not be overstated — or the "magic of dialogue" according to one behavioral expert (Yankelovich, 1999). The necessity of conversation is the fuel for trust, and it must take place both within the partnership and around it in order to increase the collective understanding of why the partnership is being undertaken, what it is aiming to achieve, and what sorts of twists and turns might reasonably be expected.

An equally essential component of learning and adaptation is the need to embrace flexible innovation as a guiding principle of partnerships. Too often in government, innovation is embraced as a goal, but the expectation is to minimize uncertainty as to how to undertake its pursuit.

Flexibility in innovation speaks to the paramount importance of relational value that can be generated through effective partnerships. Learning organizations are those that effectively align their internal decision-making processes with their external stakeholders, strengthening both in a collaborative manner. As such, there is little point in embracing partnerships unless all participants enter into any such arrangement with the firm acceptance that there is much to be discovered through collaboration along the way.

Such an emphasis may seem rhetorically straightforward, but it presents nothing short of a cultural revolution in many democratic institutions where political accountability is a recipe for clear authority and cautionary control.

Partnerships are now central to public management — and a priority for governments must be to both foster and strengthen capacities for collaborative action. E-government adds to the urgency due to the growing reality that in a digital world, as effectively dealing with more relational and fluid organizational architectures becomes the core competency of a continually renewed and enabled public service. *The unavoidable and powerful truth of e-government's emergence is that the risks of attempting to cling to what is certain far outweigh those of joining a team embracing what is uncertain.*

REFERENCES

Allen, B., Juillet, L., Paquet, G., & Roy, J. (2001). E-government in Canada: People, partnerships and prospects. *Government Information Quarterly*, *30*(1), 36-47.

Armstrong, A. A. (2000, June). Building e-partnership. *Government Executive, 32*(5), 84-86.

Essex, L., & Kusy, M. (1999). *Fast forward leadership*. Financial Times, Prentice Hall.

Globerman S., & Vining A. (1996, November/December). A framework for evaluating the government contracting-out decision with an application to information technology. *Public Administration Review.*

Guillaume, G. (1999). *L'empire de réseaux*. Paris: Descartes & Cie.

Jayes, D. (1998). Contracting out information technology services at the UK Inland Revenue. *Contracting Out Government Services.* OECD's Public Management Occasional Paper No.20.

Jelich, H., Poupart, R., & Roy, J. (2000). Partnership-based governance: Lessons from IT management. *Optimum, 30*(1), 49-54.

Langford, J., & Harrison, Y. (2001, May). Partnering for e-government: Challenges for public administrators. Paper prepared for the *Institute of Public Administration of Canada Conference*, Edmonton, May 2001. Retrieved from *http://www.ipaciapc.ca/english/menu.htm*

Lenihan, D. (2002). *E-government: The message to politicians.* Ottawa: Centre for Collaborative Government.

Mornan, R.G. (1998). Benefits-driven procurement: A model for public and private sector collaboration. *Optimum, 28*(1).

OECD. (2001, March). The hidden threat to e-government, avoiding large government IT failures. PUMA Policy Brief No. 8.

Paquet, G., & Roy, J. (2000). Information technology, public policy and Canadian governance – Partnerships and predicaments. In G. D. Garson (Ed.), *Handbook of public information systems* (pp. 53-70). New York: Marcel Dekker, Inc.

Rifkin, J. (2000). *The age of access.* Penguin Putnam.

Rosenau, P.V. (2000). *Public-private policy partnerships.* Cambridge, MA: MIT Press.

Stevenson, H. (1998). *Do lunch or be lunch.* Harvard Business School Press.

Tapscott, D., & Agnew, D. (1999, December). Governance in the digital economy. *Finance and Development,* 84-87.

Weil, P., & Broadbent, M. (1998). *Leveraging the new infrastructure – How market leaders capitalize on information technology.* MA: Harvard Business School Press.

Yankelovich, D. (1999). *The magic of dialogue – Transforming conflict into cooperation.* New York: Simon and Schuster.

Zifcak, S. (2001, June). Contractualism, democracy and ethics. *Australian Journal of Public Administration, 60*(2), 86-98.

ENDNOTES

1 At the time of the initial preparation of a draft version of this chapter for an OECD Seminar in June 2002, the authors were Senior Research Fellows of the Centre on Governance at the University of Ottawa. The authors are grateful for the assistance of numerous colleagues at the Centre, and to Ariel Lifshitz in particular, a visiting scholar in 2002 from the United Nations.

2 Outsourcing in Government: The Path to Transformation. (2002). The Government Executive Series, Accenture consulting., p. 4.

3 Continuum adopted from Wendell C. Lawther's report, Contracting for the 21st Century: A Partnership Model (The PricewaterhouseCoopers Endowment for The Business of Government: January 2002)

4 While it may seem a trite example, one good, and relatively rare illustration of success to watch for on the e-government conference circuit: government and industry officials jointly presenting the results of an IT partnership and the winding story of how failures and successes came to be.

5 Report from the Australasian Council of Auditor-General (1999:4). In S. Zifcak (2001) "Contractualism, Democracy and Ethics" (Australian Journal of Public Administration, 60(2), 86-98.

6 The Gartner Group predicts (*Why Today's Government Portals Are Irrelevant*) that by 2006, less than one-fifth of government-to-citizen transactions will take place via public sector portals. The rest will flow through mixed channels involving a range of external service providers in the private and non-profit sectors.

7 Essex, L. and Kusy, M. (1999). Fast Forward Leadership - How to exchange outmoded leadership practises for forward-looking leadership today.(Financial Times / Prentice Hall.

8 Adopted from Vision 2010 - Forging tomorrow's public-private partnerships, a survey report published by The Economist Intelligence Unit in cooperation with Andersen Consulting. The results are based on interviews with senior public servants in 12 countries from North America, Africa, Europe, and Asia.

9 It is, however, noteworthy that several large scale outsourcing projects are under way involving the transferring of entire IT architectures of governments to private-sector partners. Two notable examples are San Diego County and the Government of South Australia. A similar plan envisioned by the State of Connecticut in the United States was abandoned after nearly three years of negotiating.

10 Admittedly, such may be a predominantly North American characterization – particularly in the so-called knowledge industries where union representation is in decline.

11 Harris, B. (2000, Spring). E-Government: Beyond Service Delivery. *e.gov* (supplement to *Government Technology* Magazine).Retrieved from the World Wide Web at: egov.govtech.net

12 For examples, there are several scholarly articles critical of the Australian federal government experience with contracting out and outsourcing programs. Similarly, in 1999, CIO Magazine published a review of IT failures in the British government (failures that today, in the absence of careful and exhaustive analysis can be considered no better or worse than the IT management experiences of any large organization in the private or public sector).

Chapter XVII

What Skills are Needed in an E-World: E-Government Skills and Training Programs for the Public Sector

Alexander Settles, University of Deleware, USA

ABSTRACT

The transition to e-government applications for public service delivery and management involves significant changes to the traditional systems of public management. E-government applications modify the internal interaction between government units and private sector providers of public services and the external relations between government, citizens, and other members of the public. The use of Information and Communication Technologies (ICTs), in combination with significant policy changes and systems of operation, has the potential to provide greater transparency and democracy. By reducing information transaction, storage, and dissemination costs, ICTs allow for greater access to information and records. The evolution of interactive communication technologies has opened additional channels for the public to access public sector information, comment on public decisions, and interact with their elected officials.

INTRODUCTION

Unlike their private sector counterparts, public organizations typically are late adopters of new advances in information technology and are constrained by the public sector decision-making process. Public organizations are also subject to the outside view that business applications can be used without significant adaptations. Public sector managers face issues concerning how to utilize ICTs to improve government processes to meet efficiency, equity, and openness goals while operating within the financial and time resources available. Managers are often involved in the project management, selection, and implementation of information technology and may or may not have both the technical and political skills to choose the best outcomes.

E-government requires a change in public sector mindsets from government-centric to customer-centric. Organizational change, which breaks down the segmented "stove-pipes" of government bureaucracy and facilitates cooperation between agencies and government levels, will be crucial to pull together an interoperable virtual electronic government interface. Across the Organization for Economic Cooperation and Development (OECD) countries the public sector has been under pressure to be more responsive to a diverse set of concerns and to continue to improve the efficiency, speed, and effectiveness of public service provision. Public agencies across OECD governments have attempted to use e-government applications to integrate public services through information technologies in order to provide "single points of service" to improve the interaction between government and its constituents.

Information technology has also reduced the time period of decision cycles by placing an added condition of meeting public expectations for quick, efficient, and accurate decisions and actions. OECD governments have begun to have an appreciation for e-readiness that is apparent in the national and sub-national government efforts to reorganize the provision of ICT services through coordinated IT departments headed by chief information officers (CIOs).

The use of information technologies has the potential to improve the process of democratic decision making through increased connectivity between constituents and decision-makers, increased transparency through greater documentation and dissemination of public information, and by encouraging collaboration and consultation during the decision making process. There has been a widespread adoption of e-government solutions by OECD national, regional, and local governments in order to provide wider distribution of information concerning the activities and products of government. The development of a seamless e-government interface will require more than IT and project management skills. The public sector will face significant organizational change, coordination, and political issues and will need to develop continuous training and education.

To meet these challenges during the early stages of ICT development, governments have opened online channels for constituents to receive services and, in some cases, participate in the decision-making process. The widespread adoption of e-mail by individuals in the private and public sectors has added an avenue for communication with decision makers. Online access and dissemination of public information, government forms, legislation, and other public documents has lowered both the cost and time barriers to individuals who need to collect static public information. Transparency has also been enhanced through technologies, such as Web-casting of meetings, structured online commenting, and online comment forms. These ICT solutions have opened government to wider scrutiny and to expanded real-time review and feedback processes.

It has been argued that the adoption and use of ICTs by public organizations changes the structure of organization (Heintze & Bretschnieder, 2000) and rearranges who has information and how information is accessed and used. The development of ICTs has increased the efficiency of both private and public bureaucracies to manage data and reduce the time necessary for transactions to occur. Information technology allows for flatter organizations with decentralized decision-making processes. Information technology can be seen as an enabler of public sector organization change toward less hierarchical structure, with greater flexibility, and with the decision-maker closer to those constituents served by government.

The managerial skills necessary to meet the demands of e-government and other applications of ICTs involve the ability to: (1) understand governmental processes; (2) evaluate and utilize technology in a manner appropriate for public-sector applications; and (3) integrate technology decision-making with personnel, organization and financial management skills. In addition to technology-based skills, effective implementation of e-government solutions will require leadership, an understanding of government processes and applicability of e-government solutions to these government processes, strategic systems planning, and modifications in personnel, financing, and budget methods.

A range of skills and competencies will need to be developed in public-sector organizations in order to properly manage information technology projects. A consensus from the current literature indicates that the skills that are required to develop effective e-government solutions are based on knowledge of:

- Planning and coordinating information systems
- Evaluating information system outcomes
- Developing information policies
- Integrating information systems across organizational boundaries
- Demonstrating leadership skills
- Negotiating the political arena to build support for project implementation
- Implementing organizational change
- Legal implications of information technologies
- Risk management
- Personnel management and education
- Budgeting and financing

The Institute for Electronic Government at the IBM Corporation and Harvard's Kennedy School of Government detailed the need for focused leadership in the area of information technologies. In the publication series *Eight Imperatives for Leaders in a Networked World*, the authors state that leaders need to focus their attention on the concerns that matter to their organizations. With the current state of confusion and fear of the unknown concerning the implementation of ICTs, leaders need to apply determined and consistent attention to sort out how organizations will adopt and adapt to these new network technologies (Mechling & Applegate, 2000-2002).

The Office of the E-Envoy in the United Kingdom has outlined a skills map as part of the UK Online Strategy effort to prepare UK government agencies for e-government adoption. The E-Envoy has defined seven areas for skill development: (1) Leadership; (2) Project Management; (3) Acquisition; (4) Information professionalism; (5) IT professionalism; (6) IT-based service design; and (7) End-user skills (Office of the E-Envoy, 2000a). The E-Envoy has produced a Skills Assessment Toolkit to determine the e-readiness of each agency. This tool has been used as a self-assessment for departments to provide an understanding of skills required for planning, implementing and delivering e-government services. The assessment identifies the skills available internally to the organization through in-house technology and information professionals and identifies any skills gaps that may need to be addressed through expanded staff or out-sourcing (Office of the E-Envoy, 2000b).

The adoption of the CIO model has spread across federal, state, and local government, as the public sector struggles with adoption of technology for major IT investment and the adoption of e-government solutions. An effective CIO will use a wide range of skills that include an understanding of technology and systems planning, budgeting and finance, management and human resources, and the political and collaboration skills. National and local CIOs have been asked to steer IT and e-government implementation programs through difficult political challenges and organization reform while also attracting and maintaining a competent and effective IT staff, selecting the appropriate technology, and minimizing costs and delays. The basic skills needed for CIOs and IT managers have been defined by government organizations that provide training to these public officials. The skills identified by the Information Resource Management College of the National Defense University can be organized into the Information Technology Skills, Information Management Skills, and Information Society Skills categories (Information Resource Management College, n.d.a).

IT technical and managerial skills can be obtained through formal education, on-the job and formal training, work experience, non-formal experiences and interaction with other specialists in professional associations or working groups. Technology skills gap in the overall IT industry has been met through tertiary-level education (Lopez-Bassols, 2002). Higher education institutions are beginning to respond to formal training needs through the modification and expansion of IT specialist training programs and modification of business and public management education to include a focus on information technology. Some governments have identified the need to build a public-sector workforce with IT skills and have funded training programs that have been either government-run sessions or training provided through private-sector vendors. Another means for skill acquisition is interaction with members of the profession. Participation in professional associations and attendance at professional meeting provide real-world examples. The formation of coordinating committees or interagency project teams also provides an opportunity to build skills. Participation in these teams is analogous to the technique of problem-based learning, and provides an opportunity for managers and IT specialists within different agencies to interact and share knowledge and skills.

To harness the transformational power of ICTs, governments will need a solid base of IT skills. As part of implementing an e-government strategy, appropriate and necessary IT skills should be defined for chief or senior information officers, IT and program managers, and IT specialists. E-government implementation programs need to have an evaluation component to determine prior to engaging in e-government activities if public agencies possess IT skills. Previous experience with the implementation of major IT projects has demonstrated that insufficient leadership, business process, IT and managerial skills have led to significant failures. Training and education programs are key to building an IT skill base in the public sector. The public sector should be involved in the establishment of IT management curriculum at the university level and should encourage the addition of information technology to public management curriculum. Training should also be provided in a comprehensive manner to public-sector employees with a focus on basic IT literacy. The implementations of IT projects require strong project management and organizational change skills, and these skills should be the first priority for IT management.

The public sector has a range of options to build the necessary skill set to facilitate e-government and IT adoption. IT Skills can be acquired through: (1) recruitment and retention of IT specialists and IT managers, (2) outsourcing of or partnering with other organizations to provide IT and e-government functions, and (3) building skill sets through training of public-sector employees. Across the OECD, governments have identified the need to recruit and retain public sector employees with technology and IT management skills. Many governments have also entered into agreements with non-government partners to provide IT and e-government services. These activities will build the IT capacity, but it is important that those directly involved with the provision of government services have the skills necessary to create and manage IT projects. The use of non-government partners will increase the need for project management, business-process definition, communication, and organizational skills. Additional IT specialists and outside partners provide the IT and information management skills.

Public-sector agencies need to have a comprehensive evaluation of employee skills as part of IT implementation. National or central governments need to assist agencies to define, which skills are necessary and provide guidance to the relative importance of IT skills. An assessment of leadership, project management, and basic IT literacy should be conducted for e-government projects implemented with either internal IT staff or with outside partners.

Public management education should expose future managers to a range of IT literacy, information management, and information technology skills. A general IT literacy would include an appreciation of: (1) IT with a focus on the use of computers, the Internet, and network systems, (2) use of computers to complete work tasks, and (3) an understanding of IT deployment. An effective integration of IT into the public administration curriculum would be introducing IT skill instruction with other functional areas of public administration. Kraemmer et al. (1986) recommend that within core courses such as personnel, budgeting, financial management, and government accounting, "hard" IT skills can be taught. The integration of statistical, spreadsheet, accounting, and project management software into these core courses provides basic IT literacy and technical IT skills, such as system design, software competency, and hardware use.

Governments should consider the establishment of project management academy or training program public sector managers. New skills will need to be developed as the traditional form of monopoly government service provision gives way to the forces of decentralization, public-sector reform, or through IT implementation. Organizations face significant change and expanding partnerships with other public and private actors to provide services. Public managers across OECD countries face issues related to specifying, negotiating, and managing contracts for outside or coordinated functions and services that had traditionally been operated as single-source monopolies. Program management academies or training programs are crucial to provide these skills.

The U.S. government programs at the CIO University, the Strategic and Tactical Advocates for Results program, the Information Resources Management College, and the State of Washington's Digital Government Applications Academy are U.S. examples of government sponsored or certified training programs. These programs range from single-day training session to master's degrees in information management. These programs use a combination of government-operated training, use of outside vendors, and partnering with higher education institutions. Common themes across these programs are the definition and adoption of IT and management skills by the involved governments and the organizational "buy-in" that development of project management and IT skills are crucial to successful IT and e-government implementation.

Basic end-user skills will be needed of all public-sector agencies if governments intend to open e-government channels for a significant percent of government services. Public sector employees will need the basic skills to use e-government effectively. Project management and organizational skills are increasingly important. Public-sector officials will continue to define what services are provided, manage the legal and ethical issues, oversee the project and financing, and participate in translating political decisions into the provision of public services. The quality and availability of appropriate educational and training opportunities for managers, staff, and, perhaps, even the public, provide a critical mass for potential change. Bringing everyone along in the new e-government is essential. If the new systems prove to overwhelm rather than facilitate public administration, the potential of IT will not be fulfilled.

INTEGRATION OF INFORMATION AND COMMUNICATION TECHNOLOGIES INTO GOVERNMENT WORK PROCESSES

The adoption and implementation of ICTs by public-sector organizations continues to be a significant public management issue, since, unlike their private-sector counterparts, public organizations typically are late adopters of new advances in information technology and are constrained by the public-sector decision-making process. Public-sector officials, from street-level managers to CIOs to elected officials face issues concerning how to utilize ICTs to improve government processes and meet efficiency, equity and openness needs within the available time and funding constraints. Managers in the public sector are often involved in the project management, selection, and implementation of information technology. Therefore, as expectations for ICT savings increase, and the public demands greater efficiency and openness, these managers are increasingly facing decisions concerning the selection of hardware, software, connectivity solutions and IT consultants. The evolution of Internet and other network technologies, combined with the shift from centralized computing to decentralized client-server architecture, has shifted the focus of technology decision-making from IT specialists to the front-line and middle-level managers. These managers may or may not have both the technical and political skills to select and implement successful e-government applications.

Which IT Skills Do Managers Need?

The managerial skills necessary to meet the demands of e-government and other applications of ICTs involve the ability to: (1) understand governmental processes; (2) evaluate and utilize technology in a manner appropriate for public-sector applications; and (3) integrate technology decision-making with personnel, organization and financial management skills. Public managers will need to have more than basic technology literacy in the era of e-government adoption. Managers in the public sector, as in the private sector, will need to develop skills to understand how technology can and should be incorporated into business processes within a governmental framework.

Since the management of information technology has traditionally been the closed domain of information technologists, it has not yet been sufficiently incorporated into public administration training in a manner similar to finance, personnel, policy analysis, or organizational management. Public managers have relied primarily on internal information experts or outside technical consultants for advice on hardware, software, and applications of ICTs. This paper reviews the skills necessary for public sector managers and decision makers to better manage the implementation of ICT and to obtain the benefits of incorporating ICTs through organizational change and joined-up or integrated government practices. The goals and objectives of e-government initiatives in many OECD countries have evolved well beyond the simple opening of new information channels. Many OECD countries have combined e-government implementation activities with the continuation of public administration reform.

Information technology can assist public-sector reform by changing how the public sector provides its services, thereby changing how government relates to citizens and how it can supply new services. One view of ICT effects on organizations can be characterized as improvements in efficiency. ICT can bring cost savings through producing the same outputs at a lower cost per unit, producing more of the same output at the same cost, and producing the same outputs in less time at the same cost. Another view suggests that innovation may change the outputs favorably. The adoption of ICTs may allow an organization to produce better or higher value-added products and potentially to produce new products.

Why are Governments Different?

Knowledge of public management practices and unique dimensions of the public sector frames the management techniques that are crucial for inclusive e-government implementation. E-commerce skills may not always be appropriate for e-government applications. Public management differs fundamentally from the practice of business management in that public sector agencies serve the greater public and incorporate such values as democracy, equity transparency, and public accountability. Business administrative practices are primarily measured by accountability to the efficiency, and profitability dictates the market place. The public sector has benefited, as has the private sector, from productivity gains from the adoption of ICTs to produce greater efficiencies in data and transaction management. New Public Management theory has focused on the operational efficiency gains possible through "running government like a business" and through the adoption of private-sector practices or outright privatization of public service delivery. However, there have been some failures in this model of adoption of technology, and quality control of privatization projects has often been elusive. If, for example, a key element in a strategy depends on the private contractor delivering a service in a timely manner, and if no controls are in place, the whole program may collapse.

ICTs lend themselves to aiding in efficiency improvements, and modeling e-government applications has significant appeal when public services are tailored for citizens as customers. The use of ICTs by the public sector is significantly different when issues of equity, transparency, participation, or democracy are present. Any programs or systems will need to be analyzed in terms of their ease of adaptation to these values. It cannot be assumed that all citizens have access or the skills necessary to participate on an equal basis. Alternative delivery systems may need to be maintained for sometime in the future. Transparency may be mandated in certain programs, such as public hearings and announcements, but there may be situations in which security and privacy will be in conflict with the goals of openness and accessibility.

SKILLS AND COMPETENCIES FOR E-GOVERNMENT SUCCESS

The skills necessary for the adoption of information technology into government processes include basic technology skills and the management skills necessary to implement the reform and change in public administration. Information technology allows for a re-conceptualization of the structure of government, how and what services are provided and how government interacts with its citizens and constituents. In addition to technology-based skills, effective implementation of e-government solutions will require leadership, an understanding of government processes also required for implementation is applicability of e-government solutions to government processes, strategic systems planning, and modifications in personnel, financing, and budget methods. There can be resistance to new projects due to earlier failures of technology, individual frustration with learning new routines, and inadequate and non-intuitive new systems interfaces. The manager may need to demonstrate personal buy-in and leadership skills in order to get the parties involved in productive synergy.

The process of implementing e-government solutions requires new managerial and technical skills to plan, evaluate, manage, finance, and integrate information systems as part of government operations. The adoption of new technology, as part of a government process, does not occur merely by acquiring the software and hardware or hiring the appropriate information technology professionals. For a government service that plans to incorporate ICT, planning and management are more important than the selection of "best" or "cutting-edge" technology. Developing an interactive Web portal is not sufficient if the government process has not been planned to integrate the use of technology. The traditional hierarchical structure of government will need to be replaced to provide services integrated around functions or customers. The organization of government faces change to provide joined-up government and to take advantage of ICTs. The process of joining up different functions in government with a systems level integration may involve solving some historical and political legacies. Professional subcultures and interest group politics may undercut collaboration and integration.

How e-government applications are conceptualized and which models are selected will dictate the skills necessary for implementation. An e-government model that simply duplicates existing printed material and forms on a Web site will require only Web management and Web content skills combined with management skills to select accurate and appropriate information to be distributed. OECD governments have grown beyond the information distribution model, and a recent trend has been towards portal development by national, state, and local governments and organizations as well as integrated "one-stop shopping" sites. This approach directly challenges the traditional bureaucratic and segmented structure of government and, to some extent, all large public and private organizations. When the portal or "one-stop" models are adopted, the implementation of an e-government solution will need to address service integration issues and governmental and political process issues. The selection and implementation of technology may only be a minor part of the overall program design and implementation process. The larger contextual and organizational issues are crucial for success, and the public managers will need skills to overcome these political and organizational issues.

Public managers need to be able to integrate the process of government with emerging information technology systems. The matching of government processes with appropriate technology solutions will be central to the success of any e-government application. Technology has evolved into a required management competency similar to budgeting, strategic planning, and personnel management. No public manager should lack basic technology management skills. The public sector will need public managers capable of utilizing and evaluating technology. The adoption of e-government solutions has been hampered by the lack of knowledge about how technology can be used as a tool to accomplish or improve government processes.

A range of skills and competencies will need to be developed in public sector organizations in order to properly manage information technology projects. A consensus from the current literature indicates these skills that are required to develop effective e-government solutions are based on knowledge of:

- Planning and coordinating information systems
- Evaluating information system outcomes
- Developing information policies
- Integrating information systems across organizational boundaries
- Demonstrating leadership skills
- Negotiating the political arena to build support for project implementation
- Implementing organizational change
- Legal implications of information technologies
- Risk management
- Personnel management and education
- Budgeting and financing

SKILLS AND COMPETENCIES

Basic IT Skills: What All Public Administrators Should Know

Managers will need a basic skill set to understand how ICTs operate, how technology can be incorporated into existing government functions and how e-government applications have the potential to build new government products or open new channels of communication. Having a solid grounding in the options and their strengths and weaknesses will allow the manager to have the confidence to negotiate and to specify characteristics for developing projects that will work. Governments will need managers with technological literacy that are able to understand and apply appropriate existing, new, or emerging technologies to public-sector problems. Managers will need to have a basic ability to assess relationships among ICTs and to have the ability to assess the strength and weakness of integration of these technologies.

Managers that work directly with ICT implementation projects should, as part of technological literacy, be exposed to basic IT theory and applications. This would include a basic understanding of the methods to structure IT solutions to match government processes and of current technology applications. Managers should also have an understanding of the ICT industry by continuing to develop an awareness of the vision, strategy, goals, and culture of the information technology industry. Keeping up with this fast-paced field will require continuous attention. The management of information and technology should be as familiar as the management of personnel and finances.

Leadership Skills

The transformation of the operation of government into an integrated, joined-up, and networked organization will create a second transformation of how ICT is thought of by public managers. Information and communication technologies have been treated as a specialized service function of government. Frequently these services have been handled as separate agencies with the sub-units having special relationships and policies for information and publication. This will need to change as e-government channels and integrated systems of information and knowledge management increase efficiency and transform how government acts. Leadership perceptions of technology will need to change to incorporate e-government and ICTs. It would be easy for the technology to shape the program rather than serve the specific objectives of the governmental units.

The Institute for Electronic Government at the IBM Corporation and Harvard's Kennedy School of Government detailed the need for focused leadership in the area of information technologies. In the publication series *Eight Imperatives for Leaders in a Networked World*, the authors state that leaders need to focus their attention on the concerns that matter to their organizations. With the current state of confusion and fear of the unknown concerning the implementation of ICTs, leaders need to apply determined and consistent attention to sort out how organizations will adopt and adapt to these new network technologies (Mechling & Applegate, 2000-2002). The eight imperatives for leaders defined in the report include:

1. Focus on how IT can reshape work and public sector strategies
2. Use of IT for strategic innovation, not simply tactical automation
3. Utilize best practices in implementing IT initiatives
4. Improve budgeting and finance for promising IT initiatives
5. Protect privacy and security
6. Form IT-related partnerships to stimulate economic development

7. Use IT to promote equal opportunity and healthy communities
8. Prepare for digital democracy

Example of Leadership Skills: U.S. National Governors Association

In the U.S., state and local governments are typically the access point for governmental services and the sources of regulation and permitting for private sector activities. State governments are facing increasing challenges from citizens to provide government services more efficiently. One of the voluntary associations that promote the communication of best practices has been the U.S. National Governors Association (NGA). This group of elected officials has recognized the importance of leadership from governors to guide IT development and implementation. To address the need for viable e-government solutions, the NGA has taken a best practices approach to provide assistance to Governors and their staff. An important part of the NGA best practices approach to e-government has been recommendations for the development of a focus on IT leadership through appointment of CIOs, practical solution for recruitment of IT specialists and managers, and preparing government workforce for ICT implementation through training and skill development.

In its program *Building Better e-Government: Tools for Transformation*, the NGA has identified the significant investment state governments have made into developing online presences and automation of government processes. Important priorities for governors are meeting customer expectations, enhancing economic competitiveness, and improving public services. The NGA claims that "governments will be expected to be flexible and responsive as a service business that has increased value," and that in the "new consumer society everything is becoming a service, and service value is dependent on information quality" (National Governors Association, n.d.). State governments will need to improve public services and provide a "friction-free" environment for citizens and the private sector to access and utilize government services (NGA, n.d.). The improvement of government services, which has been characterized as either seamless, friction-free, or joined-up government will require governments to adopt new organizational structures that best take advantage of ICTs.

The appointment of a central information officer or coordinating body has been regarded by government organizations, such as the NGA or the National Association of State Chief Information Officers (NASCIO), as a crucial component of leadership development within government. A Chief Information Officer has the task to undertake enterprise-wide strategic planning and to establish a cross-agency governance and management structure to guide the development of e-government programs and policies. The roles of a CIO differ from each state to state and agency to agency, but, in general CIOs serve as focus points for decision making and policy guidance in a role similar to human resources officer or chief financial officer.

The adoption of the CIO model has spread across federal, state, and local government as the public sector struggles with adoption of technology for major IT investment and the adoption of e-government solutions. An effective CIO will use a wide range of skills that include an understanding of technology and systems planning, budgeting and finance, management and human resources, and the political and collaboration skills.

National and local CIOs have been asked to steer IT and e-government implementation programs through difficult political challenges and organization reform while attracting and maintaining a competent and effective IT staff, selecting the appropriate technology, while minimizing costs and delays. The general skills that CIOs will need include:

Soft Skills

- Political and organizational awareness and negotiating skills
- Policy awareness and understanding of government process
- Personnel selection and management

Hard Skills

- An ability to assess technology and an understanding of information systems planning and architecture
- Budget, financing and acquisition skills
- An understanding of security and privacy issues

Human Capital Skills

Successful implementation of information technologies requires a focus on retaining personnel with skills to define the government process (managers), those that can utilize the information technology applications, and those that have the capacity to design and develop technology solutions (IT professionals). Governments throughout the OECD area have identified the recruitment and retention of IT professionals in the public sector as a crucial issue. As a key person becomes knowledgeable and capable of guiding policy, decisions, and training, he or she also becomes valuable on the market outside of government, often at quite high differentials in compensation. Since most governmental programs are not set up to meet outside competition for skilled people, developing intrinsic rewards and recognition are increasingly important, if government IT is not to become simply a training organization for outside organizations. Public agencies have had to rely on outsourcing and contracting for services to meet the needs for information technologies skills and have often lacked the skill to evaluate and monitor the contracts. The lack of available skills within public agencies has led to these decisions to outsource or contract for services in the IT field, in contrast to making the decision based on the most efficient allocation of resources.

Communication skills are crucial to the development of solutions that utilize the potential of ICTs, to the integration of technical, policy, and managerial concerns, and to the necessary inter-organizational coordination. Managers need technical writing and speaking skills that allow for the translation of technical information into language that non-specialists and the general public understand. Typically, technical specialists have often prided themselves on maintaining a separate tech culture where communication with others outside the inner group has not been valued. Understanding of technology application by the general public will increase the buy-in for the development of new technology and increase participation when the technology is deployed.

Knowledge Management Skills

Public and private organizations rely on the ability to manage and analyze information to produce mission-critical knowledge. Public-sector managers must include in their management portfolio the skills necessary to manage knowledge, organize information, and build connections between pools of relevant knowledge. Having some theoretical concepts to create linkages and structures to amplify the utility of the information available could be an advantage. Increased demand from public officials and the general public for efficiency and effectiveness in public organization means that public managers will need to do more with less, reuse knowledge bases, and manage the interconnected nature of joined-up government.

The use of knowledge management techniques to take advantage of the intellectual capital of public-sector employees will require the development of skills that aid in the identification of the components of business/government process, an understanding of how to use the identified knowledge to change the operation of the organization, and an understanding of the use of information technology to accomplish the documentation and reuse of knowledge in the organization. Because the activities in government cover such a wide range of knowledge areas and, to a great extent, government may be the original or sole source of certain information, the responsibility for accuracy, updating, and accessibility is magnified.

The skills for knowledge management can be organized as:

Business process identification and analysis

- Understanding the knowledge process within the business
- Understanding the value, context and dynamics of knowledge and information
- Knowledge asset identification, creation, maintenance, and exploitation
- Knowledge mapping and flows

Change management

- Leveraging ICT to create Knowledge Management workers
- An understanding of support and facilitation of communities and teams

Project management

- Information structuring and architecture
- Document and information management and workflow
- An understanding of information management principles
- An understanding of technological opportunities

The successful implementation of e-government will be based on the ability of public-sector organizations to document and utilize organizational and individual knowledge concerning government processes and on the potential of ICTs to improve or expand public services. Public managers' use of knowledge management skills will become crucial, as demands for citizen and public official accountability increase and resources continue to be constrained.

Knowledge Management to E-Learning

An important part of implementing e-government projects will require managers to effectively use internal and external practices and to be able to differentiate between data, information, and value-additive knowledge. Data include qualitative and quantitative measures of events. When data have been placed within a context and meaning has been assigned, it becomes usable information. Knowledge is based on the beliefs about causal relationship within an organization, and information serves to measure and analyze these relationships. When an organization is able to use value-additive knowledge, it is able to gather data and information in a systematic way that generates new knowledge about activities and then is able to use this knowledge to improve the organization. A traditional organization, sends out signals downward as directives or policies and results. Feedback or resistance travels upwards. An e-learning organization differs from a traditional organization since knowledge exchange occurs dynamically and in horizontal and networked interchanges (Mitchell & Kulik, 2000). The ability to create open flows of critical value-additive knowledge is the measure of a good system for IT. Those public officials involved with IT implementation will need to use coordination, communication, and political skills to overcome old rivalries and exclusive claims to information of the separate agencies.

Knowledge management and e-learning techniques are particularly important to the public sector due to its information-dependent nature. Public agencies do not typically produce widgets or other tangible products and, where physical products, such as roads or airports, are produced typically, a private firm completes the work, and the public agency acts as a project or program manager and financier. At the street-level, bureaucrats will use e-learning organization and knowledge management techniques to accomplish what needs to be done. Where the current routines are adapted and appropriate they will be used. Often modifications will be created because of the need to solve problems. These "unsanctioned" modifications challenge the established order but form a path to implement new policy. The task for OECD governments is to harness these tendencies, select those that work, and control or terminate those practices that undermine the public agency.

Project Management Skills

State governments have also faced significant challenges attracting and developing skilled employees to manage IT projects. In a 2001 report the Center for Technology in Government recommends that the States "establish and support a project management 'academy' for both state and local managers" (Center for Technology in Government, 2001). The report explains that the traditional forms of monopoly government service provision are giving way to complex program models that involve a range of actors and may require exchanges of information between public agencies as well as private and non-profit organizations. Public managers across OECD countries face similar issues of specifying, negotiating, and managing contracts for outside or coordinated functions and services that had traditionally been operated as single-provider monopolies. The report concludes, "public managers would greatly benefit from a well-organized program of training and development that prepares them to guide projects from inception to evaluation in this complex new environment" (CTG, 2001).

Establishment of Project Management Academies

The State of Washington has developed a training academy to accelerate the deployment of digital government. The State intends to deploy a digital government framework that will allow citizens to access government services in a manner that is immediate, simple, seamless and intuitive. The methods to build cost-effective and innovative solutions have not always been intuitive the first time around for Washington state agencies. The State set up the Digital Government Applications Academy as a catalyst for "rapid and replicable development of secure, convenient, and cost-effective digital government applications" (WSDIS, 2001a).

The Washington State Academy provides an answer to the question of how public agencies can build e-government competencies and knowledge to better utilize existing technology and develop a culture of innovation. The Academy is based on a collaborative process that brings together the business experience of agencies, the knowledge of industry experts, and the input of customers and citizens to implement government services online and streamline business practices. The Academy encourages business managers, Web masters, and developers to attend Academy classes prior to implementing digital government applications to build core competencies and share information. The program allows attempts to reduce the cost and time to deploy new digital government services by exposing managers and IT professionals to easily replicable application templates. These templates represent the collaborative work and decision-making of many agencies, industry experts and customers. The Academy attempts to avoid "re-inventing the wheel" to accelerate application development by providing documentation of previous Academy course sessions as knowledge base for Washington state agencies (WSDIS, 2001a).

The building of competencies in public managers to model and outline how an e-government application would be incorporated into government processes is crucial. The Washington Academy uses an Applications Template and Outfitting Model (ATOM), as a "comprehensive and detailed roadmap for the fast and efficient way to build digital government applications" (WDIS, 2001b). This model brings together the required policies, necessary infrastructure components, and useful technologies in one place and integrates them into a task list allows manager to develop off-the-shelf e-government applications. This online guide provides managers with a step-by-step approach to developing Internet applications by mapping key issues to consider and steps to take. The model begins with project definition that guides a project manager through outlining and defining project goals and objectives. The model contains a process for assessment and evaluation of existing IT skills and resources within the agency to determine what available staff can do the project. This model also identifies the skills gap that may need to be filled through training, recruitment or outsourcing. A comprehensive list of policies and operational issues are included as part of the knowledge base that has been made available to all State of Washington agencies.

The Washington State hopes that the Academy can accelerate the development and deployment of digital government by saving time through the replication of digital government templates, saving money through increase productivity by using ICTs to create streamlined Internet-based government services, and by providing a collaborative process exploring applications of cutting-edge technologies and practices integration with government process. This type of academy or training experience provides valuable lessons in what can work, how to use an existing knowledge base to solve current puzzles, and how to avoid costly mistakes.

Modeling Skills

The ability to map out how ICTs fit into existing governmental processes and the ability to define new channels and processes will require the creation of process mapping and model building. An understanding of how automation and information integration will reduce information barriers and synchronize business processes will be crucial to the development of successful e-government applications. Reducing barriers will shift power and responses to information. The integration of ICT into governmental processes will require managers to build models to conceptualize theoretical and practical frameworks that describe complex processes and ideas in understandable, usable ways. The ability to map out a governmental process and construct models from a public management framework will allow managers to control how ICT applications are developed. Reliance on experts alone for guidance on how to model processes may revert to an off-the-shelf e-commerce solution and miss important public policy aspects of the service. Democratic decision-making, transparency, and equity are not typically values of e-commerce but will need to be included in successful e-government programs.

Skills to Deal with the Legal Implications of Information Technologies

The legal implications relating to use of information technology span from open record and public meeting legislation, to privacy issues for employees, citizens, and other entities with data on file at public agencies, to the use of intellectual property and implications of misuse by employees. Public managers have a legal, fiduciary, and personal responsibility in the proper storage and distribution of data and use of intellectual property to their respective public agency employers. The adoption of widespread use of e-mail in the late 1990s by public agencies in the USA and across OECD countries has changed how official and semi-official communications occur. The ability to trace such communications and the expectation of privacy are often in conflict. The legal requirements for documents now include e-mail and everything stored on PCs, making the employee and employer more vulnerable to scrutiny. The potential for further expansion into interactive e-government decision-making processes will further test the traditional bounds of record retention and distribution policies and the meaning of open and fair meetings. Managers involved in the implementation of e-government projects will need knowledge and skills related to a general understanding of open records and meetings laws, of how to archive and distribute public records, and of the legal rules of privacy protection. The use of a decentralized e-government framework shifts the responsibility for compliance to privacy, open records and meetings rules from central information archiving agencies to operational units.

Open Public Record and Decision Making Process Issues

The adoption of IT solutions for public record management, increased use of e-mail and desktop word processing and publication, and e-government solutions for collaborative decision-making processes increase the volume of information stored in public agencies. Public managers are facing issues related to open records procedure, privacy protection, appropriate use standards, and protection of intellectual property rights.

The U.S. federal government has set information policies through the U.S. Office of Management and Budget (OMB) and the Chief Information Officers Council. The U.S. Office of Management and Budget issued Circular A-130 in November 2000 to update and define federal information management policy and replace previous information management memorandums. The OMB Circular A-130 also defines the standards for information management and retention. Agencies are required to consider the effects of their actions on the privacy rights of individuals and to maintain appropriate safeguards. The OMB requires that an agency record, preserve, and ensure accessibility to information "to ensure the management and accountability of agency programs, and to protect the legal and financial rights of the Federal Government" (OMB Circular A-130, 2000, November). Agency IT programs should include a records management, archival and distribution function in the planning, design and implementation of these IT programs. The intention of this policy is to build in public disclosure into IT systems.

The OMB expects agencies to fulfill these goals by providing information to the public consistent with their missions that adequately describes the agency and its activities, disclosing information required by law, and complying with the Freedom of Information Act and the Privacy Act in dissemination of information. Managers in federal agencies need to strike a balance between the goals of "maximizing the usefulness of the information and minimizing the cost to the government and the public" (OMB Circular A-130, 2000, November).

Circular A-130 (2000, November) cautions against establishment of exclusive or restrictive information distribution policies that set barriers or costs for distribution that may hinder access to information. Federal agencies have been constrained to set dissemination charges at the cost rate of reproduction. Costs associated with data collection and value-added information are not to be recovered in the distribution of information. The collection of data, conversion to electronic formats, and production of information creates value. Public agencies have valuable information products but typically distribute this information at a fee level that only recovers the cost storage media and the marginal cost of transferring the information.

Privacy

The protection of privacy of individuals is a concern across the OECD countries. Decisions regarding the dissemination of public records must be made in most cases based upon an established privacy law or regulation. The OMB has set safeguards that most agencies follow to ensure that information is protected commensurate with the risk and magnitude of the harm that would result from the loss, misuse, or unauthorized access to or modification of such information. A process to correct errors in information collected on individuals is to be adopted. Agencies are limited to collecting information on individuals to that extent which is legally authorized and necessary for the proper performance of agency functions. Information on individuals may only be shared in a manner that is legally authorized and that maintains confidentiality. They should also develop and install systems that protect information from unauthorized use or access, while at the same time, ensure that individual citizen data is safely stored and transmitted while providing public services online and off-line.

Evaluation Skills

Successful IT implementation results in solid information systems planning, deployment, and post implementation evaluation. The Office of Management and Budget (OMB) has specified that agencies must plan in an integrated manner for managing information throughout its life cycle. OMB Circular A-130, Management of Federal

Information Resources, defines how federal agencies should plan for information systems. One skill that managers will need to apply includes consideration, at each stage of the information life cycle, of the effects of decisions and actions on other stages of the life cycle, particularly those concerning information dissemination. Public outreach and intergovernmental coordination are part of information system design. Organizations will need to account for the impacts on the customers, both internal and external to the agency. The OMB expects agencies to conduct integrated planning for information systems with plans for resource allocation and use, including budgeting, acquisition, and use of information technology (OMB Circular A-130, 2000, November). Although the OMB sets standards for IT implementation and evaluation, there is a gap for the managers to fill between the assertion of the standard and the training and commitment to its reality. Defining a life cycle and understanding the systems impact internally and externally are matters of higher-level problem solving and require allocation of resources on a continuing basis. In contrast, the budgeting cycle and political cycles often have much shorter-range allocations and demands for change that may impact these systems.

SKILL DEVELOPMENT AND TRAINING PROGRAMS

OECD governments have a vested interest in skill development as the knowledge societies develops and as the public sector incorporates ICTs into open new communication channels and transforms public administration. The public sector faces an IT specialist challenge in recruiting and training in the field of information technology implementation. Those managers with skills in information technology are even more difficult to find and retain.

Information technology, management, society skills can be developed through a range of processes. There has been a great deal of focus from governments and international organizations on how to provide an adequately trained information technology workforce in reports from the OECD, International Labor Organization (ILO), OMB, and the United Kingdom's Office of the E-Envoy. Recommendations typically focus on the development of IT specialists through the expansion of higher education options to increase the supply of formally trained IT workers (Lopez-Bassols, 2002). Governments are sponsoring training programs and government/academia partnerships as means to expand formal and post-graduate professional development training.

Some governments have gone so far as to establish government training academies for IT project management and e-government development. The broader educational understanding of how IT fits into democratic institutions and creative and innovative public administration requires both a theoretical and practical understanding of governmental and management practices. This context is crucial, even if training for the specific current IT options and capabilities is provided outside of the university setting. Good theory may have long-term utility and serve as a means of designing evaluation. Training is always in need of updating and perhaps is best built into the governmental institutional structures. Sharing of practical problem solving know-how is needed but not easily capture in conventional in-service education. Higher education institutions are beginning to respond to formal training needs through the modification and expansion of IT specialist training programs and modification of business and public management education to include a focus on information technology.

Some governments have identified the need to build a public-sector workforce with IT skills and have funded training programs that have been either government-run sessions or training provided through private-sector vendors. Another means for skill acquisition is through interaction with members of the profession. Participation in professional associations and attendance at professional meeting provides real-world examples. The formation of coordinating committees or interagency project teams also provides an opportunity to build skills. Participation on these teams is analogous to the technique of problem-based learning, and this interaction provides an opportunity for managers and IT specialists within different agencies to interact and share knowledge and skills.

Public Administration and Management Education

Higher education institutions face the challenge of responding to the evolution of knowledge-based economies by increasing the supply of graduates with IT competencies and skills. The modification of curriculum and program expansion is particularly acute in the area of public-sector management. Public management education has lagged behind programs at higher education institutions that have a tradition of developing such as information technology skills computer science, electrical engineering and business programs focused on management information systems. Two aspects are important for public management education. First, the development of both "hard" skills that provide a background in theoretical, applied IT, and information management skills and secondly an exploration of "soft" skills that provide an understanding of the evolving information society.

In the U.S. public administration programs have not typically offered management of information systems coursework until recently, and IT remains a secondary subject to personnel, budgeting and finance, organizational theory, and policy analysis in the typical program. Most of the computer skills that earlier graduates possess have been gained incidentally with the skills they developed to analyze data in research and application projects and in presenting their work in written and oral form. Looking at the tools for their systems management aspects has not been addressed directly. Graduates of public management programs have been expected to have a basic knowledge of IT trends and benefits of IT. This is in contrast to public budgeting and public personnel, where more training has been expected. The National Association of Schools of Public Affairs and Administration (NASPAA) and the International City/County Managers Association recommended the following basic management training in IT from accredited programs in Urban Management:

Local government administrators need to understand emerging trends in electronic systems used to compile, store, and analyze information and data. They need to be sufficiently expert in the use of such systems to understand when and how to manage such technologies, interpret the results of their use, and optimize the community's benefit from their use (ICMA/NASPAA Task Force on Local Government Management Education, 1992, Section 6, Information Technology).

How will the transforming impacts of adoption of ICTs for efficiency and innovation change how public administrators are taught? The issue of information technology was addressed in a study entitled, "Curriculum Recommendations for Public Management Education in Computing." The authors of this study recommended that graduate programs require "three levels of computer technology literacy: (1) the ability to use the technology in their own work; (2) the ability to use technology of the organizations they manage; and (3) the ability to develop policy for effective use and control of technology for strategic as well as operational advantages" (Kraemmer et al., 1986). The authors recognize that the development of IT skills provides managers with an increase in personal effectiveness and empowers managers to better understand the costs and benefits of IT investments.

Public management education should expose future managers to a range of IT literacy, Information Management, and Information Technology skills. A general IT literacy would include an appreciation of: (1) IT with a focus on the use of computers, the Internet and network systems, (2) use of computers to complete work tasks, and (3) an understanding of IT deployment. An effective integration of IT into the public administration curriculum would be to introduce IT skill instruction with other functional areas of public administration. Kraemmer et al. (1986) recommends that within core courses such as personnel, budgeting, financial management, and government accounting "hard" IT skills can be taught. The integration of statistical, spreadsheet, accounting, and project management software into these core courses provides basic IT literacy and technical IT skills such as system design, software competency, and hardware use (Kraemmer et al., 1986).

Since the completion of the Kraemmer study in 1986, technology has dramatically evolved and the importance of IT skill development for public managers has increased. Public management education programs have, in general, adopted basic IT literacy. The use of word processing, statistical, and spreadsheet software, and use of the Internet are common in a higher education setting. The question remains, though, how IT should be included in the curriculum and what should be taught. The evolution of the conceptualization of technology for automation for efficiency to use technology to produce comprehensive joined-up e-government shifts the focus from IT technical skills to information and organizational management skills. Kim and Layne (2001) envision the integration of e-government issues into the current public administration curriculum and the addition of content focusing on leadership in e-government implementation.

The management skills needed for e-government are part of the existing public administration core courses. In the public management core curriculum the development of skills relating to collaborations/partnerships, citizen participation and intergovernmental relationships as well as leadership and change management can be developed. Human resources courses provide skills necessary for recruitment, staff assessment, and training and expose students to issues relating to privacy and security of records. Coursework that gives an introduction to public administration and organizational theory provides an understanding of the current state and possible paths to reform public administration. These courses cover such topics as political skills and understanding bureaucracies. Crucial to information management are development of political and organizational skills to overcome or transform existing institutional barriers or structures.

Another approach would be the use of an additional core course focused on information technology and information management skills (Rocheleau, 1998). The design of the course may reflect the skills of faculty available, availability of resources, skill level of the students at admission. An issue for graduate education will be to divide those IT literacy skills (use of a networked computer, word processing, and Internet surfing) from literacy of uses of technology in government and other organizations, technical skills, and information management skills. It would be difficult to give graduate credit for learning to type or log on. The skills that would be important to present in an IT course would include IT implications for democracy, design of information systems, program management, database management, information resource management, legal implications of IT, and use of communication technology. Specializations in use of IT in functional areas, such as geographic information systems, budgeting and accounting, customer/citizen relationship management, procurement management, and enterprise management, would supplement these basic skill areas. The supply of public managers with IT skills depends, in part, on the skill set obtained through formal education. It is important to OECD country governments to pay attention to which IT skills are taught and to remain involved in the development of IT course curriculum.

Government Sponsored Training

The U.S. Federal government has adopted the policy to establish an interagency support structure to "improve the management and use of information technology ... by developing information technology procedures and standards and by identifying and sharing experiences, ideas, and promising practices; and provide innovative, multi-disciplinary, project-specific support to agencies to enhance interoperability, minimize unnecessary duplication of effort, and capitalize on agency successes" (Executive Order 13011, 1996, July 16). U.S. government officials have identified, as have U.S. state and other OECD governments, that the largest obstacle to e-government success has been the traditional ministerial and departmental structure that divides functions and information. According to Tony Trenkle, deputy associate commissioner, Office of Electronic Services, Social Security Administration, the biggest problem is that the federal government is "not organized to do e-government today" and the traditional "stove-piped organizations" are unable to integrate information and services to conduct e-government activities (Making e-gov work, 2002, June 3). Federal e-government programs contain both the difficulties of ICT integration and structural reform of public administration.

Federal managers, like all public-sector actors involved in implementation of e-government solutions, face significant structural and cultural barriers to successful implementation. Significant organizational barriers exist in the U.S. Federal government that prevents information and knowledge exchange and the integration of public services. Agencies' organization, rules, funding mechanisms, and culture do not reward inter- and intra-cooperation. Priorities are based on a departmental, agency, or program basis, and funding is provided through 13 different appropriation bills (Association for Federal Information Resources Management, 2002, June). Bridging these divides and overcoming natural resistance requires both personal charm and political determination. Being able to form alliances and make the case for e-government to the different constituencies requires political savvy as well as technical foundations and skills.

Training Programs

The Government Services Agency (GSA) operates the CIO University to provide professional development and training for federal CIOs. The CIO University is a "virtual consortium of universities, which offers graduate-level programs that directly address the executive core competencies adopted by the Federal Chief Information Officers (CIO) Council" (General Service Agency, 2002, March 8). Participant universities provide skill training related to policy and organization, leadership and motivation, and process and change management, program management, incorporation of ICT into government processes, security, emerging technology and technical competency. To be admitted to the CIO University a federal employee "must be a member of the Senior Executive Service (SES), or a high achieving federal employee, have the approval of your senior management, be selected or sponsored by your senior executive, and be selected by your university based on their standards for executive development programs in terms of education, position and experience" (GSA, 2002, March 8). The CIO University program focuses on skills derived from the Cohen-Clinger Act (Information Technology Management Reform Act of 1995). These skill sets are divided into management, information society, information technology management, and technical skills. A CIO is expected to have the following skills (CIO Council, 2001, September):

Managerial Skills

- Understand the organizational structure, the department or agency missions, organization, function, policies, procedures, and the governing laws and regulations, including rules concerning privacy and security
- Display leadership and managerial skills to define roles, skill sets, and responsibilities of Senior Officials, CIO, staff, and stakeholders, to build partnership and teams techniques and practices which attract and retain qualified IT personnel
- Implement process change management by applying techniques of organizational development and change, process management and control, modeling and simulation tools and methods, and business process redesign/reengineering models and methods

Information Society Skills

- Understand e-government, electronic business, and electronic commerce issues as these technologies impact the business model of government services, open new channels of communication and government by increasing the use of Web-based channels for citizen information delivery

Information Technology Management Skills

- Apply information resources strategy and planning methods and understand IT system life-cycle planning
- Conduct performance assessment to measure the business value of IT and to measure customer satisfaction with IT applications
- Engage in effective project and program management by defining project scope, setting requirements, measuring time/cost/performance, assessing quality and managing risk
- Plan for capital and assess IT investment through use of cost benefit, economic, alternative, and risk analysis methods and to properly manage acquisition

IT Technical Skills

- Understand issues related to IT security and information assurance
- Posses IT skills necessary to understand information architectures, client/server models, collaborative processing, telecommunications technology, emerging or developing technologies, information delivery technology software development, and data management
- Have basic technology literacy through the development of skills to use desktop technology tools

An important point that the CIO Council has made concerning the competencies and learning objectives for the CIO University and other training programs is the need for skills related to organizational, political and change management activities. The role of the CIO is described as the "Chief Visionary of the organization" that needs to work in partnership with executive and operating officers to produce change. Technical and technology management skills alone will not lead to IT implementation success. To gain the transforming power of IT, CIOs and IT managers need to understand the organization and be able to manage change through use of organizational development and process management concepts. The adoption of IT solutions will have significant organizational issues, including restructuring hierarchies and responsibilities, and can fundamentally change business processes. When combined with an overall reform of public administration agenda, the task of e-government becomes a process of organizational and business process change.

The skills are taught in three types of programs that are offered by four universities. The CIO University teaches as an integrated graduate degree program in information management that covers the full set of core competencies. The certificate program is offered as either a modular program that focuses on portions of the competencies or as a one-week survey course (General Service Agency, 2002, March 8). The Technology Management and Information System Science degree programs are taught as a two-year master's degree and are geared toward both private and public sector while covering the full range of CIO skill competencies. The certificate programs cover narrow range of skills and competencies focusing on Managerial and Information Management skills. These programs have less required coursework and course time and range from four to 12 class sessions per course.[1]

The GSA also offers the STAR (Strategic and Tactical Advocates for Results) training program for ICT program managers. This program focuses on skills related to project management, leadership, security, technology, and government. Each model of the program is taught by partner organizations that are experts in the respective content area. This program is open to federal employees that are project managers below the Senior Executive Service level (i.e., employees that are not CIOs). The STAR training program incorporates results based management and the use of information technology as a strategic resource. The learning objectives of the program are: "strategic management skills, strategic planning, business planning, technical infrastructure, management structures, policies and processes, program and project management skills, leadership skills, organizational culture, insight on outsourcing, oversight of organizations' functions, and technology trends" (General Service Agency, 2002, July 12a).

The Department of Defense (DoD) established the Information Resources Management (IRM) College at National Defense University post-graduate training in information technology and information management. This IRM College and the IT training programs are open to both DoD and other government agency officials. The IRM College programs also follow the Clinger-Cohen Act (Information Technology Management Reform Act of 1995), CIO model, and specified core competencies for IT specialist and managerial training. The IRM College has been designated with the responsibility to implement the senior-level educational requirement of the Clinger-Cohen Act for the DoD (IRMC, n.d.b). The IRM College operates an *e*-government Leadership Certificate Program, a CIO Certificate Program, and an Advanced Management Program (AMP). The e-government Leadership Certificate Program focuses on the information management skills, such as e-government innovation, leadership, communication and coordination, and use of information strategically (IRMC, n.d.c). The CIO certificate program provides the complete overview of the Federal CIO Council core competencies and IT skills. The course work in the CIO certificate program may be applied to selected master's degree programs at partner higher education institutions (IRMC, n.d.d). The Advance Management Program provides greater depth in training in IT management competencies. AMP graduates may also qualify for the CIO Certificate and apply the coursework to select master's degree programs (IRMC, n.d.a).

The *e*Government Leadership Certificate Program provides a basic overview of e-government activities and helps to develop basic IT management and IT technical skills to use information technologies to transform government operations and to improve effectiveness and efficiency of processes and service delivery to citizens. The program goal is to create government leaders that are systematic thinkers that foster partnerships and networks in complex environments to collaborate, integrate, and redesign processes and policies (IRMC, n.d.c). The skills that the eGovernment Leadership Certificate Program addresses include:

Information Technology Skills

- Enterprise Architecture for Managers
- Enterprise Resources Planning (ERP): Issues in Strategic Planning and Information Management Planning
- Security, Privacy, and Access Issues in e-government

Information Management Skills

- Information Technology Capital Planning
- Transforming Processes & Resource Use
- Services Planning for Improved Government Performance
- Strategic Human Resources Issues in e-government
- Measuring Results of Organizational Performance
- Using Information Strategically
- Knowledge Management: Leveraging Intellectual Resources

- Homeland Security
- Strategic Management of Web Sites
- Data Management Strategies and Technologies: A Managerial Approach

Information Society Skills

- Setting New Directions through Adoption of e-government Processes
- Transformation to e-government (IRMC, n.d.a)

The CIO Certificate Program and AMP are organized around 11 subject areas directly related to CIO competencies identified by the federal CIO Council. These competency areas include:

Application of governing IRM policies; laws and reporting requirements; information resources strategic planning that links the agency's vision, mission, and programs with performance standards and budgets; information planning strategies and modeling; capital planning and selection and evaluation of investments using established criteria; benchmarking and process analysis to ensure performance and results-based management; assessing technology trends and identifying organizational technology needs for implementing e-government solutions; applying standards and guidelines for designing architectures to align technology with organizational structure, processes, and human resources; acquiring technologies using acquisition reform to support efficient and effective government operations; and leading the organization through changes necessitated by this new way of doing business (IRMC, n.d.d).

The IRM College programs provide basic information technology literacy and information management skills to facilitate e-government implementation. The basic e-government skills include: "(1) how electronic channels differ from traditional channels, (2) the value chain implications of electronic channels for information products versus physical products, and (3) how electronic channels can augment or cannibalize traditional channels, both in the context of government and private-sector environments" (IRMC, n.d.e.).

The IRM College courses entitled, New World of the CIO, Leadership for 21st Century, and Improving Organizational Processes, build leadership, organizational, and change management skills. The training focuses on the transformational power of IT while recognizing that managers will need political, leadership, and organizational change skills to facilitate a transformation. Implementing successful IT projects, if the skills taught in DoD program are an accurate guide, does not solely rest on selecting the best technical solution and completing the project at budget. The organization will need to adapt to successfully implementing IT programs.

The CIO Certificate and the APM have incorporated a strong focus on knowledge management and strategic use of information as important IM skills. The ability "to compete in the information age, to understand the relationships between learning, change, and strategic planning, and incorporate the practices of learning organization" (IRMC, n.d.f) are key learning objectives in the program. The course work in knowledge management provides a basic understanding of knowledge management and relates examples on how organizations have implemented knowledge management techniques. An important part of knowledge management is how organizations then translates tacit into explicit knowledge, or how knowledge moves from understanding the organizational processes or structures to becoming a resource for improving the organization. The coursework also reviews information and communication technologies that support knowledge management. IT managers are prepared to "assess current knowledge management organizational practices and incentives that promote collaboration and knowledge sharing and explore alternative ways to demonstrate the value added of knowledge and knowledge management to an organization's mission tools and techniques for use in specifying, evaluating, modeling, measuring, cost justifying and redesigning business processes" (IRMC, n.d.f).

CONCLUSIONS

E-Government: Setting the Stage for Public Sector Reform

The transition to e-government applications for public service delivery and management involves significant changes to the traditional systems of public management. E-government applications modify the internal interaction between government units and private sector providers of public services and the external relations between government, citizens, and other members of the public. The use of ICTs, in combination with significant policy changes and systems of operation, has the potential to provide greater transparency and democracy. By reducing information transaction, storage, and dissemination costs, ICTs allow for greater access to information and records. While the implementation of e-government applications provides for greater efficiency, transparency, and access, the use of ICTs alone will not produce reforms in public sector management or return greater trust in government. Effective public sector use of ICTs will depended on the skill sets that public managers and IT specialists possess.

E-government requires a change in public sector mindsets from government-centric to customer-centric. Re-engineering of processes and re-organization of public services are important to take advantage of efficiency gains with the use of ICT. The realization of productivity gains from the incorporation of ICT in the private sector has been tied to implementing organizational change. Murphy (2002) indicates that private firms that have been best able to integrate ICTs into business practices have implemented organizational change to take advantage of these technologies. The private sector reorganization has consisted of the replacement of hierarchies, development of flat organizations, a focus on collaboration and alliances, and rewarding innovation. Organizational change that breaks down the segmented "stovepipes" of government bureaucracy and facilitates cooperation between agencies and government levels will be crucial to pull together an interoperable virtual electronic government interface.

Across the OECD countries the public sector has been under pressure to be more responsive to a diverse set of concerns and to continue to improve the efficiency, speed, and effectiveness of public service provision. In 2000, the OECD identified in the seminar report, "Government of the Future," that information and communications technology has reshaped the economies of developed countries and is driving societal change (Lau,

2000). Information technology has the potential to assist public agencies to provide better, faster, more efficient and diverse public goods and services. ICTs are capable of reducing the cost of services through efficiencies derived from information and knowledge management and delivering services through new online or other telecommunication channels. The application of information management techniques will allow governments to tailor services to specific user groups and individual constituents. Public agencies across OECD governments have attempted to use e-government applications to integrate public services through information technologies in order to provide single points of service to improve the interaction between government and its constituents.

The use of information technologies has the potential to improve the process of democratic decision through increased connectivity between constituents and decision-makers, increased transparency through greater documentation and dissemination of public information, and by encouraging collaboration and consultation during the decision making process. There has been a widespread adoption of e-government solutions by OECD national, regional, and local governments in order to provide wider distribution of information concerning the activities and products of government. The basic hierarchical informational structure of government has been slow to adapt to the introduction of Internet technologies. Government Web pages are a reflection of the traditional form of public bureaucracy. The initial front-page offerings of most public agencies mirrored the organization chart or phone directory, and even today, as an online user drills down through a public Web site, the underlying hierarchical and compartmentalized structure of government remains. The development of seamless e-government interface will require more than IT and project management skills. The public sector will face significant organizational change, coordination, and political issues.

Governments during this first stage of Internet adoption, 1995-2001, have opened online channels for constituents to receive services and in some cases participate in the decision-making process. The wide spread adoption of e-mail by individuals in the private and public sectors has added an avenue for communication with decision makers. Online access and dissemination of public information, government forms, legislation, and other public documents has lowered both the cost and time barriers to individuals who need to collect static public information. Transparency has also been enhanced through technologies such as Web-casting of meetings, structured online commenting, and online comment forms. These ICT solutions have opened government to wider scrutiny and to expanded real-time review and feedback processes.

It has been argued that the adoption and use of ICTs by public organizations changes the structure of organization and rearranges who has information and how information is accessed and used (Heintze & Bretschnieder, 2000). Public organizations have their roots in the traditional Weber characteristics of bureaucracy. Governments are typically divided into agencies with fixed and official jurisdictional areas, a hierarchy with graded levels of authority that exist within and between individuals and units. Office management is conducted with written documentation and by clearly defined rules of action (Weber, 1946). The formation of bureaucracies for the operation of large organizations has been a modern response to the needs of information management, knowledge assessment, and control.

Much of the literature argues that ICTs affect organizational structure. How ICTs change structure is less clear. The development of ICTs has increased the efficiency of both private and public bureaucracies to manage data and reduce the time necessary for transactions to occur. Information technology allows for flatter organizations with decentralized decision-making processes. Information technology can be seen as an enabling public sector organization change toward less hierarchical structure, with greater flexibility, and with the decision-maker closer to constituents served by government.

Organizations are structured to allow for control and implementation of rules and policies. These structures can be conceptualized in terms of the principle, the decision maker or rule setter, and the agent, the individual tasked to implement the rule. Agents react to information signals emanating from their organization and factors in the environment. The speed of information flows and the availability of data, information and knowledge combined with organization and societal defined decision rules determine how and when decisions are made. The adoption of new information technologies changes the conditions of organization.

Training and education programs are key to building an IT skill base in the public sector. The public sector should be involved with the establishment of IT management curriculum at the university level and encouraging the addition of information technology to every public management curriculum. Training should also be provided in a comprehensive manner to public sector employees. A basic focus for all public sector employees should be IT literacy. The implementations of IT projects require strong project management and organizational change skills and these skills should be the first priority for IT management.

The public sector has a range of options to build the necessary skill set to facilitate e-government and IT adoption. IT Skills can be acquired through: (1) the recruitment and retention of IT specialist and IT managers, (2) outsourcing of or partnering with other organization to provide IT and e-government functions, and (3) building skill sets through training of public sector employees. Across the OECD, governments have identified the need to recruit and retain public sector employees with IT and IT management skills. Many governments have also entered into agreements with non-government partners to provide IT and e-government services. These activities will build the IT capacity but it is important that those directly involved with the provision of government services have the skills necessary to create and manage IT projects. The use of non-government partners will increase the need for project management, business process definition, communication, and organizational skills. Additional IT specialists and outside partners provide the IT and information management skills.

Basic end-user skills will be needed of all public sector agencies, if governments intend to open e-government channels for 100 percent of government services. Public sector employees will need the basic skills to use e-government effectively. Project management and organizational skills are increasingly important. Public sector officials will continue to define what services are provided, manage the legal and ethical issues, oversee the project and financing, and participate in translating political decisions into the provision of public services. The quality and availability of appropriate educational and training opportunities for managers, staff, and perhaps even the public, provide a critical mass for potential change. Bringing everyone along in the new e-government is essential. If the new systems prove to overwhelm rather than facilitate public administration, the potential of IT will not be fulfilled.

Public sector agencies need to have a comprehensive evaluation of employee skills as part of IT implementation. National or central governments need to assist agencies to define which skills are necessary and provide guidance to the relative importance of IT skills. An assessment of leadership, project management, and basic IT literacy should be conducted whether e-government projects are implemented with either internal IT staff or with outside partners.

Public management education should expose future managers to a range of IT literacy, Information Management, and Information Technology skills. A general IT literacy would include an appreciation of: (1) IT with a focus on the use of computers, the Internet and networked systems, (2) use of computers to complete work tasks, and (3) an understanding of IT deployment. An effective integration of IT into the public administration curriculum would be to introduce IT skill instruction with other functional areas of public administration. Kramer et al. (1986) recommended that within core courses, such as personnel, budgeting, financial management, and government accounting, "hard" IT skills can be taught. The integration of statistical, spreadsheet, accounting, and project management software into these core courses provides basic IT literacy and technical IT skills, such as system design, software competency, and hardware use (Kraemmer et al., 1986).

Governments should consider the establishment of project management academy or training program for public sector managers. New skills will need to be developed, as the traditional form of monopolized government service provision gives way to the forces of decentralization, public sector reform, or through IT implementation. Organizations face significant change and partnerships with other public and private actors to provide services are expanding. Public managers across OECD countries face issues related to specifying, negotiating, and managing contracts for outside or coordinated functions and services that had traditionally been operated as single provider monopolies. Program management academies or training program are crucial to provide these skills

The U.S. government programs such as the CIO University, the Strategic and Tactical Advocates for Results program, the Information Resources Management College, and the State of Washington's Digital Government Applications Academy, are U.S. examples of government-sponsored or certified training programs. These programs range from providing single-day training sessions to master's degrees in information management. These programs use a combination of government operated training, use of outside vendors, and partnering with higher education institutions. A common theme across these programs has been the definition and adoption of IT and management skills by the involved governments and the organizational "buy-in" that development of project management and IT skills are crucial to successful IT and e-government implementation

To harness the transformational power of ICTs, governments will need a solid base of IT skills. As part of implementing an e-government strategy, appropriate and necessary IT skills should be defined for chief or senior information officers, IT and program managers, and IT specialists. E-government implementation programs need to have an evaluation component. Previous experience with the implementation of major IT projects has demonstrated that insufficient leadership, business process, IT and managerial skills have led to significant failures.

REFERENCES

Association for Federal Information Resources Management. (2002, June). *A blueprint for successful e-government implementation: Steps to accelerate cultural change and overcome stakeholder resistance.* Retrieved July 6, 2002, from *www.affirm.org*

CIO Council. (2001, September). *CIO University learning objectives.* Washington D.C. Retrieved from *http://www.gsa.gov/attachments/GSA_PUBLICATIONS/extpub/lo-matrix-2001.doc*

Executive Order 13011. (1996, *July 16*). *Federal Information Technology.* Retrieved July 6, 2002, from *http://www.fgipc.org/02_Federal_CIO_Council/Resource/17_execOrder16July1996.htm*

General Service Agency. (2002, March 8). *CIO University general information.* Retrieved July 2, 2002, from *http://www.gsa.gov/Portal/content/offerings_content.jsp?contentOID=117021&contentType=1004*

General Service Agency. (2002, July 12a). *STAR (Strategic and Tactical Advocates for Results)* Retrieved August 15, 2002 from *http://www.gsa.gov/Portal/content/offerings_content.jsp ?contentOID=113962&contentType=1004*

General Service Agency. (2002, July 12b). *STAR prework (described).* Retrieved August 22, 2002, from *http://www.gsa.gov/Portal/content/offerings_content.jsp?contentOID=113962&contentType=1004*

Heintze, T., & Bretschnieder, S. (2000). IT and restructuring in public organizations: Does IT related structural changes improve organizational performance? *Journal of Public Administration Research and Theory, 10*(4), 801-830.

ICMA/NASPAA Task Force on Local Government Management Education. (1992). *Urban management education guidelines.* Retrieved on July 15, 2002, from *http://www.naspaa.org/principals/resources/urban.asp*

Information Resource Management College. (n.d.a). *The advanced management program.* Retrieved on July 1, 2004, from *http://www.ndu.edu/irmc/programs/amp.html*

Information Resource Management College. (n.d.b). *College information.* Retrieved on August 10, 2002, from *http://www.ndu.edu/irmc/about_the_college.htm*

Information Resource Management College. (n.d.c). *eGovernment Leadership Certificate Program "Facilitating Cross-Boundary Leadership."* Retrieved July 1, 2004, from *http://www.ndu.edu/irmc/programs/egov.html*

Information Resource Management College. (n.d.d). *The chief information officer program.* Retrieved August 10, 2002, from *http://www.ndu.edu/irmc/cio.html*

Information Resource Management College. (n.d.e). *Leadership for 21st century.* Retrieved August 10, 2002, from *http://www.ndu.edu/irmc/courses2002/ldc2002.htm*

Information Resource Management College. (n.d.f). *Knowledge management: Leveraging intellectual resources (KMI).* Retrieved August 10, 2002, from *http://www.ndu.edu/irmc/courses2002/kmi2002.htm*

Kim, S., & Layne, K. (2001, October). Making the connection: E-government and public administration education. *Journal of Public Affairs Education, 7*(4), 229-240.

Kraemmer et al. (1986, November). Curriculum recommendation for public management education in computing: Final report of the National Association of Schools of Public Affairs and Administration, Ad hoc committee on computers in public management education. *Public Administration Review, 46*, 595-603.

Lau, E. (2000). *Government of the future.* Paris: OECD 42200081P1. Retrieved from *http://www1.oecd.org/publications/e-book/4200081E.PDF*

Lopez-Bassols, V. (2002). *ICT skills and employment.* STI Working Papers. Paris: OECD JT00129785. Retrieved August 11, 2002, from *http://webdomino1.oecd.org/comnet/pum/egovtf.nsf/Documents/[002]%20E-Government%20Resources/$File/DSTI_ICTSkills_V.LópezBassols@Other_Docs%20.pdf*

Making e-gov work. (2002, June 3). *Federal Computer Week.* Retrieved July 6, 2002, from *http://www.fcw.com/fcw/articles/2002/0603/mgt-egov-06-03-02.asp*

Mechling, J., & Applegate, L. (2000-2002). *Eight imperatives for leaders in a networked world: A series of guidelines for the 2000 election and beyond.* Boston. The Harvard Policy Group on Network-Enabled Services and Government John F. Kennedy School of Government Harvard University. Retrieved July 6, 2002, from *http://www.ksg.harvard.edu/stratcom/hpg/*

Overview. *http://www.ksg.harvard.edu/stratcom/hpg/eightimp.pdf*

Imperative #1: Focus on How IT Can Reshape Work and Public Sector Strategies (December 2000), *http://www.ksg.harvard.edu/stratcom/demo/hpg/imp1.pdf*

Imperative # 2: Use IT for Strategic Innovation, Not Simply Tactical Automation (January 2001), *http://www.ksg.harvard.edu/stratcom/demo/hpg/imp2.pdf*

Imperative # 3: Utilize Best Practices in Implementing IT Initiatives (March 2001), *http://www.ksg.harvard.edu/stratcom/demo/hpg/imp3.pdf*

Imperative # 4: Improve Budgeting and Financing for Promising IT Initiatives (April 2001), *http://www.ksg.harvard.edu/stratcom/demo/hpg/imp4.pdf*

Imperative # 5: Protect Privacy and Security (December 2001). *http://www.ksg.harvard.edu/stratcom/demo/hpg/imp5.pdf*

Imperative # 6: Form IT-related Partnerships to stimulate economic development (April 2002), *http://www.ksg.harvard.edu/stratcom/demo/hpg/imp6.pdf*

Imperative # 7: Use IT to promote equal opportunity and healthy communities (August 2002), *http://www.ksg.harvard.edu/stratcom/demo/hpg/imp7.pdf*

Imperative # 8: Prepare for digital democracy (August 2002), *http://www.ksg.harvard.edu/stratcom/demo/hpg/imp8.pdf*

Mitchell, C., & Kulik, T. (2000). *Knowledge management: Becoming an e-learning organization.* New York: The Conference Board.

Murphy, M. (2002). *Industry issues: Organizational change and firm performance.* Paris: OECD JT00123853.

National Governors Association. (n.d.). *Building better eGovernment: Tools for transformation.* Retrieved July 14, 2002, from *http://www.nga.org/center/egovernment*

Office of Management and Budget. Circular A-130. (2000, November 28). Management of federal information resources. Retrieved on June 8, 2002, from *http://www.whitehouse.gov/omb/circulars/a130/a130trans4.html*

Office of the E-Envoy (2000a). Skills for government, London. Retrieved June 29, 2002, from *http://www.e-envoy.gov.uk/publications/guidelines/skills/skills4iag.htm*

Office of the E-Envoy (2000b). *e-Business skills assessment toolkit.* London. Retrieved June 29, 2002, from *http://www.e-envoy.gov.uk/publications/guidelines/skills/ebusskills/overview.htm*

Partners in State-Local Information Systems: Lessons from the Field. (2001). *Center for technology in government.* Retrieved July 6, 2002, from *http://www.ctg.albany.edu/projects/lg/iisexec.html*

Rocheleau, B. (1998, July). The MPA core course in information technology: What should be taught? Why? *Journal of Public Affairs Education*, *4*(3), 193-206.
Weber, M. (1946). *Bureaucracy, extracts from essays in Sociology* (H. H. Gerth & C. W. Mills, Eds. & Trans.). In J. M. Shafritz & A. C. Hyde (Eds.), *Classics of public administration* (3rd ed., p. 51). Reprinted by permission H. H. Gerth 1973, Belmont, CA: Wadsworth.
Washington State Department of Information Services. (2001a). *The digital government applications academy.* Retrieved on June 30,2002, from *http://www.wa.gov/dis/academy/*
Washington State Department of Information Services. (2001b). *Applications template and outfitting model.* Retrieved on August 18, 2002, from *http://www.wa.gov/dis/atom/*

ENDNOTES

1 Additional information about the CIO University program can be found at the following university program Web sites: Carnegie Mellon at *http://www.mism.cmu.edu/cioi/*; George Mason University at *http://www.som.gmu.edu/techman/index.php*; George Washington University at *http://www.gwu.edu/~mastergw/programs/mis/*; and University of Maryland University College at *http://www.umuc.edu/grad/certificates/exec.html#cio*.

Chapter XVIII

Citizen Participation in Public Administration: The Impact of Citizen Oriented Public Services on Government and Citizens

Hein van Duivenboden, Capgemini Consulting Services, The Netherlands, and Tilburg University, The Netherlands

ABSTRACT

This chapter is on responsive electronic government services. Various changes in the relationship between government and citizens will be discussed by examining theory and practice of electronic public service delivery initiatives in a broad sense. The increasing complexity of society, individualization, new expectations of citizens and the use of modern ICT all influence the behavior of governments in their relations with citizens. What impact does e-government have on some of the most important principles of good governance — such as principles that safeguard "access and transparency", "accountability and legitimacy" and "effectiveness of policy- and decision-making"?

"What counts most for people is not the programs that traditionally concern political elites, such as diplomacy, defence or macroeconomic management of the economy, but programs providing education, social security, health and housing." (Rose, 1989, p. 5)

INTRODUCTION

In literature and policy regarding electronic government there is a dominant focus on service delivery. Although in policy documents electronic democracy, electronic accessibility of government information and improvement of operational management are also mentioned as important elements e-government programs, most of the attention seems to be paid to the subject of improving the relationship with citizens in their role as customers of the government. In many cases, the term e-government itself is even used as a synonym for electronic service delivery (Bekkers, 2001a; Office of the e-Envoy, 2001).

By emphasizing the one side of improvement of public service delivery as the main element of e-government programs, one seems to forget — or underestimate — the danger of neglecting the improvement of politico-administrative policy processes with the help of citizens and other stakeholders of the democratic states involved. In this political domain, public and private values are being weighed and legally binding decisions are being prepared and made on the basis of carefully balanced and often long-term processes of policy preparation and evaluation. While trying hard to improve the "economics" of government by focusing on e-government services it could be the case that — as a result of insufficient citizen participation in policy processes — the legitimacy of government is decreasing at the same time. This can be considered to be the so-called legitimacy paradox of e-government strategies: trying hard to improve legitimacy through better services and yet losing territory exactly because of that same focus (Fountain, 2000, as in Bekkers, 2001b).

Secondly, it can be questioned whether traditional democratic mechanisms like elections and referenda by themselves are still leading to an acceptable degree of translation of the needs and wants of citizens into policy and delivery processes (ICT and Government Advisory Committee, 2001; Rosenthal et al., 1996). The idea of a responsive government implies that government institutions are open for social debate and initiatives include a key role for so-called collective learning processes — based on knowledge exchange, communication and "trial and error." For that reason, it seems only logical that there is a tendency to supplement e-government projects with e-democracy initiatives (Bekkers, 2001a).

In this chapter, we will discuss electronic government services from the perspective of both government and citizens. We will focus on the changing relationship between government and citizens by examining the theory and practice of electronic public service delivery initiatives in a broad sense.

For government and its institutions, we will pay special attention to the promise of a shift from supply-driven service delivery to demand-driven service delivery and to possible changes in governmental behavior towards citizens. Is there really a tendency that government agencies are becoming more responsive through introducing and implementing electronic service delivery? What consequences do these developments have for living up to the general principles of good governance?

For citizens, we will describe and analyze the threats and opportunities to fulfil their role as participants in policy processes in combination with being treated as customers – in terms of increasing accessibility, reducing administrative burdens, providing integrated and tailored services and so on (e.g., OECD, 2001a). In this chapter we will restrict discussion to the consequences for citizen participation linked directly to electronic service delivery. As a result, we will not concentrate on changes (opportunities and threats) for citizens with regard to their specific role as voters — as indirect participants in the political domain undergoing changes as a result of e-democracy initiatives (e.g., e-voting pilots or digital debates). In other words, in this study citizens will be referred to in their position as customers (exercising certain rights), citoyens (participating in policy processes) and as subjects of the state (meeting certain legal requirements). In all three cases we will ask ourselves if citizens are being treated along the principles of good governance. Does the introduction and implementation of electronic services influence the force or content of principles of transparency, accountability, legitimacy, quality and effectiveness of policy and decision-making (OECD, 2001b)? It is exactly this question where there possibly lies some clues for changing role of government and citizens at the same time.

Structure of This Chapter

In paragraph two we will discuss the different roles a citizen plays in its relationship with government. In paragraphs three we will go into the principles of good government and the way in which governments ought to behave towards citizens and other external parties, like social movements or special interest groups. After that, we will sketch the outlines of the ongoing shift in focus from policy implementation to public service delivery (a short historical overview of the rise of attention for ICT as an enabler of service quality and responsiveness).

In paragraph five we will examine some principles and strategies in the field of responsive government services and related policy processes, to be followed by presenting a number of international cases of electronic service delivery in practice (paragraph six). We will draw some conclusions with respect to the changes that the introduction and implementation of forms of electronic service delivery bring about for government, citizens and their mutual relationship. To conclude, we will make a few recommendations for further research and debate within the OECD electronic government project (OECD, 2001a).

KEEPING UP APPEARANCES

Roles of the Citizen

One can distinguish many roles of the citizen related to government: customer, voter, taxpayer, applicant, subject, stakeholder, civil servant (employee) and so on. In this chapter we use a division in four: the citizen as customer, as citoyen, as voter and as subject of the state (Thomassen, 1979; Van Duivenboden, 1999; Ringeling, 2001). Although the role of the citizen as voter falls out of the scope of this chapter, we will discuss its characteristics in order to clearly point out the differences with the other three roles that will be addressed in the remaining parts of this study.

Are You Being Served?

In general, public-service delivery concepts tend to focus on the role of citizens as *customers* of government organizations (instead of their position as taxpayers, voters or state inhabitants). However, in most cases the public-sector customer role is much different from the private-sector customer role.

Firstly, citizens seldom are customers of government agencies on a purely voluntary basis (Lipsky, 1980). Most of the time, the relationship between citizen and government concerns specific rights and duties, which have been laid down in laws, rules and policy statements that set the standard for service delivery conditions throughout the state. Citizens cannot negotiate the price or quality of services when applying for a new driver's licence, a passport or rental subsidies — because generally the law forbids, hinders or at least doesn't stimulate government agencies to compete with one another on such matters as price, speed, quality or user friendliness.

Secondly, citizens cannot "shop around" in search of, let's say, a higher amount of subsidies or benefits. When someone is legally entitled to social security benefits, student grants or — for instance — a building permit, he can not choose the cheapest or fastest service delivery agency in the region. He will have to apply for this benefit or permit at his local municipal office or at a central state department that is legally authorized for these transactions and is, therefore, always dependent on a specific organizations's service delivery.

Thirdly, once the right to a certain public service is established, in most cases public-sector customers have an absolute right to deliverance, due to the fact that government agencies have a legal duty to ensure the particular service delivery (Berg, as in Hoogwout, 2001). Unlike private enterprises, governmental agencies can seldom refuse delivery of the services and goods they have to offer in individual cases. Public services like family allowances, road safety control, fire fighting, education or even prosecution and imprisonment cannot be held back from (certain) citizens just because the government agency involved has too many customers to deal with already or is short of personnel or money — let alone the fact that it is virtually impossible for government agencies to file one's petition in bankruptcy.

The apparent incomparability of public-sector customers with private-sector customers brings some authors to the conclusion that it would be better to not talk about a citizen as a customer of government at all. Hence, they prefer to replace the term customer-oriented government with the term responsive government (Derksen et al. in: Hoogwout, 2001). However, there are some strong arguments to stick to the use of the term customer in relation to public services.

Firstly, every public sector customer is paying for the services he receives – which is, in a way, similar to private-sector circumstances. In general, every citizen is a taxpayer as well and is therefore, though (very) indirectly, paying a certain amount of money every time the government grants him, for example, a licence or a benefit or enforces democratic

Figure 1. Roles of the citizen and key elements

Citizen Role	Key Element
Customer	Transaction
Subject of the State	Law (Enforcement) and Order
Citoyen	Direct Participation
Voter	Indirect Participation

laws and regulations. This form of indirect payment is most clearly the case in situations of so-called collective customers — as opposite from individual customers (see Tops & Van Vugt, in Hoogwout, 2001). Government is serving collective customers by building dykes, bridges or roads or by maintaining order or enforcing public safety. The individual customer is also most of the times an indirect payer, but not when he applies for a passport or a driving license and has to pay some legal dues directly.

Secondly, by using the term customer as a metaphor, government agencies will compensate for the fact that they normally don't have an external trigger for improvement of their service delivery. The bureaucratic culture of most government agencies and the fact that there is no competition with other organizations in order to survive or make a profit generally doesn't help customer friendliness to be the number one priority. It's just not a characteristic of governments by nature. Over the last few years, the rising popularity of the term customer has brought many public-service organizations to implement a quality management system that — among other indicators — forces them to evaluate the citizen's satisfaction on a regular basis (e.g., the popular Balanced Score Card method or other remains from the period of Total Quality Management).

Thirdly, there are reasons to treat a public-sector customer even better than a private-sector customer. This is what Ringeling refers to by the term "customer-oriented plus," exactly because a citizen is not a voluntary customer, he needs to be treated with the utmost respect (Ringeling, 2001). As a rule, citizens don't apply for a social benefit or a building permit for pleasure. This also stands for the help of fire brigades, police or garbage collectors. The incomparability to buying a new wardrobe or going to the movies is obvious. Furthermore, in private-sector circumstances both parties normally are satisfied about the transaction that takes place, namely trading money for something valuable. Public "services" like taxation or getting a ticket for speeding usually don't result in happiness for the citizen involved. In spite of this, in the Netherlands, the Tax Office is the one with the slogan, "We can't make it any nicer, but we can make it easier." They and several other Tax Departments worldwide even live up to that expectation by being early adopters of the Internet. Electronic tax declaration facilities are in practice in Estonia, Singapore, France and California (Van Duivenboden, Frissen, Van Lieshout & Mooren, 2002). To conclude, even when citizens are actually placed in their position as subjects of the state (see below), a customer orientation (plus) can sometimes be detected.

Are You Being Watched?

Citizens in their role as *subjects of the state* are, in short, subject to rules, regulations and decisions made by government authorities. Not complying with these rules can lead to penalties varying from (official) reprimands up to imprisonment (Thomassen, 1979). This relationship between government and citizen is the traditional vertical one, whereby the main role of government is to exercise (democratic) power over the civilian population when necessary. Opposite to this stands the increasingly more horizontal one as referred to in modern, responsive democratic perspectives wherein deliberation with citizens, the system of checks and balances and the networking society have become buzz words (Van de Donk & Tops, 1992, p. 43). However, even in a very (post) modern information society the role of the citizen as a subject of the state will not disappear. For example, it is nearly unthinkable that criminal law or law enforcement in general is absent in any democratic state (ICT and Government Advisory Committee, 2001).[2] Hence, we must describe this role in more detail to get a complete picture of the impact of responsive e-government service on citizens and government.

The perspective of citizens as subjects of the state can easily be related to the classic definition of a bureaucracy. Rules are to be enforced regardless of the person involved, and there's only very little room for things like tolerating certain expectations of introducing customer friendliness (Ringeling, 2001). Of course, in today's modern welfare states, wherein technological and social trends (like individualization and horizontalization, see paragraph 3) have altered the relationship between government and citizens drastically, citizens and governments are (both) offered many more opportunities to interact in a more informal and flexible manner. Citizens are not tolerating strong top-down measures without an adequate motivation or convincing argument anymore.[3] On the other hand, civil servants making decisions in individual cases are not the Weberian role-model servants without any room for flexibility in interpretation (discretionary powers) anymore. This is where the rise and codification of many of the principles of good governance play an important role. The practices of violent and arbitrary rule and "détournement de pouvoir" have been frustrated increasingly by principles that force governments to exercise due caution, legal equality and legal security (see paragraph 3). Furthermore, because of the growing amount of products and services that government agencies have had to deliver over the last few decades, in the relationship with citizens as subjects of the state there tends to be a growing focus on responsiveness in the area of law enforcement and surveillance, too. The above-mentioned example of the taxpayer illustrates that development, but one can also think of "the introduction" of customer friendliness in granting licences or paying tickets (e.g., online in stead of in line) or by means of offering one-stop-shop facilities in case of obligatory inspections and public insurance.[4] In closing, placing all the laws and regulations in force on the Internet helps citizens as subjects of the state to be aware of what duties and obligations rest upon them.

Who Asked You for an Opinion?

In the relationship between citizens and the (democratic) state, an important role of the citizen is his position as a *citoyen*. This role sees to his activities as a carrier of democratic rights on a (more) permanent basis (than in his role as voter once every two, three or more years). The term citoyen refers to "citizenship" of a nation state. A citoyen is an individual who is — within certain limits — able to participate directly in policy processes, political parties and social movements. By doing that, he exercises valuable democratic civil rights such as the rights to freedom of opinion and speech, to freedom of peaceful association and assembly, to demonstration and petition and — at least to some extent — the right to access to government information.

For a long time, the role of the citizen as carrier of democratic rights has been narrowed down to his role as a voter. Strong political leadership and loyal grassroots support made direct political participation of citizens less necessary, or so it seems (Ringeling, 2001). As a result, most OECD countries have a strong and dominant system of (only a few) political parties governing the nation, wherein citizens are placed in a role of spectators in stead of political participants.[5]

Nowadays, the role of the citizen as citoyen seems to get renewed attention as a result of the decreasing importance of political parties and the growing individualization, or individual involvement or political awareness, in society. For example, Van Gunsteren introduces the political ideal of a Neo-Republican Citizen: a citizen who is the subject of the state and active participant in political processes at the same time.[6] Depla illustrates the increased importance of the non-electoral role of citizens by pointing to the rise of social movements, demonstrations and the popularity of formal procedures for participation in policy processes of local democracies:

"The renewal leads to a certain shifting of roles; citizens are being stimulated to actively contribute to political and policy-making processes, councillors more or less distance themselves from the administrative process and direct themselves more at the local society, while public servants participate in networks to organize forms of co-production, so that the different actors involved can have responsibilities in the policy-making process." (Depla, 1995, pp. 47-48, 319-320)

May I Have Your Votes Please?

Citizens as *voters* can articulate their wishes and needs to government in an indirect manner: by choosing representatives at the local, regional, national or international level. The importance of voters is of course clear enough to political parties. However, in today's information society, it can be questioned if this role of voter is sufficiently guaranteeing the democratic rights of individual citizens. The horizontal network in society seems to grow in importance compared to the pyramidal structure of political hierarchy and vertical steering (ICT and Government Advisory Committee, 2001). As a result, the practice of direct communication and transaction between citizen and government is growing rapidly. Visiting a local election office every two or three years might not be in line with expectations of modern citizens anymore. A responsive government is not only judged by citizens during election periods, but during every contact it has with citizens — regardless of their specific role as voters, customers, subjects or citoyens. Furthermore, apart from the role of voter, people are not to be expected to even be aware of playing these different roles in specific circumstances. Therefore, it might be advisable to address all these roles at the same time.

In this chapter on responsive government services we will concentrate on three of the four roles: customers, citoyens and subjects. In these three roles we expect citizens to be offered opportunities to articulate wishes, comments and needs in a more or less direct way. Because the role of the citizen as a voter is one of indirect participation in policy processes, we see less direct opportunities for intensive responsiveness of government services.

GOVERNMENTAL BEHAVIOR AND PRINCIPLES OF GOOD GOVERNANCE

Changes in Governmental Behavior

In the OECD publication "Citizens as Partners" (2001, p. 73), it is stated that there are many examples of OECD member countries that "have taken steps to reinforce their legal, policy and institutional frameworks and develop better tools for information, consultation and active participation." They do so in order to live up to the principles of good governance and to further improve the quality of representative democracy. There is a growing need for that, because:

"The context in which national governments and their citizens interact is increasingly complex. Policy decisions are made at multiple levels of government. The solutions to many problems (...) require co-operation and agreement across regions, countries, or at (the) global level. Modern information and communication technologies (ICTs) have reinforced these interdependencies. (...) Governments increasingly realize that they will not be able to conduct and effectively implement policies, as good as they may be, if their citizens do not understand or support them." (OECD, 2001, p. 20)

The growing awareness of governments for the need for change with regard to their relationship with citizens has to do with several social, politico-administrative and technologic trends. Albeda and Van Bijlert (2001) sum up three important trends that raised the attention for enhancing citizen-oriented service delivery and policy making:

1. Along with a more individualistic attitude, citizens' expectations towards the services of government have changed. The confidence in "good governance" is no longer self-evident and people are getting accustomed to tailor-made services as they experience quality improvement in private-sector service delivery.
2. New forms of steering are being implemented as an answer to a more complex societal surrounding. Vertical and hierarchical forms of steering alone aren't satisfactory anymore in the new, more horizontal, information society. Government agencies have become one of many parties in horizontal relationships. Often, they have just as much influence on the outcome of policy chains as citizens, private organizations or social movements (Van de Donk, 2001).
3. New service offerings are made possible through the use of modern ICT. Integrated services, proactive service delivery and multichanneling forms of information supply are some of the new possibilities in the relationship with citizens, which in part determines the behavior of government.

These new expectations, steering forms and service offerings influence the relationship between government and citizen in an extensive way — especially when you take the influence of ICT into account. On that specific matter, the Dutch ICT and Government Advisory Committee (2001) observed various more or less radical transitions in this relationship and its surroundings: horizontalization, deterritorialization, virtualization and acceleration.

Firstly, a transition from an order-based economy to a negotiation-based economy will lead to an institutional system based mainly on more horizontal principles of checks and balances:

"Horizontalization strengthens the role of the citizen as a 'customer' of government services, as a participant in the policy- and decision-making process and as a member of society. The position of citizens also becomes more autonomous because horizontalization reduces their traditional information disadvantage. As a result, they are better placed to scrutinise the way in government performs its functions."

Secondly, the widespread use of ICT will make citizens, businesses and organizations more "footloose." Activities involving communication and the provision of information can be undertaken from any given place and have an impact on any other given place:

"Deterritorialization is undermining the foundations of government as we know it. (...) In the virtual world authority is not self-evident and must be instead acquired."

The third important trend the Committee discerns is on virtualization (immaterialization of processes, activities and products) and reliability (opportunities for manipulations):

"Information, images and meanings are seldom unequivocal in the virtual world and are also not always connected with the physical world. The opportunities for manipulation are therefore greatly increased." And, "The transparency made possible by ICT had not yet, on balance, resulted in a more transparent government organization. By contrast, citizens have become more transparent for government."

The fourth and last observed social trend with relevance to the relationship between government and citizens is on the difference in pace of technological and politico-administrative change ("acceleration and red tape"). Because the pace at which society adjusts to and copes with change is usually lower than the pace at which ICT adjusts, the Committee sees a diminishing scope for prediction and control that can result in social dislocation:

"Changes in the political and administrative system take place at a slower pace than the development of ICT. Legislation in a substantive sense is impossible if the object of regulation is in a state of flux."

To conclude, the raising complexity of society, individualization and new expectations of citizens and the use of modern ICT all influence the behavior of governments in their relations with citizens to a certain extent. The guidelines for this behavior are set out in laws and regulations, but are also to be found in the international acknowledged "principles of good governance." In the next paragraph, we will examine some of these principles in order to determine which ones are most likely to be of influence on the relationship between government and citizens regarding responsive e-government services.

Principles of Good Governance

Lyon states that "societies that claim to be democratic imply by that term that there is a degree of involvement by the citizenry in the political process. Governments thus claim to be responsive to citizens, who are viewed as political equals" (Lyon, 1994, p. 116). To establish and maintain a generally accepted degree of the involvement of citizens in all kinds of political and policy processes, it is important to assure a necessary level of public support. Such public confidence can only exist if citizens can rely on the law and policy and on the correct implementation of norms that are laid down in these laws and policies (Bekkers & Van Duivenboden, 1995). Therefore, decision making has to be in accordance with known, uniform laws and has to eliminate as much as possible arbitrary and capricious behavior. It also requires the possibility of actually exercising the right to appeal to assure that proper procedures are in fact being followed (Clarke, 1992). This is the idea of the "Rechtsstaat" — of democratic constitutional states. This idea is being made operational in at least three related principles, which complement each other: the principle of legal equality, the principle of legal security and the principle of checks and balances (Bekkers & Van Duivenboden, 1995).

The principle of legal equality sees to it that all cases, which are the same in their nature and characteristics, are dealt with in the same way, and that all cases unequal should be dealt with unequally to the extent they differ. This principle forbids discrimination in general.

The principle is of legal security implies that government interventions which affect citizens should be based on the existing laws and regulations so that in the end these interventions are predictable. People must be able to refer in their actions to these laws and regulations and should trust that the law is being executed.

The principle of checks and balances is based on the idea that, in order to protect citizens to an arbitrary execution of power by the state (power that is in one hand), this power should be divided among separate institutions. This separation of power can be safeguarded if these institutions could control each other and could keep each other in balance — which refers to the classical idea of the division of powers between the legal power, the execution and the judiciary (the Trias Politica). Specifically on the subject of the relationship between government and citizen, the idea of checks and balances refers to striving for protection of citizens against capricious interventions by the government. Government interventions should be controlled and counterbalanced. In fact, *citizens* should be able to control government. A necessary condition is that there is to some extent a transparent government.

In literature and in practice the principles of legal equality, legal security and checks and balances in literature and regulations are further worked out in several other important principles of democratic state systems, such as the principles of openness, individual participation and accountability (OECD, 1981). The umbrella term for these general and more specific democratic principles to which governments are obliged is "the principles of good governance" (OECD, 2001; Van Duivenboden, Frissen, Van Lieshout & Mooren, 2001). In this chapter, we will analyze the practice of responsive e-government services, or more precisely, their impact on government and citizens on the basis of the following clusters of principles of good governance:

- Access and transparency
- Accountability and legitimacy
- Effectiveness of policy- and decision-making

We think these clusters of principles are of specific importance because they explicitly influence the mutual balances in the democratic relationship between government and citizens, such as the balances between:

- Government's information position versus citizens' information position
- Openness of government versus transparency of individual citizens
- State surveillance versus individual freedom

- State surveillance versus individual privacy
- Citizen-oriented service delivery versus individual privacy
- Law enforcement versus flexible bureaucracy
- Power of the state versus power of citizens (or social movements)

Better *access and transparency* can offer opportunities for citizens in the sense that they can get better information on policy issues or service offerings and are able to understand the functioning of public administration better. In other words, improved openness of government implies giving the citizen more possibilities to get access to government information. Access precedes transparency and in its turn, this transparency can be considered as a form of information supply that precedes different forms of citizens' participation, for example co-production by citizens and government (Zouridis, 1998).

However, there is a downside to the issue of transparency — as already illustrated in one of the citations of the Dutch Advisory Committee. The use of ICT could also one-sidedly lead to a more transparent citizen instead of to a more open government. For instance, being able to deliver tailor-made and/or proactive services to citizens implies that within public administration there is a large amount of detailed customer information to be registered in databases. Potential loss of privacy then seems to be the price to pay for more tailored and proactive service delivery.

The *accountability and legitimacy* of the state in general and of public-service delivery organizations in specific are important issues when it comes to democratic values and good governance. After all, the power of the government ultimately depends on the faith that the people (that have given this power) have in that very same government. As stated in our introduction, the use of ICT can lead to an increase as well as to a decrease of the government's legitimacy. In the latter case, this could well be the result of a too one-sidedly economic perspective on e-government services. In other words, by considering citizens solely in their role as customer, the citizen as carrier of democratic rights is being pushed too far to the back. As a result, citizens may feel uncomfortable with public organizations as they get too little room to respond to or to participate in policy processes. This can be the case when they have too little information to base a proper judgement on or simply because there's no opportunity to give any feedback on the quality of the specific service that is being provided.

The *effectiveness of policy- and decision-making* is obviously a relevant cluster of principles of good governance to take into account when discussing *responsive* e-government services. A key element of improving the responsiveness of public services is to gear policy programs and administrative decisions more adequately to (individual or collective) problems, wants and needs of the citizens. This could mean striving for a shortage of waiting time or a reduction of costs, but it could also imply the development and implementation of a whole new (or radically changed) policy program. In other words, discussing changes in the responsiveness of government that concern the effectiveness of policy-making can vary from the way in which services are delivered to the supply of services itself. Furthermore, the stage of the policy process involved can vary from the early agenda-setting phase to an ex post evaluation of the policy implementation or service delivery.

CITIZEN ORIENTATION AND ELECTRONIC SERVICE DELIVERY[7]

Toward Citizen Orientation

Citizen orientation in the public sector is a development that results from increasing attention for policy implementation in public administration. For years, the dominant focus of government (service delivery) organizations has been supply-oriented. The basic idea was that society could be "served" most effectively through solid political decisions taken by elected officials and detailed policy plans prepared by specialized and experienced professionals. The quality of the policy design was perceived to be directly related to (intended) policy effects in society. In other words, policy implementation and, with that, the attention for the environment of government organizations was for years of minor importance in public administration.

During the 1970s a shift in focus can be seen in an increasing awareness of the value of (attention for) a carefully designed policy implementation process for policy outcomes (Pressman & Wildavsky, 1979). At the same time, the Managerialism movement gained ground in the public sector. These developments brought the functioning of public bureaucracies and their relationship with citizens into the spotlight of public administration.

In the 1980s, particularly under the flag of the New Public Management (NPM) movement, the perspective of citizens as customers gained ground in public administration. According to NPM ideologists, government needed to be reshaped in order to function better in modern times. In other words, government had to become more *responsive* to social developments and therefore had to take a more entrepreneurial position in society. According to Bellamy and Taylor (1998, p. 47), the *new* public management from earlier forms of managerialism is a new emphasis on the management and delivery of public services, and how those services are accessed and used. Consequently, one of the main principles for government organizations to become more entrepreneurial was to meet the needs of the citizen, rather than the needs of the bureaucracy. User-friendliness, transparency, and holism were therefore thought of as important policy goals (Lips & Frissen, 1997).

During the 1990s — especially with the increasing use of the Internet — many governments came to perceive ICTs as an important means to implement the NPM's range of ideas to make the customer the central focus. From various national government's strategies to improve the functioning of government with the help of ICT — which are mostly published during the second half of that decade — we may conclude that ICTs are acknowledged to offer opportunities partly to further modernize public service delivery, partly to fundamentally restructure public-service delivery and, with that, the whole of the bureaucratic organization behind the service counter (Lenk & Traunmüller, 2001, pp. 66-68; Silcock, 2001, p. 89).

ICT-Enabled Citizen Orientation

According to the OECD, there's a strong tendency "to place greater emphasis on performance or results rather than simply on adherence to prescribed rules and processes (...). Service quality initiatives represent a step beyond earlier forms. Whereas these focused mainly on improving internal process or efficiency, a focus on service quality requires public sector organizations to become more outward looking and in some cases even to justify their role and existence" (OECD, 1996).

Today, many government organizations are introducing ICT as an instrument to actually (further) shape the turnover of their work processes from a supply orientation to a demand orientation. In doing so, public institutions are confronted with a large number of new, often multidisciplinary questions that are related with electronic government or electronic governance. In practice so far, a distinction is often made between questions that primarily concern the organization of the "front office" — where most contacts with customers take place — and questions that especially focus on the organization of the "back office" of the organization. To be able to realize the organization's turnover process towards a demand orientation, a strategic vision is needed which connects both foci of attention and related questions. In this respect, we may see that many government organizations are currently developing so-called "e-government" visions in which these different organizational questions are accommodated.

Initially, many national governments introduced e-government as a counterpart or part of electronic commerce or e-business and often equated it with the deliverance of governmental services online (Kubicek & Hagen, 2001, p. 177; Bekkers, 2001b). This focus on front-office-related visions on e-government is also translated into the seemingly strict time targets for transformation into e-government organizations. Often these time targets are committed to the percentage to which service delivery at the front office is handled electronically.[8] In practice, to establish an adequate service level at the front office constrains high standards of quality in communication and data exchange in the back office of e-government. This communication and data exchange is not restricted to internal processes (intra-organizational). Often, data and information are to be obtained from databases of third parties, such as other government agencies within the policy chain (inter-organizational). For example, social security agencies cannot assess an applicant's benefit payments without verifying personal data with the data stored in the municipal (name and address) register or the registers of the Tax Authorities and the Industrial Insurance Board (Van Duivenboden, 1999). This implies that focusing on the needs and demands of citizens instead of on the regulations and organizational structure of government organizations asks for involvement of the whole chain of organizations of a policy field (i.e., the social security policy field). In other words, citizen-oriented service delivery demands transformation of the processes and organizational design of the back offices of all parties involved.

RESPONSIVE E-GOVERNMENT SERVICES: STRATEGIES

Responsiveness as a Policy Strategy

Several years ago, the OECD already identified responsiveness as "a key factor in determining the value of public services to the citizen." It was stated that "there is a general consensus that the previous orientation towards orientation of rules must be replaced by an orientation towards results generally, of which the needs of the client are an important aspect." Furthermore, "a focus on service quality is part of the general direction of public sector management reforms being pursued by the OECD Member countries, namely to improve the responsiveness of public sector institutions by requiring and encouraging a greater emphasis on performance or results." To conclude, the OECD pointed out that "there is a general acceptance of greater empowerment of clients, rather than having all key decisions made by the supplier, at least without formal and adequate consultation" (OECD, 1996). In other words, the key element of responsive e-government services is the improvement of service quality through enforcement of citizen orientation (meeting the needs of the citizen).[9] In this chapter, we concentrate on responsive government services by examining the impact of responsive e-government services on both citizens (customers, citoyens and subjects of the state) and government itself.

Expectations of Citizens

In order to meet the needs of the citizen it is obvious that government must form an adequate picture of what those (individual or more collective) needs really are. Dutch studies on the needs and expectations of the citizens themselves has pointed out that citizens expect e-government (the use of ICT in public administration) mainly to contribute to (Dialogic, 2001, 2002):

- Reduction of costs
- Improving access
- Tailoring services
- Improving transparency
- Shortening of waiting time

When asked for their opinion on the most important criteria in their contacts with government agencies in general — so not only electronically — the most popular categories are: (1) the expertise and professionalism of the civil servant and (2) shortening of waiting time.[10]

Other studies (Albeda & Van Bijlert, 2001; Leenes & Svensson, 2001; Snellen, 2001) confirm the importance of improving service delivery at these main categories of research findings by pointing specifically at:

- waiting times being too long;
- prices being too high;
- differences between quality and price for similar services offered by different (local or regional) government agencies are too big;
- physical access to simple services like providing new passports or driving licences often being problematic (in terms of opening times or accessibility);
- the presentation or provision of services in most cases being too much geared to the rationale of bureaucracy and regulations instead of to the logic of citizens.

To conclude, on the basis of citizens' expectations and research findings we can observe that there really seems to be a need for improvement of service delivery.[11] Underneath we will discuss the changes in service delivery strategies of government agencies that are closely related to the increased use of modern ICT.

Strategic Shifts in Service Delivery

Several trends can be acknowledged in the redesign of public-service delivery towards a more responsive design of the relationship between government and citizens. With the help of ICT, governments are generally trying to improve the convenience of public service provision to citizens with strategies implying a shift:[12]

- *from supply-oriented to demand-oriented public-service delivery* (focusing on the needs and demands of citizens instead of policy makers)
- *from collective to tailor-made public-service delivery* (gearing services to the specific individuals needs and demands instead of to groups of customers or citizens)
- *from fragmented to integrated public-service delivery* (implementing "single–window" policies geared to question patterns of citizens instead of based on existing laws, regulations and organizational structures)
- *from functional to holistic public-service delivery* (transforming the organizational design of service delivery to coherent policy issues instead of being bound to the judicial or politico-administrative determined borders of government organizations)
- *from specialized to general public-service delivery* (offering citizens logical and coherent "hyperlinks" to all relevant issues whenever he contacts a government agency for a specific service. For instance, when applying for a social security benefit the citizen is also provided with information on training facilities (in order to return to the labor market) or rent subsidy regulations)
- *from reactive to proactive public-service delivery* (taking into account the future demands and needs of citizens up to the situation wherein citizens are automatically informed or provided with services)
- *from passive citizen participation ("consumption") to active citizen participation ("prosumption") in public-service delivery* (taking into account the merge of different citizens roles: the participant role in the "production" of policy tends to merge with the customer role — which has to do with giving citizens (customers) more influence on policy programs, towards letting him fulfil the role of co-producer or co-director of policy programs)
- *from one service counter to "multichanneling" in public-service delivery* (offering citizens different types of channels or windows — digital or physical — in order to let him choose the most suitable one when expedient)

RESPONSIVE E-GOVERNMENT SERVICES IN PRACTICE

In this paragraph we will present a number of examples of responsive e-government services. With that, we hope to create scenery for further discussion and analysis of the impact of citizen-oriented e-services on the relationship between government and citizen.

Multi-Service Express: Easy One-Stop Shopping in Victoria

The Government of the State of Victoria, Australia, has established a target of providing all suitable services online to the public by the end of 2001. To provide easy access for customers (both citizens and businesses) at a single electronic service counter, the so-called "Multi-service Express" Web site has been established (*http://www.vic.gov.au/onlineservices.cfm*).[13] Through this Web site customers are helped to quickly find the public service they are looking for, without having to know which government department or agency is responsible (see the text in Figure 2). Additionally, they are also able to immediately conduct transactions online with the government. Services provided on this Web site are currently classified according to service type (for example, current service types include Apply for Licence/Permit — see the pop down menu in Figure 2 — Book a Service, Calculators, Change Address With, Government Tenders/Submissions, Grant Application, Monitoring Progress, Obtain Information/Action, Pay Bills or Fines, and Order Products), life and every day events (for example, Becoming a Parent, Becoming an Adult, Buying a Motor Vehicle, Buying Government Books and Publications, Buying Land and Property, Changing Contact Details, Cleaning up the Environment, and Coping with Addiction), and organizational type (for example, government departments, distinct business units within government departments,

Figure 2. Multi-service Express: online application for licences and permits

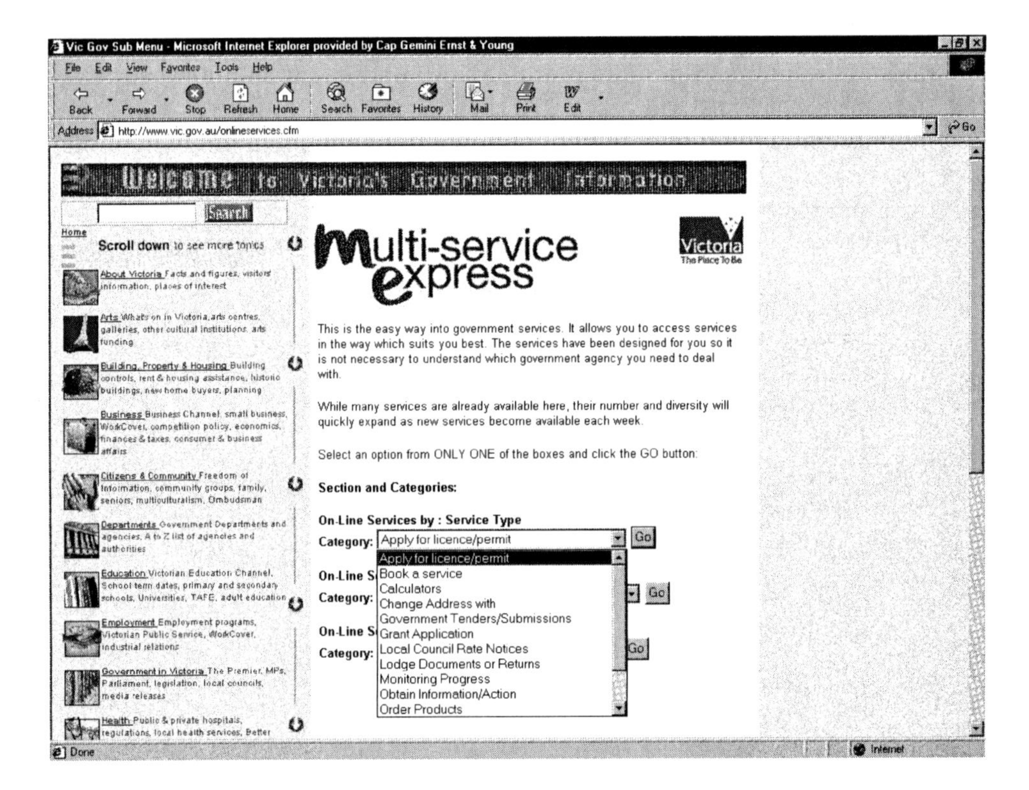

statutory bodies, and logical groupings). The Victorian government only wants to include services on the Web site, which are of a "doing/transactional nature." This implies that strict information provision is not deemed suitable for inclusion. Examples of services which are of a "doing/transactional nature" include filling out and submitting forms online, ordering publications online, paying bills online, booking a service online, and searching a database to retrieve information, and so forth.

This initiative of the Victorian State Government is an example of the general development of online public-service delivery from information provision at first to more and more online transactions.

E-Citizen: The National Service Portal of Singapore

In Singapore, more than 65% of all the public services today that can be delivered are being electronically accessible and the remaining 35% will be during the end of 2002 (Infocomm Development Authority, 2002). The crown jewel of this nation is the national so-called e-citizen service portal *www.ecitizen.gov.sg*. This is a one-stop shop, integrated Web site for all government services (information, communication, and transactions) structured in service packages around events in the course of life of an ordinary Singaporean citizen. For instance, one can apply for a birth extract online (see Figure 3), look for a job, and get information on starting a business or on retirement. With that, the

Figure 3. E-citizen: online application for extracts from register of births

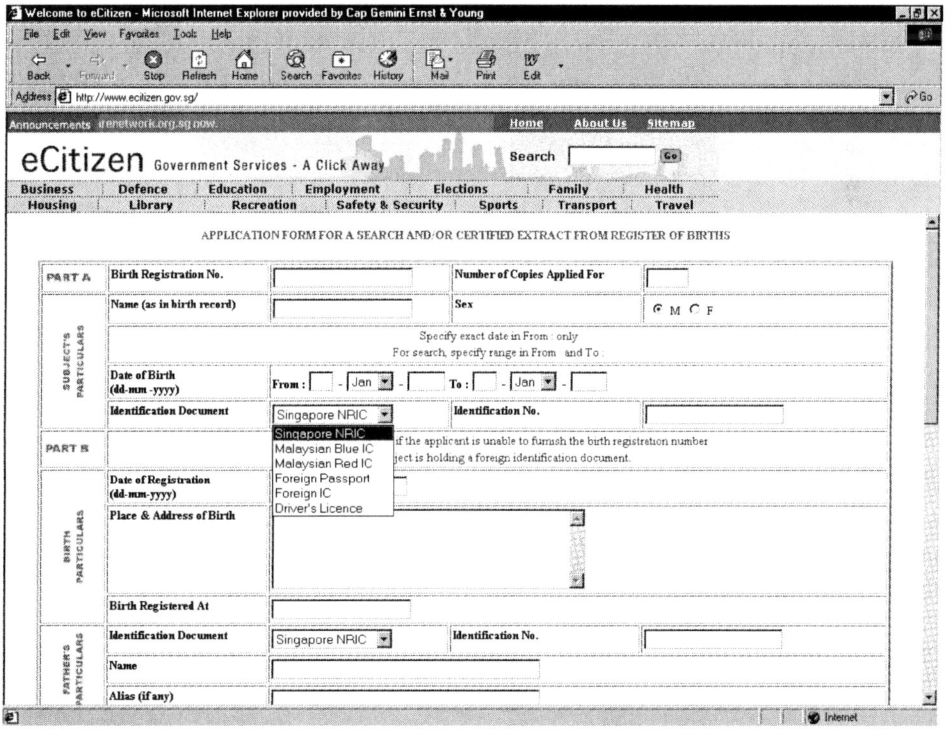

Singaporean government has a Web site through which customers can access all government departments and policy sectors in a customer-friendly way. On their Web site, the government explicitly links the task to "serve citizens" to the opportunities that ICTs have to offer:

"Changes in technology and the advent of the Internet have redefined the way citizens expect of government and its services. To keep abreast and meet these challenges, the Singapore Government is committed in its efforts to e-enable its various agencies in their service delivery to the public, and businesses. It aims to build a 'Connected Government' where services are easily accessible and delivered in an integrated and timely manner. Singaporeans will be able to enjoy the convenience, faster turnaround times and simpler procedures that integrated Government services can offer. As a demonstration of the Government's commitment, more than 680 eServices have been made available online by the various government agencies. The Government to Citizen portal, the eCitizen Centre, presently has 50 eService Packages and 170 eServices in the eCitizen portal."

Eos-Program: Proactive Rental Subsidy Service in The Netherlands

The Dutch Housing Department offers citizens the possibility to calculate their possible right to rent subsidy — and the exact amount if applicable (*http://www.minvrom.nl*). Furthermore, in 2000 the first 120.000 cases of automatic continuation of rent subsidy payments have been established on the basis of information already available at the department or partner organizations in the policy chain. In that, there is no need for the applicant to fill in forms year after year as long as neither his situation nor the legislation has changed (Agterhorst & Thaens, 2000; Mettau, 2001). The department states that two reasons lay behind the idea of automatic continuation. Firstly, tenants used to apply for rental subsidy every year and were confronted with a long lasting paper procedure through a chain of landlords, municipalities and the Housing Department. As a result, on average it took four months to receive payments if applicable. Secondly, tenants used to initiate the process and provide the department with all kinds of data that in fact were already known to (other parts of) government. The department acknowledged this to be ineffective and now gathers all information directly from the different sources involved (landlords, population register and the Tax Authorities).

An interesting development is that the Housing Department and its yearly forms to be filled in seem to be disappearing along with the development of this automatic continuation system based on the data this "e-government organization" already possesses. Over time, the average customer will be less aware of the existence of a specific back-office organization that is accountable for the assessment of rent subsidies. In order to continue receiving — or in the future maybe even applying for — rental subsidies, there will not be any need for personal (non-virtual) contact with a government agency.

Quality Cards: Information Service on School Results in The Netherlands

The Dutch Education and Science Department offers an information service on the Internet for parents to be able to compare the performance of schools in detail. Among other things, this site gives access to "quality cards" of all primary and secondary schools of the country (http://www.kwaliteitskaart.nl). Next to these quality cards, that enable comparison on national and local level (e.g., all schools within a bicycle's ride) a detailed report on the results of every school is accessible online. One can get immediate insight into results, student guidance, facilities (computers, buildings) and for example extracurricular activities. In this way, parents can get easy access to many ins and outs of the quality of the greater part of education services available in the neighborhood – which is most convenient when a decision must be taken on which school their precious children will attend over the next few years.

Project TOM: Direct Citizen Participation in Estonia[14]

In Estonia, an interesting pilot project in the field of direct facilitating, direct participation of citizens in public decision- and policy-making is TOM (Today I Decide). This project aims at decreasing the gap between government and citizens by giving citizens full opportunity to generate ideas and suggest changes in — existing *or* non-existing — laws and regulations. The government guarantees to respond to any actually given idea and citizens or social movements can bring forward their own enactments and vote on official bills. Furthermore, citizens are offered the opportunity to comment on bills in a special chat room prior to the moment that it is actually being put forward in Parliament. If a majority of votes is in favor of the bill, the Prime Minister will sign the bill (as a "draft" for legislation). From that moment on, a clock will start running and visitors will be able to see online who's conducting the bill and what time this person has left for finishing off.

Do-It-Yourself: Online Transaction Forms in the United States

The Web site *www.dot.gov* of the United States Federal Department of Transportation (DOT) provides so-called do-it-yourself (DIY) access to a database of online forms. It offers citizens and businesses the opportunity "to pay registration fees, insurance, and fines online with commonly used credit cards with its secure security system and data protection" and "allows citizens to make payments using DIY whenever they want" (OECD, 2002, p. 13). On the Web site, the Department explicitly mentions the advantage of using new ICT in service delivery: "The Department of Transportation now provides customers the option of reaching DOT at their convenience through the Internet. (…) By using the Internet, customers will reduce processing time and eliminate burdensome errors." An interesting observation in an OECD study (2002) is that this form of electronic service "also helps public servants avoid mistakes (e.g., misplacing the forms) and save time from extra work of entering users' information into databases." In other words, both citizens and government itself is served through increased access and transparency, shortening of waiting time and higher effectiveness of policy- and decision-making at the same time.

Maps on Demand: Tailoring Services of the US Environmental Protection Agency

The United States Environmental Protection Agency (EPA) gives access to a tailoring service called Maps on Demand (MOD) through the Web site http://maps.epa.gov/enviromapper/index.html. It consists of mapping applications (the EnviroMapper) to generate maps that display information for the entire United States. An interactive geographical information system using EPA's spatial data allows citizens to view data on national, state and county levels as well as to utilize several advanced functionalities which enable to view multiple spatial layers, zooming, identifying features and queerying single points.[15] The services also include searching toxic release inventory data, which allows citizens to find out about environmental safety of their own neighborhood (OECD, 2002).

Burgerklacht.nl: Dutch Portal for Citizens' Complaints

In The Netherlands, a consulting company has taken the initiative to offer citizens the opportunity to air their grievances on municipal services at a one stop-shop on the

Figure 4. Do-it-yourself: Online transactions (US Department of Transportation)

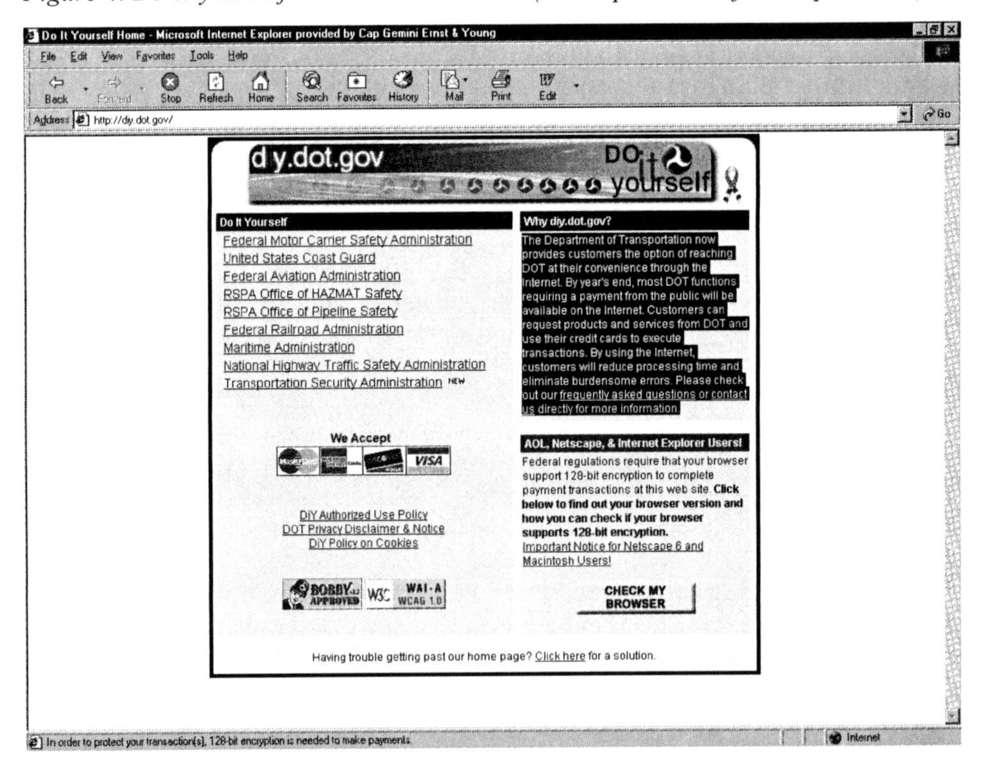

Figure 5. MOD: Tailoring services of the US Environmental Protection Agency

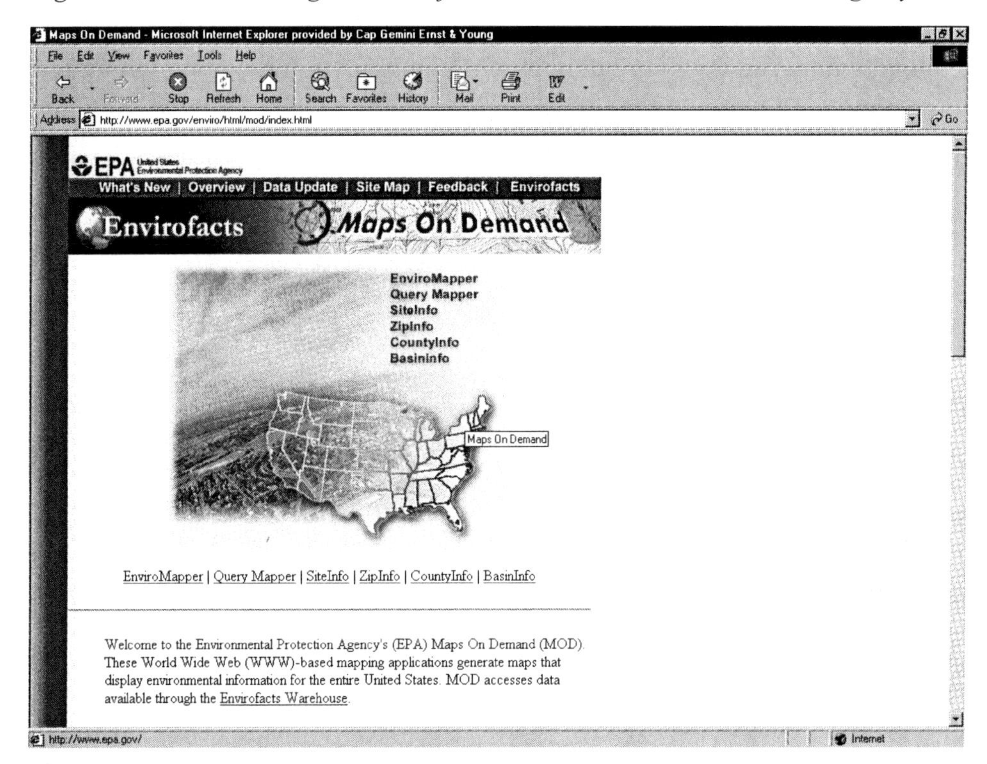

Internet called *Burgerklacht.nl* (in English: *citizenscomplaint.nl*). Complaints and other reports will be redirected to the responsible local civil servant, so that he can deal with it immediately.

Only municipalities that authorized access through this particular portal are responsive to this service. Citizens that wish to register a complaint about services of municipalities that are not (yet) registered can ask the Web master to let that be known to that municipality. In that way, Dutch municipalities are put under pressure to authorize *Burgerklacht.nl* to function as a national intermediary between citizens and local authorities. In other words, a private initiative is stimulating governments' responsiveness to complaints and suggestions of citizens on their living environment 24 hours a day, seven days a week.

INSTITUTIONAL INNOVATION AND CITIZEN PARTICIPATION

Theoretical Exercise

In our introduction, we set out to analyze the impact of the increasing use of ICT in the public sector on the relationship between government and citizens on the basis of theory and practice.

In paragraphs two and three we've discussed changes in the attitude and position of citizens towards government in general and with regard to the development of e-government. New expectations (decreasing self-evidence of good governance and getting accustomed to tailor-made services), steering forms (networking, horizontalization) and service offerings (integrated, pro-active and multichanneling) can lead to more or less radical changes in the relationship between government and citizen. We've pointed out that this relationship gradually becomes more equally balanced (reduction of traditional information disadvantage of the citizen) and that governments are forced to deliver their services more citizen-friendly (integrated, tailored and regardless of time and place). Furthermore, it can be questioned whether ICT mainly enables transparency of government itself or transparency of (individual) citizens. What effect do e-government services have on government's compliance with the principles of good governance? In particular, what influence is noticeable as a result of:

- Providing government information and services in new and multiple ways (access and transparency),
- Giving more room for direct participation in policy processes (accountability and legitimacy), and
- Altering which services and the content of what services are delivered (effectiveness of policy- and decision-making)?

In paragraphs four and five we elaborated on this theme by discussing the background of the increasing attention for (ICT-enabled) citizen orientation and presenting some relevant policy strategies, citizens' expectations and trends. As a policy strategy, responsiveness involves a major but gradual shift in government orientation from rules and policy design to service delivery and the needs and wants of citizens. The expectations of citizens seem to confirm the need for concrete improvements such as reduction of costs, shortening of waiting time, and better and more tailored access to services while increasing transparency of government its policy processes. Several strategic shifts in public policy and policy implementation regarding service delivery show that governments are actually trying to meet these expectations in practice. For example, a great number of OECD countries are implementing one-stop-shop service delivery geared to question patterns of citizens (from fragmented to integrated), are planning or cautiously experimenting with proactive services (taking into account future demands of citizens automatically) or are offering different types of delivery channels for the same product simultaneously (multichanneling).

In the paragraph above, by presenting eight examples of e-government services we've tried to lay a cautious foundation for a better insight into today's' state of affairs regarding ICT and responsiveness of government. In the following, we will analyze these eight "best practices" in order to put on trial our basically theoretical exercise on the question of whether government is actually becoming more responsive through provision of e-services.

ANALYSIS ON THE BASIS OF BEST PRACTICES

Access and Transparency

On the question whether e-government services lead to better access to information or policy issues and public service offerings and better understanding of the functioning of public administration, several examples show evidence that this is indeed the case.

The one-stop-shop cases of Singapore and Australia are clearly enhancing access to a great extent. They both are on the way to e-service delivery on an almost maximum scale, especially where it even extends to opportunities to doing all kinds of transactions online, regardless of time and place.

In the other cases, better access is given on a less extensive scale, but some of them give insight in very interesting possibilities to help improve the citizen's ability to gear the information provision to his own needs and demands. For example, the example of the Maps on Demand enables tailoring services on spatial and environmental data on national, state or county level. The Quality Cards, as well as the Eos-project, make it possible to gather detailed information geared to one's own specific right to subsidies (Eos) or the quality of education in one's own neighborhood (Quality Cards).

Special cases like the TOM project and *Burgerklacht.nl* enable direct access to decision- and policy-making (TOM) or to civil servants responsible for these policy processes (*Burgerklacht.nl*). TOM actually touches upon the issue of direct participation of citizens by allowing them to bring forward their own bills and promising them serious consideration. Furthermore, this project seems to give concrete opportunities to citizens to play the role of a co-supervisor of legislation processes, from consumer to prosumer and even maybe beyond that.

The co-supervisor role in TOM obviously greatly improves transparency of government information and processes. It can be questioned whether projects like Eos and e-Citizen are. On the one hand, the transaction process is better accessible and more transparent because services are presented in an easy way and options are given to fill in forms online or — in the Eos-case — calculate the height of payments receivable. On the other hand, the "virtualization" and "immaterialization" of government could lead to a situation wherein citizens ultimately have no idea which government agency is actually providing the service or handling their applications (with possibly consequences for the issue of accountability). Furthermore, for example in the Eos-case, individual citizens could relatively become more transparent than government agencies as they are mutually exchanging detailed information on their personal situation.[16]

Accountability and Legitimacy

As stated in paragraph three, accountability and legitimacy of the state in general and of public-service delivery organizations specifically are important issues when it comes to democratic values and good governance. The issue of faith of citizens in government and its exercise of power directly refers to the question whether government is adequately accounting for one's behavior and activities. Are citizens being sufficiently informed and facilitated to exercise their rights (as customers), participate in policy processes (as citoyens) and meet the legal requirements (as subjects of the state)?

The TOM project in Estonia as well as the Dutch *Burgerklacht.nl* initiative — though a private initiative, it is stimulating government agencies to respond electronically — potentially make a strong appeal to the accountability of public institutions. In Estonia, government employees and people's representatives commit themselves to responsiveness on concrete ideas and suggestions and can even be "watched" during the performance of this task. Municipal civil servants in the Netherlands are — once subscribed to the services of *Burgerklacht.nl* — answering citizens quickly and directly in individual cases.

With the Quality Cards, the Dutch Ministry of Education and Science opens up when it comes to detailed information on performance and policy results in the field of education.[17] In that way, government is accounting for policy and policy results online.

The subject of legitimacy of the state and its institutions is a somewhat difficult issue to analyze and judge profoundly without having performed a targeted survey of citizens' perspectives. However, it is to be expected that the multi-service windows of Singapore and Victoria, as well the tailored and/or online transaction based service delivery of respectively the US Environmental Protection Agency and the Federal Department of Transportation, contribute to some faith in government where it concerns economic transactions.

On the other hand, the one-sided focus on economics instead of (also on) policy participation might ultimately have a reversed influence on the rate to which people trust government and politicians. As mentioned earlier in our introduction, making economics the one and only target of e-government can result in a neglect of principles of good governance such as a proper balance between citizens' interests and the interest of public-service delivery organizations.

For example, a fully automated tax declaration process might drive out options for taking into consideration special circumstances of individuals that would legitimize exceptions to the rules that were incorporated in the processing information system. In this instance, along with the introduction of e-government the individual policy freedom of the traditional "street-level bureaucrat" is replaced by standard and automatically processed treatment of virtual "system-level bureaucrats" (Bovens & Zouridis, 2002). In other words, by one-sidedly implementing the "economics" of e-government (considering citizens solely in their role as customer), the citizen (as citoyen) could get uncomfortable with government agencies while having not enough options left to respond to or to participate in policy processes. Too little information to base a proper judgement on a shortage of feedback options lay on the basis of that situation. Having said that, we immediately conclude that in the case of *Burgerklacht.nl* and especially in the case of TOM there seem to be explicit opportunities for government to increase legitimacy in stead of decrease it. After all, these cases are specifically based on participation ideas, and not dominantly focussed on "economics" or online transactions.

Effectiveness of Policy- and Decision-Making

One of the key elements of improving the responsiveness of government agencies is gearing policy- and decision-making more adequately to the actual problems and demands of citizens. Shortening waiting times, reduction of costs and tailoring services are examples of concrete expectations of citizens where it concerns the contribution of ICT to public services. In most cases, e-service delivery practices all three of them to a certain extent. For example, the multi-services approaches of one-stop shops (Victoria and Singapore) and the tailored (Maps on Demand) or transaction-focused (Do-it-yourself) e-service examples all are concrete alternatives for long waiting lines during standard opening times of the traditional physical government windows. In the Eos-case, the Dutch Housing Department explicitly mentions cost reduction as one of the main goals to initiate the project. In virtualizing the government's back and front offices involved (municipalities, tax authority and the department itself) and implementing a system of automatic continuation, a great part of the costly traditional policy chain is gradually becoming obsolete.

Citizens that make use of the do-it-yourself service of the US Department of Transportation help reduce processing times and eliminate "burdensome errors" themselves. Public servants are making fewer mistakes because they don't have to fill in personal information on the forms anymore. They are also no longer responsible for entering this information into the databases, which saves time and money, too.

On the particular subject of effectiveness of policy-making, the TOM project is an example of how citizens can work on policy and legislation in close co-operation with government and people's representatives. In that way, the needs and wants as well as practical ideas derived from the actual "shop-floor-level of society" can be processed in the process of policy- and decision-making. To a lesser extent, this also applies to the case of *Burgerklacht.nl*.

Innovation of Government-Citizen Relationships: Co-Active Service Delivery

In this chapter, we discussed theory and practice of e-government services with a special focus on changes in the relationship between government and citizen. For government, the use of ICT seems to be improving its relationship with citizens a great deal, especially when it comes to the dominantly economic relations it has with citizens in their role as customers. On the other hand, some of the presented "best practices" show that the roles of the citizens as "citoyen" and "subject of the state" can also be facilitated if special attention is paid to access, transparency and the opportunities for citizens to give online feedback on policy programs, legislation processes or services. In order to avoid neglecting the democratic rights of citizens, governments seem to act wisely if they systematically take into account the consequences of using ICT for their compliance to all of the principles of good governance at the same time.

In practice, there seems to be a tendency to either implement e-government concepts on the sole basis of economic rationale or to experiment with e-services that aim more or less one-sidedly at direct citizen participation in policy-making or decision-making. Taking into account the preference for economics — which is rather logical when only addressing the subject of service delivery — we conclude that there is a need for institutional innovation in the sense that there should be a broadening in precisely that public task. After all, "e-government" consists of more than improvement of service delivery. It is important to use ICT to improve *all* relationships of government with citizens — customers as well as citoyens (direct participants), voters (indirect participants) and subjects of the state.

For that, a transformation of the structure of government to a more horizontal, flexible and responsive institution seems in place. Integrated, tailoring and proactive services as well as an increased participation of individual citizens and social movements require further co-operation of government agencies and its business partners (mainly concerning their back offices). Governments should simultaneously pay attention to: (1) both politico-administrative accountability and social responsibility, (2) both citizens as customers and citizens as participants and (3) both aspects of policy-making and policy implementation (service delivery, law enforcement and supervision). In that way, e-government implies receiving the benefits of economic and of democratic improvement at the same time.

In other words, the motto ought to be that e-services initiatives cannot work without paying attention to aspects of participation and legitimacy — to the citizen as a "whole person." In this so-called concept of *co-active service delivery,* co-production of government and citizens has a central place (Van Duivenboden & Lips, 2001). The idea is that all stakeholders — that in practice have a more horizontal and thus in many instances a more direct relationship anyway — co-operate more closely while entering into clear agreements on the division of specific responsibilities that suit the continuously developing principles of good governance (Poland & Keulards, 2001). In fact, co-active service delivery implies that government agencies and citizens do each other a service in turn every time they contact. When citizens are provided with a permit, a subsidy or relevant information — or even when they are given a ticket for speeding — they should be facilitated to give specific feedback or suggestions on the services delivered, the policy program that they are based on or the way services are provided.

CONCLUSIONS

The concept of co-active service delivery is based on the observation that the strategic policy programs and implementation of e-government can maybe cause a counterproductive effect in the sense that democratic states will be confronted with a legitimacy crisis. There seems to be a need for institutional innovation since "upscaling and downscaling trends are taking place simultaneously in society, and at the same time there is a shift from vertical to horizontal. The functioning of the traditional system of public administration based on scale and hierarchy could therefore become problematic. This could lead to a creeping crisis in the form of loss of legitimacy and authority and a marginal role in public debate" (ICT and Government Advisory Committee, 2001).

Therefore, a concrete question for further research and debate can be how the issue of electronic service delivery can be permanently connected to responsiveness and to digital participation (Bekkers, 2001b, p. 63).[18] This asks for a broad perspective on citizen orientation such as the concept of co-active service delivery as in short presented above. This subject includes more profound research on a issue such as "reinventing" good governance by aiming specifically at the impact of ICT on the relationship between government and citizens as customers *and* as participants (citoyen, subject and maybe even as a voter). Thinking through the opportunities of maybe combining e-governance (policy making), e-democracy (citizen's indirect consultation) and e-service delivery is another issue that may deserve extra attention.

Finally, the issue of transparency is especially interesting when conducting research into the possibilities and necessity of connecting electronic service delivery to digital participation. Social and technologic trends and developments ask not only for more transparency of government and government information in general. Even more important is the question whether the use of ICT in public administration can help making law and policy (processes) understandable on *individual* level. A focus in research on so-called *individual transparency* within the further development and implementation of the concepts of e-governance and e-government can give more insight into the opportunities to closely stick to the shift in service delivery from collective to tailor-made. At the same time, this could give citizens more room for playing the role of direct participant.

REFERENCES

Agterhorst, J., & Thaens, M. (2000). Veranderkundige aspecten van uitvoeringsketens. Casus uitvoering van de Huursubsidiewet. In H.P.M. van Duivenboden, M.J.W. van Twist, M. Veldhuizen & R.J. in 't Veld (Eds.), *Ketenmanagement in de Publieke Sector* (pp. 231-247). Uitgeverij Lemma: Utrecht.

Albeda, J., & Bijlert, V. (2001). Oude Klanten Verwachten Inspanningen, Nieuwe Klanten Verwachten Resultaten. In H.P.M. van Duivenboden & A.M.B. Lips (Eds.), *Klantgericht Werken in de Publieke Sector. Inrichting Van de Elektronische Overheid* (pp. 119-134). Uitgeverij Lemma BV: Utrecht.

Bekkers, V.J.J.M. & van Duivenboden, H.P.M. (1995). Democracy and datacoupling. In W.B.H.J. van de Donk, I.Th.M. Snellen & P.W. Tops (Eds.), *Orwell in Athens. A perspective on informatization and democracy* (pp. 213-223). Amsterdam: IOS.

Bekkers, V.J.J.M. (2001a). Virtuele Beleidsgemeenschappen. Over Responsieve Democratie en Digitale Participatie. *Bestuurskunde*, *6*, 252-261.

Bekkers, V.J.J.M. (2001b). De strategische Positionering van e-Government. In H.P.M. van Duivenboden & A.M.B. Lips (Eds.), *Klantgericht Werken in de Publieke Sector. Inrichting Van de Elektronische Overheid* (pp. 49-64). Utrecht: Uitgeverij Lemma BV.

Bellamy, C., & Taylor, J.A. (1998). *Governing in the information age.* Buckingham: Open University.

Beus, J. de (2001). *Een Primaat van Politiek.* Inaugurele Rede aan de Universiteit van Amsterdam. Amsterdam: Vossiuspers.

Bovens, M.A.P., & Zouridis, S. (2002). Van Street-level Bureaucratie Naar Systeem-level Bureaucratie. Over ICT, Ambtelijke Discretie en Democratische Rechtsstaat. *Nederlands Juristenblad (NJb)*, afl. 2/2002.

Clarke, R. (1996). Computer matching by government agencies: The failure of cost/benefit analysis as a control mechanism. *Information Infrastructure and Policy*, *4*, 29-65.

Commissie Docters van Leeuwen. (2001). *Burger en Overheid in de Informatiesamenleving. De Noodzaak van Institutionele Innovatie.* Rapport van de Eenmalige Adviescommissie ICT en Overheid. Den Haag: Ministerie van Binnenlandse Zaken en Koninkrijksrelaties.

Depla, P.F.G. (1995). *Technologie en de Vernieuwing van de Lokale Democratie. Vervolmaking of Vermaatschappelijking.* Den Haag: VUGA.

Dialogic. (2001). *E-government: de Vraagkant aan Bod. Een Inventarisatie van de Wensen en Verwachtingen van Burgers Over de Elektronische Overheid.* Den Haag: Ministerie van Binnenlandse Zaken en Koninkrijksrelaties.

Dialogic. (2002). *Burgers aan Het woord. Oordelen en Klachten Over de Elekronische Overheid.* Den Haag: Programmabureau burger@overheid.

Donk, W.B.H.J. van de. (2001). *De Gedragen Gemeenschap. Over Katholiek Maatschappeliijk Organiseren de Ontzuiling Voorbij*, oratie. Den Haag: SDU Uitgevers.

Donk, W.B.H.J. van de, & Tops, P.W. (1992). Informatisering en Democratie: Orwell of Athene? In P.H.A. Frissen, A.W. Koers & I.Th.M. Snellen (Eds.), *Orwell of Athene. Democratie en samenleving*, Nota. Den Haag: SDU.

Duivenboden, H.P.M. van. (1999). *Koppeling in Uitvoering. Een Verkennende Studie Naar de Betekenis van het Koppelen van Persoonsgegevens Door Uitvoerende Overheidsorganisaties Voor de Positie van de Burger als Cliënt van de Overheid.* Delft: Eburon.

Duivenboden, H.P.M. van., & Lips, A.M.B. (2001). Klantgericht Werken in de Publieke Sector: Naar een Co-actieve Publieke Dienstverlening. In H.P.M. van Duivenboden & A.M.B. Lips (Eds.), *Klantgericht Werken in de Publieke Sector. Inrichting van de Elektronische Overheid* (pp. 481-490). Utrecht: Uitgeverij Lemma BV.

Duivenboden, H.P.M. van., & Lips, A.M.B. (2003). Taking citizens seriously. Applying Hirschman's Model to various practices of customer-oriented e-governance. In A. Salminen (Ed.), *Governing networks*. EGPA Yearbook. Amsterdam: IOS.

Duivenboden, H.P.M. van, Frissen, V.A.J., van Lieshout, M.J., & Mooren, P.A.M. (2002). *Onderschat Debat. Een Internationaal Vergelijkend Onderzoek naar Beleidsvisies op Informatie - en Communicatietechnologie en de Democratische Rechtsstaat.* Den Haag: Ministerie van Binnenlandse Zaken en Koninkrijksrelaties.

Fountain, J.E. (2000). Paradoxes of public sector customer services. *Governance, 14*(1), 55-73.

Hoogwout, M. (2001). Leuker Kunnen we Het Niet Maken, Maar Willen we het wel Makkelijker? Waarom Overheden Geen Haast Hebben Met het Verbeteren van de Dienstverlening. In H.P.M. van Duivenboden & A.M.B. Lips (Eds.), *Klantgericht Werken in de Publieke Sector. Inrichting van de Elektronische Overheid* (pp. 149-166). Utrecht: Uitgeverij Lemma BV.

ICT and Government Advisory Committee. (2001). *Citizen and government in the Information Society. The need for institutional change.* The Hague: Ministry of the Interior and Kingdom Relations. (English version of Commissie Docters van Leeuwen, 2001.)

Infocomm Development Authority. (2002). the eGovernment Newsletter: Singapore. Retrieved from *www.ida.gov.sg or at www.egov.gov.sg*

Kubicek, H., & Hagen, M. (2001). Integrating e-commerce and e-government. The case of Bremen Online Services. In J.E.J. Prins (Ed.), *Designing e-Government. On the crossroads of technological innovation and institutional change.* The Hague: Kluwer Law International.

KWIZ. (2001). *Pro-actieve Dienstverlening. Van Concept Naar Uitvoering.* Onderzoek in Opdracht van het Ministerie van Binnenlandse Zaken en Koninkrijksrelaties. Groningen.

Lenk, K., & Traunmüller, R. (2001). Broadening the concept of electronic government. In Prins, J.E.J. (Ed.), *Designing e-Government. On the crossroads of technological innovation and institutional change* (pp. 63-73). The Hague: Kluwer Law International.

Lips, A.M.B., & Frissen, P.H.A. (1997). *Wiring government. Integrated public service delivery through ICT.* NWO/ITeR series Vol. 8, Samsom Bedrijfsinformatie: Alphen aan den Rijn/Diegem, pp.67-164.

Lipsky, M. (1980). *Street-level bureaucracy. Dilemma's of the individual in public services.* Mew York: Russell Sage Foundation.

Lyon, D. (1993). *The electronic eye.* Canada.

Ministry of the Interior and Kingdom Relations. (2004). *Op Weg Naar de Elektronische Overheid.* Den Haag.

Mettau, P. (2001). Procesinnovatie bij Publieke Uitvoeringsorganisaties. Het Vernieuwen van de Uitvoering van de Huursubsidie. In H.P.M. van Duivenboden & A.M.B. Lips (Eds.), *Klantgericht werken in de Publieke Sector. Inrichting van de Elektronische Overheid* (pp. 303-314). Utrecht: Uitgeverij Lemma BV.

OECD. (1981). Guidelines for the protection of transborder data flows of personal data.

OECD. (1996). *Responsive government. Service quality initiatives*, Public Management Service (PUMA). Paris: OECD.

OECD. (1998). *Impact of the emerging information society on the policy development process and Democratic quality*, PUMA (98)15, Public Management Service (PUMA). Paris: OECD.

OECD. (2001a). *Project on the impact of e-Government*, PUMA (2001)10/REV2, Public Management Service (PUMA). Paris: OECD.

OECD. (2001b). *Citizens as partners, information, consultation and public participation in policy-making.* Public Management Service (PUMA). Paris: OECD.

OECD. (2002). *From 'in line' to 'on-line': Delivering better services.* Draft, Public Management Service (PUMA). Paris: OECD.

Office of the e-Envoy. (2001). *Benchmarking electronic service delivery.* London.

OL2000. (2001). *Naar een Pro-actief Werkende Overheid. Een Handreiking Voor Gemeenten die Hun Burgers Pro-actief van Dienst willen Zijn.* Programmabureau OL2000 & Ministerie van Binnenlandse Zaken, Den Haag.

Poland, P.M., & Keulards, S.L.M. (2001). De Democratische Rechtsstaat in het ICT-tijdperk: Nieuwe Burgers in Samenspel Met een Nieuwe Overheid? In H.P.M. van Duivenboden & A.M.B. Lips (Eds.), *Klantgericht Werken in de Publieke Sector. Inrichting van de Elektronische Overheid* (pp. 429-444). Utrecht: Uitgeverij Lemma BV.

Pressman, J.L., & Wildavsky, A. (1984). *Implementation.* Revised Edition. Berkeley: University of California.

Ringeling, A.B. (2001). Rare Klanten Hoor, die Klanten van de Overheid. In H.P.M. van Duivenboden & A.M.B. Lips (Eds.), *Klantgericht Werken in de Publieke Sector. Inrichting van de Elektronische Overheid* (pp. 33-48). Utrecht: Uitgeverij Lemma BV.

Rose, R. (1989). *Ordinary people in public policy. A behavioral analysis.* London: Sage.

Rosenthal, U., Ringeling, A.B., Bovens, M.A.P., Hart, P. 't & van Twist, M.J.W. (1996). *Openbaar Bestuur. Beleid, Organisatie en Politiek.* Samson H.D. Tjeenk Willink: Alphen aan den Rijn.

Silcock, R. (2001). What is e-government? *Parliamentary Affairs, 54*, 88-101.

Snellen, I.Th.M. (2001). Administratieve Lastenverlichting: Wie is er voor het Algemeen Belang? In H.P.M. van Duivenboden & A.M.B. Lips (Eds.), *Klantgericht Werken in de Publieke Sector. Inrichting van de Elektronische Overheid.* Utrecht: Uitgeverij Lemma BV, pp. 335-346.

Thomassen, J.J.A. (1979). *Burgers in Twee Gedaanten.* Enschede.

Zouridis, S. (1998). Information technology, openness and democracy. In I.Th.M. Snellen & W.B.H.J. van de Donk (Eds.), *Public administration in an information age. A handbook* (pp. 179-193). Amsterdam: IOS.

ENDNOTES

1 The author would like to thank Miriam Lips from Tilburg University for her valuable contribution to some of the paragraphs.

2 Some researchers and politicians even observe sort of a comeback of the traditional vertical relationship between government and citizens, pointing to the growing demand for "strong leadership," security measures and

- as a result of '911'
- the "war on terrorism" (cf. Ringeling, 2001, p. 40).

3 As illustrated at the end of 2001 in Argentina at the time the president had to resign almost immediately after having taken radical financial measurements in order to deal with the poor economic situation of the country.

4 For example, the Dutch Road Traffic Agency has introduced what they call a McDonalds-concept: car owners can let their local garage carry out the annual state inspection and can register changes in car ownership at their local post office or

- when necessary
- local scrap yard (Van Duivenboden, 1999).

5 For this, De Beus (2001) has introduced the term spectator democracy.

6 In Dutch: "neo-republikeins staatsburger," as stated by Van Gunsteren, cited in Ringeling, 2001.

7 Parts of this paragraph are derived from Van Duivenboden & Lips, 2003.

8 For example, in the Netherlands at least 65% of all public services have to be provided electronically before the end of 2007 (Ministry of the Interior and Kingdom Relations, 2004). Canada and the United Kingdom have even set a target at offering 100% of their public services electronically by respectively in 2004 and 2005 (Office of the e-Envoy, 2001).

9 Some researchers place responsive service delivery in the middle of two other forms of service delivery: re-active and proactive service delivery. Re-active services are triggered by an explicit request of a citizen, whereas proactive services are delivered on government's own initiative (where there's basically no activity lrequested from citizens themselves). Responsive services are the ones whereby the citizen is provided with several alternatives as an answer to a particular question. He's being actively informed and government's continually striving for better insight in the individual's question patterns (KWIZ, 2001). The Dutch Citizen Counter Program OL2000 sees these three forms of public service delivery as a road uphill to the ideal situation: from re-active to responsive to the more or less utopian proactive form (OL2000, 2001: 13). In this chapter, we will consider both responsive as proactive service delivery to contribute to the responsiveness

of government. After all, meeting the needs of the citizens should be attained in proactive service delivery as well.

10 Remarkably, though 60% of the respondents are expecting that the use of the Internet will decrease the gap between government and citizens, there's no significant percentage of no or yes answers resulting from the question whether ICT will help improve democracy.

11 For example, in an OECD study that is based on a survey of online service delivery undertaken in 1999 and on earlier OECD studies, more or less the same core service delivery objectives are summed up: improving access, reducing administrative burdens, reducing costs to administration, providing integrated services, improving quality of services, tailoring services, incorporating citizen feedback, ensuring privacy and security, ensuring oversight and control and adapting to change (OECD, 2002).

12 This classification of shifts is derived from Van Duivenboden & Lips (2003), which in turn is partly based on Hoogwout (2001).

13 The Multi-Service Express site was decommissioned in January 2004. The functionality it provided has now been incorporated into the Victoria Online Portal and is available at: http://www.vic.gov.au/doitonline.

14 This example is derived from a study on policies in "ICT and the Democratic State," which was carried out under the authority of the Dutch Ministry of the Interior and Kingdom Relations (Van Duivenboden, Frissen, Van Lieshout & Mooren, 2002).

15 Originally, the project only aimed at creating "a common interface for the various environmental databases of various EPA programme offices (…) The nature of the project changed to provide broad public electronic access to environmental information" (OECD, 2002).

16 However, the presentation of the examples given in paragraph six offer too little information to verify these kind of threats to the compliance with the principle of transparency or openness of government. For that, more profound empirical research is needed.

17 Remarkably, it was a journalist that stimulated this government initiative by appealing to the Law on Openness of Government. In that particular case he wanted to publish the results of individual schools in the newspaper he worked for. After this, the Ministry decided to initiate this comprehensive information provision on the Internet.

18 It can be expected that the research findings will probably vary strongly depending on the type of policy implementation process that is chosen as main object of study (e.g., large "standard" benefit or subsidies programmes versus small "tailor-made" e-government services at local level). Previous research shows that although there is an enormous amount of e-government initiatives, the vast majority of these initiatives are driven by technological and economic innovation logics – as also mentioned in the analysis of this chapter. This research confirms that the focus is most of the times one-sidedly on government's internal efficiency and/or on citizens in their role of customers (Van Duivenboden, Frissen, Van Lieshout & Mooren, 2002).

About the Editor

Mehdi Khosrow-Pour, D.B.A., is currently the executive director of the Information Resources Management Association (IRMA) and senior academic technology editor for Idea Group Reference. Previously, he served on the faculty of the Pennsylvania State University as a professor of information systems for 20 years. He has written or edited over 30 books in information technology management, and he is also the editor-in-chief of the *Information Resources Management Journal*, *Journal of Electronic Commerce in Organizations*, *Journal of Cases on Information Technology*, and *International Journal of Cases on Electronic Commerce.*

About the Authors

Barbara Ann Allen (bacallen@rogers.com) is a lecturer, researcher, and consultant in public policy. Her doctoral thesis is focused on Canadian government procurement and the impact of digital technologies and trade agreements on procurement.

Frank Bongers (1971) is a senior policy researcher and advisor at Dialogic Innovation & Interaction (Utrecht, The Netherlands). He studied policy sciences at Tiburg University. In 2000 he finished his doctorate research into the contribution of group support systems to the quality of participatory policy analysis. In recent years, he often participated in Dialogic research projects on e-government, broadband infrastructures and services, innovation policies, information technology and society, and (mobile) telecommunications. He is also a member of a local Court of Audit and a member of the scientific committee of the e-Society conferences of the International Association for the Development of the Information Society (IADIS). He has published articles in *Information & Management, Journal of Decision Systems, International Journal of Technology Management,* and several Dutch journals.

Tony Bovaird (BSc, Econ, Belf; MA, Lanc) Professor of Strategy and Public Services Management (Bristol Business School, University of the West of England), has researched and published widely on performance management, policy evaluation and assessment of public management and governance initiatives. He has undertaken research projects for ESRC, the European Commission, UK government departments, the Local Government Improvement and Development Agency, the Audit Commission, and many other public bodies. He is currently chair of the Evaluation Partnership, set up by the Office of the Deputy Prime Minister (ODPM) in the UK to evaluate the Local Government Modernisation Agenda. He is also co-chair of the Local and Regional Governance Research Network which advises ODPM on the policy implications of current research in this field. Recently directed a series of evaluation case studies of the Civil Service Reform Programme, commissioned by the Cabinet Office. He is the author of *Public Management and Governance* (London, Routledge, 2003) with Elke Loeffler.

Georges Chatillon is the director of the advanced graduate diploma, Internet law for government and business at the University Paris I Pantheon Sorbonne, where he teaches classes in electronic commerce law and intellectual property law. In addition, Dr. Chatillon serves as a consultant for various institutions including European Commission; OECD; French government; German government. He has published in the proceedings of European and Compared Internet Law, Paris, 25 and 26 September 2000; International Internet law, Paris, 19 and 20 November 2001; and, eGovernment for the Benefits of citizens, Paris, 21 and 22 January 2002. He is author of the books, Public Internet Law (LGDJ, forthcoming, 2004) and From red tape to smart tape, administrative simplification in OECD countries (OECD 2003).

Marcella Corsi (mcorsi@luiss.it) is a professor of economics (II level) at LUISS G. Carli in Rome, where she teaches macroeconomics at the Faculty of Economics and Business. She has recently worked as consultant for the public management (PUMA) division of OECD and for the Department of Innovation and Technologies of the Italian Government (DIT). At the moment, she is coordinator of the research unit "E-Citizenship: Measuring the Impact of ICT on the Relationship of Government to Citizens" in the context of the MIUR (2003) project "European Citizen in e-Governance: Legal-Philosophical, Legal, Computer Science and Economical Aspects." She is the author of papers, books and reports concerning technical change, labour economics, distribution of income and economic growth, often in a gender perspective.

Stuart Culbertson is a principal in the Public and Institutional Sector Consulting with TkMC, a Canadian-based management consultancy with a focus on organisational and service transformation in public sector agencies. He has consulted extensively in the field of "e-government" and in public sector IT and service strategies, program design and development. His clients have included the government of Canada, the government of British Columbia, Canadian intergovernmental CIO and service delivery councils and international organisations such as the OECD. Mr. Culbertson has held several deputy minister and assistant deputy minister positions in the government of British Columbia – including over three years as chief information officer where he helped establish the province as the national leader in electronic government and electronic service delivery (as ranked by Accenture, 2000, 2001). He has also had extensive governmental experience in the development of successful sector development strategies, programs and organizations in the science and technology, fisheries and agri-food sectors and international trade policy.

Valerie Frissen (1960) is currently working as senior researcher and consultant for the Dutch research organization TNO. TNO "Strategy, Technology & Policy" specialises in strategic policy research on the social and economic implications of technological innovation processes. Professor Frissen is leading the research team "ICT and Social Change." One of the areas in which this unit is carrying out research is on the implications of ICT for government and governance. She also holds a part-time chair on ICT and Social Change at the Erasmus University Rotterdam. Before she started working at TNO, she was a reseacher and lecturer at the University of Amsterdam, Department of Communication Studies. She holds a PhD in social sciences (1992) and an MA in communication studies (1987) from the University of Nijmegen.

Alison Hopkins leads the Consumer Connections Team at the UK National Consumer Council. She also holds responsibility for commissioned research within the Council and has a special interest in how information society services are designed and delivered, as well as the implications for individual consumers and different user groups. Her previous publications include Consumer Concerns, a series of surveys published each year from1990 to 1999, and e-commerce and consumer protection — real needs in a virtual world (2000). As well as working with Consumers International on reports about Internet shopping, online privacy and Web credibility, she has contributed to several working groups convened by government, most recently working with other consumer experts on a report for the Minister of State for Culture, Media and Sport considering criteria for switching from analogue to digital TV signals.

Luc Juillet (ljuillet@uottawa.ca) is associate professor in the Department of Political Science and Associate Director of the School of Political Studies at the University of Ottawa.

Donald G. Lenihan, PhD, MA, BA, is CEO of the Crossing Boundaries National Council (www.crossingboundaries.ca), a non-partisan group of about 40 elected officials and department heads from across Canada. The Council's mission is to act as a champion for the transformation of government and governance in Canada through the responsible use of information and communications technologies. It is responsible for a variety of research initiatives and pilot projects to examine contemporary issues in governance, public policy and public administration and to promote change. Dr. Lenihan has more than 20 years of experience as a researcher, writer and analyst in areas ranging from electronic-government to citizenship and diversity. Before coming to the Centre, he was the Director of Research at the Institute of Public Administration of Canada (IPAC) and, prior to that, worked for The Network on the Constitution as Director of Research and Editor of The Network/Le Réseau, a national publication on national unity and constitutional issues. Over the last decade, he has developed, organized, directed and contributed to dozens of national research projects involving senior public servants, academics, elected officials, journalists and members of the private sector from across the country. He is the author of numerous articles and studies and a columnist with the Hill Times newspaper in Ottawa.

Valentina Mele (valentina.mele@unibocconi.it; valentina.mele@uniparthenope.it) is lecturer at Naples University in Naples and at the Public Administration Division of Bocconi School of Management in Milan. After earning an MPA at Columbia University, NY, and a PhD at Rome University on Electronic Government, she has been working as consultant for local and central governments, as well as for international organizations. She published several contributions on the adoption of ICT in public and non profit organizations.

Susan M. Pandy is director of the Internet Council at NACHA - The Electronic Payments Association, the leading organization in developing electronic solutions to improve the payments system. The mission of the Internet Council is to facilitate the development of global electronic commerce by enabling businesses, governments, and consumers to utilize present and future payments over open networks in a secure and cost-effective manner. Through multiple projects and working groups, the Internet Council is addressing issues related to Internet security, authentication, fraud, and payments over open networks. Prior to joining NACHA, Pandy directed the Center for eGovernance at the National Academy of Public Administration, a congressionally chartered think tank in Washington, DC, where she was responsible for developing a grassroots effort to address the challenges posed to government by the rise of digital technologies and the Internet. Ms. Pandy has been published with the General Accounting Office and The Public Manager. She holds a Masters of Public Administration from Cleveland State University and is a PhD candidate in public administration & policy at Virginia Polytechnic Institute & State University.

Gilles Paquet is professor *emeritus* and senior research fellow at the School of Political Studies of the University of Ottawa, and a senior partner of INVENIRE4. For more information, please visit his Web site at www.gouvernance.ca.

Salvador Parrado is associate professor of political science at the Spanish Distance University. His research interests and publications are related to comparative administrative systems, local governance, human resource management and e-government in the public sector. He is a consultant to Spanish local and regional authorities on management issues, to SIGMA (for Central and Eastern European countries) on e-government and to WMO (World Meteorological Organisation) on water management and governance. He is also a member of the OECD Task Force on e-government.

Franklin S. Reeder writes, consults and teaches on information policy and public management issues with The Reeder Group, a firm he formed after a career of more than 35 years in public service. His column on managing technology has appeared in *Government Executive* magazine. He is chairman of the Center for Internet Security, a not-for-profit established "to help organizations around the world effectively manage the organizational risks related to information security ..." [http://www.cisecurity.org]. He also chairs the Information Security and Privacy Advisory Board of the National Institute of Standards and Technology, a federal advisory committee [http://csrc.nist.gov/csspab/]. He has served at the U.S. Office of Management and Budget for two stints totaling more than 20 years between 1970 and 1995 where he was chief of information policy, deputy associate director for veterans affairs and personnel, and assistant director for general management. Among his accomplishments while a member of the information policy staff and later as its chief, he represented the Administration in negotiating and securing enactment of the Privacy Act of 1974 and the Computer Security Act of 1987 and wrote the guidelines on implementing the Privacy Act. While at OMB he was the U.S. delegate to the Organization for Economic Cooperation and Development's Public Management Committee (OECD/PUMA) from 1992-1995 and he chaired that committee from 1993-95. From 1977-80, he was deputy director of House Information Systems, the computers and telecommunications support arm of the U.S. House of Representatives. From 1995-97, he served as director of the Office of Administration of the Executive Office of the President. Frank served on the adjunct faculty at Syracuse University and the Georgian (that's the country, not the state) Institute for Public Affairs.

He has also taught at the University of Maryland and the George Washington University. He has received numerous honors, including the Presidential Rank Award as a Meritorious Senior Executive and induction into the *Government Computer News* Information Resources Management Hall of Fame. He is a principal of the Council for Excellence in Government and a fellow and member of the board of trustees of the National Academy of Public Administration.

Jeffrey Roy (roy@management.uottawa.ca) is associate professor of the School of Management at the University of Ottawa and associate editor of the *International Journal of E-Government Research.*

Alexander Settles is an assistant policy scientist at the Institute for Public Administration, University of Delaware. His public service and research activities have focused on e-government, comparative public administration, information technology, geographic information systems (GIS), land use planning, local government management, and state growth management policies. Mr. Settles has been a consultant to the E-Government Project, directorate for Public Governance and Territorial Development, Organization for Economic Co-operation and Development (OECD). He has been involved in the development of GIS applications for land use planning and public participation and was a founding member of the Delaware Geographic Data Committee.

Rens Vandeberg (1976) studied science and policy (Utrecht University) and specialized in quantitative sociology. He was an innovation researcher at Dialogic Innovation & Interaction (2000-2004), conducting research on innovation policy and user involvement in e-government. Vandeberg joined the Department of Innovation Studies (Utrecht University) in 2004 as a PhD researcher on user-producer interactions in nutrigenomics innovations (funded by the Netherlands Organization for Scientific Research (NWO)). He is coordinator of the Utrecht Network on Innovation, Corporations and Economies in Space (UNICES).

Robbin te Velde is a founding partner at Perquirimus and researcher at Eindhoven University of Technology, Dept. Technology Management. He has wide experience in the theoretical and practical aspects of social research and has been alternately working at universities and consultancies. He has taught methodology and philosophy of science at Twente University, was S&T policy specialist at the European branch of the Rand Corporation, researcher on information economics and telecommunications regulation at Delft University of Technology and senior researcher at Zenc, a small consultancy dedicated to ICT-innovations in the public domain. Mr. Te Velde conducted many international comparative studies on ICT-related matters on behalf of national and supranational public institutes. He has also been technology advisor to several multinational firms and has hands-on experience with the design and implementation of information systems. He has written a large number of scientific articles on a wide range of areas such as international politics, philosophy, knowledge management, business administration, technology policy and information management.

H.P.M. (Hein) van Duivenboden (1966) is vice-president and member of the Policy Board of Capgemini Consulting Services Netherlands. He also works for the TIAS Business School as a professor in ICT and interorganisational collaboration. He obtained his PhD at Tilburg University in 1999 on the impact of ICT on policy implementation and service delivery. His research and publications focus on Knowledge Management, Chain Informatisation and e-governance. In 2001 he won the Professional Publication Prize of the Dutch Organisation of Management Consultants (ROA). He was in charge of and/or participant in evaluation research on themes such as ICT and Democracy, Knowledge and ICT Innovation, e-service delivery, ICT and e-democracy, Chain Informatisation in Environmental Policy, Streamlining of Key Data, National PIN-Policy, Dutch Health Register, Dutch Population Register and Dutch Privacy Law. He participates in the Strategy Academy, the European Group of Public Administration and the Centre for Public Innovation.

Index

A

B

C

Q

R

S

T